THE CHURCHILLS

A Family at the Heart of History –
from the Duke of Marlborough to Winston Churchill

MARY S. LOVELL

ABACUS

ABACUS

First published in Great Britain in 2011 by Little, Brown
This paperback edition published in 2012 by Abacus

Boer poster on p. 178 and letter on p. 251 courtesy of the Churchill Archives.

A CIP catalogue record for this book
is available from the British Library.

ISBN 978-0-349-11978-6

Typeset in Garamond by M Rules
Printed and bound in Great Britain by
Clays Ltd, St Ives plc

Papers used by Abacus are from well-managed forests
and other responsible sources.

MIX
Paper from
responsible sources
FSC® C104740

Little, Brown
An imprint of
Little, Brown Book Group
100 Victoria Embankment
London EC4Y 0DY

An Hachette UK Company
www.hachette.co.uk

www.littlebrown.co.uk

This book is dedicated to my friends
Anne Biffin
and
Nell Whiting

CONTENTS

PREFACE

It is no easy task to write about a family that produced so many strong and active personalities, some of whose lives were so colourful that they provided source material for bestselling contemporary novelists such as Anthony Trollope, Edith Wharton and Henry James. Even so, everyone in this extraordinary family is overshadowed by one of the most remarkable men in modern history. There is very little not already well known about him, and yet his life was so full that if twenty historians sat down to write a biography of him and all were given exactly the same source materials, twenty quite different books would result.

In addition to the scores of books written about Winston Spencer Churchill, he produced a mini-library himself; fifty-odd titles, some multivolume, all written in prose that could hardly be bettered. And there remains an enduring fascination with the man. What made him so special? Many of the books about Churchill are heavyweight political biographies in which the private man is lost to the average reader amid the history of the great events of the twentieth century. But in a book about the Churchill family it is impossible to provide an in-depth account of Winston Churchill's political career – and this is not my intention. Churchill appears here as a family man, a pivot around whose activities, to a greater or lesser extent, other family members live out their lives. I hope to give readers easier access to these individuals, especially those of the nineteenth and twentieth centuries. It is the way Winston's personality and activities impinged on the lives of his family members that is important here, rather than those events which made him a household name and a national hero.

Despite all the reading I have done on Churchill over the years, there is always more to read. Even in the last year, 2009/10, newspaper articles have raised questions about aspects of his life and the lives of some of those close to him, such as the true cause of his father's early death; and it has been claimed that his mother Jennie had over two hundred lovers, that his younger brother Jack was the result of an affair between Jennie and a lover in Ireland, that Winston and Clementine were estranged for a good deal of their marriage, that Churchill was a bully; and, more recently, that Jennie 'robbed' her two sons of their inheritance. Sir Winston's last Private Secretary wisely wrote in his memoir of Sir Winston's final years, 'History is history and nothing portrayed or written of Winston Churchill can diminish his stature.' All the same, are there any facts behind these allegations?

Some reviewers may take me to task for adopting a gossipy approach to my subjects. And I should like to make it clear from the outset that this is not unintentional. In my experience – and I approach the allotted biblical span of human years – the world has always thrived on gossip, and provided contemporary gossip is presented with appropriate explanation and is properly sourced, then it can have a place even in serious biography.

When I first conceived this book I had in mind a record of the whole family, from the 1st Duke onwards, but the Churchills are a prolific and multitalented lot, and I soon saw that this was beyond the scope of one volume. Winston Spencer Churchill's father, Lord Randolph, was one of the eight children of the 7th Duke of Marlborough who survived to marry and have children. From the marriages of his paternal uncles and aunts alone, Winston had thirty Churchill first cousins. And then there were seven maternal cousins, the Leslies and the Frewens, in Ireland. In his children's generation there were over eighty Churchills, Guests, Felloweses, Leslies, Sheridans, Frewens and others. And in the following generation there were over a hundred. So in order to keep this book to a manageable size, I quickly revised my brief to include only extraordinary deeds, behaviour, achievement in the Churchill family during the last 150 years. Even then, for reasons of space I have had to cull hard – for example, the Guest family had many fascinating adventures in East Africa in the Thirties that would make a book on its own.

Winston Churchill did not become a leader by accident. He set out quite deliberately as a very young man to reach the top in British politics, and he dominated world politics in a way that any British politician would find impossible to do now. He always believed he was bound for greatness, and because of this sense of destiny, from his childhood onwards he and his family kept every scrap of paper – from important letters and other documents to ephemera such as theatre programmes and invitation cards. Partly as a result of this, Churchill's life, his daily activities, his successes and his failures, his loves and dislikes have been pored over, forensically dissected and, recently, often criticised. I freely admit that Winston Spencer Churchill was a hero to me as a child growing up in a heavily blitzed Liverpool during and after the Second World War. I well recall the sense of leadership and confidence he exuded through his radio talks – 'Winnie's on tonight!' – to which we all listened avidly on a crackly wireless that had to be constantly tuned in, becoming fainter and fainter as the acid batteries wore down.

Nothing I have read or discovered about Churchill since then has essentially changed my opinion of him. He was undeniably impulsive and impatient at times, and not all his strategies, conceived under stress, were thought out as thoroughly as they might have been; these characteristics were with him from childhood. But his failings were more than balanced by his boldness, the use he made of his experience of fighting in the field, his sound understanding of government and of the political system, his sense of dedication and duty to his country and his utter honesty, and – at the last – his absolute refusal to give in to Britain's enemies. Unquestionably he made mistakes, some major ones, but so did every other commander throughout history. And in any case, the occasional error makes him more human, more engaging. When I have felt it necessary within the terms of this family history I have – with the benefit of hindsight that Churchill did not possess, of course – discussed such errors. But irrefutably, Churchill's achievements far outweighed his failings; a recent BBC poll showed that the great mass of British people still regard him as 'the greatest Briton'.

One of the problems I experienced while writing this book was how to refer to Sir Winston. One clearly cannot refer to a baby or child as 'Churchill'. However, at the point in the story where he became a man, and a fighting soldier, it seemed over-familiar to call him 'Winston' so I took my problem to his daughter Mary (Lady Soames) and asked her advice. She told me to use my biographer's instinct and refer to him in whatever way felt comfortable. In the political arena, for example, 'Churchill' was preferable. In a family setting, featuring Clementine or his children, 'Winston' was the obvious choice.

Mary S. Lovell
Brockenhurst, Hampshire
June 2010

www.marylovell.com

The Churchills

Selective family tree of those mentioned in the text

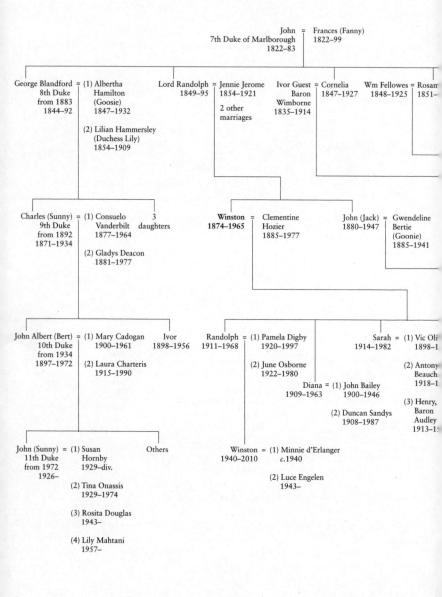

John
7th Duke of Marlborough = Frances (Fanny)
1822–83   1822–99

George Blandford = (1) Albertha
8th Duke   Hamilton
from 1883   (Goosie)
1844–92   1847–1932

                   (2) Lilian Hammersley
                   (Duchess Lily)
                   1854–1909

Lord Randolph = Jennie Jerome
1849–95   1854–1921

                2 other
                marriages

Ivor Guest = Cornelia
Baron   1847–1927
Wimborne
1835–1914

Wm Fellowes = Rosam
1848–1925   1851–

Charles (Sunny) = (1) Consuelo   3
9th Duke   Vanderbilt   daughters
from 1892   1877–1964
1871–1934
                   (2) Gladys Deacon
                   1881–1977

Winston = Clementine
1874–1965 Hozier
           1885–1977

John (Jack) = Gwendeline
1880–1947   Bertie
              (Goonie)
              1885–1941

John Albert (Bert) = (1) Mary Cadogan   Ivor
10th Duke   1900–1961   1898–1956
from 1934
1897–1972   (2) Laura Charteris
                    1915–1990

Randolph = (1) Pamela Digby
1911–1968   1920–1997

            (2) June Osborne
            1922–1980

Diana = (1) John Bailey
1909–1963   1900–1946

        (2) Duncan Sandys
        1908–1987

Sarah = (1) Vic Oli
1914–1982   1898–1

        (2) Antony
        Beauch
        1918–1

        (3) Henry,
        Baron
        Audley
        1913–1

John (Sunny) = (1) Susan   Others
11th Duke   Hornby
from 1972   1929–div.
1926–
                  (2) Tina Onassis
                  1929–1974

                  (3) Rosita Douglas
                  1943–

                  (4) Lily Mahtani
                  1957–

Winston = (1) Minnie d'Erlanger
1940–2010   c.1940

            (2) Luce Engelen
            1943–

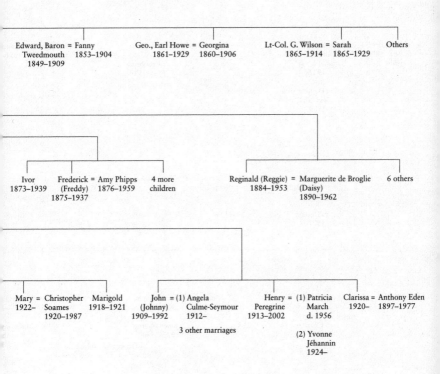

Edward, Baron = Fanny
Tweedmouth   1853–1904
1849–1909

Geo., Earl Howe = Georgina
1861–1929   1860–1906

Lt-Col. G. Wilson = Sarah
1865–1914   1865–1929

Others

Ivor
1873–1939

Frederick = Amy Phipps
(Freddy)   1876–1959
1875–1937

4 more
children

Reginald (Reggie) = Marguerite de Broglie
1884–1953   (Daisy)
1890–1962

6 others

Mary = Christopher   Marigold
1922–   Soames   1918–1921
1920–1987

John = (1) Angela
(Johnny)   Culme-Seymour
1909–1992   1912–

3 other marriages

Henry = (1) Patricia
Peregrine   March
1913–2002   d. 1956

(2) Yvonne
Jéhannin
1924–

Clarissa = Anthony Eden
1920–   1897–1977

1650–1750

'Thou art a rascal, John Churchill'

The surname Churchill is an honoured one, legendary in our time, owing to the vision and achievements of one of history's greatest men, who sprang from a ducal line and, though born without a title, was always conscious of his aristocratic heritage.

The first Churchill to come to the notice of modern history was John Churchill, born in 1650 during the turbulent years of the Civil War. He was the elder son of Mr Winston Churchill of Ashe House* near Axminster in Devon,[1] although this family of minor West Country gentry hailed originally from the village of Churchill in the neighbouring county of Somerset.† Royalist to the core, they were heavily penalised under Cromwell's administration, but even before the Civil War they were never rich. By 1660, when the monarchy was restored, money was tight and there were twelve Churchill children to bring up. Matters improved marginally when Winston Churchill became Member of Parliament for Weymouth, in what is now known as the Cavalier Parliament, and was later given a minor government job in recognition of his loyalty. Even so, young John

---

*Ashe House was destroyed by Parliamentary troops who left only a burned-out wing standing. John Churchill was born at Little Trill, a house belonging to his mother's family. Later, he purchased Minterne House in Dorset (now the home of Lord and Lady Digby). He left Minterne to his son Charles Churchill. In the family they still say, 'Charles got Minterne and poor Marlborough had to make do with Blenheim.'

†There is a legend that the family descended from Lord Courcelle, a Norman knight who came over to England with the Conqueror, but this is incorrect.

Churchill had to surrender his entitlement to the entailed family property, to allow his father to raise a mortgage on it.

Approaching manhood, John always knew he would have to make his own fortune, and that his only assets towards achieving this goal were his brains and singular good looks. Tall, with an excellent physique, he had fair hair, blue eyes and classically handsome features. His enemies (of whom there would eventually be many) would say that he began the process of advancement on the coat-tails of his older sister Arabella, a beauty by the standards of the day. At the age of sixteen Arabella became a maid-of-honour to the Duchess of York, and subsequently mistress to her employer's husband, James, Duke of York and heir to the throne, to whom Arabella bore a son.* It was said that her influence provided her brother John with his first position in the entourage of the Duke and, in 1667, a commission in the footguards.† The Duke's friendly patronage would not have proved unhelpful, though there is some historical evidence that John's father (who was knighted in 1664 to become Sir Winston Churchill) had written to an important friend at court to secure John's first appointment as a page to the Duke; and it is equally possible that a few years later Sir Winston somehow raised the money to buy the lowly commission for his eldest son. What is certain, and somehow endearing at such a distance, is that John made his public debut by cuckolding his King.

Twenty-nine-year-old Barbara Villiers, the voluptuous, tempestuous and sexually insatiable Lady Castlemaine, was still *maîtresse en titre* to King Charles II in 1670 when twenty-year-old John Churchill first appeared at court wearing his ensign's uniform. By then he had spent a few years in service in the Mediterranean, probably at Tangiers, one of the many parcels of land that the Queen, Catherine of Braganza, had brought to her marriage.[2] John Churchill and Barbara Villiers (who had been newly created Duchess of St Albans) were second cousins,‡ and before long the

---

*The child was created Duke of Berwick and became one of King Louis XIV's most famous generals.
†Commissions in regiments had to be purchased, and could be sold on retirement.
‡John's mother, Elizabeth Drake, of the same family as Sir Francis Drake, was the granddaughter of Elizabeth Villiers and Lord Boteler.

new Duchess and the handsome ensign were also lovers. One afternoon the King, having heard that he had acquired a youthful rival,
decided to pay an unscheduled visit to his mistress, whose apart-
ments on King Street faced Whitehall.

There are two contemporary accounts of the event. In one, John
escaped through a window and shinned down a drainpipe clutch-
ing his clothes, in full view of interested members of the court
who were strolling below. In another version (favoured by the
Marlborough family), on hearing his monarch approaching, John
dived into a wardrobe, where he was discovered and sent packing.
Both versions, however, agree that the following day when the
two men met, Churchill bowed apologetically and the King is
reputed to have quipped magnanimously, 'Thou art a rascal, John
Churchill, but I forgive thee for I know 'tis how you earn your daily
bread.'

The King did not quite forgive John Churchill: he banished his
young rival from court, although the affair with Barbara lasted for
some time afterwards. But it is an appealing image – young John
making his entrance into history naked and in flight – and some
elements of the story are probably factual. Within a short time the
penniless young man mysteriously acquired the large sum of
£5000.* Not being brought up to squander money he used this sensibly to purchase an annuity of £500, a sum that would be paid to
him annually for the remainder of his life. Most people at court
believed that this money was a *douceur* from the amorous Duchess,†
and her last child, born in 1672 – at about the same time as John
Churchill received his windfall – was generally accepted as Churchill's
daughter.[3] Ever resourceful, after the safe delivery of the baby the
Duchess sent a messenger to the King to tell him of the birth of
yet another royal bastard. The King, not himself renowned for
constancy, replied with characteristic nonchalance: 'You may tell my
lady that I know the child is not mine, yet I will acknowledge it
for old times' sake.'[4] The little girl bore the name Barbara Fitzroy

---

*The value in today's currency, based on Retail Price Index tables, is over £415,000.
†As did Sir Winston S. Churchill in his biography of his ancestor.

and was sent to board in a convent in France. As an adult she became a nun and was known as Sister Benedicta.[5]

John subsequently served aboard HMS *Prince*, the Duke of York's flagship, which lost a third of her company in the first naval battle of the Third Anglo-Dutch War at Solebay in June 1672. For this service John Churchill was promoted to captain in what we would now call the Marines. His next posting took him to Maastricht, where in hand-to-hand fighting he acquitted himself so bravely that on his return to London he was introduced to Charles II (who had, surely, not forgotten him?) by the Duke of Monmouth* as 'the brave man who saved my life'. As a result, John was given command of an English battalion and posted to allied France to fight for King Louis XIV. With this responsibility came a French colonelcy, but the position was no sinecure, for in one battle, at Enzheim, Churchill lost half of his twenty-two officers. The English cavalry fared even worse; half of all their troops were killed or wounded. 'No one in the world,' the dispatch to London reported, 'could possibly have done more than Colonel Churchill.'

John was still only twenty-four when he returned in some triumph to the English court, and among his personal possessions were two packing cases full of silver taken in prizes. Probably the last thing on his mind was marriage – until he met sixteen-year-old Sarah Jennings. Sarah and her elder sister Frances were ladies-in-waiting to the Duchess of York, but unlike Arabella Churchill the Jennings sisters were virtuous girls and there was no pillow talk to aid their advancement. Sarah, tall, fair-complexioned, clear-eyed and with an abundance of red-gold hair, was also an attendant to

---

*Though he had no legitimate offspring Charles II had numerous bastards, the eldest of whom was James, the son of Lucy Walter. Born in 1649 while the King was in exile, James was his supposed father's favourite. Soon after the Restoration, fourteen-year-old James was created Duke of Monmouth and married to a rich heiress. He was only twenty-one when Charles made him Captain-General of his armies. Perhaps it is not surprising, given this apparent favouritism, that when Charles II died Monmouth believed himself the true successor. With massive West Country support he proclaimed himself King and marched towards London. He got no further than Bridgwater in Somerset, where his army, mostly peasants and yeomen, was summarily defeated. Monmouth was taken, tried and executed.

the teenage Princess Anne, who was a stepdaughter of the Duchess of York.*

John first noticed Sarah Jennings dancing a saraband at a ball, and at their subsequent meeting he found her so bright and intelligent, so vital, that he was instantly smitten – a state of being that would prevail until the day he died. But Sarah was not a good catch for a young man making his way in the world by any means he could find. She had no dowry, no splendid connections, and though striking she lacked the outstanding beauty of her elder sister. Furthermore, at the age of sixteen this unusually independent young woman was in no particular hurry to settle down. John was in a torment, sending her flurries of letters expressing his devotion to her:

> I beg you will let me see you . . . which I am sure you ought to do if you care for my love, since every time I see you I still find new charms in you . . . when I am not with you the only joy I have is hearing from you . . . give me leave to do what I cannot help, which is to adore you as long as I live . . . I take joy in nothing but yourself . . . I love you with all my heart and soul.[6]

It was a stormy courtship, Sarah professing to doubt his protestations of love perhaps because initially John felt he could not afford a wife so early in his career. 'If it were true you would find out some way to make yourself happy – it is in your power,' Sarah retorted. 'I find all you say is only to amuse me and make me think you have a passion for me. As for seeing you I am resolved I never will, in private.'[7] When they quarrelled at an assembly ball he wrote telling her how, after she had pointedly walked away from him in full view of onlookers, 'I stood near quarter of an hour, I believe, without knowing what to do.' Instead of taking advantage of the sedan chair he had reserved, he had walked home in order to be able to stand under her window, 'to see the light in your chamber, but I saw

---

*Anne was the second daughter of the Duke of York (later James II) by his first wife, Anne Hyde. The elder daughter, Mary, was married to William, Duke of Orange.

none'; and since then he had twice gone to Whitehall to see her attend the Duchess of York, though Sarah had ordered him not to.

Believing that John could now make his choice from a number of heiresses and that when he married it should be for money, his parents were opposed to the relationship with Sarah and dangled other girls before him. He was not interested. Sarah teased him for eighteen months – then they were married, secretly and without fuss. At first the young couple were so short of money that they had to live with John's parents, but Sarah never regretted the marriage, for theirs was that enviable partnership, a genuine love match, though Sarah's fiery temperament ensured that their years together were never humdrum. John was a devoted husband and father, and the couple had seven children, five of whom survived infancy, but the major sorrow in their lives was the death of their only son at the age of seven. Their devotion to each other survived all problems, however, and, perhaps partly because of his frequent military absences, remained always passionate. Sarah on one occasion in middle age wrote to confide to a friend that on her husband's return from an overseas campaign he had 'pleasured' her before removing his boots.

When the Duke of York ascended the throne as King James II in 1685, he created John a baron – Baron Churchill of Sandridge – and sent him as Ambassador to the French court. It was probably at Versailles that John conceived a desire for a house as grand as that of Louis XIV. Despite his indebtedness to James II, Churchill could not accept the Roman Catholicism that James was attempting to impose on the kingdom, and he switched loyalties to support the invasion of the Protestant William of Orange.* Since Churchill took most of the army with him to participate in the 'Glorious Revolution', James (the last Stuart King) had little option but to flee the country. Parliament declared that he had abdicated by deserting his kingdom, and in 1689 invited his son-in-law William of Orange, along with William's wife the Princess Mary who was James's elder daughter, to take the throne as joint monarchs. Queen

---

*William was a grandson of Charles I.

Mary died a few years later, in December 1694, of smallpox, leaving William sole ruler of England, Scotland and Ireland.

King William III created John the Earl of Marlborough, made him a Privy Councillor, and later appointed him Commander-in-Chief of the armies in Flanders. But the new King never entirely trusted Churchill, and this is not surprising, for it was soon discovered that John was still in secret communication with the exiled King James. Churchill was disgraced and stripped of his court offices, and was lucky not to have fared worse. For some years he was out of the public eye and during this time he served as Governor of the Hudson's Bay Company, lending his name to the town of Churchill in Manitoba (which is still thriving).

In 1701 the Spanish King died without an heir. Louis XIV of France immediately put forward his grandson, the Duke of Anjou, as Spanish successor and made it clear that France would go to war to advance this claim. A coalition of European states and governments, concerned about French plans to encompass Spain, backed a rival claimant, the Austrian Archduke Charles.

Despite his misgivings about Churchill's loyalty, before King William's sudden and unexpected death (which occurred when his horse stumbled on a mole hill at Hampton Court),* the King had confided to his sister-in-law and heir to the throne, the Princess Anne, that there was only one man capable of stopping the French from taking over the whole of Europe, and that man was Marlborough. This advice was heeded, and when the War of Spanish Succession began Churchill was appointed to command the English and Dutch armies for an annual stipend of £10,000. He was a brilliant tactician, and in the first of ten successive campaigns he captured Kaiserworth and all the territory between the Rhine and Meuse Rivers. In recognition of this Queen Anne gratefully conferred a dukedom upon him and, as he was heading into his mid-fifties (then considered to be old), it seemed he had reached the

---

*King William was so unpopular that the mole was toasted all over London with the words: 'To the little gentleman in black velvet'.

summit of his career. Yet John Churchill's finest hour still lay ahead of him, and though he was an avaricious man and an undoubted time-server, his record as a commander has never been equalled – not even by the great Wellington.

Even without that direct commendation from the late King William, and had he not been the greatest military strategist in England, John Churchill – by then Duke of Marlborough –might well have been selected to lead the armies, for Queen Anne was completely in thrall to the dictatorial Duchess, Sarah Churchill. The two women had known each other since childhood, and Anne had always been fascinated by the older girl, who had advised her on how to act, how to dress and how to deal with court officials. By the time she ascended the throne, Queen Anne would never make a decision before consulting her best friend Sarah. There was only one way, besides conquest, that anyone could hope for social and financial advancement at court, and that was through royal patron-age. The entire court schemed endlessly and shamelessly for positions, pensions, sinecures and titles, but no one rivalled Sarah in the art of machination and self-promotion.

While they were still teenagers, Sarah had groomed Princess Anne to look to her for guidance in all things. And after Anne came to the throne Sarah collected a number of titles and honours for herself, to each of which was attached an annual stipend: Groom of the Stole, Mistress of the Robes, Keeper of the Privy Purse and Ranger of Windsor Park. More importantly, she was able to manip-ulate the Queen as she wished. It was Sarah, for example, who ensured that Churchill's good friend Earl Godolphin was made First Minister, the equivalent of today's Prime Minister. And it was rumoured that Sarah received a gift of £10,000 from the Duke of Kent when he was appointed to the position of Lord Chamberlain in 1704, through her influence.

So while her able husband led his armies and worked towards glory (he never lost a battle and he took every fortress he besieged), Sarah, from her start as a lowly handmaiden, had by her own efforts made herself a woman of immense power, able to influence state policy, and perhaps to change the course of history. To all intents and purposes, through Sarah, the Churchill 'set' ran the country for a while – one pamphleteer wrote that although Anne wore the crown, it was Sarah who reigned. It was said of her that 'No woman not of royal rank has ever held before, or is likely to hold again, such a position as was hers during the critical years of the eighteenth century, when the map of Europe and the constitution of England were in the making.'[8]

Churchill's sensational victory at Blenheim in 1704, where his cavalry broke the French line on the left bank of the Danube and made Europe safe again from French ambitions (until the rise of Napoleon almost a century later), was a cause for massive nationwide celebration.* Sarah made the most of it. Churchill became a national hero and in his absence honours were showered upon him. He was made a Knight of the Garter, a Prince of the Holy Roman Empire and Master General of the Ordnance, and he received other sinecures as well as a lifetime grant of £5000 a year from the Civil List. But the biggest reward of all was the gift of the 2700-acre royal estate at Woodstock in Oxfordshire† which generated £6000 a year. Furthermore, the Queen asked Parliament, on behalf of a grateful nation, to grant funds to build 'a castle' for the Duke at Woodstock, to commemorate his glorious victory. Parliament voted the huge sum of £250,000.

The Duke's ideas for this building were always more grandiose than were his wife's, especially when her power over the Queen began to wane. But Churchill – who spent all his summers

---

*Churchill sent a message, known as the Blenheim Dispatch, to advise Sarah of his victory. It was scribbled in pencil on the back of a tavern bill.

†Woodstock has many royal associations. Saxon, Norman and Plantagenet kings had held court at Woodstock Manor, where Henry II is supposed to have lived with his lover Rosamund Clifford ('the fair Rosamund', whose son by Henry was the great knight Sir William Longespée). It is said that the lovers hid in a maze when the Queen (Eleanor of Aquitaine) visited Woodstock, but she found her way to the centre of the maze by following a thread of embroidery silk that had attached itself to her husband's spur, and Rosamund ended her days in a nunnery. The Black Prince and King Richard the Lionheart were born at Woodstock, and Queen Elizabeth I, when a princess, was imprisoned there by her sister Queen Mary ('Bloody Mary'). Elizabeth scratched on the windowpane of her room the message: 'Much suspected by me, Nothing proved can be, Quoth Elizabeth, prisoner'. Chaucer and his son had both known the property well. Unfortunately, the building was much damaged by Parliamentarian soldiers during the Civil War.

campaigning in Europe – was happy to leave most things, including his advancement, to Sarah. For a while, she seems to have believed she *was* the Queen, and was witnessed not only correcting the Queen in public but shouting her down and dictating to her which jewels should be worn on state occasions. In time Sarah was supplanted by her young relative, Abigail Hill, whom Sarah had placed in a lowly position in the Queen's household. Abigail knew how to comfort the Queen and to listen to her; where Sarah stormed and threw tantrums, Abigail soothed. To Sarah's astonishment and impotent fury she saw her influence ebb away in favour of her inconspicuous relative. She was not so upset emotionally, for she had begun to find the dumpy Queen vapid, boring and lacking in taste, but the loss of her power base was a major shock to her.

Much to everyone's surprise – since it had been assumed that Sir Christopher Wren (whom Sarah chose to design their London home, Marlborough House, on the Mall) would oversee the prestigious project of what was then referred to as Blenheim Castle – the Duke chose the architect John Vanbrugh. Sarah always preferred Marlborough House, where her husband's successes were celebrated in the marbled fabric of the house but where it was her own taste that prevailed – 'my taste always having been to have things plain and clean from a piece of wainscot to a lady's face,' she wrote.[9] The Duke dreamed of 'an English Versailles', not so much as a family home but as a national monument to the glory of the victory at Blenheim, and he had been deeply impressed by Castle Howard, designed by Vanbrugh. So, in 1705, it was Vanbrugh he chose to build his dream house.

In fact the generous amount provided by Parliament proved inadequate for the grandiose building plans and the equally lavish interior. Sarah 'managed' the project herself, at constant loggerheads with Vanbrugh, so that everything took longer than necessary. When the money ran out, the fifteen hundred workmen went unpaid. Had it not been for Vanbrugh's efforts to protect the building over the winter (he moved in and lived there), it would have inevitably fallen into ruin. Meanwhile, Sarah had quarrelled irrevocably with the Queen and was stripped of all her court offices. Given that Sarah was unable to watch over the Duke's interests, his enemies at court had the best of it, and despite having led the British armies victoriously for a decade he was now accused of having prolonged the wars in Europe for his own interests. Realising that there was no longer a future for them under Queen Anne and a Parliament resolutely opposed to the Duke, the Marlboroughs decided to move to Europe, where they became close to the Electress of Hanover and her son George, who were next in line to the English throne after the childless Anne.* It was clearly a symbiotic relationship.

When, on 1 August 1714, Queen Anne died, the Marlboroughs returned immediately to England as part of the retinue of King George I, and were cheered heartily by crowds who recalled the Duke's great victories. The enemies of the Churchills were duly routed and everything went smoothly for the couple until, in the following year, their daughter Anne (her father's favourite child) died at the age of thirty-two from smallpox, and within days the Duke suffered a major stroke. He had scarcely recovered when he suffered a second stroke, which robbed him of speech. During these years the great building site at Woodstock was slowly evolving into a palace, while Sarah fought daily battles with the designer, builders and craftsmen, shaving a penny off here and sixpence off there, a hundred guineas anywhere she could, while always demanding the highest quality and being slow to pay the bills.

In the summer of 1719 the Marlboroughs finally moved into Blenheim, which had been furnished without regard to cost – the Duke, renowned for being parsimonious since he was a youth, never begrudged money spent on his pet project. Sarah hated the building, finding it unwieldy as a home: 'That wild unmerciful house,' she once wrote of it, 'which not even a vast number of feather beds and quilts, all good and sweet feathers, even for the servants, could tame.' She had penny-pinched, scolded and raged at everyone as she drove the project to completion. Her friend Alexander Pope, when he visited Blenheim, agreed with her assessment of it:

---

*Anne had eighteen pregnancies, but only one child, Prince William, lived more than a few months. He died at the age of eleven in 1700.

The chimneys are so well designed
They never smoke in any wind.
This gallery's contrived for walking,
The windows to retire and talk in;
The Council Chamber for debate,
And all the rest are rooms of state.

'Thanks, sir,' cried I, ''Tis very fine,
But where d'ye sleep, or where d'ye dine?
I find by all you have been telling
That 'tis a house, but not a dwelling.'

So unpleasant and dictatorial had Sarah become by now that even her two surviving daughters refused to visit Blenheim while their mother was in residence. When informed that the Duke was dying in June 1722 and they had little choice if they wished to see their father alive, they called to see him. But they paid their mother 'no more attention', Sarah wrote, 'than if I had been the nurse to snuff out the candles'. Incensed, she demanded that they leave, and they did so. The Duke died the following morning at dawn. Sarah said she knew the exact moment of his death, for she felt her soul 'tearing' from her body.

John Churchill, Duke of Marlborough, was buried in Westminster Abbey at his wife's expense, though she subsequently went carefully through the invoices, totalling £5000, and had the cost significantly reduced. Later, the Duke's body would be moved to Blenheim to lie with Sarah's; but meanwhile, given her personal fortune, she was regarded as a great catch and was courted by several dukes. To one, the Duke of Somerset, who had proposed marriage, Horace Walpole maliciously wrote that Sarah replied: 'If I were young and handsome as I was, instead of old and faded as I am, and [if] you could lay the empire of the world at my feet, you should [still] never share the heart and hand that once belonged to John, Duke of Marlborough.' In fact her reply was far more diplomatic. Having thanked him for the great compliment, she advised: 'I am resolved never to change my condition and . . . I would not marry the Emperor of the world though I were but thirty years old.'[10]

By special royal assent, because there was no living son the title was, unusually, allowed to pass through the female line to John and Sarah's eldest surviving daughter, forty-two-year-old Henrietta.* The new Duchess of Marlborough and her mother, now the Dowager Duchess, were estranged for many years, although Sarah was very upset when Henrietta predeceased her. In fact Sarah outlived all but one of her children, as well as a number of grandchildren including her favourite granddaughter, Lady Diana Spencer, for whom Sarah plotted a secret marriage to the Prince of Wales.† Henrietta's son William, Marquess of Blandford, had died before his mother, which was, Sarah decided, no bad thing, for he was a spendthrift.

The title then passed to Charles Spencer, the eldest son of Sarah's second daughter Anne.‡ Thus in 1733, when Charles Spencer became the 3rd Duke, the family surname became Spencer and remained so until the 5th Duke added the name Churchill, and the family became the Spencer Churchills. Some years earlier on the death of his elder brother, Charles had succeeded to Althorp, the family seat of the Spencers in Northamptonshire, but when he became Duke of Marlborough, in fulfilment of a family pact he handed Althorp to his younger brother John. It is John who is the ancestor of the present Spencer family.

Once Blenheim was finished (mostly from public money), Sarah carefully garnered her income and, like many self-made people, she hated the thought of her descendants squandering the fortune she and the Duke had made.§ Although she had spent lavishly on Blenheim to glorify her dead husband, she always made sure that

---

*In other words, she effectively replaced any 2nd *Duke* of Marlborough.
†Prince Frederick Louis, the hapless son of George II. Best known to history for the rhyme 'Poor Fred, who was alive, but now is dead . . .'.
‡Anne, who died in 1716, was the wife of Charles Spencer, 3rd Earl of Sunderland.
§When John Churchill, the 1st Duke, was ill towards the end of his life, even though he was then a rich man, he would walk rather than take a sedan chair in order to save a shilling. And it was said of him that he neglected to dot his i's and cross his t's in order to save on ink.

she got twenty shillings' value for every pound spent, whereas her grandsons were so profligate that they would pay a sedan chair-man with a golden guinea (the fare was usually less than a shilling) and refused to take change because they were too grand to be seen handling silver coins. Sarah was worth considerably more than a million pounds (£120 million today) in her final years, which made her one of the richest women in the country, and unusually her money was within her own control. She spent much of her long old age writing innumerable revisions to her complicated will, and in the last year of her life alone she rewrote it twenty-five times. As a result she left enough to sustain her descendants through several generations. She died at the age of eighty-five, having been a widow for over two decades. Of her two spendthrift noble grandsons, John ('Jack') at Althorp and Charles at Blenheim, she preferred Jack. So it was to Jack Spencer that she left most of the family property and treasures that were within her own control (not entailed). Consequently, Althorp was always the more richly endowed of the two properties.

Sarah's death on 18 October 1744 at Marlborough House in London was recorded by her contemporary, the writer Tobias Smollett: 'In October the old Duchess of Marlborough resigned her breath in the 85th year of her age, immensely rich and very little regretted either by her own family, or by the world in general.'

2

1850–74

Randolph and Jennie

It was almost inevitable that any dynastic line stemming from two such powerful personalities as John and Sarah Churchill would carry a strain of strong individualism. And so it proved, down through more than two centuries in the Spencer Churchill family, while six generations successfully established themselves in Britain's ruling elite. The marriages of all Churchill children, whether in the direct ducal line or not, were more often than not 'arranged' with the progeny of other leading aristocrats, for both dynastic and financial reasons.

By the mid-nineteenth century this family was, without question, among the top five arbiters of national policy, law, fashion and society. But beneath the splendour of this success lay the fact that instead of following the prudent example of the first Duke and Duchess, most of those who succeeded to the dukedom were profligate.

Henrietta, daughter of John and Sarah, succeeded as Duchess of Marlborough on the death of her father, but she died before her mother and had little time to make her mark. When Henrietta's nephew Charles Spencer succeeded her as 3rd Duke, to his grandmother's horror he had already managed to squander over half a million pounds in gambling and high living. He inherited from his father the Earl of Sunderland a wonderful collection of books, which by 1703 numbered twenty-four thousand volumes and was already described by some as the finest library in Europe.[1] So the 3rd Duke's contribution to posterity, and to Blenheim, was to create the Sunderland Library. He died, aged fifty-two, of dysentery while campaigning in Germany.

His son George became the 4th Duke at the age of eighteen. When he married the daughter of the Duke of Bedford, the new Duchess – who had been raised at Woburn Abbey and so was undaunted by the size of Blenheim – was the first member of the family to see Blenheim as a potential family home. Not only did she furnish it, regardless of expense, with the finest Chippendale pieces, but the Duke commissioned Capability Brown to re-landscape the park, a project that took ten years and included the creation of the great lake which forms what the family still regard as 'the finest view in Europe'. He also purchased the collection known as the Marlborough Gems, carved gemstones and other precious items, for the palace. By 1766 the Duke, who all his life had spent money without a thought for the morrow, was struggling to pay his bills. He was forced to reduce the household staff from eighty-seven to seventy-five, and to sell one of the grand Spencer houses, Langley Park. As he aged he became a recluse, and when he died in his sleep aged seventy-seven the estate passed to his eldest son, George.

It is true that George Spencer Churchill, the 5th Duke, who adopted Spencer Churchill as the family name, inherited mainly debts when he succeeded in 1817; but he had been a wild and spoilt young man, a Regency buck who had borrowed money recklessly upon his expectations and lived a riotous life in London, estranged from his parents. Rather than retrenching when he inherited, he thought up the novel solution of spending his way out of his debt problems.

In order to raise money for his favourite pastimes – which included enhancing the gardens and his beloved library – the 5th Duke began selling off family assets that were in fact entailed in perpetuity, and not his to sell. At one point this included the melting-down of valuable items of gold; the gold was then sold and the original objects replaced with cheap ormolu look-alikes in an attempt to fool the estate's trustees. But the trustees were not fooled, and took the Duke to Chancery Court where they obtained an injunction to prevent him 'selling, pawning or disposing' of any further items. The Duchess moved out to a grace-and-favour apartment at Hampton Court, while the Duke holed up in a few rooms in a remote corner of the palace and lived off game and fish from the estate while drinking his way through the vast cellars. He then scandalised society by selling fishing and shooting rights at Blenheim 'by the hour' to anyone who could afford the fees. By the time he died in 1840, the 5th Duke was penniless. Bailiffs moved into Sarah's wonderful state rooms and Blenheim survived him, but only just, in a desperate state of repair. Nine years later, when the Duke of Wellington visited Blenheim with his mistress Harriet Arbuthnot, she observed that the family had 'sadly gone to decay and are but a disgrace to the illustrious name of Churchill . . . the present Duke is overloaded with debt'.[2]

His eldest son, also named George, succeeded as the 6th Duke. He had not been a happy child and is chiefly remembered for having organised a pupil revolt at Eton and for marrying four times – if one includes a bogus marriage with a beautiful innocent teenager (an affair which reflected no honour on the family name). When he inherited a bankrupt Blenheim, the vast sum of £80,000 (£3.4 million today) was urgently needed for vital repairs, against an annual income of £10,000. His response was to raise mortgages, which – since the estate's trustees had little option but to concede – he did by changing the conditions of the trust. Had the 6th Duke been a prudent man he might have changed the fortunes of the family, but he was yet another feckless individual who lived to enjoy himself, and while he made some improvements at Blenheim (such as under-floor heating in the freezing corridors) and carried out necessary repairs, they were all financed on borrowings that he could hardly service. One cannot help reflecting that the family motto, coined during the Civil War, 'Faithful but Unfortunate', was not entirely apposite, for clearly it was not bad luck but bad management that caused most of the ill-fortune.

Present-day genealogists of the British peerage have speculated that dominant Spencer genes are responsible for many of the

Churchill family's misfortunes, since the Spencers were not only renowned for their brilliance and charisma, but also, as already noted, for their profligacy and their emotional problems.[3] According to one eminent scholar, most of the Dukes of Marlborough from the 3rd Duke to the 8th Duke suffered from a reported 'melancholia', which we would today call 'depression'.[4] So it was fortunate for Blenheim that the son who succeeded to the title in 1857 did not share his father's and grandfather's thriftlessness. The 7th Duke of Marlborough, thirty-five-year-old John Winston Spencer Churchill, and his Duchess, the former Frances ('Fanny') Anne Emily Vane, third daughter of the Marquess of Londonderry, were well matched – a stolid, high-minded, dutiful and deeply religious couple who wholly espoused the worthy Victorian ideals demonstrated by Queen Victoria and Prince Albert. Under the 7th Duke's hand, by his policy of spending only income, the estate's fortunes began to revive.

Duke John worried a good deal about 'the Catholic threat' (he had been educated by an anti-Catholic clergyman) and the lack of morals of the working classes, and entertained a constant fear that the masses might enjoy themselves inappropriately on the Sabbath. He was educated at Eton and graduated from Oriel College, Oxford, sat as MP for Woodstock – still a tied borough in those days – and worked hard during a rather unremarkable political career to strengthen the power of the established Church. His appointments were due to his inherited position rather than his ability, but he was a dutiful and hard worker; he became Lord Steward of Her Majesty's Household and Lord President of the Privy Council, and has been described by one historian as 'a complete full-blown Victorian Prig'.[5] Some of his letters to his children are a lesson in pomposity, although to be fair to him, he was remembered by his grandchildren as a kindly man.

His wife Duchess Fanny produced eleven children, eight of whom survived infancy, but the size of her brood did not trouble her unduly since they were raised and cared for by servants, and she rarely saw them except in Blenheim's chapel each morning when almost every inhabitant – family, friends and servants alike –

compulsorily attended a nine o'clock service. Duchess Fanny was slightly deaf, and perhaps as a consequence she was also shy in company. She made little attempt to conduct introductions at her dinners, and conversation with her was something of a purgatory for her dinner partners.

The mid-nineteenth century, when the 7th Duke presided over Blenheim, was a period of extraordinary prosperity in English history for the well connected. Prince Albert's sudden death in December 1861 at the early age of forty-two may have left his widow in permanent mourning and condemned her to years of seclusion, but the country was the axis of a vast Empire upon which the sun still blazed, and it was managed for the absent Queen by statesmen of vision. Agricultural income was at its zenith, and although income tax was just a few pence in the pound the rich bristled about this abomination until in 1874 Gladstone proposed its abolition. There was an explosion of technical achievement such as the country-wide railroad system,* and at sea sail gave way to steam. All this wealth and power was mainly vested in the great landowners, who lived in vast and stately country homes and enjoyed opulent town houses in London.

It was a way of life designed by, and for, the rich and titled; a world in which the working classes and the poor were set as far apart from the aristocracy as if they had been a different species. Just a few members of the successful meritocracy – brilliant writers, engineers, orators, architects, musicians, artists and so on – managed to scale the greasy pole that divided the classes, for the family histories and antecedents of the privileged were well chronicled, and without suitable provenance, acceptance into the upper ranks was rare. In the countryside and in the burgeoning cities, the huge mass of the working population described by contemporary writers such as Charles Dickens worked a ten-hour day, six and a half days a week (once a month they had a whole day off), in return for what was barely a living wage. There was no concept of leisure time for this

---

*Wellington famously opposed the railway infrastructure because it would affect foxhunting territories, called 'countries' (which it did), and because, he claimed, 'it will encourage the lower classes to travel unnecessarily'.

class; Sundays were spent church-going and praying, there were no annual holidays other than Christmas Day, and no pensions. Those in service with the great families often fared slightly better. The assistance of scores of willing servants was essential to run the great houses, gardens and stables smoothly, and to provide the lavish entertainments which were a necessary part of that society. Then, too, these country houses were not used continuously and were often empty for months, so work was lighter at those times. Meanwhile, those employed there were comparatively well housed and fed.

It was into the very top of this world of rank and privilege that the children of the 7th Duke were born – the sons, George in 1844 and Randolph in 1849, and the daughters: Cornelia in 1847, Rosamund in 1851, Fanny in 1853, Anne in 1854, Georgina in 1860 and Sarah in 1865.

The Duke and Duchess entertained regularly but within their income, and some of their entertainments showed financial prudence taken to what sounds like an extraordinary degree. Among the comments of visitors in the guest book was one from a Lord Chief Justice, who said that he was happy to share almost everything in life, *even his wife*, but felt that being served half a snipe for dinner was a step too far. The menu for a dinner and dance thrown for the Prince of Wales indicates that offerings were not always shaved quite so thinly, for there was lobster soufflé and stuffed quails and truffles in champagne, but the chronicler on this occasion also mentioned that at a dinner given that November the guests needed 'furs and hot water bottles' in order to eat in comfort in the chilly palace.[6]

The 7th Duke's heir, George, who was always known as Blandford* to his intimates, even after he succeeded to the title, was a disappointment to his parents. He was a rebellious, unhappy boy, and whatever maternal love Duchess Fanny could bring herself to demonstrate was all directed at her favourite child, the second son, Lord Randolph. Both boys were educated at Eton, where Latin and

---

*The eldest sons of the Dukes of Marlborough hold the title Marquess of Blandford, and the eldest sons of the Lords Blandford hold the title Earl of Sunderland.

Greek as well as maths and science were crammed into unwilling heads. Though children from comfortable and happy homes might well regard a boarding school in Victorian England as a form of imprisonment, the two Spencer Churchill boys found instead a freedom they had not realised existed.

Their rank and titles made it almost inevitable that they could get away with much: they ran wild, and recruited multiple 'fags' from among younger fellow pupils whom they treated as servants.* Eventually Blandford went too far and was expelled. Randolph, rebellious of rules and arrogant to the point of imperiousness,[7] could, however, exert extraordinary charm when he wished, and it was this, plus frenzied intervention by the Duke, that saved him from the same fate. He went on to Merton College, Oxford, where he continued his career of rule-breaking: windows were meant to be broken, sobriety was a joke, and he was fined for such misdemeanours. Nevertheless, the university exerted some good influence on Randolph and his tutor stated that he was 'much impressed with his . . . ability and mental alertness'. He read for honours in jurisprudence and modern history, which led to a deep lifelong interest in British history; and he cannot have been entirely feckless, for in the Michaelmas Term of 1870 he obtained a good degree, only narrowly missing out on a First. He also developed a love of the historian Edward Gibbon, and memorised long passages of text from *The Decline and Fall* which he could recite at will.

In 1869 at the age of twenty-five, Blandford – under pressure to marry suitably and produce an heir – dutifully allowed himself to believe that he had fallen in love with Albertha ('Berthe'), a daughter of the Duke of Abercorn.† Although their subsequent marriage, happily accepted by all the parents, quickly produced an heir, Charles Richard (universally known as 'Sunny' because of his title Earl of Sunderland), the mild affection – for that is more descriptive

---

*The 'fagging' system still exists in some public schools.
†Albertha Frances Ann, Marchioness of Blandford, was the sixth daughter of the Duke of Abercorn and his wife Louisa, daughter of the Duke of Bedford. One of fourteen children (seven boys and seven girls), all of whom married into the peerage, Berthe was part of an intricate web of aristocratic families.

of Blandford's feelings for Berthe – was short-lived and the relationship became not merely loveless but one of intense irritation on the part of the young husband. Poor Berthe, who did not know how to cope with Blandford's animosity, bumbled unhappily about, playing endless childish and tiresome practical jokes on visitors which took the form of cutting pieces of soap into lifelike wedges and introducing them on to the cheeseboard at dinner parties, balancing pots of ink on the tops of guest-room doors, as well as making apple-pie beds, to name but a few. She is said to have been beautiful as a young woman, perhaps to explain Blandford's initial attraction to her, but photographs show this to be exaggeration, and 'handsome' is probably the most generous description for her. She was kind-hearted but had received almost no education, and her nickname 'Goosie' probably says it all. In any case Blandford very soon tired of her and began seeking his sexual comforts elsewhere, to the shock and dismay of his parents.

By the time Randolph reached twenty-four years old, though not under the same pressures as Blandford, he was nevertheless expected to find a suitable wife from within the peerage. Because of his rank he could expect to marry someone with sufficient money to keep them both in the manner in which, as the son of a duke, he had been raised, and not to be a financial burden on his father. He had devoted his life so far to the pleasures of hunting his own pack of harriers, reading 'omnivorously' (his son would later write), and the delights of society and London's all-male clubland. He was welcome in most company for his intelligent conversation, and he moved easily within the exclusive Prince of Wales circle known as 'the Marlborough House set'. It was in this context that in 1873 Randolph joined the annual pilgrimage of English 'society' to Cowes.

For fifty weeks each year the small town of Cowes on the Isle of Wight is a sleepy backwater on the shore of the stretch of water called the Solent, which separates the island from the south coast of England. The Solent has four tides a day with highly complex tidal patterns, huge sandbanks which dry out sufficiently to allow the odd short cricket match to be played on them, and channels deep enough to accommodate the world's largest liners making for the port of Southampton. These tidal anomalies provide some of the best yacht racing in the world, and for a brief period, in early August each year, the famous Cowes Regatta propels the town and its harbour into international importance. The event is almost two hundred years old in its present form, and was already well entrenched by the middle of the nineteenth century when Albert, Prince of Wales, a keen yachtsman, became a regular visitor and competitor.

It was then that the lavish balls, parties and concerts, still held today during the Regatta, became an intrinsic element of the English social Season,* attracting yachtsmen, the cream of society and the socially ambitious. Yacht clubs burgeoned, but only one really counted: membership of the Royal Yacht Squadron, housed in an ancient fort built by Henry VIII at the mouth of the River Medina as part of the Solent defence system, alone conveyed the social cachet that is beyond purchase. With typical Victorian confidence, numerous large hotels as well as villas and boarding houses sprang up to accommodate the Cowes Week visitors; then as now, these commanded almost enough income during the Regatta to cover their running costs for the entire year.

In 1873, an American family called Jerome rented Villa Rosetta for the hot summer months. They had stayed there in the previous two years and enjoyed its location on the seafront, a pleasant half-mile walk from the town. There was no esplanade then and the lawns of Villa Rosetta ran down to the footpath skirting the beach, where the occupants could sit and watch the yachts racing. Mr Leonard Jerome, whose Huguenot ancestors had taken shelter on the Isle of Wight before emigrating to America in 1710, was a clever entrepreneur. Brought up on a family farm in Syracuse, Upper New York

---

*The 'Season' lasts from April to August, after which the action moves to Scotland for grouse shooting, and thence to houses in the shires for foxhunting during the winter. Many events of the Edwardian Season survive, including the Chelsea Flower Show, the Rose Ball, Derby Day, Trooping the Colour, tennis at Wimbledon, polo at Windsor, the Henley Regatta, croquet at Hurlingham and Royal Ascot.

State, Leonard had attended Princeton before going into law. He was twenty-seven when he bought the local newspaper, the *Daily American*, with one of his brothers. In 1849 he married Clarissa Hall, an orphaned heiress whose elder sister was already married to Leonard's brother Lawrence.* Clarissa – always called Clara – was darkly good-looking, and the couple moved to New York where their first child, Clarita, was born. Here Jerome rapidly made and lost the first of two fortunes on the stock exchange where he was known by journalists as 'the King of Wall Street'.

In New York, fashionable society was run by 'the Patriarchs', the old Knickerbocker† families who occupied the most fashionable areas of Manhattan. They were headed by a formidable grande dame, Mrs William Backhouse Astor (known as *the* Mrs Astor). So proud was Mrs Astor of her ancestry that she made it her life's work to ensure that no 'outsiders' were admitted to the select circles of the old families. Fabulously rich (she had been fortunate – or designing – enough to marry a hugely successful man who indulged her whims), she was the undoubted queen bee of Society. Her ballroom held four hundred people – all those who 'mattered', in fact. If you were not listed among these four hundred you were 'new money', an *arriviste*. Any Patriarch hostess, sympathising with someone newly arrived in New York, no matter how cultured or rich, was castigated if she dared to invite a man or woman outside the four hundred to a function. Naturally, every woman wanted to be on Mrs Astor's list, including Clara Jerome, who unfortunately was not considered acceptable. Imagine if this clique, to whom Clara so badly wished to belong, had discovered she had Native American blood.‡ This was a sufficiently good reason for Clara to keep her

---

*Lawrence's son William became District Attorney of New York and stood unsuccessfully for Governor in 1906. Had he won, there was a good chance he would have been nominated by the Democrats for President in 1912 rather than Woodrow Wilson.

†A reference to the voluminous knee-length garments worn by the Dutch – the first settlers in the area. Many of those in the top echelon of mid-nineteenth-century New York traced their ancestry back to these Dutch settlers, so it was a term of pride.

‡Clara's mother Clarissa Wilcox was the granddaughter of one Eleazor Smith of Dartmouth, Massachusetts, and his wife Meribah, who was believed by their grandchildren to have been an Iroquois Indian. Clarissa died in childbirth when Clara was two years old.

antecedents secret, only confiding the information to her daughters when they were adults.*

Leonard Jerome was not daunted by Mrs Astor's snubs, though he was undoubtedly annoyed when it caused his Clara such distress. Supremely confident and energetic, he was happy to lead his own set, and if necessary to outdo the Knickerbockers. He built great new houses at the most prestigious addresses, the latest being in ultra-smart Madison Square on the corner of 26th Street, cheek by jowl with the Knickerbocker houses. A few doors away he built a six-hundred-seat theatre for private operatic productions, and his three-storeyed marble-faced stables, erected even before the house was completed and said to be the finest in the world, were stocked with the best bloodstock and the latest design in carriages. When he entertained, newspaper reports revealed that huge indoor fountains cascaded with champagne or eau-de-cologne amidst banks of scented hothouse flowers, and every woman guest found a gold bracelet with a jewelled pendant concealed in her napkin. He was a founder of the American Jockey Club, built Jerome Park – one of the most important racecourses in the United States, near what is now the Bronx – and owned Kentucky, arguably the greatest racehorse of his day. An expert horseman, Jerome rode mettlesome horses with ease and drove a four-in-hand, always with his trademark nosegay of flowers in his lapel or attached to the handle of his whip.

Apart from horses Leonard Jerome loved the opera, and, at a more personal level, opera divas, for he was an inveterate womaniser. Among the many ladies to be seen on his arm were the singers Jenny Lind (called 'the Swedish Nightingale', and an international sensation), Adelina Patti, who was only seventeen when she met Jerome, and Fanny Ronalds (a long-term mistress),† all of whom gave solo performances to invited audiences in Jerome's private

---

*From recent research into Clara's family tree, there seems to be no existing proof either way, but certainly Jennie, her children and her sisters and their children firmly believed that Clara was part American Indian.

†When Clara and Fanny Ronalds met at a party and everyone present held a collective breath as the wife was introduced to the mistress, Clara calmly took Fanny's offered hand, and said: 'I don't blame you. I know how irresistible he is.'

theatre, as did Minnie Hauk (born soon after Jenny Lind's visit to New York, which may or may not be significant), who was probably Jerome's illegitimate child. Clara, who loved Minnie and helped to educate her, described her as 'so like Jenny, but less good-looking'. Jerome's other serious passion was sailing, and he owned a succession of fast racing yachts which he had built to his own extravagant designs, rivalling even William Astor's vessels.

In 1851 Jerome was appointed American Consul at Trieste, then part of the Austro-Hungarian Empire, and it was while her husband occupied this post, from April 1852 until November 1853, that Clara developed an infatuation with court life and the glamour of European royalty and aristocracy. Here she was accepted as an equal in the very top levels of society, even by royalty. A change of government in the United States meant that Jerome was recalled along with all political appointees, and the family returned to the USA, travelling via Paris. Clara, who was seven months into a pregnancy, wanted to stay there and even make her home in Europe, but Jerome insisted they return to New York where his financial affairs – which had been in the care of a brother – were in a poor way. He promised, however, to bring his wife back to Paris. The couple's second daughter, Jennie (named after Jenny Lind), was born on 9 January 1854 in New York.* By 1858 Jerome had fully restored his fortunes and bought a substantial shareholding (25 per cent) in the *New York Times*.

In 1860 during the visit of the nineteen-year-old Prince of Wales, the Jeromes – one of the few New York families with a ballroom large enough to accommodate three hundred people – hosted a ball in his honour. Even Mrs Astor could not circumvent this, and Clara had no difficulty in getting Knickerbocker matrons to accept her invitations. It was a triumph for her. Jennie was six at the time, and

---

*Owing to Jennie's habit of deducting years from her age as she grew older, there has been some doubt in biographies as to her true age. There are two letters written when she was younger which give her correct age – one to her husband dated 8 January 1883, and one to her mother on 9 January 1888. Added to this there is a christening mug in the family engraved with the words: 'Jennie Jerome 1854'. Jennie's statement in her memoir (*Reminiscences of Lady Randolph Churchill*) that she spent her early childhood in Trieste and spoke mainly Italian until the age of six, cannot be true.

not allowed to meet the man who would become one of her great-est friends in later life.

Although her social life improved in New York, Clara had never forgotten her dream of returning to Paris to live. She visited it for a large part of each year and her third daughter Leonie was born there,* but it was 1867 before Clara decided that although she loved her husband, she could handle his serial love affairs with more dig-nity if she lived permanently in Europe. Announcing that she needed to consult French doctors, she and her daughters moved to Paris. She took an apartment at 71 Boulevard Malesherbes in the exclusive eighth arrondissement, within easy walking distance of the Champs-Élysées, the Jardin des Tuileries, the shops in Boulevard Haussmann and the foremost museums and art galleries. Jerome visited them almost at once, and would continue to do so several times a year.

The Paris of the 1860s was the city of the Impressionists; the only traffic in its wide, tree-lined boulevards was horse-drawn, so there was no noise or petrol fumes to detract from the lovely parks and architecture. Each spring when the warm sunshine turned the chestnut-flower buds into candles, visitors flocked to the city to walk beneath the scented blossom in the Champs-Élysées and the Bois de Boulogne. At night the two-mile-long Rue de Rivoli lead-ing to the Place de la Concorde was illuminated by lamps hanging in every arch of the famous arcades, creating a 'river of light' known as *le cordon de lumière*, giving the impression that the city never slept. For Clara one of the greatest pleasures was shopping in the Rue de la Paix, where the leading fashion houses, the great names such as Worth and Doucet, had their shops, hidden behind modest exteri-ors. 'Inside,' one visitor wrote, 'the array of lovely dresses, expensive furs and diaphanous lingerie fairly took one's breath away.'[8]

Clara was not the only socially aspiring American matron in Paris. There were two other American women in precisely the same predicament. Rich and equally snubbed by New York society, Ellen

---

*Another daughter, Camille, born between Jennie and Leonie, died of a fever in Newport when she was seven years old.

Yznaga and, later, Marietta Stevens had moved to Paris for similar reasons. Each had beautiful daughters who were educated to a high level; each was ambitious for her daughters' prospects, and each had a score to settle with Mrs Astor. All would succeed spectacularly.*

Clara's girls adored Paris and all three spoke faultless French and fluent German. Clara held a successful salon, and as an ultra-rich American she and her girls were absorbed without difficulty into the life of the court of the Emperor Napoleon III and Empress Eugénie, experiencing little social snobbery. Clara began to write her surname 'Jérôme', Clarita made her debut into adult society at a glittering ball at the Tuileries before the Emperor and Empress, and Jennie became 'Mademoiselle Jeannette'.

The major Wall Street crash of Black Friday 1868 forced Jerome to return hastily to New York, where he sold the Madison Square house and retreated from other investments. This crash hardly affected Clara and her daughters because before she left for Paris Jerome had made her a substantial financial settlement, giving her independence from his investments; the women probably did not even know there was any difficulty, for they lived as they had always lived – as though money did not exist. Nor had Jerome discouraged them: he was a man who lived life to the full, and when he had money he spent it just as fast as any Spencer Churchill heir would have done. He *expected* his wife and daughters to dress in gowns from the top Paris couturiers.

The girls had been educated in the same manner as the daughters of Clara's aristocratic friends. They had private tutors who specialised in languages and music; they rode in the Bois, learned to dance and ice-skate with precision, to play the piano under the tutorship of a master pianist (Stephen Heller, a friend of Chopin),† and regularly attended matinées at the opera. In 1871, during the

---

*One of Ellen's daughters, Consuelo Yznaga, would marry Lord Mandeville, later Duke of Manchester, and Marietta's daughter Minnie Stevens would marry a grandson of the Marquess of Anglesey who was on first-name terms with the Prince of Wales. How the mothers must have gloated when the *New York Times* duly carried extensive articles about these prestigious marriages.
†He once told Jennie she had the ability to attain concert standard if she continued to work hard. 'But,' he added with a sigh, 'you won't!'

Franco-Prussian War, when Paris was besieged by Prussian troops, Clara and her girls fled to England. Jerome met them and set them up in London's Brown's Hotel for the winter, but for the summer months he rented the seaside house Villa Rosetta in Cowes. Here, Jerome could race aboard a friend's yacht, the *Dauntless*, which had crossed the Atlantic. Soon after Jerome departed for New York* aboard the *Dauntless* it was deemed safe for Clara and the girls to return to Paris. But the great city had not recovered from the uprising and everything was changed for the worse: the Emperor had been deposed, there was no court, and life seemed very dull. The following year Clara and the girls again travelled to the Isle of Wight for the summer, where the delights of Cowes Week with its racing and the cream of English society offered them a full social life. Furthermore, Clara's friend the former Empress Eugénie was also spending the summer there. So, it seemed quite natural that the family would return to Villa Rosetta for the third year in a row.

It was an unusually brilliant Cowes Week in 1873. Apart from the Prince and Princess of Wales, who never missed Cowes because the Prince was an avid yachtsman, Queen Victoria's second son Alfred, Duke of Edinburgh, and his new bride the Grand Duchess Marie, daughter of the Tsar of Russia, also attended. The bride's brother, the Tsarevich (later the ill-fated Tsar Alexander III), who had visited England for the wedding, was invited to stay with the Queen for several weeks at Osborne House in East Cowes with his wife Maria Feodorovna. And as Maria Feodorovna was the sister of Alexandra, the Princess of Wales (later Queen Alexandra), it was very much a family gathering.

By Jerome family standards Villa Rosetta was tiny. After their mansion in New York and a palatial apartment in Paris, the hall and stairs of the villa were almost impossibly narrow to accommodate the crinoline dresses required for formal occasions in the early 1870s. But the reception rooms were of a reasonable size, and the women

---

*Where he found that, along with others such as John Jacob Astor III, he had been the victim of embezzlement on a grand scale. As a result he had to sell everything for what he could get in order to survive, and his second fortune all but disappeared; what he most minded losing was his major shareholding in the *New York Times*.

were prepared to play at living in a sweet little seaside cottage. For large parties Mrs Jerome cleverly added a marquee to the side of the house to extend its floor space, accessed through the french doors of the dining room.

That year, 1873, was also a special one for the Jeromes' second daughter Jennie (now known as Jeannette), because it was her first year 'out' in Society. Of course, she had not been able to experience the joys of a Paris season at the imperial court, as Clarita had done a few years earlier, but it was still exciting. The two girls were formally presented to the Prince and Princess of Wales at a ball at the Royal Yacht Squadron, after which Jennie was officially regarded as an adult and allowed to attend, in the company of Clarita, all the entertainments that Cowes Week had to offer; but both girls were always under the careful chaperonage of their mother. Jennie was raven-haired and dark-eyed, while Clarita – who favoured her father – was fair with blue eyes. The two exceptionally beautiful young women offered a remarkable contrast in colouring, and, as a consequence of their mother's strict insistence that they practise the piano daily, they played duets to concert-hall standard. Not for them the glazed expressions of fellow guests when a young lady, asked if she would like to play something, would inevitably reply coyly: 'Well, I do *happen* to have brought my music with me.' When the Jerome sisters sat down to play the other guests tended to sit up and listen, and even demand an encore.

The girls were so busy enjoying themselves that they forgot to write to their father, who unbeknown to them, though not ruined, was daily battling against financial troubles in New York while still regularly sending cheques to Clara. On 7 August he wrote a plaintive note to remind them that two weeks had elapsed since he had had a letter from them:

I have no doubt that you will see many nice people and will have Cowes all to yourselves as far as Americans are concerned . . . Do you make it lively and have you secured the Villa Rosetta for another year? etc. I rather like the idea of Cowes next summer and a yacht. Don't forget, while sitting under your own vine and eating up your own fig tree, that I am awfully disappointed if I don't get my weekly letters.[9]

The ball that everyone wanted to attend at Cowes that year was held on Tuesday 12 August. Usually the Cowes Week balls were, and still are, organised by and at the various yacht clubs. But this ball, held in honour of the Tsarevich and his wife, took place on board the naval vessel HMS *Ariadne* at the personal request of the Prince and Princess of Wales. The *Ariadne* was acting as guard ship to the Regatta and to the royal yacht *Victoria and Albert*. Guests were ferried out to the ship from the Royal Squadron jetty in fleets of launches, and around the *Ariadne*'s deck the national flags of England and Russia were draped. Unusually, it was a late-afternoon function,* from 3.30 to 7.30 p.m., but it was warm and dry – outdoor balls were always a worry for organisers – so the canvas canopy was not required.

That Clara had made a sufficient impression on Society for her daughters to be invited was, in itself, something of a coup, for invitations to royal occasions were limited, and even very rich Americans were regarded with a certain amount of suspicion – after all, what was known about them? Of course, there had been the ball for the young Prince at the Jeromes' home in Madison Square in 1860, and Clara assumed the manner of an exiled French aristocrat who had every right to be included in the most refined society. Perhaps the former Empress Eugénie had introduced her? The coveted gilt-edged invitation read: 'To meet Their Royal Highnesses the Prince and Princess of Wales and Their Imperial Highnesses the Grand Duke Cesarevitch and the Grand Duchess Cesarevitch' (later Tsar Alexander III and the Empress Maria Feodorovna).† No one knew it, but the scene was set for a momentous meeting.

Dressed in a cloud of white tulle adorned with fresh flowers,

---

*This information came as a surprise to the author, since previous biographies describe this ball as occurring under the stars with the moon shining on the sea and a deck lit by lanterns – an impossible scenario, given the time and date.

†Under the printed words 'To meet' Jennie wrote in bold handwriting: 'Randolph'. Randolph also kept his invitation to the ball. After his death it was found among his most treasured effects.

Jennie was determined to dance every dance. According to her, she was dancing a quadrille – a 'set' dance – when she caught the eye of Lord Randolph Spencer Churchill. As he watched her dancing, Randolph evidently experienced a *coup de foudre* not unlike that experienced by his illustrious ancestor two hundred years earlier, when John Churchill had spotted Sarah dancing a saraband at court, and he acted with similar alacrity. No doors were closed to the son of a duke; Randolph immediately engineered an introduction to the delectable American debutante. He secured the next dance too, but – because he was a poor dancer (the spins of the Viennese waltz apparently gave him vertigo) – after an initial circuit of the deck the couple 'sat out' and chatted, though always in full view of the chaperones, while the famous Royal Marines Band provided the background music. The instant attraction was mutual.

Jennie was nineteen – older than many English debutantes experiencing their first Season – and her looks were unusual. Her face was framed by her dark, almost black hair and she had black arched brows over large, lambent brown eyes; her full red lips required no colouring and her high cheekbones made her instantly appear more exotic than the fair complexion and blue eyes of many English girls. Clara was secretly proud of her Native American inheritance from which Jennie's looks derived, but knew that it would not go down well in either American or British society. When she told her daughters of their heritage because 'it might help you to understand yourselves', she also cautioned them never to speak of it to others, as it was 'not chic'.*[10]

Both Clarita and Jennie were always beautifully dressed, usually in creations by Monsieur Worth, Clara's favourite fashion house in Paris; and Jennie was slender, with the much admired hourglass figure and 'wasp' waist that could usually be obtained only by strict lacing. In Jennie's case, though, not much lacing was required. On her small capable hands with their long fingers she wore the de

---

*In recent books about Jennie this Iroquois strain has been queried, but Anita Leslie, granddaughter of Jennie's sister Leonie, was given this information by her mother and it is still believed within the family.

rigueur tight white kid gloves that had to be eased on like a second skin, stretching each finger of the gloves in succession, until when in place they fitted so perfectly that the outline of the fingernails was evident. Once worn and stretched these costly and exquisite items were ruthlessly discarded, as they never looked so good on any subsequent wearing.* Jennie habitually used a French *parfum* and always moved in an aura of mild fragrance. But looks and dress aside, what chiefly made her stand out was her vivacity. She had an energy that gave her an unusual radiance, a characteristic that she possessed until her death and which was much commented upon. Furthermore, she was not only naturally intelligent but had received a wider education than that afforded to the average upper-class English girl.

Randolph was five years older than Jennie; tall, boyishly slim and slightly pop-eyed (although this feature was not so pronounced then as it would later become), he wore the drooping moustache which was the fashion of the day (later he would wear it waxed and twirled) and he dressed beautifully. His manner was casually confident – that of an aristocrat at home among his own kind, but quietly reserved with those outside this tight milieu. He was clearly mesmerised by the vibrant and beautiful American girl, but what immediately attracted Jennie to him was his conversation. She was spellbound as soon as he began to speak, and just as quickly he realised that Jennie was not just a fashion-plate but was well educated, intelligent and not afraid to voice a well considered opinion. Randolph, regarded as one of the most eligible bachelors of the day, was never short of dance partners, but there is no evidence to suggest that before meeting Jennie he had ever been seriously involved with any woman. Enough was said within minutes of their first meeting to intrigue each of them, and at some point, to judge from later correspondence, they must have discussed Randolph's hopes for his future, to which Jennie had responded with enthusiasm.

The couple would not have been allowed to spend the entire ball

---

*The small size of Jennie's hands could be judged from some of her gloves, which were on display in 2007 at the American Museum near Bath in the exhibition *The Dollar Princesses*.

together. Nor would they have expected to do so. After the time taken for a set of country dances, and perhaps a discreet waltz – half an hour at most – Mrs Jerome would have politely broken up the tête-a-tête and whisked Jennie away to dance or talk with someone else. To be the object of too marked an interest by an unattached gentleman was considered unbecoming to a girl; it compromised her and marked her as 'fast'. The couple would have been able to manage another short chat later, over an ice, perhaps, or a glass of champagne, but otherwise they would have had to be content with looking out for each other on the crowded deck.

Before the ball ended, at Jennie's strong urging, Clara was persuaded to invite Randolph and his companion Colonel Edgecombe* to join them after the ball for a late dinner at Villa Rosetta.† Small the seaside villa may have been, but Mrs Jerome kept house in style, and she had brought over her own chef from Paris so that her dinner parties were not only smart but exceptionally well catered. Jennie recalled how that evening she and Clarita played duets for their guests and how they had all 'chatted merrily'. We know that Randolph was already badly smitten, for during dinner, only a few hours after he first clapped eyes on her and while watching the sisters play a duet, he told Colonel Edgecombe of his intention to make 'the dark one' his wife. And Jennie evidently knew very well what was happening, for when she was undressing that night she confided in her sister that she thought Randolph would propose to her. Clarita hooted derisorily: Jennie had never yet shown any particular interest in a man, Clarita did not consider Randolph 'dashing' enough, and they had only just met.

The next day (a Wednesday) the pair contrived to meet while Jennie was taking her morning walk with her sister and Randolph exercised his little pug dog, 'Puggles', which had travelled with him to Cowes. Reporting this supposedly accidental meeting, Jennie prevailed upon her mother to invite her new friend to dinner again

---

*In his book *My Early Life* Sir Winston Churchill spells this name 'Edgecumbe'.
†Now called Rosetta Cottage, the villa is owned by the National Trust and is used as a holiday rental.

the following evening, and, because of the long English summer evenings when it is daylight until 10 p.m., they were later allowed to walk together in the garden. It was only their third meeting, and the first time they were alone together without a chaperone. Randolph took full advantage of this unexpected bonus and proposed to Jennie, whom he was still addressing as 'Miss Jeannette'. It was a whirlwind that had each of them in thrall and she accepted him without a moment's hesitation.

Randolph was due to leave on the following day (Friday), but he deliberately missed the ferry so that he was effectively marooned on the island and had no alternative but to stay over until Monday morning. This enabled him to see Jennie and her family in church on Sunday morning. Again he was invited to dine at Villa Rosetta, although Clara told her daughter somewhat grimly: 'That young man has been here rather a lot.' When he finally sailed from the island aboard the 7 a.m. ferry on Monday morning, Randolph spent the entire eighty-minute voyage writing to 'Dearest Jeannette' and promising to break their news to his parents. Jennie, meanwhile, told her mother and wrote to her father. Perhaps the dewy-eyed couple anticipated no obstacles, but they soon realised what they were up against when they encountered strong opposition from both sets of parents.

Mrs Jerome, first to hear the news, told her daughter briskly that their betrothal was all nonsense, over-hasty and not properly thought out. Without doubt, marriage to the son of a duke conferred social cachet, but he was only a younger son, after all: the heir had a healthy son; and Mrs Jerome valued her lovely and talented daughters highly. She immediately wrote to her husband asking him to return to England by the next available ship. Probably by the same mail, Mr Jerome received a letter from Jennie explaining that she had become engaged, but omitting the name of her fiancé. He replied at once, saying that he hoped that it would work out for her:

> I always thought that if you ever did fall in love it would be a very dangerous affair. You were never born to love lightly. It must be way down or nothing . . . Not so Clara [Clarita]; happily not so. Such

natures [as yours] if they happen to secure the right one are very happy but if disappointed they suffer untold misery. You give no idea of who it is . . . Do you apprehend any serious opposition from me supposing it comes to that? Hardly. Yet you know my views. I have great confidence in you and still greater in your mother and anyone you would accept and your mother approves I could not object to. Provided always he is not a Frenchman or any of those continental cusses.[11]

After days of begging her mother to be allowed to correspond with Randolph, Jennie was given permission to write to him just once. She wrote lovingly, saying that she had told her mother and, even though she liked him a great deal, she did not agree to the engagement, but Jennie was sure they would win her over in the end.

Randolph found his happy news was not well received at Blenheim, either. His mother Frances, Duchess of Marlborough, the proud and virtuous daughter of the Marquess of Londonderry, could not conceive of anything so low as her son marrying an American, a foreigner whose antecedents were unknown to English society. Apart from Blandford, whose marriage was now something of a farce, Randolph was her only surviving son,* and not only was he her favourite child but she wanted him to marry well, by which she meant to an English heiress from within the ranks of the peerage. The Duke had gone away for a few days, so Randolph wrote him an extremely long letter, hoping to elicit a more favourable reception from his father. He enclosed a photograph of Jennie and stressed that he loved her 'better than life itself'.[12] He apologised for not telling his father in advance, but explained that the night before he left Cowes, his feeling of sadness at their parting was more than he could bear, and he had confessed his love for her and proposed marriage. He had not spoken to Jennie's mother, he wrote, but Jennie had done so, and she had since written him a note to say that her mother would not hear of the engagement, which he found difficult to understand.

---

*Three other sons, Frederick, Charles and Augustus, had all died in childhood.

The Duke could not understand it, either – after all, he must have reasoned, what mother would not look kindly on an offer of marriage from the son of a duke? But that did not mean he approved of the match himself. Far from it.* He made a few inquiries in London from which he learned that Leonard Jerome was considered something of a financial buccaneer in New York, and that he had recently lost almost everything in a stock market venture, only managing to hold on to some properties by heavily mortgaging them. The Duke immediately wired Washington, requesting a full report on Jerome from the British Ambassador there, and wrote to Randolph telling his son that he was acting without wisdom, that his judgement was completely paralysed by his emotions, and his feelings uncontrolled – 'Never was there such an illustration of the adage "love is blind", for you seem blind to all consequences in order that you may pursue your passion.'[13] As for Leonard Jerome, the Duke wrote, '[he] seems to be a sporting, and I should think vulgar kind of man . . . I hear he drives about 6 and 8 horses [*sic*] in N.Y. (one may take this as an indication of what the man is) . . . it is evident he is of the class of speculators.'[14] In the circumstances the Duke was, understandably, not inclined to give his blessing.

Leonard Jerome had by this time received a long letter from Jennie, explaining her engagement and revealing the identity of her fiancé, and he responded to his wife by cable that he was delighted with the proposed match and would arrange to endow Jennie with £2000 a year. He then replied to his daughter: 'Best of all you think, and I believe, he loves you. He must. You are no heiress and it must have taken heaps of love to overcome an Englishman's prejudice . . . I like it in every way.'[15] But when Randolph wrote telling Jennie of his father's pejorative comments about Jerome, Jennie was deeply offended and soon afterwards Leonard Jerome, too, withdrew his consent.

---

*The Duke's reaction mirrored exactly that of Anthony Trollope's fictional character in the *Palliser* series in *The Duke's Children*, written in 1879, when the Duke of Omnium's son and heir Silverbridge fell in love with the rich daughter of visiting Americans. In this case there is no doubt that art was imitating life, for it all fell out in the novel exactly as it did in real life. Trollope even used some of the same phrases as the real-life protagonists, and his best-selling novel was published only five years after Randolph and Jennie's courtship.

Even Randolph's siblings were against the match. The sisters –
ranging in age from twenty-six-year-old Cornelia, who was married
with a child, to the youngest girls Georgina aged thirteen and Sarah
aged eight, who were both still in the schoolroom – not unnaturally
followed their mother's line. Blandford wrote at great length deplor-
ing his brother's news: 'With a rashness that even I was never
capable of, you run *tête basse* [head first] into the wildest superlative of conceivable folly . . . you really only want to marry because
you are in love with an idea . . . You are mad, simply mad.'[16] It was
a pure fantasy, Blandford went on, all based 'on a six-day seaside
holiday romance'. He also enclosed some bad poetry that he had
written about it, which warned Randolph of perambulators, baby
food and a whining wife, all the ills that he forecast would
inevitably follow the proposed marriage. His ode ended with the
words:

> So go you forth on your appointed way
> And treat my poor advice with slight.
> Still will I for a golden future pray,
> 'May I be wrong' and 'You be right!'[17]

With everyone ranged against them, and even Jennie now recon-
sidering her feelings in the light of the criticism of her beloved
father, Randolph's response was to return to Cowes for two days.
Here, thanks to Mrs Jerome relaxing her disapproval, the couple
were able to meet briefly on both days, during which they renewed
their vows of love. The Prince of Wales was still in town, staying
with his mother at Osborne,* and Randolph presented Jennie to the
Prince as the woman he hoped to marry. The Prince liked Jennie
from the start and counselled Randolph to stand firm in the face of
parental opposition.

Soon, more detailed information about Leonard Jerome's fortunes
came to light. It was reported that he had indeed suffered reverses,

---

*At Osborne House, overlooking East Cowes, Queen Victoria retired into semi-seclusion after
her husband's death. Today it is open to the public.

but these had been no fault of his own, and before his financial problems arose he had already ring-fenced money for his wife and daughters.

Randolph also had an ace to lay down in the negotiations. With high rank but without money, there were few career opportunities open to him. He could waste his life in Society as his elder brother was doing (to the disapproval of their parents), he could go into the Church or the Army, become a master of hounds, or he could enter politics. He had already more or less accepted that he would follow his father into politics, a solution much desired by the Duke, who had arranged for his son to stand as candidate for Woodstock in the forthcoming general election.

The result of this election was almost a foregone conclusion. Any member of the Duke's family who stood as candidate at Woodstock was bound to be elected, but the proprieties must be observed. Randolph must at least appear to fight the borough, in other words meet the electors and give a speech. Knowing how much his father wanted him to go into politics, Randolph now used this as a lever to change the Duke's mind about Jennie. No engagement – no electioneering. He wrote to his father that he could not do as his parents wished without help. On the other hand, he continued, if he had a wife such as Jennie, who would be sure to take an interest in his career, and who would encourage him to pursue his ambitions and assist him, he might achieve far more than his parents had ever envisaged for him.[18] This worked: the Duke gave his reluctant consent but insisted that Randolph must get his career under way first – and they must wait a year before marrying.

Leonard Jerome was now brought round too, and pronounced himself 'delighted ... more than I can tell. It is magnificent.' However, it remained a difficult time for the lovers – Jennie was allowed by her mother to write only infrequently ('she does nothing but sermonise me on the subject,' Jennie complained), though she was permitted to receive letters from Randolph and he wrote faithfully to her almost daily. At last, six weeks to the day after their meeting aboard the *Ariadne* – by this time Mrs Jerome and her daughters had returned to Paris* – Randolph was able to write to Jennie that their problems were over. And although he seemed to have lived six years since they met, rather than six weeks, despite all the worries and bother that had occurred since – he still blessed the day of their meeting. He regretted that their plan to marry in December was not now possible but he was confident that it would not be very long before they were able to.'[19] To his future mother-in-law Randolph wrote that he had been anxiously awaiting a reaction from Mr Jerome to their engagement and was relieved and delighted to hear that Jennie's father had given his consent to the marriage. He ended by writing that he was well aware of the great treasure that was being consigned into his care.[20]

All he had to do now was get himself elected which, with the help of some experienced supporters, he proceeded to do. There was no sign at the public meeting that the nervous and stammering young man, who could not even remember all of his speech, was to become one of Parliament's greatest ever exponents. In his speech he opposed any reduction in naval and military establishments: 'An economical policy might, however, be consistently pursued,' he said, 'and the efficiency of our forces by land and sea completely secured without the enormous charges now laid upon the country.'[21]

He was elected with a majority of 165 votes over his opponent, and cabled Jennie: 'I have won a great victory.' He set out for Paris at once to see her, but as he reached Dover he was recalled because one of his aunts, Lady Portarlington, was dying in Ireland and his presence was needed there with his family. He was made to kick his heels in Ireland for three long weeks, but as soon as his aunt was buried he rushed off to Paris for a few days – all the time he could spare because he had to be back in London to take his oath in the House and his seat as a supporter of Disraeli's new administration.

That visit was frustrating. The couple were never allowed to be alone together; at every meeting Mrs Jerome sat at her desk in the

---

*The couple had met briefly in London on 15 September as the Jerome women passed through the city en route to Paris.

same room, pretending to deal with her correspondence. When they went for a walk they were trailed by a chaperone. For a while the parents were at odds over the marriage settlement – Leonard Jerome having very strong feelings that the man in the family should be the provider, and the Duke believing that if his son was marrying a so-called heiress the least to be expected was that she bring with her a sufficient sum to enable the couple to live in an appropriate style. The fact that he had allowed Randolph to marry Jennie was surely enough? Even after he and the Duchess had travelled to Paris and met Mrs Jerome and her daughters, had been 'charmed' by Jennie and pronounced themselves satisfied, the Duke had to be more or less forced by Leonard Jerome into settling an annual allowance on Randolph. To be fair, the Duke had many other obligations – not only the crippling upkeep of Blenheim but the need to provide decent dowries for his flock of daughters. What he, and none of the other protagonists, realised at that time was that Jerome was not in any position to finance what they thought he could manage easily.

It was all very sticky for a while, and Randolph wrote to the Duke that he and Jennie's parents were now barely on speaking terms. He could not see how it would all work out but he thought their behaviour 'perfectly disgraceful' and Jennie was in entire agreement with him.

In the end Jerome settled a capital sum of £50,000 on the couple, invested to produce £2000 a year, but he stipulated that £1000 of this amount must be Jennie's personal allowance, under her own control. His insistence on this clause outraged the Duke and the Marlborough lawyers, but eventually the Duke agreed to pay off Randolph's debts (£2000), increased the annual allowance he made his son to £1100 and accepted Mr Jerome's wishes. The impression is left of the Duke and Duchess having been driven into giving their approval, and this is almost certainly the reason why they did not attend the marriage ceremony in Paris – held on the Duchess's birthday. Six days before the wedding Leonard Jerome wrote to the Duke: 'I am very sorry you will not be able to come over to the wedding . . . Under the circumstances, however, we must of course excuse you.'[22] (Unfortunately, the page of the letter containing the explanation of 'the circumstances' cannot be found.) On the eve of the wedding the Duke wrote to Randolph to wish him well. 'Your wife . . . is one whom you have chosen with less than usual deliberation but you adhered to your love with unwavering constancy and I cannot doubt the truth and force of your affection . . . I am very glad that harmony has been restored and that no cloud obscures the day of sunshine but what has happened will show that the sweetest path is not without its thorns and I must say ought not to be without its lesson to you.'[23]

The absence of the ducal couple notwithstanding, the wedding of Randolph and Jennie on 15 April was the event of the 1874 Season. Huge weddings had not yet become fashionable, but an announcement in *The Times* ensured that magnificent presents began to arrive from everyone from the Prince and Princess of Wales down. The Marlboroughs were represented by Blandford, three of Randolph's sisters* and an aunt, while Francis Knollys, Private Secretary to the Prince of Wales, was Randolph's 'supporter' (best man). Mrs Jerome had not stinted: apart from the white satin and Alençon lace wedding dress, Jennie's trousseau included twenty-five gowns, mainly from Maison Worth.

Jennie's younger sister Leonie described the day in a letter to a schoolfriend:

We had to get up very early having to be at the British Embassy at 11.15. Jennie was dressed in white satin, a plain long train behind and a great many lace flounces in front. She wore a long tulle veil which covered her entirely. Clara [Clarita was now called Clara in the family] and myself were bridesmaids and were dressed in blue silk with white embroidery. We received charming bridesmaid's lockets – a crystal heart with pearls and diamonds around it. We drove to the English Embassy, Papa and Jennie in one carriage, and Mama, Clara and myself in another. [She describes the short service by the Revd Forbes] . . . Then, not being quite married, [Jennie] took Papa's arm

---

*Ivor Guest, husband of Lady Cornelia, signed the marriage certificate as witness.

and went with him to the American Legation. The service was performed again, and then Randolph and Jennie drove off together to the house where our friends came to attend the wedding breakfast. The drawing rooms were full of pretty white flowers. Randolph and Jennie had their breakfast upstairs – in the little drawing room by themselves – a European custom. When everyone was present they came down but not for long as Jennie had to change into a very pretty blue and white striped dress for travelling and a white hat with a white feather. At 2 she bid us goodbye. A beautiful carriage with four grey horses and 2 postilions . . . waited to carry them off to a chateau called Le Petit Val. Before 4 we were alone.[24]

Château Petit Val was just an hour's drive from Paris, and had been built for the Marquis de Marigny, the brother of Madame de Pompadour. An avenue of tall poplar trees still stood between the old chateau and Madame de Pompadour's home, Choisy-le-Roi. Petit Val was renowned for its gardens, designed by the same architect who laid out the park of the Petit Trianon, and it contained an arboretum, grottoes, waterfalls and fountains, winding paths, pavilions, aviaries and terraces but also a wall about twenty feet high which made residents feel very private. It was a perfect location for a honeymoon.

3

1874–5

The Birth of Winston

Three weeks later, in early May, the newly-wed couple arrived by train at Woodstock. Waiting for them was a horse and carriage to take them the short distance to Blenheim Palace. Jennie was not prepared for the old tradition whereby the horses were taken out of their harnesses, the men of Woodstock replacing them in the traces to drag the coach through the arch and along the drive. She wrote in her memoirs that it was a shock to her – evidently, she would never fully understand that this was done not from some sense of feudal obligation but as a freely offered compliment and a sign of approval by the local people who could not afford wedding gifts. As the carriage rolled towards the palace, Randolph waved an arm towards the lake and declared confidently to her: 'This is the finest view in England.' The Duke and Duchess and their daughters were waiting for them on the steps.

Years later Jennie would freely admit that she was 'awed' by Blenheim,[1] but at the time she was determined not to be patronised by the women there, particularly her sisters-in-law. She had a superior education and musical ability on her side; moreover, she had been further into the wider world than the Blenheim ladies. She was a more accomplished pianist, dressed more elegantly, spoke more languages, was as well read and articulate; and she rode at least as well, if not better, than they did. The Duchess appeared almost a leftover from a bygone age, with her large aquiline nose and prominent eyes (which she passed on to her sons), and her firm conviction that there was no greater calling in life for a non-royal woman than to be an English duchess. She may have been shy in company, but at the rustle of the Duchess's silken skirts, Jennie wrote, 'the entire household trembled'.

With everyone except the Duchess, Jennie adopted a feigned arrogance as a cover for her true feelings. When the glories of Blenheim were pointed out to her, she would compare them with the Château de Compiègne (which she had visited once). She did not actually criticise the entertainments laid on at Blenheim, but she could not help telling stories of the wonderful balls and parties she had been to in Paris. She found the afternoons spent sitting over needlework with the Duchess and her daughters a bore, and complained frequently about them in letters to her mother and sisters.

Her attitude gained her no friends among the Spencer Churchill daughters, but probably no demeanour that Jennie could have presented would have done so. She was resented by the unmarried sisters-in-law because she had enjoyed an independence they did not, and never would; and then there were those twenty-five new Parisian gowns in which she paraded – perhaps not as extravagant as it sounds, since ladies were required to change their dresses at least three times a day. Jennie in turn deprecated the frumpy, locally made country clothes and sensible shoes of her sisters-in-law* and the informal domestic arrangements at Blenheim, such as the plain glass tumblers used as water glasses when dining *en famille*: 'the kind we use in bedrooms,' she told her mother. But in her memoirs, written years later, she had the grace to admit that her high heels, sweeping skirts and plumed hats had been out of place in the country and probably constituted a hazard, and that shorter skirts and thick-soled shoes offered more advantages in such circumstances.

In her memoir, Jennie described a typical day:

---

*In a letter to Mrs Jerome about a ball she attended in May 1874, Jennie stated that her sister-in-law Frances was dressed in a monstrous fashion. Frances was ugly enough anyway, Jennie confided, but she had chosen at this event to dress in a bright green dress with pink accessories, lots of gold jewellery and a black veil. In another letter she reported that she had caught the Duchess looking at her 'jealously', evidently disapproving because Jennie had been laughing too much.

When the family were alone at Blenheim everything went on with the regularity of clockwork. So assiduously did I practise my piano, read or paint, that I began to imagine myself back in the schoolroom. In the morning an hour or more was devoted to the reading of newspapers, which was a necessity if one wanted to show an intelligent interest in the questions of the day, for at dinner conversation invariably turned on politics. In the afternoon a drive to pay a visit to some neighbour or a walk in the gardens would help to while away some part of the day. After dinner, which was a rather solemn full-dress affair, we all repaired to . . . the Vandyke room. There one might read one's book or play for love, a mild game of whist . . . No one dared suggest bed until the sacred hour of eleven had struck. Then we would all troop out into a small anteroom, and lighting our candles, each in turn would kiss the Duke and Duchess and depart to our own rooms.[2]

This routine lasted only a fortnight, but the lively Jennie found it stultifying. In the third week of May the newly-weds moved to a rented house in Curzon Street in Mayfair, while waiting for their own house at 48 Charles Street, Westminster, so that Randolph could make his maiden speech and to enable Jennie to be presented at court. When Randolph got to his feet in the House on 22 May, his speech was impromptu, and it answered rather than supported a member of his own party, which caused some offence. Even Disraeli, who had known Randolph since he was a small boy and actively backed him, in a note to the Queen described it as 'imprudent'. However, reflecting that a great deal of licence is given to a maiden speech, Disraeli continued: 'The House was surprised, and then captivated, by his energy, and his natural flow, and his impressive manners . . . it was a speech of great promise.'[3] From this minor success Randolph recognised at once how intoxicating it would be to really rouse the Commons – which assembly, wrote his contemporary Anthony Trollope, 'by the consent of all men is the greatest in the world'.[4]

The London Season had begun. In Jennie's own words, 'it was looked upon as a very serious matter which no self-respecting persons who considered themselves "in society" would forgo, nor of which a votary of fashion would willingly miss a week or a day'.[5] From early May, each evening, the great mansions of Belgravia and the embassies opened their doors for a series of flower-bedecked balls, dinners and parties organised by hostesses who vied with each other in elegant excess. During the day the fashionable flocked to Hurlingham,* to Wimbledon, to flower shows, to garden parties with brass bands playing or to the races – many of these are still features of the Season today. It was important to be seen at Rotten Row[†] in Hyde Park. To parade each day in 'the Row' at the fashionable hours between noon and 2 p.m., on foot, in a carriage or – best of all – on a well-groomed showy hack, was an essential element of the diary. Here friends and acquaintances could meet informally; clandestine lovers could exchange notes or longing glances. Horsewomen like Jennie, dressed in severely cut riding habits that perfectly fitted the upper body but hid the hips and legs under sweeping skirts, showed themselves on mettlesome thoroughbreds to advantage, envy and admiration. Only on Sundays did the constant round of pleasure cease, for the Lord's Day was kept with strict observance – or so, at least, it must appear; all entertaining then was done in private.

In June Jennie made her curtsey to the Queen, as all young married women in her position must do. Also present in that drawing room were the Prince and Princess of Wales, to whom Jennie had already been formally introduced at Cowes the previous August. The Prince was always kind to Jennie, and bearing in mind his reputation as a serial womaniser there is at least a suspicion that, even then, he may already have had an ulterior motive. Every day throughout June and July there was at least one daytime event as well as one grand function to attend at night, and Jennie rose to every occasion with zest – always beautifully dressed, always with

---

*Hurlingham was then, and remained until the Second World War, the polo headquarters of the British Empire.

†The name 'Row' derives from the old Carolean name, 'The King's Road'; and the French translation '*Route du Roi*' is believed to have become 'Rotten Row' when pronounced locally.

a fund of witty, intelligent remarks. She was already demonstrating that she was the perfect wife for an ambitious new politician, even though as an American in English society she was a *rara avis* and was watched carefully for gaffes. Then there were the races – Ascot, the Derby and Goodwood. For her first visit to the Royal Enclosure at Ascot Jennie wore (as was traditional) her wedding gown, altered for the occasion and trimmed with pink roses to match her bonnet, and carried an exquisite lace parasol which her father had given her as a wedding gift. The Prince of Wales offered her his arm in the Royal Enclosure, sealing her success. Later she would recall how they used to drive down to Ascot in summer frocks and feathered hats, 'and stay to dinner, driving back by moonlight'.

Her entry into Society, successful as it was, was necessarily brief. Already Jennie and Randolph knew that they were to become parents; they announced that the child was due in mid-January – exactly nine months from the date of their wedding. Mrs Jerome visited from Paris, bringing a layette of baby clothes, and during her frequent visits to Blenheim Jennie was now forced to take things easy and go for sedate rides in a carriage with the Duchess instead of joining Randolph riding in the park. She found this routine stulti-fying, but it was not improved even when they had guests. On one occasion, returning from a drive, she found the drawing room full of visitors having tea. Jennie escaped as soon as she could, making the excuse that she had to write to her mother. The first hour, when no one knew each other, was always stiff and uncomfortable, with long silences. But she knew from experience that the house guests would soon make themselves at home, and – she wrote to her mother – they would shortly be exchanging slanderous gossip. Everyone in society and politics was pulled to pieces, and it was not only the women who were guilty of this, Jennie wrote, the men were equally to blame.[6]

In late November, when Jennie was seven and a half months pregnant, the couple visited Blenheim for a shooting party. Jennie enjoyed these parties, with their friendly outdoor picnics and enlivening conversation. Most of the women guests walked out to join the men for lunch, but Jennie used a pony trap. On Friday 27 November she decided to walk with the other ladies, but during luncheon she felt very tired so she elected to use the trap to return to the house. During the bumpy drive she began experiencing labour pains, and because the baby was supposedly not due for a further six weeks the local GP, Dr Frederick Taylor, attempted to stop the pains by ordering complete bed rest. The pains continued spasmodically throughout the Saturday night and all day Sunday, by which time Jennie had risen and joined the family. On Sunday evening at 6 p.m., however, it became obvious that she was in full labour and the birth was imminent. The London obstetrician who had been booked for Jennie's confinement could not get down to Oxford in time as there were no trains on Sunday evenings, and an Oxford specialist was busy elsewhere, so Dr Taylor was called in from nearby Woodstock to deliver the child. When the worst pains started Jennie had been hurried into a small, bleak bedroom along a passage leading from the Great Hall to the Long Library. It had formerly been allocated to the Duke's chaplain, Dean Jones, and latterly to an organist who had come to play the organ in the library. It was (and is) chiefly notable for lacking any pretensions to ducal grandeur.

Attended by the Duchess, Randolph's aunt Lady Clementine Camden* and Berthe, Lady Blandford, at 1.30 a.m. on 30 November Jennie had a son, to whom they gave an old family name, Winston.

In view of the date of the birth, six weeks earlier than anticipated, the question has inevitably been asked – was Jennie pregnant before they married? Did Randolph use this fact to force the hand of the Duke into agreeing to their marriage? It might explain his sudden capitulation, and also perhaps why he and the Duchess did not attend the wedding of their favourite son. Mrs Jerome's recorded care of the reputations of her three daughters makes it difficult to surmise how and when the couple might have consummated their love, but it is possible that, given their engagement and with wedding plans well advanced, Randolph and Jennie might have stolen a short time together alone. We know from their letters how much in love they were, and being thwarted almost always stimulates passion.

---

*Daughter of the 6th Duke of Marlborough by his second wife. She married the 3rd Marquess Camden by whom she had four children, and was widowed in 1872.

Before their marriage on 15 April, Jennie and Randolph had last met on 3 March, when he left Paris after a short visit. Winston was born 272 days later. Given that gestation is approximately 266 days, had they consummated their relationship on 2 March this would mean that Jennie was actually a week past full term when Winston was born. But had she indeed been at full term, would it not have been apparent to her doctor? And would she have really gone out for a long walk, then travelled over rough ground in a pony trap when she would have been hoping to hang on to her baby as long as possible to avoid inevitable gossip? If she was close to full term it was brave of her to have gone to Blenheim for a shooting party, away from London doctors and knowing that there were no preparations for the baby's arrival; yet she could hardly have made the necessary arrangements without advertising the fact that she expected the birth imminently.

We shall never know the answer. When Winston was asked about his birth he responded with typical humour: 'Although present on the occasion I have no recollection of the events leading up to it.'

Whether premature or not, the fact of his birth occurring at Blenheim was always something of which Jennie's first child was immensely proud, and he joked as an adult that he had deliberately timed it to ensure he was born there. Randolph wrote immediately to Mrs Jerome of the surprise element of the confinement, hastening to assure her that 'everything went well' and Jennie was fine. The Duchess also wrote to her about more practical considerations. No baby clothes or cradle had been available.* The beautiful Parisian layette presented by Mrs Jerome was waiting in the nursery of Randolph and Jennie's home in London (even had she anticipated going into labour on that visit to Blenheim, carrying a baby's layette around with her would have aroused suspicions). Fortunately, the necessary items could be borrowed from the wife of a Woodstock

*The then nineteen-year-old Princess of Wales had had a similar experience in 1864. She had insisted on being taken by horse-drawn sledge to watch her husband play ice hockey. During the game her pains began and she was rushed to nearby Frogmore, where she gave premature birth to her first child, Albert (later Duke of Clarence). There was nothing to hand in which to dress the baby but some cotton wool.

solicitor, Mr Thomas Brown, who had prepared in advance for her own forthcoming confinement in January. Meanwhile, baby Winston's own things were sent for from 48 Charles Street. Mrs Jerome professed to be shocked when a horse-racing friend wrote about the new baby that he had 'interesting breeding, stamina goes through the dam, and pace through the sire'.[7]

The main thing was that the little boy was fine and described as 'healthy' (a word not normally applied to a very premature baby in that era), as was his mother. He was baptised in the Blenheim chapel with the names Winston Leonard Spencer Churchill, and both families rejoiced.

In those days few upper-class women nursed their own children, and a nurse and wet-nurse were found within hours of Winston's birth. Most doctors would have been able to recommend a respectable local woman who had recently given birth and had milk to spare, or perhaps (since infant mortality was so high) someone who had lost her own baby. Jennie was soon on her feet again and on returning to London a nanny was recruited. Miss Elizabeth Everest,* always called 'Mrs Everest' by courtesy, was to be fully responsible for all aspects of the nursery. Jennie had done her duty, so to speak, and after the months of enforced rest during her pregnancy she could now enjoy herself again. And Jennie, twenty years old, with all her remarkable energy threw herself into the whirl of gaiety that beckoned. 'Many were the delightful balls I went to,' she wrote in her memoirs, 'which . . . invariably lasted until five o'clock in the morning. Masked balls were much the vogue. Holland House [a Jacobean mansion in Holland Park, destroyed by bombs in 1940] with its wonderful historical associations and beautiful gardens was a fitting frame for such entertainments, and I remember enjoying myself immensely at one given there. Disguised in a painted mask and a yellow wig, I mystified everyone.'[8]

---

*Elizabeth Ann Everest (1833–95) was born in Chatham, Kent, and her first job as a nanny had been with the Revd Thomas Phillips of Carlisle. When her first charges outgrew the nursery, she was employed by Jennie. She had been so much loved in the Phillips household that she had a standing invitation to visit whenever she wished and she sometimes spent her holidays with them.

At dinner parties she was often, as a lady of high status, seated next to Disraeli, who had a soft spot for Randolph, or even beside the Prince of Wales who would tease her that she was seeking some preferment for Randolph when she monopolised the Prime Minister. Indeed, promoting Randolph now became Jennie's chief aim; her own dinner parties were well patronised and she was soon regarded as a successful hostess. Lord Blandford's well bred wife Berthe did not shine socially and the couple were never seen together in London. Despite his early opposition to his brother's engagement, after he met her Blandford conceived a great fondness and respect for Jennie, for she possessed every characteristic that he most admired in a woman. He saw his younger brother happy in his marriage, the proud father of a healthy son, and apparently not only succeeding in a career in politics but also basking in parental affection.

Most of this Blandford put down to Jennie's influence, and one day he presented her with a ring as a token of his affection and regard. In November 1875, a year after Winston's birth, when Jennie was visiting Blenheim, probably to illustrate the fact that she had made friends with Blandford she innocently showed off this ring to her mother-in-law and sister-in-law Rosamund, only to be faced by appalled accusatory stares from both women. The ring was part of the entailed family jewel collection, and should never have been given to anyone except the wife of the Duke or the wife of the heir. Technically, the ring belonged to Goosie during her lifetime, and it was not Blandford's to give away. Jennie immediately made Randolph write to Blandford explaining what had happened and asking him to take the ring back as their friendship needed no demonstration. Suddenly Jennie was treated to a spectacular family row.

Randolph and Blandford were quite happy to quarrel vehemently with their parents, and the Duke and Duchess seemed equally happy to fling bitter accusations of treachery and lying at their sons. But Jennie was at the centre of it all – and, not brought up to family enmity, she was made deeply unhappy.

It was three months before the row blew over, and meanwhile she and Randolph had been unable to spend Christmas at Blenheim as planned. Randolph fell ill over the New Year and could not accompany Jennie and baby Winston on a hastily arranged trip to Paris to visit Mrs Jerome, so he went instead to stay with one of his married sisters, Frances ('Fanny').* Within days he wrote to say Fanny had thrown him out because he had insisted that he was in the right in the family quarrel, and he had gone to stay in a hotel.

Jennie stayed on in Paris, ice-skating and enjoying herself, well away from Churchill family feuds. The Duchess would always blame Jennie for alienating the affections of her favourite son, and her antagonism towards her daughter-in-law, although never overt, was to become a lifelong dislike.

---

*Frances, the third daughter of the 7th Duke, married in 1873 the politician Edward Marjoribanks (1849–1909), eldest son of the 1st Baron Tweedmouth. He succeeded to the title in 1894. He was Liberal MP for Berwickshire from 1880 until 1894 and held the offices of Chief Whip, Lord Privy Seal, Chancellor of the Duchy of Lancaster, First Lord of the Admiralty and Lord President of the Council.

4

1875–80

A Dysfunctional Family

'As every skoolboy knows', after being widowed in December 1861 the forty-two-year-old Queen Victoria retreated into a life of seclusion primarily at Osborne House on the Isle of Wight, with occasional visits to Windsor and Balmoral. So when, two years after Prince Albert's death, Edward, Prince of Wales, married the elegant and beautiful Danish princess Alexandra (who had been preselected by the late Prince Albert), the newly-weds immediately became the leaders of Society and fashion. The public adored them and thronged the streets, cheering loudly, whenever they made an appearance. The image of Prince Edward as a stout old roué is so fixed in our collective minds that it is difficult to think of him as he was then, at twenty-two, slender, handsome and full of energy. His Princess was just eighteen, and these young royals were not predisposed to follow the example set by his staid middle-aged parents. A constant whirl of balls, parties and other festivities thrown in honour of the couple made the 1864 Season a particularly glamorous one, and set the standard for future Seasons.

Edward and Alexandra moved into Marlborough House on The Mall, which would be their home for another forty years and would subsequently pass to other members of the royal family. It had been built in red brick with stone quoining by Duchess Sarah as a sort of mini-Blenheim, but the building had long since been lost to the

Churchill family.* The Marlborough House set, friends of either the Prince or the Princess of Wales but only rarely of both, surrounded the royal couple. Blandford and Randolph Churchill were part of this coterie, without ever being among the Prince's confidants. However, following their marriage, Randolph and Jennie became for a while part of the inner circle.

Blandford was an erratic personality: he was a clever scientist but he suffered from the Churchill arrogance without the Churchill charm, was ham-fisted in relationships and always prone to ungovernable flashes of temper and impulse, and he possessed no financial sense whatsoever. The six-year union between him and Goosie had been a disaster almost from the outset, and although they had four children between 1870 and 1875 he had come to despise her simplicity and infantile humour. Soon after the birth of his fourth child, at about the time of the family dispute about the ring, he began a passionate love affair with Edith Lady Aylesford whose lively husband Lord Aylesford, popularly known as 'Sporting Joe', was a close friend of the Prince.† Blandford and Edith were gossiped about, of course. Who was sleeping with whom – discreetly – was an essential, even an enjoyable, part of their world. And had Blandford been content to live within the rules set by Society, all would have been well with the arrangement, despite the strong disapproval of his parents. The problem arose when the Prince made an official visit to India and, against the Queen's counselling, included Lord Aylesford as a member of his entourage.

---

*Marlborough House was purchased by the Crown in 1817, soon after the death of the 4th Duke of Marlborough. It was from there, in 1936, when it was the home of the widowed Queen Mary, that King Edward VIII announced his intention to abdicate in order to marry his mistress Wallis Simpson.

†In that rarefied stratum marriages were often arranged for dynastic or financial reasons rather than love. It was a sine qua non that a woman should be a virgin on her marriage, but once she had provided an heir, she might discreetly look for emotional gratification elsewhere. Divorce, obtainable only by husbands at that point, was unthinkable for many reasons. Until the Married Woman's Property Act of 1882 a wife owned nothing – everything belonged to her husband from the date of the marriage. A wife in a divorce case was extremely unlikely to be given custody, or even access, to her children. And social ostracism was absolute for both parties, innocent and guilty. As a result divorce was rare, and was still only in double figures annually in the entire kingdom.

Aylesford's months of absence left the field clear for Blandford, who moved into a hotel near to the Aylesfords' country house at Packington near Coventry. Ostensibly, he was there for a season's foxhunting, but Edith gave him a key to a side door of the house so that he could come and go at night without having to be admitted by servants. This did not fool anyone, especially after footprints in the snow provided clear evidence of his nocturnal visits. The affair flamed into passion, and within a short time the pair decided they could no longer live apart. They proposed to run away and live together, each asking for a divorce.

It is impossible today to convey the shock that was felt by the respective families of the lovers at this news. The Prince's party was in Nepal when Aylesford received Edith's letter – the first time he had heard from his wife in five weeks – advising of her intention to elope with Blandford. Aylesford acted swiftly, cabling* his mother with instructions to collect his children at once and keep them secure until his return. He then told the Prince and asked for permission to return home immediately. The Prince, furious because his hunting party was being prematurely broken up (he had been loaned a thousand elephants for his trip), roundly castigated Blandford as a 'rabble' and a 'blackguard' before Aylesford, seated on the back of an elephant, left the royal camp to make the six-week journey home.

Randolph and Jennie were stunned too, though to Randolph's credit – despite the opprobrium that would cling to him because of it – he both wanted to help his brother and also try to prevent him doing anything that would cause permanent damage to the family name. Not knowing that Aylesford had already left India, Randolph cabled the Prince of Wales, requesting that he persuade Aylesford not to agree to a divorce. The Prince's response was to wire Lord Hardwicke, who held the title Master of the Queen's Buckhounds, instructing him to call on Randolph and directly convey his profound indignation at Blandford's conduct.

When Randolph subsequently visited his brother he faced the

---

*England was linked to India by electric cable in 1864.

full blast of Blandford's passion for Edith. He vowed he would 'never give her up' whatever happened and that he intended to marry her. Randolph pointed out that the Prince was utterly opposed to the union, and that every member of both families faced social ruin if this course of action was pursued; he suggested that the lovers simply remain in their marriages and continue their affair discreetly, which was what the Duke and Duchess counselled. Blandford railed against the hypocrisy of this suggestion, and in support of his indignation he produced a bundle of letters which he handed to Randolph. Apparently, some years earlier Edith Aylesford had enjoyed a relationship with the Prince of Wales, during which the Prince had written these letters to her, and some of them, apparently,* were indiscreet enough to be embarrassing.

When Aylesford was within days of reaching London, bent on thrashing Blandford and divorcing Edith, Blandford – probably bowing to family pressure to put some distance between himself and Edith, at least temporarily – left for the Low Countries. Perhaps he was fleeing from his wife, as much as anything. Goosie's sad attempt to bring some humour into the situation had been to place a small pink celluloid doll on Blandford's toast at breakfast. Anticipating his usual poached egg, when he lifted the domed cover what he saw there proved the last straw – he walked out of the house and would not return for many years.

Randolph's interview with Lord Hardwicke revealed that the Prince was in favour of Aylesford's plan to divorce Edith, and this prompted Randolph to make one of the gravest mistakes of his life. In an attempt to persuade the Prince not to goad Aylesford into divorce, Randolph impulsively took the Prince's love letters to his wife, Princess Alexandra, telling her that if there was a divorce case the letters would be produced in evidence, to prove that Aylesford had condoned his wife's former relationship with the Prince. If this happened, he said, the Prince would never be allowed to sit on the

---

*The contents have never been revealed, but there is enough correspondence in the public domain between the Queen and her advisers to indicate that they would have been damaging to the Prince.

throne. It was a suicidal move. Surely only someone with Randolph's arrogance would have attempted to blackmail the heir to the throne.

The Princess, by now no stranger to her husband's supposedly discreet extramarital affairs, wisely called in Prime Minister Disraeli, who in turn informed the Queen. Victoria had accepted long ago that her thirty-five-year-old son fell far short of her late husband's standards. She was chiefly concerned that the throne be protected. Having been told that the letters were 'innocent' but contained 'chaff that could be misinterpreted',[1] the Queen wrote to the Prince: 'What a dreadful disgraceful business about Lady Aylesford and Lord Blandford! And how unpardonable . . . to draw dear Alix [Alexandra] into it! Her dear name should never have been mixed up with such people. Poor Lord Aylesford shd not have left her [to go to India]. I knew last summer that this [affair] was going on.'[2] What had begun as an amorous fling was now a full-blown state crisis.

Neither of the Churchill brothers came out of it well – Blandford was now an acknowledged adulterer who appeared to be skulking in Holland to avoid facing the irate husband, and Randolph was attempting to blackmail the Prince through his wholly innocent wife. Blandford refused to accept any blame; he wrote to Randolph that as soon as the Prince turned up he intended to come back and tackle him. 'I shall lick HRH within an inch of his life for his conduct generally,' he wrote, 'and we will have the whole thing up in the Police Court!'[3] Despite a heavy cold Randolph travelled over to The Hague to discuss the matter with Blandford, but he found his brother's harangues 'wearying'. He wrote to Jennie that he would be glad to get back home to her and that she and the baby were always in his thoughts.[4]

Jennie, meanwhile, was trying hard to cool the situation in London, fully aware that unless she was successful the social life that she adored was as good as dead. She dined with Randolph's sister Fanny but found no support there; 'Fanny is the most "bottled up" creature I have ever met,'[5] she wrote to Randolph, also warning him that Blandford had raved at his parents who were now staying in Paris for the time being, to avoid any confrontations. 'You have displayed to me an untold cruelty of intention,' Blandford wrote to them in an angry fifteen-page letter. 'What can it affect you who I marry and who my children may be? In what manner do they come into the circle of your life? . . . For what considerations of a worldly character have you thought fit to step in to sacrifice my whole life?'[6]

Randolph, meanwhile, had been writing furious letters to Lord Hardwicke, and in one of Jennie's letters to Randolph she warned against doing so, telling him that she knew Hardwicke would 'abuse us'.[7] She knew and disliked Lord Hardwicke, who had apparently once attempted to force his attentions on her during her first Season in London, before she met Randolph. Now, as Jennie forecast, Hardwicke mischievously worked against them at court.

When the latest situation was relayed to the Prince he was so annoyed at Randolph's behaviour, and particularly because he had involved the Princess, that he ordered his friend Lord Charles Beresford to travel home ahead of him, at speed, and challenge Randolph to a duel on his behalf. In fact it was Lord Knollys, who had been Randolph's best man two years earlier, who delivered the challenge. Randolph accepted, but after naming his second (Lord Falmouth) he wrote an arrogant and insulting private letter to the Prince, suggesting that the challenge had been made in the full knowledge that a duel could never take place. Not only had duelling been made illegal by the Prince's late father, but they both knew that no British subject could take up arms against the heir to the throne.

By now, having acted very foolishly, Randolph was beginning to tire of the matter and wrote to Jennie that he would be pleased to return home because he loved her and hated it when they were parted, but also because his brother had become 'a horrid bore'. Blandford had raged at him because Lady Aylesford had been advised by her lawyers that she should try to reconcile with her husband. Randolph had been very short and the brothers had quarrelled violently. He signed off lovingly, asking her to kiss the baby for him.[8]

By the time the Prince returned from India, the Aylesford matter had leaked into Society and gossip was rife. It was essential that it be dealt with urgently. The Princess met her husband's ship at Portsmouth and at his express instruction she went on board '*first* and *alone*' before he made any public appearance. The royal couple were then alone together for some time while, presumably, he told her about his old affair with Lady Aylesford. They were then closeted with Lord Hardwicke, who advised what steps must be taken to limit the damage, since gossip was by now widespread. Only then could the Prince's siblings go aboard the ship and begin the formal welcome. There was a triumphal procession through London as the couple returned to Marlborough House, and within an hour they left again for a gala performance at Covent Garden Opera. It was a brave test of the Prince's popularity, but as they entered the royal box (late) the couple were cheered to the rafters – and between every act there was renewed cheering.[9] So the matter was handled with the smoothness of today's spin doctors.

Aylesford made the decision not to divorce Edith, the royal letters disappeared – presumably into the fire or into the deepest recesses of the royal archives – and the Prince declared that henceforth he and the Princess would boycott any function to which the Churchills were invited. This proved very inconvenient for Cornelia, the eldest Churchill daughter, who was married to Sir Ivor Guest, since her long-planned ball in honour of the Prince and Princess was imminent. She was very severe with Jennie about it, and Jennie was made to realise that she and Randolph were not even to *think* of attending. But the whole of Society closed ranks, and despite a worried Sir Ivor being dispatched to speak to the Prince's secretary after Cornelia's invitation was declined, her ball had to go ahead without the royal couple.

Edith had now joined Blandford on the Continent and the couple began a series of travels about Europe that would last for some years. Lord Aylesford found himself punished as thoroughly as were the guilty parties; he subsequently travelled to America where he bought some land and settled. He died a few years later of drink-related problems at the age of thirty-six.

Quickly realising how impossible it was to remain in London where they were nothing less than pariahs, Randolph and Jennie decided that they should also absent themselves for a while, and they too travelled to America. Jennie's father still lived there and she had not been 'home' since she was a child. It was no great punishment for her.

In the autumn of 1876 the Duke of Marlborough was summoned by the Queen, who was anxious to help her old friend. Disraeli had suggested a solution. After insisting that Randolph must make a formal apology for his attempt to involve the Princess,* the Duke was offered the post of Lord Lieutenant of Ireland. Goosie's father, the Duke of Abercorn, was the retiring incumbent and it was a viceregal post; but the Duke could not regard the office as an honour, having already refused it a few years earlier on the grounds that he could not afford it. This time Marlborough felt obliged to accept. It meant selling off a number of works of art to fund the necessary expenditure, but at least the family could remove themselves with some vestige of dignity from an insupportable situation. In Ireland they would be not merely acceptable in Society, but the formal representatives of the Queen.

Appalled and hardly able to believe the mess in which his sons had landed the family, the Duke insisted (again at Disraeli's urging) that when Randolph and Jennie returned from America they and little Winston must join himself and the Duchess, their three unmarried daughters and Goosie and her children in Dublin. There, Randolph was to work as his father's unpaid private secretary. It was essential, they felt, to present a united family front.

On the night before they left England in January 1877 for what would prove a costly three-year exile in Ireland, the Duke and Duchess stayed at Windsor with the Queen, who noted in her diary that the poor Duchess (the same one who made servants tremble when they heard the rustle of her skirts) had been so distressed and wretched that she could scarcely control her tears.[10]

As an adult, Winston Churchill's first memories would be of the

---

*Randolph complied, with gritted teeth, signing a letter worded by his father and the Lord Chancellor. But he added a postscript of his own, and the Prince did not feel it was a genuine apology.

years his family lived in Ireland when he and his parents occupied a lodge in Phoenix Park, Dublin. Mostly these memories were of playing with his cousin Sunny, son and heir of his Uncle Blandford, and of his mother dressed for hunting in her severely cut riding habit, often mud-spattered as she blew into the nursery exhilarated after a day spent following the hounds. For anyone who enjoyed fox-hunting, Ireland was the place to be. It was not a wholly elite activity even then, and though one was likely to meet a good sprinkling of the aristocracy in the field, anyone of any class who had a horse capable of galloping and jumping could be a foxhunter. A bold-riding farmer was as respected as any other member of the field.

It was just as well that Jennie enjoyed hunting, for there was little else to occupy her time. As representatives of the sovereign the Marlboroughs were virtual rulers of Ireland and obliged to entertain despite the constant drain on the Duke's purse. But Jennie found these balls and drawing rooms parochial. She later wrote that she found the women, in their 'home-made clothes', boring. However, there is perhaps another clue to her character in that she also wrote that in the three years she lived in Ireland she could not recall meeting one dull man. She had her own court of admirers when out hunting, which included Colonel Forster, who was Master of Horse to the Duke, and Viscount Falmouth, who was the Duke's military adviser, as well as Lord d'Abernon.

When Randolph was not working as his father's secretary he was paying one of his increasingly regular visits to London where, during the next few years, he would find his feet in politics. Amazingly, considering his first stumbling speech to the House, he would emerge as one of the greatest political orators of his day and perhaps of any era in English history, excelled only by his son.

With hindsight Jennie realised that his post as his father's secretary played a large part in creating this new Randolph, for his isolation diverted his mind 'from the frivolous society to which he had till then been rather addicted, and which now had ceased to smile upon him'.[11] It also brought home to him the appalling lot of the Irish peasantry. The country was still feeling the effects of the potato famine, during which a million people died and another million emigrated.

Now, twenty-five years on, there was a smouldering resentment that the country was still governed by mainly absentee English landlords. There were two words on everyone's lips: 'Home Rule'.

Having this opportunity to study the Irish problems at first hand, Randolph found himself in great sympathy with those affected, and though opposed to Home Rule he favoured a form of local self-government that would mitigate the damage caused by short-sighted British politicians and officials. He soon became known in Parliament for his views on the subject and for his confidence in his political opinions. On 7 March 1878 he made some enemies when he launched a furious attack on some of the respectable but perhaps not very able ministers in Disraeli's government, to whom he referred as 'the old gang', who were, he said, characterised by having a double-barrelled name, almost always 'a badge of intellectual mediocrity'. Clearly, he did not feel this extended to the name Spencer Churchill; nor did he include Disraeli in his onslaught, for he admired his leader; but the speech nailed Randolph as a Young Turk.

For Jennie, the only alternative to hunting lay in assisting her mother-in-law with a fund aimed at alleviating the dreadful hardships of the poor. Called the Irish Relief Fund, it was a huge success and raised £135,000 (£6.5 million today), and the Duchess was decorated by the Queen not only for her fund-raising but for the commonsense manner in which she distributed the money.* But Jennie preferred hunting, often riding to hounds four or five days a week. Later she would claim that during this period she had hunted with every pack in Ireland. She was a brave rider and did not mind falls, which won her more admirers. Once, when she fell and was knocked unconscious, she woke to find that Randolph had believed her dead. In his relief at seeing her move he grabbed the flask of a friend 'and emptied it'. It became a family joke that Jennie had the bad fall and Randolph had the whisky. It was while out hunting

*When she lay dying, the Duchess sent for the 9th Duke and gave him the Queen's letter of commendation to remind him that although she was now 'a useless old woman' there was a time when she was 'of some importance and did good in my day'.

that Jennie met the beautiful Empress Elizabeth of Austria, generally accepted as the best woman rider in Europe. With her famous 'pilot' (and, some say, lover), the dashing, hard-riding Bay Middleton, the Empress hunted six days a week during her visit to Ireland and caused deep offence by not making time to visit the Marlboroughs at the viceregal court in Dublin.

In 1879 Jennie was pregnant again, and on 4 February 1880 she gave birth to another seven-months child whom they named John Strange Churchill. Eyebrows have been raised about this child: Jennie was said by a number of biographers to have enjoyed a friendship with John Strange Jocelyn, 5th Earl of Roden, in the year before the baby's birth. Although it is not impossible that she was unfaithful to her husband, the content and loving tone of their correspondence at this point in their marriage make it extremely unlikely. Also, Lord Roden was godfather to this baby who bore his Christian names, and surely if Jennie had had anything to hide she would not have advertised the possibility quite so blatantly? And would Colonel Roden – a Crimean War veteran more than thirty years older than her and sometime confidant of the Queen – have been so cool about participating in the baptism had the child been his? Again, it is very unlikely – especially as the gentleman was also a very close friend of the Duke and Duchess of Marlborough. In fact, the 5th Earl was not even in Ireland at the time Jack was conceived.[12] He had inherited the title only a month earlier from his sickly thirty-three-year-old nephew – a friend and supporter of Randolph in Parliament, who had died childless – and it was this much younger deceased Lord Roden (the 4th Earl), a leading light in the Conservative Party despite his frailty, with whom Jennie had been friendly before the Randolph Churchills left for Ireland.

The baby, always known as 'Jack',* was heartily welcomed by five-year-old Winston into the small almost separate household of

---

*It is true, as several of Jennie's biographers have noted, that as an adult Jack bore no facial similarity to his brother Winston. However, he did resemble Lord Randolph (which Winston never did), and Jack's son John looked far more like Winston than did Winston's own son.

the children and the nursery staff. He would always recall the moment when his father came into the nursery to tell him that he had a baby brother, and throughout Jack's life Winston loved him dearly and was never slow to tell people this.*[13] Winston saw almost nothing of the grown-ups beyond the daily formal visit to see his parents in the time after tea and before they dressed for dinner. His mother was remote to him: 'My mother always seemed . . . a fairy-princess: a radiant being possessed of limitless riches and power . . . she shone for me like the Evening Star. I loved her dearly – but at a distance.'[14] Children of their class were not cuddled by their mothers; such a thing would have been regarded as certain to spoil. Jennie was always prepared to rebel over something she did not like or really want, but she was clearly happy to adopt this nursery regimen and so the conclusion must be that it did not especially bother her. Despite her happy personality and ability to charm the opposite sex it is difficult for a modern-day researcher to regard her as other than an extremely self-centred young woman at this time.

There is a good eyewitness description of Jennie during her time in Ireland. She was, recalled her admirer Lord d'Abernon,

a dark, lithe figure, standing somewhat apart and appearing to be of another texture to those around her, radiant, translucent, intense. A diamond star in her hair, her favourite ornament – its lustre dimmed by the flashing glory of her eyes. More of the panther than of the woman in her looks, but with a cultivated intelligence unknown to the jungle. With all these attributes of brilliancy [she possessed] such kindliness and high spirits that she was universally popular. Her desire to please, her delight in life, and the genuine wish that all should share her joyous faith in it, made her the centre of a devoted circle.[15]

Other male admirers noted this pantherine quality in Jennie, and she never lost it.

---

*In 1946 Winston told the Prince of the Belgians: 'I have a brother who is five years younger than me and whom I dearly love and have always cherished.'

When the Conservatives were routed by the Liberals under Gladstone in the general election of April 1880, the Duke and Duchess were recalled from Ireland. No one in the Churchill family was sorry that the viceregency had ended, and against the national trend Randolph was returned as MP albeit with a small majority of sixty votes. As his son wrote many years later, 'his hour had come'. The Conservatives were in disarray after a long period in office and Disraeli (now Lord Beaconsfield), already ill with the condition that would soon kill him, had practically retired. The Tory backbenchers were discouraged and the former ministers, 'the old gang' as Randolph had labelled them, were rudderless. Randolph seized the day, boldly advocating a new, more aggressive and resolute type of Toryism. He attacked and harried not only the new Liberal government but also, frequently, his own party, ably backed by a trio of supporters whose actions were so concerted and focused in the first session of the House after the election that the foursome began calling themselves 'the Fourth Party'. It is clear that Randolph had correctly gauged the feelings of this parliament because some of his suggestions were even backed by the Liberals. And Disraeli, always a supporter of Randolph, wrote: 'I am glad he is to speak about Ireland. He will speak on such a subject not only with ability but with authority.'[16] Gladstone, however, held quite another view: 'There never was a Churchill from John of Marlborough down, that had either morals or principles.'

Jennie was delighted to return to London, where Randolph rented a house at 29 St James's Place in Mayfair, and although they were still not accepted in court circles she joined wholeheartedly in the excitement of her husband's burgeoning career. Politics energised her. They lived next door to the house belonging to Sir Stafford Northcote (later the Earl of Iddesleigh), who was then leader of the Conservative Party. He would have been horrified to know what went on in the neighbouring house, where Randolph and his political cabal were plotting to upstage the despised 'old gang' of which Northcote was chief protagonist.

For little Winston it was a bad time. At the age of seven, on a dark winter day, he was uprooted from his comfortable nursery

routine, his beloved Nanny Everest, his baby brother and his growing collection of lead soldiers – which occupied him for hours every
day – and packed off to a boarding school, St George's Preparatory
School at Ascot. There he would endure several years of a personal
hell during which, in the short periods he spent at home each year,
everyone except Nanny Everest was far too busy to notice the
misery of a small boy.

It is well known that for Winston, Nanny Everest was the centre
of his world, his sole confidante. He never forgot her, and years later
wrote: 'Mrs Everest it was who looked after me and tended to all
my wants. It was to her I poured out my many troubles.' When he
was in his seventies he would tell his nephew Johnny: 'Children
very often like their nurses better than their parents. My own nurse,
Mrs Everest, was my closest and dearest friend.'[17] During Winston's
and Jack's entire childhoods Jennie was merely a beautiful fleeting
luminary, paying flying visits to the nursery dressed to go riding or
hunting or in her evening clothes, scented, sparkling with diamonds –
untouchable. Small wonder she appeared to her sons as a goddess-
like creature to be adored rather than loved. Winston accepted this
as normal, and never resented her emotional neglect. And it is
important to recognise that this behaviour of Jennie's was entirely
normal for her time and her class. It was also entirely normal to send
a seven-year-old boy away to boarding school.

Undoubtedly, Randolph and Jennie had done some research and
believed they had chosen a good school for Winston. All the masters there were highly qualified, it was bright and modern, had
electric light (still considered a wonder and installed in very few
homes, let alone in schools), a swimming pool and good sports
grounds, and the boys were taken on regular outings. What they
could not have known was that the respectably married headmaster,
the Revd H.W. Sneyd-Kynnersley, was a sadist. According to the
witness statement of a fellow pupil[18] (forced by the demands of self-
protection to assist the headmaster in these sessions by holding
down the terrified victims), Kynnersley took positive pleasure in
flogging small boys until they bled, or even excreted through fear
and pain. This punishment was administered for the slightest

indiscretion – for being late, or performing badly in an exam. Winston was renowned for unpunctuality and regularly had the lowest marks in his class throughout his school career.* He was also, even at this early age, bombastic, self-opinionated and possessed of his fair share of pugnacious Churchill arrogance, which would have marked him out to his ghastly headmaster.

The following is one of the milder extracts from a fellow pupil's description of those years at St George's: 'The swishing was given with the master's full strength and it took only two or three strokes for blood to form everywhere and it continued for 15 or 20 strokes when the boy's bottom was a mass of blood.'[19] Winston never complained to his parents – indeed, his letters home (which would have been scanned by masters for spelling, composition and presentation) invariably included a sentence such as 'I am very happy at school'; but in fact he was one of those regularly singled out for corporal punishments.[†]

Not surprisingly, Winston's work suffered, despite the optimism in his letters in which he wrote about how well he thought he was doing. His poor reports show that he was regarded by his teachers as lazy, arrogant, wilful, naughty and unpunctual, with comments under the heading 'Headmaster's Remarks' such as 'Very bad – is a constant trouble to everybody and is always in some scrape or other. He cannot be trusted to behave himself anywhere'; and, remarkably in view of his subsequent career, 'He has no ambition.'[20] He had a few friends but he was not generally popular. Can his parents never have wondered why this exceptionally bright child was such a duffer at school? Their only reaction was to reprimand and criticise him by letter throughout his school career. His letters to them were a constantly recurring theme (apart from regular requests for more pocket money), begging them, especially his mother, to visit him.

---

*He suffered from extreme anxiety, shaking, sweating and nausea before any exam, lest he should not do well and disappoint his father.

†Winston nurtured dreams of revenge against his torturer for many years. As a robust young military cadet at Sandhurst, he felt he was at last fit enough to face Sneyd-Kynnersley in order to exact physical retribution. He rode to the hated school and with mixed feelings received the news that Sneyd-Kynnersley was dead and the school was now in new hands.

Jennie very occasionally made a visit – perhaps once a year – and her replies to Winston were full of excuses such as 'I can't come down on Wednesday, darling – I am far too busy.' Randolph visited his son no more than three times during his years at school.* All this small boy had to look forward to between the ages of seven and nine was the school holidays and half-term breaks, and he counted the days until the end of each term – '30 days more and the *Holidays* will be *here*'[21] – while daydreaming of the sanctuary of his nursery and the loving care of Nanny Everest, of his brother Jack and his collection of toy soldiers on the rug in front of the fire.

Even during school holidays he saw little of his parents. It was not unusual for Randolph and Jennie to spend most of the holidays visiting friends in their great country houses, or on trips abroad. In the summer the two small boys were often left at Blenheim with Mrs Everest, it being thought better for them to breathe fresh country air than stay in London; they would also often spend two weeks at the seaside with her. Sometimes neither Randolph nor Jennie was even home for Christmas. When Mrs Everest wrote to Winston at school, two or three times a week, she addressed him as 'My Precious boy' and 'My own darling boy'. In her less frequent letters Jennie wrote 'Dearest Winston'. In June 1884, nine-year-old Winston wrote forthrightly to his mother, 'It is very unkind of you not to write to me before this. I have had only one letter from you this term.'[22]

Following the return to London of the Duke and Duchess, the Duke had resumed his seat in the Lords. He had soon realised that he faced a horrendous financial position. It should be explained that the Marlboroughs had never owned extensive income-producing lands as did those much older aristocratic families who had amassed great swathes of land and properties in the fifteenth and sixteenth centuries, especially during the Dissolution. In the mid-nineteenth century, for example, the Earl of Derby had an annual income of £150,000; the Duke of Northumberland, £160,000; and the Duke

---

*Winston had been at Harrow for eighteen months before his father visited him at school, and there were two further visits before he left there for Sandhurst at the age of eighteen.

of Norfolk netted £231,000 a year.[23] By contrast, the Marlboroughs' income was only £40,000 a year, and out of this the 7th Duke had to maintain a palace covering seven acres and requiring a huge staff, provide significant dowries for six daughters, and periodically bail out his two spendthrift sons.[24] The Irish viceregency had been a financial disaster, and he was now forced to adopt a desperate measure. He contacted a friend, Earl Cairns, who was Lord Chancellor, and with his assistance an Act was put through Parliament called 'The Blenheim Settled Estates Act'. Effectively, this Act dismantled the 'entail' created by John Churchill's will in 1722, which had protected the most valuable contents of Blenheim since the death of the great Duke. Immediately, the 7th Duke began to sell off some of the books in the Sunderland Library and the Marlborough Gems,* as well as a collection of pictures and Limoges enamels.

Blandford, waiting in the wings for the time when he would become the 8th Duke, was especially interested in the spectacle of his parsimonious father selling off heirlooms to raise money. He filed the information away for future use.

---

*A collection of 730 engraved gemstones and cameos that were miniature works of art, rather than individual jewels as the name suggests. Some were of great antiquity, amassed by the 4th Duke. The most famous cameo (the 7th Duke's favourite) was *The Marriage of Cupid and Psyche*, which was reproduced by Josiah Wedgwood for his Wedgwood cameo ware.

5

1880–7

A Career Thrown Away

Having redeemed himself with his parents, Lord Randolph was busy furthering his reputation in Parliament as architect of what he called 'Tory Democracy'. Between May and August 1880 he made seventy-four speeches and asked twenty-one questions in the House. Boyishly slim, he would be dressed in his customary beautifully tailored grey frock-coat and coloured waistcoat. His waxed and twirled moustache and his protruding eyes distinguished him from his colleagues, and his ironic jay-like laughter 'in its weirdness was merriment itself'.[1] Although still a backbencher, with characteristic aplomb Randolph had already made the move to a seat on the front benches, below the gangway beside his 'Fourth Party' cohorts Arthur Balfour, Sir Henry Wolff and John Gorst. Together, nightly, they harried and teased Mr Gladstone, and whenever Randolph caught the Speaker's eye the word would go out, 'Churchill's up!' and the Chamber would rapidly fill in the hope of a firework display of wit, sarcasm and perfect delivery. He was also a persistent heckler, always delighting in waking up the House with an interjection such as the following, recorded in Hansard, when a member was droning on during his speech about there being 'two great parties in the State'. The response from the Chamber:

Mr Parnell [Leader of the Irish Party]: 'Three!'
Lord Randolph Churchill: 'FOUR!!'
(laughter)

Randolph was master of the short, memorable phrase, and one such, which stuck and did the victim little good, was his description of Gladstone, the 'Grand Old Man', as 'an old man in a hurry'.

Jennie now came into her own as a political hostess, and in this guise she made her own impression on British politics. True, her father-in-law worried about her guest lists. He believed she too often invited the wrong ones – 'dangerous radicals' like Joseph Chamberlain and Charles Dilke* who, he felt, exerted the wrong kind of influence on Randolph (Dilke was rumoured to have made advances to Jennie that were not entirely unwelcome). But Jennie was sure-footed, and she made certain her salon also included leading artists, journalists and writers – people who had a say in shaping public opinion. She flirted – of course she did – but her work in the background helped Randolph immeasurably – even busy important men did not decline her invitations. Her life was not entirely happy, though. She was sometimes obliged to take the two boys to Blenheim and she came to detest her visits to her worthy but dreary parents-in-law who still disapproved of her, or at least made her feel they did. During one stay at Blenheim, in November 1880, she wrote frankly to her mother in Paris, who had proposed that she come to visit Jennie in London. 'I'm so delighted . . .' Jennie replied. She sometimes quite forgot what it felt like to be with people who loved her and longed to have someone in whom to confide. Of course Randolph always backed her, but she felt she could hardly abuse his mother to him when the Duchess was totally devoted to him and would do anything for him.

'The fact is I *loathe* living here,' she wrote. Not because it was deadly dull – she could tolerate that – but it was no use denying the truth. It was, she said, 'gall and wormwood' to accept hospitality and to be living within a family she hated and who hated her. She believed the Duchess disliked her just because she was what she was:

---

*Sir Charles Wentworth Dilke, 2nd Baronet (1843–1911), was a reforming Liberal politician who supported causes such as women's suffrage, workers' unions, the improvement of working conditions, the reduction of hours in factories and shops and education for all children.

prettier and more attractive than the Duchess's own daughters. Everything she said and did was noted and found fault with, she wrote. They were all always studiously polite, but the atmosphere was like a volcano, just waiting to erupt.[2]

One of the biggest problems for Jennie, attempting to make a reputation as a political hostess at that time, was the fact that she and Randolph were still *personae non gratae* with the Prince of Wales, which meant that the most important doors were closed to them.

But there was a greater reason for Jennie's unhappiness than she admitted to her mother. At some point in 1880 or 1881, shortly before she returned from Ireland, Randolph had – in the tactful words of Jennie's great-niece Anita Leslie in her memoir – 'separated himself from her physically'.[3] Jennie had come to accept that for all his declarations of love early in their relationship, for all the small 'kisses' he still enclosed at the bottom of his letters to her, Randolph was not capable of love in the generally accepted meaning of the word, or at least as she interpreted it and hoped for. Randolph unquestionably still admired and respected her, and would always come to her defence and wrote dutifully that he loved her. Furthermore, he had come to rely upon her support and help. He was proud of her beauty, and her abilities, proud that other men admired her. But in their relationship there was none of the close affection, the loving intimacies and shared laughter, the gentleness between lovers that she had seen even between her own mother and father when she was a child. And any passion in the bedroom had fled even before he deserted Jennie's bed. Yet it is clear that they had not fallen out, for in one of a series of tender letters when she was unwell over the New Year in 1883 he wrote that she must take the very greatest care of herself and not be careless with her health. If anything were to happen to her, he told her, his life would be ruined.[4]

Randolph did not even show affection to his children, appearing to be little interested in them: when forced to confront Winston and Jack during 'the children's hour' he treated them, one of Jennie's sisters noted, like a general reviewing his troops. So although she remained proud of him and loyal, Jennie simply accepted that Randolph was a physically cold man, totally absorbed in his political world. At first when he stayed away from her bed she had, not unnaturally, suspected an affair with another woman, but with the benefit of hindsight it seems more likely that Randolph had already been told that he had been infected with a form of venereal disease and had been given the usual advice by his physicians to abstain from sexual relations with his wife. Jennie was not taken into his confidence for some years. Anita Leslie – granddaughter of Leonie – later wrote that it was known that Randolph had been keeping a mistress in Paris at the time,* and it was believed in the Leslie family that it was from this woman that he had acquired venereal disease.[5]

It must be said that while she was in Ireland the passionate and impulsive Jennie, so attractive to men, had herself engaged in a number of friendships which may or may not – according to which gossip one believes – have resulted in discreet love affairs. Hunting weekends were an ideal cover for such interludes. It is quite possible that Randolph somehow heard of one or more of these and that this is what lay behind his self-exile from his wife's bed. Jennie was distressed that her marriage was in trouble and confided in her sisters, but there was little, apparently, that she could do about it, for Randolph simply refused to discuss the matter with her, and to outward appearances all was well with the couple. Randolph was the rising star in Parliament, with a beautiful, charming and able wife at his side and two healthy sons. Family rumour suggests that the couple were never sexually reconciled after this date. Jennie was not yet thirty.

Blandford was still the black sheep. He had been living for some years with Edith Aylesford in Paris where they called themselves Mr and Mrs Spencer, to the distress of the Duke and Duchess who managed to avoid the couple whenever they travelled on the Continent. Other members of the family met them, and every time that Jennie and Randolph holidayed in France, Blandford always

---

*Randolph and his friend Tom Trafford each kept a mistress in a shared flat in Paris, to save costs.

managed to join them, whether they wanted him to or not. He was still very attracted to Jennie.

On 4 November 1881 at 8 Avenue Friedland in Paris, Edith gave birth to a son, Guy Bertrand Aylesford, whom Blandford professed to love more than all of his other four children. Somewhat cheekily, two years later they bestowed upon him the title of Lord Guernsey, belonging to the Aylesford family. Unsurprisingly, since Aylesford had not clapped eyes on his wife for several years before the birth of the child, the Aylesford family contested the matter. It was taken up in the House of Lords,* with the result that Guy Bertrand was formally declared illegitimate and the title was disallowed.

During the eighteen months of legal infighting over this matter, which caused yet further inevitable gossip distressing to the Marlboroughs, Blandford's passion for Edith unaccountably cooled. Soon after the verdict was reached by the House of Lords about baby Guy Bertrand, Blandford ignobly abandoned Edith and his son in Paris, and with the encouragement of the Marlboroughs he returned permanently to England.

Meanwhile, Lord Aylesford had died in America, where he had fled after the scandal of Edith's desertion and their separation. In his will he left a small pension to her but this was all she had to live on, and for her it was poverty. It evidently assuaged Blandford's conscience, however, and he did nothing else either for her or for the son he had professed to love. Edith's reputation was totally destroyed: a return to her family and her life in England was simply not possible. This did not disturb Blandford; he did not even mention Edith in his will, though he rather sensationally included another mistress. He died before Edith; there was no wreath from the Churchill family at her funeral in 1897, but there was one from the Prince and Princess of Wales. There must have been some contact, however, for immediately after his mother's death sixteen-year-old Guy Bertrand went to stay at Blenheim for a short time.

---

*In July 1885 the House of Lords ruled that the 7th Earl of Aylesford was not the father of Guy Bertrand, and that the child had no right to the title.

It is difficult to know how and where he fitted in there, but he soon left to make his own way in the world and lost touch with the family.*

At the strong urging of the Duke and Duchess, and probably because he was – as usual – very short of money and being pressed by creditors, and because Goosie was persuaded it was her duty, Blandford and his wife were reunited for a short time. But this relationship was long dead and Blandford soon returned to his old ways and adulterous affairs. It ended with him being named as co-respondent in the sensational Lady Colin Campbell divorce case. Her portraits depict Lady Colin as a seductive and sultry beauty. When he was asked under oath what he had looked for in so continually seeking her company, Blandford coolly replied, 'Her conversation', which statement caused great merriment in the courtroom.† A year or so later he bought Lady Colin a Venetian palazzo on condition that she allowed him to make an annual visit to her there.

Goosie had now come to the end of her considerable tolerance, and she decided to divorce Blandford for infidelity and cruelty. It was not the first time she had decided upon this course, but she had previously been talked out of it. With her husband's reputation so irreparably damaged, she was advised that she would have little difficulty in obtaining a decree. Blandford, however, counter-sued, surprisingly citing Goosie's infidelity with the Duke of Alba. In the early summer of 1883 this was the talk of London, and Randolph was not best pleased at the adverse publicity which reflected badly on him; nor were his parents and sisters, who all felt stained with the flying mud.

It all proved too much for the sixty-one-year-old Duke. On 4 July that year, though ill and tired, he spoke passionately in the House of Lords on the unfortunately named Dead Wife's Sister's

---

*In a recent book, the present Duke's daughter stated that Guy was last sighted by a member of the family just after the Second World War. Nothing was heard of him subsequently.
†When he died, Blandford (by then the 8th Duke of Marlborough) left the then huge sum of £20,000 to Lady Colin Campbell as evidence of his 'friendship and esteem'.

Bill,* which he bitterly opposed; indeed, he is credited with helping to ensure its defeat. Afterwards, he took the train to Oxfordshire
and that evening dined at Blenheim with Randolph and Jennie. He
seemed in good spirits over dinner but during the night, possibly
worn down by long-term worries and the stress and shame of the
scandal surrounding Blandford's divorce case, the 7th Duke suffered
a massive heart attack and died.

The death of his father removed all vestiges of restraint on
Blandford as he succeeded to the title of 8th Duke of Marlborough,
with poor Goosie his very unwilling Duchess. Eventually, her evidence prevailed in the courts and the Marlboroughs' marriage was
duly annulled on 20 November 1883. Although she was legally entitled to the title of Duchess, Goosie spread it about that she wished
to be known by the name she had used throughout most of her
married life, Albertha, Marchioness of Blandford.

The evidence revealed by Goosie's lawyers during the divorce
hearing, together with the fact that Blandford was still not recognised by the Prince of Wales, was sufficient to ostracise the new
Duke from polite society, but now he had access to the Blenheim
coffers he lived even more extravagantly than before. His twelve-
year-old son Charles Richard, formerly known as Lord Sunderland,
became the new Lord Blandford, but the Duke continued to be
called 'Blandford' by his friends and Charles continued to be known
as 'Sunny' (from his former title 'Sunderland'). Sunny's sisters
Frances, Lilian and Norah remained with their mother after
their parents divorced, but Sunny was made to live with his
father. There is a sustained pattern of unhappy elder sons throughout the Marlborough family history and Sunny did not escape
it. He had already endured a wretched childhood due to his
parents' long estrangement, and as an adult he would claim that
from the time he embarked on his adolescent years and went to live
at Blenheim with his father he was 'given no kindness and was
entirely crushed'.

---

*Which enabled a widower to marry the sister of his late wife. Such an incongruously named
bill was snapped up and used by writers and novelists for years; it was passed a few years later.

Blandford, the 8th Duke of Marlborough, is known to history as 'the wicked Duke', and very little has been written about him outside of his disposal of Blenheim's assets. So it comes as rather a surprise to find that in spite of his personal problems, Blandford regarded himself as an economist, and a number of well written papers by him were published in magazines of the day.[6] He was intelligent, but unfocused in his thinking. Nor did he have the gift of great oratory, but the scandals in Blandford's life would anyway have prevented his going into politics as Randolph had done. Had he done so, however, the result would have been interesting, since he disagreed with his brother on almost every point of policy. Had Blandford not been born into the Churchill family he might have made a first-rate scientist, but he was too privileged to have ever needed to make the most of his innate abilities. Nevertheless, there is evidence that some of his later inventions with electricity and the telephone predated those of Thomas Edison, and were developed by him in parallel.

He soon realised that the estate income could not meet the expenses of the lifestyle he espoused and the laboratories and equipment he needed for his scientific experiments, as well as the cost of running Blenheim. His late father's action in contravening the entail made it conveniently easy for him to dispose of further art and literary treasures to meet the increasing demands of his creditors.[7] Consequently, he is mainly remembered now for the items he sold off: eighteen Rubens paintings, three of which were purchased by the Rothschild family; ten Van Dycks including the renowned equestrian portrait of Charles I;* and dozens of exquisite works by Raphael, Rembrandt, Brueghel, Gainsborough, Claude, Watteau, Stubbs and Reynolds among others were sacrificed along with most of the fine china collection – all to the dismay of every other member of the family. Only family portraits were kept. This massive sale raised £400,000 (over £19 million in today's values) and helped to underwrite projects that would occupy the remainder of Blandford's life: modernising his farms, building hothouses for his

---

*It was purchased by the National Gallery in 1885 for £17,500.

collection of orchids and laboratories for his experiments, and installing electricity at Blenheim. Randolph unsuccessfully attempted to prevent the sale, and later complained that as he travelled around the world he was frequently confronted with one of the former Blenheim works of art with which he had grown up.

Soon after the death of his father, Randolph had taken Jennie and nine-year-old Winston to the spa town of Bad Gastein in Austria for the summer months. Winston, always prey to chest complaints, had been seriously ill and it was thought that the air would do him good. Both Randolph and Jennie also had serious health problems. In 1882, Randolph had succumbed for months to a mystery illness that his previous biographers have concluded was possibly an early stage of syphilis. The features of this phase of the disease are flu-like and include headaches, fever, sickness, loss of appetite and lack of energy, lasting from a few weeks to many months. Randolph was unwell from March to September 1882 and unable to attend the House, although his parliamentary colleagues visited him at home where he spent his days lying on a sofa while he recuperated. He made several trips abroad for convalescence that summer, but returned home no better. It would be October before he made his return to the House. But while he was holidaying in Nice in December, Jennie contracted typhoid. She had no idea how dangerously ill she was when Randolph wrote affectionately to her advising her to join him in Nice to recuperate. Jennie replied that she was eager to join him, but not immediately for she had been forbidden to wear stays,[8] and she also hoped that Randolph would not spread it about that she would be twenty-nine years old on 9 January: '26 is quite old enough!'[9] In all their letters it was tacitly acknowledged that he was the more unwell of the two of them.

So the trip to Bad Gastein that spring was intended for the health of all three: Randolph, still mourning his father, Jennie recovering from typhoid, and Winston. Winston always recalled meeting Bismarck and his sense of awe when it was explained to him who Bismarck was. They also met the German Emperor who was staying there, and Jennie sat next to the Emperor at tea one day, charming him and as usual trying to advance Randolph's career, but apparently without success. Writing to a friend, Randolph joked that, although it was humiliating to admit, he believed the fame of the Fourth Party had not yet reached the ears of the Emperor.[10]

Soon afterwards Blandford came out to join them at Bad Gastein. At his invitation, Jennie took Winston home to spend the summer months with Jack and Sunny at Blenheim under the supervision of their respective nannies. Jennie spent this time alone in London. Blandford's divorce case was still to come to a conclusion, but that autumn he asked Jennie if she and Randolph would move in with him so that she could act as his hostess now that the Dowager Duchess had moved out with her unmarried daughters. Jennie came to appreciate Blandford at last, and in her memoir she wrote that she enjoyed that winter at Blenheim 'enormously' even though apart from hunting parties not a great deal of entertaining was done. She said it was the first time she had ever felt comfortable and 'wanted' in the great palace. Winston, having recovered his health during the summer, was packed off back to the hated St George's School.

Despite being short of money Randolph had decided during the previous year that he needed larger accommodation in London, and with two growing boys this made even more sense, so the couple disposed of 48 Charles Street and bought number 2 Connaught Place, which although more spacious cost less. The back of this house overlooks Marble Arch and Hyde Park, and is just a few steps away from the site of the Tyburn gallows.* When the couple had some work done on the cellars they found some ancient mass graves. Jennie was more than pleased to accept Blandford's suggestion that they should 'electrify' the house and place the noisy dynamo down there. For the two little boys nothing changed: whenever they were home they still lived in the nursery with Everest – which house they were in was almost irrelevant. The way

---

*The public gallows were located beside what is now 49 Connaught Square. The first recorded execution took place in 1196 and the last in November 1783 when the highwayman John Austin was hanged.

the Churchill family (and most others of their social class) dealt with their children was the same whether they were at Blenheim or in town: the children were kept strictly isolated from the grown-ups in a nursery suite 'well out of earshot',[11] except for the prescribed hour about tea-time when, washed and dressed in best clothes, they might spend some time politely chatting with their parents or with visitors.

Not long after their move to Connaught Place, the long period of ostracism by the Prince of Wales came to an end when he agreed to attend a dinner at the Attorney General's house at which Prime Minister and Mrs Gladstone and Randolph and Jennie were to be guests. Gladstone disliked Randolph (the feeling was mutual), but he enjoyed Jennie's company. The other guests must have held their collective breaths on 9 March 1884 when the Prince first came face to face with the Churchills, but he was willing to be charmed, and since Randolph had the full quota of Churchill panache and allure, the evening was a glorious success. Other royal dinner invitations followed, and Jennie was always ready to fascinate and amuse the Prince.

It would be another two years – May 1886 – before the Prince actually dined at Connaught Place with Blandford as a fellow guest, and thereafter it became not unusual for the Prince to call there. It was as if the old ill-feeling between them all might never have arisen, but Jennie was always on the alert lest something should occur that might return them to social purdah. She was not slow to see that the Prince was kinder to, and paid more attention to, her two boys than did their father. Jennie's younger sister Leonie, who stayed at 2 Connaught Place before departing for New York where she would marry a young Anglo-Irish Guards officer, John Leslie, son of the baronet Sir John Leslie, could not help noticing how whenever the children dared to approach their father he would shoo them away, waving his newspaper at them whenever they were brought in to see him. 'Two pairs of round eyes, peeping round the screen,' she remembered, 'longed for a kind word.'[12]

The school holidays of summer 1884 provoked a small crisis in the Churchill household at Connaught Place. It is believed in the family that it was while Winston was being examined by the family physician Dr Robson Roose that Dr Roose and Nanny Everest observed the physical evidence of corporal punishment on Winston's backside, and Everest persuaded the boy to tell her about it. It seems he had taken some lumps of sugar from the pantry and had been given a routine beating for it. Far from this making him contrite, he took the headmaster's straw hat from its peg and kicked it to pieces. He would have known that he could not hope to escape retribution, and he was flogged severely. When an old man, Winston would tell Anita Leslie about his experiences at the school, saying that had his mother not finally listened to Everest and taken him away from there, he believed he would have broken down completely. 'Can you imagine a child being *broken down*?' he asked her.[13] Winston, who had not been in full health for months,* was removed from St George's immediately and enrolled in a less pretentious establishment in Brighton, where the air was said to be better for him. This new school, an old-fashioned 'dame school', was run by two ageing spinsters, the Misses Thompson, and was recommended by Dr Roose whose own son of a similar age to Winston attended there. Winston would later recall that 'there was an element of kindness and of sympathy which I had found conspicuously lacking in my first experiences. At this school I was allowed to learn things which interested me: French,† History, lots of Poetry by heart, and above all Riding and Swimming. The impression of those years makes a pleasant picture in my mind, in strong contrast to my earlier schoolday memories.'[14] His school reports improved immediately.

Jennie continued to give her utmost loyalty and support to Randolph, but her heart was elsewhere. In that same year, when Winston changed schools and began his famous stamp collection, Jennie embarked upon a passionate relationship with Count Charles Kinsky, the man who was destined to be the love of her life. He was a handsome and debonair Austrian nobleman, a former

---

*He had suffered from chest infections and asthmatic attacks since the age of five.
†In fact, Winston was always notoriously poor at French.

cavalry officer turned diplomat who had everything Jennie sought in a man: good looks, breeding, charm, education, a love of music – and he was a dashing sportsman. Randolph, too, possessed many of these qualities, but he lacked the romantic passion that Kinsky had in large measure. Kinsky was not only an accomplished horseman when hunting, but to the astonishment of their circle he had won the Grand National the previous year, riding as an amateur on his own hunter. He had bought the horse, Zoedone – an unexceptional-looking chestnut mare with short legs – from a hunting stable at Oakham, to add to his string of hunters. Quickly recognising her jumping ability and determination, he put the mare into training, doing much of it himself. His unexpected win made him the toast of the town. Now he and Jennie were head over heels in love, but they were always discreet – so discreet, indeed, that whenever Kinsky visited their home he was heartily welcomed by Randolph as well as the two boys.

Conveniently, Randolph now decided he needed a long holiday to recuperate from his persistent illness. It is probable that the Conservative leader Lord Salisbury* had already hinted at a specific Cabinet position for him in his next administration, for Randolph chose to go to India and made the holiday an opportunity for some major research. Leonie and Jack (John Leslie), who had just returned from honeymoon in the USA, moved into Connaught Place 'to keep Jennie company', and helped to observe the proprieties when Kinsky was often to be found breakfasting there.[15] When Jennie's mother wrote from Paris in December 1884, she said that Randolph richly deserved his trip to India:

> I hope he will come back well & strong to enjoy life for many long years. He has made himself such a good name so early in life . . . I suppose the dear children are with you for the [Christmas] holidays. Clara writes me that Winston has grown to be such a nice charming boy. I am so pleased. Will you give him my best love, and

---

*Robert Cecil, 3rd Marquess of Salisbury, had assumed the leadership of the Conservative Party after Disraeli's retirement.

my little Jack . . . I am dying to see them again. What a delightful surprise it must have been for Jack and Leonie to be with you at Connaught Place . . . such a nice house & such a lot of jolly little people living together.[16]

Although Randolph's letters to his family were full of reports of tiger shoots, he also spent a good deal of his time investigating India's political system and the problems there. Because he was not afraid to voice his opinions he became popular in the Indian press, and when after six months he returned home, in April 1885, he was invited to speak at an important banquet. He chose India as his subject, and his speech was powerful enough to mark him henceforward as an expert on Indian affairs as well as on Irish problems.

In June 1885 Gladstone, harried and baited beyond endurance on the issue of Home Rule, was beaten in the House by twelve votes. He immediately resigned and Salisbury agreed, with understandable reluctance, to form a minority government.* All members of the 'Fourth Party' were given important Cabinet posts: Arthur Balfour (Salisbury's nephew) became President of the Local Government Board, Sir Henry Wolff was sent to Egypt on a delicate diplomatic mission, and John Gorst became Solicitor General. Randolph had made such a good impression in the Commons that no Conservative government could be formed without him in some significant position. Soon after his return from India he was offered the post of Secretary of State for India, which embodied membership of the Privy Council and gave him a salary of £5000 a year.

Any other man would have jumped at such an offer, but – typically – Randolph laconically made his acceptance conditional. He stated that he could not serve in any government containing Sir Stafford Northcote, leader of 'the old gang' of Conservatives which he accused of having brought the great party to its present low ebb. The Queen was shocked, and told Salisbury that as Randolph had never yet held office he should not be allowed to dictate terms. But

---

*A minority government can only work with the cooperation of another party or parties, possibly in the form of a coalition.

Randolph held out and won – Salisbury needed every vote in the House and could not afford to have Randolph's followers against him. As a result, the Queen found it difficult to approve of the appointment, but since she could find no insuperable objection she agreed to it, hoping that 'the India Council would be a check on him'.

Before he could officially take up his new post, however, it was necessary for Randolph to resign his seat at Woodstock and stand again for election, and since he was, he wrote, 'overwhelmed' with work in London, Jennie offered to do the local canvassing for him. Her campaign speeches – written by herself – were the same brand of democratic Toryism that Randolph supported, and she was arguably the first woman of any significance to play such an active role in politics.

Randolph's sister Georgie,* who was a noted horsewoman and whip, brought down her famous tandem-drawn trap, decorated in Randolph's racing colours of pink and brown, and in this smart rig the two women toured the countryside, local factories and even workers in the fields, day after day. Georgina had been brought up locally and knew many of the constituents by first name, but Jennie's approach was more basic – she simply begged people to vote for Randolph. 'Oh please won't you vote for my husband?' she would say endearingly. 'I shall be so unhappy if he doesn't get in.' When some factory workers grumbled about her invading their work break asking for votes, Jennie replied, 'But I want your votes, how am I to get them if I don't ask you?' – which simple logic seemed to placate the grumblers.

Randolph won the Woodstock seat with an increased majority, but it had been no walkover, as in his previous contest; the two women had been obliged to fight hard for every vote. The main reason for this was that Blandford, a committed Liberal, had offered his support to the opposing candidate. In Woodstock the support of the Duke was no light matter. Seeing the success Jennie and

---

*Georgina, Lady Curzon, nicknamed by Randolph 'the stud groom' because she spent so much time in the stableyard.

Georgina were having, the other side hastily put up two women canvassers, but they competed in vain. Dinners at Blenheim during this period, when Jennie and Georgina were staying at the palace but working each day from an office in Woodstock, must have been lively. Jennie always considered that election contest as one of the most satisfying periods of her life.

For Randolph, the time he spent at the India Office was a high-water mark. His first real test in office came when a palace coup took place in Burma. Thibaw, a younger son of the late King, massacred twenty-seven of his brothers together with their families. Two brothers escaped and applied to the British for asylum, but other members of the royal family remained in hiding and were in grave danger. The British declined to hand over the two princes to the self-declared King Thibaw, and demanded that the killing and intriguing stop at once. Queen Victoria refused to acknowledge the new King. The Foreign Office was deeply concerned that if not checked this affair could damage the stability of the Indian Empire, and Randolph was consulted for advice. He recommended that an ultimatum be issued to the Burmese, and that if it was rejected, force should be used '*at once* and in such strength as to be over-whelming from the very start'. This advice was carried out to the letter by the Viceroy, Lord Dufferin, and when the period of the ultimatum expired the British advanced immediately, occupying Mandalay. Within seven days they had taken the King prisoner, and annexed all of upper Burma. The cost of the campaign to the British in casualties was four men – one officer and three other ranks.

Fulfilled and fully occupied, Randolph seemed not to notice that Jennie was deeply involved with Kinsky; they were undoubtedly discreet. Perhaps he simply accepted it. Possibly, he was just too busy to see what was under his nose, for the minority administration could not hold out for long and in November 1885 Salisbury was forced to call another general election.

Since the previous election new legislation had given the vote to another two million householders and redrawn electoral bound-aries. Woodstock was one of the constituencies swept away, so

Randolph needed to look for another seat. He could have chosen a safe constituency but instead he arbitrarily decided to contest the Liberal stronghold at Birmingham, held by the great radical and reformer John Bright. Bright was arguably the only other man in Parliament who could lay claim to the title 'the greatest orator of his generation', and the contest was hard-fought.

It was characteristically rash of Randolph to attempt to take a major safe seat from the opposing party, especially when he was in poor health and the election was fought in November and December, cold months in which to canvass. An acquaintance, Wilfrid Scawen Blunt,* wrote that when he visited him Randolph was quite exhausted and could only climb a short flight of stairs with great difficulty.[17] Another wrote that Randolph was 'in a very bad way, the action of his heart has given way and he takes a lot of digitalis'.[18] As before, he was ably supported by Jennie, and this time even his mother the Dowager Duchess was brought in to help, sometimes sitting on the platform beside Randolph while Jennie went off to give a talk elsewhere. There was no question, this time, of Jennie wafting about on a tandem and flirting with prominent constituents for votes; it was a bitter contest, Randolph filling the halls every night with working men whom he could bring to their feet with his stirring rhetoric. He recognised before anyone else that the Conservative Party needed new policies that would appeal to the new grass-root voters who were not traditionally Tory supporters. And he was somehow able to convince these men† that he would better champion them than the Liberals, who claimed to be the party of the people. He did not win the seat, but to everyone's surprise in this largely working-class constituency he greatly reduced Bright's majority.

It was during this time that the rapprochement occurred between the Prince of Wales and the Randolph Churchills. Immediately, the couple were bombarded with invitations, and they were never

---

*1840–1922, diplomat, writer, traveller and poet. Blunt's gossipy diaries (some still unpublished) offer a fascinating insight into the upper classes of the Victorian and Edwardian eras.
†It should be remembered that women did not have the vote at this time.

without somewhere to stay when Randolph travelled around the country speaking on social reform: 'The Conservative Party will never exercise power until it has gained the confidence of the working classes,' he opined, 'and the working classes are quite determined to govern themselves, and they will not be either driven or hoodwinked by any class or class interests.' His frequent castigation of the Tory Party as being led by a cabal of old aristocrats sounds strange from the son of a duke, but it won him many votes from the working people, who would shout encouragement such as 'Give it to 'em hot, Randy!'[19] It did not, of course, win him many supporters within the senior ranks of his own party.

Ten-year-old Winston followed his father's career closely through the newspapers, and was keenly disappointed when Lord Randolph failed to take Birmingham by only a slim margin. However, a fellow MP who was an admirer stood down from his own safe seat in South Paddington in Lord Randolph's favour. The voters seemed to approve of the replacement, so he was back in Parliament the day after the election. The Liberals had assumed that the two million new voters from the working and lower-middle classes would return them with a good working majority, but they too were disappointed. In February 1886, Gladstone was again the leader of the party with the most votes, but there was no overall majority and the Irish Nationalists held the balance of power. Gladstone, a supporter of Home Rule, was backed by the Irish party led by Charles Stewart Parnell, but it was a shaky coalition at best and many Liberals were opposed to it. Randolph opposed Home Rule and his practical knowledge of the Irish question had enabled him to capitalise on what was a very confused situation, taking votes from the other side of the House to the maximum advantage of the Tories. That month he made the most memorable speech of his life on the subject and his deeply held opinions were summed up in his famous slogan, 'Ulster will fight, and Ulster will be right.'

Randolph's and Jennie's busy life came to a halt a month later when Winston suddenly fell seriously ill. Predisposed to colds – he seemed to have one every month during the winter – one led to a lung infection which deteriorated to pneumonia. In those pre-antibiotic days pneumonia was a killer, and the boy's life hung in the balance. On 14 March 1886 Dr Roose, whose practice was close to the school, was quickly called in. He advised in a note, 'This report may appear grave yet it merely indicates the approach of the crisis which, please God, will result in an improved condition should the left lung remain free. I am in the next room and will watch the patient during the night – for I am anxious.'[20]

Randolph and Jennie hurried down to Brighton with Nanny Everest. They were allowed only brief visits, to see their son from a distance, and on the following day Dr Roose isolated himself with his patient and wrote them a series of frightening progress notes: 'I shall give up my London work and stay by the boy', 'We are still fighting the battle for your boy', 'Your boy is . . . holding his own.'[21]

By the 17th, Winston seemed out of danger but was still very ill, and Dr Roose impressed upon Randolph and Jennie 'the absolute necessity of quiet and sleep for Winston and that Mrs Everest should not be allowed in the sick room today – even the excitement of pleasure at seeing her might do harm! And I am so fearful of relapse.'[22]

The Prince of Wales interrupted a levee to inquire about Winston's progress, and on 24 March when writing to Lord Salisbury, Randolph mentioned that Winston had almost died the previous week but was now out of danger. In fact from now on it was all good news for Winston. Since Nanny Everest had firmly expressed the opinion that his illness was due to unhappiness as much as to anything else, his mother paid him a great deal more attention, even occasionally taking him around with her during the school holidays. Her friend the Duchess of Edinburgh (married to a son of the Queen) invited Winston to play with her children at Buckingham Palace, and again later that year while they were all visiting Cowes for Cowes Week, at Osborne House.

After a short visit to Paris that spring with a party of friends which, somewhat surprisingly, included Count Kinsky, Randolph continued his constant attacks on Gladstone's government, and at last his rhetoric bore fruit.

There was another general election in June, and this time the

Conservatives romped home with a clear majority of 118 over all other parties. This victory ended the Liberals' long dominance of Parliament – they had held power for eighteen of the previous twenty-seven years but would hold it for only three of the next twenty. It was generally agreed that Randolph Churchill, with his able oratory and grasp of the Irish problem, had facilitated the rout and that this must be recognised. He was duly appointed Chancellor of the Exchequer and Leader of the House of Commons. When the Queen was told of the appointment by Lord Salisbury she wrote in her diary of the visit: 'Lord Salisbury . . . feared Lord Randolph Churchill must be Chancellor of the Exchequer and Leader, which I did not like. He is so mad and odd & also has bad health.'[23] She had not forgotten his behaviour over the Aylesford letters. All the same, Randolph was only thirty-seven and already being roundly tipped as the next Prime Minister. It was heady stuff for Jennie.

By the end of the year Winston was back to normal health, writing confidently to Jennie about his progress in swimming: 'I am in good health. It is superfluous to add that I am happy.' As usual, most of his letters contained a request for a visit from his mother, or from Everest. He *was* much happier – that can be easily seen from the chatty weekly letters he sent, filled with details of concerts and plays, cricket matches and horse-riding, what he wanted for Christmas, almost always a request for money to build up his stamp collection or his platoons of lead soldiers, and inquiries after the various pet dogs that the family always owned.

The seeds of his literary ability and his love of words can already be seen emerging from the ink-blotted copperplate script: 'My Darling Mama, I hear that you are greatly incensed against me! I am very sorry – But I am hard at work & I am afraid some enemy hath sown tares in your mind.'[24] 'Please excuse all these blots; this ink is as thick as cream and I have only one flickering candle.'[25] But what comes across most strongly from his weekly letters is that he was still a young boy who missed his family a good deal. In one letter to Randolph during 1885 in which he requested some autographs for his fellow pupils (which he secretly sold to increase his pocket money) he wrote, 'I cannot think why you did not come to see me, while you were in Brighton . . . I suppose you were too busy to come.' A year later he used almost the same words: 'You never came to see me on Sunday when you were in Brighton.'[26] He makes no complaint, but the disappointment rises up from the page. Eleven-year-old Winston could not know, of course, of the major problems that would soon lead to the end of everything for which his father had worked.

There is no doubt that Randolph reached his exalted position at the early age of thirty-seven by sheer hard work, real ability and his genius for oratory. But he was always idiosyncratic in his behaviour, and – as the Queen had privately noted – he had been in poor health for some time. Now, suffering from persistent insomnia, he had become chronically irritable and irrational, living on his nerves and chain-smoking; he drove himself and his staff to exhaustion. His very able secretary collapsed from the strain of it all and was sent away to convalesce, but the man died two months later.

Practically everyone now, especially Jennie and the Churchill family, regarded Randolph as a Prime-Minister-in-waiting. But his family did not know that during that autumn of 1886 Randolph had begun behaving very erratically at work, often losing his temper, and was increasingly viewed as a handicap by his Cabinet colleagues. He was not a team player and would never listen to the opinions of others. Having been raised to consider his views were important, he believed he was always right. His speeches were often critical of Salisbury's administration. Even his friend Arthur Balfour could not help but be sadly aware of the damage Randolph was doing to his reputation, and to that of the government. Balfour wrote to his uncle Lord Salisbury: 'At present we ought to do nothing but let Randolph hammer away . . . we should avoid all . . . "rows" until R. puts himself entirely and flagrantly in the wrong by some act of Party disloyalty which everybody can understand and nobody can deny.'

Jennie, still immersed in her affair with Kinsky, had merely noticed a new coldness and a quickness to anger in Randolph, and that nothing she did could please him. It appears from extant correspondence between Jennie and others that during the autumn there was a major row, when Randolph moved out of 2 Connaught Place. Jennie must surely have suspected that he knew of her now long-standing affair with Kinsky, but when Lady Mandeville whispered to her that Randolph was involved with Gladys, Lady de Grey,* she concluded that this must be the reason for his behaviour. At no point did she consider, apparently, that there might be any connection between her own unfaithfulness and Randolph's coldness. She probably had Blandford's scandals in mind, and was in a state of great distress when she eventually confided in her mother-in-law, the Dowager Duchess Fanny. The two women had never been close, but to the credit of the Dowager Duchess she did try to help Jennie at this point.

'I cannot make it out,' Duchess Fanny replied, 'have you told me everything? Can anything have got to his ears, or some diabolical mischief have been made? . . . Write to him . . . Even if he does not answer he must read your letter & you could tell him how miserable you are and appeal to him not to break your heart . . . I cannot understand his being so hard if he realises all you suffer. Perhaps he is full of other things. I *cannot* believe there is any other woman.'[27] Duchess Fanny wrote again on 8 September 1886 at great length from her home at Huntercombe Manor near Maidenhead:

Dearest Jennie,
I thought so much about you . . . Rely on one thing . . . I may not be able to do any good but I will do no harm & not like my poor Cornelia put the fat in the fire in my desire to help you. Meantime I *pray* you [that] you do not breathe thoughts of revenge against *anyone*. It will bring you no blessing. Accept your present worry & anxiety patiently . . . avoiding the [company] of those friends who while ready enough to pander to you would gladly see you vexed or humbled as they no doubt are jealous of your success in society . . . I wish so much you had your sisters for they are to be trusted & I really would trust no one else. Try dear, to keep your troubles to

---

*Gladys, Countess de Grey, was often called the most beautiful woman of her generation. Oscar Wilde dedicated his play *A Woman of No Importance* to her.

yourself – this is hard for you as you have a telltale face – though you do tell little fibs at times.

It is a horrid time of year for you to be in town . . . dear Jennie do come and vegetate quietly here. Bring Jack and we will try to make you as happy as possible. I am sure it will show R[andolph] you care for him & he has a good heart and will give you credit for it. If I were you I would not, if it killed me, let the heartless lot you live with generally see there was 'a shadow of a shade of a shred' wrong, only HE should know it & feel that it makes you miserable . . . He hates trouble . . . Oh dear Jennie you are going through a great *crise* of your life & on yourself will depend whether your hold & influence become greater than ever or not . . . I have no doubt of your success for I *know* in his heart he is truly fond of you – & I think I ought to know.

Sunny came yesterday & . . . gives a good account of your boys. Perhaps it will be as well for you to go there [to Blenheim] for next Sunday. But pray be careful with Blandford. He is so indiscreet to say the least of it . . . I daresay there is some ground for Lady M[andeville]'s story. I can believe anything of those sorts of women. They seem to like to spoil a ménage. I pray that God may . . . watch over dear R. and keep him straight.[28]

In another letter, after she had spoken to Randolph but avoided asking him outright if he was being unfaithful, Duchess Fanny cautioned Jennie about her affair with Kinsky:

Life cannot be all pleasure, & oh dearest Jennie, *before it is too late* I pray you to [take] my advice to heart & give up that fast lot you live with, racing, flirting & gossiping . . . As to other matters I feel sure you have no cause for jealousy in that quarter. But I feel there is a great deal of talk & I fear, dear, you have not been able to conceal things as you should have done. Mrs Stirling, L[ady] Mandeville, L[ady] Londonderry and others have talked & it has come to me from Mary & my children. I do pray you to be *very* discreet this week & I hope and trust for both your sakes that nothing will be observed at Newmarket.[29]

There was more in this vein, hinting that Jennie's own behaviour was unacceptable, and especially her continued extravagance. Visitors to 2 Connaught Place recalled that there was a constant stream of deliveries to the house of hats and dress boxes, all bearing exclusive and expensive names. It was almost unavoidable, given that Jennie ran with what the Dowager Duchess called the 'fast lot' who peopled Marlborough House parties. And Randolph was in deep water financially at that point, partly because of the extravagant manner in which both he and Jennie lived. But the fact remains that though they kept up appearances and were socially in great demand, both parties in this marriage were engaged in extramarital affairs. The Duchess could see the inherent dangers, but it was useless for her to ask Jennie to give up everything she most cared for in life.

In November the Queen invited them to dine at Windsor, a great honour, as well as to visit Sandringham (one of several such invitations that year), where the Prince and Princess of Wales held their alternative and far livelier court. And there were always house parties, which Jennie attended usually with Randolph; but sometimes she went alone, and on these occasions Kinsky was often to be found among the guests. Jennie adored these house parties – 'Do come from Friday to Monday . . .' (the word 'weekend' was not then in general use). A large wardrobe was required, and a maid; and a gentleman required a valet. So a hostess not only had her guests to accommodate and feed but the same number of servants, at least; for a woman might bring her dresser as well as her maid. It is difficult today to appreciate the sheer number of clothes such a woman of the Victorian era would have to pack, besides the voluminous underclothes worn in those days.

For breakfast, while the men wore either hunting clothes or plusfours, the women could dress casually in a tweed skirt and blouse with a tweed jacket (unless they were riding to hounds). The morning would be spent writing letters or chatting and then they would invariably set off in pony traps to join the shooters for a substantial hot picnic set out in tents or buildings somewhere on the estate. By 5 p.m. they had to be back at the big house, bathed and dressed in elaborate tea gowns for tea, and they would perhaps be asked to play the piano or sing. At seven the dressing gong would sound and all the guests trooped to their rooms, to be dressed in formal attire – white tie for the men, and for the women low cut, tightly laced evening dresses and whatever jewels ('never diamonds in the country') were appropriate. A woman could not travel to one of these three-night house parties with fewer than three tea gowns, three evening gowns (which must not have been seen before), plus walking clothes and the correct shoes and accoutrements that accompanied all this paraphernalia. For Jennie, chatting, charming the male guests, playing the piano – this was her element.

In November the Dowager Duchess Fanny wrote to her, again on the subject of Randolph: 'My heart aches for you but I feel you intensify matters and worry yourself in vain. If you could only be quiet and calm – I feel sure everybody at Sandringham saw your jealousy . . . there is much talk about it. And people will not pity you. The idea is that you who have led so independent a life are foolish *now* to be so jealous. And you have been too successful and prosperous not to have made enemies.'[30]

By December the Churchills' personal difficulties seem to have subsided somewhat, for Jennie gave out in her letters, at least, that she anticipated Christmas 1886 would be an especially happy one. Randolph's career seemed to be going from strength to strength; her boys, now twelve and six and both away at school, were coming home for the holidays; and on 20 December Randolph was again invited to Windsor to dine with the Queen and stay overnight.

During their conversation there the Queen noted that Randolph looked 'low', and she told him she hoped the new Parliament would be a happier session for him than the previous one when he had appeared so tired. She recorded in her diary that he answered her evasively. In fact Randolph was in serious trouble, probably aggravated, as ever, by poor health and, at this time, by his emotional and domestic problems. The financial demands of the War Office (headed by W.H. Smith[*]) and the Admiralty (headed

---

[*]William Henry Smith, grandson of the founder of the W.H. Smith newsvending shops. He was a leading politician and served as a minister in several Tory governments.

by Lord George Hamilton) could not be met from the national budget. The Queen could have had no idea that on his way to Windsor Randolph had already made the decision to issue what amounted to an ultimatum: when he retired that night he wrote to Lord Salisbury, on Windsor Castle writing paper, stating that, as Chancellor, he could no longer be responsible for the country's finances since neither Smith nor Hamilton would reduce their estimates for the coming year.

This was a major miscalculation on Randolph's part – the greatest mistake of his political life, in fact. He was confident that he acted from a position of strength, believing (as many great men before him have done) that the government could not succeed without him, and that his implied resignation would ensure Salisbury's support. But although he had flashes of brilliance, Randolph had often been more of a hindrance to the government than an asset. He had on occasion leaked information to *The Times* and spoken frankly against government policies; he frequently threw tantrums and behaved in a manner which many of his colleagues thought out of keeping with the expected behaviour of a minister of state. If this was not enough, he appears to have alienated many Tories by his open ambition to head the party. As well as the rumours of his liaison with Lady de Grey, new rumours were circulating that he was mentally unstable, certainly very unwell. With a clear majority in the House, Salisbury no longer needed to pander to Randolph and his diminishing band of supporters. The letter played straight into his hands.

Randolph travelled back to London on the train with one of the two chief protagonists of his political troubles, the First Lord of the Admiralty, Lord George Hamilton. Randolph told him that he could no longer go on as Chancellor because of the exorbitant estimates of the cost of the Army and Navy for the coming year. He then showed him the letter he had written and Hamilton was stunned. Although he was one of those most concerned in the matter he urged Randolph to consult someone else – or at least talk to Duchess Frances – before sending it to the Prime Minister. Randolph ignored this advice and later that day sent the letter by special messenger. It arrived at Hatfield House* during a ball at which Randolph's mother was present. Salisbury did not mention the matter to her. In fact he did not mention the matter to anyone, not even the Queen, while he took time to consider all the implications. Two days later he wrote to W.H. Smith telling him that he considered Randolph's letter as offering his resignation, which he had accepted.

Still having heard nothing from Salisbury himself, Randolph went to lunch with Smith, who told him of the content of Salisbury's letter, which he had just received. Later that day when he took Jennie to the theatre, Randolph was fidgety, and shortly after the first act he left her, saying he was going to the club. It was there, at the Carlton Club,† that Randolph received Salisbury's formal reply unequivocally accepting his resignation. Randolph's instant reaction was that he would have his letter published, to demonstrate that he had not actually resigned (later he would insist that it had been intended merely as 'the beginning of a correspondence' on the subject), and he went immediately to see George Earl Buckle, editor of *The Times*. Having read the letter Buckle was aghast and told him, 'You can't send that.' Randolph said it had already been sent, told him of the outcome and asked for Buckle's support in a leader article, in return for publishing it. Buckle refused, saying, 'You can't bribe *The Times*.' But the next edition carried the dynamite letter anyway.

Jennie had no idea that all this was going on. Probably it is a measure of how far apart their personal lives had grown that all had seemed quite normal to her, with Randolph coming and going, attending the theatre, visiting his club as usual. He had allowed her to carry on organising a big party at the Foreign Office, merely saying to her at the theatre when she queried something about the

---

*Historic stately home built by Robert Cecil, 1st Earl of Salisbury, in 1611. In 1558 while she was living in the old palace at Hatfield, Elizabeth I learned of her accession to the throne.
†The Carlton Club was founded in London in 1832 by leading Conservatives as a venue where party policy and events could be coordinated. The premises in Pall Mall were destroyed in the Second World War and the clubhouse, still the heart of the Conservative Party, is now in St James's Street. For men like Randolph it was a second home.

guest list, 'Oh I shouldn't worry about it . . . it probably will never take place.' Puzzled, she had asked him what he meant, but he declined to explain as he left for the club. The following day, 23 December, when Jennie's breakfast tea and newspaper were delivered to her bedroom, she read Randolph's resignation letter. Their personal lives may have been in turmoil but she had become so sure of his political brilliance that, though dumbfounded at what she read, even then she believed there was some rational explanation – that it was a ploy of Randolph's to gain greater control. She wrote of that morning in her memoirs: 'When I came down to breakfast, the fatal paper in my hand, I found him calm and smiling. "Quite a surprise for you," he said. He went into no explanation, and I felt too utterly crushed and miserable to ask for any, or even to remonstrate. Mr Moore [Randolph's private secretary] . . . rushed in, pale and anxious, and with a faltering voice said to me, "He has thrown himself from the top of the ladder, and [he] will never reach it again!"'[31]

It was a political sensation, of course, and the main topic of conversation at social events that Christmas. Salisbury at last informed the Queen, who was furious with him because – like Jennie – she had been left to read Randolph's letter in *The Times*, and with Randolph too, because he had abused her hospitality by writing his resignation letter on Windsor Castle paper.

Randolph spent the entire Christmas lying prostrate on the sofa at home, chain-smoking. Jennie, having ascertained that there was probably no way back into government for him, was very bitter, for apart from anything else, what Randolph had done was tantamount to financial suicide. It is probable that she took the two boys away to spend Christmas with her sisters or perhaps even her mother-in-law, since callers at No. 2 Connaught Place who wrote about Randolph's demeanour did not mention Jennie. The letters and accounts of this period in the Churchill archive suggest that Randolph knew very well that he was critically ill, and that – tired and depleted – he was trying to come to terms with this while affecting nonchalance. It is impossible to believe that a man of Randolph's sagacity and means had not consulted all the eminent specialists in the field of his illness; he undoubtedly knew the prognosis only too well. He would not have been human had his health problems and his shattered career not depressed him.

No one in the family has written of what that Christmas was like, although Winston was then twelve and would no doubt have recalled it when he came to write his memoir of his early life. When he returned to school he undoubtedly had to face the questions and even the jeers of his contemporaries. However, he was a child who had already shouldered more emotional stress than most children are ever required to do, and his letters home in January 1887 did not touch on the domestic situation, merely recording his good health, that his marks were 'not bad for me' and that he had managed to get into the first eleven at football. By the first week in January, however, London was buzzing with rumours that Lady Randolph was about to file for divorce citing Lady de Grey, and that Lord Randolph was to counter-sue citing John Delacour,* a dandyish sportsman with whom Jennie sometimes hunted. If there was an affair between Jennie and Delacour it was brief and unrecorded.

Count Kinsky was immediately recalled to Vienna, to avoid a diplomatic crisis. Lord Derby wrote in his diary that he had been told Randolph was 'taking steps to get rid of his wife whom he accuses of playing tricks with four men. A pleasant disclosure of manners in that set.'[32] Newspaper reporters were given short shrift by Randolph, but one contemporary diarist wrote of the *on-dit* going round the London clubs and dining rooms:

Question: Why did Lord Randolph leave the Government?
Answer: Because he did not approve of the Austrian alliance.

It was exactly the sort of scandal that terrified the Dowager Duchess, and even Jennie.

Randolph had banked on there being no one else in the Conservative Party qualified to take on the post of Chancellor. And, indeed, it was extremely difficult for Salisbury to replace him.

---

*Chiefly recalled now for the *Vanity Fair* cartoons of him by 'Spy' and 'Ape'.

6

1887–95

Lilian's Millions

Having effectively wrecked his career, Randolph's reaction was to crave some winter sun and warmth. He left almost immediately for North Africa, with a few male companions.* Jennie seems to have undergone a sudden change of heart towards him. Was this because of a realisation of the distance between them, or was it possibly at this point that she was told by his physicians of their diagnosis and prognosis? Her letters to him, addressed to 'Dearest R.', became friendly and affectionate again. She kept him informed of what was happening on the political scene and what was being said about him, though her accounts of the latter were abridged versions. She certainly seems to have grasped how serious his illness was, and her letters became bolstering in tone.

Jennie refused to go into retirement and went about as normal, but she took a good deal of flak socially, most of it good-natured; undoubtedly a lesser woman would have found it hard to face. She gave as good as she got, and with the Prince of Wales and other good friends supporting her she coped, on one occasion unhesitatingly accepting an invitation to a party thrown by the Salisburys. Both Lord and Lady Salisbury were nervously attentive, skirting

---

*He went first to Constantine in Algeria, but it snowed there so he moved to Biskra, a small city in the north-east of the country at the northern edge of the Sahara Desert, renowned for winter warmth and hot sulphur springs.

round the subject of Randolph, but eventually the conversation turned to winter sunshine and Jennie said that Randolph was enjoying his trip. Later she reported the incident, writing to Randolph that Salisbury had remarked, 'I am sure the rest will do him good, Randolph's brain works so quickly that it must wear out his nervous system.' Jennie responded that it was certainly true that his brain was so quick he usually reached a conclusion six months before most other people. Her assessment was that Salisbury wanted to remain friendly but that he would not help Randolph politically.[1]

At one dinner party when someone asked her mischievously if she would be offering to sell Randolph's robes (the Chancellor's costly robes of office) to Mr Goschen, she answered hotly that she could not, as Randolph would need them again before too long. The Liberal Unionist leader Lord Hartington gallantly interrupted to say, 'Randolph won't want them in the future, as he will be P.M. next time.'[2] Other friends rallied round but they were in the minority, and Jennie watched bitterly as people whom she had regarded as close friends deserted Randolph now he was out of power.

Winston was not spared. After he returned to school in January he was taken to a pantomime in Brighton where Lord Randolph's resignation was referred to in a sketch. The audience booed and hooted and Winston, who seldom saw his father – but was immensely proud of him – was livid with rage. Turning to the man immediately behind him, he hissed: 'Stop that row, you snub-nosed Radical!' Randolph was delighted when he heard of his son's loyalty and asked Jennie to send him a sovereign with her next letter.

Writing of all this to her sister Leonie, Jennie gave a franker version of London gossip and her meeting with Salisbury than she had reported to Randolph. She knew now that Salisbury would never reinstate Randolph in his Cabinet and said she sometimes felt sick at heart that Randolph had thrown away such a splendid position. He had flown too high and convinced himself that 'he could do anything' with impunity. However, there was a compensation, for Randolph had been much nicer to her since the crisis, she wrote. His letters were very affectionate and she had hopes that their relationship would be better when he returned.[3]

Jennie saw little of Blandford, who came to London rarely. The stigma of his divorce still clung to him and he was a lonely figure. He began making regular annual trips to America, where he was not shunned – in fact, the reverse, for he found himself lionised by Society hostesses despite adverse newspaper comments. One disclosed the fact that the Duke had arrived with thirty-five pieces of luggage: 'Everything His Grace of Marlborough [*sic*] brought with him was clean, except his reputation.'[4]

It had not taken Blandford long to run through the money he had raised from the sale of Blenheim's finest art treasures. Within four years it was clear that he had to find another huge sum to keep himself and Blenheim afloat. Now, at the suggestion of an acquaintance, an obvious solution presented itself: during his visits to America he was introduced to an apparently endless supply of rich American girls – why not marry an heiress? Perhaps secretly he hoped to find someone like Jennie, who had been such an asset to Randolph, but with money.

Leonard Jerome was happy to introduce the forty-four-year-old Duke to New York's rich set, as a result of which, in the early summer of 1888, the Duke met Mrs Lilian Hammersley, a widow. Lilian was hardly a girl, at thirty-three years old,* but in addition to a significant legacy from her father she had been left a fortune of $5 million by her late husband. Her claim to fame seems to rest on the fact that she festooned the small room behind her box at the opera with expensive orchids, and that she changed her name to Lily because Lilian rhymed too easily with 'million' for copywriters to resist. She was no great beauty – indeed, she had a faint moustache, which was widely commented upon. She

---

*No date of birth is given for Lilian in the peerage guides but she declared her age as thirty-six in the 1891 UK census returns. She gave birth to a son in 1897, in her third marriage, so this could be correct.

did not dress fashionably, and she was not witty or bright in conversation, but she was an intelligent, kind person with a pleasant nature, and the Duke was not looking for a love match.

Within weeks Leonard Jerome was writing to Clara, who was in London, that he rather thought the Duke would marry Mrs Hammersley. 'Don't you fear any responsibility on my part. Mrs Hammersley is quite capable of deciding for herself, besides I never set eyes on the lady but once. All the same I hope the marriage comes off as there is no doubt she has lots of tin.' Less than a month later he wrote to tell his wife that the introduction had worked, and that the Duke and Lily Hammersley were already married. 'I went with him to the Mayor's office in the City Hall at 1 o'clock today,' Jerome confirmed, 'and witnessed the ceremony.'[5] That was the civil part dealt with, but there was great difficulty in arranging a religious marriage because of the Duke's divorce. Eventually they found a kindly Methodist minister who consented to marry them. Afterwards there was a grand dinner and two days later Jerome waved them off as they sailed for England aboard the Cunard Line's three-masted steamship *Aurania*.*

The new Duchess was in for a series of shocks as she settled into Blenheim. The 'courtship', if it could be called such, had been so fast that she had hardly had time to organise a trousseau, and she knew little of her husband's reputation or his past. The first thing that confronted her was the life-sized nude of Lady Colin Campbell, painted by Whistler, which hung in the Duke's dressing room. The second thing she noted was the chill of Blenheim and the lack of bathrooms. The third was the fact that she and her husband were not received at court. Jennie had been the first American woman to marry into the British aristocracy; one might say she led the charge. The next American heiress to capture an English lord was the glamorous Consuelo Yznaga who had married Lord Mandeville in New York in 1876 (two years after Jennie married

---

*In those early days of steam-powered ships, owners were reluctant to commit entirely to steam because of frequent engine trouble. The *Aurania* completed the voyage between Liverpool and New York under sail on a number of occasions.

Randolph), to become eventually the Duchess of Manchester when Lord Mandeville succeeded to the dukedom in 1890. So Duchess Lily had several supportive countrywomen willing to give her advice and tell her what she should expect of her bargain.

Jennie worked at getting Lily accepted into society: she introduced her to the Prince and Princess of Wales, and persuaded five of her sisters-in-law to arrange various entertainments and invite the new Duchess. This was no small favour, as the Churchill women consti-tuted a large swathe of the peerage. Cornelia, Lady Wimborne, was the wife of the 1st Baron Wimborne, and had the vast Guest fortune behind her; Anne was the Duchess of Roxburghe, Fanny was the wife of the 2nd Baron Tweedmouth, Rosamund was married to the 2nd Baron Ramsay of Ramsay Abbey, and Georgina had married Richard George Curzon, 4th Earl Howe.* Duchess Lily was thus successfully introduced into society without the need to curtsey to the Queen.

Meanwhile, she was happy for Blandford to spend some of her money on the palace, and when Randolph visited Blenheim in the following year he described some of the new works to his mother. He had looked over the reparations and improvements and was not especially impressed, considering the amount of money spent. He admitted that the electric lighting and heating in the stables had been 'well-done', but thought that the huge amount of money lavished on refurbishing the drawing room was rather wasted. He was bored during his visit as Duchess Lily only wished to talk about and praise her husband, who – as a consequence – had come to believe he was a 'beneficent genius'. The domestic arrangements also left much to be desired, Randolph wrote, since they breakfasted at 11 a.m., lunched at 3 p.m. and dined at 9 p.m.; hours which did not suit his digestion. He could not help remark-ing that Duchess Lily's 'moustache and beard' were 'becoming serious'.[6]

This was unfair, and indeed Randolph would later regret this

---

*The sixth and youngest sister, Lady Sarah, was still unmarried at this point but would marry Lt-Col. Gordon Chesney Wilson in November 1891.

snap assessment of his sister-in-law; Duchess Lily had also paid to have the palace roof releaded to prevent leaks, as well as for central heating and electricity to be installed. But there was no doubt that she was unused to running an establishment like Blenheim and it was difficult for her to please the Marlborough clan.

Despite these problems the marriage seemed to be a reasonably happy one, which was a rare enough event in the Churchill family. Blandford seemed content at last, pottering around Blenheim free of money worries and unhampered by his compliant Duchess. This was more than could be said for Goosie, who in 1891 went to court to petition her former husband for money for their son's education. She lost her case, but as the boy was still able to go through Cambridge, probably her family stepped in to help. Blandford's new-found sense of ease was, though, to be short lived. To everyone's great shock, on 9 November 1892 at the early age of forty-eight, he was found dead in his laboratory on the top floor of Blenheim with – as the housekeeper told members of the family – 'a terrible expression on his face'.[7]

This left Blandford's son Charles – universally known as 'Sunny' – to succeed as the 9th Duke. It was a week before his twenty-first birthday and he was still up at Cambridge. Described as 'proud, off-hand and frequently offensive',[8] no one could have been less prepared to take on the onerous task of looking after Blenheim. Needless to say, his coming-of-age celebrations had to be delayed for some months because of the requisite period of mourning, but one of his first visitors at Blenheim was his cousin Winston, who became a frequent guest thereafter and a close friend for the next forty years. At his belated birthday party the new Duke received his guests with his mother at his side. Goosie was still regarded as faintly ridiculous by most of the Churchill family, and almost immediately after the party it was his grandmother, Dowager Duchess Fanny, who took on the task of finding Sunny a suitable wife.

Apart from Duchess Lily, Randolph was probably the person most affected by Blandford's death. Upon receiving the news he had gone immediately to Blenheim to help, if he could, and the following day he wrote from there to Jennie admitting he had been wrong about Lily: 'Nothing could exceed her goodness and kindness of disposition,' he wrote. He also prepared Jennie for possible scandal, because Blandford's will contained a large bequest to his former mistress, Lady Colin Campbell. Duchess Lily seemed genuinely broken-hearted at her loss. Jennie later told her sisters that the widow had torn Blandford's collection of photographs of Lady Colin into shreds and posted them without any explanatory note to her rival in Venice. The Whistler nude was never seen or heard of again. It was generally assumed that it had been burned.

The shock of his brother's death seems to have precipitated the final chapter of Randolph's worsening health. The symptoms of the third stage of syphilis can last from a few months to many years, and are so varied, resembling those of so many other illnesses, that physicians used to call syphilis 'the great mimicker'. This final phase can take up to twenty years to develop, so that many older patients never suffered some of the symptoms. But those who did would have experienced rashes and ulcers on the skin, and lesions on ligaments, joints and bones causing reduced and painful mobility. But the worst feature, and the one that all syphilis patients feared before the discovery of antibiotics, was the threat of madness, which doctors referred to as 'a general paralysis of the brain'. It was a good descriptive term, given that tertiary syphilis attacks the entire nervous system as well as the heart and blood vessels. Sufferers often become blind, paralysed in various parts of the face and body, and speech becomes slurred. Mood swings and violent anger lead to, at worst, clinical insanity. One of the features is a sort of hypermania in which the patient experiences great optimism alternating with depression. Randolph was noted by his physicians, family, friends and acquaintances as showing all these symptoms.

As early as 1888 'Randy' Churchill's increasingly slurred speech was beginning to cause comment; 'indistinct utterances' was how journalists put it, and he began apologising during his speeches for his poor hearing and articulation. However, this was still only the beginning of his problems.

During that year, when he visited the nursery on Winston's fourteenth birthday, Lord Randolph found his elder son confidently recreating a famous battle with his huge collection of lead soldiers, including all the accoutrements of war that he had been amassing since the age of seven. After watching this for twenty minutes, he had smiled at Winston, an unusual event on its own, and asked if he would like to enter the Army as a career. Carried away by the moment, Winston said he would – and that was his career decided upon, to Winston's later regret.

By 1893 Lord Randolph was suffering the onset of paralysis of his extremities – a recognisable symptom to Dr Roose, given the patient's history. In the five intervening years those closest to Randolph – Jennie, Winston and Jack, Duchess Fanny and his sisters – had had to watch him inexorably failing as he attempted to carry on with his career. In his biography of his father written many years later, Winston, who was occasionally present when Randolph gave a speech and studied them in the newspapers, loyally contended that his father's performances were just as brilliant and hard-hitting as always. Contemporary evidence does not bear this out. Randolph may well have still been capable of putting his thoughts on paper in a cogent manner, but he could no longer present them to the House in a fashion that impressed his listeners. Even his letters to *The Times* had become rambling and lacked his former incisiveness. His insistence on attending the House, punctuated by frequent visits to European spas for 'convalescent' treatments, made his gradual breakdown very public. His bursts of bad temper were legendary. Friends who did not see him for a few months were invariably shocked at the deterioration. He was forty-four and looked twenty years older, with thin greying hair and his skin hanging in folds.

Randolph's behaviour towards Winston after his illness took hold was colder than ever, and usually critical. Of Jack he often said, 'He is no trouble', but Winston came in for a cascade of angry notes for his lack of achievement at Harrow, his spendthrift habits, his carelessness and lack of application generally. Randolph even wrote to his mother to complain about him: 'He has little [claim] to cleverness, to knowledge or any capacity for settled work. He has a great talent for show-off exaggeration and make-believe.' This, he wrote, was proved by Winston's 'total worthlessness as a scholar . . . at Eton or Harrow' (he seemed not to know at this point which school Winston attended). 'He need not expect much from me . . . I will not conceal from you it is a very great disappointment to me.'[9] In fact, Winston's reports were above average, but there were frequent comments that he was not performing to his full capacity, although he shone at history, English and fencing. His compositions showed an original mind, and hints of the great writer and orator he was to become. His biggest crime was unpunctuality – and he was obstinate, rebellious of authority and very mischievous. Alas, when Winston was in trouble for joining other boys in breaking the windows of an abandoned factory, his father evidently failed to recall that as a student at Oxford he had himself been in trouble for breaking windows, and he came down hard on the boy.

Mrs Everest was still the centre of Winston's and Jack's world. Invariably they spent Christmas with her while Jennie visited grand friends and Randolph recuperated somewhere in the sunshine. Randolph and Jennie were on a visit to Russia together when Winston wrote to his mother in December 1887: 'I must tell you about Christmas Day. Aunt Clara [Clarita] was too ill to come so Aunt Leonie and Uncle Jack were our only visitors. We drank the Queen's health. Your health and Papa's, then Everest's . . . It is very dull without you. But after all we are very happy.'[10]

When, after Jack went away to school and the nursery was empty, Randolph sold the house at Connaught Place and he and Jennie moved in with Duchess Fanny in her leased mansion at Grosvenor Square, Mrs Everest moved with them as housekeeper, and although the two boys were upset at the sale of their own home the presence of Everest at Grosvenor Square made the move bearable. Before long, however, the Dowager Duchess decided to end this arrangement so as to save money – a sixty-year-old woman was unlikely to be able to do the work of a thirty-year-old in those days before household appliances.* Indeed, Mrs Everest had already left

---

*There has been some doubt about Everest's age, but in the 1891 census she gave her age as fifty-nine.

the family some weeks before Winston heard about this decision, but when he did he raged at his mother in a letter:

> At her age she is invited to find a new place & practically begin all over again . . . I think such proceedings cruel and rather mean . . . The Duchess has every right to discharge a servant for whom she has 'no further use'. But I do think that you ought *to arrange that she remains at Grosvenor Square – until I go back* to Sandhurst & Jack to school. In the meantime she will have ample time to make up her mind where to go – to find a place & resign herself to a change . . . Then, when a *good* place has *been secured for her* she could leave and be given a pension which would be sufficient to keep her from want & which should continue during her life . . . It is in your power to explain to the Duchess that she *cannot* be sent away until she has got a good place . . . I cannot bear to think of Everest . . . being got rid of in such a manner.[11]

Jennie's conscience must have been pricked, because soon afterwards Randolph sent Everest a gift of £17 (six months' salary); it was little enough reward for a loyal servant of almost twenty years, who had acted as mother to his two sons. Jennie would have paid as much for a new hat. Mrs Everest found herself some rooms and thereafter Winston regularly sent her small sums of money, although he was himself always overdrawn on his allowance. 'My darling Precious Boy,' she wrote on 1 April 1895. 'I have just received £2.10s from Cox & Co [bank], Charing Cross on your account. I thank you very much indeed dearest it is awfully kind and thoughtful of you. My dear dear Boy you are one in ten thousand but I am afraid you will find your income [insufficient] . . . for your expenses dear. It really is too good and kind of you I don't know how to thank you enough.'[12]

In June 1894 Randolph insisted on making what he termed a round-the-world fact-finding trip. Not only could he not afford the expense of such a trip, but Dr Robson Roose and Dr Thomas Buzzard, the specialist who was treating him for syphilis, had written him a letter signed by them both, advising against such a plan.[13] When Randolph rejected their concern out of hand they wrote again, this time to Jennie, advising her that if the trip went ahead she must take a private physician in the party.[14] Jennie went along with Randolph's wishes reluctantly, convinced by what Dr Roose told her, that her husband would probably die during the journey. Consequently they not only travelled with a full-time doctor and nurse, but during the final stages of their trip their mountain of luggage included a lead-lined coffin. During the early stages of the journey Randolph had good remissions, periods of normal lucidity during which he wrote long letters to friends as if there was nothing wrong with him. And amazingly, he survived the long journey – just.

Jennie behaved with supreme patience. She put her life on hold to nurse Randolph through his terminal illness and she was touchingly devoted and loyal to him, but later she would say that it had cost her 'everything'. During the year before their departure her life had become extremely complicated. Charles Kinsky had given her an ultimatum – either she leave Randolph for him or their relationship was over. The first she could not do in the circumstances and instead, during one of Kinsky's long absences from England, she embarked upon a new sexual relationship, this time with a young man called Freddy Wolverton who begged her to end her relationship with Kinsky. It must be remembered that the Churchill marriage was an 'open' one, that Randolph and Jennie had ceased all sexual relations many years earlier, and that Jennie was a passionate woman who needed a man in her life and in her bed. But with all her domestic troubles she could evidently not juggle her lovers as well. When she embarked on the world trip in June she had simply hoped that her tangled affairs would wait in limbo until her return to London.

Five months later, in November, the couple had reached Rangoon when Jennie heard from Charles Kinsky that he had become engaged to a young Catholic countess from an eminent Austrian family, Elizabeth Wolff-Metternich. It was a massive shock to Jennie, and she wrote to her sister Leonie that she was entirely 'crushed'. It was an outcome for which she had not prepared, for although she had recently taken another lover she still regarded Kinsky as the great love of her life. She assumed he felt as she did, and perhaps he did share Jennie's passion, but financial constraints inevitably obliged him to agree to marry as his family wished. It is arguable whether he would have married Jennie, anyway; she was not a Catholic and was unlikely at forty to give him children.

Jennie wrote in a fit of anxiety to Leonie, frantically begging her to contact Kinsky and plead with him to wait for her return to England. 'Oh, Leonie darling,' she scrawled, her pen dashing across the page in her frenzy, 'do you think it is *too late* to stop it . . . can't you help me? For heaven's sake write to him . . . use all cleverness & all strength & urge him to put off his marriage. Anyhow until I have seen him.'[15] It would be only about another month, she added. The news from Charles Kinsky, she explained to Leonie, had come on top of a lesser blow that had nonetheless affected her badly because she now saw it as all part of a contraction of her options. It concerned Freddy Wolverton. She had not written to him since leaving England, and when she and Randolph reached Hong Kong there had been a cable from him, advising in abrupt telegraphic jargon that he considered their relationship at an end. There was little she could do, as she escorted her dying husband around the world.

It was only a matter of time, she reflected, before she was left a widow, and as Randolph could not leave her much to live on she would be a widow in very reduced circumstances. Jennie knew that it was all her own fault for not writing to Freddy and the only thing she blamed him for was his insisting on her giving up Charles Kinsky when he did not intend his own relationship with her to be a long-term one. Charles was the only man she could ever envisage starting a new life with, and if she had lost him then she had been well punished for her treatment of him. She was convinced that Charles had cared for her in the same way until recently, and that if she was only given another chance she would make up for her past mistakes. She believed that society would soon forgive Kinsky if he ended his engagement, and that the girl – knowing how he felt about her – would surely be willing to give him up.[16]

Randolph and Jennie arrived back in England in late December. Randolph was in a coma. Once home he rallied one final time, but he was in great pain and distress. As long ago as 1 October Jennie had warned Winston that his father was seriously ill. In early November nineteen-year-old Winston, suspecting from what he heard from friends that he had not been told all there was to be told about his father's illness, confronted Dr Roose and insisted on being given the truth.* 'He told me everything,' Winston wrote to Jennie, 'and showed me the medical reports. I have told no one.'[17] Years later he confirmed to Anthony Montague Browne, his Private Secretary, that Roose had informed him that his father suffered from '*locomotor ataxia*,† the child of syphilis'.[18]

Three weeks after returning to England, on 24 January 1895, Lord Randolph died.[19] He had suffered greatly with attacks of acute mania and delusions lasting for several hours at a time, alternating with comas. His end came quickly when he developed pneumonia and his lungs filled up. Jennie was with him.

On the day of the funeral the body was transported by train to Oxford, and he was buried in the family plot at Bladon churchyard near Blenheim. It was so cold that the Thames almost froze over. Winston, who had spent his entire childhood and early youth attempting to please his father in order to forge something approaching a normal father–son relationship, was devastated at the loss. Most of their recent exchanges had consisted of angry tirades from Randolph criticising Winston for his lack of application and his failure to achieve, yet Winston was still proud of his father. Probably their last intimate moments together had been when Randolph took him to the races and then to Lord Rothschild's house at Tring in Hertfordshire in October 1893. Winston was then a cadet at Sandhurst, and his father wrote to the Dowager Duchess that he had smartened up considerably and was quiet and well

---

*For Lord Randolph's condition and other theories as to his death, see Appendix 2.

†*Locomotor ataxia* or *Tabes dorsalis*, one of the common symptoms of syphilis, is a disorder of the spinal cord which causes dysfunction of the nerve pathways and a characteristic shuffling gait.

mannered. This was against the usual trend of bulletins about Winston, for he was normally reported as being badly behaved, while Jack, a gentle and tractable child, was generally praised. On the day their parents set out on the world trip, 27 June 1894, Winston and Jack had accompanied Randolph and Jennie to Southampton, where they were to sail for New York. Lord Rosebery, then Prime Minister, was also there, and even then Winston could see that his father was seriously ill. 'His face looked haggard and worn with mental pain,' he recalled. 'He patted me on the knee in a gesture which however simple was perfectly informing . . . I never saw him again except as a swiftly-fading shadow.'[20] In *My Early Life* Winston mused that he would rather have been born to a plumber, a grocer or a bricklayer – for then 'I should have got to know my father, which would have been a joy to me.'[21]

As an old man, Winston told his nephew Johnny that when he was told of his father's death he was prostrate with grief for a day and a half. Even then he spoke of Lord Randolph as a dashing hero, whose certain path to the position of Prime Minister had been prevented only by his early death at forty-six; Winston still disregarded the errors Randolph had made.[22] 'All my dreams of comradeship with him, of entering Parliament at his side and in his support, were ended,' he wrote in a memoir of that period. 'There remained for me only to pursue his aims and vindicate his memory.'[23]

This ambition was to be the driving force in Winston's future life. He already knew that he wanted to go into politics rather than the Army, but he had no money to campaign; and even assuming he could gain a seat, backbench Members of Parliament were not salaried in those days, so first he needed to find some means of supporting himself. He concluded that he would have to 'do something' to gain public acclaim, but at least any plans he might make were no longer dependent upon his father's likely reaction: 'I was now in the main the master of my fortunes.'[24]

This romantic, idealistic and, above all, ambitious young man would never lose his feelings of love for his father. Lord Randolph's political downfall, the diagnosis of syphilis, his often cold-hearted treatment of Jennie – Winston knew of all these things, but neither they, nor the fact that he and Jack had had no emotional relation-ship with their father, ever affected his lifelong pride in Randolph. Similarly, he identified strongly with his father's heritage; Blenheim was not merely his family home but his spiritual base, and his descent from the famous 1st Duke of Marlborough was always there for him as a sort of bastion when life got tough. On one occasion, when he was checking on the construction of the War Rooms in London, he jumped over a steel girder only to land in a pool of liquid cement. His Secretary humorously remarked that Winston seemed to have met his Waterloo. 'Certainly not,' Winston replied. 'My Blenheim.'

There were no surprises in Lord Randolph's will: he left £500 and his personal effects to Jennie, and the residue to his sons with a life interest to Jennie in the income. Had Randolph outlived his mother, the Dowager's estate would have come to him and even-tually to Jennie, with the intention that it would filter down to their sons. But now, on the demise of the Dowager, that capital would go directly to Winston and Jack, skirting Jennie. There was some £75,000 invested in South African mines which should have set his sons up nicely in life, but unfortunately Randolph and Jennie had continued their old lavish lifestyle funded by loans raised during his illness, and these loans were secured against the South African shares. After all debts were paid there was very little left to be shared between Winston and Jack, and Jennie now depended solely on the settlement made by her father on her marriage.

Winston received his commission a month after his father's death, and it cost just under £1000 to join his regiment, the 4th Hussars, buy a charger (he was given another horse by Aunt Lily and her husband Bill Beresford*) and a couple of polo ponies. He was never, throughout his Army career, out of debt, and for some years after that money was a struggle. This was a young man who had to make his own way, and in a hurry. He burned with

---

*In 1895 Duchess Lily married (her third marriage) Lord William Beresford VC (1847–1900). The marriage was a happy one and in 1897 – to everyone's great surprise, including Duchess Lily's – she gave birth to a son.

ambition, though no longer with the military world in his sights, for his every instinct was to follow his father into politics. He knew, though, that his youth was against him – he was still only twenty – and he wrote to his mother that 'four years of healthy and pleasant existence, combined with both responsibility and discipline, can do no harm to me – but rather, good. The more I see of soldiering the more I like it, but the more I feel convinced that it is not my *métier*. Well, we shall see.'[25] Meanwhile, he took seriously the fact that he was now the senior male in the family and, as far as he was able, took responsibility for his mother and younger brother.

After the funeral and a month spent with her mother-in-law in the deep mourning prescribed for widows, Jennie travelled to Paris. She had reserved a suite in the Hotel Imperial and was still travelling in some style, accompanied by her maid and butler. Did she know that Charles Kinsky and his bride were honeymooning in the same hotel? Did she, even now, think that she could revive the relationship that had meant 'everything' to her for the past eleven years? She was addicted to Kinsky, she wrote to Leonie, as some people were to opium or drink although they would not wish to be so.[26] It seems an impossible coincidence that of all the hotels in Paris Jennie hit upon that very one by accident.

Jennie and Charles met in Paris, but it was clearly too late for them, and Jennie quickly moved from the hotel into an apartment where Leonie and her children came to join her. It is probable that Jennie was never again alone with Kinsky and her misery over losing him could be explained away as mourning for Randolph. But the pain of the parting was not confined to Jennie, for in a letter written many years later by Kinsky's cousin to Anita Leslie, it appears that when Charles Kinsky heard of Randolph's death he attempted to break off his engagement, and 'it was only under heaviest pressure from his family that he gave in'.[27] In the event his marriage was not a happy one; there were no children and Charles was said to be always *agacé* (irritable) with his wife. Winston remained his admirer, and in his rooms he always hung a picture of Count Kinsky riding his Grand National horse Zoedone.

Jennie did not stay long in Paris; within a few weeks she and

Leonie hurried to Tunbridge Wells in Kent, to join sister Clarita at the bedside of their dying mother. Clara Jerome died on 2 April 1895.

There was a further death that year but it affected Jennie's sons more than Jennie herself. In July their old nanny, Mrs Everest, became seriously ill. Winston was summoned by wire and she was 'delighted' to see him, but her condition was grave and he called in Dr Keith, the physician who had accompanied Randolph on the world voyage, and engaged a nurse. It was a hopeless case; Everest sank rapidly and died of peritonitis. Winston never left her for two days and nights, and he thought his presence at her bedside had made her happy at the last. Although it had been shocking for him to witness, he thought the old lady did not suffer greatly when she died at 2.15 a.m. on 3 July. 'Her last words were of Jack,' he wrote to Jennie. 'I shall never know such a friend again ... I feel very low – and find that I never realized how much poor old Woom* was to me.'[28] In his next letter he wrote that he was still 'very despondent and sad'.[29] It had been the third funeral, after his father's and Grandmother Jerome's, that he had attended in five months. Everest had continued to write lovingly to her 'dear precious boy' up to a few weeks earlier. Jennie felt it was not her concern, Jack was still at school on a schoolboy's allowance, so after the funeral it was Winston who paid for the headstone and for a local florist to maintain Everest's grave.†

By this time Jennie was back in Paris, living in a rented apartment at 34 Avenue Kléber.‡ Winston wrote to her that he had been to see his grandmother, the Dowager Duchess Fanny, who looked 'very pale and worn . . . She carped a little at your *appartement* in "the gayest part of the Champs Élysées" but was otherwise very amiable – or rather not particularly malevolent.'[30] Duchess Fanny might have done more than carp a little had she known that within weeks of

---

*Nanny Everest was nicknamed 'Woomany' or 'Woom' by Winston and Jack.
†The headstone on the grave at the City of London cemetery, Manor Park, reads: 'Erected in memory of Elizabeth Anne Everest who died 3rd July 1895 aged 62 by Winston Spencer Churchill and Jack Spencer Churchill'.
‡Still in existence and still an exclusive apartment building.

Randolph's death Jennie was already involved in a passionate fling in Paris. The man was Bourke Cockran, a brilliant silver-tongued orator, lawyer and American Congressman. Both had recently been widowed, and they spent all their time together. Leonie, also staying at Avenue Kléber that summer, was attracted to Cockran too, but she generously 'stepped back' because 'poor Jennie' who had been so unhappy was in desperate need of a 'romance'.

Jennie's family were fully aware that she had an affair with Cockran that summer, and in any other newly widowed woman this would have been regarded as more than shocking. But in Jennie's case she had lived with Randolph platonically for so many years that her undeniable sadness at his death was not linked in any way to her sexual needs; and she was on the rebound from Kinsky. This latest affair between two tempestuous individuals was passionate but not necessarily very comfortable – a niece described it as 'the clash of two cymbals'.[31] But by the time Cockran returned to the USA in late summer the liaison had run its course; the couple parted fondly but without any deep regret, and would remain friends.

In October, Winston was granted leave from his regiment and on the spur of the moment he decided to visit the USA and Cuba with a fellow subaltern, Reggie Barnes. They planned to travel cheaply, by mail boat, and it would cost only £37 return, he told his mother, which would be 'less than a couple of months hunting at Leighton Buzzard by a long way' as well as being safer than the stiff fences in the Vale of Aylesbury. Although she quibbled a little on the grounds of cost, cash-strapped, Jennie gave in and provided the return ticket as a birthday present. She also obtained some useful introductions for him, because, she advised, 'New York is very expensive.' Bourke Cockran was one of these contacts, perhaps the longest-lasting, for not only was he a generous host but he would prove to be a role model for Winston for many years.

1892–5

Consuelo, the Dollar Princess

When Sunny became 9th Duke a few days before reaching the age of twenty-one, he inherited empty coffers and an estate whose finest art treasures had been plundered over two generations. He was still studying at Trinity College, Cambridge, when his father died, and because it was a totally unexpected event he was unprepared for his new role. However, he had been educated to have immense pride in his heritage and in Blenheim Palace, and he took on the burden as his birthright.

He was an unhappy youth despite his nickname (which clung to him for the rest of his life), who in many ways felt that he had drawn the short straw. Partly this can be attributed to his parents' long estrangement during his childhood and their subsequent divorce, after which he was placed in the custody of his father. Sunny later stated that in his entire childhood he never received a single kind word from his father. In this he shared the experience of his cousin Winston, whose correspondence with Lord Randolph makes uncomfortable reading for present-day researchers.

The disagreements between Randolph and Blandford had resulted in an estrangement that had caused Sunny to lose touch with Winston, but after his father's death when the widowed Duchess Lily moved out of Blenheim, one of the first things Sunny did was invite Winston to stay. Although Goosie stayed there in the first few weeks, Sunny, as the 9th Duke, lived in the great palace alone, supported by visits from his two sisters and his grandmother Dowager Duchess Fanny, who showed great fortitude, if not much empathy. It was the old Duchess who convinced Sunny that it was his duty to marry for money for the sake of Blenheim, and there was much trawling through the lists of eligible young women.

Winston spent the first Christmas of Sunny's dukedom at Blenheim with Sunny and Aunt Berthe (Goosie), 'who has really gone out of her way to make me comfortable,' he reported to his mother. The two young men became firm friends and Winston was a frequent weekend visitor: 'I rode in the park [at Blenheim] chiefly with Lady Angela* – who is not bad company,' Winston told Jennie on one occasion. 'I think she is trying all she knows to captivate Sunny – but it appears to me that her efforts will be fruitless.'[1]

Lady Angela was the seventeen-year-old third daughter of the 4th Earl Rosslyn; her two elder sisters had married well – one to a duke and the other to an earl – but while she was perfect in every other way (and it is probable that Sunny came to love her), Lady Angela's dowry would not have enabled Sunny to run Blenheim. Indeed, there was no English girl both rich enough and eligible enough, and eventually the reluctant conclusion was reached that the only way out of Sunny's dilemma was to marry an American heiress – not a minor heiress, as Jennie had seemed to be, but some well brought up girl to whom the upkeep of Blenheim would be a mere fleabite. Jennie was consulted as to the most likely candidates and, curiously, Goosie's sister, Maude, Lady Lansdowne, had already met one of the leading contenders, sixteen-year-old Consuelo Vanderbilt, daughter of William K. Vanderbilt and his wife Alva.

Mrs Alva Vanderbilt had been a childhood friend of Consuelo Yznaga and Minnie Stevens, and Jennie knew her reasonably well as a member of the coterie of American expats in Paris. Like Jennie, Consuelo and Minnie, Alva (*née* Erskine Smith) had been partly educated in Paris and had absorbed a taste for European grandeur and design, but her family, who had been plantation owners in

---

*Lady Angela Selina St Clair-Erskine was probably the inspiration for the character of Lady Mabel Grex in Anthony Trollope's novel *The Duke's Children*.

Alabama, were ruined by the Civil War and had been obliged to return to America in the hope of recouping. They never recovered their former wealth, so Alva's marriage in 1875 to the young William Kissam Vanderbilt, following an introduction by Consuelo Yznaga, was a real triumph for her. William K (as he was known) stood ultimately to inherit a $50 million share (worth multi billions today) in the fortune built by his grandfather 'the Commodore', Cornelius Vanderbilt, in steamships and the New York Central Railroad, and expanded by the Commodore's son, William Henry Vanderbilt (known as William H).

The young William Ks lived in New York, but neither Alva's Southern pedigree nor the riches of her Vanderbilt in-laws were acceptable to Mrs Astor – still the acknowledged leader of New York's society. They had too many connections in trade. Consequently, the William Ks were never invited to the really important social occasions populated by Knickerbocker families of 'the old four hundred'.

The pugnacious Alva adopted an apparent lack of concern at being sidelined, but in reality she simmered over it before deciding on a long-term strategy, knowing there was no alternative to a waiting game while the old Commodore was still around reminding New Yorkers of his rough-and-ready background.* Meanwhile, Alva produced two sons and a daughter. The daughter, a child of striking appearance from the moment of her birth on 2 March 1877, was named after Alva's friend Consuelo Yznaga. And when Consuelo Yznaga married Viscount Mandeville, Alva conceived a plan for her daughter who, she decided, would never be excluded from *any* society. No ifs or buts – little Consuelo would marry a European title, just like her namesake. Having herself married for money, this probably seemed no more than a reasonable ambition to Alva.

After the old Commodore died, his multimillionaire heirs began to build homes in New York that were the size of European palaces. In fact, William K's and Alva's new construction at 660 Fifth

---

*In fact, the Vanderbilts had an American pedigree at least as old as the Astors. The first Vanderbilt arrived in the New Netherlands from Utrecht c.1650.

Avenue, faced in limestone, boasting a pitched roof with copper decorations, elaborate dormers, flying buttresses and a steep tourelle topped with the fleur de lis, was easily as grand as any European palace. Its design was based on the sixteenth-century Château de Blois near Chenonceaux, and indeed was always called in the family 'the chateau'. The ballroom was a replica of the one at Versailles, and there was an eight-foot malachite vase that came from the Winter Palace at St Petersburg.

Next to the chateau were two equally large and imposing, though more conventionally designed, mansions. These were also Vanderbilt residences; one was the home of William H, Alva's father-in-law, and the other had been built by William H for his daughters. These three buildings occupied a massive site opposite what is now St Patrick's Cathedral. Alva's house was completed in 1883. While it was still under construction she organised a magnificent costume ball as a house-warming party, letting it be known that the guest of honour was the woman all New Yorkers wanted to meet, Alva's good friend, Consuelo, Lady Mandeville. The ball was to be held on a Monday – the normally 'quiet' evening on which Mrs Astor customarily held her 'at home' – which was considered a very daring move.

Alva sent out more than a thousand invitations, and the guest list included 399 of New York's finest families. Only one family was not invited: that of Mrs Astor, for by Mrs Astor's own dictate she must always make the first move towards any 'newcomer'. The whole of New York was agog with leaked stories about the magnificence of the forthcoming ball in the fairy-tale white palace that had magically appeared among the brownstone houses on Fifth Avenue. Few declined the opportunity to attend what was certain to be the social event of the decade, let alone the chance to rubberneck inside this amazing building. It might be supposed that the aloof Mrs Astor would ignore such parvenu entertainment, but she had a debutante daughter whose dearest wish was to attend the costume ball at the chateau along with her debutante friends, who were already rehearsing a quadrille for the occasion. It was not long before Mrs Astor sent her footman to 660 Fifth Avenue with a calling card, thus conveying that Alva had been 'recognised'. Game, set and match to Alva. On the following day an engraved invitation to Alva's ball was duly dispatched to Mrs Astor.

More like a ball at a European court, the event was a triumph. No one had ever seen such an ostentatious parade of jewels and wealth in New York. The gowns and costumes, costing small fortunes by the standards of ordinary families, had mostly been commissioned months earlier, amid great rivalry as to whose outfit would be the most beautiful or inventive. Alva and the Vanderbilts were thereby launched into a leading position among New York's elite families. This was the foundation stone of Alva's plans for her daughter.

Another requirement was an appropriate rural setting. The William Ks already owned a huge rambling summer mansion called Idlehour, constructed a few years earlier on the banks of a river on Long Island. It was wooden-framed and built in the style of Queen Anne, and William K and his children liked it. There they could dress in more comfortable clothes, crab and fish, sail and ride; but it was too folksy for Alva. This was not the home of a future European princess.

So her next great building project was a mansion in Newport, Rhode Island. Her husband had very little hand in it other than to pay the bills, but Alva's brother-in-law, Cornelius, was also building there and they both employed the same architect, Richard Morris Hunt. The seventy-room house Cornelius built was called 'The Breakers' (after the small wooden beach house it replaced), and Alva's house was appropriately named 'Marble House'. These were perhaps the grandest of the Newport mansions, referred to by their owners as 'cottages'. Marble House, inspired by the Petit Trianon at Versailles, cost $11 million in 1887 (over $200 million now), and more than half the cost (over $7 million) went on the 500,000 cubic feet of marble used in the construction.* Alva's thirty-ninth birthday coincided with the completion of Marble House, and as her birthday gift William K gave her the title deeds.

---

*Marble House and The Breakers survive in their full glory and are open to the public at Newport, Rhode Island.

As might be supposed, little Consuelo had a very privileged childhood, at least materially. With her parents and brothers she travelled all over the world, along with her own nurse, English governess and tutors. As well as being instructed in English literature by her governess, the various tutors taught her French and German in which she was fluent (she was widely read in the literature of both countries), Latin, mathematics, science, art and history. In addition, the curriculum included the all-important 'deportment'. Consuelo had ponies, carriages, servants, a sensational bedroom with an en-suite playroom large enough for her few carefully selected friends to ride their bicycles around, and wonderful clothes, but her memoirs do not mention any love or the companionable family background so essential to a happy childhood.

Alva later claimed to have 'sacrificed' the years when her children were growing in order to nurture them herself – that is when she was not building or planning some great project – disregarding entirely the staff who waited on and taught Consuelo and her brothers. Consuelo admitted that her mother probably did love her, but in the same way that she loved her great houses built in French Renaissance style, in which everything had to be perfect. In fact, the decor at Marble House was planned down to the last detail, with items such as pens, cutlery and dressing-table toiletry items so precisely placed on their allotted surfaces that, when she eventually moved in, Consuelo felt unable to use them for fear of disturbing the symmetry. She believed that her mother had 'created' her, just as she created her beautiful houses, in an image she had conceived of 'the perfect lady' – which to Alva meant a wife suitable for an English duke or a European prince.

Consuelo was allowed very few playmates so that she had no opportunity to meet anyone unsuitable. She was a sweet, sensitive and submissive child, quite unlike her mother. She never rebelled against the spinal brace that Alva decreed her daughter must wear daily while studying. This was an iron rod, strapped to her body at the waist, shoulders and head, to encourage an upright carriage. In order to read she had to raise her book almost to eye level and it was almost impossible to write when wearing it, but it did – she conceded as an adult – achieve its objective since she was known for her upright carriage. Even when out on informal pleasure outings the growing girl wore clothes of her mother's choosing: ankle-length skirts, tight corsets and high collars stiffened with whalebone, skin-tight gloves and large beribboned hats skewered to her piled-up hair with long steel pins. Certainly no romping in these outfits. Her mother was a disciplinarian and would never relax her standards: Consuelo and her two brothers were 'switched' on their bare legs with a riding whip for even minor infringements. As a child, Alva had been punished in the same way, and she felt it had done her no harm but it *had* made her behave well. To the more sensitive and introspective Consuelo, though, the terror of these beatings was to haunt her long into adulthood.

Consuelo's recollection was that as a teenager she was profoundly unhappy, not least because her parents were continually quarrelling and she was sometimes made the bearer of hurtful messages from Alva to her husband. William K took to spending most of his time on his magnificent yacht the *Alva*.* His children saw little of him after this. It is hardly surprising that after receiving such a superior education Consuelo assumed she would be allowed to go to university, but although Alva sent for the entrance application to Oxford for her, this was not to be. Alva merely wished to ensure that Consuelo was well enough educated to be accepted, were she to apply.

When she was sixteen, in 1893, Consuelo and her parents left the USA for an extended world tour in their second yacht the *Valiant* (the *Alva* had sunk after being rammed in fog). At all their ports of call they were received as visiting dignitaries, and treated accordingly by ambassadors and state leaders. In Bombay, the Vanderbilts stayed at Government House, where they were welcomed by the Viceroy and Vicereine, Lord and Lady Lansdowne, the uncle and aunt of the twenty-two-year-old Sunny, Duke of Marlborough.

---

*285 feet long at the waterline, the *Alva* was the largest private yacht in America. She was launched by Alva's sister Jenny (who had married the brother of Consuelo Yznaga), and regularly sailed with a crew of over fifty.

Years later Alva would confess to Consuelo that it was during that meeting that she was able to focus her ambitions and decide that she would marry her daughter to either the Duke of Marlborough or his cousin, Viscount Curzon's heir. Consuelo spent the visit in the company of the younger daughters of the Lansdowne family. When they compared the books they were reading Consuelo was shocked at the Lansdowne girls' lack of education. No Homer, no Virgil, no Gibbon. She did not realise, then, that an academic education was considered wasted on upper-class English girls, who needed only to know how to behave well, to have sufficient knowledge in English literature, geography and history to converse well in polite company (in English *and* French), and enough arithmetic to check the household accounts. They simply accepted that their principal role was to produce healthy heirs and entertain. Consuelo said nothing, of course, but she privately wondered how girls brought up under such restrictions were expected to converse on the same level with men educated in English public schools.

When the Vanderbilts reached the Mediterranean in the spring of 1894 the *Valiant* docked at Nice. By then it had become abundantly clear to their many guests on the yacht, as well as to international gossip columnists, that the Vanderbilt marriage was at an end. The atmosphere during the previous weeks between Alva and William K had been frigid.

What had happened? In subsequent months William K was paired in the press with a number of other women, one a French courtesan. But much later it transpired that she was merely a screen for the really important new relationship in William K's life, who was none other than the woman Alva always considered her best friend, Consuelo Yznaga, now Duchess of Manchester. Somehow, Alva may have got wind of this fact during the cruise. But she too had her 'walker', one Oliver Belmont (whom she would later marry), who was a guest on the *Valiant*. So perhaps this was the problem? There were certainly widespread rumours about Alva and Belmont. However, they were both discreet, and this relationship was never even raised in the subsequent divorce proceedings – probably William K was too much of a gentleman to have it brought out in court. As a result Alva was the injured party in the sensational divorce case, in which she appeared so innocent of any blame that even Mrs Astor supported her.

After the party aboard the *Valiant* broke up, William K. travelled to England to watch the Derby. Oliver Belmont sailed for New York. And Alva took Consuelo to Paris, where they stayed for two months. There, Consuelo attended a number of 'white balls' where the young maidens were all dressed in white, radiating innocence and purity, while Alva commissioned a suitable wardrobe for her daughter from leading designers before they left for London.

Alva received five proposals of marriage for Consuelo while they were in Paris, but only one, from a middle-aged German prince, seemed worth Alva's consideration. Consuelo was told about the offer, and she wrote later that for a short time her mother's intentions to marry her to an English duke faltered at the possibility of a royal crown. But Consuelo shuddered at the thought of marriage to this much older man, whom she described as 'a prejudiced German Princeling' for whom she felt only aversion and to whom, she realised, she was simply a means to an end: 'It seems I was about to exchange one bondage for another. Such a marriage could only mean unhappiness . . . how could I reconcile myself to such a life?'[2]

When they reached London Alva launched divorce proceedings. They moved into Brown's Hotel, which was respectable and comfortable, if a little dull. Consuelo thought longingly of the bright, glamorous suite in the hotel in Paris overlooking the Tuileries Gardens. The first thing Alva did – in a smart carriage and accompanied by a footman – was to visit her old childhood friend Minnie, Lady Paget (the former Minnie Stevens), in Belgravia Square.* The outcome of this meeting was that Consuelo's debut was placed in the hands of Lady Paget who, though financially strapped, was worth cultivating because she had a direct entrée to the Prince of Wales's circle. Lady Paget offered to 'bring Consuelo out' – almost

---

*Minnie Stevens married Arthur Henry Paget (later Sir Arthur), grandson of the Marquess of Anglesey, in July 1878. Among the wedding guests were the Prince of Wales, Consuelo Viscountess Mandeville and Lady Randolph Churchill.

certainly for a fee. She not only ordered a wardrobe of sophisticated new clothes for the teenager, in satins and with daring décolletages, to replace the demure white tulle debutante gowns bought in Paris, but she insisted that Consuelo receive elocution lessons to improve her French accent and public speaking voice. Consuelo heartily disliked this hard, worldly woman, likening her to the fictional Becky Sharp.

Within weeks, seventeen-year-old Consuelo was introduced to twenty-three-year-old Sunny Marlborough at one of Lady Paget's dinner parties. Consuelo felt that she was so pointedly thrown together with the Duke that it must be obvious to everyone what Lady Paget intended, and this made her feel gauche and embarrassed. Her impression of him was that he was intelligent and good-looking enough, though with a large nose and prominent blue eyes, and that he seemed very proud of his beautifully shaped small hands. But she was not overly impressed, perhaps because, at five feet eight inches, Consuelo was some six inches taller than the diminutive Duke; and although he had an undoubted charm when he wished to exert it, he was somewhat morose by nature. He seemed to hide any personality behind a veneer of icy reserve: his eyes were slightly hooded so that one could not read his feelings, and he wore a neatly trimmed moustache which turned down at the corners, accentuating his supercilious expression.

We do not know what the Duke thought of Consuelo because he never recorded his feelings. What he would have seen was a quiet, thoughtful young woman, tall and slender with a noticeably erect carriage. She had high cheekbones, large doe-shaped eyes and an extraordinarily long and slender neck around which she often wore a simple ribbon. In earlier times she would have been called 'swan-necked', but one friend who was extremely fond of her later said that the length of her neck was actually only just short of being a disfigurement.[3] She had an inquisitive expression and habitually held her head on one side as she listened. She was naturally intelligent, and had been taught to entertain with her conversation; moreover, she was always exquisitely dressed, thanks to her mother's training. So she would not have bored him. But

John Churchill, the 1st Duke. Blenheim Palace was a gift from a grateful nation. (Painting by Sir Godfrey Kneller, Blenheim Palace)

Sarah Churchill was imperious and arrogant, but her husband adored her. (Blenheim Palace)

Duchess Fanny, Jennie's mother-in-law: 'at the rustle of her silken skirts the whole household trembled'. (Blenheim Palace)

John, the 7th Duke of Marlborough, who reined in the family expenditure. (Blenheim Palace)

'Blandford', later the 8th Duke. (Blenheim Palace)

Blandford's first wife, Lady Albertha 'Goosie' (Hamilton), was renowned for her childish practical jokes. (Blenheim Palace)

Lady Colin Campbell, Blandford's mistress, for whom (despite his large debts) he bought a Venetian palazzo. (Giovanni Boldini, c.1897, National Portrait Gallery)

Duchess Lily (Hammersley), second wife of Blandford. She quickly installed central heating at Blenheim. (Blenheim Palace)

Jennie Jerome – one admirer described her as 'more panther than woman'. (Getty)

Lord Randolph at the time he met Jennie. (Corbis)

Jennie and Randolph:
an engagement portrait.
(Churchill Archives).

Lady Randolph: Jennie at the height of her beauty. (Getty)

Jennie with her two sons, Jack (left) and Winston (right). (Getty)

Jennie's family: Jennie standing with Winston. From left to right: her sister Clarita, holding Oswald Frewen; her mother Mrs Leonard 'Clara' Jerome, holding Claire and Hugh Frewen; Jack Churchill (standing in front of Jenny); Norman Leslie (standing); Shane Leslie seated on Leonie Leslie's lap. (Private collection)

Nanny Everest – the most important woman in Winston's young life. (Churchill Archives)

Winston aged seven – ready to take on the world. (Corbis)

Winston aged six with his Aunt Leonie. A little-known photograph. (Churchill Archives)

Lord and Lady Randolph and Dr Keith in rickshaws on their world trip. Randolph is looking cadaverous and was the greatest worry to Jennie and his doctor; it was feared they would not get him home alive. (Churchill Archives)

Lord Randolph in 1890, when his illness had taken its toll (Corbis)

Jennie aboard the hospital ship *Maine* at Durban with Jack, one of her first patients. (Private collection)

Winston as a young subaltern in the 4th Hussars. (Getty)

Marlborough was almost certainly already captivated by Lady Angela St Clair-Erskine, so perhaps he was not in the mood to be charmed by Consuelo.

Rumours were already rife, however. On 19 July when the Dowager Duchess Fanny wrote Jennie a letter containing family gossip, such as that she had given Winston permission to attend the Sandown Races on condition that he did not bet – 'he is thoughtless about money' – she added: 'I was amazed at the "news" of Marlborough's marriage. Mrs Paget has been very busy introducing him to Miss Vanderbilt and telling everybody she meant to make up a marriage between them. But he has only met her once and he does not seem inclined to pursue the acquaintance.'[4]

Nevertheless, Alva believed that she had moved her campaign along, and soon after this dinner she and Consuelo sailed for New York. They did not see the Duke again before leaving, and Consuelo thankfully assumed that her mother's notion of marrying her to the young nobleman had been abandoned, along with any other plan for a 'foreign alliance'. Now she could look forward to the forthcoming season of balls and parties; and she even allowed herself to hope she might continue a budding relationship that had begun before she left home, with a Newport man of impeccable family.

Winthrop Rutherfurd was a descendant of the first Governors of New York and Massachusetts, Peter Stuyvesant and John Winthrop. Educated as a lawyer, he was rich in his own right (though not as rich as Consuelo), and a keen sportsman. 'Wintie', as he was known to his familiars, was regarded as 'the handsomest bachelor in society'.[5] He was much older than Consuelo, thirty-two to her seventeen, but she was in love with him and there are good grounds for believing that the attachment was genuine on his part, too. Their relationship had been noted in Newport society, and on Valentine's Day 1895 it was even hinted at in gossip columns. Alva was clearly aware of Rutherfurd's attentions to her daughter, for she began dropping contemptuous remarks about him into her conversation.

Rutherfurd's courtship was a gentle one, necessarily so because

Consuelo was so carefully chaperoned; the only time the couple were ever alone was when they danced together under Alva's watchful eye. We can be sure that this was never more than two dances at each event, and that after each dance Consuelo would have been whirled away from anyone who appeared to be paying her too much attention.

Consuelo had her eighteenth birthday on 2 March 1895. That morning she received masses of flowers, and among the lavish baskets, bouquets and sprays was a long slim box, lined with green wax paper and containing a single red 'American Beauty' rose.* There was no card but Consuelo knew instinctively who had sent it. Later that day, when her invited birthday guests took a cycle ride along Newport's Riverside Drive, Winthrop and Consuelo managed briefly to outdistance the other guests. During the short time they were alone together they confessed their mutual love and he asked her to marry him. Consuelo breathlessly assented, agreeing to keep their engagement secret from her mother who – they both knew – would put a stop to it. Consuelo and Alva were due to leave for Paris within a matter of days and Winthrop swore he would follow them and try to see her there. Surely Alva would allow a fellow Newport resident to call on them? Somehow, he would find a way to see her and then, when Consuelo returned from Europe, he said, they would find a way to elope. At this point Alva, pedalling furiously and red-faced, caught up with them, and the conversation necessarily ended. But Alva was too late and the damage was done. Consuelo considered herself secretly engaged and had given her heart.

It could be argued that Alva was looking after her daughter's best interests by not allowing her to consort with a much older man, who was perhaps after Consuelo's fortune. But Winthrop Rutherfurd would be independently very rich until the end of his life despite a high-rolling lifestyle, so that at least could not have been her

---

*Bred and launched by an American nursery in Washington in 1883, the long-stemmed 'American Beauty' was named after the 'Dollar Princesses'. It became popular both sides of the Atlantic and its high cost, at $2 per stem, was part of its appeal.

objection. He was supremely eligible and was never a noted womaniser. His age *was* against him, but this did not bother Consuelo (although her main objection to the German prince had been that he was so much older).

Before they sailed for France in April, Alva announced that she would be throwing a ball at Marble House in August. She had spent the previous months divorcing William K and keeping her own affair with Oliver Belmont out of the papers. A few months in Europe now would enable her not only to 'settle' Consuelo appropriately but also to miss the huge wave of adverse gossip in the New York papers when the divorce was granted. Consuelo was content that somehow she would soon see her secret fiancé. But Alva was no fool; she suspected from her daughter's unusually happy demeanour that there was trouble brewing.

During the five months that Consuelo was in Europe she heard nothing from Winthrop. There was no reply to her letters to him, nor did he call on them. Only much later did she learn that he had followed her to Paris, but though he had tried on a number of occasions to see Consuelo, he was always thwarted. He had written frequently but his letters never reached her and her own few letters never reached him. After two months he returned home to await Consuelo's return in August and make plans for an elopement. It is not hard to understand how this would have affected Consuelo. She was eighteen years old, with the naivety of a naturally submissive girl raised in very sheltered conditions in an age when women were not noted for their rebelliousness. This was her first love, and even if it was only a teenage crush (and we don't know that it *was* only a crush), it is easy to sympathise with this lonely girl in her gilded cage.

Alva had the measure of her daughter, and Consuelo later said that soon after they arrived in Paris her mother was so confident that her plan would succeed that she secretly ordered a wedding gown for her. As the weeks wore on with no word from Winford, Consuelo became anxious, pale and withdrawn, submitting like an automaton to the numerous dress fittings, allowing her mother to choose her clothes and accessories without offering any input. She did not suspect that Alva was responsible for the silence from Winthrop, so she did not rebel; she simply became unhappy and introspective.

In late May Alva and Consuelo travelled to London, where Lady Paget had prepared the way for them with a sheaf of invitations. Of these the one Consuelo recalled best was a glittering ball given by the Duke and Duchess of Sutherland and, knowing nobody else, she was grateful when the Duke of Marlborough wrote his name on her card for several dances. A few days later Sunny invited Alva, Consuelo and Minnie Paget to Blenheim for a weekend visit. They travelled to Woodstock on a Saturday in June, to find that the gathering was a family party consisting of Sunny, two male cousins (one of whom was the son of Lord Lansdowne and had been in Alva's matrimonial sights at one point), together with Sunny's two sisters, Lady Norah and Lady Lilian. 'Lilian, a pretty blonde a few years my senior, immediately won my heart by her simple unaffected kindness,' Consuelo wrote, and this helped her to enjoy her first experience of the great house.

The following day, the Duke suggested that he drive Consuelo around some of the villages on his estate. In June Blenheim would have been at the height of its beauty, and he would have had every right to be proud of it. Consuelo had never previously been allowed to be alone with a man but, unusually, Alva made no objections to this proposal, so that Consuelo immediately scented danger. 'I felt I was being steered into a vortex that was to engulf me,' she wrote later.[6] Yet she felt hardly able to refuse, and on the drive she conversed intelligently; unafraid, when villagers curtsied or touched their caps as they rode by, to discuss his social obligations to them. Sunny appeared to find this amusing. Alva's proposals had been conveyed to him by one means or another – perhaps through Lady Paget and his Aunt Lansdowne. His grandmother had apparently indicated she was in favour, and perhaps Sunny assumed that Consuelo knew of and condoned the plan. Marrying her would mean ending his existing romantic relationship, but the terms offered by Alva were so favourable for Blenheim that they could hardly be refused. It was stated in a contemporary newspaper that

Marlborough's income was £8000 ($40,000) a year, whereas it cost him £74,000 ($370,000) to run Blenheim.[7] Consuelo's dowry was rumoured to be about $10 million.*

'It was that afternoon,' Consuelo stated in her memoirs, 'that he must have made up his mind to marry me and to give up the girl he loved . . . For to live at Blenheim in the pomp and circumstance he considered essential, needed money, and a sense of duty to his family and to his traditions [required] the sacrifice of personal desires.'[8]

Consuelo, though, had already firmly decided that she would not marry the Duke. She intended to marry Rutherfurd, even if it meant doing battle with her mother over the issue. 'I did not relish the thought, but my happiness was at stake,' she wrote.[9] Nevertheless, she was nervous when she learned that Marlborough had accepted an invitation to Alva's grand ball at Marble House in Newport in August, now only six weeks away. How was she to contact Rutherfurd?

Once again Alva anticipated her daughter's reaction and Consuelo's tiny spark of independence was snuffed out. 'On reaching Newport my life became that of a prisoner, with my mother and my governess as wardens.' Try as she might, there was no way she could get a message to Rutherfurd and no way he could get a message to her. 'Brought up to obey, I was helpless under my mother's total domination,' she recalled.[10] Then, amazingly, Consuelo and Rutherfurd came face to face at a ball that he gate-crashed. The lovers managed just one short dance before Alva 'dragged me away'. But during that dance they had the opportunity to reassure each other that their feelings had not changed. Rutherfurd explained how hard he had tried to contact her in Paris and since, and Consuelo realised the full extent of Alva's treachery.

When they reached home there was a resounding row between mother and daughter. Consuelo bravely insisted she had a right to

---

*On their marriage, stock in the New York Central Railroad, which was valued in 1895 at $2.5 million (about $7 million today), was settled on the Duke. This gave him a guaranteed income of $100,000 a year for life, even if the marriage subsequently ended in death or divorce. Consuelo was also provided with a lifetime income of her own of $100,000 a year.

choose her own husband. At this, Alva's wrath exploded. She used every invective against Rutherfurd that she could think of, shouting at Consuelo that he was a fortune-hunter determined to marry an heiress (incorrect), that there was madness in his family (unproven), that he was impotent (incorrect), that he was a womaniser (incorrect) and that he was known for his relationship with a married woman (doubtful). Ironically, some of these accusations could have been truthfully applied to Marlborough. But Consuelo had no defence; she did not know whether her mother was speaking the truth or not and she did not know how to defend her lover. They argued all night and Consuelo eventually went to her room, still insisting she would marry Rutherfurd or no one.

The next day Consuelo felt desolate. No one came near her, not even a servant, and she felt the house was strangely quiet. She was left to endlessly rerun her mother's accusations. Late in the afternoon Alva's best friend of the time, a Mrs Jay, came to Consuelo's room and told her that Alva had suffered a heart attack, brought on, said Mrs Jay, by Consuelo's callous indifference to her mother's feelings. 'She confirmed my mother's intentions of never consenting to my plans for marriage,' Consuelo recalled. Indeed, Alva had vowed to shoot Rutherfurd if Consuelo eloped with him. Consuelo asked to see her mother and was refused – with the excuse that the doctor had warned that another scene might cause a stroke or even kill Alva. Believing every word of this, not least that to proceed might mean the death of her mother or of Rutherfurd, 'in utter misery' Consuelo capitulated and agreed to allow Mrs Jay to advise Rutherfurd that she could not marry him.*[11]

In the days that followed, Consuelo's English governess, a Miss Harper, undoubtedly acting on Alva's instruction, convinced Consuelo that because of her privileged station in life, duty and a

---

*Winthrop Rutherfurd (1862–1944) remained a bachelor until 1902, when he married Alice Morton. Alice died in 1917, leaving Winthrop with six small children. The couple had converted to Catholicism shortly before Alice's death, and in 1920 Winthrop married fellow Catholic Lucy Mercer, the secretary and later the mistress of Franklin D. Roosevelt. Lucy was with the President when he died.

higher idealism should override her personal wishes. Once she noted her daughter's return to her usual submission, Alva made a miraculous recovery, arranging the forthcoming ball and fêtes at Marble House with all her old energy and verve.

When Marlborough arrived in Long Island Consuelo was again propelled into society, attending every ball and party of note of that Newport season. There were daily carriage drives along Bellevue Avenue (then Newport's equivalent of London's Rotten Row) and to polo matches, escorted by the Duke and always chaperoned by her beaming mother. There was no danger of meeting Rutherfurd; on being given Consuelo's message he had withdrawn from society (probably he went to Europe), so her anxious scanning of the guests at each event was in vain.

'It was in the comparative quiet of an evening at home that Marlborough proposed to me in the Gothic Room, whose atmosphere was so propitious to sacrifice,' Consuelo wrote in her memoirs. 'There was no need for sentiment. I was content with his pious hope that he would make me a good husband.'[12] She immediately went upstairs to her mother and told her. Next day the news was out in the papers, a date announced for the marriage, and Marlborough left on a pre-planned visit to New York and a proposed tour of the USA. This was, after all, his first trip to America, and for all the financial advantages involved it is quite likely that the Duke felt as trapped by circumstances as did his helpless fiancée. Consuelo's twelve-year-old brother Harold greeted the news scathingly with a typically brutal sibling comment: 'He is only marrying you for your money.' At which point Consuelo burst into tears.

The next eight weeks flew by. In New York the Duke's lawyers met with the Vanderbilt lawyers to thrash out a prenuptial agreement. Consuelo played no part in planning her trousseau – indeed, most of it had been ordered in Paris months earlier. Only when the Parisian wedding gown was presented to her, an exquisite creation of white satin and Brussels lace, with a high collar and skin-tight sleeves, did Consuelo realise that her mother had conceived the entire plan a long time earlier.

Brought up chastely, she was embarrassed to read in the papers details of her bridal underclothes and the startling exaggeration that her garter buckles were made of solid gold. Consuelo's quiet musings must have been bitter – certainly she recalled this agonising period with great clarity when, as an elderly woman, she was writing her memoirs. Even the eight bridesmaids were selected by Alva, without any consultation with the bride. And there was yet further distress for Consuelo when she found that her Vanderbilt relatives, demonised by Alva because they had naturally sided with William K during the divorce, were not invited to the wedding. Furthermore, the presents sent by them were returned unopened, without thanks, in Consuelo's name. Surely, the Vanderbilts would have had to be very gullible not to have realised who was responsible for this particular piece of spite?

Marlborough might have hoped to have his favourite cousin Winston among his small party at the wedding. He would certainly have been aware that Winston was on his way to New York that week aboard the Cunard Royal Mail steamship *Etruria*. But a mail boat is not a passenger liner with a strict schedule to meet, and bad weather made the voyage some days longer than expected. The passengers had chosen this cheapest manner of travelling for obvious reasons, and did not expect luxuries such as public rooms or entertainments. 'There are no nice people on board to speak of – certainly none to write of,' Winston wrote to Jennie as the ship struggled to reach its destination. 'The days have seemed very long & uninteresting . . . I shall always look upon journeys by sea as necessary evils which have to be undergone in the carrying out of any definite plan.'[13]

Winston arrived in New York on 9 November, having missed the big event by three days. He and his companion Reggie Barnes were met at the dock by Bourke Cockran, who accommodated them in style in his apartment at 763 Fifth Avenue on the corner of 58th Street. Cockran went out of his way to ensure the young men were entertained, amused and instructed, and introduced them to anyone who might be useful to them. On the 14th, Sunny arrived in New York from the Vanderbilts' Long Island home Idlehour, in Oakdale, where he and Consuelo were spending the first days of their honeymoon.* Consuelo had decided to remain at the mansion while Sunny visited his cousin. 'He is very pleased with himself and seems very fit,' Winston reported to Jennie.[14] It was a week full of new experiences for Winston and he wrote home glowing accounts of his impressions. There were plenty of people happy to entertain generously a young man who was a protégé of Cockran, a cousin of the Duke of Marlborough and the grandson of Leonard Jerome. Among them were Winston's new connections by marriage – the Cornelius Vanderbilts.[15]

Cockran was impressed with the young man's grasp of politics and his ambition, and the two would correspond for many years. Winston regarded him as 'perhaps the finest orator in America', and there is ample evidence that he modelled his own oratorical style on that of Cockran. In 1946, when Churchill gave his 'Sinews of Peace' speech, usually referred to as 'the Iron Curtain speech' and arguably his greatest ever,[†] he would say: 'I have often used words which I learned fifty years ago from a great Irish-American orator, a friend of mine, Mr Bourke Cockran.'[16]

Much later, Winston's son would write that as the relationship between the two men grew over the coming years, 'Cockran in some way fulfilled a role that Lord Randolph should have filled if he had survived.'[17] This seems unlikely, because while Cockran had a real affection for Winston and a respect for his abilities and ambition – which he demonstrated in many ways – Lord Randolph was always hypercritical of his son.

He arranged for Winston and Reggie to visit West Point, where Winston professed to be horrified at the discipline imposed, compared with that at Sandhurst. 'The Cadets enter from 19–22 & stay 4 years,' he wrote to his brother Jack. 'They are not allowed to smoke or have any money in their possession nor are they given any leave except 2 months after the first two years. In fact they have far less liberty than any private school boys in our country.'[18] From

---

*Idlehour was destroyed by fire in April 1899.
†Delivered at Westminster College in Fulton, Missouri, on 5 March 1946.

New York the two young men went on to Cuba, looking for adventure. Winston would not see Sunny again for almost six months, and had not yet met Consuelo. Missing Winston's visit by only a day or two, she followed Sunny to New York before the couple left for Europe.

Consuelo had spent the entire morning of her wedding day alone in her room, in tears. No one came near her – even her governess was not allowed to call on her. A footman was stationed outside her door to turn away any member of the family or staff. Only 'a lowly maid' was allowed in when it was time for Consuelo to dress, to help her into the bridal ensemble. The exquisite court train, encrusted with seed pearls and silver embroidery, was clipped to her shoulders and fell 'in folds of billowing whiteness'. Having patiently stood while the headdress and veil were fitted, and in abject misery, Consuelo then descended the stairs to see the upturned faces of her father and her eight bridesmaids turn from gaiety to anxiety. Alva had only just left for the church, waiting until the last possible moment. She was apparently concerned that in her absence Consuelo might find the spirit to revolt.

William K was under orders from Alva to escort his daughter to the church, officiate at the ceremony, and disappear afterwards; but one can imagine his concern when his daughter made her appearance. Having wept for hours, her face and eyes were red and swollen. Ice water was sent for and her eyes bathed by one of the bridesmaids. It is some measure of Alva's steely personality and her explosive temper that William K, for all his riches and love of his children, did not feel able at this stage to stop the wedding on his daughter's behalf. The delay in making Consuelo's face presentable made the bridal party twenty minutes late at the church. This was possibly the longest twenty minutes in Alva's life as, trapped in the front pew, she feigned a smiling unconcern as she awaited her daughter's arrival and the fruition of her long-nurtured plan. New York reporters, expecting to see a radiant bride and a proud and beaming father, commented in puzzlement on the serious look on William K's face and the sadness of the bride, 'who appeared to have been crying,' wrote one.[19]

The Duke of Marlborough, with his cousin Ivor Guest, waited patiently in the opposite pew, and like all the guests could not help turning occasionally to gaze down the aisle of the Church of St Thomas towards the open doors, as the organist attempted to keep the throng entertained with impromptu pieces he had not anticipated any need to practise. At last a cheer from the crowded street outside signalled the arrival of the bride. Consuelo was now calm. She recalled being glad of the protection of her veil from the prying eyes, and that she squeezed her father's arm to slow down their procession up the aisle, as she had been rehearsed to do.

After the ceremony, William K carried out his final allotted task and signed the register before removing himself, as ordered. The *New York Times* reported that he spent the afternoon at his club. Then the Duke and his new Duchess entered their carriage, which had virtually to force its way through the ranks of excited onlookers to get to Alva's new house on 72nd Street. They stood in a bower of white roses to receive their guests, among whom Mrs Astor was a guest of honour. Alva's wedding gift to her daughter was the magnificent string of pearls that had once belonged to Catherine the Great, which William K had given her early in their marriage.

When the wedding breakfast and speeches were over, the couple changed and left for their honeymoon at Idlehour on Long Island. As their carriage drew away, Consuelo looked up at the façade of her mother's latest house. She saw Alva, half hidden behind the curtains, but clearly in tears. Years later Consuelo bitterly reflected that, having at last achieved all her ambitions for her daughter, Alva now felt free to indulge in sentimentality.

After the journey to her once-loved childhood home which had been beautifully prepared with cheerful log fires blazing, she found that her mother's large suite had been prepared for her, with the adjoining room allotted to Marlborough. Consuelo then faced that great hurdle of her wedding night with a man who was still a virtual stranger. 'A sudden realisation of my complete innocence assailed me, bringing with it fear. Like a deserted child I longed for my family,' she recalled. She wrote movingly that deep in her memories of that night lay 'sorrows too deep to fathom'.[20] Matters could

1895–9

The Unhappy Duchess

No matter what one thinks of Alva Vanderbilt's motives and actions, the manner in which she educated her daughter, in a prim, almost convent-like environment and with able tutors, undeniably fitted Consuelo well for her adult life as Duchess of Marlborough. In addition to her unusual beauty and graceful carriage, there was a natural nobility coupled with a modest simplicity about this young woman. She lacked Jennie's sparkle and energy, but this was not considered necessarily a handicap by her new family. Even members of the old aristocracy, predisposed not to like Consuelo because she was a rich American who – everybody knew – had been married for her fortune in order to save Blenheim, found themselves drawn to her. During the Marlboroughs' honeymoon tour of Spain, France and Italy, where she met European royalty, British ambassadors and numerous high-born travellers, she acquitted herself well. Marlborough quickly saw that he would never have cause to blush for his teenage duchess.

But the four-month honeymoon was anything but happy. The quarrels that characterised this marriage seem to have begun almost immediately. Consuelo and Marlborough were totally different in outlook, and by the time they had reached Italy and were ensconced in the expensive but cheerless hotel suite in Rome where they were to spend Christmas, Consuelo was listless and depressed. A doctor, called in to check her over for a life insurance policy, declared that she was seriously ill and would probably not live longer than six months. A London doctor, hurriedly summoned out to Italy for a second opinion, was more cheerful: he opined that there was no organic problem – she had merely 'outgrown her strength' and needed rest. Undoubtedly the stress of the previous few months, about which the doctor knew nothing, was chiefly responsible. And few doctors would ever have been called upon to treat acute misery in a honeymooning bride.

Now, removed from Alva's smothering influence, for the first time Consuelo began to think about what her life was about and 'to chafe at the impersonal role I had so far played . . . first a pawn in my mother's game and now, as my husband expressed it, "a link in the chain"'.[1] By this Sunny Marlborough meant that Blenheim and the family were their first priority; that he and Consuelo were merely the present incumbents in the family's long history and had to hand it on in good order. From his point of view he had secured enough money to see Blenheim safely through the next decades, but at considerable personal sacrifice; indeed, the reason for their extended honeymoon tour of Europe was that the marriage settlement had enabled him to set in progress some much needed work at Blenheim. He made it clear that he saw 'no need for sentiment' and did not waste his time trying to coax Consuelo into an affectionate relationship, but he insisted that their paramount duty was to produce a son.

Perhaps this lay at the root of their first quarrels? Could there be anything more painful – physically and emotionally – for an eighteen-year-old girl raised modestly, presumably still in love with another man at that point, than to be regularly used to produce a child, by a man who made no secret of the fact that he had no love for her and that any sentiment was out of place? She wanted to do her duty and appreciated that she needed to become pregnant quickly, but her illness made this unlikely. She had no one in whom to confide or to turn to in this crisis. For companionship she had only Joanne, the chic French maid chosen by Alva, who accompanied her on the honeymoon. Consuelo does not say whether she liked Joanne or not, but it appears she was never a confidante.

Perhaps Alva had instructed Joanne to report back to her. But anyway, Marlborough thought Joanne totally unsuitable as she had no knowledge of 'the English way of doing things'. He wired his mother to recruit a suitable person for their arrival in England.*

While Consuelo spent days resting in her rooms, Marlborough went on a spending spree, 'ransacking' (as she described it) Rome's antique shops. He was anxious to fill the gaps left by the indiscriminate sale of art treasures by his father and grandfather which had denuded many rooms at Blenheim. Occasionally Consuelo was allowed to accompany her husband on these shopping trips, but he complained that whenever she appeared in her furs the prices rocketed. From Italy they went on to Egypt for a cruise along the Nile, where Consuelo retired to her cabin in dismay when nautch dancing girls were summoned to perform after dinner.

From Cairo they travelled to Paris to stay at the Hotel Bristol. Consuelo had always enjoyed Paris, and at last she found herself looking forward to something. She was to complete the purchases for her trousseau and it would be the first time she had ever shopped for herself, for Alva had always chosen her daughter's wardrobe. But even here she was to be disappointed: 'Marlborough took it upon himself to display the same hectoring rights [Alva] had previously exercised in the selection of my gowns,' she wrote. 'Unfortunately, his taste appeared to be dictated by a desire for magnificence rather than by any wish to enhance my looks.'[2] Curiously, when Consuelo was able to buy her own clothes, they were the simple, modest styles preferred by Alva. One evening at their hotel they met Angela St Clair-Erskine who was in Paris with her mother to buy her trousseau, and Marlborough invited the two women to dine with them. Having lost Marlborough it had not taken Angela long to find another suitor but it was an awkward moment for Consuelo, knowing that this beautiful English girl was Marlborough's real love. Angela noted waspishly: 'Consuelo was very pale, rather shy, and with only the promise of the good looks

---

*The woman recruited, a middle-aged, dour Swiss, worked loyally for Consuelo for twenty years and died in her service.

she afterwards developed . . . She was quite the thinnest person I have ever seen and she used to wear her pearls sewn up in a horsehair bag as a bustle tied around her waist – this was partly to insure their safety, and partly to make her look fatter.'[3]

Meanwhile, Consuelo was being equipped for her new life with sophisticated gowns and furs and amazing jewels at Marlborough's dictate. The magnificent tiaras gave her a headache, and she instinctively felt that the jewels he bought were not so much gifts for her pleasure as a display of his newly acquired riches. Princess Alexandra had initiated a fashion for rows of pearls worn tightly clasped around the neck – 'dog collars', they were called – and many Society women adopted this item of jewellery, wearing up to a dozen rows at a time. Marlborough seemed to know about women's fashions and commissioned one for Consuelo's slender neck that contained eighteen rows. She wore it, and though she must have known it suited her, she disliked it because it rasped her skin when she moved her head; also, it was symbolic of what she increasingly felt was her entrapment.

Only when she was properly equipped did Marlborough consider she was fit to meet his family. In March 1896 the couple travelled to London, where a group of Churchills and friends had turned up at the boat-train platform to welcome the newly-weds home. Consuelo had celebrated her nineteenth birthday the previous week but, she later revealed, she still felt like a schoolgirl as she disembarked from the train and faced the scrutiny of many pairs of eyes. There was her mother-in-law Berthe (Goosie), and Marlborough's two sisters Lilian and Norah (whom Consuelo had already met during her visit to Blenheim the previous year); Ivor Guest, who had been her husband's best man at their wedding; Lady Sarah Wilson,* Sunny's hard-eyed, cynical aunt, whom Consuelo instinctively disliked; and Jennie (widowed just over a year earlier) with Winston, now a twenty-one-year-old subaltern in the 4th Hussars, at her elbow. Numerous other friends made up the party, all chattering at once in their distinctive clipped English accents, which

---

*Youngest of Lord Randolph's sisters.

instantly made Consuelo feel different and excluded. Surrounded by the strangers who were now her closest family she felt lonelier than ever, but she recognised that she would have to make friends with these people if she was ever to make a life for herself.

As an onlooker, she saw straight away that there were factions among the group, and noted how most of the Churchills patronised her mother-in-law, who was, in turn, deeply aggrieved that her son had refused to pay the fare for her to attend his wedding in America. But Consuelo instantly liked Winston, describing him as 'a young red-headed boy a few years older than I'. She had heard much of this young cousin of Sunny's whom Sunny regarded as his best friend. He had only just missed their wedding and had gone on from New York to Cuba in search of adventure, and found it by involving himself in the Spanish attempt to quell an insurgency there and sending back dispatches to the *Daily Graphic*, for which he received his first journalist's fee.*

On his twenty-first birthday Winston had attached himself to the Spanish commander, General Valdez, and found himself 'in the most dangerous place in the field' during the fighting. 'For the first time,' he wrote in a memoir, 'I heard shots fired in anger and heard bullets strike flesh or whistle through the air.'[4] He acquitted himself so well that he was decorated by the general (a decoration he was never allowed to wear on his Army uniform), but his *Graphic* reports of the battle were not received with universal approval by rival newspapers. 'Sensible people,' grumbled one leader editorial, 'will wonder what motive could possibly impel a British officer to mix himself up in a dispute with the merits of which he had absolutely nothing to do . . . Spending a holiday in fighting other people's battles is rather an extraordinary proceeding even for a Churchill.'[5] Winston was nevertheless happy to have made his first small mark on the world.

Knowing that Winston was Marlborough's heir until she produced a son, Consuelo had wondered before meeting him whether

---

*In old age, Winston would say that what gave him most pride in his life was his ability to have earned his living by his pen.

he would be her enemy, but his open, friendly and self-confident welcome invigorated her. And after all, she reflected, he was half-American. 'He struck me,' she wrote, 'as ardent and vital and seemed to have every intention of getting the most out of life, whether in sport, or in love, in adventure or in politics.'[6] During the years Consuelo spent at Blenheim, Winston would be one of the most regular visitors, staying there at least several days each month and always taking centre stage in conversation. She enjoyed the fact that his views were sharp and well informed, and not delivered with the sense of self-importance that her husband's were.

Consuelo's relationship with her mother-in-law was also comforting. 'Her outlook was limited, for she had received an English girl's proverbially poor education,' she wrote. And she was more amused than shocked to find that Goosie believed all American families lived on large plantations with slaves for servants, and 'that there were Red Indians ready to scalp us round every corner'. But she quickly realised that Goosie was not as stupid as was usually suggested: 'She possessed shrewd powers of intuition and observation, and . . . she liked me.'[7]

The following day Consuelo was formally presented to Marlborough's formidable grandmother, the Dowager Duchess Fanny* who had caused Jennie so much heartache in her early years among the family. Still dressed in mourning for Randolph, and using an ear trumpet, the Duchess made the meeting resemble a royal audience. She had been strongly in favour of Sunny's marriage because of the financial advantages, but she was eager to see what the bargain was like and frankly inspected Consuelo, her clothes and demeanour. She was apparently not dissatisfied with the slim, tall girl, who had a modest grace, and she told Consuelo how she hoped to see Blenheim soon restored to its former glory. 'Then,' Consuelo wrote, 'fixing her cold grey eyes upon me she continued, "Your first duty is to have a child and it must be a son, because it

---

*At this point there were no fewer than five women entitled to style themselves 'Duchess of Marlborough': Berthe, Marchioness of Blandford, former wife of the 8th Duke; Jane, widow of the 6th Duke; Frances (Fanny), widow of the 7th Duke; Lily, second wife and widow of the 8th Duke; and Consuelo, the present Duchess.

will be intolerable to have that little upstart Winston become Duke. Are you in the family way?"'[8]

This recollection sits oddly with the fond letters in the Churchill archive written by Duchess Fanny to Winston from his childhood onwards. She was certainly annoyed with him on occasions because she thought he spent his small allowance too freely, and she loathed the fact that after he left school he liked going to the races and gambling (a trait shared by most Churchill men). Her affection may have changed during Lord Randolph's final illness when Winston could do nothing to please his father, and – almost emotionally estranged from Jennie – it had been to Duchess Fanny that Randolph frequently wrote to complain about Winston and express his disappointment in his elder son. Randolph had been Duchess Fanny's favourite child, the star in her brood, and she never recovered from his early death. She may have blamed Winston for causing his father such worry, but on the other hand she often invited him to stay and reported to Jennie that he was 'affectionate and pleasant'. Her letters to Winston at that time certainly did not lack warmth: 'Do be careful dear of bathing not to catch cold or otherwise come to grief,' she had written a few months earlier, signing herself 'Ever your affectionate Grandmother'.[9] Perhaps she had intended her remark to Consuelo to be taken humorously? No other explanation makes sense.

After the ordeal of meeting the Churchills, Consuelo was taken to meet Marlborough's maternal family, the Hamiltons, at the home of Berthe's brother the Duke of Abercorn. Consuelo liked the Hamiltons better than the Churchills and was pleased to note that Marlborough was more Hamilton in appearance and mannerism than Churchill. But again, the conversation was soon brought round to the subject of an heir and Consuelo found herself infected with everybody's anxiety on that topic. Berthe's sister the Marchioness of Lansdowne, whom Consuelo had met in India, was a surrogate mother to Marlborough – and indeed he told Consuelo he much preferred this aunt to his mother. Lady Lansdowne was very like Berthe 'but much better looking', and she, like her sister, showed some kindness to the newcomer.

With the introductions over, Marlborough took Consuelo home to Blenheim. The whole of Woodstock and nearby villages turned out to greet them. Consuelo recalled standing tired and cold, though dressed in fabulous furs, in the sharp April wind, waiting while the Mayor and every other local dignitary welcomed her with what each considered an appropriate speech. At the railway station the Mayor suggested that the Duchess might be interested to know that Woodstock had a mayor and corporation before America was discovered. Consuelo recalled that she 'seethed' with an unspoken riposte, which seems an oversensitive reaction to an obviously well meant piece of information, but again she felt patronised. Each speech delivered along their route under triumphal arches bedecked with early spring blooms was cheered by flag-waving crowds, enchanted by the youth and beauty of the new Duchess. And after each speech Consuelo was presented with a bouquet, until her arms were full of flowers.

At last they were in the carriage for the drive to Blenheim, and – just like Jennie before her – Consuelo was taken aback when the horses were unhitched and 'our employees proceeded to drag us up to the house'.[10] Although touched by the warmth of the welcome, Consuelo was 'discomfited by this means of progress, at which my democratic principles rebelled'. The last time she had seen Blenheim had been on her first visit as an awestruck guest who had nevertheless disdained the domestic arrangements, which were not up to Alva's standards. Now it was her home, under her management, and she had to make the best of it.

She was relieved to get to her room, where her new maid had a hot bath ready and had laid out her gown for dinner. But she was not much impressed with her accommodation. High above her, a plaster frieze of garlands held by golden cupids seemed to suggest that some thought had been given to cheering the new occupant; but her bed faced a fireplace upon which the inscription 'Dust, Ashes, Nothing' was carved in black letters. It was the first thing that greeted her each morning, and Consuelo often thought longingly of her own bright, modern, warm suite in New York.

That evening was the first of the dinners *à deux* that were to become a purgatory to Consuelo over the years. Cartoons depicting a long table with a diner at either end, unable to converse with each other because of the distance between them, were simply art imitating life as far as Consuelo was concerned. She wrote of Marlborough's curious habit of loading his plate with food before dismissing the servants. Then he would move his plate away, along with all the cutlery and the glasses, and push his chair back, while twirling his signet ring and contemplating some train of thought, often getting up and walking about the room for five or ten minutes. Afterwards he would return to his place and eat his dinner very slowly, complaining that the food was cold. 'As a rule neither of us spoke a word. I took to knitting in desperation.'[11] Their butler – equally bored – used to sit outside the door reading detective novels.

The strict hierarchy of the servants was something else that Consuelo had to learn, and to survive. This was quite as rigid as the English class system itself, and Consuelo, used to Alva's well run homes, knew what was needed but found it hard at first to achieve. Quarrels between the chef and the housekeeper were frequent, and required careful adjudication. Each servant had their allotted tasks and for one to do the work of another – perhaps someone lower in the pecking order – was to cause a loss of face. Hence, if Consuelo wanted someone to set a match to the fire in her sitting room, the butler, who might be in the room at the time, would have to gravely send for a footman to do so. On one occasion, at least, Consuelo lost patience and sprang up to light the fire herself rather than wait. We do not know what the butler thought of this act of *lèse-majesté*.

Fortunately, whenever Marlborough made one of his frequent trips to London, his sisters Lilian and Norah stayed with Consuelo so that she was not always left alone, and Consuelo tried to learn from these two women who had spent their childhood at Blenheim. She was quick, bright and dutiful – 'watchful as a child is watchful' is how one visitor described her – so that although she received no formal instruction she began to pick up the running of the great household. She learned to live with its inconveniences – though always inwardly resentful about all the same things that Jennie had complained of years earlier: the insularity of life at Blenheim, the stuffiness and arrogance of the family, the acute discomfort of a house with impossibly high ceilings, insufficient heating and limited bathroom facilities. To fill her days she visited the sick and elderly in the neighbouring villages (not, one would suppose, an occupation any nineteen-year-old newly-wed would choose willingly). But with a resilience typical of her youth, Consuelo came to terms with her bad bargain and began to look forward to weekends when visitors came and alleviated the dullness. As far as she was able she worked at her marriage and came eventually to believe that she had stimulated some affection in Marlborough, if not love. She concluded that a woman could only really be happy living at Blenheim if she were in love with the Duke, but that never happened to Consuelo.

The London Seasons of 1896 and 1897 were, it is generally accepted, the most brilliant ever known and eclipsed those of other European capitals by the sheer diversity and extravagance of the entertainments and events laid on. These were the days of the great town mansions – Devonshire House, Lansdowne House, Apsley House and Montagu House,* to name a few – and of legendary hostesses such as Lady Londonderry and Lady de Grey (Jennie's one-time rival). But the centre was Marlborough House. The Queen, who was nearly eighty, celebrated the sixtieth year of her reign in June 1897, and the Diamond Jubilee celebrations were the chief reason for the lustre and quality of that London Season. With Victoria living mostly in seclusion at Osborne and Windsor, Society in London revolved around Marlborough House.

Consuelo and Marlborough were invited everywhere, and as she got to know people she was less intimidated and even began to enjoy herself. Full of youthful energy, she took pleasure in the wonderful balls, peopled, she recalled, by 'beautiful women and distinguished men' who danced energetic polkas and graceful waltzes by Strauss and Waldteufel, to orchestras brought over from Vienna, as well as old-fashioned set dances such as quadrilles – far

---

*Belonging, respectively, to the Dukes of Devonshire, the Marquesses of Lansdowne, the Dukes of Wellington and the Dukes of Buccleuch).

less lively, but requiring knowledge of the intricate steps and patterns if one were not to cause embarrassing chaos. 'We dined out nearly every night and there were always parties, often several, in the evening . . . one had to exercise discretion in one's acceptances in order to survive the three months,' she wrote.[12] All this was without counting the races, the riding in Hyde Park, afternoon parties at Ranelagh and Roehampton, and inter-regimental polo matches at Hurlingham. On Fridays the Marlboroughs generally returned to Blenheim where they entertained twenty or thirty guests until Monday, then all travelled back to town. For Consuelo the chief worry was the minefield that was etiquette – not mere manners, in which Alva's training had been first-class, but knowing the order of precedence for prickly aristocrats who knew to a semicolon what their place was in society. Allow one titled matron in to dinner ahead of her rightful place, and a hostess would never be forgiven by anyone displaced by the error. Eventually Consuelo was lucky enough to obtain an order of precedence with the names of all those of rank printed in the correct order. It became her bible. Otherwise, for such a young woman not raised in this closed society she appears to have been amazingly sure-footed.

After the fruit course it was the role of the hostess, or the senior woman present, to rise, and at this signal all the ladies would follow her, leaving the gentlemen to their port and cigars. At Consuelo's first major dinner party she was about to rise when Sunny's youngest aunt, Lady Sarah Wilson – who had patronised Consuelo from the day she arrived in England – rose to her feet. All the ladies followed her example. Consuelo stiffened, immediately aware that it was a deliberate attempt by Lady Sarah to assert her dominance. She heard her neighbour, Lord Chesterfield, say: '"Never have I seen anything so rude; don't move!" I nevertheless went to the door and meeting her, inquired in dulcet tones, "Are you ill, Sarah?" "Ill?" she shrilled. "No, certainly not, why should I be ill?" "There surely was no other excuse for your hasty exit," I said calmly. She had the grace to blush; the other women hid their smiles, and never again was I thus challenged.'[13]

For such a novice Consuelo seems to have sailed with aplomb

through the difficulties of hosting royal weekends with all the potential tripwires in matters of etiquette and precedence. Other than this, royal house parties were not very different from ordinary 'Friday to Monday' visits during the winter months when there was a strict routine which Consuelo followed – though always, it seems, she was on the outside looking in:

> The number of changes of costume was in itself a waste of precious time. To begin with, even breakfast, which was served at 9.30 in the dining room, demanded an elegant costume of velvet or silk. Having seen the men off to their sport, the ladies spent the morning round the fire reading the papers and gossiping. We next changed into tweeds to join the guns for luncheon, which was served in the High Lodge or in a tent. Afterwards we usually accompanied the guns and watched a drive or two before returning home. An elaborate tea gown was donned for tea, after which we played cards or listened to a Viennese band or to the organ until time to dress for dinner when again we adorned ourselves in satin, or brocade, with a great display of jewels . . . one was not supposed to wear the same gown twice. That meant sixteen dresses for four days.[14]

Her next hurdle was a Churchill family Christmas at Blenheim, when generations of brothers and sisters, aunts and cousins all came together. Consuelo could not decide which occasions were more traumatic – the royal visits or the family gatherings.

In January 1897 she conceived her first child and it was a great relief to know that at last she had 'done her duty' towards forging the next link in the chain. But it meant that when the couple moved to Melton Mowbray in Leicestershire for the foxhunting season Consuelo was unable to ride, so while Sunny hunted most days, she spent the interminable months reading German philosophy. Her sitting-room window overlooked a pond where a former butler had drowned himself. 'As one gloomy day succeeded another,' she wrote, 'I began to feel a deep sympathy for him.'

Marlborough leased Spencer House, overlooking Green Park in London, for Consuelo's confinement, and on 18 September their first son John Albert Edward (named after his godfather, the Prince of Wales) William (after Consuelo's father, also a godfather) John (after the 1st Duke) was born. As the heir he was always called 'Blandford', of course, but Consuelo called him 'Bert'. At Blenheim the staff were jubilant, firing off salutes from the roof as though for a royal birth and donning their most formal dress at a celebration ball given for the servants and villagers. The Dowager could heave a sigh of relief that the ducal line was safe. Winston was now out of the equation, and Jennie, writing to tell him that Consuelo had given birth to a son, reminded him to write to congratulate Sunny. 'He is very fond of you,' she added.[15] At the time Winston was working on his first book, a novel that has been described as a 'Ruritanian romance', into which he poured many of his romantic ideals and ambitions and invested his hero, the eponymous Savrola, with a good number of his own characteristics, ambitions and beliefs.*

While Consuelo was recovering from Blandford's birth, Marlborough met a young woman called Gladys Deacon who was visiting London from Paris, where she lived with her mother and three sisters. Gladys (she pronounced her name to rhyme with 'ladies')[16] was only sixteen and not yet 'out' in society, but she was extremely beautiful, bright and entertaining. American by birth, she was wholly European in upbringing, and Marlborough was captivated by her. When he introduced Gladys to his wife, thinking they had much in common and that Gladys might cheer up Consuelo, he could have had no suspicion of the impact Gladys would have on their future lives.

Gladys had been raised amidst trauma, dissension and scandal. Her mother Florence was said to be so beautiful that when she entered a room it had the same effect as if a crystal chandelier had crashed to the ground.[17] Florence had married for money a rich and handsome millionaire, Edward Parker Deacon, whom, however, she

---

* *Savrola* was published in 1899, when he had already published two other books. Had it not been written by Churchill it would undoubtedly have been lost to history among the other romantic novels of the day. Now it stands as a useful insight into the thoughts of the young Churchill. It was his only work of fiction.

did not love, and the marriage was always stormy. It eventually ended when Deacon shot his wife's lover in Paris. The man died, but Deacon was only convicted of unlawfully wounding his victim 'but without intent to cause death'; he was sent to prison for a year. Gladys was eleven years old. The family split up at this point but when Deacon was released he took custody of the children – except Gladys, who was kidnapped by her mother from her boarding school. These scandalous events, in addition to divorce proceedings in which Deacon accused his wife of 'criminal adultery',* were played out in newspaper headlines of which Gladys was not left in ignorance. Eventually, she was returned to her father, who took her to New York to be reunited with her sisters. Her education continued in Newport and Boston, and though their home in Newport was almost opposite Alva's Marble House the Deacons did not move in the same circles as the Vanderbilts, so Consuelo and Gladys had never met there.

Gladys had been fourteen when the Marlborough engagement made headlines; probably it never occurred to her that Consuelo might be an unwilling bride, since Gladys saw the marriage to the young Duke as a fairy-tale, exactly the sort of happy ending she dreamed of for herself. She wrote to her mother on the subject: 'If I was only a little older I might catch him yet. But *hélas*! I am too young though mature in the arts of woman's witchcraft and what is the use of one without the other . . .'[18] It seems a curious letter for a girl to write to her mother; but then, Florence had done the same thing as a teenager. When she was fifteen and about to leave the convent, Gladys was allowed to go to France on vacation with her mother. She preferred this to visiting New York, where she felt she was always gossiped about as 'the daughter of those Deacons'.[19] She was still living in Paris with her mother three years later when her father, who had become insane, died of a 'general paralysis of the brain' (syphilis).

In the autumn of 1897 Mrs Deacon took sixteen-year-old Gladys

---

*Adultery was a criminal offence in the USA (and still remains so in a few states), carrying terms of imprisonment and fines for those found guilty.

to London, and there they were introduced to the Duke who had figured largely in Gladys's girlish daydreams. He could hardly have known of her fantasies, of course, and it is surprising that he was not put off by the scandal that still clung to Florence. However, the attractive women and their innate good manners were hard to over-look, and the fact that Gladys had been almost a neighbour of Consuelo's in Newport and so might have a lot in common with her may have been a deciding factor. Anyway, Sunny was taken enough with Gladys to invite her to stay at Blenheim. Consuelo, still convalescing from the birth of Blandford and glad of a confi-dante, even one four years younger than herself, was charmed: 'Gladys . . . was a beautiful girl endowed with a brilliant intellect. Possessed of exceptional powers of conversation, she could enlarge on any subject in an interesting and amusing manner. I was soon subjugated by the charm of her companionship and we began a friendship.'[20] Soon, however, Gladys had to return to Europe for the final stage of her education, which included the study of German, Latin, Italian and mathematics. Her classical beauty attracted the most famous artists of the day – Paul-César Helleu, Giovanni Boldini, Jacques-Émile Blanche – all of whom portrayed her and became her friend. There is no doubt that she was highly intelligent. At this point she began to collect books and read all the poetry she could lay her hands on. She and Consuelo corresponded, but it would be another four years before Gladys again entered the lives of the Marlboroughs, when she was invited to Blenheim for a six-month visit.

Ivor Spencer Churchill, Consuelo's second and always her favourite son, was born in October 1898. And having provided the 'heir and spare' (the phrase she is credited with having coined), Consuelo lay back after her travail and basked in the knowledge that she would now be allowed 'a certain measure of the pleasures of life'. Goosie was thrilled, greeting her daughter-in-law cheerily with the words: 'You are a little brick! American women seem to have boys more easily than we do!'[21]

In the following months Consuelo was able to join her husband foxhunting in the shires, acquitting herself well under supercritical

9

1896–9

Looking for Trouble

In September 1896 Winston sailed for India, but with reluctance. He had been closely watching events unfolding in South Africa for the past six months and rightly foresaw that there would soon be major problems there with the Boers. And he was actively looking for trouble – some fracas in which an ambitious young subaltern might get noticed and marked out for rapid promotion. Without any financial resources behind him, such a record – perhaps with a medal or two, he reasoned – would help him enormously in the future when he intended to stand for Parliament. So before his regiment embarked for India he attempted, frantically but unsuccessfully, to get a transfer to South Africa.*

In letters to his mother he gloomily forecast that his time in India would be wasted and he would simply vegetate there unless he could 'get hold of the people' who might further his career. He had already decided that he had made a serious mistake in joining the Army and should have gone directly into politics, though he knew his father would never have sanctioned this at the time. 'Had I come to India as an MP – however young and foolish,' he wrote to Jennie, 'I could have had access to all who know and can convey. As a soldier my intelligent interests are supposed to stop short at Polo, racing & Orderly Officer.'[1] Later he would write, 'You can't realise

---

*He also tried unsuccessfully to get himself posted to the Sudan and Matabeleland.

how furiously intolerable this life is to me when so much is going on a month from here.' One letter must have puzzled Jennie, who had thrown in her lot wholeheartedly with the Tory Party. Winston revealed that his political views were Liberal in all but name, and that he sometimes caused mayhem in the mess when he expressed them. 'Were it not for Home Rule – to which I will never consent – I would enter Parliament as a Liberal,' he wrote. 'As it is, the Tory Democracy will have to be the standard under which I shall range myself.'[2]

Historians might reasonably reflect that Winston's period in India was far from wasted, since it provided him with time to think about what he really wanted from life and started him on his literary career. However, it seems he had already decided upon his ultimate ambition, for it was at this point that he began telling people that one day he expected to be Prime Minister.[3] Mostly his listeners laughed, thinking he was joking, and yet most would agree later that there was something special about this unusual young officer.

Meanwhile, he occupied himself with a butterfly collection, a growing library, racing, polo (a sport he loved – he rarely played fewer than eight chukkas each evening) and some roses he had planted, among them varieties called 'Gloire de Dijon' and 'La France'. 'Every morning I can cut about 3 great basins full,' he wrote to his mother one January day. He also mentioned that he had met the daughter of the Resident of Hyderabad, Pamela Plowden. 'I must say she is the most beautiful girl I have ever seen – "bar none" – as the Duchess Lily says. We are going to try and do the City of Hyderabad together – on an elephant,' he wrote.[4]

Pamela was Winston's first love; he held her image in his heart for years, and had he been able to afford to marry then, it seems certain he would have done so. A letter to her at that time shows him laying down a marker: 'I have lived all my life seeing the most beautiful women London produces . . . Never have I seen one for whom I would for an hour forgo the business of life. Then I met you . . . Were I a dreamer of dreams, I would say . . . "Marry me – and I will conquer the world and lay it at your feet" . . . [But] for marriage two conditions are necessary – money and the consent of both parties. One certainly, both probably, are absent. And this is all such an old story.'[5] He had first to make his name and his fortune, but for the next three years he wrote frequently to her and they met whenever possible.

Having been a diffident student at school he now developed a keen desire to learn. He spent most mornings reading voraciously, his juvenile taste for the works of Dickens, Thackeray and Wordsworth having given way to Plato, Gibbon, Darwin and Aristotle as well as Hart's *Army Lists,* Jane's *Fighting Ships* and transcripts and reports of political speeches. He had been fond of Thomas Babington Macaulay at Harrow, where he could recite pages of the *Lays of Ancient Rome.*[*] Now he tackled Macaulay's multivolume *History of England.*[†] He admired the rolling phraseology, and there can be no doubt that Macaulay's work coloured Winston's perception of history. He could recite from *The History* verbatim, but in later life, when critics occasionally queried factual details in his own books, he would admit ruefully that without a tutor to warn him of the drawbacks he had simply accepted Macaulay's racy accounts as wholly fact.

As part of this self-education process he asked Jennie to send him printed parliamentary records. To her dismay she found there were a hundred volumes at fourteen shillings each: she sent him twenty-seven. Once embarked upon this course of study Winston began to regret not having obtained the gloss of Oxbridge, but he admitted to Jennie that he was reluctant, now, to spend time learning the necessary Latin and Greek, so that was not an option for him.[6] And when Jack expressed a wish to go to Oxford, Winston wrote that he was greatly in favour and would be prepared to take out a personal loan of £500 for the purpose, proposing that Jack could repay him

---

*Then out spake brave Horatius, the Captain of the Gate:

'To every man upon this earth, Death cometh soon or late.

And how can man die better, than facing fearful odds,

For the ashes of his fathers, and the temples of his gods . . .'

†Macaulay's *History of England* was a massive endeavour, well researched and colourfully written. It is not sufficiently accurate for the academic, but general readers found a good trade-off in sheer readability, sweep of subject and forceful opinion.

at some later date. 'I envy Jack the liberal education of a University,' he wrote. 'What a strange inversion of fortune – that I should be a soldier and Jack at college.'[7]

Money was a constant worry for both Winston and Jennie. Although Jennie had a life interest in the trust established by Randolph's will, the income seldom reached the £800 annually required to pay Winston's and Jack's allowances. She had received nothing from her mother's will,* her main income being £2000 a year from her marriage settlement. Nevertheless, after Randolph's death, having tasted freedom during her fling in Paris with Bourke Cockran, she had no wish to return to living with the Dowager Duchess. And when she looked for a new house there was no sign of any financial retrenchment. She leased 35a Great Cumberland Place, a seven-floor mansion a block from Connaught Place, close to Hyde Park and Park Lane, and continued to live as though money was of no concern. She wrote to Winston in March 1897 that from her total annual income of £2700 (about £162,000 today) she provided the allowances of £400 a year each to him and Jack. Then there was over £400 for rent of the house and stables, leaving her only £1500 for everything else – taxes, servants, food, dress, travelling. In addition, she now had to pay interest on the money she borrowed.[8] It is possible she worried about her finances in the dark hours of the night, but she never allowed this to impede her very full life at the apex of court society. Encompassing numerous flirtations and love affairs, her life went on almost as it always had, by virtue of raising loans and by accepting gifts from her many admirers and friends.

At the end of that year Jennie found that she needed £17,000 (today, £1.1 million) – more than six years' income – in a hurry, in order to repay some fixed-term loans that were coming to an end and to satisfy those creditors who would wait no longer. Her solution was to insure her own and Winston's life and use these life policies as

---

*Clara Jerome, knowing that Jennie was provided for by her marriage settlement, had left the small amount she still owned at the time of her death to Jennie's two sisters, Leonie and Clarita, both of whom had financial problems.

guarantees against new loans. The drawback was that she needed Winston to guarantee the premiums of £700 a year, should she default, and she was fully aware that this would be an impossible sum for him to meet if it came to it. When Winston received her letter – the mail took two months between England and India – he felt he had little option but to agree. But he too had borrowed extensively:

Speaking quite frankly on the subject – there is no doubt that we are both, you and I, equally thoughtless – spendthrift and extravagant. We both know what is good – and we both like to have it. Arrangements for paying are left to the future. My extravagances are on a smaller scale than yours. I take no credit to myself in this matter as you have kept up the house & have had to maintain a position in London. At the same time we shall vy soon come to the end of our tether – unless a considerable change comes over our fortunes and dispositions. As long as I am dead sure and certain of an ultimate £1000 a year – I do not care as I could always make money on the press – and might marry. But at the same time there must be a limit . . . I sympathise with all your extravagances – even more than you do with mine – it seems just as suicidal to me when you spend £200 on a ball dress as it does to you when I purchase a new polo pony for £100. And yet I feel that you ought to have the dress and I the polo pony. The pinch of the whole matter is that we are damned poor.[9]

He also wrote to Jack and suggested that he should take on a share of the family financial burden when he left university, to which Jack agreed.* Winston thanked him, admitting to his brother that money was the only thing in life that really worried him – that is, his own extravagant tastes versus his 'diminished resources'.[10] Despite the diversions he mentions in his letters – which for his fellow officers endowed with adequate funding and being waited on hand and foot no doubt made life in India under the Raj an extremely pleasant one – Winston felt every hour that passed was an hour wasted. He constantly pressed Jennie to help him with

---

*In fact, Jack never attended university.

introductions and push his name with her important friends. 'I cannot believe,' he wrote, 'that with all the influential friends you possess and all those who would do something for me for my father's sake . . . You really ought to leave no stone unturned . . . it is a little thing for you to ask and a smaller thing for those in authority to grant – but it means so much to me.'[11] A few months in South Africa, he maintained, would inevitably lead to a few medals, which – in a year or two – he could put to good use: he would 'beat my sword into an iron despatch box', as he put it. Every letter he wrote at this time harped on the same theme: advancement – not glory for glory's sake, but as his passport into the political arena.

Eventually Jennie complied – or so Winston thought* – by travelling to Egypt to tackle Lord Kitchener, the Commander-in-Chief of the army there, in person about Winston's requests for transfer. In reality Jennie's journey to Egypt was not solely to aid her son's ambitions. By coincidence her latest lover Major Caryl Ramsden, regarded as the handsomest man in his regiment, the Seaforth Highlanders – an attribute for which he was nicknamed 'Beauty Ramsden' – had just been posted there.

Perhaps worn down by Jennie's stream of letters (her close links to the Prince of Wales could not have harmed her petition, and she got friends in Parliament also to write on Winston's behalf), Lord Kitchener at last agreed to put Winston's name down for a posting to the Sudan. At the same time he advised that there were no immediate vacancies in the cavalry. So Winston was still left kicking his heels while he waited for this promise to bear fruit. While he waited he managed to find some action in skirmishes along the North West Frontier, an area that included the strategic Khyber Pass, the site of constant struggles between British forces and local warriors. He pulled every string he could to get himself attached as a special correspondent to the regiments involved there. In one battle, to his gratification, he received

---

*He wrote on 16 February 1898: 'I feel vy grateful indeed to you for going to Egypt. It is an action which – should I ever have a biographer – will certainly be admired by them. I hope you will be successful. I feel almost certain you will. Your wit & tact & beauty should overcome all obstacles.'

a mention in dispatches praising his courage and resolution: 'He made himself useful at a critical moment,' the report read. His CO forecast that 'if he gets a chance [he] will have a VC or a DSO'. In fact it was held by many senior field officers that the only reason Winston did not get a VC was because he had made too many enemies among the staff because of his pushiness. To his mother he wrote that he was noticed less because of anything he had actually done in that skirmish than for having ridden a grey pony, thus making himself conspicuous among the brown ponies ridden by his fellow officers, chosen so as to provide a less obvious target for snipers. But the reports and diaries that covered this battle, and another that would follow, show that Winston was always in the front line, that he fought bravely and seemed heedless of his personal safety. In his letters to Pamela Plowden he happily recounted all the bullets that narrowly missed him.

Jennie's love affair that winter came to an unexpected end. She and Caryl Ramsden parted tenderly before he rejoined his regiment in Wadi Halfa, and Jennie set off for England. When, on reaching Port Said, she was advised that her ship would be delayed for several days, she impulsively rushed back to Cairo hoping to spend a final few hours with Ramsden. On entering his hotel room unannounced, in order to surprise him, it was she who was surprised, for she discovered her lover in a compromising situation with Louisa, Lady Maxwell, wife of his commanding officer. The hotel was filled with interested British visitors who were subsequently treated to Jennie's opinion of Ramsden at full volume. The story inevitably reached London and even the ears of the Prince of Wales. He, finding it amusing, wrote to Jennie reminding her: 'You had better have stuck to your old friends than gone on your Expedition of the Nile! Old friends are best!' Jennie was in fact deeply hurt by Ramsden's betrayal, and when she received this note on her arrival in London she fired off a robust reply to the Prince, citing a similar thing that had happened to him. Fortunately her sister Leonie, having offered to post the note, wisely destroyed it. And later, when he understood how truly upset Jennie had been by the affair, the Prince would apologise: 'I must ask your pardon if my letter pained. I had no idea *que c'était une affaire si sérieuse* [it was such a serious affair],' he wrote.[12]

Jennie was a frequent guest at Sandringham and was always welcome at Marlborough House entertainments, which indicated that Princess Alexandra approved of her. Hostesses wishing to make up a house party to include the Prince often invited Jennie because she knew how to charm and please him, in addition to whoever happened to be the *maîtresse en titre* of the moment. Photographs dated 1898 show Jennie sitting beside the Prince when he had his first drive in an early motor car. He regularly made informal late-afternoon calls at her home, when the servants were likely to be off duty after the ritual of tea and before that of dressing for dinner. By common consent this was the 'safe time' for a gentleman to call upon a mistress. Adultery was widespread among the upper classes because, as noted earlier, divorce was unacceptable – it would play havoc with the estates and money of those concerned. But provided the succession of an estate was secured, a discreet affair was regarded as a safe outlet for passions and boredom. The practice of afternoon visits was even given a code-name by the cognoscenti: the *cinq à sept* (the five-to-seven).

After Jennie's death hundreds of letters and notes from the Prince were found among her papers. After Randolph's death all these letters begin '*Ma chère Amie*', but none was compromising – the Prince had obviously learned that lesson from his youthful experience with Lady Aylesford – and although there are some obvious coded phrases, they offer no evidence that the couple ever had a sexual liaison.[13] Yet from what we know of Jennie's attitude to men and from the historical evidence of the Prince's serial womanising, it would have been uncharacteristic for them not to have slept together at some point. Also, it is known that in 1889 Randolph forcibly ejected the Prince after finding him alone with Jennie 'unchaperoned'. So it is not unreasonable to conclude that Jennie and the Prince were at times sexually intimate.

The Prince would have been entitled to regard an affair with Jennie as 'safe' because she was known to have a number of lovers, most of them younger than herself. Indeed, during her lifetime she was rumoured to have slept with more than a hundred men, though one must make allowances for gossip and plain jealousy. During the twentieth century this figure seems to have escalated to two hundred, which seems a little excessive, but there was nevertheless a small squadron of men either recognised by her intimates to have been Jennie's lovers, and/or about whom Jennie wrote to Leonie. Apart from those already mentioned – Charles Kinsky, Freddy Wolverton and others – among the rest were Hugh Warrender, Henry de Breteuil, Baron Hirsch, Kinkaid Smith, Paul Bourget, Sir Edgar Vincent, William Waldorf Astor, Lord Dunraven, Thomas Trafford, Norman Forbes-Robertson and Harry Cust. From her correspondence can be gleaned others whose full names are not given – someone called Simon, and another – an Italian – called Casati. Then there was John Delacour, whom Randolph intended to cite as corespondent if they were to divorce, and a number of men in Ireland who were written about but unnamed in her correspondence. And besides her lovers, Jennie seemed to be able to attract and impress men of power and character who never hopped into her bed, and these – Lord Salisbury, the Duke of Cambridge and Lord Cromer to name three – were all grist to Winston's mill, contacts to be exploited to achieve his ends.

The question must be asked: Was Winston ever aware of his mother's numerous lovers? The answer is unequivocally yes. An observant teenager, he once noted that when Jennie went out to lunch there was a tiny run in her stocking near the ankle; when she returned after tea the run had transferred to the other ankle. And in a letter to Jack when their father was in South Africa, Winston reported that while enjoying a rare exeat and instructed to stay with his grandmother he had gone home first to surprise his mother, to find her breakfasting with Charles Kinsky.[14] He was sixteen, not so young that he could not guess what this implied. There is also the story that Winston once challenged a fellow officer to a duel after his mother's reputation was called into question; but he must have been aware that she was something of a sexual predator. On one occasion, after reading a racy book entitled *An Englishwoman's Love Letters*, he wrote to Jennie, 'Are all mothers the same?'[15] To Winston, though, whatever her faults, Jennie remained the perfect woman. Her early neglect of him seemed never to have affected his feelings for her; he was tolerant of her peccadilloes, and when he bullied and cajoled her that was simply part of his relationship with her – he loved her deeply. It is very probable that Winston's chaste behaviour as a husband owed something to his disapproval of his mother in this one respect. But watching his father die slowly from a diagnosis of syphilis must also have been an object lesson.

Certainly, Jennie managed to stay friends with the Prince of Wales for the rest of her life, indicating a genuine affection between them that was more than simple lust. From the Prince's view point, she was a friend of long standing who was discreet and who knew how to keep him entertained at boring parties. The relationship provided Jennie with a social cachet that few widows in her financial position could match and that ensured her a constant flow of invitations. She often spoke to the Prince about Winston; she mentioned such conversations in her letters to Winston and passed on short messages to him from the Prince.

When Winston published his first book, *The Story of the Malakand Field Force* which detailed the 1897 military campaign on the North West Frontier, he had been working against time, having learned that a fellow officer was also writing a book on the subject. Clearly, there was no market for both, and he knew his had to be published first. It was Jennie who found an editor and got the book out quickly. She presented a copy to the Prince and to top politicians, all of whom were complimentary about it, though Winston himself was in an agony of despair. Because of the time it took for the mails to get to India and back he had decided to forgo checking the proofs himself and asked an uncle* to read them for him. In the event the book contained dozens of typographical errors, and Winston feared this would reflect badly on his work. 'I blame myself and myself alone for this act of folly and laziness,' he wrote miserably to Jennie, 'which has made me ridiculous to all whose good opinion I would have hoped for.' But the editorial errors were overlooked; the book sold more than twelve thousand copies and provided him with some much needed income.

Meanwhile, he was hard at work on another book, to be called

---

*Moreton Frewen, the handsome but hapless husband of Jennie's sister Clara (Clarita). He was known in the family as 'Mortal Ruin' for his unsuccessful business schemes.

The River War: An Historical Account of the Reconquest of the Soudan.
In a letter to his mother he made a self-revealing remark: 'I think
what is written is really good. Let me quote you one sentence – it
is about the Mahdi [the Sunni Muslim leader] who was left while
still quite young an orphan: "Solitary trees, if they grow at all, grow
strong: and a boy deprived of a father's care often develops, if he
escape the perils of youth, an independence and a vigour of thought
which may restore in after life the heavy loss of early days."'[16] One
cannot help but wonder whether it dawned on Jennie that he was
writing from personal experience.

It was Jennie who got Winston a regular column in the *Daily
Telegraph*, though he considered she had not tried hard enough to
get him the fees he thought his pieces were worth, and he was furious to find that he was being published over the byline 'From a
serving officer' instead of 'From Winston S. Churchill'. He welcomed the income, but he wanted his name put constantly before
the British public; it was all part of his long-term plan.

At this point, in July 1898, Jennie received an invitation from
Daisy Warwick* to spend a long weekend at Warwick Castle.
Among the guests was a twenty-four-year-old Scots Guards officer,
George Cornwallis-West,† a godson of the Prince. One of George's
sisters, Daisy, was married to Prince Heinrich of Pless, and the
other, Shelagh, to Hugh Grosvenor, 2nd Duke of Westminster.
The two girls were exceptionally attractive, and George was said to
be 'one of the handsomest men in England'. It was expected of
George that he would marry as well as his sisters had done, since
although the family owned two properties – a 10,000-acre estate at

---

*Frances 'Daisy' Greville, Countess of Warwick (1861–1938), was a mistress of the Prince of
Wales and also of his confidant Lord Charles Beresford, who probably fathered her fourth son
Maynard, born in 1898. At this point the Prince dropped her and she soon became known as
'the Babbling Brook' owing to her husband's former title (Lord Brook) and her constant indis-
creet gossiping about her love affairs. The music-hall song 'Daisy, Daisy, Give Me Your Answer
Do' was written about her. Many years later, in financial distress, she demanded of King
George V the massive sum of £100,000 not to sell intimate letters from Edward VII (King
George's father) to an American newspaper. Instead her mountainous debts were settled by
Tory MP Arthur du Cros, who subsequently received a barony.
†The original family name of West had been changed to Cornwallis-West in 1886 under the
terms of a will.

Ruthin in North Wales and Newlands Manor near Lymington, Hampshire – there was no money. George's parents had been badly hit by the agricultural recession of the 1870s, and the Ruthin estate had been rented to tenants while the family lived between the smaller Newlands Manor and their London house. George knew all this but by his own account he took one look at forty-three-year-old Jennie – 'Still beautiful,' he recalled; 'she did not look a day more than thirty, and her charm and vivacity were on a par with her youthful appearance' – and fell headlong in love.[17]

Jennie's initial interest in George is likely to have been that he was an exact contemporary of Winston's, the two having been born within a fortnight of each other, so she was especially kind to the young officer. Over the weekend at Warwick Castle he took her boating on the river and she told him all about Winston. Thereafter, he bombarded her with notes, letters, gifts and declarations of love until she succumbed and, against her better judgement, fell in love with him. As we have seen, it was not unusual for men to fall in love with Jennie and some became her lovers, but although many of them were younger than Jennie, George was so much younger that the affair was bound to cause gossip, and it did. The Prince of Wales was soon writing to her rebuking her for being 'up to your old game again . . . it is a pity you have got yourself so talked about – and remember you are not 25'.[18]

While Jennie was in the throes of this affair, Winston heard from the War Office that his long-awaited posting to the Sudan had been approved. Delighted, he packed hurriedly, anxious to catch a steamer about to depart. In his haste he left unpaid a small bar bill of 13 rupees at the Bangalore United Services Club. The amount was recorded in the club books as an 'irrecoverable sum' and is still proudly shown to visitors. Winston caught the steamer and reached Egypt just in time to participate in what is known as the last great cavalry charge at the Battle of Omdurman.* The Anglo-Egyptian forces, twenty-five thousand strong and led by Kitchener, had

---

*This was not in fact the last cavalry charge; there were others after Omdurman, but they were smaller affairs.

assumed this would be a mere skirmish with a few thousand men crouched in the scrubby bushes, which appeared as a large black smudge ahead of the British lines. As they rode towards the enemy, however, the 'bushes' turned into men, and immense numbers of tribesmen appeared over the crest to join them until Kitchener's men found themselves facing a dense living wall four or five miles wide. It was the entire army – sixty thousand dervishes – of Khalifa, successor to the Madhi. And while Winston watched, amazed at the sight, a deafening wave of sound hit the British forces as the enemy host called on the Prophet for victory. Winston declared: 'This is an hour to live . . . talk of fun . . . where will you beat this! They think they are going to win. We shall see about that . . . The masses . . . defined themselves into swarms of men, in ordered ranks bright with glittering weapons, and above them danced a multitude of gorgeous flags. We see for ourselves what the Crusaders saw . . .[19]

As the enemy swept towards them, as inexorable as the incoming tide, Winston chose his place and galloped his troops forward into the mass of 'blue-black bodies'; it was what they had been trained for. Men either side of him were killed – shot, or hacked to death with spears and gleaming curved swords – but Winston's star held good. 'My dearest Mama,' he wrote on 4 September 1898, two days after the battle, 'you will have been relieved by my telegram which I sent off at once. I was under fire all day and rode through the charge. You know my luck in these things. I was about the only officer whose clothes, saddlery, or horse were all uninjured. I fired 10 shots with my pistol – all necessary – and just got to the end of it as we cleared the crush. I never felt the slightest nervousness.'[20] He anticipated that he would get leave immediately and would be home in a matter of weeks, so he asked her to arrange some political meetings for him in Birmingham and Bradford. 'Sunny will help,' he added confidently.

When Jennie showed this letter to the Prince of Wales he replied: 'It is a most interesting letter and he indeed had a charmed life to escape out of that charge without a scratch.' But he was strongly of the opinion that Winston should remain in the Army and not go into politics.[21]

Jennie was staying with relatives of Leonie's husband on the Isle of Mull* when she received Winston's note. George Cornwallis-West was also staying there, indicating that Jennie's family, at least, had accepted the unlikely liaison. During the months after her return to London, George wrote daily letters of love which also detail his hunting, fishing, racing and shooting exploits and his participation in regimental races. They are the letters of a very young, very active man of the archetypal Victorian squirearchy. Jennie read his rather boastful reports – 'We had a good day – about 1100 head all told, 700 pheasants and the rest rabbits and hares . . . my horse won the Regimental race in a common canter' – in tandem with the letters from Winston who was now back in India and writing in much the same vein about sporting activities. But whereas Winston regarded these as mere pastimes and had visions for his future, as time went on George was still wedded to his youthful pleasures as if they were his *raison d'être*. And when Winston audaciously resigned his commission and returned to England in the spring of 1899 (at about the time that his formidable grandmother, Duchess Fanny, died[†]) he unfurled his colours by casting himself at once – if unsuccessfully – into a campaign for the vacant parliamentary seat of Oldham. Quite how he proposed to manage financially is unknown, for even had he been successful, MPs in those days received no salary.[‡] He had hopes of some income from his writing but he was still deeply in debt with only the annual £400 from his father's trust, which did not cover his Army expenses. However, he believed that he had done all he could usefully do in the Army; it was time to move forward.

From the start Jennie knew that her relationship with George Cornwallis-West was impossible; she knew, too, that their liaison was the talk of London Society. The Prince good-naturedly advised her to end it; she was spared criticism from one quarter, at least, by the death of her mother-in-law. George was warned off by his superior officers, by his parents and by his godfather the Prince, but he

---

*At Duart Castle, now renamed Torosay Castle.
†Duchess Frances died on 16 April 1899 aged seventy-seven.
‡Members of Parliament first received recompense in 1911.

would have none of it, saying that he wanted to marry Jennie – to the distress of his parents and of Jennie herself. She kept telling him to marry a young heiress (though probably without naming anyone). Jennie fell in love easily and she was genuinely in love now; her youthful lover made her feel young and desired. They saw each other constantly, though she continued to insist that marriage was out of the question.

By the autumn of 1899 a war in South Africa was inevitable. Having failed to gain the seat at Oldham, Winston, though now a civilian, was suddenly on fire to join the British troops sailing for Cape Town and Durban. Alfred Harmsworth, the proprietor of the *Daily Mail*, cabled him asking if he would act as their war correspondent; Winston promptly used this offer to obtain a far more lucrative contract from the *Morning Post** of £250 a month, which was then a record sum. With his military training, his natural ability as a strategist, his VIP contacts and his burning ambition, Winston was a new and different sort of war correspondent. One of his first actions, when appointed, was to write personally to the Colonial Secretary Joseph Chamberlain, requesting introductions to people of importance in South Africa. Chamberlain duly obliged, saying he would do so 'for the son of my old friend'.[22]

While he waited to leave for Cape Town, Winston found time to coach Consuelo, who – without any qualifications – had agreed to give a talk about technical education to a club for the blind. Afterwards he bolstered her confidence, telling her that a professional speaker could not have done better. In this way Winston was an enabler, for his encouragement helped Consuelo to find her own path into public life, something Sunny would never have bothered to do. The continuing close link with Blenheim was important to Winston, and he was always affectionately tied to his family. He also maintained close links with the Dowager Duchess Lily, and often stayed with her at her seaside estate, Deepdene, on the Dorset coast.

---

*The contract stipulated £1000 for four months' work, £200 a month thereafter. All expenses 'shore to shore' were to be paid, and the *Post* kept the copyright of Winston's dispatches.

The first shots of the Boer War were fired on 10 October and within two days Winston was on his way to South Africa rejoicing, despite being seasick for most of the early part of the journey. With him went his valet – his father's former manservant, Thomas Walden – and a huge quantity of luggage including seventy-two cases containing fine French wines, vintage port, Vermouth, ten-year-old Scotch whisky, eau de vie, fruit brandy and Rose's lime juice. As Winston's son Randolph would later write, 'He never believed that war should be needlessly uncomfortable.'[23] His fellow passengers aboard the ship *Dunottar Castle* included Sir Redvers Buller, commander of the British troops in South Africa, accompanied by his ADC Lord Gerard, who by serendipity had been one of Lord Randolph's closest friends. Winston intended to ask Lord Gerard for a temporary commission in the Yeomanry.

Fourteen days into the voyage he was cast into despair when they passed a homebound ship from which they obtained news that three battles had been fought in which the Boers had been easily defeated. He worried that it might be all over before he even arrived. But he realised his fears were unjustified when he and two fellow journalists disembarked at Cape Town and started asking questions. From the answers they received the three men concluded that there was plenty of fighting still to be done, and that they could yet make a name for themselves if they grasped every opportunity. This was all Winston asked.

1899–1900

National Hero!

As a result of the intelligence they gleaned, Winston and the other two journalists agreed to leave the ship and make the remainder of the journey together overland by train and steamer. This would enable them to reach Durban a full three days before Buller and his staff. When Winston arrived he found his old friend Reggie Barnes, with whom he had travelled to Cuba, wounded in the thigh and resting aboard a hospital ship waiting to be shipped home. Barnes told him that the Boers were courageous, skilful and successful fighters – an opposing view to the received image of the Boers in England that was not lost on Winston.

Realising that Buller would need to spend time, when he arrived, in establishing a general headquarters before moving towards the front at Ladysmith, Winston and his companions decided to go on immediately, before the enemy could consolidate their gains. J.B. Atkins of the *Manchester Guardian* was one of the two fellow journalists travelling with Winston. He left a useful sketch of him: 'skin, slightly reddish – hair, pale, lively'; he walked about 'with neck out-thrust' and often sat in deep meditation folding and unfolding his hands 'as though he were helping himself to untie knots'.

When the prospects of a great career like that of his father, Lord Randolph, excited him, then such a gleam shot from him that he was almost transfigured . . . it was as though a light was switched on inside him which suddenly shone out through his eyes. I had not before encountered this sort of ambition, unabashed, frankly egotistical, communicating its excitement and extorting sympathy. He had acquired no reverence for his seniors as such and talked to them as though they were of his own age or younger.[1]

Atkins recalled that from Pietermaritzburg they had hired a train to take them on to Ladysmith, but they were still many miles short of it, at a 'tin township' called Estcourt where a small British force was camped, when their train was halted. The line ahead of them was closed because the Boers were in control of most of the area as far as Ladysmith and they held the bridge over the Tugela River between Estcourt and Ladysmith. Ladysmith itself was blockaded and the Boers were not far ahead of them. 'At any moment,' Winston wrote, 'ten or twelve thousand mounted Boers might sweep forward to attack us or cut off our retreat. Yet it was necessary to hold Estcourt as long and in as firm a posture, as possible.'[2]

Wars were fought at a different pace in the nineteenth century, and Winston's ample stores were evidently put to good use. 'We pitched our tents in the railway yard,' Atkins wrote:

> We found a good cook and we had some good wine. We entertained friends every evening, to our pleasure and professional advantage . . . one memorable evening we entertained the officer commanding . . . While we were dining the clang of field guns being loaded into trucks went on unceasingly . . . the officer, as he told us, had decided the position at Estcourt could hardly be held and that a retirement . . . was necessary.
>
> As dinner proceeded, Winston, with an assurance which I partly envied and partly deprecated, argued that [Piet] Joubert [the Boer commandant] was probably too cautious to advance yet; that he was no doubt delighted with the security of the Tugela River; that it would be a pity to point the way to Maritzburg, and so on. Shortly after our guest had left us the clanging in the trucks, which had ceased, began again. The trucks were being *unloaded*. Winston gleamed. 'I did that!' he said; but added gracefully, '*We* did that!'[3]

Within a short time Winston had met two old acquaintances at Estcourt. One, Leo Amery* the correspondent for *The Times*, had been a fellow pupil at Harrow, where Winston had once pushed him into the swimming pool; they were never friends. The other man was a close friend and a fellow polo player from Winston's days in India, Captain Aylmer Haldane. Haldane had just been ordered to take an armoured train and reconnoitre the line towards Ladysmith, and he asked Winston to accompany him. Winston was not at all sure that an armoured train would provide much protection if they were trapped on it, but he agreed to meet Haldane at dawn next day.

The expedition soon ran into trouble: the Boers had sabotaged the line and the rear part of the train was derailed. Under heavy fire Haldane, Churchill and about fifty men escaped from the upturned section and put up a brave fight, but they were captured – in Winston's case by a Boer commander named Louis Botha.[†] Winston had already reached a position of safety by the engine, but had hurriedly returned to assist those left behind in the fighting, accidentally leaving his pistol lying on the engine plate. The captives were transported 'hundreds of miles into the heart of the enemy's country'[4] to a prisoner compound at the officers' camp based in the State Model School in Pretoria, the capital of the enemy-held Transvaal.

Winston was held there for three weeks, hating every moment – 'more than I have ever hated any other period in my whole life,' he wrote.[5] He described his surroundings vividly in letters to Jennie and Pamela (whose lucky charm he still wore, at her request), ending his letter to Pamela with the words: 'I write you this line to tell you that among new and vivid scenes I think often of you.' On 30 November

---

*Leopold Charles Amery (1873–1955) was a Conservative politician and journalist, noted for his military knowledge. He is probably best remembered for his intervention during the Norway debate in 1940 when he attacked Chamberlain's government, blaming it for the recent military and naval defeats. This heralded the downfall of the government and the formation of a national government under Churchill.

†Many years later this account of Winston's capture was queried by a former serving Boer, who said it could not have been Louis Botha who personally captured him, although he was undoubtedly the CO in charge of that area and Churchill would have been taken before him for questioning. Churchill, however, insisted that his captor had been Botha in person.

he added a postscript to a letter to Bourke Cockran: 'I am 25 today – it is terrible to think how little time remains.'[6]

His first inclination was to try to talk his way out of what he saw could be a lengthy and ignominious incarceration, by presenting his credentials as a civilian war correspondent and claiming to have been an 'unarmed non-combatant' when captured. This failed, because he had been widely reported by those who had escaped as not only leading the fighting but rousing the men on the train to fight. So he and Haldane hatched an escape plan with a fellow prisoner who knew the country well and spoke Afrikaans and Dutch. In the event, on 11 December Winston hopped over the wall using a ledge in the latrines to give him a spring, and was waiting on the other side when a sentry became suspicious and the other two men had to give up their escape attempt.*

It does not take a great deal of imagination to work out what thoughts must have raced through the young man's mind at that moment, as he crouched alone in the night under leafless thorn bushes. He could not return unnoticed because there was an overhang at the top of the wall on his side and no ledge to help him get back. He had only recently arrived in the country so he had no reserve of knowledge, and his only assets were some English money and bars of chocolate in his pockets. He had no maps, no compass, no supplies or weapons, and no knowledge of Afrikaans or Dutch. He concluded that he had two options: to give himself up and risk spending the war in even closer confinement as a would-be escapee, or try to make his way alone to the border with Portuguese East Africa, taking him three hundred miles through hostile territory. He made his decision instantly and began to make his way through the darkened streets of Pretoria by the simple expedient of walking confidently in the centre of the road, humming a tune, appearing as though he knew where he was headed. There were townspeople about but no one looked at him twice and he judged his direction

---

*Haldane escaped a few months later and included a report of his first escape attempt which matched Winston's in every detail. Years later, though, Haldane became embittered and wrote a different account, accusing Winston of abandoning his fellow escapees in the prison.

by the stars, until he reached the railway line which, he reckoned, must run towards the East African coast.

After hiding in the freight yard, Winston scrambled aboard a train going in the right direction. He abandoned it just before dawn and spent the day hiding in undergrowth and drinking from pools. When night fell he walked along the railway line hoping to repeat his success of the previous day, but no trains came. He became very dehydrated until eventually, near dawn, seeing a house near a mine he tentatively knocked at the door. By almost incredible luck the house was occupied by a pro-British manager – the only non-Boer sympathiser for miles – who hid and fed him. While he was eating his first meal Winston discovered that one of his protectors came from Oldham, and having listened to Winston's story of his defeat in the election there, the man pressed his hand and said he was not to worry – 'They'll all vote for you next time,' he promised.

Winston then spent over a week uncomfortably hiding deep in a mineshaft, mostly in the dark, with rats – who ate his candles – for company, during which the countryside and every building was scoured for him. Posters offering a reward of '£25* dead or alive' were everywhere, and ensured the search was very thorough. He was described as 'about 5 ft 8" or 9", blond with a light thin moustache. Walks with a slight stoop, cannot speak any Dutch'. When at last the hunt for him moved on, he was transferred to a remote safe-house for a further few weeks while his protectors organised his escape route. Eventually he was told he was to stow away under bales of wool on a train bound for Lourenço Marques,† where he would be met by a trustworthy contact. It was a crude and simple plan – Winston was afraid even to fall asleep during the overnight stops in case he snored and was heard – but it worked. Having learned by heart the names of all the stations en route, he knew when he was near his destination; but he was still not safe, for even though he had reached Portuguese territory he had been warned that Lourenço Marques was crowded with Boers and Boer sympathisers.

---

*Twenty-five pounds would have represented several months' income, at least, to most workers.
†The former name of Maputo, the capital of Mozambique.

However, he was met and safely guided to the British Consulate and by that evening was on board the weekly ferry to Durban, where he was able to read the news. A few weeks later he sent fifteen suitably engraved gold pocket watches to the men who had helped him evade recapture, and his 1930s memoir of his adventures still provides a beautifully written and thrilling read.[7]

In the month that had elapsed since Winston was taken prisoner, the British forces under Buller had suffered serious reverses as well as casualties on a scale unknown since the Crimean War: three thousand deaths occurred in seven days, which the newspapers dubbed 'Black Week'. As an antidote to this dire news, in order to bolster public morale desperate editors had fastened on Winston's '*Boy's Own*' escape and in triumphant headlines blazoned the story and the unsuccessful search by the Boers. In the absence of any news of him

Boer Poster announces reward for capture of Mr. Churchill. This was put up outside the Government House in Pretoria

he was variously reported as recaptured or dead, but he was always portrayed as the daring English fox with a price on his head, evading the Boer hounds. The question on everyone's lips was 'Where is Churchill?' As a consequence, when Winston arrived at Durban, much to his gratification he was given a hero's welcome. 'The harbour was decorated with flags. Bands and crowds thronged the quays,' he wrote. 'The Admiral, the General, and the Mayor pressed on board to clasp my hand. I was nearly torn to pieces by enthusiastic kindness . . . whirled along on the shoulders of the crowd.'[8]

The popular press in England went wild with the story – how the young, good-looking, patrician officer had single-handedly defied the Boers. Within days he was back with the British Army promoted to the rank of lieutenant by Buller, without having to abandon his role as war correspondent, and posted to the South African Light Horse Regiment. In those few weeks since his capture and escape Winston had become a household name not only in South Africa, but – far more importantly for his future ambitions – in Britain. Two items of correspondence dating from that moment stand out among the mass of documentation. One is a letter from General Buller who wrote to Winston's great-aunt Lady Londonderry, thus confirming that Winston's objective to 'be noticed' had succeeded: 'He really is a fine fellow . . . I must say I admire him greatly. I wish he was leading regular troops instead of writing for a rotten paper.'[9] The other is a telegram to Jennie from the girl with whom Winston had 'an understanding', which read simply: 'Thank God – Pamela.'[10]

But Winston was not the only Churchill involved in the Boer War. Recognising where their duty lay, other family members plunged into the fray with alacrity. The dire news of Buller's difficulties prompted the British government to send out a larger force under the most famous military commander of the day, Lord Roberts, together with his chief of staff Lord Kitchener, the hero of Omdurman. It was Lord Roberts's brief to split the Boer front, taking some of the pressure off Buller at Ladysmith, by attacking in the west from the direction of Bloemfontein and Mafeking.

Among the newcomers bringing reinforcements, to Winston's 'great joy', was his brother Jack who had arrived on board the hospital ship the *Maine*. The idea of going to Oxford seems to have been forgotten, and Winston had suggested Jack come to South Africa believing at the time that the worst of the fighting would be over before he arrived. When they met again, however, he worried whether he had done the right thing in encouraging Jack to get involved. Nor need it be supposed that while Winston was out in South Africa Jennie had sat around wringing her hands about the unknown fate of her missing elder son. Far from it. As well as her two sons, her lover – George Cornwallis-West had sailed two weeks after Winston but had a longer voyage, so missed him in Cape Town – and many of the other men she knew were already involved in the war, and she wanted to be of help. Now, with her remarkable energy, she decided to involve herself in the war effort and to make use of her network of rich and powerful people. But not for her knitting parties or fund-raising teas. Winston describes her activities succinctly: 'Within months,' he wrote, 'she had raised a fund [£41,597 – today, £2.4 million], captivated an American millionaire, obtained a ship, and equipped it as a hospital with a full staff of nurses and every comfort.'[11] After a stormy voyage she had arrived at Cape Town, in January 1900, where Jack was able to join her for the voyage to Durban. There she was to collect a consignment of wounded and Jack was to rejoin his unit.

Later Jennie would admit that she did not know how she would have 'got through' the time when Winston was missing had she not been totally absorbed in getting the ship equipped and ready to sail. But her reward for all the effort came quickly: one of the first casualties to be carried aboard the hospital ship *Maine* at Durban was none other than Jack from whom she had only recently parted.

Soon after Jack's arrival in Cape Town, where Jennie and the brothers had been briefly reunited, Winston had left to move forward with the main force, but Jack and Winston met up again a few weeks later, on 12 February, at the Battle of Hussar Hill. It was Jack's first time in action and he was resting in his tent when he was wounded in the leg by a stray bullet. Winston, who was actively involved in the fighting, was unscathed (a fellow war correspondent commented that it was almost as though Jack had 'paid his elder brother's debts'). It was by an extraordinary stroke of luck that Jack was taken to Jennie's hospital ship, and as soon as he could be spared Winston rushed to join him and their mother there, spending several days on board the *Maine*. Before leaving he wrote a note to Pamela, telling her his news: 'Oh why did you not come out as secretary . . . in the *Maine*?' he wrote, 'so that I should be going to meet you now? Perhaps you are wise.'[12]

There were some who believed that Jennie's main reason for organising the hospital ship was to join her young lover. If so, she was disappointed, for Cornwallis-West fell ill with ophthalmia, severe sunstroke and enteric fever and had been shipped home shortly before she arrived in Cape Town.[13] He regarded his service in South Africa as a few exciting months that were 'rather like an Aldershot field day' but with live bullets. However, he remembered enough to feel uncomfortable about fighting the Boers, who he quietly concluded were simply fighting to protect their own country from invasion. Later he would report to the Prince of Wales that the British lacked the mobility of the Boers, but he did not dare to reveal his sympathy for the enemy.

Sunny Marlborough already held the post of Paymaster General in Lord Salisbury's administration when the Boer War had begun in the latter months of 1899. Like many patriots he wanted to serve his country in the crisis, sailing for South Africa on 10 January 1900 as a lieutenant with the Imperial Yeomanry. The *on-dit* in London's drawing rooms was that he was glad to go because his marriage was in serious difficulty and he was now leading a bachelor life apart from his Duchess. Consuelo's mother came over from Paris that month to stay with her at Blenheim, and as Alva was fiercely pro-Boer, Consuelo would have been among the few to hear both sides of the dispute. She attended dinners for local units departing for South Africa, but Consuelo never joined in the flag-waving, tub-thumping patriotism of the British over the war. And she had to be persuaded by Alva to go to Southampton and wave her husband goodbye for the sake of public appearances.

Before he sailed Sunny was appointed Assistant Military Secretary to Lord Roberts, but after his departure there was criticism in the British press because he had no military training. It was also noted that Lord Roberts's staff read like a precedence list in *Debrett's*: as well as Marlborough, it included the Dukes of Westminster and Norfolk. The government were already feeling the lash of disapproval over South Africa and consequently, when Roberts and the brigade marched north from the coast, the Duke of Marlborough was diplomatically left behind at Cape Town. But Sunny had not sailed to South Africa to be an office wallah, and he asked Winston to get him into the fighting.

Winston's unpaid post in the South African Light Horse Regiment, which he described as 'a roving commission', enabled him to send back daily streams of dispatches to the *Morning Post*.* He made sure always to be where the main action was and he took an active role in the fighting with various units, in return for a regular supply of adequate horses. 'I stitched my badges of rank to my khaki coat and stuck the long plume of feathers from the tail of the *sakabulu* bird in my hat, and lived, from day to day, in perfect happiness,' he wrote.[14] Cock-a-hoop with the success that his corps was enjoying – unlike most, they moved fast and light, tackling the Boers with a like-for-like mobility – he had dared to write in one of his columns: 'More irregular corps are wanted. Are the gentlemen of England all foxhunting? Why not an English Light Horse?' He received a cable by return: 'Best friends here hope you won't go making a further ass of yourself.'[15]

But he did not make an ass of himself when he was present at the battles of Tugela River, Spion Kop and Hussar Hill. Rather, he was generally seen where the fighting was hottest, seeming to lead a charmed life. From Spion Kop he wrote to Pamela Plowden that he had endured five 'very dangerous days – continually under shell and rifle fire and once the feather in my hat was cut through by a bullet'. Pamela (they always addressed each other as 'My Dearest') urged him to return home – there was no need, she wrote, for him to place himself in further danger. Winston replied that he would forfeit 'my

---

*Winston's columns were eagerly read by those at home avid for news. Only once did he raise hackles when he wrote sympathising with the Boers, whom he admired as brave enemies. With his easy grasp of the essential facts he could already see both sides of the affair, and despite his utter loyalty to Britain he dared to comment that had he been a Boer he too would have been fighting the British.

self-respect for ever if I tried to shield myself like that behind an easily obtained reputation for courage . . . but I have a good belief that I am to be of some use and therefore to be spared'.[16] This life-long prescience of his place in history, which he called 'my star', would sustain him through many crises, only deserting him late in life. 'I have faith in my star,' he wrote to Jennie at this point – 'that is, that I am intended to do something in the world.' Meanwhile, men all around him were hit and killed by bullets and shrapnel.

When Ladysmith was relieved by the British on 28 February, Winston rode in with the first column to enter the town, jauntily carrying with him a food parcel for Pamela's brother-in-law.* Later he wrote to Joseph Chamberlain: 'You will understand how keen were our feelings of joy and triumph to at last succeed in relieving Ladysmith, and in bringing food to our starving friends. I expect that your satisfaction at home was even greater than ours, for it is more painful to read of disasters at a distance when one cannot do anything to restore them and cannot accurately measure their extent, than it is to sustain them on the spot.'[17]

Temporarily assigned to the staff of General Sir Ian Hamilton thanks to the influence of Colonel Neville Chamberlain,† who was Private Secretary to Field Marshal Roberts ('Lord Roberts desires me to say he is willing to permit you to accompany this force as a correspondent – for your father's sake'), Winston met Sunny in Cape Town. There he was able to wangle a transfer to get his cousin out of headquarters, and the two men served together for the next few months. Then, as the city of Pretoria was falling to the British, he and Sunny broke away and galloped directly to the prisoner-of-war camp from which Winston had earlier escaped. His aim was to liberate his former fellow prisoners before they could be shipped out by the Boers, 'perhaps in the very last train' with the retreating army. His fears that he might be too late were unfounded, he wrote:

---

*In the event her brother-in-law was too unwell to eat the provisions Churchill carried, so he ate them himself.
†Prime Minister at the outbreak of the Second World War.

As we rounded a corner, there was the prison camp, a long tin building surrounded by a dense wire entanglement. I raised my hat and
cheered. The cry was instantly answered from within. What followed resembled the end of an Adelphi melodrama. We were only
two, and before us stood the armed Boer guard with their rifles at
the 'ready'. Marlborough, resplendent in the red tabs of the staff,
called upon the Commander to surrender forthwith, adding by a
happy thought that he would give a receipt for the rifles. The prisoners rushed out of the house into the yard, some in uniform, some
in flannels, hatless or coatless, but all violently excited. The sentries
threw down their rifles, the gates were flung open, and while the last
of the guard (they numbered 52 in all) stood uncertain what to do,
the long penned-up officers surrounded them and seized their
weapons. Someone produced a Union Jack, the Transvaal emblem
was torn down, and amidst wild cheers from our captive friends the
first British flag was hoisted over Pretoria. Time: 8.47, June 5.[18]

Sir Ian Hamilton, who saw action in that war, wrote many years
later that had Winston been a serving officer rather than a war correspondent during his time in South Africa he would undoubtedly
have received a VC, for he was several times commended in dispatches for conspicuous gallantry.

Another member of the Churchill family who saw a form of service in the Boer War was Lady Sarah Wilson, the younger sister of
Lord Randolph and aunt of Winston and Sunny. She was nine years
older than Winston, and in the spring of 1899, aged thirty-three, she
had travelled to South Africa with her husband Lieutenant Colonel
Gordon Chesney Wilson on a holiday tour of South Africa and
Rhodesia. Lady Sarah was probably the perfect wife for a soldier,
but the Churchill wives – Goosie, Jennie and Consuelo – regarded
her as a trouble-maker and a cruel gossip. Consuelo loathed her,
describing her as 'hard and sarcastic', particularly to Goosie who
had not sufficient wit to register the barbs of her adversary. It was
Lady Sarah who had attempted to upstage Consuelo by giving the
signal to the ladies to retire after dinner at Blenheim. Jennie also
disliked this sister-in-law, and the feeling was mutual. Hence, in

family biographies, especially those by Consuelo and Jennie, Lady Sarah does not show to advantage.

However, in October 1899 she was unwittingly to become the first ever woman war correspondent. When war looked likely that autumn she and her husband had abandoned their holiday and proceeded to the small garrison at Mafeking, where Lieutenant Colonel Wilson was appointed ADC to Colonel Robert Baden-Powell. For a while he rode with his chief on the western borders, raising two regiments of irregular horse (later known as the Protectorate Regiments), recruited principally from the district between Mafeking and Bulawayo, while Lady Sarah busied herself with setting up a field hospital.

On 13 October an army of three or four thousand Boers threatened to storm Mafeking, which was protected by only 378 British soldiers under Baden-Powell. Lady Sarah did not wish to leave, but she felt she could hardly refuse when Baden-Powell asked her to go and arranged transport for her in a Cape cart drawn by six mules making south for Cape Town. She set off with her maid and the following day the Boers began shelling Mafeking.

With the countryside in uproar, Lady Sarah was forced to break her journey at an isolated farm called Setlagoli at Mosita, about twenty-five miles from the border. There she was marooned for weeks, but at least she was able to collect intelligence about the Boer movements from the occasional horseman passing through, such as the *Daily Mail* correspondent who called in on his way south to cable his dispatches to London. She inserted a microscopic note into an old cartridge case and recruited an ancient servant on the farm to go to Mafeking to give the beleaguered garrison news of the surrounding country. This worked, so it was occasionally repeated, and during the first two months of the siege it was practically Baden-Powell's sole means of receiving information from outside.

Eventually food ran out at the farm, and there was no way of replenishing stores since the railway line was cut. So Lady Sarah rode out alone to the local Boer commander, and with Churchillian self-confidence offered herself as a hostage in exchange for food and supplies. She suggested that they could exchange her for a Dutch woman in Mafeking who, she had learned, was anxious to leave the town. Instead, the Boers offered to exchange her for a Boer fighter whom they were anxious to see freed. Lady Sarah thought this infra dig, and on 2 December she wrote her husband a message which was passed between the Boers and the British. 'My dear Gordon, I am at the laager. General Snyman will not give me a pass unless Colonel Baden-Powell will exchange me for a Mr. Petrus Viljoen. I am sure this is impossible, so I do not ask him formally. I am in a great fix as they have very little meal left at Setlagoli or the surrounding places. I am very kindly looked after here.'

Her husband replied the following day: 'My dear Sarah, I am delighted to hear you are being well treated, but very sorry to have to tell you that Colonel Baden-Powell finds it impossible to hand over Petrus Viljoen in exchange for you, as he was convicted of horsestealing before the war. I fail to see in what way it can benefit your captors to keep you a prisoner. Luckily for them, it is not the custom of the English to make prisoners-of-war of women. Gordon Wilson.'[19]

Eventually, though, Baden-Powell agreed to the exchange, and Lady Sarah galloped into Mafeking during the handover to ringing cheers from the men in the trenches. Her departure from Mafeking had been unnecessary, for the town had not been stormed as feared. Baden-Powell had some brilliant officers and engineers on his staff, and during her absence the British had not only held out but had constructed over six miles of trenches, which enlarged the town to the extent that even with their superior force the Boers did not have the ability to storm it on all sides. There were also eight hundred bomb shelters to protect the residents, and the entire network of trenches and shelters was connected by field telephones. The Boers were unaware that the town had been restocked with food, fuel and other supplies shortly before 13 October, so that with rationing they could hold out for months yet. There was also a belief among the Boers, learned of much later by the British, that the town was stocked with dynamite and that the entire perimeter had been mined by the British, so the Boer chiefs were reluctant to move forward.

But after five months food was indeed becoming short, and on 3 April 1900 Sarah got a message to her sister in London: 'Breakfast to-day – horse sausages; lunch – minced mule, curried locusts. All well.' Occasionally, she was allowed a tiny bread roll for breakfast, but it had to last for dinner too. 'No dogs or cats were safe . . . but all the while we were well aware our situation might have been far worse. The rains were over, the climate was glorious, fever was fast diminishing, and, in spite of experiencing extreme boredom, we knew that the end of the long lane was surely coming.'[20] She decorated the mud walls of her dugout with huge Union flags and African spears captured in the Matabele War, and held dinner parties for six whenever she could find the rations.

After the unidentified *Daily Mail* correspondent was captured by the Boers Lady Sarah wrote via the occasional courier to Alfred Harmsworth, and was consequently commissioned to keep a diary for the *Mail* about life in the beleaguered town. Although she had no training as a journalist and her dispatches were necessarily irregular, the resulting column gained a large following of readers who approved of her no-nonsense style and avidly followed the fortunes of their besieged countrymen. 'The Boers have been extremely active in the last few days,' she wrote briskly in March 1900. 'Yesterday we were heavily shelled and suffered eight casualties . . . Corporal Ironside had his thigh smashed the day before and Private Webbe of the Cape Police had his head blown off in the brickfields trenches.'[21] She described how, by force of personality, Baden-Powell generated sufficient loyalty and trust to overcome the great hardships, the worry over dwindling supplies of food and medicines, and a frightening outbreak of typhoid during which the Mafeking hospital was attacked with great force by the enemy. Somehow, with a grit and determination that thrilled the *Daily Mail*'s readers, the garrison held out for 217 days.

The end came on 17 May when British forces arrived to relieve the town and people gathered to sing 'Rule, Britannia!'. At home in London when the news broke the city went wild with jubilation, dancing in the streets and letting off fireworks. Indeed the celebrations were so exuberant that a new verb – to maffick – was added to the language, meaning to make extravagant public demonstrations of joy. Lady Sarah's weekly dispatches describing life in Mafeking as the town held out against the Boers seemed to symbolise British determination in the face of great adversity, and she was subsequently decorated with the Order of St John of Jerusalem.

She left soon after for England, stopping en route at Pretoria where with difficulty she attempted to obtain a room at the fully booked Grand Hotel. The manager suggested that one apartment might soon be free as the gentleman was packing to leave, so with Lady Sarah in tow he politely knocked on the door of the suite:

> Great was my surprise [Lady Sarah wrote] at discovering in the khaki-clad figure, thus unceremoniously disturbed in the occupation of stowing away papers, clothes, and campaigning kit generally, no less a personage than my nephew, Winston Churchill, who had experienced such thrilling adventures during the war, the accounts of which had reached us even in far-away Mafeking. The proprietor was equally amazed to see me warmly greet the owner of the rooms he proposed to allot us, and, although Winston postponed his departure for another twenty-four hours, he gladly gave up part of his suite for our use, and everything was satisfactorily arranged.[22]

It was the final note in Winston's Boer War. Later, his fellow prisoner Haldane (who as Lord Haldane would serve as Secretary of State for War from 1905 to 1912) wrote an assessment of Winston at that time which shows how he saw himself, and how easy it was for him to make enemies as well as friends: 'He is always unconsciously playing a part – an heroic part. And he is himself his most astonished spectator . . . He thinks of his great ancestor . . . [and] thus in this rugged and awful crisis will he bear himself. It is not insincerity; it is that in that fervid and picturesque imagination there are always great deeds afoot with himself cast by destiny in the Agamemnon role. Hence the portentous gravity that sits on his youthful shoulders so oddly.'[23]

As for Winston, now leaving South Africa for England with high hopes of making his mark in British politics, he believed it was the last time he would hear bullets fired in anger.

II

1900–4

The Young Lion

When they celebrated the relief of Mafeking so enthusiastically in London, most people thought the Boer War was over. Certainly, most volunteers such as Winston and Marlborough had begun returning home by July, leaving the long task of mopping up the remaining guerrilla fighters to the regulars. In fact, the Boer War was to wear on for a long time yet and claim many casualties, but except for Jack the Churchills were out of it by then.*

Winston was a driven man, keen to kick-start his career on the back of his recent deeds. 'I need not say how anxious I am to come back to England,' he wrote to Jennie. 'Politics, Pamela, finances and books, all need my attention.'[1] During his return voyage he dashed off another book, *Ian Hamilton's March*, an edited compilation of his dispatches as a war correspondent. Together with *London to Ladysmith via Pretoria*, these two volumes were to sell twenty-two thousand copies in the first year.

When he arrived back in England in late July 1900, he headed for

---

*Lady Sarah's sister, Georgina Curzon (Countess Howe), also involved herself in the war, raising money and organising field hospitals. Heading a committee of titled women, she bullied, harried and begged, slicing through red tape with the self-confidence of the daughter of a Duke, adroitly managing harassed War Office officials and keeping her committee unanimous and contented. Within three months a fully equipped base hospital containing over five hundred beds (subsequently increased to a thousand) was shipped from England. She worked herself to a standstill and damaged her heart. She died aged forty-six.

London to stay with his mother, naturally regarding her home as his own. To his chagrin he found she had let the house at Great Cumberland Place, an economy suggested by George Cornwallis-West who had pointed out that it was far less costly for her to stay at the Ritz when she was in London than to run the house and maintain a full staff in order to entertain there. This meant that Winston had nowhere to stay until Sunny stepped in and offered to lend him an apartment he had formerly used himself at 105 Mount Street,* which had a short lease, two years remaining. It was an excellent address in Mayfair, close to what is now the Connaught Hotel.† Winston took the apartment as his first flat, and later bought a new lease on the property and lived there for five years very comfortably. It was an ideal arrangement for a bachelor, as the hotel sent waiters out to nearby residences, providing meals from their regular menus. Winston asked his Aunt Leonie to arrange the furnishing and decor for him, telling her that he was not fussy as long as he had a clear table and plenty of writing paper. Leonie, however, did not allow his new home to become a monk's cell. The flat was well furnished with items retrieved from Jennie's home, including Lord Randolph's desk and chair and his massive brass inkwell. Comfortable old leather chairs were supplemented with newly purchased items. On the walls, Spy cartoons of Lord Randolph were aligned with a painting of his most successful race-horse, Abbesse de Jouarre (called by bookies on racecourses and by many of the race-going public 'Abscess of the Jaw').

A few days after moving in, on 28 July, Winston attended the wedding at St Paul's Church in Knightsbridge of forty-six-year-old Jennie to twenty-six-year-old George Cornwallis-West. Sunny Marlborough, who had only just returned from South Africa in the company of his Aunt Sarah, gave the bride away; and there was, Winston noted, 'a solid phalanx' of Churchills[2] among the guests, as well as Jennie's own family, to throw a cloak of respectability over

---

*Off Park Lane, it was a few steps to Lansdowne House, owned by his second cousin the Marquess of Lansdowne.
†The Connaught, then called the Coburg (after Prince Albert of Saxe-Coburg), was built in 1897. The name was changed during the First World War.

the ceremony. There was no one at all from the bridegroom's family. The reception was held at the house of Jennie's sister Clara Frewen in Chesham Place, and the couple were loaned Broughton Castle in Oxfordshire for the first days of their honeymoon. There had been much criticism of Jennie's relationship with George West, but their marriage shocked Society and George's resignation from his regiment was 'requested' soon afterwards. Even the Prince of Wales was annoyed at this coupling of one of his favourite women with his own godson, and it was some weeks before Jennie was able to wheedle him round. Eventually the Prince met George privately and told him that the large age difference was his only objection to the marriage. But George's father wrote a blistering letter to Leonie, whom he accused (incorrectly) of promoting the match:

> I wish seriously to ask you if you consider a marriage . . . between Lady Randolph and my son can possibly lead to the happiness of either? To begin with she is older than his own mother . . . and she will find herself married to a young man of such an impressionable nature that only a few weeks ago he proposed marriage to a young and pretty girl who refused his attentions – not withstanding his protestations of love and his repudiation of your sister. The life of a couple so ill-assorted is doomed, is painful to think of . . . I can only add that if this marriage takes place, it will estrange the whole of my family from my son and so I have told him.[3]

In a letter to Winston, George addressed him as 'my dear friend', and clearly Winston accepted the relationship stoically for his mother's sake. He was always on friendly terms with his young step-father, but still there is a hint of disapproval in a letter he wrote to Jack: 'The wedding was very pretty and George looked supremely happy in having at length obtained his heart's desire. As we already know each other's views on the subject, I need not pursue it.'[4] Jack, still in South Africa, wrote morosely that he felt like 'the prodigal son who is sent away to these horrible colonies with instructions never to be seen or heard of again'.[5]

Perhaps hoping the gesture would prove the genuine love behind her marriage, Jennie let it be known that she would drop the title 'Lady Randolph'. It was announced in the newspapers thus:

> The Papers give this information
> At Lady Randolph's own request
> That now her proper designation,
> Is Mrs George Cornwallis-West.

Winston had already set about his main objective. Ignoring his mother's honeymooning status in Scotland he bombarded her with tasks and requests, just as before. He was still targeting the parliamentary seat of Oldham, where he was greeted by the town band as a conquering hero and where he delivered some of his most stirring speeches. When he asked Jennie to come and help him with the electioneering, she obediently left her husband with friends and went to her son's aid. Winston had a fight on his hands because the Liberal incumbent was not only popular but well financed. When one man declared that he would rather vote for the devil than for Winston, he disarmingly responded: 'But since your friend is not running can I count on your vote?' On 1 October 1900 Winston was returned as the Member for Oldham; true, his majority was modest – only 230 votes – and he won only because the Liberal vote had been split by an independent candidate, but Winston's political career had begun. Now he had to sort out his finances, make enough to live on, and ask Pamela to marry him. He wrote to Jennie: 'I think a great deal of Pamela, she loves me very dearly.'[6]

What remained of his earnings as a journalist in South Africa had been used to fight the election (together with a donation by Sunny of £400 to his campaign chest). He needed to earn money fast and all he could rely on, apart from his allowance, was the anticipated royalties on his two books. Now, in an attempt to capitalise on his South African adventures – and on a fame he feared might prove transitory – he arranged a punishing series of lecture tours in Britain, America and Canada to build up his financial reserves before Parliament resumed in the spring. This worked well in the

UK – in one month he earned £4500; but he found American audiences sparse, sometimes even hostile. He had Bourke Cockran to support him on his tour and he was thrilled to meet Mark Twain, who introduced him at one event. But his talks were not generally well accepted in the USA; the audiences had only a passing interest in the Boer War, while a significant number sympathised with the Boers. He went on to Canada and spent Christmas in Ottawa at Rideau Hall with the Governor General, Lord Minto.* Here he was briefly reunited with Pamela, who was also a guest of the Mintos.[7] From the financial point of view, Winston's goal of marriage to Pamela was at last within sight. In five months he had spoken every day, six days a week, for an hour or more and sometimes twice a day. He had also written articles. All sold well and at the end of his tour – though that date had not quite come when he saw Pamela in Ottawa – he had earned his target amount, the then huge sum of £10,000 (worth over £570,000 today) which he sent to his father's old friend the financier Sir Ernest Cassel,[†] asking him to 'feed my sheep'.[8]

Curiously, the meeting in Ottawa between Winston and Pamela, which both had evidently looked forward to, was not satisfactory. Jennie had clearly expected to hear the announcement of an engagement during this time; she had written months earlier to Winston that Pamela was devoted to him, and she was convinced it was merely a question of time as to when they would marry.[9] But all was not well. Pamela evidently felt neglected, and before Winston's departure for

---

*Gilbert John Elliot-Murray, 4th Earl of Minto (1845–1914), served as Governor General of Canada from 1898 to 1904 and as Viceroy of India from 1905 to 1910.

†Born in Germany to Jewish parents, Sir Ernest Joseph Cassel (1852–1921) arrived penniless in England at the age of seventeen. He found work in banks, rapidly gaining promotion, where his industry, ability and cosmopolitan outlook made him a shrewd investor. He became one of the country's wealthiest men. He was a friend of King Edward VII and of leading politicians such as Asquith and Churchill. After his marriage he converted to Catholicism and following the early deaths of his wife and his only daughter he raised his two granddaughters, one of whom, Edwina, was to marry Lord Louis Mountbatten. Churchill later wrote about Cassel: 'He fed the sheep with great prudence. They did not multiply fast, but they fattened steadily, and none of them ever died. Indeed from year to year they had a few lambs, but these were not numerous enough for me to live on. I had every year to eat a sheep or two as well, so gradually my flock grew smaller.'

the USA she had complained to him that he was 'incapable of affection', to which Winston coolly replied: 'Why do you say I am incapable of affection? Perish the thought. I love one above all others. And I shall be constant. I am no fickle gallant capriciously following the fancy of the hour. My love is deep and strong . . . Who is this that I love? Listen – as the French say. Over the page I will tell you.' And on the following sheet he wrote mischievously: 'Yours vy sincerely, Winston S. Churchill'.

After Winston left Ottawa, a puzzled Lord Minto wrote to Jennie that the relationship between the young couple, about which she had forewarned him, had shown no sign of romance – indeed, 'everything seems to me . . . platonic'. On 1 January 1901, after leaving the Mintos, Winston wrote to his mother but he did not mention Pamela, choosing to write instead about his success: 'I am very proud of the fact that there is not one person in a million who at my age could have earned £10,000 without capital in less than two years.' Three weeks later, though, he was writing to Pamela while on a train to Winnipeg that he had heard that 'the Queen is dying, is perhaps already dead'. If this 'momentous event' occurred, he wrote, his cross-Canada lecture tour would be automatically cancelled and he would have to return home.

Queen Victoria died two days later on 22 January, at the age of eighty-one, after a reign of sixty-three years which had seen the expansion of the Empire and the continuing industrialisation of Britain. Winston was twenty-six years old; his values and mores had been forged in the Victorian era, and like everyone else who had known no other monarch he wondered how the country would fare. Unlike most people, he was acquainted with the new King: 'Will it entirely revolutionise his way of life?' he wrote to Jennie. 'Will he become desperately serious? Will he continue to be friendly to you? Will the Keppel* be appointed to 1st Lady of the bedchamber? Write to me all about this.'[10] On the day of the Queen's funeral, 2 February, Winston sailed from New York for London in

---

*Mrs Alice Keppel, the new King's mistress, was the great-grandmother of Camilla, present Duchess of Cornwall.

order to take his seat in Parliament. He had arrived back in a capital in which everyone was clad in black and the streets were still respectfully hushed.

On 14 February he wrote his mother a cheque and sent it with a note that made her weep: 'I enclose a cheque for £300. In a . . . sense it belongs to you; for I could never have earned it had you not transmitted to me the wit and energy which are necessary.'[11] He also formally surrendered his right to the annual allowance which, under the terms of his father's will, he should have been paid from the interest on the capital sum in which Jennie had a life interest. He then made his way to Westminster to take his seat in the House.

Against the advice of experienced MPs who cautioned him to wait before drawing attention to himself, Winston had attended Parliament for only four days before he rose to his feet. He wanted to make his maiden speech count. Knowing that the swashbuckling Liberal MP David Lloyd George – who was pro-Boer – was to move a contentious amendment, Winston applied for, and was granted, the opportunity to reply to him. Lloyd George, having got wind of this plan, declined to move his amendment, and was careful to answer all his own questions, leaving Winston with no hook to hang his response on. Instead he sat down suddenly, stating that he 'would curtail his remarks as he was sure the house wished to hear a new member'.

Winston, who had taken a seat immediately behind the front bench, was appalled at this turn of events and saw disaster staring him in the face: all the notes he had so carefully made for days about the amendment were suddenly irrelevant. His mother and many women friends were sitting expectantly in the gallery, and members were streaming into the Chamber to see how 'Randy's boy' would do. Luckily, sitting next to him was the experienced and sympathetic parliamentarian Thomas Gibson Bowles.* Quickly appreciating Winston's position, Bowles whispered a possible riposte.

---

*Thomas Gibson Bowles was the maternal grandfather of the Mitford sisters. See Mary S. Lovell, *The Mitford Girls* (Little, Brown 2005) and *The Sisters* (W.W. Norton, New York, 2005). As well as being an MP, he was a successful entrepreneur and among his ventures was the founding of the magazines *Vanity Fair* and *The Lady*. The latter is still going strong and is still owned by his descendants.

Winston accepted it desperately, he later wrote, as 'manna in the wilderness'. He rose to his feet and rephrased the sentence Bowles had given him:* 'When we compare the moderation of the amendment with the very bitter speech which the honourable member has just delivered, it is difficult to avoid the conclusion . . . that it might have been better on the whole, if the honourable member instead of making his speech without moving his amendment, had moved his amendment without making his speech.' This was heartily cheered, and gave Winston the space and confidence to lead into the situation in South Africa, a subject upon which he had, after all, spoken about publicly every day for five months. 'I do not believe that the Boers would attach particular importance to the utterances of the honourable member. No people in the world received so much verbal sympathy and so little support. If I were a Boer fighting in the field' – he paused and looked around the Chamber, then said emphatically – 'if I were a Boer then I hope I should be fighting in the field.'[12] His own front bench stirred uncomfortably while the Liberals cheered, but Winston continued, neatly placing a small stiletto under the ribs of the Liberals: 'I would not allow myself to be taken in by any message of sympathy, not even if it were signed by a hundred honourable members.'

His speech was well received, and afterwards he was in 'a happy coma' when approached by Lloyd George who, after complimenting him, noted that Winston had caused a 'ruffle' on the Conservative front bench. He warned him amiably: 'You are standing against the light.' Thus began a political relationship that was to last many decades.

It is not the purpose of this book to follow Winston's political career in detail, but his reputation rose steadily despite his lack of height and a lisp, both drawbacks that were noticed by political pundits. His lisp caused him to slur the pronunciation of the letter 's' and made him a target for mockery by those who did not like him – and

---

*Bowles had whispered: 'You might say "Instead of making his violent speech without moving his moderate amendment, he had better have moved his moderate amendment without making his violent speech."'

these were many. Sometimes *sotto voce* imitations of the lisp disconcerted him while he was speaking.[13] Within a month, though, he was already addressing the House regularly on major topics with the fluent and colourful oratory for which he became renowned, and which could be depended upon to turn votes in his party's direction.

He left nothing to chance. He spent as much time as he could with fellow MPs, and whenever he heard of a debate coming up that he wished to participate in he worked through the night, often for several nights running, writing a speech on the subject. This became his modus operandi, and his speeches, which sounded so impromptu, were in fact all written in advance and learned by heart. Take one,* for example, that he delivered a few months after his debut. He took six weeks to prepare it, and he learned it so thoroughly that it hardly mattered where he began or what questions he was asked. Like his father before him, in order to ensure that an important speech was reported correctly the following morning, he often sent copies of the text to major newspapers, before delivering it.

The speech just referred to firmly established his future in the House of Commons. In addition to his regular appearances in the House, his engagement diary for that period shows that he was in constant demand as a dinner guest; he also hunted a couple of times from Sunny's hunting box at Melton Mowbray; and in March of that year alone he delivered lectures at Nottingham, Exeter, Plymouth, Torquay, Hastings, Bournemouth, Southampton, Portsmouth, Folkestone, Dover and Chester.†

This single-minded pursuit of his career jeopardised his personal life, for at one point Jennie wrote to Jack that she could not think what Winston was about: 'He has not written to Pamela for 8 weeks.'[14] She could have known this only from Pamela herself, and when Winston continued to neglect her Pamela evidently considered herself a free agent. Yet Winston clearly loved Pamela deeply – his letters to Jennie during the previous three years had been littered with

---

*Known as the 'Mr Brodrick's Army' debate, it was a scheme for Army reform proposed by St John Brodrick, Secretary of State for War.
†He earned for these talks a total of £586.

remarks about his love and admiration for her, and he had said that he hoped to marry her. That summer, though, a deeply concerned Jack visited George Cornwallis-West and told him he had learned that Pamela 'is the same to three other men as she is to Winston'.[15] Winston knew that Pamela had been branded a flirt since the earliest days of his relationship with her; he had defended her to his mother* when Pamela was accused of spoiling the career of an acquaintance by ending their relationship soon after meeting Winston.[16] 'I am sorry for Winston,' George reported to Jennie, 'as I do not think he would be happy with her.'[17]

When, that month, Winston finally proposed to Pamela in a punt on the river while they were staying at Warwick Castle, he considered himself secretly engaged.[18] But evidently he was too late, for almost immediately he returned to London he learned that two other young gentlemen also regarded themselves as secretly betrothed to Pamela. Not surprisingly, he was distraught. After a sleepless night pacing his bedroom at 105 Mount Street he went to see his Aunt Leonie and told her about it. Straight away she summoned her carriage and drove to confront Pamela, telling her firmly: 'You *can't* do this to my nephew.'[19] When Jennie wrote later to Leonie to say she was concerned about Winston and Pamela's relationship, Leonie replied: 'Oh how I hope he won't marry Pamela. She is not the wife for him although she is so pretty and attractive.'[20] And one of Winston's former senior officers,† writing to Leonie from South Africa, agreed: 'I think Winston is quite right to have put off with dear little Pamela. She ought to be a rich man's wife. But in any case she ought to be someone's wife soon as Pamela must be "getting on".'[21]

Within days Pamela had accepted a proposal from Victor, Lord Lytton,‡ and the marriage was announced. There is no record of

---

*'Now she loves me,' he wrote in August 1899, '[and] if there be any possibility of marrying she would marry me.'

†Colonel J.P. Brabazon, who had ensured Winston's commission in the 4th Hussars. Winston was 'devoted' to him.

‡Victor Alexander Bulwer-Lytton (1876–1947), 2nd Earl of Lytton, was a politician and served as Under-Secretary of State for India during 1920–2 and as Governor of Bengal during 1922–7.

Winston's reaction to this, but his earlier hurt suggests that it was an extremely painful episode for him. Pamela told Winston she hoped he would be 'our best friend', and he attended the wedding and continued to write to her affectionately for the remainder of their lives. Probably his duties as an MP and the sheer energy he threw into this task absorbed much of his emotional capacity. And now he was about to embark upon an ambitious literary project.

Soon after Pamela's marriage, the diarist Wilfrid Scawen Blunt* met Winston at a luncheon at the Lyttons' home, and he recorded his impressions:

> I stopped to luncheon with Victor and Pamela and met there . . . Winston Churchill. He is a little, square-headed fellow of no very striking appearance, but of wit, intelligence, and originality. In mind and manner he is a strange replica of his father, with all his father's suddenness and assurance, and I should say more than his father's ability. There is just the same *gaminerie* and contempt of the conventional and the same engaging plain-spokenness and readiness to understand. As I listened to him recounting conversations he had had with Chamberlain I seemed once more to be listening to Randolph on the subject of Northcote and Salisbury . . . I should not be surprised if he had his father's success. He has a power of writing Randolph never had, who was a schoolboy with his pen, and he has education and a political tradition. He interested me immensely.[22]

After her first meeting with Winston, the teenage Violet Asquith† told her father, H.H. Asquith, that 'for the first time in my life I had seen genius'. Asquith was tolerant and amused at his daughter's enthusiastic description. 'Well, Winston would certainly agree with you there,' he replied. 'But I am not sure you will find many others of the same mind. Still, I know exactly what you mean.

---

*His only daughter Judith was the wife of Victor Lytton's younger brother, who succeeded as 3rd Earl because Pamela and Victor's two sons would both predecease them.

†Later Helen Violet Bonham Carter, Baroness Asquith DBE (1887–1969). Her father Herbert Henry Asquith, the Liberal politician, was Prime Minister from 1908 to 1916.

He is not only remarkable but unique.'[23] When she asked which of the two Asquith rated higher, Lord Randolph or Winston, he told her that it was not possible to compare them: 'Randolph was irresistible. He had incomparably more charm, more wit. But – Winston is by far the better fellow of the two.'[24]

Winston never set out to charm. It was not in him. With women he was inept, and he knew it. He spoke to them as he spoke to men, which did not always work. He noticed how confident Sunny was around women: 'He is quite different from me, understanding women thoroughly, getting into touch with them at once, & absolutely dependent upon feminine influence of some kind for the peace & harmony of his soul.'[25] Apart from his mother, female family members and the occasional girlfriend, there were few women in Winston's life, and this possibly disadvantaged him in forthcoming confrontations with the women's suffrage movement. Perhaps a more typical reaction than Violet Asquith's was that of a new aunt-by-marriage, Daisy, sister of George Cornwallis-West, who met Winston at Jennie's wedding. She wrote that she met him with mixed feelings, for what she had heard about him was not complimentary, and she was not won over. 'I cannot say I ever cared for him much.'

But without question, even in these very early days of his career, Winston possessed some special qualities that were evident to anyone who met him, whether they liked him – and these qualities – or not. Equally without question, his overt ambition, his bombast and his vigorous criticism of his own party's policies set many fellow MPs against him. At times he seemed to enjoy causing resentment, and some thought he was merely carrying on where his father had left off. Others believed he was out to get anyone who had crossed his father, and he certainly appeared to carry a chip on his shoulder on account of his father's treatment by the House. It is possible that the anger he felt at his father's rejection of himself found an outlet in his fury at his father's critics.

It was at this time, in the summer of 1902, that Winston approached his father's literary executors and told them he wished to write a political biography of Lord Randolph. With hindsight at least, there could have been no one in the world more qualified, yet the request threw the executors into confusion as they were unsure as to the precise extent of their duties. Would they have to strictly control what was written about the subject? Would they be responsible for editing the proposed book? Winston was firm with them, as usual finding apposite words and argument: 'I strongly incline to the belief that the duty of the literary executors is discharged when, to the best of their judgement, they have selected a suitable biographer. Questions of style, of literary taste, of the scope of the work . . . are all matters upon which opinion will very often be divided. A syndicate may write an encyclopaedia, only a man can write a book.'[26] The executors gave in gracefully. For the next three and a half years Winston would devote every spare moment to this task, which in many ways would prove cathartic. After its completion he would seem at peace in relation to Lord Randolph's memory, as though he had done all he could to answer his father's enemies and lay all the ghosts.

Sunny Marlborough, meanwhile, having played a major role on Jennie's wedding day, had returned from South Africa to dissension in his own marriage. He and Consuelo were scarcely on speaking terms, not helped by rumours that during his absence Consuelo had enjoyed a relationship (and almost certainly a discreet affair) with the fashionable Society portrait artist Paul Helleu, who had gone to Blenheim in May 1900 to produce a series of portraits of Consuelo. At the very least, 'a great friendship'[27] had resulted, which involved the exchange of gifts such as engraved silver cigarette cases. While not believing Consuelo had actually committed adultery, the Duke found it unpleasant to have his wife the subject of gossip. But he was far more angry when he was overlooked for the post he coveted of Lord Lieutenant of Ireland because, as he came to believe, Consuelo had made it known in Society that she would dearly like to be Vicereine. Her remarks were commented upon in the press and when the Queen got to hear of it she was annoyed, so Marlborough's name was removed from the list of possibilities. When the Marlboroughs travelled abroad that year, the papers noted that they did not even sleep in the same buildings, let alone the same rooms. This was a marriage in deep trouble.

In her letters Consuelo noted how much respect the Duke had

for his younger cousin when he visited Blenheim: 'Sunny is still attentive to Winston's every remark – a great sign of friendship,' she wrote. 'Winston is still on the talk – never stops and really it becomes tiring.'[28]

It was against this background that Gladys Deacon paid her second visit to Blenheim. Since her first visit there as a teenager, she had subjugated a number of men in Italy. With her long slender legs and exquisite slight figure, she was described as 'more like a nymph than mortal . . . her fine red-gold hair framed her face and illuminated her fair skin; her eyes were blue fires. The fascinating little kink at the bridge of her nose added poignancy to her beauty – an endearing hint of imperfection which saved it from being too classically severe.' She was also endowed with wit, intelligence and radiance, and a cosmopolitan sophistication. Full of spontaneous gaiety, she illuminated the Blenheim house parties – even, to Consuelo's surprise, teasing Sunny into laughter. She now proceeded to enthral not only Sunny but his cousin (and former best man) Ivor Guest, who was a fellow house guest. Confused and jealous, realising that he had no right to fall in love with his wife's friend, Marlborough left and went to Harrogate 'for a health cure' from where he wrote a series of letters to Gladys in French, frankly expressing his feelings for her while deprecating his chances of any reciprocation.

When he returned to Blenheim to host a visit of the nineteen-year-old Crown Prince of Germany, who was accompanied by the German Ambassador, Count Metternich and a number of courtiers, Sunny had to watch the Crown Prince suffer the same fate as himself and his cousin Ivor. The Prince fell instantly in love with Gladys, who appeared unaffected by all the adulation flowing in her direction. The Prince was speedily removed from her vicinity so as to avoid a diplomatic incident, but not before they had exchanged tokens of jewellery. But there was a leak, and an 'exclusive' story, that the Prince and Gladys were engaged, appeared in *Paris Matin*. It was promptly denied by the German government, but soon afterwards, when Consuelo and Gladys travelled together on a tour of Dresden and Berlin, they were escorted everywhere by a high-profile German nobleman. Consuelo was not slow to realise that the purpose of this escort was to prevent a meeting between Gladys and the Crown Prince, rather than a mark of courtesy. Consuelo had never had a close woman friend and during this trip she too fell under Gladys's spell. Afterwards, the two women sent each other daily letters in which they used pet names (Consuelo was 'Coon') and exchanged locks of hair. Gladys confided to a friend at this time that Consuelo was in low spirits because Marlborough insisted on his marital rights, and made 'wild' love to her.[29] Perhaps this was the reason why, soon after her return from Germany, Consuelo visited her mother in Newport – for the first time since her marriage.

The end of that year, 1901, was to have tragic consequences for the twenty-four-year-old Consuelo. While she and Sunny were visiting Russia she caught a head cold, which led to an ear infection that left her slightly deaf. Unfortunately, this deafness did not clear up and successive specialists were unable to help. Until the invention of miniature hearing aids many years later, this was the beginning of a life increasingly spent on the periphery of conversations and excluded from the whisperings and gossip-mongering among family and friends. She wrote that she felt more isolated and unhappy than ever at this time, although some months later George Cornwallis-West's sister, Princess Daisy of Pless, reported that Consuelo, while in Vienna for treatment for her deafness, had been 'flirting outrageously' with an Austrian prince. 'She is looking very well,' Princess Daisy noted, 'and I think fascinatingly pretty, with her funny little turned up nose and big brown eyes . . . She leaves here tomorrow for England and from there goes to India* for the Durbar.'[30]

After the Marlboroughs had left for India as the personal guests

---

*In 1902 British Imperial India was at its apogee, and the coronation of Edward VII as King–Emperor was celebrated in a show of pomp, spectacle and pageantry never seen before or since. Organised by the Viceroy Lord Curzon, the Delhi Durbar lasted two weeks, and more than a million people lined the streets jostling to see the state processions of maharajas, ambassadors and national leaders who attended. On painted elephants and tasselled horses, in howdahs and carriages, they paraded between massed ranks of marching soldiers, bands and functionaries. Special medals were struck, and there were firework displays, exhibitions and glamorous balls, culminating in the Coronation Ball presided over by Lord Curzon representing the King, and Lady Curzon wearing a stunning gown of peacock feathers. (As these feathers are considered unlucky in India, few among the local community were surprised when the beautiful young Vicereine died suddenly less than two years later.)

of Lord Curzon, Gladys went to stay with her mother where she suffered a nervous breakdown. She was admitted to a Paris clinic where she spent days lying on a bed and gazing at her face in a mirror. While there, she commissioned some cosmetic surgery, which was to be the biggest mistake of her life. Admiring reports of her physical appearance up to this point are so numerous that her beauty may be taken for granted. However, she disliked the small imperfection on the bridge of her nose and aspired to the pure aquiline 'Grecian' look of her sister. Perhaps it seemed to her a good opportunity, with her friends so far away, to correct this. So she underwent a process whereby warm paraffin wax was injected into her nose to smooth over the imperfection. Visitors at the time noted that her nose was red and swollen, but in correspondence they seemed more concerned with her mental state. Just before the Marlboroughs were due to arrive in Paris in April Gladys appeared to make a complete recovery, and discharged herself from the clinic. For some years the cosmetic procedure worked, but Gladys's apparently minor decision, made at a time when her mental health was fragile, was to haunt her in later years.

Sunny was as besotted as ever and sent her a flurry of agonised notes; but Gladys had plenty of men at her feet, among them several dukes, one of whom was the widowed Duke of Norfolk, the premier nobleman* in England. Marriage to him would place her above Consuelo in order of precedence, but Gladys seemed happy merely to flirt with him. Other admirers were as obsessed as Sunny, but she remained unaffected, emotionally, by any of them.

Winston spent most of the summer at Blenheim in a suite of rooms made over to him in order to allow him to work quietly on Lord Randolph's biography. His Aunt Cornelia's sons Ivor and Freddie Guest visited, as did Jack, and Sunny's mother Goosie whom Consuelo liked. The stream of visitors at least made it easier for Consuelo and Sunny to live in the same house. When the visitors departed, Consuelo was often lonely there, but the gift of a new electric brougham from her father enabled her to drive around

---

*The oldest English dukedom, it was established in 1483.

the estate without a groom, giving her a degree of freedom she had hitherto never known.

In 1903 Sunny was appointed Under-Secretary for the Colonies in Arthur Balfour's government, at about the time that the Marlboroughs took possession of their newly built London home, Sunderland House, in Curzon Street. This was a gift to Consuelo from her father (now happily remarried to Anne Rutherfurd* and living in Paris), and was built on the site of the old Curzon Street chapel. Here Consuelo was able to enjoy the modern heating, bathrooms and plumbing that were lacking at Blenheim. And she was at last able to furnish a home with the French antique furniture that she – and her mother – loved.

With the Duke's political career taking off, the London house was in constant use for entertaining. This gave Consuelo a *raison d'être* for a while, but though she liked political debate and attended sessions in the gallery of the House of Lords where she had a seat, her poor hearing impeded her enjoyment. Also, she was not a born political hostess and lacked the flair for it that came so naturally to Jennie. Jennie and her new sister-in-law Princess Daisy, who were both frequent guests at Consuelo's dinners, receptions and soirées in London, considered the dining room at Sunderland House 'pokey'. The ceiling was too low, they thought, and as it was on the ground floor and overlooking the street the windows had to be screened. After the novelty had worn off, Consuelo found the receptions 'by no means a pleasure'.[31] Not only did she find them tedious, but she grew to feel that her taste was being criticised. Left alone for a good deal of the time between these entertainments, she was searching for a life of her own; and that, for a woman of her class at that time, meant only one thing: charitable work. She had helped Jennie equip the hospital ship the *Maine* for the Boer War, but she could not leave her two boys to accompany Jennie to South Africa. Perhaps it was just as well, since both Jennie and her sister Clara were united in feeling that while Consuelo was a willing

---

*Daughter of a banker, Oliver Harriman; her former husband was the cousin of Consuelo's first love, Winthrop Rutherfurd.

recruit she was also something of a handicap, except for her bottomless purse. However, by now Consuelo's deafness was getting worse, and at just the time when her marriage was at a lower ebb than ever.

Both Marlboroughs wrote regularly to Gladys, and from their letters it is clear that neither knew what the other wrote. When Gladys's sister died, the Marlboroughs each wrote fondly to her – in Sunny's case, the tortured letter of a man coming to terms with rejection after Gladys had refused to allow him to visit her in Italy at her mother's home. He had 'experienced such difficulty in resigning myself to the position of one who no longer may claim to be included in the inner circle of your . . . thoughts and emotions'.[32] He pleaded with her not to treat him merely as just another of her many admirers; yet she was a young single woman and he was a married man – and married, moreover, to her supposed best friend. How was she to answer? The Duke's letter suggests that there may have been some intimacy in the past, which, he now realised, would no longer be allowed.

Consuelo wrote: 'I love you, & feel for you and you want love and sympathy now . . . Gladys dear I want you too, I long for your clever and deep thoughts [and] . . . all that makes you so attractive and dear.' By now neither of the Marlboroughs was attempting to make their marriage work or even pretending to. They would be seen together at balls and dinners, but only for the sake of appearances. Consuelo still had few friends, and Gladys was clearly very important to her. Love between women friends, she wrote, was purer than that between man and woman because a man's love for a woman was selfish and self-interested. She had been unhappily married for nine years, had done her duty and provided the next links in the chain. Now, needing her freedom, it is likely she had broached the matter with her father, who was building up his stable of racehorses in Paris. He was sympathetic to Consuelo's misery.

That year, 1904, Winston's life took an unexpected direction. In favour of free trade, increasingly now he found himself at odds with the Conservative government's policy of protectionism and in sympathy with Lloyd George's Liberals. He had, in any case, long

been a closet Liberal, and on the last day of May, feeling powerless
to make any impact on his own party's direction he crossed the floor
of the House and sat with the Opposition. It was not a dramatic
occasion, although the newspapers would later make it one: he
simply entered the Chamber and, instead of making for the government benches, walked towards his father's old seat on the front
bench below the gangway. The seat next to him was occupied by
Lloyd George, who grasped Winston's hand. This defection, his
daughter Mary would write, 'caused him to be regarded as a rene-
gade in the eyes of his own party, and by many others as a traitor
to his class'.[33] Most incorrectly believed that he was succumbing to
a fit of the sulks because he had not been given high office by the
Tories, and even at the end of his life after a glorious career this act
of defection would still be held against him by his critics. Certainly,
it was sensational in Winston's circles – a strange parallel of his
father's behaviour and a protest against superiors who would not
listen to him. It could easily have ended his political chances.
Winston was now twenty-nine, and the career that had looked so
promising appeared to have stalled. His cousins Ivor and Freddie
Guest, both Conservative MPs, defected to the Liberals at the same
time – to the fury of their mother, Winston's aunt Cornelia. In fact,
Winston was able to steer the matter in a positive direction in his
speeches by pointing out that his actions had been dictated by his
conscience and by the people who elected him to speak for them,
rather than slavishly reflecting the party line.

Many of the old Tory grandee houses were now closed to him,
but he was welcomed – even lionised – at Liberal functions, and
soon afterwards he attended a ball with Jennie at the home of the
Marquess and Countess of Crewe, both Liberal supporters. Among
the guests that night was a young woman who caught his eye. Her
name was Clementine Hozier.

Since Pamela had married two years earlier, Winston had dated a
number of women friends from time to time. He even proposed to
two of them: first, to the beautiful and talented twenty-two-year-
old American actress Ethel Barrymore, a member of the famous

acting family. She was on her first visit to London, but it is possible that Winston had already met her in New York. He besieged her with flowers and notes, taking her to dinner each evening at Claridge's after her shows. In July 1902 he even took her to Blenheim. Did he think, perhaps, that another American woman might emulate his mother? Ethel would go on to have a successful career in movies and is famous for her pithy sayings – among them, 'To be a success an actress must have the face of Venus, the brain of Minerva, the grace of Terpsichore, the memory of Macaulay, the figure of Juno . . . and the hide of a rhinoceros.' She told Winston, though, that she felt she would never be able to cope with his world of politics.

The second was Muriel Wilson, heiress to a shipping magnate. She attempted to help Winston overcome the lisp of which he was so self-conscious, making him regularly practise the line: 'The Spanish ships I cannot see for they are not in sight.' It has long been assumed that Winston's interest in Muriel was pecuniary, not least because while touring Europe in Lionel Rothschild's car, accompanied by Muriel and another girl, he described his relationship with her in a note to Sunny as a *banalité*. In 1994, however, some letters came to light that he had written to her after he had proposed to her in early 1904 and been rejected, from which it appears that he was rather taken by her. In one he said he had written 'a long letter three days ago, but decided to burn it', declining to reveal what he had said in it 'because you would think me tiresome . . . Don't slam the door . . . I can wait – perhaps I shall improve with waiting. Why shouldn't you care about me some day? I have great faith in my instinct . . . Time and circumstance will work for me . . . I love you because you are good & beautiful.' He goes on to say that he has not taken her no for a final answer and that the more she opposes him the stronger his feelings will be: 'I am not going to be thrust back into my grey world of politics without a struggle.'

Later he would write 'Of course you do not love me a scrap', yet he believed there must be a key 'if I could only find it – if you would only let me look for it – which would unlock both our hearts'. He felt 'mysteriously drawn' to her, he wrote, yet 'you dwell apart – as lofty, as shining & alas as cold as a snow-clad peak . . . I do love to be with you – to watch you, to study you, to come in contact with your nature . . . I always feel that I am not hateful or ridiculous in your eyes & that no impenetrable veil hangs between us.' Sixty years later the woman whom Winston would marry wrote to the Wilson family, revealing that Winston had admitted to her that as a young man 'he was very much in love with [Muriel]'.* At the time, though, Muriel felt his prospects were not good enough and that he had no future.

Later that year he was observed escorting around town nineteen-year-old Helen Botha, daughter of his old enemy, the Boer leader Louis Botha of South Africa. Soon there were widespread rumours of an engagement. The *Manchester Guardian* offered congratulations, and Muriel Wilson wrote to Winston teasingly, but there was no engagement. Winston was still a free man, all his mental energy given over to politics. And then there was Violet Asquith, who would be a lifelong friend. Winston courted Violet briefly and there were several people who thought they would make a match of it. A friend at that time, Lord Dalmeny (later the 6th Earl of Rosebery), believed that Winston had been devoted to her, and later Winston had confided, 'I behaved badly to Violet because I was practically engaged to her.'[34]

Clementine Hozier was different from the other women in his life, but it would be years before she resurfaced to play the greatest role of all.

---

*Muriel Wilson eventually married an Army officer, who is reputed to have loved fast cars more than his wife. She kept Winston's letters even before he became famous, which may suggest that she cared for him more than her casual rejection implied. The seven letters from Winston to Muriel were auctioned by Christie's in 1994 by her family.

1904–7

My Darling Clementine

Clementine Hozier was the second of the four children of Lady Blanche Hozier (née Ogilvy), who was the daughter of an earl but the possessor of a questionable reputation. Hugely attractive but wayward, Blanche had married in her late twenties. Considered 'on the shelf' by then, she had accepted, perhaps with relief, a proposal from a much older, divorced man, Sir Henry Hozier,* who was not of noble stock and therefore believed by Society to be beneath her. The marriage was a disaster that quickly revealed itself when Sir Henry insisted that he wanted no children while Blanche had hoped for a large family. Blanche, or 'Natty' as she was known in the family, was subsequently credited with nine lovers. After five years of marriage, in 1883 she gave birth to her first child, Kitty. Two years later Clementine was born, and three years after that came twins, Nellie and Bill. It is doubtful that Sir Henry fathered any of his wife's children, although he somewhat unwillingly accepted the first two as his own.

It was known, even within her family, that one of Natty's most attentive lovers was her brother-in-law 'Bertie' Mitford, 1st Baron Redesdale,† the husband of her sister Clementine. Jennie Churchill

---

*A professional soldier, Sir Henry Hozier (1838–1907) acted as Assistant Military Secretary to Lord Napier of Magdala. He served with the Royal Artillery in China and was a war correspondent during the Austro-Prussian War of 1866. He was Secretary of Lloyd's of London for thirty-two years.
†Grandfather of the well-known Mitford girls.

met both Bertie Mitford and Natty when they all hunted in Ireland and she certainly knew of their affair in London, for she wrote about it in her diary and had many cosy chats with Natty.* It was openly believed in their circle that it was Bertie Mitford rather than Sir Henry who was Clementine's natural father; in fact, Natty confided in a close friend a few weeks before Clementine's birth that Lord Redesdale was indeed the father of her forthcoming baby. This seemed to be confirmed when the baby was born with the distinctive blue eyes that were characteristic in the Mitfords, and she named the baby Clementine after his wife. However, in his secret diaries Wilfrid Scawen Blunt, who had an affair with Natty soon after Clementine's birth, wrote that Natty had confessed to him that her first two daughters were both fathered by Captain George ('Bay') Middleton,[†] known by his foxhunting contemporaries as 'the bravest of the brave' and to history as the dashing escort, and perhaps the lover, of the exquisite but tragic sporting empress, Elizabeth of Austria. Jennie had met all the protagonists while hunting in Ireland.

Whoever her father was,[‡] Clementine had grown up in a fractured family. Her parents separated in 1891 when she was five years old, but Sir Henry appeared at the family home from time to time, breathing wrath and vengeful threats of removing the two elder daughters from their mother. Eventually, Natty moved to Dieppe, to evade his threats but also for economic reasons, since Sir Henry regularly defaulted on the allowance he had agreed to pay her. Hardly had Natty and her children settled in their new home than sixteen-year-old Kitty contracted typhoid. Clementine and her young sister Nellie were sent to stay with their grandmother in Scotland and there, a fortnight later, they heard of Kitty's death. The funeral was held at Batsford in Gloucestershire, the home of Natty's sister and her husband Bertie.

---

*Her diary entry of 24 February 1882: 'Took Winston [then aged seven] and had tea with Blanche Hozier in her lodgings.'
†Captain Middleton was red-haired and had hazel eyes.
‡It is still not known for sure. Lady Churchill only discovered in middle life that Hozier was not her natural father and at first she was very upset, but later accepted it. In 2002 Clementine's daughter Mary Soames, having read the Blunt diaries, felt that Bay Middleton was probably Clementine's father.

Kitty and Clementine had been devoted to each other, and were the closest of friends in their unusually peripatetic life. Furthermore, Kitty was a confident and outgoing girl and had been a role model to Clementine. Given that many of the diseases now defeated by antibiotics and modern medical techniques were still prevalent and that childhood mortality was more common than it is now, Victorian and Edwardian families almost expected to lose children to infections, but this did not make Kitty's death any easier for Clementine to bear.

Natty was broken-hearted at the death of her favourite child and for a while Clementine was left to wander around unchaperoned, during which time she formed an unlikely, and wholly innocent, friendship with the artist Walter Sickert* who was living in Dieppe with his mistress. Sickert used to send Clementine home in an electric brougham.[1] When Natty moved her family back to England she devoted all her attention to the twins, Bill and Nellie, who were still small. Clementine, devastated by Kitty's death, felt even more isolated at a time when an adolescent is most in need of a confidante. She developed a very protective relationship towards little Nellie but she was never close to her mother and, unusually for girls of her class, she was now sent to a grammar school (in Berkhamsted, Hertfordshire) instead of being educated at home by a governess. This provided her with a wider circle of contemporaries than she had previously known, but she remained shy and reserved, and though she mixed well enough with her schoolfriends she did not forge any lasting friendships.

She grew up deeply troubled by her mother's chaotic and unconventional, almost bohemian, lifestyle, and disapproved of Natty's male friends as well as of the drinking and gambling she witnessed. And she developed what would become a lifelong tendency to worry constantly about how the household bills were to be paid. There seems to have been considerable tension between the high-minded, disapproving teenage Clementine and her carefree mother,

---

*Sickert's paintings were often explicit nudes, and he took a deep interest in the crimes of Jack the Ripper. In 2002 the crime writer Patricia Cornwell wrote a book in which she stated that Sickert *was* Jack the Ripper.

which made Clementine withdraw into herself even more. When she was eighteen various members of the Ogilvy family were recruited to help 'bring her out', and one of these, a rich great-aunt, Lady St Helier, invited her to a ball at her home, Crewe House, in the spring of 1904. It was here that she was introduced to the controversial young MP Winston Churchill.

By his own account, Winston asked his mother to effect an introduction to a particular girl he found stunning, and Jennie went off to make inquiries. When she returned she told him, 'How very interesting: she is the daughter of a very old friend of mine, Blanche Hozier, whom I haven't seen for years.'[2] The introduction made, Winston was, most unusually, struck dumb. His daughter Mary would later retell his recollection of the event: 'He stood rooted to the spot staring at her.' Highly embarrassed, Clementine signalled to a male friend, who came up and asked her to dance. As they moved away, her partner warned her about speaking to 'that frightful fellow Winston Churchill'.[3]

It was hardly a propitious meeting, and neither gave too much thought to it at the time. Possibly, Winston noted some time later the announcement of Clementine's engagement in *The Times*, followed shortly afterwards with a notice that 'the marriage will now not take place'. He could not know that she had almost suffered a nervous breakdown over it. She had accepted the proposal of a much older man at a time when she badly wanted to get away from her mother, for whom she had little admiration. But probably when she thought of what marriage involved her innate sensitivity got the better of her.

In April 1904, when she was in Paris to consult doctors about her loss of hearing, Consuelo refused to return to Blenheim at Sunny's request to act as hostess at a weekend party for some important guests. Sunny was reduced to apologising for her absence through Winston, who announced that 'the special treatment' she was receiving from her consultant in France could not be interrupted – 'She particularly desired the party to go on.'[4] That summer the Marlboroughs were together in Paris for some weeks, joined there by Gladys Deacon. Both were delighted to see her, though having recently lost her much loved sister from a heart condition, Gladys was upset and appeared on edge the entire time. If her behaviour was slightly erratic, her recent loss seemed an adequate explanation. When Gladys returned to her mother in Italy, the Marlboroughs each wrote to her affectionately. Sunny, clearly still love-stricken, was worried about her health and longed to see her again. He spent an entire day at Blenheim reading through all her letters to him, but her latest caused him great pain, for she had insisted that their relationship must be henceforth platonic (which appears to confirm that it had not always been so). She had been right to be so frank with him, he wrote, and he was glad in a way that she had been, because he had been living in a fool's paradise. Yet the pain and anxiety of their long separation was too much to bear, and he almost wished they had never met. Later that year when he visited Italy he kept his word not to attempt to see her, though he could not resist calling on her mother to inquire about Gladys's health. Meanwhile, the terrible spectre of divorce faced Sunny and Consuelo, but both were reluctant to embark upon such a course because of the inevitable social ramifications.

Once again Winston spent most of the parliamentary recess in September 1904 at Blenheim, working on his biography of his father. He had made himself a portable office and archive in a series of three-foot-square tin boxes, each divided into compartments. At least one of these boxes accompanied him on every journey so that even on the train or when spending a weekend with friends he could continue his work. Invariably he would ask his hostess to provide him with a large table, where he would set out his sheaves of papers, lists, notes and letters in order to utilise every spare moment to advantage. 'I have moved a greater part of my tin boxes here and am now settled down in the Arcade Rooms which are most comfortable,' he wrote to Jennie. 'Consuelo is quite alone here . . . I have been working most assiduously at my book and the great thing to avoid is unnecessary movement . . . I may as well remain here where I can ride each morning.'[5]

When Sunny returned to Blenheim Consuelo took herself off to her father in Paris, where she found a welcome normality in a house alive with the laughter of a happy family and a couple at peace with each other. 'I rejoiced in the happiness he had found in his second marriage,' she wrote in her memoirs. 'My stepmother had a gay and gentle nature. Entirely engrossed in her husband and the four children her two previous marriages had given her she lived the life that suited my father . . . my father had his racing stable and a small house at Poissy, a short drive from Paris. We sometimes spent the night there and in the early morning went out to his private track to see the horses gallop.' Seeing her father so content, and recalling the ghastliness of his divorce from her mother, it is no surprise that Consuelo wondered whether she might find a similar contentment away from Sunny. The major drawback was that the law as it stood required a husband to prove unfaithfulness in his wife – which would, of course, bring such disgrace on the woman that her social life would be utterly destroyed. In those days even an innocent party, along with all the members of their family, would also be tainted by the stigma of divorce.

Once having crossed the floor, Winston began to feel that Oldham was no longer the right constituency for him, and having done his research he had concluded that Manchester, the home of the free-trade doctrine, would suit him better. His son would note many years later: 'It is not without significance that many of his leading supporters in Manchester were Jews. The names of Nathan Laski, Chaim Weizmann, Israel Zangwill, Joseph Dulberg and Barrow Belisha stand out among his early adherents and supporters. No wonder that he so early was indoctrinated in the cause of Zion.'[6] Winston threw himself in on the side of 'the simple immigrant, the political refugee, the helpless and the poor', and he opposed the Aliens Bill of 1904 on the grounds that 'it will commend itself to those who like patriotism at other people's expense. It is expected to appeal to insular prejudice against foreigners, to racial prejudice against Jews, and to labour prejudice against competition.'[7] On this platform he made his first speech from the Opposition bench and established his reputation as a champion of minority groups, or what he called 'the left out millions'. He was also active concerning a new Army bill and a licensing bill, and on one occasion caused uproar in the Chamber by accusing the Prime Minister of orchestrating an attempt by the Conservatives to howl him down when he was attacking the government.

The Chamber was never dull when Winston was on his feet. His thinking was original, his grasp of politics – whether one agreed with him or not – all-encompassing. His speeches, carefully prepared and delivered to devastating effect, often against Joseph Chamberlain who was vehemently opposed to free trade, were also aimed at showcasing himself. He was going to succeed spectacularly, on the fast track, or die in the attempt; everyone in the House knew it, and en route Winston made lots of enemies because of his blatant opportunism and shameless ambition. He was even blackballed by the Hurlingham polo club. Nevertheless, this would have been less of a blow to him than having to formally resign from the Carlton Club, which he did on 14 April 1905. He was still playing polo, his favourite recreation, whenever he could spare the time: 'I am going to spend the Sunday with Ivor [Guest] at Ashby [Ashby St Ledgers, Northamptonshire],' he wrote to Jennie on 6 April, 'with polo on Sat[urday] and Monday. I have begun electric treatment to tighten my dislocated shoulder.* It is rather pleasant. We shall be together either at Blenheim or Salisbury Hall the whole of the Easter holiday.'8

Since she had let her house in Cumberland Place, Jennie hated not having a house of her own where she could repay some of the entertainment she and George regularly accepted. She was always looking for somewhere they could settle, outside London but within easy reach of it. In January 1905 she had found Salisbury Hall, a beautiful moated, red-brick Tudor house near St Albans.†

---

*Caused by an accident as he jumped from his troopship for a ladder set into the wall in Bombay harbour. He always had the shoulder strapped up when he played polo.

†The house was extensively remodelled in 1668, after which it was used as a *petite garçonnière* ('bachelor pad') by Charles II; but he may have used it years earlier as a hiding place when he was on the run from Cromwell's troops. Nell Gwynne was installed at Salisbury Hall for some years by the King. It was there in 1670 that she gave birth to his illegitimate son Charles. Legend has it that on the arrival of the King soon after she had given birth, Nell Gwynne called for her child and holding out her arms, said: 'Come here you little bastard and greet your father.' When the King laughingly rebuked her, she replied: 'Your majesty has given me no other name to call him by', whereupon the King created the baby the Earl of Burford. Subsequently, he was created Duke of St Albans.

By car it was seventeen miles from the centre of London, but felt deeply rural.

George and Jennie moved to Salisbury Hall that spring. Jennie always had the knack of making a comfortable and impressive home and the Hall gave her ample scope. George had already realised that in money matters Jennie was even less adept than he was. 'The value of money meant nothing to her,' he wrote. 'What counted with her were the things she got for money, not the amount she had to pay for them. If something of beauty attracted her, she just had to have it; it never entered her head to stop and think how she was going to pay for it . . . her extravagance was her only fault.'[9] Hence, with Salisbury Hall she acted as though she was as rich as the grand names she regularly entertained there, from the King and his entourage (including his mistress, Mrs Keppel) to the Dukes of Connaught, Marlborough, Manchester and Roxburghe, Lords Curzon, Lennox and Lytton and a myriad other glittering Society names. It quickly became a much loved second home to Winston and Jack, somewhere they could respectably take any girl-friends or repay hospitality.

Their Guest cousins, Ivor and Freddie, became engaged that year. Ivor was a special friend, often forming a trio with Winston and Sunny to travel in Europe. He was, like Winston, in favour of free trade and stood as a candidate for Cardiff on that platform, with Winston's strong support.[10] Both brothers were politically knowledgeable, and they were often at Blenheim when Winston visited. In June 1905 Freddie married an American heiress, Amy Phipps, at St George's Church, Hanover Square. All the Churchill cousins were there.

Freddie was an Army captain serving in India when he first met Amy, who was touring with her father Henry Phipps, the steel indus-trialist turned philanthropist, and the multimillionaire partner of Andrew Carnegie. Having crossed the floor at the same time as Winston, Freddie would make a successful career as Liberal MP for East Dorset, much to his mother's annoyance, for Cornelia (who had been a close friend of Disraeli) was an arch Tory. She tried hard to persuade Winston to return to the Conservative benches and blamed him for Ivor's Liberal views, but in fact Ivor was more

Liberal than Churchill.* It is to his Aunt Cornelia's credit that though she deprecated Winston's political ideology, she was generous with her support and not only invited him often to stay at Canford, her home in Dorset, but several times sent him cheques at critical moments. 'You know how much we care for you and your career, not only for your dear father's sake, but also for yours, for you are always very dear to us and we want to be of a little help to you,' she wrote affectionately in April 1905. 'Now I know elections & Parliament in general all mean a great deal of expense & so we want . . . to send [you] a little present.† When the heiress is found, I think the good fortune will not be only on your side.'[11] Freddie, having already found and married his own heiress, would later attain high office in government, and at various times act as Private Secretary and confidant to Winston. Ivor would later become 2nd Baron Wimborne, a junior minister and Lord Lieutenant of Ireland.

It is difficult to know why, in view of his failing marriage, Sunny Marlborough decided soon after Freddie's wedding that summer to commission John Singer Sargent to paint a family portrait as a companion piece to one of the 4th Duke painted by Sir Joshua Reynolds. At first glance, though stunning, it seems a fairly conventional representation. But knowing the emotional stress the main subjects were experiencing at the time, one perceives the sense of estrangement. Consuelo's swan-like beauty draws the eye first, as intended. She stands gracefully wistful in a dark gown with a fur trim which, although opulent, manages not to detract from its wearer. She wears no jewellery. The artist has placed her at the top of a short flight of steps in the great hall, the others grouped around her. Sunny is to the left of her, dressed in his Garter‡ robes and

---

*'I am not a socialist, in the sense of believing that communistic effort can replace individual inducement,' Ivor Guest wrote to Winston in November 1905, 'although I have a great deal of sympathy for those who get crushed in the modern machine.'
†£1000. Churchill sent it to Cassel to invest for him.
‡The Most Noble Order of the Garter is the oldest order of knighthood still in existence, and the most senior order of chivalry in the British honours system. Membership of the Order (a male member is known as a Knight Companion and a woman as a Lady Companion) is strictly limited. The sovereign and the Prince of Wales hold office by birthright, and membership (never more than twenty-four, in addition to certain members of the royal family and certain 'strangers') is conferred by the sovereign alone.

standing on a step below Consuelo to disguise the fact that he was considerably shorter than his Duchess. Between them, held against his mother, is the heir, Lord Blandford, and to the right is the younger son Ivor with his Blenheim spaniels* – both children are dressed in costumes that would not have been out of place two centuries earlier. The only cohesion between these subjects is that between Consuelo and her elder son (in fact Ivor was her favourite child), and there is a general sense of unease despite – perhaps highlighted by – the sumptuous background, the beauty of the composition and the genius of the artist. '[Sargent] was very self-conscious,' Consuelo recalled, 'and his conversation consisted of brief staccato remarks of a rather caustic nature . . . as I got to know him better, I came under the spell of his kind-heartedness, which not even his shyness could disguise.' It was almost the last thing Sunny and Consuelo would do together. After the portrait was completed Consuelo spent most of her time at Sunderland House and unless Sunny was away, she returned to Blenheim only when required to act as hostess there.

When the parliamentary session was over, Winston relaxed as the guest of Sir Ernest Cassel at his Swiss villa perched at seven thousand feet in the mountains near the Italian border, and in early September he travelled to meet Sunny in the Massif du Mont d'Or near the French–Swiss border. The two men were still the best of friends, and they spent some time together before returning to London. Ahead of them, they knew, was a period of hard electioneering for a general election in which Winston was to stand as Liberal candidate in the Tory stronghold of Manchester. When

---

*A strain of King Charles Cavalier spaniel said to have been brought back to England by the 1st Duke. These chestnut-and-white dogs are renowned for their faithfulness and good temperament. The lozenge, or spot, on the head of true Blenheim Cavaliers has a charming legend attached to it. It is said that while Sarah Churchill waited anxiously for news of her husband fighting at the Battle of Blenheim, to calm her nerves she sat with her pregnant bitch for company. As she fondled the little dog's head and ears her thumb was continually pressed against its head. When the bitch whelped each of her puppies had a spot (or 'thumbprint') on the top of their heads.

Sunny returned from Switzerland Consuelo went to America to have a minor operation on her throat which, it was believed, might relieve her deafness. She stayed with her mother, and soon the American papers were gossiping that all was not well between the Marlboroughs, that Consuelo was badly treated by the Duke, and there were hints of divorce. The gossip was echoing around London too, but the papers there would not have dared to be quite so open. At Christmas Consuelo tried to fill Blenheim with family members whom she could rely on to support her and help lighten the atmosphere. 'Consuelo tells me she is going to bid you to Blenheim for Christmas,' Winston wrote to Jennie. He was going there himself, and he begged her to join the party;[12] Jennie's bright conversation and her musical contributions were always a welcome addition to any country house party.

By the end of 1905 Winston had completed his masterly biography of his father, and recognising that publishing was outside his area of expertise he had contacted the Irishman Frank Harris,* a literary agent who had formerly been editor of the *Evening News*, the *Fortnightly Review* and *Vanity Fair*; he had also been one of the first to detect the genius of George Bernard Shaw and H.G. Wells. Winston had hoped to sell the book for as much as £5000, but Harris told him: 'Properly worked this book should bring you in £10,000, or I'm a Dutchman.' In fact Harris achieved £8000, and Winston was delighted. 'I could certainly never have made such a bargain for myself,' he wrote to Jennie. On 2 January 1906 the two volumes were published to critical acclaim, and remain the standard work on the subject. One of those who had opposed Winston when the project was initially suggested was Lord Rosebery, a close friend of Lord Randolph. Now he wrote that to his surprise the book had enthralled him. It had seemed to him an almost impossible book to write, but having read it,

---

*Perhaps now best remembered for his notorious four-volume autobiography, *My Life and Loves*, which included sexually explicit descriptions of Harris's numerous relationships, and for his exaggerated view of his own role in history. It was published in the 1920s, and until recently shelved under 'banned books' in the British Library.

I must congratulate you without qualification or reserve. I am I think naturally a cold-blooded critic. But here I can only dwell on one long monotonous note of praise. The plan was beset with difficulties. A son, who hardly knew his father as a public man or not at all, writing his father's life; the story only ten years old and full of delicacies & resentments; many survivors of those times, whose toes it was impossible to avoid treading upon, still in existence. Moreover the career to be written about was full not merely of dazzling successes, but of perturbances and infirmities. . . . And what is the result? I cannot find a fault.[13]

January 1906 was an important month for Winston's political life, too. With polling day a mere nine days off, he arrived in Manchester on the 4th. Having checked into the Midland Hotel, he went immediately to tour the worst slums of the city. 'Fancy living in these streets,' he remarked to a companion, 'never seeing anything beautiful – never eating anything savoury – *never saying anything clever!*' The last phrase being most important to Winston, he stressed it.*

Manchester was the home of the women's suffrage movement led by the remarkable Mancunians Emmeline Pankhurst and her daughter Christabel who founded the Women's Social and Political Union (WSPU). A bill for women's suffrage had been filibustered in May of the previous year, after which Emmeline Pankhurst and other WSPU members began a loud protest outside the Parliament building. The bill was lost but Pankhurst considered it a successful demonstration of the organisation's power to capture public attention. At the time of the 1906 election she declared: 'We are at last recognized as a political party; we are now in the swim of politics, and are a political force.' One of their earliest attempts to infiltrate a public meeting had occurred at one of Winston's addresses three months earlier, and from a publicity viewpoint it

---

*In 1999 when I interviewed Churchill's cousin Diana Mosley for another book, she reminded me of this passage. She already knew of it when she was incarcerated, without trial, in appalling conditions in Holloway for the duration of the Second World War. She never forgave Churchill for separating her from her small children, nor for subjecting her to the experience which, she said, was perfectly summed up by this quotation.

had been a huge success. Accordingly, they now ignored most other candidates and concentrated on Winston's higher-profile speeches, waving 'Votes for Women' banners and repeatedly heckling him – 'Will you give us the vote?' – which irritated the mostly male audience and at times even disconcerted Winston. At one meeting he invited a woman on to the platform to have her say. Before being forcibly ejected by the chairman she was given a rough time by the audience, especially the few women there: 'Be quiet!' – 'You are disgracing us!' – 'Leave it to the men!' When finally allowed to speak she asked Winston if, as a member of the Liberal government, he would 'give a vote to the women of this country'. He replied: 'The only time I have voted in the House of Commons on this question I have voted in favour of women's suffrage, but having regard of the perpetual disturbance at public meetings in this election, I utterly decline to pledge myself.' The term 'henpecking' came into popular usage as one consequence of these demonstrations.

Winston's prime platform, however, was free trade, and it was on this issue that he carried the day. He was returned with a clear majority of 5639 votes over his opponents' collective 4398, but of the nine parliamentary seats in the Manchester and Salford constituencies his was the only Liberal victory, all the others remaining resolutely Tory. Outside the Manchester area, though, the Liberals under Henry Campbell-Bannerman swept to victory with a landslide majority of 125 seats over all other parties, while the Tories under Arthur Balfour lost more than half of theirs.*

If Winston ever needed any justification for having crossed the floor (though there is no evidence that he agonised about it), this must have settled the matter. Some months before the election he had been offered an important Shadow post. And he knew what victory in the election meant for him – it was a stepping stone to his main goal, a Cabinet post. Now, with his election victory, he assumed for the Liberals the position that Sunny formerly held for the outgoing Tories, Under-Secretary for the Colonies. Originally he

---

*The Labour Representation Committee was third, winning 29 seats. After the 1906 election it was reformed as the Labour Party under the leadership of Keir Hardie.

had been offered the post of Financial Secretary to the Treasury, and though this was technically a superior post it would have meant working under the formidable Herbert Asquith, giving him little chance to shine. At the Colonies, however, even as an under-secretary Winston would have as his chief Lord Elgin with whom he knew he could work in harmony, but who was also frequently absent visiting his Scottish estates. This would provide Winston with a far greater degree of autonomy. Elgin had been Viceroy in India when Winston was a lowly subaltern there, and since then a mutual respect had developed. Elgin would write later that he knew at the outset that it would be no easy task to work with Winston, but he had taken a keen interest in the younger man's ability, and liked him.

Sunny wrote in a note of congratulation: 'I am truly glad . . . You don't realise yet what a position is now offered to you. Your speeches will be read throughout the Colonies, and you alone will be the mouthpiece of the Govt.' On the contrary – Winston, having engineered it, fully realised what he had been offered. Acceptance put him in need of a good Private Secretary, and the two women whom he trusted above all others, his Aunt Leonie and Pamela Lytton, each separately encouraged him to select a man just a little older than himself – Edward ('Eddie') Marsh. The two men had first met at a dinner party in December 1905, and later in the evening Marsh saw Winston sitting on a sofa with Leonie. They were obviously discussing him, Marsh thought, because they kept looking over at him and nodding. Marsh had heard of the appointment but the gossip about Winston was not flattering. 'Next morning [Churchill] paid his first visit to the Office,' Marsh recalled, 'and asked the Permanent Under-Secretary* to appoint me as his Private Secretary! This was quite out of the ordinary course, as I was no longer in the class of "Juniors" to whom such posts, with their extra pay, are a perquisite.'[14]

Without knowing of her championship, Marsh took himself off to Pamela Lytton to voice his misgivings and ask her advice. 'Her answer,' he wrote, 'was one of the nicest things that can ever have

---

*Charles Stewart Henry Vane-Tempest-Stewart, Lord Castlereagh (1878–1949), elder son of the Marquess of Londonderry, who succeeded his father to the title in 1915.

been said about anybody. "The first time you meet Winston you see all his faults, and the rest of your life you spend in discovering his virtues"; and so it proved.' Marsh was to work for Winston as his Private Secretary on and off throughout his working life, one of the handful of totally trusted people in Winston's inner circle.

It was soon after the election that Consuelo began a passionate affair with Charles, Viscount Castlereagh, who was a friend of Winston's and also his second cousin. Charles was married to Edith ('Edie') Chaplin,* but he already had a reputation as a ladies' man. Like Sunny and Winston, he had been busy electioneering in January 1906 and had been elected MP for Maidstone, but by springtime people in their own close circles had become aware that Charles and Consuelo were involved in a romantic relationship. For Consuelo it was not her first affair. There had almost certainly been Paul Helleu, and there may have been other harmless flirtations. But she was now twenty-nine, a vulnerable, unfulfilled and lonely woman, deeply in need of tenderness. When she fell in love with Charles Castlereagh, all common sense was ignored in the thrill of passion. The lovers were spotted together in Paris at the end of March. But they had not been very discreet before that, in London, and when Consuelo returned home to Sunderland House, apparently after receiving a telegram from Sunny telling her not to bother to return at all, it was to face not only his wrath but that of Charles's formidable mother, Theresa, Lady Londonderry.

Sunny had not remained faithful, but he did not believe that his wife should be granted the same privilege. Lady Londonderry had had at least two notorious liaisons, one of which permanently estranged her husband who, although they continued to live together, never spoke a word to her again for the rest of his life. This, however, did not make her especially sympathetic to the position in which Consuelo now found herself; rather, her chief concern was to avoid

---

*Edith Chaplin, daughter of the 1st Viscount Chaplin and granddaughter of the Duke of Sutherland. She married Charles, Viscount Castlereagh, in 1899 and eventually became Marchioness of Londonderry.

Lady Sarah Wilson: an acid-tongued aunt, loathed by Jennie and Consuelo. She acted with great bravery under fire at Mafeking and became the first woman war correspondent. (Getty)

Major Jack Churchill during the Boer War – both he and Winston wore this dashing uniform of the Light Horse and both grew moustaches. (Churchill Archives)

Winston as a belligerent prisoner-of-war. Captured on 15 November 1899, he soon escaped and went on the run, later writing, 'I hated my captivity more than I have hated any other period in my life.' (Churchill Archives)

The instant hero: Winston addresses the cheering crowds at Durban following his escape. (Churchill Archives)

An unusual photograph of Winston in front of his 'rowtie' tent during the Boer War. (Private collection)

'Sunny' Marlborough,
the 9th Duke. (Getty)

The family portrait
Sunny ordered less
than a year before he
and Consuelo parted.
(Blenheim Archives)

Consuelo Vanderbilt, Duchess of Marlborough,
forced by her mother into a marriage distasteful
to her. She had an affair with the artist Paul
Helleu, who painted this charming portrait.
(Private collection)

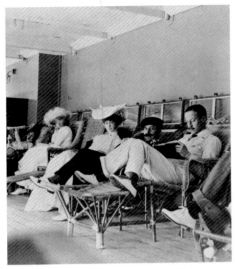

Consuelo and Sunny en route
to the Delhi Durbar. (Getty)

Consuelo and Winston. The
two were always great friends.
(Churchill Archives)

Winston with the Kaiser during military manoeuvres in 1909. Few war leaders have been on first-name terms with the leader of the enemy as Winston was during the 1914–18 war. (Getty)

Vanity Fair cartoon of Winston delivering a speech in the House. He deliberately adopted the confident 'hands-on-hips' stance of his father. (Mary Evans Picture Library)

Sisters: Lady Clementine and Lady Blanche Ogilvy. Lady Clementine's husband Lord Redesdale may have been the real father of Blanche's daughter, Clementine Hozier.
(Churchill Archives)

An engagement picture of Winston and Clementine after he proposed to her in the Grecian temple at Blenheim. (Churchill Archives)

A portrait of Clementine at the time of her marriage to Winston. (Getty)

Winston shortly before his marriage. (Corbis)

The bridesmaids await the bride. (Mary Evans Picture Library)

Jennie, arriving at Winston and Clementine's wedding. (Mary Evans Picture Library)

Winston arriving at the church with his best man, Lord Hugh Cecil. (Mary Evans Picture Library)

Clementine's arrival: thousands waited to see the couple married.
(Mary Evans Picture Library)

Winston and Clementine leaving for their honeymoon. Nellie and Lady Blanche Hozier are
on the right. (Mary Evans Picture Library)

a scandal that would put an end to the political career of her son, who had recently been made a permanent under-secretary.

Theresa Londonderry apparently asked the Prince of Wales to bring pressure on the lovers to break up the affair. She also remonstrated with Consuelo who, notwithstanding their disagreement, continued to admire and like the older woman for many years afterwards. Consuelo was so smitten that she would have been willing to sacrifice her loveless marriage for this relationship, had it not been for her children. But letters between Charles and his wife Edie make it clear that, if not love, at least a great affection still existed between them. Edie was deeply hurt by the affair and took a long time to forgive her errant husband, despite letters from a contrite Charles pleading with her to pardon him. At the end of May a chastened Charles travelled to Spain with his wife to attend a royal wedding and Consuelo, wounded by the fact that Charles had chosen to return to his wife, was left to face Sunny.

There is no formal record of the clash between the Duke and Duchess after Consuelo returned from Paris, but there evidently was one, and letters within the family mention the worsening situation between them throughout that time.[15] A visitor to Blenheim in May, at the height of the trouble, without knowing the cause, wrote to a correspondent: 'There is no affection in the atmosphere [here]; the poor Duke looks ill and heartbroken.'[16]

Later that year American Society columns reported several incidents that had apparently occurred during the summer of 1906. At a dinner party at Blenheim, it was reported, Consuelo had mentioned casually that she was intending to go to Paris to order her wardrobe for the following winter. The Duke – perhaps suspicious that she was planning to meet Charles there – flew into a temper and roared that she ought to go to Paris and stay there. It was also claimed that during that same summer Consuelo and Gladys Deacon had met in Paris and had quarrelled violently after Consuelo had accused Gladys of improper behaviour with her husband. From that date onwards Consuelo and Gladys were estranged.

How could the papers have known about these incidents – which, with hindsight, have the ring of veracity – unless someone had primed them? It would not have been the Duke, or Consuelo or Gladys; but in all probability it was Alva, who had heard Consuelo's side of the story and was now as keen on her daughter obtaining a divorce from the Duke as she had once been that they should marry. Alva and the Duke were no longer on speaking terms – he now referred to her in his correspondence as 'the old hag'. It is probable that Alva saw no reason why bad behaviour on the part of the Duke should be kept secret, and her contacts with Society-column editors were such that it was said of her that 'she could write her own headlines'.

Winston considered both Sunny and Consuelo as his friends and he tried hard to effect a reconciliation, but in mid-October he accepted defeat and wrote to Jennie from Blenheim: 'Sunny has definitely separated from Consuelo . . . Her father returns to Paris on Monday. I have suggested to her that you would be vy. willing to go and stay with her for a while, as I cannot bear to think of her being all alone during these dark days. If she should send for you, I hope you will put aside other things & go to her. I know how you always are a prop to lean on in bad times. We are vy. miserable here. It is an awful business.'[17] But Jennie had heard the news and had already joined Consuelo at Sunderland House, from where she wrote to Winston, saying that it was a very painful experience. Mr Vanderbilt was also staying with Consuelo in order to work with the solicitors on his daughter's behalf. A few days were still needed before the legal separation could be signed and although Consuelo was being dignified and calm, she was utterly miserable. Jennie wrote that she avoided asking any direct questions because she felt as sorry for Sunny as she did for Consuelo. She was inclined to believe that Consuelo had brought this all about by her affair with Charles Castlereagh, but she was sympathetic to the fact that Consuelo would be ostracised by women who had had twenty lovers, but had behaved discreetly and kept their husbands.[18]

Winston was in the difficult position of trying to support each of the parties while wishing to retain the friendship of both. He discussed the matter with Lord Hugh ('Linky') Cecil, a confidant of his and Sunny's,* who wrote that Sunny was placing himself in a difficult position which pleased 'neither the Christians, nor the fast set'. The Christians, he said, felt that whatever Consuelo had done the Duke was equally to blame as he had himself been unfaithful. On the other hand, the 'fast set' around the King were annoyed because the usual discretion about such affairs was not being observed and this cast their own behaviour into focus.

> [Sunny's] position, that his wife is unfit to live with him because she went wrong before he did & because the standard for women in these things is higher than for men, is not defensible . . . I am sure he will do himself harm . . . A much higher consideration is his children: to break up the home is ruinous to them – sooner or later it will dawn on them what it means – & there will be a third generation of shame. I do feel this very strongly: the children are the only people concerned who are innocent – their well-being ought to be the dominant consideration.[19]

But matters had gone far beyond the reconciliation urged by their friends. When George Cornwallis-West returned home, Jennie took Consuelo with her to Salisbury Hall. 'Poor little Consuelo is here,' George wrote to Winston. 'I do pity her with all my heart, what a tragedy . . . Take my advice & if ever you do marry, do it from motives of affection & none other. No riches in the world can compensate for anything else.'[20]

The following day, however, George was writing again to

---

*Lord Hugh R. Cecil (1869–1956) was a younger son of the 3rd Marquess of Salisbury and became Tory MP for Greenwich in 1895, a seat he lost in the Liberal rout of 1906. In 1910 he became MP for Oxford and remained so for twenty-seven years. He had been close to Churchill since they were young backbenchers critical of the leadership of Arthur Balfour. Then, together with F.E. Smith, Arthur Stanley and Ian Malcolm, they had formed a group of young Tory politicians calling themselves 'the Hughligans', based loosely on Lord Randolph's 'Fourth Party'.

Winston, angrily this time, about some gossip that had just been repeated to him. The Marlboroughs' separation was on everyone's lips that week and Sunny and Winston's aunt, the redoubtable Lady Sarah Wilson, was in the thick of it, disseminating rumour and innuendo via her friend Minnie Paget. Naturally, most of the Churchill family ranged themselves squarely behind the head of their family, and it was variously alleged that Consuelo had been unfaithful with from three to six lovers. George Cornwallis-West was stunned to hear from someone who had obtained the information directly from Lady Paget that he himself was being mentioned by Sarah Wilson as one of these lovers.

'Sarah has behaved like a perfect beast,' he wrote furiously to Winston, 'and the sooner she is told the better . . . I naturally did not discuss the case, but merely denied any knowledge of such details. If Sarah thinks she is championing Sunny's case by casting mud (some of which will undoubtedly come back to him) she is much mistaken. Surely the obvious line for all your family to take is to decline all discussion on the matter, let alone volunteering disgusting gossip with the most renowned of gossip mongers. She actually had the impudence to tell Consuelo,' he had now discovered, 'that she was not certain whether I was her lover, and that the only reason she had any doubt about it was because I had borrowed money from Sunny . . . I am sorely tempted to go and tell Sarah what I think of her . . . what a liar that woman is.'[21]

This matter might have been the cause of the serious fallingout between Consuelo and Jennie that week. A month afterwards Jennie wrote to her that she had been 'deeply wounded' by Consuelo's recent treatment of her. Reminding Consuelo that she had always been a 'true friend', she continued, 'had you been a sister [I] could not have shown you more loyalty or affection.' She did not regret this, Jennie wrote, and 'God knows you are not in a position to alienate a friend – therefore I will still call myself one.'[22] However, the two women were not reconciled and two years later they would still avoid parties and weekends if they learned the other was to be present. The entire family were dragged into the affair in one way or another. Following George's letter, Winston, who attempted to be scrupulously fair to both parties throughout this marital mayhem, had tackled his Aunt Sarah, and they had also quarrelled. Sunny wrote and told him wearily to drop the matter, which he claimed had all been caused by Consuelo being mischievous and malicious.[23] Anne Vanderbilt, Consuelo's stepmother, in Paris, however, told another member of the Vanderbilt family: 'The real problem is that [Consuelo] is physically repulsive to [Sunny] and that he cannot bear to be near her.'[24]

Of course the problem was not quite as clear-cut as that, for the Duke was still in love with Gladys Deacon and wanted no one else. From correspondence between Winston and Lord Hugh Cecil it appears that Sunny and Gladys were lovers and that Consuelo had been willing to bolt with Castlereagh. Furthermore, although no names are mentioned in this correspondence it seems that Consuelo's dalliance with Paul Helleu was known about and pre-dated Sunny's first adulterous liaison. 'The fact that Sunny had married her without loving her,' Cecil wrote, 'is not and has not been absolved now by her misconduct, and therefore his unfaithfulness is a thing of which he ought to be seriously ashamed.'[25]

By Christmas, with Winston's assistance, it looked as though the matter had been settled reasonably amicably with a legal separation. Their lawyers had agreed that neither party would accuse the other of infidelity, and that they would have equal access to the children who would spend half a year with each. Sunny and Consuelo each wrote to Winston thanking him for this help, but at the beginning of January 1907 any progress achieved had dissipated. Alva (now Mrs Belmont) became involved, insisting on a clause that would prevent Marlborough, under threat of legal enforcement, from making allegations in public about Consuelo, and allow her to visit Blenheim for the sake of appearances. These new terms, which Winston thought reasonable, were read out in the office of the Duke's solicitors. Infuriated, Marlborough backed down on all the agreements he had made so far and refused to sign. Winston became very angry, went home and wrote his cousin a stern letter. If he would not cooperate with those who had his best interests at heart, he told him, 'I cannot save you from yourself. If you will not fight and will not make peace you will be hunted down and butchered.' It made him heartsick, he said, when they were so close to a satisfactory settlement,

> to see you cast away your last chance of a decent life by folly and weakness . . . All you were asked to do was give up the pleasure of blackguarding your wife. Rather than surrender that you will immerse yourself in such shame and public hatred that no one will ever be able to help you any more . . . if you are not equal to the task of settling this social difficulty why won't you entrust it to Cecil or to Ivor? Let them talk to Mrs B[elmont] . . . why on earth can't you face the situation like a man? Do your best to help Consuelo to have a fair chance in life, under the new conditions, and forget for the moment your petty pride, your shoddy consistency . . . and the damned fools to whom you listen.[26]

The above draft may or may not have been sent, but either way it provides valuable insight into how matters stood; and Winston may well have realised that such frankness could easily lose him Sunny's friendship, which meant much to him. The following day he wrote a somewhat less frank letter, offering to come to Blenheim to discuss the problem. Sunny's answer came indirectly via a note to Winston from Mr Angus at the Blenheim estate office asking if he would suggest a date for the removal of his three polo ponies from the Blenheim stables. After that there was nothing for two weeks until Winston wrote again, asking Sunny if he now felt he had a quarrel with him. The Duke replied at great length:

> No, I have no quarrel with you and nor if I had would it be of long duration. I will initiate your suggestion not to enter into a long argument. I will make only one or two brief comments on your communication.
>
> I deny that I gave you previous authority or knew that you were going to suggest . . . that a visit to Blenheim by Consuelo should be one of the terms of the agreement. But then neither you nor anyone else excluded from the area of possibility that at some future date

when I deem it right and proper, I may invite her to visit the children. That invitation will depend on circumstances but it will be at my pleasure and convenience . . .

I cannot help feeling that if you consulted your political associates and tell them the advice which you offered me, explaining at the same time that you were cognisant of the reasons which induced me to ask Consuelo to leave Blenheim, that they would reverse their belief in the capacity and probity of your judgement . . . Your abilities are considerable but my mind is sufficiently active to detect the appearance of infirmities in your case. That is why I would not accept the proposals . . . though my refusal mostly inflamed you and induced you to leave me in anger . . . there was policy in my method. I knew that Mrs B . . . believed that she had intimidated you and she relied on your influence to work on me. The moment she was informed about that broken communication with Ivor and Cecil she dropped all her excuse of social clauses . . .

My dear, you tried to bring pressure on me to do as you wished, but not what I wanted. You must forgive me if in order to have my way and not submit to pressures I had to pretend to be estranged from you. It was the only way I could triumph over that old Hag. She is now entirely deflated . . . The hand of reparation you ask for I give you with both of mine, and I suppose that in order to celebrate the termination of my bothers, and the reinstatement of the aims I had in view when these threats began, that we journey to Paris at once . . .[27]

Consuelo had already left England by then with their sons, to cruise in the Mediterranean with her father. In the autumn of 1907 she visited her mother. Disembarking at New York she was mobbed by crowds and press. Jennie wrote to Winston when she heard of this, saying that it was far too soon for Consuelo to go back while she was still headline news.[28]

1907–8

Couples

In the spring of 1907 Winston was rumoured to be on the brink of marriage. A Colonial Conference was held in London in April and among the delegates was Louis Botha – the same who had taken Winston prisoner during the Boer War after the train wreck seven years earlier. Now he was General Botha of the Transvaal, and accompanied by his striking and intelligent daughter, Helen. A valued friendship and mutual esteem had grown between these former adversaries, and Winston was so flattering about Botha in his eloquent speeches and so much in Botha's company that it elicited press comment about the true nature of his interest. This rumour reached Winston's former girlfriend Muriel Wilson, who wrote both to congratulate him on his engagement to the elegant Miss Botha and also on being made Privy Councillor, a signal honour for such a young man. 'I hope [you] and Miss Botha, and all the little Bothas will come and see me,' Muriel wrote teasingly.

The engagement rumour was not true, though Winston had been seen with Miss Botha a few times; but the elevation to Privy Councillor was fact. The King wrote to Winston: 'We have known your parents for many years (even before their marriage) & you & your brother since your childhood. Knowing the great abilities which you possess – I am watching your political career with great interest.'[1] One outcome of the new friendship offered to Botha by the British was the gift from the people of Transvaal of the Cullinan diamond to the King on his sixty-sixth birthday. It was the largest ever discovered, at over 3025 carats (uncut).*

But it was twenty-seven-year-old Jack, not Winston, who found a marriage partner that year. Jack was an unusual Churchill in that he possessed what few of his male relatives did: namely, an endearing and gentle humility. And he was proud to be known as Winston's brother. Although Jack had once hoped to go to Oxford, his son has written that he 'was not what I would call intelligent',[2] and his love of music and books was more a flirtation than a deep commitment. Unlike Winston, who had begun to prepare himself for leadership in his teens, Jack had no ambitions other than to marry and be happy and to earn enough to decently maintain a family. Consequently he was content to work 'laboriously' for a London stockbroker, enduring a routine that Winston could never have accepted: 9 a.m. until 5 p.m. each day, Monday to Friday, with three weeks' annual holiday. Although he was earning £500 a year – quite sufficient, when added to his parental allowance, to enable him to live comfortably and elegantly as a bachelor – it would not provide for a wife and family.

It has been suggested by several biographers that the girl Jack fell in love with, Lady Gwendeline Bertie, was interested at first in Winston, and he in her. She wrote a number of spirited letters to him during 1907, but they are simply that – spirited, but with no hint of romance. It is evident from her girlish prattle that she would never have suited Winston as a wife. It would seem that there was probably a sort of youthful hero-worship on her part, except for one microscopic piece of evidence. John ('Jock') Colville, who knew Churchill intimately in later life, suggested in one of his books, but without providing any explanation, that Winston had 'succumbed to her charms' before he met Clementine Hozier.

Nowhere in her letters to Winston does Lady Gwendeline hint that she and Jack were romantically involved, although later the two would state that they had been secretly in love for six months

---

*The diamond was later sent to Holland for cutting into nine smaller stones. Of these, the largest was a 530.2-carat tear-shaped diamond called the Star of Africa Number 1, which fits into the royal sceptre but can be removed and worn as a piece of jewellery. Star of Africa Number 2 is a 317.4-carat cushion-shaped diamond in the front of the British imperial state crown.

(which covered the period she was writing to Winston), and even earlier before they had told each other. Jack had felt he could not honourably make overtures to Gwendeline because he could not support a wife, and also there were religious differences. Gwendeline (universally known as 'Goonie') was the daughter of the 7th Earl of Abingdon, who expected his daughter to marry suitably – that is, someone with prospects, but, primarily, a Catholic. It looked hopeless, and Jack told Winston he had not been able to see any way forward.[3] A friend who knew Goonie when she was a debutante described her thus: 'Her alluring mermaid beauty has a strange translucent quality . . . Her wide-opened eyes are like blue flowers . . . [her] enigmatic loveliness casts so subtle and so lasting a spell . . . A gift for making whatsoever she might choose to wear seem exactly right, was part of Goonie's magic.'[4] John Singer Sargent caught these qualities in a family portrait of her.

One biographer has suggested that Winston vanished to Paris at this point so as to avoid any romantic complications with Goonie; however, his trip had been planned for a long time beforehand and could not have been connected (though it may have been convenient). Winston had worked hard and efficiently that year and had organised a five-month overseas fact-finding trip beginning with his official participation in a series of Army manoeuvres in France, which would have fascinated him. He had correctly calculated that Lord Elgin's social and domestic commitments in Scotland meant that he himself effectively ran the Colonial Office. The archives of that department clearly demonstrate Winston's energetic and knowledgeable leadership; and his command of the English language is evident even in his routine interdepartmental memoranda.

From France he travelled on to Italy, where he met Sunny in Venice before setting out for East Africa, a region only recently colonised and about which Winston was curious. There was a warm letter from Pamela Lytton to speed him on his way, addressed to 'Winston mine'. She told him that she had been to Doncaster races with Goonie: 'We talked about you. There were endless cats . . . chief among them sly Sarah – whose evil eye shines ever brighter and harder.'[5] Sarah Wilson, whose undertakings in South Africa had proved her to be brave, intelligent and resourceful, took huge pleasure, as already noted, in spreading stories about Consuelo. Her constant mischief-making suggests that she may have been bored with life in peacetime England.

Winston replied to Pamela, referring to her as a 'kitten' and thanking her for her always constant friendship. 'I have vy few friends', he wrote from Venice:

> I could make more, but . . . alas with my busy selfish life – I fear, as it is, I fail too often in the little offices which keep friendship sweet & warm. But you always understand me & pardon, because you know me & care about me; & upon my word you are almost the only person who does – except Jack & my mother – which is different: & Sunny, who also is different again . . . Sunny is vy glad to get me here. All his old friends are in the canals [in Venice] – but he does not dare to go to see any of them except for a minute or two because of gossip. He is all alone: & quite embittered. But he has only to keep his head high & to hold firm for two or three years – for all to come right for him.[6]

Among Sunny's friends in Venice that year was Gladys (to whom Winston referred as 'a strange glittering being'). She and Winston spent a morning together in a gondola, but he reported that he had nothing in common with her. Did he realise what was going on between Sunny and her? For all his political precocity, Winston was rather naive in emotional terms. Perhaps he was simply being diplomatic, but he was one of the very few men who did not fall at Gladys's feet. The only time Sunny ever lived up to his nickname was when he was in her company. Sunny's misery at his situation was compounded by jealousy. He was only too aware that he was merely one of a legion of admirers, which included Marcel Proust* and the Russian philosopher Hermann Keyserling – who had asked Gladys to marry him, but his proposal was left unanswered for a year. Others were Hugo von Hofmannsthal, the Austrian playwright and

---

*Proust told Count Loche Radziwill that he had never met a girl 'with such beauty – such magnificent intelligence, such goodness'.

poet who wrote libretti for some of Richard Strauss's operas, and even the seventy-year-old sculptor Auguste Rodin. Winston did not dislike Gladys, but he was not attracted to her and did not know how to react to her. Probably, too, his loyalty to Consuelo affected his reaction. As for Gladys herself, her dislike of Winston may have stemmed from her failure to enslave him. In conversation with Hugo Vickers, one of her biographers, she delivered a scathing attack on Winston, claiming that he was cold and self-obsessed. 'He was incapable of love,' she said. 'He was in love with his own image . . . he took an instant dislike to me . . . he was entirely out for Winston.'[7]

From Venice, Winston travelled via Vienna to Malta, where he rendezvoused with his other travelling companions. He had originally organised this trip with his cousin Freddie Guest and his secretary Eddie Marsh. But Freddie's wife Amy was about to give birth to their first child and refused to be deserted, so Freddie cancelled, offering his car to enable Winston to proceed as planned – he was to send back the car before he joined his ship. In Freddie's place Winston invited Colonel Gordon Wilson, the husband of his Aunt Sarah. The fourth member of the party was Winston's manservant, George Scrivings.

Sailing leisurely via the Red Sea aboard the cruiser *Venus*, which the Admiralty had placed at Winston's disposal, the party arrived at Mombasa in November. At Cyprus and Somalia and every other stop on the way, Winston leapt into action, and little escaped his attention. He fired off lengthy memoranda and reports to his department on his findings, causing considerable annoyance (and jealousy, judging from scribbled comments on some of the reports) among senior civil servants confined to their Whitehall desks, and thereby fostering further long-term enmities.

By one postbag he received welcome news from his brother. 'I am writing to tell you that a very wonderful thing has happened,' Jack wrote. It was to say that Goonie and he were in love. In fact he had loved her for a long time, but because he could not afford to marry he had been unable to tell her, and also he did not know how she felt about him. However, six months earlier the two had confessed their love to each other, even though they knew they could not marry, and a week afterwards Goonie had written promising to wait for him. That very day, Jack wrote, he had seen Goonie in London and they had become secretly engaged. One minute he was head over heels and thrilled at having won this wonderful girl as his potential life partner, and the next he was plunged into despair at the difficulties that lay ahead of them. These were chiefly money (he had none), religion (Goonie was Catholic) and her parents, who he felt would be 'very angry' when they were told. Unlike Winston, he said, he had no great ambitions; all his dreams were wrapped up in Goonie, so he begged Winston to keep their secret.[8]

Jennie was also told and she wrote at once to Winston to say that she had sometimes wondered whether he had designs on Goonie himself – though she thought not serious ones for she knew that Goonie had always cared for Jack. In the same letter she broke the news that she and George had reluctantly decided that they must let Salisbury Hall and take a small flat in London. While her husband believed that her extravagance was to blame for their present financial crisis, Jennie claimed it was George's disastrous business dealings that had brought them to the edge: 'I am making the best of it for it preys dreadfully on poor George who is getting quite ill over it all.'[9] When George was eventually ordered to St Moritz by his doctor on account of an asthmatic illness, Jennie reported that they simply could not afford for her to accompany him. In reply Winston said he was glad that Jack had 'not married some beastly woman for money . . . how happy he must be'.[10]

Following two days of lavish official receptions given by the small band of white settlers in Mombasa, Winston and his friends travelled up country to Nairobi on the now fabled Uganda Railway 'Lunatic Express'. They sat, as all visiting VIPs did, on a bench strapped to the cow-catcher on the front of the locomotive, with an unobstructed view of this Garden of Eden.

'One can see literally every animal in the Zoo,' Winston wrote to his mother wonderingly. 'Zebras, lions, rhinoceros, antelopes of every kind, ostriches, giraffes – often five or six different kinds are in sight at the same moment.' In the 'White Highlands' there was unlimited hunting. At one point while stalking a wounded antelope they suddenly came upon a rhino, quietly grazing. 'I cannot describe to you the impression produced upon my mind by the sight of the grim black silhouette of this mighty beast – a survivor of prehistoric times – roaming in the plains as he & his forerunners had done since the dawn of the world.' But in this era of the white hunter, despite his awe Winston shot the rhino,* along with another smaller one they found nearby, as well as several lions. Later they rode to Embo, a new cattle station opened only months previously: 'We rode [twenty-six miles] through all this beautiful country . . . having nothing but what we stood up in & only a banana inside us . . . the two white officers there were properly astonished . . . to see us swoop down upon them with the night. But they gave us a most excellent dinner & we all slept on floors and chairs & blankets utterly but naturally tired. What a difference to the fag of a London day. My health bounds up with every day I spend in the open air . . . Joyous times.'[11]

Even the beauties of Kenya were later eclipsed by his impressions of Uganda. Here Winston met the boy-king, eleven-year-old Daudi Chwa, who, he wrote to Jennie, looked 'exactly like Consuelo in his expression'. He commented in a short postscript on his youthful stepfather's financial difficulties: 'George ought not to gamble.'[12]

Consuelo had returned to England for Christmas, which she had arranged to spend with Sunny's cousin Rose and her husband Matthew Ridley† at their comfortable Elizabethan manor, Blagdon,‡

---

*An image of him with the rhino was used on the front jacket of his book about the East African journey.

†Matthew White, Lord Ridley (1874–1916), married in 1899 Winston's first cousin the Honourable Rosamund (Rose) Guest, youngest daughter of Viscount Wimborne and Lady Cornelia (Guest née Spencer Churchill).

‡The Blagdon estate, Northumberland, has been in the Ridley family since the seventeenth century. One famous family member was Bishop Ridley, the scholar who was burnt at the stake by Bloody Mary in 1555 and to whom Bishop Hugh Latimer addressed the words: 'Play the man, Master Ridley. We shall this day light such a candle by God's Grace in England as I trust shall never be put out.'

ten miles north of Newcastle upon Tyne. Jennie, George and Jack had also been invited, but when Jennie heard Consuelo was to be one of the party, she was not particularly enthusiastic.[13] She had only seen Consuelo at a distance since her return from the United States, and she was looking remarkably well, Jennie wrote, indeed quite chubby for Consuelo. Where Sunny would spend the holidays, Jennie had no idea. She had heard he was trying to let Blenheim and felt that he might as well try to let a white elephant.[14] Then Consuelo announced she would not be able to go to Blagdon if Jennie was also there, and Jennie immediately cancelled, as did Jack.[15] 'It really is too idiotic,' Jack wrote angrily to Winston. In the event Jennie and Jack joined Sunny, F.E. Smith* and a few other guests hastily gathered together for a quiet Christmas at Blenheim where, 'looking thin and seedy', Sunny confided to Jennie that he was terribly lonely.

Meanwhile, from East Africa Winston's party travelled by train and steamer to Khartoum, which he had last seen when he participated in the cavalry charge at Omdurman. The four men arrived in high spirits on 23 December, but within hours Winston's manservant George Scrivings became seriously ill and had to be rushed to hospital. He sank rapidly and died the following day of choleric dysentery, which devastated Winston, who wrote to Jack that it had 'cast a gloom over all the memories of this . . . wonderful journey . . . We passed a miserable day, and I had him buried in the evening with full military honours as he had been a Yeoman. The Dublin Fusiliers sent their band and a company of men and we all walked in procession to the cemetery as mourners, while the sun sank over the desert, and the band played that beautiful funeral march.'[16] To Jennie, who had been notified immediately by cable of the unexpected death, fell the unenviable task of breaking the tragic news to Mrs Scrivings.

---

*F.E. Smith (1872–1930), always called 'F.E.', had served as a Yeomanry officer with Winston in the Oxfordshire Light Hussars (before Winston was posted to the 4th Queen's Own Hussars) and was a brilliant lawyer, MP and wit. Although they were often politically opposed – F.E. was a protectionist – the two men were the best of friends and gambled, drank and dined together. He was created Viscount Birkenhead in 1921; he introduced Winston to Max Beaverbrook.

Jennie was working on a new literary project at this time: her memoirs, entitled *Reminiscences of Lady Randolph Churchill*, which skate so lightly over her life as to be virtually useless to modern researchers. 'Cleverly but cautiously written,' George Cornwallis-West recalled; 'there was not a line in it to which any of her many friends could take exception.'[17] She sent chapters to Winston to vet from time to time, but he was a brutal editor for a first-time author. About the chapter on George Goschen ('the forgotten man' in the matter of Lord Randolph's resignation) he advised frankly that he did not think it could be published in the manner his mother had written it without giving offence: 'It would cause a great deal of offence, not only to the Goschens but to Jews generally.' On another occasion he simply scribbled a bald 'No' alongside a paragraph of political reminiscences. Jennie bristled – the book was still 'in the rough', she said, and would never have been sent to the publishers in the form in which he saw it. But Jennie's life had been gossiped about for so long that as soon as it was published it became a bestseller, and it brought in some much needed income at a difficult time, for George had recently been swindled out of a large sum of money by a crooked stockbroker.

Winston and Sunny met in Paris on the homeward leg of his East African tour in mid-January 1908. Scrivings's death had made Winston very depressed. His manservant had not eaten anything that the others had not also eaten, and although it could have happened to any of them Winston felt miserably responsible. 'I cannot bear to think of his wife & children looking forward to his return,' he wrote to Jennie. 'Letters [arriving from him] by every post and then this horrible news . . . I must from ever-straitening resources make some provision for her future.'[18]

As usual Winston relied on his pen to bolster his ever-straitening resources. From his notes of the trip he produced articles totalling thirty-five thousand words for the *Strand* magazine, which more than covered his expenses; and within months he published a book containing sixty photos called *My African Journey*, which has seldom been out of print since its first publication. But the benefit was not merely personal – Winston returned bursting with ideas

and plans to help the countries he had visited, including an exten-
sion of the rail link into the African interior.

He had purchased his first house at 12 Bolton Street in 1905, and
as an economy he had let it for six months while he was away. It was
not yet available, and the Ridleys (perhaps to make up for the
Christmas clash of Consuelo and Jennie) loaned him their London
flat in Carlton House Terrace for a few months so that his work
could resume as soon as he arrived back in London. He attended
the House of Commons almost every day, ran the Colonial Office,
wrote numerous personal letters, lunched and dined regularly with
friends and political contacts, wrote his articles and worked on his
book. His output was prodigious; his name was never out of the
newspapers. Although he had his critics, he was not generally
unpopular. He was never at rest on account of his conviction that
he would not live to an old age but was meant to make a mark on
history, so he regarded time as his enemy. He told more than one
person, 'We Churchills die young, and I want to put something
more on the slate.'[19] To his family, though, he had truly picked up
his father's baton, and all believed it was merely a matter of time
before he was given a Cabinet post. To Jennie, who adored powerful men, the son who had been largely ignored as a child had now
become her *raison d'être*.

Some weeks after Winston's return to England, Prime Minister
Campbell-Bannerman* was forced to retire after a heart attack. He
was succeeded by the former Chancellor of the Exchequer,
H.H. Asquith, who recognised that Winston's ability and energy
could not be overlooked. Asquith offered him a choice: the
Admiralty without a Cabinet seat, or the Local Government Board
which carried a Cabinet post. Winston replied that while he
wished more than anything to have a Cabinet post he would prefer
to stay in the Colonial Office working under Elgin than move to
the LGB:

---

*Sir Henry Campbell-Bannerman (1836–1908), a Liberal, was the first man to be called 'Prime
Minister'. Before this the leader of the party in power was known as First Lord of the Treasury
(which is still the formal title of the Prime Minister). Bannerman served from December 1905
until his resignation on 3 April 1908. He died three weeks later.

There is no place in the Government more laborious, more anxious, more thankless, more choked with petty & even squalid detail, more full of hopeless and insoluble difficulties . . . I would rather continue to serve under Lord Elgin at the Colonial Office without a seat in the Cabinet than go there . . . Five or six first-class questions await immediate attention – Housing, Unemployment, Rating Reform, Electoral Reform, Old Age pensions administration . . . On all of these I [should] be confronted by hundreds of earnest men who have thought of nothing else all their lives, who know these subjects – as I know military & Colonial things – from experience learned in hard schools, or else men who have served for many years on local bodies.[20]

He went on to outline the sort of reforms he would want to make concerning the exploitation in the workplace – and even in the Army – of teenage boys, and concerning maximum standard working hours for unskilled labour, matters upon which he felt strongly. But he insisted: 'I am sure you will find people much better qualified than I for service in this arena. No condition personal to myself shall prevent me serving you where you wish.'[21] The Admiralty, Winston wrote longingly, was the most glittering prize, and he yearned for it, but he felt he could not accept it because the post was presently held by his uncle, Lord Tweedmouth.

A week later, however, on 10 April, he accepted the post of President of the Board of Trade. Asquith advised that he could not offer an increased salary for the time being, at which Winston prudently renounced any increase at all – a gesture eagerly accepted by Asquith and later ruefully regretted by Winston. Asquith's wife Margot wrote remarkably frankly to the thirty-three-year-old Winston:

There are a few moments in life when unwilling decisions seem forced on one. I know them well, they make one feel sick & rebellious but I've had luck with mine. I knocked a great love out of my life to make room for a great character & do you suppose we ever

reminding her how kind her great-aunt had been, bringing her out into Society at her own expense. Meanwhile, at 12 Bolton Street Winston was soaking in his bath, having decided that dinner at Lady St Helier's would be a bore and he had better things to do with his evening. When Eddie Marsh found him there, he reminded him how helpful Lady St Helier had been to him over Omdurman and how ungenerous it would be now to let her down at the last minute. Winston reluctantly got dressed, and presented himself an hour late at Lady St Helier's door, full of apologies.

Although everyone had reached a main course by then, his place at the table had been left empty, between the guest of honour Lady Lugard (wife of Sir Frederick Lugard, a noted African explorer) and Clementine Hozier. As soon as he saw her, Winston determined not to appear an idiot to this woman, whose beauty had struck him dumb at their first meeting. To Clementine's embarrassment, after Winston was seated he spent the entire time talking to her, ignoring Lady Lugard, who had been invited especially for Winston's benefit. But Clementine succumbed totally to his brilliant conversation. He set out to charm her, and she was charmed. He made one mistake – he promised to send her a copy of his biography of his father, and evidently forgot. She thought badly of him for this, not realising that one of the most exciting periods in his life was unfolding.

If the book slipped his mind in this drama-packed week, his dinner partner had not, and a few days later Winston asked his mother to invite Clementine to Salisbury Hall. The date arranged was that pivotal weekend in April when he was appointed to head the Board of Trade. And it was the only date available for Clementine and her mother; they were leaving on the Monday for a six-week trip to the Continent. Lady St Helier warned Natty Hozier she was 'mad' to let her daughter go away when Winston was so obviously showing an interest in her, but the trip was not merely a holiday. They were to collect Clementine's younger sister Nellie, who had been receiving treatment for tuberculosis in a German clinic. During their brief time together that Sunday at Salisbury Hall the couple hit it off, and although Winston was already involved in the by-election and in taking over his new department, he made time to write a long letter to her on Thursday 16 April from 12 Bolton Street:

> I am back here for a night and a day in order to 'kiss hands' on appointment, & I seize this fleeting hour of leisure to write & tell you how much I liked our long talk on Sunday, and what a comfort & pleasure it was to me to meet a girl with so much intellectual quality & such strong reserves of noble sentiment. I hope we shall meet again and come to know each other better and like each other more: and I see no reason why this should not be so. Time passes quickly and the six weeks you are to be abroad will soon be over . . . Meanwhile I will let you know from time to time how I am getting on here in the storm.[23]

He invited her to write to him, and she did, ten days later: 'If it were not for the excitement of reading about Manchester every day in the belated newspapers I should feel as if I were living in another world than the delightful one we inhabited together for a day at Salisbury Hall.'[24]

Usually, by tacit agreement, in such circumstances the Opposition party did not contest a by-election seat. But in the 1908 by-election at Manchester the Tories had nothing to lose and everything to gain by throwing all their resources into the contest to defeat Winston. It was their first opportunity to regain some credibility after the rout of 1906, when seven Tory grandees including their leader, Balfour, had lost their seats. Furthermore, there was entrenched hostility towards Winston on the part of many senior Tories, who still regarded him as a traitor. It was a contest hard-fought on both sides, and against all expectations the Tories won by a majority of 429 votes. The reasons were complex but apparently the nine hundred Catholic voters in Manchester were a significant factor: an imminent but ill-fated Education Bill threatened the closure of Catholic schools (as well as some Church of England ones), and they were persuaded at the last minute not to vote for Churchill.

Winston's defeat was a triumph for the Conservatives, and they made the most of it. Elated Tory supporters sold 'Churchill memory cards' in Manchester. But one staunch Liberal, offered one of these, responded: 'It's a little too soon for that, my friend, you have not done with Mr Churchill yet. We have lost him for Manchester, like we lost John Bright before my time, but he will be a great figure in English politics . . . Manchester will be sorry for what she has done today.'[25] Meanwhile, Parliament and the Stock Exchange buzzed with the joke: 'What is the use of a WC without a seat.'

Winston wrote to Clementine on 27 April that he had been comforted by the knowledge that she had followed his fortunes from afar with sympathy. 'It was a vy hard contest & but for those sulky Irish Catholics changing sides at the last moment under priestly pressure, the result would have been different. Now I have to begin all over again – probably another long & exhausting election. Is it not provoking!'[26] Subsequently he was offered a safe seat at Dundee, where the incumbent had been elevated to the peerage. Safe or not, given the result at Manchester and the interest that fight had aroused in the newspapers, the other parties put up opponents so that it became a four-way fight, and – as Winston forecast – an exhausting business. In his rousing speeches he launched fierce attacks on the Tories: 'old doddering peers, cute financial magnates, clever wire pullers . . . all the enemies of progress . . . weaklings, sleek, smug, comfortable, self-important individuals'. His appearances were attended by thousands of appreciative voters who seemed not to realise that many of the people he spoke of were his own relatives. But they could applaud his intention of 'unfurling the old flag of civil freedom and social justice under which your fathers conquered, under which you, in your turn, will be unconquerable'. Driven to his best performances by the sting of his recent defeat, he was said by the *Manchester Guardian* to have evoked with his magnificent oratory the great days of Gladstone. And on 9 May he polled a convincing majority of votes over the Conservative candidate.* Winston was back on track and he could now take his place in the Cabinet.

By now Jack had persuaded his senior stockbroking partner to

---

*Churchill (Liberal) 7079; Baxter (Conservative) 4370; Stuart (Labour) 4014; Scrymgeour (Prohibition) 655.

guarantee him a salary (including bonuses) of £1000 a year, and together with the £400 allowance from his father's trust he was able to persuade Goonie's father that they could, with prudent management, live respectably on this. It was agreed that there would be both a civil and a Catholic ceremony. During the early nineteenth century Catholic services alone did not satisfy all the legal requirements, and it was still common practice by Catholics well into the twentieth century either to have a registrar present in church or to hold a civil service as well as a church service, so as to satisfy the civil authorities. The wedding was planned for 7 August. In keeping with their financial status it was not to be a grand affair.

A few months earlier Jennie had written to Winston about Jack, saying now that her younger son had 'gone off' she supposed that he, Winston, would soon get married, as that was often what happened in families. Sure enough, Winston already had the matter very much in mind. Clementine's cool English beauty, her presence, simplicity and intelligence entranced him. It seemed to him that it would be appropriate to propose to her at Blenheim, which he regarded as his ancestral home. On the day of Jack's wedding he wrote to her:

> This is only to be a line to tell you how much I am looking forward to seeing you on Monday. But I have a change of plan to propose wh. I hope you will like. Let us all go to Blenheim for Monday and Tuesday & then go on, on Wednesday to Salisbury Hall. Sunny wants us all to come & my mother will look after you – & so will I . . .
>
> Jack has been married today – *civilly*. The [church] service is tomorrow at Oxford: but we all swooped down in motor cars upon the little town of Abingdon and did the deed before the Registrar – for all the world as if it were an elopement – with [Goonie's] irate parents panting on the path . . . Afterwards . . . back go bride and bridegroom to *their respective homes* until tomorrow. Both were 'entirely composed' & the business was despatched with a celerity & ease that was almost appalling.[27]

In this letter he also reported that the previous night, while staying at Freddie and Amy Guest's house, Burley-on-the-Hill near

Oakham in Leicestershire, a fire had broken out. Much damage was done to the seventeenth-century mansion and the occupants were lucky to escape with their lives. Dressed in his pyjamas and overcoat and a fireman's helmet, Winston had directed operations standing on the tiny (and inadequate) fire engine that had rushed from Oakham: 'My eyes smart still & writing is tiring,' he wrote. Most pictures and valuable items of furniture perished but Winston had lost nothing, having instructed his servant to throw everything out of the window as soon as he was roused; but Eddie Marsh lost all his papers, his entire wardrobe – even his watch, a family heirloom – 'through not packing up when I told him . . . It was vy lucky that the fire was discovered before we had *all* gone to sleep – or more life might have been lost than one canary bird.'[28]

Clementine had seen in the papers that the house had burned down: 'My heart stood still with horror,' she wrote. She was in Cowes for the Regatta – just as Jennie and Lord Randolph had been thirty-five years earlier – when she received the cable from Sunny inviting her to Blenheim. Clementine was at first reluctant to go directly from Cowes to Blenheim since she did not have an appropriate wardrobe with her (she would later recall that she was down to her last cotton frock) and she had no maid. Winston's plans looked as though they might be scuppered, but he replied to her cable with another: 'I do hope your reluctance is only due to not quite understanding the change [of plan] and fancying there was to be a great function or to very naturally requiring some more formal invitation, & not to any dislike of Sunny . . . perhaps on imperfect information . . . He is my greatest friend, & it would grieve me very much if that were so. . . . You know the answer I want to this. Always yours, W.'[29]

Clementine admitted that her reluctance was born only of shyness, and duly arrived at Blenheim on Monday 10 August. Winston was waiting for her at the railway station at Oxford, and at Blenheim Jennie acted as chaperone and provided a maid. Perhaps Jennie recalled her own awe when she first arrived at the great house, and her pretence at sophistication in the face of the cool reception she had received from Randolph's mother and sisters. Anyway, she was kind and motherly to Clementine.

Winston had made such a point, the day before, of asking Clementine to walk with him the following morning after breakfast that it was apparent to her that a proposal was on the cards. She must have lain awake that night working out what her reply would be. She had come down to breakfast expecting him to be waiting, but he was noticeable by his absence. Winston was never an early riser, but Clementine could be excused for having expected him, on that day at least, to make a special effort. She herself was always punctual. When breakfast was over and he had still not put in an appearance, she started to look annoyed and hint at returning to Cowes. Sunny, more attuned to feminine sensibilities than his cousin, immediately sent a servant to rouse Winston and tell him to come down at once before Clementine decided to leave. Then he suggested that she come for a short drive with him, to give Winston time to dress.

Eventually, the couple set off for their walk. When it began to rain they rushed to take shelter in an ornamental Greek temple a few hundred yards west of the palace. There, Winston proposed to Clementine and she accepted.

With characteristic enthusiasm, he swept her along; they must get married at once – no need for a long engagement. He agreed, however, that they should keep the matter secret until Clementine's mother had been informed, and that Clementine would return to London the following day by train to tell her. Plans made, they left the little temple, and as they walked across the lawn they saw F.E. Smith coming from the house. Besides Jack and Sunny, he was probably Winston's best friend. Winston rushed up to him, threw his arms around him and, well within earshot of servants, announced his engagement. That was the end of the secret. It was hardly to be expected that he could have kept his feelings in check and not tell the other members of the Blenheim family. His letters to friends, telling them his news, so radiate with joy that there can be no doubting that this was a man in love and thrilled that his love was returned.

That night, Clementine sent Winston the first of a lifetime's love letters. It was a note containing the drawing of a heart with the word

'Winston' written in it. It was enough to make him rise early the next morning in order to write a fond response to her and pick a bunch of dew-drenched roses for her to take back to London. And after breakfast he wrote a letter for her to take to Lady Blanche Hozier:

> Clementine will be my ambassador today. I have asked her to marry me & we both ask you to give your consent and your blessing. You have known my family so many years that there is no need to say much in this letter. I am not rich nor powerfully established, but your daughter loves me . . . I think I can make her happy and give her a station & career worthy of her beauty and her virtues. Marlborough is very much in hopes that you will be able to come down here today & he is telegraphing to you this morning. That would indeed be very charming & I am sure Clementine will persuade you.

In the event this letter, the first of many he scribbled that morning, was not needed. When the engaged couple reached the station Winston could not bear to be parted from Clementine, so at the last minute as the train moved off he leapt aboard and accompanied her to London; then, task accomplished, he returned triumphantly to Blenheim that evening accompanied by his fiancée and her mother.

'Yesterday,' Lady Blanche wrote to Wilfrid Scawen Blunt from Blenheim, 'he came to London to ask my consent, and we all three came on here. Winston and I spoke of you and of your great friendship with his father. He is so like Lord Randolph, he has some of his faults, and all his qualities. He is gentle and tender, and affectionate to those he loves, much hated by those who have not come under his personal charm.'[30] Blunt noted in his diary: 'It is a good marriage for both of them.' To mark their engagement Clementine gave Winston a small gold heart with a ruby in the centre, to hang from his watch chain.

When Winston said they should not wait, he meant just that. It was important to have the wedding and honeymoon within the summer parliamentary recess, so he at once appointed his best man, his friend Linky Cecil (who proposed himself for the office), and the date of the wedding was fixed for 12 September, barely a month away. The two mothers, Blanche and Jennie, now had to organise a Society wedding – 'the wedding of the season' it would be called – in a very short time. The church they had in mind was found to be already booked, but a couple being married earlier that day obligingly moved their time forward at Winston's request, to allow the Churchill–Hozier marriage to be performed that afternoon.

One of the first letters Winston had written on the day after his engagement was to his first love: 'Pamela, I am going to marry Clementine & I say to you as you said to me when you married Victor – you must always be our best friend.' There is no record of Pamela's response – she was travelling in Norway, but her husband sent a cable: 'A thousand congratulations . . . I can wish you nothing better than to find in marriage all the happiness which it has brought to me.'[31] The signs were all good: '*Je t'aime passionément,*' Clementine wrote to her fiancé, adding that she felt less shy expressing herself in French.

Among the hundreds of congratulatory letters – from everyone in Society, it seems, from the King and Queen down – was one from Muriel Wilson, who had once turned him down because she thought he had no future. She wrote: '[Clementine] is so extraordinarily

beautiful I did not think you could help falling in love with her . . .
I only hope she realises *how* lucky she is . . . Bless you dear
Winston.'[32]

Winston evidently tried to persuade Sunny to attend the wedding with Consuelo, but Sunny made it clear there was no chance
of that. Although the news had given him great pleasure, he said,
he felt he could not – in his own sad circumstances – stand the pain
of witnessing his cousin's happiness at the ceremony and so: 'Alas,
I shall be unable to be present at your wedding . . . I hope you will
allow me to spare myself the mingled pleasure and pain of such a
ceremony . . . I have made arrangements that [Blenheim] be at your
disposal from the date of your wedding until you wish to journey
elsewhere.'

Halfway through the frantic preparations, despite writing frequently of how passionately she loved Winston, Clementine
considered calling the whole thing off. Her brother Bill stepped in
to remind her firmly that she had already broken off one engagement and that as head of the family (he was twenty, and a naval
officer) he could not allow her to embarrass such an important
public figure as Winston. This steadied her, and the plans went
ahead – Winston may not even have heard of it until long after the
marriage. But Clementine was not alone in suffering from nerves.
Jennie apparently took it upon herself to prepare her son because
he was anxious about the sexual aspect of marriage. Winston was a
romantic, never a womaniser. This was not an era when promiscuity
among unmarried people flourished anyway, and although he may
not have been a virgin on his marriage (few men returned in that
state after service in India), he could not have been described as
experienced. It seems he asked Jennie's advice on the subject, probably because he was concerned about Clementine. Or maybe Jennie
raised it, worried that the highly strung Clementine might need
special consideration on her wedding night.

Wilfrid Scawen Blunt, one-time lover of the bride's mother,
described the wedding day in his diary: 'It was quite a popular
demonstration. [With] Lord Hugh Cecil Winston's best man, and
the great crowd of relations, not only the Church [St Margaret's,

Westminster*] was full, but all Victoria Street . . . I arrived late when all the seats were taken, but Blanche Hozier found me one in the family pew . . . the bride was pale, as was the bridegroom. He has gained in appearance since I saw him last, and has a powerful if ugly face. Winston's responses were clearly made in a pleasant voice, Clementine's inaudible.'[33] The bride wore a high-waisted ivory satin gown, and among her five bridesmaids were her sister Nellie, her cousin Venetia Stanley and Winston's cousin Clara Frewen. Seated among the eight hundred guests, family, friends and political colleagues, was Clementine's uncle (and perhaps her natural father), Bertie Mitford. And as a very special wedding gift to Winston, Sunny and Consuelo Marlborough attended, sitting together with their elder son between them. Among the wedding gifts the couple found twenty-two silver inkstands.

They left by train for Blenheim in a private compartment, and as the train slowly pulled out of the station Winston took his bride in his arms. When they next looked up it was to find that their train had halted and another was slowly passing alongside, from which a stream of fascinated passengers were gazing at them.

From Blenheim next morning Winston sent his mother a note: 'Everything is vy comfortable and satisfactory in every way . . . & Clemmie [is] vy happy and beautiful . . . there was no need for any anxiety. She tells me she is writing you a letter. Best of love my dearest Mama. You were a great comfort & support to me at a critical period . . . we have never been so near together so often in a short time. God Bless you! What a relief to have got that ceremony over! & so happily.' He opened the letter to add a generous post-script: 'George said he could wish me no better wife, or happier days, than he had found in you.'[34]

A week later he wrote to say they had done little at Blenheim except to loiter and love there – 'a serious occupation,' he added.[35]

---

*The parish church of the House of Commons.

1908–14

The Next Generation

Churchill once wrote: 'I married and lived happily ever after-wards.'[1] From the start his marriage was a success, and the romantic in Winston was boyishly thrilled with his beautiful bride whom he habitually called Kitten, Cat or Kat, while she called him her Pug or Pig, and they would continue to do so throughout their long lives. And it was a marriage of opposites, for Clementine was reserved and austere, while Winston was outgoing, bombastic and self-confident. Perhaps one reason for the success was that Clementine accepted that Winston's main life was away from home and that her role was to provide a restful and secure environment for him when he returned. They always had separate bedrooms, and often sent each other loving notes before rising. When they were apart they wrote to each other, and these notes and letters record the bond between them.

Neither had ever come first with anyone before they married, and they blossomed emotionally with each other. Like all couples they would encounter difficulties from time to time, but it is clear that, like Winston's famous ancestors John and Sarah Churchill, these two people remained in love for the rest of their lives. A friend wrote after their deaths, 'No woman would have found it easy to be married to Winston . . . despite his devotion and his affectionate nature . . . she was . . . sufficiently self-assured to be able to cope with his demands and his idiosyncrasies.'[2] Clementine adored

Winston above anyone else on earth. She furnished their various homes with exquisite taste, made them comfortable and efficient as well as beautiful. But life with Clementine was not always easy, Jock Colville said: 'Her standards were consistently high and her husband, her children, her friends and her domestic staff often fell short of them. She could then display an acidity of tongue before which the tallest trees would bend, and she would occasionally give vent to uncontrollable temper. The storms were terrifying in their violence, but the more usual calms were beautiful and serene.'[3]

One immediate effect of the marriage was that Winston used Clementine as his sounding board, confidante and emotional support, which largely cut Jennie out of the picture. From his entry into the Army until his marriage, Jennie had been the biggest single influence in her son's life (indeed, she had always been so if one counts the one-sided relationship of the child adoring the all-too-often absent mother). But though Winston remained devoted to Jennie and still consulted her about important issues from time to time, their once close relationship naturally tailed off.

After the honeymoon the couple moved into Winston's bachelor flat, which Winston had asked Jennie to redecorate as a surprise homecoming for his bride. But Jennie's taste, 'sateen and muslin covers trimmed with bows', was too florid for Clementine – indeed, so was Jennie, whose lifestyle too closely resembled her own mother's for Clementine to approve of her. For the moment, she made the new bride's attempt to get on with her mother-in-law but privately, as she later told her daughter Mary, she thought Jennie's taste vulgar (and the covers cheap and tawdry).[4] In the early months of 1909, when they knew that Clementine was to have a child, due in July, the Churchills bought a lease on a family house at 33 Eccleston Square. There, Clementine, only ever called 'Clemmie' by her intimates, was careful to insist upon choosing her own interior design.

While Clementine created their new home, Winston was working harder than ever. At the Board of Trade he had succeeded Lloyd George (who had gone to the Exchequer), and he intended to carry on with his predecessor's programme of welfare – the forerunner of the welfare state, in fact. Among Winston's immediate problems was a series of dock strikes in the main ports; he was also concentrating on legislation to standardise working hours in the 'sweated labour' trades of tailoring and dressmaking as well as stevedores. Later, it would remain a source of pride to Churchill that he had helped lay the foundations of state-funded old-age pensions and unemployment insurance, but at the time he and the Chancellor were pushed to fund these laudable aims. It was done by raising death duties and imposing punitive taxes on alcohol, tobacco and petrol, and an even more controversial 'land duty'. Middle- and upper-class landowners were appalled at the harshness of these measures and Winston received frantic appeals from his closest relatives. 'I suggest death duties should not be made retrospective but that past transactions, carried on in good faith under the law and often embodied in marriage settlements, should be respected,' wrote his cousin Ivor Guest, who sent figures to prove that if he paid all the new taxes he would not be able to keep his estate; yet nor, by the law of entail, was he able to sell it. So angry was Ivor that Winston worried he might resign his parliamentary seat. Considering his social milieu, his remarks to his mother on these taxes are interesting: 'I never saw people make such fools of themselves as all these Dukes and Duchesses are doing. One after another they come up threatening to cut down charities and pensions, sack old labourers and retainers, and howling and whining because they are asked to pay their share, as if they were being ruined.'[5] Perhaps Winston's crusade was even more difficult for Jennie, who spent all her time with those who would be most affected by the proposed land duty. Unfortunately, her response does not survive.

Between selling the flat at Bolton Street and the completion of works in the Eccleston Square house, Clementine lodged at the Carlton House Terrace flat of Freddie and Amy Guest, spent the month of April at Blenheim, and visited her cousins the Stanleys at Alderney. She was at Blenheim when Winston was in the thick of a fight with the unions, and she wrote appealingly that she was missing him: 'Do try & come down here tomorrow instead of Friday – it is perfectly lovely but I can't enjoy it properly without you, whereas Lloyd George can quite well manage his Disestablishment Bill alone.'[6] Their letters now began to be illustrated with cartoons of pug dogs and cats – appropriately pregnant in Clementine's case.

On 30 May there was family news to report. 'Jack and Goonie have had a son,'* Winston wrote:

> . . . Jack like a little turkey-cock with satisfaction. 'Alone I did it', sort of air. It seems to have been a most smooth & successful affair. Goonie dined out, walked home [and] slept soundly until 2. Then felt premonitory sensations . . . and at 4 or 5 all was gloriously over . . . she hardly had any pain. My dear Bird – this happy event will be a great help to you & will encourage you. *I* rather shrink from it – because I don't like your having to bear pain & face this ordeal. But we are in the grip of circumstances, and out of pain joy will spring & from passing weakness new strength arise.[7]

Clementine replied confidently: 'It is wonderful Goonie having her Baby so easily – I feel it is *nothing* now & only wish there was not another month to wait.'[8]

The couple's first child, Diana, who immediately became 'the puppy kitten' (and often 'the P.K.'), was born on 11 July 1909. The healthy baby remained in London with father and nanny, while Clementine went to convalesce with her mother and sister and brother at a seaside cottage belonging to Wilfrid Scawen Blunt. It was 'wild, savage and altogether delightful', she wrote, and 'the Kat' was being waited on hand and foot by her family and servants so that she was 'purring loudly – occasionally she gives a plaintive mew for her Pug and PK (especially for her Pug) but except for that she is very happy'. In fact, although Winston had determined that his children would never suffer the neglect that he and Jack had experienced, Clementine would always put her husband ahead of her children in her list of priorities.

In September Winston was invited by the Kaiser to attend

---

*John George Spencer Churchill.

German Army manoeuvres, which meant that Clementine was staying alone at Alderney with her Stanley cousins on their first wedding anniversary. 'My darling,' she wrote, 'how I wish we were together – it is just 5 o'clock. This time last year we were steaming out of Paddington on our way to Blenheim – The Pug was reading an account of the wedding . . . aloud to the Kat! Then the Pug embraced the Kat, but unfortunately another train was just passing us quite slowly & its occupants caught him in the very act.'[9] On the same day he wrote to her from Strasbourg: 'A year today my lovely white pussy-cat came to me . . . my precious & beloved Clemmie my earnest desire is to enter still more completely into your dear heart & nature & to curl myself up in your darling arms. I feel so safe with you.'[10]

These military manoeuvres could not be other than fascinating. Here was a man whose favourite toys had been armies of model soldiers which he had drilled and endlessly manoeuvred into the precise formations of the Battle of Blenheim and other set-piece conflicts fought by his ancestor the 1st Duke, and who grew up surrounded by tapestries and other images of John Marlborough leading his forces on a rearing horse with guns blazing. Winston was rapt by what he saw in Germany, especially when they visited the battle site of Blenheim ('Sunny should make this pilgrimage,' he wrote to Clementine). But more importantly he now saw at first hand the military might the Kaiser had created, and in view of his later career it is worth noting his reaction. 'This army is a terrible engine,' he wrote. 'It marches sometimes 35 miles in a day. It is in number as the sands of the sea – & with all the modern conveniences . . . Much as war attracts me & fascinates my mind with its tremendous situations – I feel more deeply every year . . . what vile & wicked folly & barbarism it all is.'[11]

Jennie's fortunes looked up somewhat that month. She had been through a rough time during the previous two years. Her marriage to George was now punctuated by many arguments and several short separations. There are a number of notes extant from that period in which George apologises to her for misdemeanours that have upset her and driven him away. His sister, Princess Daisy, knew things were not going well for the couple; she wrote in her diary that Jennie was 'uncommonly nice and still very handsome' and that she loved George 'immensely . . . but of course the difference in age is a sad and terrible drawback (no babies possible)'.[12]

With Salisbury Hall still rented out to pay for its upkeep, Jennie attempted to economise after Winston's wedding by renting the Asquiths' London house in Cavendish Square, where she spent the winter trying to get a play she had written (called *His Borrowed Plumes*) on to the stage. She had tempted the legendary Mrs Patrick Campbell into producing it and playing the lead, but this was not enough to make the play a success. Not only was it a financial disaster but, to add to Jennie's distress, Mrs Patrick Campbell (Stella) began a love affair with George. In the spring of 1909 there had been word of Charles Kinsky, who had been widowed. She had seen him several times since his marriage, and once he and his wife had been to stay at Salisbury Hall. Jennie wrote a letter of condolence, but Kinsky's reply put an end to any secret hopes she might have nurtured that his wife's death would reopen their once passionate relationship.[13]

In August 1909 Jennie made a large profit on a house she had bought, redesigned and redecorated, then sold on. Although Clementine did not admire Jennie's taste in decor, she was in the minority; most people liked her ability to present a house in the manner of a modern show home. Winston, who had just helped to resolve a major coal strike, wrote cheerfully:

Dear Mama

I am so glad to hear of your excellent stroke of business. The utility of most things can be measured in terms of money. I do not believe in writing books which do not sell, or plays which do not pay. The only exceptions to the rule are productions which can really claim to be high art, appreciated only by the very few. Apart from that money value is a great test. And I think it very creditable indeed that you should be able after two or three months' work, which you greatly enjoyed, to turn over as large a sum of money as a Cabinet Minister can earn in a year . . . [He urged her to repeat the project]. . . your knowledge and taste are so good and your eye for comfort and elegance so well trained, that with a little capital you ought to be able to make a lot of money and if you sell a few more houses, you will be able, very nearly, to afford to produce another play. I am sure George admires your great cleverness over this house as much as I do.[14]

He, Clementine, Jack and Goonie and the babies, he told her, were all off to Blenheim for two or three weeks. Jennie, meanwhile, set off for France on a spending spree. Buying new gowns always cheered her up. At the end of the family vacation Winston had to go to Dundee to deal with some constituency matters. His speeches were coming under pressure from suffragettes and it was clear he was still being targeted by them. Winston was not opposed to women's suffrage, as already noted, and he never voted against it. But he could not bring himself to support the movement because he despised the tactics and behaviour of the militants, which seemed to him to be beneath contempt. There can be no question where Clementine's sympathy lay, confirmed in a letter Winston wrote to her in October 1909:

I hope you will not be very angry with me for having answered the suffragettes sternly. I shall never try to crush your convictions [but] I must claim an equal liberty for myself. I have told them I cannot help them while the present tactics are continued. I am sorry for them. The feeling here is vy hot against them. The women's meeting I addressed later – 1500 – absolutely orderly & enthusiastic – was unanimous against the rowdyism. The Women's Lib[eral] Association has doubled its membership in the last 12 months. They were full of solicitude for you: & I told them you would be at their head on the day of battle. My sweet cat – my heart goes out to you tonight. I feel a vivid realisation of all you are to me; & of the good & comforting influence you have brought into my life. It is a much better life now.[15]

That their marriage was a success is evident from the affectionate remarks that peppered his letters: 'I would so much like to take you in my arms all cold & gleaming from your bath . . . Sweet Kat – I kiss your soul.'[16] Yet the short separations began to tell on Clementine's imagination and – perhaps understandably, given the world in which they moved – she tackled her husband about what he did during his frequent periods away from her. Winston was shocked and upset by her 'wounding doubts':

> Dearest, it worries me vy much that you should seem to nurse such absolutely wild suspicions wh. are so dishonouring to all the love & loyalty I bear you, & please God will bear you while I breathe. They are unworthy of you and me. And they fill my mind with feelings of embarrassment to which I have been a stranger since I was a schoolboy . . . they depress and vex me – & without reason. We do not live in a world of small intrigues, but of serious & important affairs . . . you ought to trust me for I do not love & will never love any woman in the world but you . . . your sweetness and beauty have cast a glory upon my life.[17]

Soon after this letter was written, in mid-November, the couple had just alighted from a train at Great Western Station in Bristol when a suffragette wielding a whip leapt out of the crowd and attacked Winston. She grabbed his coat and hit him in the face shouting, 'Take that you brute. I'll show you what Englishwomen can do.'* Brandishing the whip again, she drove him backwards on the platform in an attempt to force him on to the line in the path of an oncoming train. It happened so quickly that both Winston and the men in his party were taken by surprise, but Clementine – her senses sharpened at the imminent danger to her beloved Pug – jumped over a pile of luggage and pulled him away from the edge of the platform to safety.[18]

In the early months of 1910 a general election was in the offing,

---

*When Theresa Garnett was arrested, she defiantly countered: 'Has it hurt him much?' Christabel Pankhurst excused her behaviour: 'Moved by the spirit of pure chivalry, Miss Garnett took what she thought to be the best available means of avenging the insult done to womanhood by the Government to which Mr. Churchill belongs.' Churchill did not press charges, but Theresa Garnett was sentenced to a month in prison for disturbing the peace.

and perhaps because she was able to assist him in a practical way at last, Clementine felt happier than at any time since their marriage; in any event, there were no further expressions of doubt in her letters. Against the national trend Winston held his seat, and in the new government he was appointed Home Secretary, the youngest holder of that post since Sir Robert Peel.* So much did Clementine enjoy electioneering that when another Guest cousin, Henry, stood for Parliament in East Dorset and Winston could not be spared from his ministerial duties, Clementine went down to Canford to help Henry's campaign. Although she had made it her job to provide a home that was a place of refuge for Winston, Clementine was not a natural stay-at-home woman. Quick and intelligent, she too felt strongly about political matters and, like Consuelo, was strongly in favour of women's suffrage; but, like her husband, she could not support militant tactics. When a pompous article appeared in *The Times* opposed to giving the vote to women on grounds of psychological and physiological differences, Clementine's dry wit was shown to best advantage when she replied through the letters page, signing herself 'CSC':

Sir, After reading Sir Almroth Wright's able and weighty exposition of women as he knows them, the question seems no longer to be, 'Should women have votes?', but 'Ought women be abolished altogether?' I have been so much impressed . . . that I have come to the conclusion that women should be put a stop to. We learn from him that in their youth they are unbalanced, that from time to time, they suffer from unreasonableness and hyper sensitiveness . . . and . . . later in life they are subject to grave and long-continued mental disorders, and, if not quite insane, many of them have to be shut up. Now this being so, how much happier and better would the world not be if only it could be purged of women? . . . Is the case really hopeless? . . . Cannot science give us some assurance, or at least some ground of hope, that we are on the eve of the greatest discovery of all, ie: how to maintain a race of males by purely scientific means?[19]

*

*Peel was thirty-four when he first held the post in 1822. Churchill was thirty-five.

The end of the Marlborough marriage did not signal the end of Sunny's and Consuelo's troubles. Following the separation order the Duke was formally advised by the courtier and equerry Lord Knollys, writing on the instructions of the King, that henceforth neither he nor the Duchess should attend any form of entertainment where the King and Queen were likely to be present. In top circles this meant they were launched into the sort of social limbo that had stultified Jennie's and Lord Randolph's lives for so many years. Sunny felt the effects of exclusion more keenly than Consuelo, especially in his role of Knight of the Garter: now, after attending the occasional chapter meetings of the order at St George's Chapel, he had to slink away early while his companions went on to dine with the King. Seeing how much this depressed his cousin, Winston eventually used his influence to alleviate it. He wrote to the King:

> I venture to write to Your Majesty upon a private matter. It concerns my cousin the Duke of Marlborough. Owing to the fact that he and his wife are living apart neither is invited to the regular ceremonies of Your Majesty's court . . . But the Duke of Marlborough is a knight of the Garter. He has been summoned to attend the Chapter of the Order to be held at Windsor . . .
>
> On the last occasion when he obeyed this summons he was alone excepted and excluded from the entertainment in the Castle which followed the Service. Your Majesty will I am sure see that an incident of that character is wholly different from the general exclusion from Court functions . . . [and] the base press of the United States was filled with insulting references to the Duke and highly coloured accounts of his treatment at the Castle and a great deal of unkind comment was excited in London . . .[20]

The King agreed with Winston in the matter and an invitation to luncheon at the Castle was issued to the Duke. But, Lord Knollys wrote, 'he is sure the Duke of Marlborough will understand that in taking this step it must not be supposed that His Majesty proposes to abrogate the general rule, which affects him in regard to his coming to Court'.[21]

In the United States the Duke of Marlborough had become the epitome of caddish behaviour, a reputation that had even penetrated the White House. Theodore Roosevelt opined that 'the lowest note of infamy is reached by such a creature as this Marlborough, who proposing to divorce the woman when *he* at least cannot afford to throw any stone at her, nevertheless proposes to keep and live on the money she brought him.'[22] All public sympathy was with Consuelo. Her friends, her parents and their new spouses, and even Goosie her mother-in-law and Sunny's sisters, rallied round her at Sunderland House to bolster her. Although she could not attend any royal functions, she was not short of invitations. In her diary (kept at the suggestion of Prime Minister Asquith) in 1908 she wrote: 'Every night one is bidden to three or more balls. Today there were six parties.'[23] But since leaving Sunny, a more serious side of Consuelo's nature had come to the fore. She threw herself into philanthropic ventures aimed at helping poor women, and by 1907 she had become deeply committed to women's suffrage – though she too was in favour of a conservative approach to gaining the vote, 'rather than in the distressing exhibitions of martyrdom . . . typified by Mrs Pankhurst in gaol being forcibly fed'.[24] She believed that such behaviour demeaned women and could ultimately cost them the possibility of success in England.

In 1908 she interested her mother in this cause, little knowing at the time that Alva would take up the banner and become a leading fighter for women's suffrage in the United States (what, in fact, Alva has become best known for). Unsuspected by Consuelo, in the years that followed, Alva became one of the main financial supporters of the Pankhursts and the WSPU. She had them to stay at her house in France on several occasions when they were in danger of arrest in England, or to recuperate after spells in prison. On one occasion the thirty-two-year-old Christabel spent the entire summer with Alva, and when Consuelo paid a visit she could not help noticing that they got on together more amicably than did she herself with her mother. As a result of that visit, while constantly maintaining her support for women's emancipation, Consuelo publicly distanced herself from the militancy of the Pankhursts and made a

statement to that effect in the American press. However, that did
not prevent her from appearing, at her mother's request, at a high-
powered suffrage rally organised by Alva at Marble House in
Newport. Alva knew that Consuelo would not only command press
acreage, but would provoke interest in those women who had been
distanced from the cause by militancy.

Meanwhile in London, Consuelo had her literary admirers, who
could be counted on to keep her amused at dinner parties: H.G.
Wells, George Bernard Shaw, W.B. Yeats, John Galsworthy – whose
Forsyte Saga was a bestseller of the day – and Sir James Barrie,
who told a friend of Consuelo, 'I would stand all day in the street to
see Consuelo Marlborough get into her carriage.'[25] The plain fact was
that for Consuelo, life was far happier outside her marriage than in it.

Sunny fared less well. He truly felt the stigma of his situation,
and he tried to cope with his misery by travelling. In 1907, after a
meeting in Venice with Winston, he made a long summer tour of
France accompanied, somewhat surprisingly, by Jennie and her
sister-in-law Daisy. Then, when Gladys Deacon moved to London
and took a flat in Savile Row,* gossip was rife about the relationship
between her and the Duke. But it was not until 1912 that they would
openly become lovers and travel together on holidays. Between these
trips, whenever it was Sunny's turn to have his sons the Duke lived
at Blenheim and Gladys lived in her Savile Row flat or at an apartment owned by her mother at 25 Quai Voltaire on Paris's Left Bank.
Because she was always surrounded by friends there, this was a way
of life more suited to Gladys, for though she was a snob she mixed
well in a wider range of society than did Sunny, and she was invariably drawn to the artists and writers of the *belle époque*. It was
noticeable that whenever he was with Gladys the Duke was happy
and outgoing, and that when they were apart he was morose, often
sliding into one of his habitual depressions. He yearned for the unattainable goal of marriage to Gladys. However, he was able to make
legal arrangements to ensure that she would be cared for financially
in the event that he died suddenly or accidentally.

---

*At number 11, over the premises of Huntsman the tailors.

Edward VII died in May 1910. Jennie, who had first met him as a young man in Cowes in 1873,* was very upset, and she knew it would change her life for ever. She wrote to the widowed Queen that the late King had shown her and her family the greatest kindness for thirty-five years and she had a host of pleasant memories to look back on. She said that he had not only been a great King but a lovable man.[26] Her own marriage struggled on: she was often in misery over George's extramarital flirtations, if not affairs. She constantly forgave him and welcomed him back, but after her play *Borrowed Plumes* closed and he departed with the great actress in full view of everyone, Jennie realised there was nothing left in the marriage for either of them. The beautiful Mrs Patrick Campbell was older than George, but only by twelve years to Jennie's twenty, and she was a widow, her late husband having died gallantly in battle during the South African War.

In August 1910 Jennie drafted a dispirited letter to George's mother Patsy Cornwallis-West in which she crossed out some telling phrases, such as 'There is much I could say but will refrain'. Patsy was already aware that she and George (Patsy's only son) had been experiencing difficulties because of his relationship with Mrs Patrick Campbell, Jennie wrote, and now she was prepared to let him have his freedom, to remarry if he wished and thought it would make him happy. She believed she had done her best in their marriage and failed. George blamed Jennie's extravagance for their financial difficulties, but she rejected this, saying that if their accounts were to be examined she would almost certainly be proved the less extravagant, although she admitted she had faults – her shortcomings were 'many' she wrote. Yet she swore she had always been totally faithful and loyal to George and she loved him more than anyone else on earth.[27] George handled the crisis by taking a long trip to Mexico. When in April 1911 he wrote asking if he could return to her, Winston – totally happy in his own marriage, so perhaps biased – advised her to welcome him if he returned of his own free will. George returned to the marital home – although,

---

*At Edward VII's coronation in 1902 Jennie had been seated in a private box with other ladies who were or had been 'special friends' of the new King. It was called 'the King's Loose Box'.

Winston reported to Clementine, 'He did not like my letter.' Clementine was unsure of the wisdom of advising George's return, saying that unless he behaved himself and made Jennie happy there wasn't much point in a reconciliation. Secure in Winston's affections, Clementine had begun to appreciate Jennie for her own sake, seeing beyond the lifestyle of her mother-in-law that had at first been so distasteful to her.

Winston survived both of the general elections of 1910, but with diminished majorities. His tenure at the office of Home Secretary was, on the one hand, enjoyable; he had much to occupy his mind and his abilities in what he believed were the best interests of his country. On the other hand, he was responsible for deciding the fate of condemned murderers. This caused him great anguish, in case any decision made by him should take the life of someone later found to be innocent. Much later in life he would confide to his daughter Diana, when she was suffering from depression, that he too suffered from what he famously termed 'the black dog', and that his first experience of it was while he was at the Home Office. None of his many letters of the time reflect this; rather, he appears from the surviving paperwork to have been just as confident and fulfilled as before. But in a letter to Clementine in July 1911 he mentions his 'black dog', telling her that Ivor Guest's wife Alice has just been successfully treated for depression by a German doctor: 'I think this man might be useful to me – if my black dog returns. He seems quite away from me now – It is such a relief. All the colours come back into the picture. Brightest of all your dear face – my Darling.'[28]

Winston met crises such as the South Wales miners' strike and the Sidney Street siege* head on, with aplomb and energy, despite

---

*A notorious gunfight in January 1911 between the police and a politically motivated gang of criminals under a leader known as 'Peter the Painter'. The gang had been tracked to their HQ at 100 Sidney Street in Stepney; they were known to have stocks of weapons and ammunition with which to fight off any attempt to arrest them. The gun battle began at dawn and lasted six hours, watched by Churchill. A heavy artillery gun had just been placed in position, on his orders, when the house caught fire. Suspecting a ruse, Churchill refused to allow the fire brigade to enter the building but the men made no attempt to escape. The remains of only two bodies were later recovered. Peter the Painter seemed to have somehow escaped. Churchill's action sparked a major political row.

a good deal of open criticism in the press. He was used to criticism, and could take it now that he had Clementine as his cushion against the world. He also had a small circle of trusted friends. The Tory politician, eminent lawyer and wit F.E. Smith was probably at that time closer even than Sunny, Ivor or Freddie Guest, for they shared many characteristics and political beliefs despite being in opposing parties. It would probably be fair to say that each sharpened his wits on the other. Together the two men founded a political dining club known as 'the Other Club'* – to dissociate it from 'the Club', the ancient and venerable dining society founded in 1764 by Sir Joshua Reynolds and Dr Johnson, but whose members had blackballed both Smith's and Winston's applications to join. Winston belonged to the Other Club until his death, and its high-spirited, intelligent conviviality was always a joy to him.

In the summer of 1911, coronation year, Clementine gave birth to another child. There was only one name for this much longed-for son: Randolph (although his parents usually referred to him as 'the Chumbolly', a word Winston had picked up in India which means 'a chubby happy child'). The new King's eldest son was invested as Prince of Wales, and Winston attended the ceremony in his official capacity to read out the patent. 'He is a vy nice boy,' he told Clementine of the future Edward VIII, 'quite simple, & terribly kept in order.'[29]

Winston was one of only a handful of men, including Lloyd George and F.E. Smith, in that hot and happy summer of celebration who gave much thought to the possibility of an imminent European war. He had been alerted when he was with the German Army on manoeuvres two years earlier, and had wondered why such might could be needed by a friendly nation. Now a frisson of suspicion resurfaced when the Kaiser sent a warship into the

---

*Founded 18 May 1911. The original membership was 12 Liberals, 12 Conservatives and 12 non-political 'distinguished outsiders'. Churchill is believed to have contributed rule 12: 'Nothing in the rules or intercourse of the Club shall interfere with the rancour or asperity of party politics.' Virtually every noted twentieth-century politician belonged to the club at one time or another – from Lloyd George to Oswald Mosley. It met fortnightly at the Savoy Hotel when Parliament was in session.

French-controlled Moroccan Atlantic port of Agadir in a show of force. Winston was both excited and disturbed by the affair. He fired off a flurry of warning letters, as well as writing a government paper on the subject: 'If Germany makes war on France . . . we should join France.' He was not in favour of carte blanche support of the French, but if Morocco was to be carved up between Germany and France he wanted Britain to have some say in the matter. As a Cabinet Minister he was involved in all the discussions although it was outside his remit as Home Secretary.

For years Winston had been advocating economies for the Royal Navy, but this had been based on the fact that Germany was largely seen as a friendly nation. Now the dangers in being outgunned by an unfriendly Germany were only too apparent. 'Are you sure,' he wrote to Asquith on 13 September 1911, 'that the ships we have at Cromarty are strong enough to defeat the whole German High Sea fleet? If not they shd be reinforced without delay. Are 2 divisions of the Home Fleet enough? This appears to be a vital matter.'[30] The incident at Agadir was serious enough to prompt Lloyd George to suggest it might be a pity if war did not now occur, and he told the shocked King as much when he visited him at Balmoral. Winston kept similar opinions to himself – after all, there were many family connections with Germany's royal house. But the paper he wrote on how and where a European war against Germany might be fought was so prescient that when it was recirculated three years later, in September 1914, Balfour wrote to Eddie Marsh that it was 'a triumph of prophecy'.[31] From the summer of 1911 on, Winston never lost sight of a possible war, and he gave considerable thought to such a likelihood.

The Moroccan incident passed over with nothing more than some ruffled diplomatic feathers, and soon afterwards Winston landed the post he had long coveted when Prime Minister Asquith appointed him First Lord of the Admiralty. He had a happy marriage, two healthy children, his beautiful Clementine and his new post: Winston's star was riding high. And not the least of his acquisitions was the yacht *Enchantress*, attached to the post. It was smaller than the royal yacht *Victoria and Albert* but built on the same lines, and Winston took full advantage of this privilege. During the next three years he spent a total of eleven months aboard the *Enchantress*. Much of the time he was visiting dockyards, naval sites and ships. But when the yacht was not required on Admiralty business the First Lord was allowed to entertain private guests at his own expense, so his family and friends such as the Asquiths and Lloyd George were invited to sail on her, and he made several long cruises in the Mediterranean and around Britain. But mainly Winston used the yacht as it was intended, as an essential means of permitting the First Lord of the Admiralty to be on intimate terms with the ships of the British Navy.

Another privilege that went with the post of Admiral of the Fleet was the right to live in Admiralty House, and Winston longed to live in a spacious house again. But for Clementine the proposition was more a worry than a treat. She was the one responsible for managing their domestic finances, and Winston always lived by his famous maxim, 'I am easily satisfied by the very best.' She knew they could not afford to live at Admiralty House, and for some time she was able to oppose Winston's wish to move there. Eventually he won the day, but with a compromise insisted upon by Clementine: the fourth floor would remain sealed off for the sake of economy. That meant they could run the house with only nine servants instead of twelve. And they must pull in their horns in other ways, too. Furnishings were supposed to be chosen from a Civil Service catalogue, which Clementine looked at and described as 'grim . . . I really think they ought to have a woman at the head of the office of Works – someone like your Mama'. (Her opinion of Jennie's interior design abilities seems to have undergone a U-turn.) Winston, aboard the *Enchantress* while the removal was happening, wrote: 'It will be nice coming back to the Admiralty . . . I am sure you will take to it when you get there. I am afraid it all means vy hard work for you – Poor lamb. But remember I am going to turn over my new leaf! That I promise – the only mystery is "What is written on the other side?" – It may be only "ditto, ditto"!'[32]

Winston was fascinated by new technology, and there was little from submarines to torpedoes and new forms of heavy artillery that did not come under his close scrutiny, so it was hardly surprising that the new science of flight excited his interest. Aviation was less than a decade old,* and aircraft in 1912–13 were still flimsy and highly unstable. Three years earlier Louis Blériot had made the first successful crossing of a body of water by flying across the English Channel, although aeroplanes were still renowned more for their crashes than their successes. But Winston recognised the military advantages of aerial reconnaissance and even of arming aircraft with guns. He began establishing an 'Air Department of the Admiralty', which initially met considerable opposition from the Treasury. But Winston insisted on it, pointing out that they could not afford to fall behind other countries in developing this potential new weapon. Out of this came the Royal Naval Air Service (RNAS), formed 'for the aerial protection of our naval harbours, oil tanks and vulnerable points', he wrote, 'and also for a general strengthening of our exiguous and inadequate aviation'.[33] Under his leadership in 1913 the first torpedo was dropped from a British plane, night flying was practised for the first time, and HMS *Hermes* was converted to carry floatplanes, which could take off and land on water.

With characteristic enthusiasm he arranged to take flying lessons, telling his first instructor, 'We are in the Stephenson age of flying. Now our machines are frail. One day they will be robust, and of value to our country.'[34] When Winston gave his attention to something, it was with his complete commitment. On days set aside for flying instruction he would make as many as ten flights. It was normal then for a learner-flyer to go solo within twenty hours of instruction, and Winston was a good pilot, always fascinated by the few available instruments. But his instructors (he had several) were afraid to let him go solo in case he killed himself (they were concerned, not least, for their own careers).[35] When he had done thirty-five hours he began clamouring to be allowed to fly solo. But many deaths occurred in those early days of flying, and his family

---

*Wilbur and Orville Wright made the first controlled heavier-than-air human flight on 17 December 1903.

were horrified; Sunny Marlborough wrote, 'I do not suppose that I shall get the chance of writing you many more letters if you continue your journeys in the Air. Really I consider you owe it to your wife, family and friends to desist from a practice or pastime – whichever you call it – which is fraught with so much danger to life. It is really wrong of you.'[36]

These fears were compounded when his latest instructor, the highly qualified Captain Lushington, side-slipped while making an approach into Eastchurch airfield in Kent and could not recover in time. The aircraft crashed and Lushington was killed. Soon afterwards, in May 1914, Winston was among those waiting at Portsmouth to receive the flying ace Gustav Hamel, who was flying from Paris at Churchill's invitation to give an air display to Royal Flying Corps pilots. Hamel never arrived, and no trace of him was ever found. Fatal aviation crashes were sensational news, and special editions of the newspapers were rushed out to record his disappearance while flying the Channel. Almost immediately Winston flew to a Yeomanry camp about eleven miles away. 'We got a great reception,' he wrote that evening to Clementine from *Enchantress*, berthed at Portsmouth, 'the men all running out in a mob, as if they had never seen an aeroplane before.'

F.E. Smith wrote to him: 'Dear Winston, Why do you do such a foolish thing as fly repeatedly? Surely it is unfair to your family, your career & your friends. Yours ever, F.E.'[37] But in the end it was Clementine's distress that persuaded him to give up flying. She was pregnant again, after a miscarriage the previous year had left her ill and low for some months. Her frequent requests that he stop flying had little effect until, finally, she described to him in a letter a terrible nightmare she had had, which brought Winston up short because he had not until then realised the extent of her concern:

My darling one
I will not fly any more until at any rate you have recovered from your kitten: by then or perhaps later the risks may have been greatly reduced. This is a wrench, because I was on the verge of taking my pilot's certificate. It only needed a couple of calm mornings; I am

confident of my ability to achieve it vy respectably. I shd greatly have liked to reach this point wh wd have made a suitable moment for breaking off. But I must admit that the numerous fatalities of this year wd justify you in complaining if I continued to share the risks – as I am proud to do – of these good fellows. So I give it up decidedly for many months & perhaps forever. This is a gift – so stupidly am I made – which costs me more than anything wh cd be bought with money. So I am vy glad to lay it at your feet, because I know it will rejoice & relieve your heart. Anyhow I can feel I know a good deal about this fascinating new art . . . I have been up nearly 140 times, with many pilots, & all kinds of machines, so I know the difficulties, the dangers & the joys of the air – well enough to appreciate them . . . This poor Lieutenant whose loss has disturbed your anxieties again, took me up only last week in this vy machine! You will give me some kisses and forgive me for past distresses – I am sure. Though I had no need & perhaps no right to do it – it was an important part of my life during the last 7 months, & I am sure my nerve, my spirits & my virtue were all improved by it. But at your expense my poor pussy cat! I am so sorry.[38]

Jack and Goonie had also increased their family in the past year with the birth of a second son, Peregrine. The two sisters-in-law had decided to spend the summer of 1913 at the seaside, so the children could play together. Accordingly they rented two neighbouring properties, Pear Tree Cottage and Beehive Cottage at Overstrand, a quiet cliff-top village with fine sandy beaches near Cromer in Norfolk. Winston and Jack usually joined them at weekends.

By this time Jennie and George Cornwallis-West had parted for good. Unable to obtain any formal financial settlement because George was bankrupt, Jennie accepted his word that he would pay her £1000 a year after the first £2000 (which he would need to live on) of any income. She sued for a divorce in January 1913 and the matter went to court that July. Jennie's case was handled by F.E. Smith, who told the court that his client sought a divorce on the grounds of 'desertion and misconduct'. The proceedings were brief, taking only seven minutes because George admitted his guilt in a letter, and a decree nisi was issued. Two hours after the decree was made absolute, on 6 April the following year, George married Mrs Patrick Campbell at Kensington register office. The bride wore black silk for the wedding, and there was no long honeymoon, for she was in rehearsals to play Eliza Doolittle, the starring role that was written for her, in George Bernard Shaw's *Pygmalion*, which was due to open at His Majesty's Theatre a few weeks later. Shaw cabled Winston: TWO TICKETS RESERVED FOR OPENING NIGHT PYGMALION. BRING A FRIEND. IF YOU HAVE ONE. Winston replied: CANNOT MAKE FIRST NIGHT. WILL COME TO SECOND. IF YOU HAVE ONE.

Jennie had known in advance about George's wedding but it was nonetheless deeply wounding, despite the sympathetic messages with which she was showered, including from George's sisters. Princess Daisy cabled: JENNIFER DEAREST YOU DID YOUR BEST IT IS AWFUL AND HE WILL REGRET JUST READ NEWS IN PAPER AM MISERABLE HOPE SEE YOU SOON MUCH LOVE DAISY. His other sister Shelagh, married to the Duke of Westminster (known as 'Bendor'*), told Jennie how much she had felt for her during the last months: 'I knew all the time what you were going through; and I admired what you did for him more than I can say.'[39] Her words were not mere idle sympathy, for Bendor was also involved with another woman, and soon after Shelagh wrote this letter they parted. Bendor did not discuss the matter with Shelagh, but wrote her a letter saying that he could no longer live with her and she must leave the house. He offered to make her an annual allowance of £13,000, which she refused, saying she would do 'nothing that would reflect upon her position as [his] wife and mother of his children'. A year later there was a formal separation agreement and they lived thereafter much as Sunny and Consuelo did. The papers took the part of the wronged wife, and for

---

*The 1st Duke (grandfather of the 2nd Duke (1879–1953), had owned the winner of the 1880 Derby, Bend Or, who was thought to have been a ringer. Shelagh Cornwallis-West was the first of the 2nd Duke's four wives in a life crammed with drama, extravagance and excess. A right-wing Tory, he hoped to bring the Liberal Party into disrepute by 'outing' his bisexual brother-in-law (the 6th Earl Beauchamp – a Liberal peer whom Evelyn Waugh characterised as Lord Marchmain in *Brideshead Revisited*). Homosexuality was illegal then, and the horrified King had exclaimed: 'I thought men like that shot themselves.'

a while Sunny was quite cheered to know that Bendor was now taking the sort of critical flak that he had endured for several years.

In the spring of 1913 Sunny paid one of his regular trips to the French Riviera. Unusually, Gladys did not accompany him, and soon after his arrival at a hotel in Beaulieu-sur-Mer he met one of his numerous cousins, Reggie Fellowes,* who was also a grandson of the 7th Duke. The meeting was not a friendly one, as Marlborough had good cause to believe that Reggie was either Consuelo's lover or was about to become so, and he suspected that the pair had intended to rendezvous at this very hotel. He cut Reggie dead in public, considered a great insult in Edwardian society, and wrote to Gladys: 'I have spoilt this plan for the moment . . . I ought really to have him watched. I must do so when I get back.'[40]

Whether or not he did so is unknown. The world they knew, in which such events as divorce had seemed of major importance, was nearing its end. By the early summer of 1914 Winston was practically sure that there was to be a war in Europe. He has often been called a warmonger, but his papers and letters make it obvious that war was positively not what he wanted. Yet he was not going to allow Britain to be caught unawares.

---

*Reginald Fellowes (1884–1953), second son of Rosamund Churchill (a sister of Lord Randolph) and her husband William Fellowes, 2nd Baron de Ramsey.

15

1914–16

A Fall from Power

That the Navy and the infant Royal Naval Air Service were fully prepared when war was declared on 4 August 1914 was arguably attributable to Churchill's prescient grasp of politics and his determination in the face of severe opposition from others in the Cabinet.

His aim before 1914 was to ensure that Britain's Navy remained superior to the German Navy in case of war. His plans were unpopular. Even his ally Lloyd George, now the Chancellor, opposed him, announcing in the newspapers as late as 1 January 1914 that he deprecated the increase in the naval estimates* announced by Churchill. Had the old (1887) levels been adhered to, he stated, the tax rate could have been slashed dramatically. It was a safe argument: tax cuts were always popular and nobody really believed Germany would attack Britain. Winston was shooting in France with the Duke of Westminster at the time this discord reached the headlines, and he maintained a dignified silence. But from this point onwards Clementine watched Lloyd George, and she warned Winston on numerous occasions that he was not someone who could be relied upon and that Winston should not wholly trust him, as he had hitherto. Clementine seemed now to be taking upon herself the role of guarding Winston's public image.

---

*Naval estimates provide Parliament with full details and costings of new ships that have been either commissioned or accepted into service during the current financial year.

The naval estimates row almost cost Winston the Admiralty, for at one point he threatened to resign over the matter, causing his Aunt Cornelia to write reminding him of his father's 'great error of judgement' and the tragic consequences that resulted from it. 'Because I love you and care so much for your career I have an instinct that you are going wrong,' she warned. 'Even the ablest of men may wreck their political life.' Characteristically Winston held on, with almost everyone against him, insisting that the number of ships and aeroplanes must be increased for the nation's safety, which also meant that of the Empire. Most other members of the Cabinet were by now fully aware of Germany's aspirations in Europe, but were still hoping that the difficulties could be dealt with by diplomacy.

Winston set out the problem in simple terms for the King:

The burden of responsibility laid upon the British Navy is heavy . . . All the world is building ships of the greatest power, training officers and men, creating arsenals, and laying broad and deep the foundations of future permanent naval development and expansion . . . we are witnessing this year increases in expenditure by Continental Powers of armaments beyond all previous experience. The world is armed as it was never armed before. Every [diplomatic] suggestion for arrest or limitation has so far been ineffectual.[1]

It was his duty, Winston said, to ensure the Navy was ready for any eventuality. Fortunately, the King agreed with him.

Eventually, Lloyd George suggested that Winston should come to breakfast at No. 11 Downing Street to 'settle the matter'. Winston accepted, fully anticipating that he might have to resign that morning. After Lloyd George had greeted him, he said: 'Oddly enough my wife spoke to me last night about this Dreadnought business. She said, "You know, my dear, I never interfere in politics; but they say you are having an argument with that nice Mr Churchill about building Dreadnoughts.* Of course I don't understand these things,

---

*The dreadnought was a battleship armed with guns all of the same big calibre and noted for its great range and power.

but I should have thought it would be better to have too many rather than too few." So I have decided to let you build them. Let's go in to breakfast.'[2]

By the spring of 1914 it was no longer a secret that members of the German General Staff were braying for war against France and Russia. In June Archduke Franz Ferdinand, heir presumptive to the thrones of Austria and Hungary, and his wife were assassinated at Sarajevo in Bosnia by a Serbian nationalist. Germany leaned on Austria to demand an Austrian-led search inside Serbian borders, to seek out those responsible for the murder. The wording of the deliberately offensive message, in effect an ultimatum, was considered so threatening that the governments of Europe were shocked by its open hostility. Winston immediately wrote to Clementine to tell her that Europe was trembling on the brink of a European war, 'the Austrian ultimatum to Servia [*sic*] being the most insolent document of its kind ever devised'.

Even at the height of the direst crisis or when he was inundated with work, on board the *Enchantress* or at Balmoral with the King and Queen – whenever they were apart Winston wrote daily to Clementine, never forgetting to add an affectionate remark and usually rows of kisses. One letter ended: 'Here are three kisses, one for each of you. Don't waste them. They are good ones.' Clementine replied: 'I have kept the three precious kisses all to myself, as I appreciate them more than the P.K. & [the] C.B.'* Not to be outdone, Winston countered: 'Since you have kept the three kisses for yourself, I send you 2 more for the P.K. and [the] C.B. **XX**, and out of a store that will never be exhausted send you an additional six.**XXXXXX**'[3]

But his letters to Clementine, written as they were to someone with whom he never needed to prevaricate or hedge, are above all an important historical source as well as providing a record of Winston's devotion to his wife. He produced beautifully written books about the events leading up to 4 August 1914, but it is arguable that the best record is contained in the letters he wrote at the time to Clementine.

---

*Puppy kitten and Chumbolly.

There were no traditional summer naval manoeuvres that year, for economic reasons; instead, Winston ordered a test mobilisation of the Third Fleet. The review by the King was held at Spithead on 17–18 July. It consisted, Churchill would later write, of 'incomparably the greatest assembly of naval power ever witnessed in the history of the world'. He knew the event would not have been lost on the Kaiser, Wilhelm II, and this deliberate show of strength by Churchill was an attempt to halt the deepening threat of war. The Fleet was never dispersed after this exercise, though some of the crews were sent on leave, for on Sunday 26 July, the Cabinet learned that Austria had rejected Serbia's diplomatic reply to their ultimatum. That weekend Winston was at Cromer with Clementine, Jack, Goonie and all the children. They suspected that this was likely to be the last time in the foreseeable future they would all spend together. Winston's second-in-command, Prince Louis of Battenberg,* kept him up to date with the news by telephone and as the cottage did not have one, some neighbours obliged by allowing Winston to use theirs. As the situation deteriorated, he decided to return early to the Admiralty, and by the time he arrived there, Prince Louis had already taken the decision to halt the planned dispersal of the naval ships to home ports. Winston ratified this order. Later he wrote to Clementine:

28th July 1914   Admiralty
Midnight

My darling one & beautiful,
Everything tends towards catastrophe and collapse. I am interested, geared up & happy. Is it not horrible to be built like that? The preparations have a hideous fascination for me. I pray to God to forgive me for such fearful moods of levity. Yet I wd do my best for peace, & nothing wd induce me wrongfully to strike the blow. I

---

*Making Prince Louis First Sea Lord was Churchill's first appointment at the Admiralty, but in October that year the Prince became the subject of a press hate campaign because of his German background, and was forced by public demand to resign from a post he had filled with great ability.

cannot feel that we in this island are in any serious degree responsible for the wave of madness wh has swept the mind of
Christendom. No one can measure the consequences . . .

The two black swans on St James's Park lake have a darling
cygnet – grey, fluffy, precious & unique. I watched them this
evening for some time as a relief from all the plans & schemes. We
are putting the whole Navy into fighting trim (bar the reserve).
And all seems quite sound & thorough. The sailors are thrilled and
confident. Every supply is up to the prescribed standard.
Everything is ready as it never has been before. And we are awake
to the tips of our fingers. But war is the Unknown and the
Unexpected! . . . You know how willingly & proudly I wd risk – or
give – if need be – my period of existence to keep this country great
& famous & prosperous & free. But the problems are vy difficult.
One has to try to measure the indefinite & weigh the imponder-
able. I feel sure however that if war comes we shall give them a
good drubbing. My darling one – this is a vy good plan of ours on
the telephone . . . Ring me up at fixed times. But talk in parables –
for they all listen. Kiss those kittens & be loved forever only by me.
Your own, W[4]

Winston had no Cabinet authority to mobilise the Navy; in fact,
when the matter had last been discussed his request to do so had
been refused. He recalled that when he told Asquith he intended to
mobilise the Fleet the Prime Minister merely 'looked at me with a
hard stare and gave a sort of grunt'. So he knew only too well that
he was taking a colossal risk when he gave the order; had war not
been declared, he would have had to answer to a furious House of
Commons, and his forced resignation would have been a matter of
course. But he was utterly convinced that he was doing the right
thing, and on the following night under cover of darkness, without
showing a light, the First Fleet passed quietly through the straits of
Dover into the North Sea. Two days later it was on station at Scapa
Flow, Cromarty and Rosyth. The Second Fleet was ordered to
assemble at Portland. All naval harbours were cleared, all bridges
and stations were guarded; ferries and steamers were boarded by

armed men. Observers were in place along the south and east coasts, and all reservists were summoned for a total mobilisation. That done, he wrote to Clementine.

31 July 1914.   Admiralty
Secret – Not to be left about but locked up or burned.

My darling,
There is still hope although the clouds are blacker & blacker. Germany is realising I think how great are the forces against her & is trying tardily to restrain her idiot ally. We are working to soothe Russia. But everybody is preparing swiftly for war and at any moment now the stroke may fall. We are ready.

The City has simply broken into chaos. The world's credit system is virtually suspended. You cannot sell stocks & shares. You cannot borrow. Quite soon it will not perhaps be possible to cash a cheque. Prices of goods are rising to panic levels. Scores of poor people are made bankrupts . . . but I expect the apprehension of war hurts these interests more or as much as war itself . . .

Fondest love my darling one – your devoted husband, W[5]

Jack and Goonie were among the 'poor people' who stared ruin in the face. Jack had carefully reinvested anything left over from his living costs since his marriage, but now all was wiped out by the stock-market collapse. Goonie told Jennie that they had not a shilling left in the world. 'I do not know what the future holds in store for us,' she wrote gloomily. Jack's job as a stockbroker was now superfluous.

While trying to regularise his mother's tangled affairs at this point, he had been alerted by the family solicitors, recently appointed by himself and Winston in case either should be killed in the forthcoming conflict, to a clause in his father's will that had previously escaped everyone's notice. Under this clause, the arrangement whereby Jennie had received the income from the capital left by Lord Randolph changed if she were to remarry. In this event, Jennie would receive only 50 per cent of any income generated, and the other 50 per cent over and above their allowances was to be shared by Winston and Jack 'towards their advancement in the world'. In the event of their deaths it was to be distributed to their respective children.

Jennie was so deeply in debt, with loans made against her future income, that Jack knew there was no point in trying to reclaim any of the monies that should have come to him in the fourteen years that had elapsed since her marriage to George Cornwallis-West in 1900. However, he could not resist pointing out to his mother that the oversight had meant a delay in his marriage to Goonie, had prevented him from going into the Army as he had wished and even from going to Oxford, because there had not been the money available at the time. There was no suggestion that this was a deliberate attempt by Jennie to defraud her sons of their inheritance – the will had been drawn up by the old Duke's solicitor and the man responsible had since left the practice. Jack himself was at a loss to explain how this significant passage could have been missed by all the solicitors who had examined the document – especially as the terms would have improved his financial standing in his marriage discussions. The clause had apparently even been missed by the Marlborough-appointed trustees whose job it was to administer the trust and pay Jennie's annual trust income. That Jennie herself would have been familiar with all the terminology of a complicated trust is extremely doubtful; it had probably never been explained to her in full and the 'new discovery in the will' undoubtedly came as much of a surprise to her as it had done to Jack and Winston. They were each earning their own living and as long as they could do so, Jack wrote, neither of them would make any claims, although he believed that were they to do so they were entitled to a further £300 a year each. So the discovery would make very little difference to Jennie, except that it significantly altered the security she had offered against her borrowings: her guarantees were not nearly as safe as she had believed. In summary, Jack said that while it would not immediately affect Jennie, it gave himself and Winston considerable comfort that should they die before Jennie, their children would immediately inherit from their grandfather, under the terms of the will.[6]

Touchingly, although there had been a pecuniary effect due to the oversight, the discovery was chiefly important to Jack and Winston because it indicated that their father had not forgotten them. It made a considerable difference to them, Jack wrote, to discover that their father's will was not made – as they were always led to suppose – without any consideration of his sons.[7] Jack then went on to lecture his mother severely about her continued spending (Jennie was still buying herself expensive and unnecessary jewellery, furs and new dresses, despite the fact that her creditors were pressing hard), pointing out that she had an income of over £2000 a year, larger than his own, yet she had no family or family home to finance. If she started running up bills again, he admonished, nothing could save her from the bankruptcy courts.[8]

Jennie was shocked and depressed at the lecture; she was too old to change her ways and she could not see how to begin to retract and change her entire lifestyle. After a while, though, she realised that the national news was so serious that 'this is not the moment to lament about one's personal affairs'.[9]

Jack was one of the first men to get into uniform, leaving immediately to join his voluntary Yeomanry unit at Banbury. Goonie was relieved that at least he had something to occupy his mind rather than sitting at Cromer worrying about finances over which he had no control. 'I wish he had not had to go, but I am proud that he is serving his country!' she wrote.[10]

On 2 August the Cabinet learned that Germany had declared war on Russia. 'I cannot think that the rupture with France can be long delayed,' Winston told Lord Hugh Cecil. 'And the course of events is likely to be very serious as regards Belgium.'* Clementine, who had stayed at Cromer with Goonie and the children, was still encouraging and urging diplomacy, but her hopes were dashed when she received the following note:

---

*That night Churchill dined at the Carlton Hotel in the Haymarket with Lloyd George and a few other members of the Cabinet. A little-known fact of history is that a trainee chef at the hotel at that time was a young man called Ho Chi Minh, who in 1941 became leader of the Viet Minh independence movement which established the Communist government of North Vietnam.

2 August 1914 1 a.m.   Admiralty

Cat – dear – It is all up. Germany has quenched the last hopes of
peace by declaring war on Russia, & the declaration against France
is momentarily expected. I profoundly understand your views – But
the world is gone mad – & we must look after ourselves – & our
friends. It wd be good of you to come for a day or two next week.
I miss you so much – Your influence when guiding & not contrary
is of the utmost use to me.

Sweet Kat – my tender love. Your devoted W[11]

Two days later, at 11 a.m. on 4 August, Winston sent out the general signal to the Navy: COMMENCE HOSTILITIES AGAINST GERMANY.

At first, no one imagined that Britain would be confronted with
an all-out world war that would last for the next four years. The
Triple Entente alliance entered into with France and Russia in 1907
against the Central Powers of the German and Austrian empires
assumed that the brunt of the fighting on land would be carried out
by the Russian and French armies, which – with strategic assistance
from the British Army in the form of a British Expeditionary Force
(BEF) – would be able to stop the German Army from annexing
the rest of Europe as Napoleon's armies had done. The Kaiser had
spent the seven years before the war feverishly building warships in
an attempt to enable the Germans to take on the British Navy.* So
Britain's main role was to be the containment of the German Navy,
and in particular her much vaunted new dreadnought battleships
which were thought to be superior to those of the British Navy.

For two days Winston had been impatient to attack the German
warship the *Goeben*,† in the Mediterranean, on the grounds that
she was faster than anything in the French Navy and was therefore
a danger to French troopships. But the Cabinet had held him to the

---

*There were rumours that this all began after the Kaiser's racing yacht was roundly beaten at
Cowes by that of his uncle, King Edward VII.
†A heavy battlecruiser, the *Goeben* was among the fastest and most powerful warships of its
day. Manned by over a thousand crewmen, she was armed with thirty-four guns of various
sizes, the largest of which could accurately target ships up to fifteen miles away.

strict terms of a declaration of war, and to his utter frustration the *Goeben*, together with the *Breslau*, slipped away to Constantinople beyond the reach of British ships. The Germans then announced that they had sold the two ships to Turkey (who at that point had not taken sides). Winston's bitterness over this lost opportunity was only assuaged by the success of the Navy in transporting the entire British Army across the Channel to Calais, Boulogne and Le Havre without the loss of a single man. Three days later the British Expeditionary Force, the best-equipped and well-trained force that had ever left Britain, was successfully attacking the German Army at Mons, where they were ordered to defend the canal even though outnumbered by six German fighting divisions to four British. Only when the French Army retreated did the British begin a general retreat, which over the next two weeks took them back as far as the outskirts of Paris.

The Secretary of State for War was Winston's former chief, sixty-nine-year-old Lord Kitchener.* Their last meeting was in September 1898 at Omdurman, when Winston had been a subaltern reporting the advance of the dervish forces to his commanding officer. Their experience of each other was unfortunate: Winston had little patience with the Sirdar, and in his book *The River War* had openly criticised Kitchener for not stopping the killing of wounded members of the opposing army and for allowing the destruction of the Mahdi's tomb at Khartoum. Likewise, Kitchener had disapproved of Churchill because he suspected that he did not intend to make the Army his career and was therefore usurping opportunities that rightly belonged to men who did. Now these two men, the only Cabinet members with any experience of actually fighting a war, were forced to work in tandem. It was an uneasy truce, but at least Kitchener recognised that Winston's interest and experience in aviation were greater than his own. The Army's Aviation Division was fully

*Field Marshal Horatio Herbert Kitchener (1850–1916; later 1st Earl Kitchener of Khartoum) had in 1892 been appointed Sirdar of the Egyptian Army, then been made a major general in the British Army. It was he who had led the British and Egyptian forces up the Nile to defeat the Sudanese at the Battle of Omdurman, for which he was acclaimed as a national hero.

occupied in France with the planned counter-attack on the Marne, so on 3 September Kitchener invited Winston to take over responsibility for the aerial defence of Britain. Winston eagerly accepted this, for he was convinced there would be attacks on London from the air by Zeppelins. His days were already long – from 9 a.m. to 2 a.m., broken only by an afternoon power nap. He would have been perfectly justified in believing that this moment in history was the destiny he had so long believed was his and was the reason why he had been saved in so many dangerous circumstances.

The Churchills, like families all over Britain, were directly and immediately affected by the war. Only eight weeks after the outbreak of hostilities the first family casualty was reported. Jennie's sister Leonie was staying at her London house when she received news that her second son, twenty-eight-year-old Norman, had been killed in France at Armentières. The family asked Winston to confirm through the War Office that this was correct. Norman had been leading his unit across a railway embankment, carrying in his hand the sword that had been given to him by the Duke of Connaught* (a former lover of Leonie's), when a sniper positioned in a signal box killed him outright. Leonie was so shocked that for days she hardly took in what had happened. Everyone said to her what is always said to women survivors of war dead – 'Better to die quickly and cleanly, than of typhoid in a filthy hospital', and so on – and though there may have been some comfort to be found in these words the fact remained that her beautiful young son was never coming back. Jennie, who was very close to Leonie, believed that her sister never fully recovered from this loss.

Leonie's elder son Shane had suffered a nervous breakdown some time earlier, and was deemed not fit to fight. Nevertheless, a month after the tragedy he travelled to France determined to locate his brother's body. He found it buried a mile behind the trenches and

---

*Prince Arthur (1850–1942), third son of Queen Victoria. He was appointed Governor General of Canada in 1911 and remained there until 1916.

within the sound of the guns of both armies. Some planks had been placed over the body so that when they were removed 'he looked just as he had been', he reported to Leonie. 'His clothes were unsoiled and clean.' He double-checked for a broken tooth that Norman had chipped with a billiard ball fifteen years earlier, then cut a lock of his brother's hair for Leonie and arranged for his body to be placed in a coffin and buried formally. A modern-day onlooker might conclude that this action of Shane's was in its way as brave as his dead brother's had been. The body would not fit in the coffin with the boots on, so they were removed. 'I did not cry,' Shane wrote, 'till I saw that lonely pair of boots on the field for they had the shape and look of so many other pairs of his [that] I had seen outside his room.'[12]

Jennie herself was depressed. Apart from feeling the loss of her nephew, she had never been alone before; there had always been a man on the scene to whom she could turn. Now that she was sixty she felt the stigma of her divorce, and she could not manage within her budget; many of her oldest friends had died, the world had changed beyond recognition, and the war meant the end of her constant trips to Paris. Moreover, she had put on weight and had stopped colouring her hair which was by now quite grey though always elegantly styled. And she was in debt yet again, despite Jack's lectures.

Although he had not actually lectured her on her extravagance, a letter from Winston a little later must have concerned her: 'The world has gone mad – the whole financial system has completely broken down . . . Be careful with what you have got – Gold will soon be unobtainable.'[13] Winston and Jack both led the lives of busy young family men, and though Jennie appreciated this the fact that she saw comparatively little of them made her feel isolated and lonely.[14] The part she had once played in Winston's political career, which had so thrilled her, had now been taken over by Clementine. But at the outbreak of war she threw herself into fund-raising for the American War Fund, and worked in various ways for the American hospitals in London and Devon. Later she would organise piano concerts and matinées for military charities.

Goonie felt it was rather exciting to be still living on the east coast at Cromer, as it was considered to be a possible danger zone, and she wrote to Jennie that there was a chance that the Germans might fly over and bomb Overstrand.[15] Clementine wrote something similar to Winston. When Goonie returned to London on 1 September, she called on Jennie at 72 Brook Street, a house that Jennie had redecorated as a 'project', and there she was treated to a seven course dinner – pre-war style – which hardly appeared to reflect a woman trying seriously to 'live within her means'. Goonie reported each detail to Jack – the exquisite platters of luscious fruits, served after the meal in a sumptuous dining room, the walls of which were decorated with beautiful paintings. Afterwards they had sat in the 'pickled-oak' drawing room, well-lit with concealed lighting; both of these features were previously unheard of in England at that time. The house was filled with expensive bibelots, furniture, rugs and flowers, and seemed to Goonie to be very opulent and comfortable. Upstairs, she wrote, there was a silver bedroom, a blue dressing room and a white bathroom. Downstairs, she had noticed several pieces of new furniture such as writing tables, chairs and occasional tables, but she thought that perhaps some of these had been exchanged for her older larger furniture.

More important to Goonie though, was learning from Jennie (who had it from Winston) that the Yeomanry would soon be going to the front line. She wrote that every woman was going to be unhappy in 1914, and she was no exception, but she felt it very cruel that Jack had to be away at a Yeomanry camp at Churn* in Oxfordshire, when she wanted to be with him every moment until he was sent overseas. She was trying to be brave, and clung to the hope that he might be needed in England, and so not have to expose himself to slaughter by the enemy. Winston had told her he might run down to Churn to see Jack that day, but he had refused to take her with him, as he said it was 'all men' and she would be in the way. Jennie had generously invited Goonie and the children to come and stay with her during the war, but Goonie

---

*The Yeomanry camp, near Didcot.

declined at this stage, perhaps preferring to be her own mistress. Soon afterwards, Jack was commissioned as a major and transferred into the Queen's Own Oxfordshire Hussars.

For Consuelo the thought of war was terrifying. She had two teenage sons, the elder of whom, Blandford, had recently completed his schooling at Eton and was about to start an officer-training course at Sandhurst. She was still in America staying with Alva and speaking at women's suffrage meetings when the crisis flared in July, and she hurried back to England where she threw herself into war work. She was a sad figure, living mostly alone in Sunderland House apart from her servants. Winifred Beech* was the seventeen-year-old daughter of a Woodstock clergyman who had come to live in London at Consuelo's suggestion to study acting. She had rooms close to Consuelo's home, and as Consuelo liked to keep a friendly eye on her she was a regular visitor at Sunderland House. In her memoirs, written after she had achieved renown as an actress, Winifred recalled Consuelo's life in the period leading up to the war: 'Her loneliness . . . tore my heart. She had everything in the world except the things that matter most. After she had kissed me farewell I hated to hear those little heels of hers clicking away from me across the marble floors into the dim desolation of that great French palace, fragrant with lilies and incense and lovely with antique brocades and priceless porcelain.'[16] Yet the dreadful war years would eventually bring Consuelo the happiness that had so far eluded her.

Like most MPs of the right age, at the outbreak of hostilities Ivor and Freddie Guest were quickly into uniform. Ivor was appointed to the staff of the newly formed 10th Irish Division under Lt-General Sir Bryan Mahon at the Currah, and Freddie, who before entering Parliament had been a professional soldier, returned to active service as an aide-de-camp to Field Marshal Sir John French

---

*In 1914 she married John Fortescue (later Sir John), who was the King's librarian and archivist at Windsor and later known for his standard history of the British Army. He was twenty-eight years older than Winifred but the marriage was happy. As well as being a noted actress, she went on to become a writer (her bestselling books included *Perfume from Provence* and *Crushed Lilies*) and a fashion designer.

who was commanding the British Expeditionary Force in France. Because of his fluent French, Freddie was quickly put to work performing confidential missions for the French and liaising with political leaders in both countries. He rather enjoyed his war, having led a somewhat subjugated life at home under the domineering personality of his redoubtable wife Amy. A year earlier when Clementine had stayed with Freddie and Amy at their home, Burley-on-the-Hill (renovated after the great fire on the eve of Jack and Goonie's marriage), she noted: 'The wind whistled round this great gloomy barrack of a house . . . Amy is kind, but more Suffragetty, Christian Science & Yankee Doodle than ever. Poor Freddie is a Sheep in Lion's clothing.'[17]

Bill Hozier, Clementine's brother, was in the Navy, in command of a torpedo destroyer. But it was Bill's twin Nellie, of whom Clementine was especially fond (she was known as 'the Bud' or 'Mlle Beauxyeux'), who was causing her most concern. In late July it was arranged that Nellie would come from Dieppe to join Clementine at Cromer, bringing their mother. But Lady Blanche arrived alone announcing that Nellie had joined a nursing unit as secretary and interpreter and was headed for Belgium. Angry – as much as anything because she was then into the third trimester of her pregnancy and did not feel up to looking after her mother on her own – Clementine had written crossly to Winston that as her sister was not trained 'She'll be just one more useless mouth to feed in that poor little country.' But Clementine was very anxious about her, and with reason. On 20 August Nellie and her little group were in Brussels when it was occupied by the Germans. They were able to get to Mons, but there they were taken captive. The Germans allowed the unit to treat British captives and Belgian casualties for several months, but when Nellie's group refused to treat German wounded they were repatriated – via Norway, in mid-November, and wearing only the clothes they had worn to travel in August. There was great joy when a half-frozen Nellie arrived without warning at 41 Cromwell Road, Goonie's London home.

Meanwhile in Winston's absence Clementine's baby, a daughter she called Sarah, had been born on 7 October at Admiralty House. When Lloyd George remarked that baby Sarah looked just like her father, Winston famously replied that 'all babies look like me'. The period of rejoicing was short, for Winston was at the centre of a row over the defence of Antwerp. The Germans saw the port as a main objective, but their sweep through Belgium to take the city was halted by the British Army at the River Marne. Winston was sent to Antwerp to persuade the Belgian King and Queen and the government not to evacuate the city, as they had advised they were about to do. Once there, he became so involved with Antwerp's plight that he telegraphed Asquith and asked if he could resign from the Admiralty to direct the defence there. His request was denied, and he was relieved of his post at Antwerp on 6 October by Sir Henry Rawlinson. The city capitulated four days later. Winston travelled to London overnight on the 6th and after attending on the King at Buckingham Palace he went straight to Admiralty House, where Clementine proudly introduced him to baby Sarah.

By November 1914, when the Turks entered the war on the side of the Central Powers, Russia was hard-pressed in the Caucasus. The German armies blocked Russia's land routes to Europe and no easy sea route was available, so when Russia appealed to Britain for help against the Turks it was decided to send a military force to Gallipoli to secure the Dardanelle Straits.* The war chiefs, horrified that the war in Europe, which should have been 'over by Christmas', had descended into stalemate in the Flanders trenches, and with growing daily lists of dead, welcomed a plan for a second front that might offer a hint of victory. Jack was one of the first to be sent out there. As Goonie and the family saw him off at Charing Cross in February 1915, they could little have envisaged the disaster that lay ahead. Probably they were relieved that he was not going to Flanders.

---

*The Dardanelles (formerly called the Hellespont) are a forty-mile-long narrow strait in north-west Turkey connecting the Aegean Sea with the Sea of Marmara. It separates the Gallipoli Peninsula from the mainland of Asia (see map).

The original plan to attack Gallipoli and capture the Dardanelle Straits was not Winston's (though usually associated with him). It had been proposed many months earlier by Vice-Admiral Carden,* and Winston initially ignored the idea, believing that all military efforts should be concentrated in northern Europe: 'It is not until all the Northern possibilities are exhausted,' he wrote, 'that I wd look to the S of Europe as a field for the profitable employment of our expanding mil[ita]ry forces.'[18] However, when he looked at the matter again he saw that the Dardanelles were a possible Achilles heel and worth exploiting. From the start of the war the War Cabinet had repeatedly discussed ways to occupy the Gallipoli Peninsula in order to allow a naval penetration of the Turkish-held Straits. But it was accepted that it would take time and organisation before an army could be landed there to open a second front. Winston now conceived a bold strategy to strike hard and fast and force the Straits. Having cruised to Constantinople in 1910 with

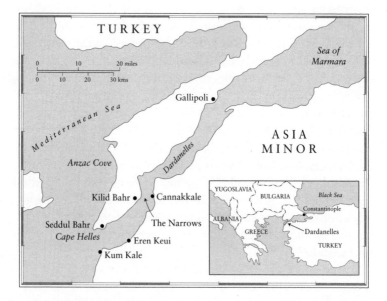

---

*Later Admiral Sir Sackville H. Carden (1857–1930).

F.E. Smith, he appreciated the geography of the area, and this helped his formulation of a plan to capture the Straits using naval power alone, with the Army following afterwards for a land assault on Gallipoli. Success there would not only give the Triple Entente powers access to the Black Sea – providing a means of supplying the Russians – but would place Constantinople, the capital of the Turkish Empire, at their mercy. Victory would eliminate Turkey as an ally of the Germans, and would almost certainly bring Greece and Bulgaria into the war against Germany. If successful it could precipitate the end of the war.

But it was not quite as straightforward as it might sound, given that the northern bank of the Dardanelles (up to seven miles wide in places) was formed by the Gallipoli Peninsula, and Asia Minor protected the southern bank. Furthermore, the Straits ended in a narrow passage between high cliffs that were easily defended. Here at the narrows the Turks had constructed heavily armed fortresses backed up with portable howitzer gun stations. And any fleet forcing the Straits would have to run the dual gauntlet of heavy bombardment from the shores, as well as mines.

In order not to call on the Fleet, which was protecting home waters, Winston proposed to use old 'spare' warships to capture the Straits, with help from the French Navy and a Russian warship. His second-in-command, Lord Fisher, who had replaced the retired Prince Louis of Battenberg as First Sea Lord and had himself been First Lord of the Admiralty until 1910, agreed to this plan, if reluctantly. Though Fisher would later claim that he had never supported Churchill's plan there is no record of his having opposed it at the time. And Churchill, believing he had the full approval of the government and of Fisher, went ahead. Lloyd George said he liked the plan. Kitchener, who had control of land forces, certainly approved the idea, moving the single surplus British infantry division into readiness to attack on land at the Gallipoli Peninsula following the naval attack, and in addition he diverted seventy-five thousand Australian and New Zealand troops stationed in Egypt, bound for the Western Front, to the Dardanelles instead. Jack Churchill was there serving on the HQ staff of the ANZAC forces.* The French added a further corps (which, however, arrived too late to assist in the grim first battle).

The first naval attack on the Dardanelles took place on 19 February 1915, with an Anglo-French fleet comprising a battleship, 3 battlecruisers, 16 old dreadnoughts, 4 cruisers, 18 destroyers, 6 submarines, 21 trawlers and the *Ark Royal* carrying seaplanes. The massive bombardment from this fleet took out the closest forts, but many seemed out of range (although much later it would transpire that greater damage had been inflicted on the Turkish defence system than was recognised at the time). The fleet advanced six miles into the Straits before finding it impossible to proceed further because the channel had been mined. Minesweepers were sent in, but were forced to withdraw under fierce bombardment. The weather then closed in, so a second attack had to wait six days, until 25 February. This was equally unsuccessful, so the fleet again withdrew.

With hindsight it is evident that such an attack could only work given an element of surprise – the shock-and-awe technique – and Churchill began frantically agitating for an immediate third attack. Had it gone ahead as he demanded, there is, again with hindsight, a possibility that it might have succeeded.† But the War Cabinet had been badly frightened, and it was decided instead that a combined land and sea attack was needed to achieve success. Almost a month was allowed to elapse while the necessary preparations were made for Allied landings at Cape Helles and Anzac Cove. Those valuable weeks allowed the Turks to repair the severe damage inflicted in the earlier assaults, to lay more mines and significantly to improve their defences, under the command of a German officer who brought in eighty thousand troops to boost the Turkish Army. The Allied fleet attacked again on 18 March, when eighteen battleships entered the Straits. Three British ships hit mines and

---

*Jack Churchill was mentioned in dispatches and was later awarded the DSO for his part in this action.

†What would have happened if they had been able to force the Straits and reached Constantinople without any land forces in place is another matter. Churchill had mooted this, but then opted for the purely naval operation.

were sunk or disabled, and the fleet retreated for a third time, with the loss of seven hundred men. Grave as this was, it was an insignificant number compared with the daily losses on the battlefields of the Western Front.

After much argument and changing of mind in the War Council, the failure of the naval attack gave birth to a new proposal: to send in land forces behind the forts that protected the Straits in order to capture Constantinople. This idea gained great support in the Cabinet, and on 25 April the Gallipoli Campaign began, with significant naval support. Kitchener had been warned by the Greeks that 150,000 men would be needed to take Gallipoli by land, but he believed only half that number would be needed.

The subsequent land battle at Gallipoli was to be a disaster for the Allied forces, with some 60,000 British and Commonwealth troops killed and over 200,000 other casualties before the Allies finally retreated. But long before that retreat occurred, in December 1915, Churchill found himself pilloried by public opinion, by the War Cabinet and by the Tories for the failure of the naval attack. Fisher resigned, after making two public speeches claiming he had been opposed to the plan all along. Churchill alone was held to blame for the fiasco.

The failure of the Dardanelles attack was the single greatest error, and certainly the greatest setback, of Winston's life. With his usual enthusiasm for the task in hand, he had reached out too far and had lost. Asquith would have retained Winston in a Liberal administration but he was now heading a coalition government, and he had no option but to remove the Admiralty from Winston to satisfy outraged public opinion and to quell the anger of the House of Commons, but mainly to save his own neck in the face of the Tory hatred of Winston. To retain Winston's valuable expertise in the War Cabinet he offered a face-saving minor office, the chancellorship of the Duchy of Lancaster – 'a bone,' Sunny Marlborough commented succinctly, 'on which there is very little meat'. Prime Minister Asquith, who knew very well how the campaign had come about as well as the support that had been given to Winston's plan, could easily have saved Winston's career by revealing the facts, and Winston initially assumed he would do so. But what he did not know was that Asquith had recently suffered a major tragedy in his personal life and was not operating with his usual perspicacity.

For years Asquith had been in love with his daughter Violet's friend Venetia Stanley (who, curiously enough, was Clementine's best friend). Venetia was his sounding-board, adored and unattainable, a trusted confidante with whom he shared the pressures of his high office. She encouraged him through bouts of depression and self-doubt, advised and cautioned him, and – ironic though it is, given that women were not even allowed to vote – the Prime Minister had come to rely utterly on her counsel. It was during the Dardanelles attacks that Venetia had informed Asquith that their friendship must end, as she was to marry Edwin Montagu, Under-Secretary of State for India. It was a blow from which Asquith would never recover. Racked with jealousy, desperately trying to persuade Venetia to maintain contact with him, he was unable to focus on the political crisis in hand; and though he held on to office he had lost the will to fight without Venetia, whom he called the 'soul of my life'. 'You alone of all the world,' he wrote to her, 'to whom I have always gone in every moment of trial & trouble, & from whom I have always come back solaced and healed & inspired – were the one person who could do nothing wrong . . . To my dying day [this] will be the most bitter memory of my life.'[19]

Winston was bewildered by his fall from such great power. Now his role was little more than that of an onlooker. Having controlled great fleets, he now found himself appointing county magistrates. He fell into a deep depression, regarding Asquith as his enemy because the Prime Minister refused to make known the whole truth behind the ill-fated expedition. Winston had made mistakes in strategy, and he accepted that.* But he refused to accept that in

---

*He is said to have once remarked: 'Show me a man who never made a mistake and I'll show you a man who never made anything.'

rushing to grasp the glittering prize of Constantinople – the romantic-sounding goal that had fired his imagination and that would have given him a glorious victory to rival that of the Battle of Blenheim – he had omitted to ensure that adequate preparations were in place for failure. Had the initial naval action been carried out some weeks later with the support of the Army, had he obtained better intelligence about the mined areas of the Straits, the operation would have stood a better chance of succeeding. Had the Navy returned immediately after the first attack and cleared the mines, the later attacks would also have stood a better chance of success. Certainly, the lapse of almost a month between the second and third attacks had been a fatal error.

But the fact remains that Churchill was made a scapegoat, for while he and Kitchener had joint responsibility for the campaign, all the blame for the failure in the Dardanelles and at Gallipoli was laid at Churchill's feet. Such was his misery in the aftermath of this fiasco that his friends were concerned that he might commit suicide, and Clementine told a friend later that she thought he might die of grief. For the remainder of his life hostile hecklers at his talks, probably with no knowledge of the facts, would shout out: 'What about the Dardanelles?'

Nor was it only his career that was affected. His domestic circumstances altered greatly and immediately, too. With the loss of high office his salary fell from £4500 to £2000 a year. The Churchills had rented out Eccleston Square in 1913, and had lived at Admiralty House ever since. Now Asquith wrote kindly to say he would allow them to stay on there, but Clementine would not hear of it. Her pride would not allow them to be pensioners of Asquith. After a short stay at Ivor Guest's house in Arlington Street, they moved in with Goonie and her children at 41 Cromwell Road opposite the National History Museum. 'Instantly,' Goonie's son Johnny would later recall, 'our cozy home became Uncle's war head-quarters. The most important statesmen of the day, Lloyd George among them, knocked for admission at all hours; I recollect that dispatch boxes cluttered the hall and stairs, and we used to open doors to find the most unlikely rooms crammed with secretaries banging at typewriters. Telephones were installed at strategic points.'[20]

Fortunately for Goonie and Clementine, soon afterwards a Cabinet decision to pool all Cabinet salaries, then divide the total equally, resulted in Winston's income being raised again, to £4360, and he decided to lease a small farmhouse, Hoe Farm near Godalming in Surrey, for a year. From there he could commute to London, and the rural location gave him a measure of rest from the stress he now lived with day and night. He also considered it a safer place for his family to be. And even during the worst times, Winston could always be diverted by beauty. Now he wrote of Hoe Farm to Jack:

How I wish you could be there. It really is a delightful valley and the garden gleams with summer jewellery. We live vy simply – but with all the essentials of life well understood & well provided for – hot baths, cold champagne, new peas & old brandy. The war is terrible and carnage grows apace, & the certainty that no result will be reached this year fills my mind with melancholy thoughts. The youth of Europe – almost a whole generation – will be shorn away. I find it vy painful to be deprived of direct means of action, but I bear the pangs because I see and feel the value of my influence on general policy. I do not think the present arrangement will last forever, and I hope to regain a fuller measure of control before the end of the year.[21]

It was just at this point, when he needed some relaxation from a situation out of his control, that he discovered painting. He had become interested while watching Goonie sketching, and in an attempt to give him some solace of mind Clementine had rushed out and bought him the necessary materials. Equipped with oils, easel, brushes and palette, he set out to paint a small pond in front of the farmhouse, but found the virgin canvas intimidating. He had just cautiously applied a tiny patch of blue for the sky when he was disturbed by the slamming of a car door. He wrote:

From this chariot there stepped swiftly and lightly the gifted wife of Sir John Lavery.* "Painting! But what are you hesitating about? Let me have a brush – the big one." Splash into the turpentine, wallop into the blue and the white, frantic flourish on the palette – clean no longer – and then several large, fierce strokes and slashes of blue on the absolutely cowering canvas. Anyone could see that it could not hit back. No evil fate avenged the jaunty violence. The canvas grinned in helplessness before me. The spell was broken. The sickly inhibitions rolled away. I seized the largest brush and fell upon my victim with berserk fury. I have never felt any awe of a canvas since.[22]

Over the years his artistic output would be prodigious;[23] he used art, Jennie once wrote, 'as an opiate'.[24]

As the months rolled on and Britain made no headway, Jack suggested to Winston that he visit Gallipoli as an observer, and this fired Winston's imagination. He applied for permission, but to his fury he was refused. And when Asquith wound up the Dardanelles Committee, making himself, Kitchener and Balfour solely responsible for that theatre, Winston no longer had a role in the War Cabinet. There was only one avenue remaining that would allow him to participate in the war, and that was to join the fight in the trenches. This meant giving up his Cabinet salary and a sinecure post. But he felt there was no honourable alternative and so he drafted a resignation letter to Asquith:

I agree with the principle of a War Executive composed of the Prime Minister & the heads of the two military departments. But the change necessarily deprives me of rendering useful service. After

---

*Lavery (1856–1941), the Irish portrait painter, once said of Churchill's artistic ability: 'Had he chosen painting instead of statesmanship I believe he would have been a great master with the brush.' He married his second wife Hazel Martyn, a beautiful and spirited Irish American, in 1909, and she was his model in over four hundred paintings. She also posed as the allegorical figure of Ireland, painted by Lavery for the Irish government to appear on Irish banknotes. No mean artist herself, Hazel Lavery is also noted for her many extramarital affairs. When her lover Michael Collins, the Irish revolutionary, died, she attempted to throw herself into the grave and thereafter wore 'widow's weeds'.

leaving the Admiralty five months ago I have only remained in the Government at your request in order to take part in the War Council. It would not be right for me at this time to remain in a sinecure . . . Nor could I conscientiously accept responsibility without power.

The long delays in coming to decisions have not been the only cause of our misfortunes. The faulty & lethargic executions and lack of scheme and combination over all military affairs & of any concert with our Allies are evils wh[ich] will not be cured merely by the changes indicated in yr memorandum . . . I therefore take leave of you not without many regrets on personal grounds but without any doubts. There is one point however on which it would perhaps be well for us to have a talk. It is now necessary for the truth to be made public about the initiation of the Dardanelles expedition.[25]

He made his farewell speech to the House of Commons on 15 November, and used the traditional courtesy shown to members on such an occasion by delivering a long speech about the Dardanelles, which he referred to as 'a legitimate gamble', knowing that he would not be interrupted. But because of the great loss of life that had been incurred his opinions shocked some of his listeners and gained him few supporters.

The next day a group of his closest friends gathered in Jack and Goonie's house in the Cromwell Road to say goodbye to Winston. Among them were Margot and Violet Asquith, Clementine's younger sister Nellie Hozier who was staying with Clementine, and Edward Marsh, Winston's Private Secretary. Max Aitken (later Lord Beaverbrook), who called later, found 'the whole household was upside down while the soldier statesman was buckling on his sword'. Marsh was in tears and Jennie, remembering how long her nephew Norman Leslie had lasted after he was shipped out to France, was 'in a state of despair at the thought of her brilliant son being relegated to the trenches. Clementine seemed to be the only person who remained calm and efficient.'[26] She was behaving as she knew Winston would want her to behave; only her subsequent letters to her husband reveal that she was as frightened as the others.

Three days after his resignation speech Winston was on his way to France, commissioned, like Jack, as a major in the Queen's Own Oxfordshire Hussars. Soon after his arrival he was attached to the 2nd Battalion of the Grenadier Guards which was about to go into the line. This gratified his sense of history, for the 1st Duke of Marlborough had once commanded the same unit. Lord Cavan the commanding officer told him, 'If you come and lunch with me . . . at one o'clock, you will be in plenty of time.'[27]

'I am sure I am going to be entirely happy out here, and at peace,' he wrote to Clementine. 'I must try to win my way as a good & sincere soldier. But do not suppose I shall run any foolish risks or do anything wh[ich is] not obviously required.'[28] A few days later he sounded almost jaunty when addressing Clementine as 'My dearest Soul' and remarking, 'This is what the great Duke of Marlborough used to write from the Low Countries to his cat.' Then: 'I cannot tell the rota in wh we shall go into the trenches. But I do hope you will realise what a vy harmless thing this is. To my surprise I learn they only have about 15 killed & wounded each day out of 8000 men exposed! It will make me vy sulky if I think you are allowing yourself to be made anxious by any risk like that.'[29]

In fact his immediate anxieties were not connected with the risks of battle. Having been dropped at the Grenadiers HQ near Laventie some twelve miles west of Lille and close to the Belgian border, he had been greeted coolly by the officers in his unit, who were clearly suspicious of him. 'I think I ought to tell you,' his CO told him coldly, 'we were not at all consulted in the matter of your coming to join us.' Winston recognised that only time and example could deal with this matter. And it was not too long before he realised that he had not brought the right equipment with him. He wrote to Clementine asking for another pair of trench boots – one pair was not enough (and henceforward he would always advise soldiers in the trenches to have two). Also, he asked for a sheepskin sleeping bag – this was late November in the Low Countries, after all – and other personal items such as a bath towel. Clementine did what she could, but found that the London shops had sold out of waterproof trench wading boots. She sent him all she could find – a pair of wellingtons – until she could locate some trench boots. He was able from time to time to speak to Jack, who, to Goonie's massive relief, had been transferred to Staff HQ.

Winston served with honour, often in the thick of the fighting, until May 1916. At one point in February that year he was placed in charge of his brigade, commanding five battalions and 4000 yards of trenches in the front line. He hoped this meant he would get a brigade of his own and in fact the French Commander-in-Chief wanted this, but it was merely a temporary appointment while the brigadier was away. Drawing on his experience in the trenches and his knowledge of what was required, Winston designed what he called a 'caterpillar', the first-ever rudimentary 'tank', which was shown to the Prime Minister and Army chiefs ('foolish slugs and dawdlers', Winston called them); it 'performed miracles'. He was critical of the technical support given to the men in the front line. 'Take the telephone system for example,' he wrote:

> It is grotesque. You cannot get through. When you do you cannot hear. There is always a dog fight going on, on the wires. They have stuck in the main to the same little field instruments that an army on the move uses, instead of making a perfect system wh cd so easily be done. And how vitally important it might be in a battle! If we had been content at the Admiralty to paddle along at that feeble pace, we shd never have mastered the German submarines. Then of course there ought to be 10 times (at least) as many light railways on the front. This war is one of mechanics & brains & mere sacrifice of brave and devoted infantry is no substitute, & never will be. By God I wd make them skip if I had the power – even for a month.[30]

While Winston was in France and Belgium* he wrote several notes to his small son, and he and Clementine wrote to each other continually. He kept her up to date with his life as a fighting officer,

---

*He spent some months at Ploegsteert in Belgium, two miles north of the French border, where the fighting was very fierce. The soldiers nicknamed it Plug Street. It is now the site of a military cemetery.

and she informed him of family matters and the affairs of friends. Meanwhile, at his request she attended lunches and dinners with his old political contacts to keep doors open. 'Don't let them . . . think I have resigned the game,' he instructed.

Property sales in London were sluggish, so as an economy Jennie planned to let her house in Brook Street and to join Goonie and Clementine at Cromwell Road, an arrangement that suited all three women. 'Your mother is being very generous and contributing £40 a month to the upkeep of this establishment until she comes to live with us,' Clementine wrote. Jennie was also funding some of Johnny's school fees, as Goonie could not manage them all. At one point Jennie had an inflamed toe amputated and was in great pain. While she was recuperating her house was burgled and she lost most of the pretty and valuable items she had collected over the years, among them gifts from Lord Randolph, the Prince of Wales and other friends and lovers. They were never recovered. 'It is cruel,' Clementine wrote, but Jennie put a brave face on it, saying it relieved her of a lot of worry. During her convalescence she knitted a scarf for Hugh Warrender, a young admirer who had once hoped to marry her and was now in the trenches. The scarf was so huge that he was able to use it as a blanket. But this was a mere kindness by Jennie, for though she was fond of Warrender there was a new man on the horizon. As usual, he was much younger than her.

Nellie Hozier became engaged at the end of 1915 to Bertram Romilly. He had formerly been a lieutenant in the Scots Guards attached to the Egyptian Camel Corps, and they met when he was invalided home with a serious head injury. His long-term prognosis was poor, and he would never be entirely free from headaches and other pain. So, far from this being a joyous occasion Clementine, always very protective of Nellie, was anxious because she believed her sister was marrying Bertram out of pity. The two women discussed it heatedly, Clementine advising a postponement of the wedding, which upset Nellie. 'She has hardened into a mule-like obstinacy & says with a drawn wretched face that she loves him, is divinely happy & [she] will marry him on the 4th [of December],' Clementine wrote

to Winston. 'She . . . says that if I say one word against her marriage . . . she will leave the house & never come near me when she
is married. Goonie thinks the marriage should not take place but
we can do no more.'[31] The newly-weds rented a small cottage near
Taplow from the Astors for a peppercorn sum, and went to live
there after honeymooning in the New Forest. Clementine saw them
six weeks later in London and reported: 'They look very happy and
cannot be parted for one moment.' By April 1916 Nellie was pregnant and suffering from morning sickness, and as the couple had
just rented a little house near Eccleston Square, Clementine could
keep an eye on her.

For a break from the boredom of living on almost nothing,
Goonie went to Dublin to enjoy a few weeks of 'royal splendour'
with Ivor and Alice Guest, where he was Lord Lieutenant of
Ireland. Clementine was left in charge and it was helpful for her to
have Jennie on hand, for although there was a nanny and a nursery maid at Cromwell Road Clementine was kept busy running
errands for Winston; and she had become involved in 'war work',
managing canteens for munitions factory workers.

When Winston returned to England in the summer of 1916 he
took his seat on the Opposition back benches, where he joined an
angry and articulate group pressing for a more efficient management of the war. He could speak from a position of strength, having
suffered at the sharp end from the delays and poor leadership.
Bad news rattled in daily, from Jutland or the Somme, each battle
theatre bringing lengthy lists of fatalities and wounded. But Winston's
main aim was still to clear his name over Gallipoli so that he could
take office again. He could not persuade Asquith to publish the
official papers on the matter, but under pressure the Prime Minister
agreed to appoint a commission to investigate the Dardanelles action.
With this Winston had to be content for a while. Throughout the
next six months he attended hearings, where he was called upon to
justify and explain his every action, but eventually an interim report
was published in March 1917, which (without ever revealing the
complete story – it was still considered too sensitive for the public
domain) cleared Winston's reputation by concluding that he had not

acted alone in taking the decision that had led to the disaster. Winston was reasonably content with the outcome, feeling that he had been publicly absolved and could therefore honourably take up his career in politics again. But this technical ruling was little consolation to the parents and wives of men who had died in an unwinnable action, particularly in Australia and New Zealand. The odium remained.*

In December 1916 Lloyd George finally wrested control of the government from Asquith, which gave Winston hope that he would be offered a Cabinet post as soon as the true facts about Gallipoli were made public. With this slight hint of cheer in the air, Winston, Clementine and the children, Goonie and her children, Jennie and the F.E. Smiths were all bidden by Sunny to Blenheim for Christmas. It was a warm interlude set against the bleakness of the current news – a reminder of what it was like not to be at war and of what the country was fighting for.

---

*In 2009, over ninety years later, when the Cabinet Papers were available to researchers, an Australian writer on the subject insisted: 'Churchill was, in fact, *the architect*, which is why his fall from grace was so marked.'

1917–21

The Armistice and After

With the Dardanelles report partially restoring Churchill's reputation and after a twenty-month interim, Lloyd George felt able to offer him the post of Minister of Munitions, despite the inevitable criticism this decision would provoke. The appointment necessitated another by-election at Winston's Dundee constituency, and when ministerial work detained him in London Clementine took to the platforms in his place and campaigned for him. During the decade she had lived with Winston, the shy Clementine had become a woman who could address a crowd and even beard a Prime Minister at No. 10. The election was held on 29 July 1917 and was a resounding victory, giving Churchill a majority of 5226. In order to make visits to the Front he took to flying again, but only as a passenger and only in order to carry out his duties. He tackled the new position with characteristic verve: 'I found a staff of 12,000 officials organised in . . . fifty principal departments each claiming direct access to the Chief, and requiring a swift flow of decisions upon most intricate and interrelated problems,' he wrote. 'I set to work at once to divide and distribute this dangerous concentration of power.'[1]

Winston and Clementine had returned to Eccleston Square at the end of 1916 and would live there until the lease ended two years later. Meanwhile they had leased another country house, a small farm called Lullenden near East Grinstead. Winston, who worried about the Zeppelin raids on London, was happier when Clementine moved 'the kittens' out of the city.

The year 1917 was arguably the worst of the war for most people. The country had now been fighting without any good news for three years, and there was still no end in sight. The casualty lists seemed endless, and there was probably no family in the country who was not affected in some way. On 10 December Winston delivered a defiant speech at Bedford, exhorting his audience to be steadfast in the fight and not to be misled by pacifist suggestions of 'treating with the enemy'.

Britain's main food imports came from America and Canada, but in 1917 the Germans introduced all-out submarine warfare aimed at merchant ships. The resulting losses had a major impact on supplies, especially on bread, and at one point the country had only six weeks' supplies of wheat. Food prices rose dramatically, and coal had to be rationed. This basic fuel for heating and cooking was in short supply because of lack of labour and the requirements of factories involved in munitions. Initially, a voluntary code of food rationing was introduced. People were encouraged to limit their intake, and the royal family led the way. However, this did not work because munitions factory workers especially, who needed large amounts of energy foods, were not getting enough to eat, while anyone with money could buy as much food as they wanted on the black market. In early 1918 a formal system of rationing was brought in. And in an attempt to increase home food production the Women's Land Army was formed to take the place of farm workers who had gone to the trenches. Recruits were instructed: 'Remember you are doing a man's work and so you are dressed rather like a man. But remember that because you wear a smock and trousers you should take care to behave like an English girl who expects chivalry and respect from everyone she meets.'

Strategic offensives in the later phases of the war such as Passchendaele placed even greater strain and responsibility on Winston's department. He pushed the development of the tank with more than a professional interest. He visited aeroplane and munitions factories, and resumed his visits to France in order to see for himself the needs of the Army there. Invariably he flew, and he had a number of narrow escapes when his various aircraft developed engine troubles over the Channel. He regarded these incidents as adventures, and was exhilarated rather than intimidated by them. For him, they were infinitely preferable to an office desk. In March 1918 on a visit to the Front he met the commanders Foch, Haig and Pétain as well as Georges Clemenceau,* and he was also able to visit Jack who was at Staff HQ near Ypres. He was still warning that 'a most formidable struggle' lay ahead of them. He wrote grimly to Clementine: 'Nearly 800,000 of our British men have shed their blood or lost their lives here during 3½ years of unceasing conflict! Many of our friends & my contemporaries all perished here.' And he noted on the way back from a tour of the trenches: 'We passed the lunatic asylum blown to pieces by the sane folk outside!'[2]

That spring Jennie's friend Montague Porch came home on leave from Nigeria where he worked for the Foreign Service as an Intelligence officer. During a previous leave he had proposed to Jennie. She did not take him seriously, probably because of the age difference: three years younger than Winston, even younger than George Cornwallis-West. Furthermore, Winston was in the trenches at the time and she was distracted by worry about him, but she had agreed to correspond regularly with Porch, and had done so ever since.

By 1918 Jennie was tired by her war work and the unremitting grimness. She was a keen fund-raiser for the American Women's War Relief Fund, and honorary head matron of a hospital for officers in London and of a convalescent home in Paignton, Devon.† She sometimes toured barracks and hospitals entertaining the men with her piano-playing, and helped Clementine and Goonie when called upon to entertain the children. Former patients recalled that she was

---

*Georges Clemenceau (1841–1929) was Prime Minister of France from 1906 to 1909 and 1917 to 1920, and one of the prime movers of the Versailles Treaty.
†She had talked Paris Singer, of Singer sewing-machines, into allowing his palatial home near Paignton to be used as a convalescent home for officers for the duration of the war. It is now open to the public.

quite unlike the other Lady Bountiful types who called on them, and that her visits were a real boost to injured and sick men. Often she would say winningly, 'And when you get better you *must* vote for my son Winston', leaving them in no doubt that they would recover.[3] Many evenings she dined alone, not bothering to dress for dinner any more, and sometimes she would phone Leonie's youngest son Seymour to come and play the piano with her, for company. There were occasions when he found her in tears, so despondent was she. So when Porch came to London on leave it seemed a good idea to invite him to go with her to Castle Leslie, at Glaslough in County Monaghan, Leonie's home in Ireland, away from the resumed bombing raids on London and away from the war, where they could eat a meal of pre-war standard without feeling guilty.

Porch was a handsome young man, and fun to be with. When he proposed again Jennie accepted, on two conditions: that she would not be required to go and live in Africa, nor change her name from Lady Randolph Churchill. Neither of these provisions bothered Porch, and Jennie wrote to Winston and Jack to tell them her news. Porch also wrote to his prospective stepsons. He was forty-one and had never been married. He wrote of his total happiness at winning Jennie, but he was careful also to put their minds at rest about her financial situation. 'Your mother's financial affairs are understood. I love your mother, I can make her happy. Her difficulties & obligations from henceforth will be shared by me – so willingly.'[4] The thought of their mother's extravagances being taken over must have been one of the more attractive aspects of this surprising development. Winston is said to have commented: 'I hope this doesn't become a vogue; I am feeling rather old.' He was going to France that week anyway, and when he met up with Jack, as he did on such visits, they discussed the matter. There was little they could do about it, and it was left to Jack, who had never heard of Porch or met him, to write kindly to Jennie of his surprise at the news, which he had received by a letter recently forwarded to him. He joked that every time he went off to war she got married, but he knew how lonely she had been since her divorce from George Cornwallis-West, and he realised that with both Winston and himself married with young families, it was inevitable that she would be alone a lot of the time. If Porch made her happy, then he was sure that he and Porch would soon be firm friends and it was a great consolation to him to know that she would no longer be on her own.[5]

No researcher of Jennie's life can fail to be impressed at her ability to attract younger and younger men, even though she was no longer a slim young woman. Her body may have thickened with middle age and her jaw line was no longer fine, yet she could still command a room, and – clearly – she had retained her sexual magnetism. With Porch's return and his open admiration she had bloomed like a bud in sunshine. The marriage was held quietly at Kensington register office on 1 June 1918.

Porch's mother was as opposed to her son's marriage as the Cornwallis-West family had been at Jennie's marriage to George. Once again none of the groom's family were present, but Winston, his first cousin Jack Leslie, his Aunt Clara, Clementine and Goonie all witnessed the entry in the register. Even Lady Sarah Wilson, mistress of the withering remark, was there. Montague Porch and his bride then spent a week in London before travelling to Castle Leslie for their honeymoon. The marriage was much talked about in London drawing rooms – the 'May and November' factor attracted inevitable arch comments. And the joke went around that Jennie had been seen in the park, peering into prams – when asked what she was doing she replied that she was looking for her next husband. Jennie's reaction was merely a shrug; she was a trend-setter, not a follower of fashion. 'I have a past and he has a future,' she responded lightly, 'so we should be all right.' Early in the war, when all the young males among her servants went off to fight, she had the butler's and footmen's uniforms remodelled for young women, and thereafter had managed her house with a wholly female staff. Though Society breathed in deeply at first, it was soon regarded as a patriotic gesture rather than a bohemian one. Her third marriage was happy, although Sunny Marlborough reported to Gladys that it was said in town of Jennie that she looked 'exhausted' after three days with her new husband. Theresa Londonderry had apparently met the newly-weds at the opera and asked Porch openly why they had bothered to get married. 'How furious these old cats must be,' Sunny wrote, 'to find that the eldest of their gang can get hold of a ring.'[6] Shane Leslie later reported that Jennie had confided to a member of the family that Porch was the best lover she had ever known. 'But,' he added, somewhat ungallantly, 'she must have been grateful for any mercies at 63.'[7]

There is no question but that the relationship had rejuvenated Jennie; she was as scintillating and charming as she had been before the war. Her friends noted that she looked years younger – and, as always, she had celebrated by buying a new wardrobe. His leave up, Porch had to return to Nigeria for the duration of the war, but Jennie had someone in her life again and that was enough to make her happy. She still had her war work, and before he left England Porch sold some land in Glastonbury and gave her the money to buy a house in Berkeley Square as a renovation and investment project. She would hardly have been human not to have felt a touch of *schadenfreude* when she heard that the marriage of George Cornwallis-West and Mrs Pat was in trouble and they were to part.*

While Winston was engaged in one of his regular ministerial trips to France in August 1918, Clementine, who was expecting their fourth child that November, did the rounds of friends with large country houses. 'Paying visits in War time in August,' she wrote to Winston, 'must be like what visits were like in Miss Austen's time. No bustle, no motors, very few fellow guests, walks in the shrubbery, village tittle-tattle.' From a gabled Tudor manor house, Mells Place, near Frome in Somerset,† she wrote: 'This is a delicious place to rest and dream & I feel my new little baby likes it – Full of comfort, beautiful things, sweet smelling flowers, peaches ripening on old walls, gentle flittings

---

*Stella (or Mrs Pat, as she was known) refused to give George a divorce. After her death in April 1940 he married for a third time, but this marriage failed too. Stricken with Parkinson's disease and alone again, he committed suicide in 1951.

†Owned by the Horner family for many generations. An early member of this family, John Horner, is reputed to have been the 'little Jack Horner' of nursery rhyme fame.

& hummings & pretty grandchildren. But under all this the sadness & melancholy of it all – Both the sons dead, one lying in the little Churchyard next to the house, carried away at sixteen by Scarlet Fever, and the other sleeping in France . . . as does the Husband of the best loved daughter of the House, Katherine Asquith.'[8]

Winston was out in France again in September. He scented victory by now and in contrast to the chilly suspicion of the previous year he was thrilled to be greeted with jubilation and friendliness by officers and soldiers at the Front. On his return journey, in the Ritz in Paris on the tenth anniversary of his marriage to Clementine, he ran into Muriel Wilson. His old girlfriend was there to meet her husband who was on leave, and though Winston considered that the husband looked a 'very average specimen' he concluded that Muriel seemed happy with him.

By this time Clementine was only two months from giving birth and had had to stop her canteen work (for which she would later be decorated). Knowing from Winston that the end of the struggle now lay within sight, she pleaded with him to return from France as soon as he could, wisely looking ahead: 'My Darling do come home and look after what is to be done with the Munitions Workers when fighting really does stop. Even if the fighting is not over yet, your share of it must be, & I would like you to be praised as a reconstructive genius as well as for a Mustard Gas Fiend, a Tank juggernaut and a flying Terror. Besides the credits for these Bogey parts will be given to subordinates and not to my Tamworth.'[9]

On 15 November, four days after the end of the war, Clementine had her fourth baby, a girl with her father's red-gold hair. They called her Marigold. The relief brought by the end of the war combined with the safe delivery of the new baby made this a specially joyous time. And with the end of the war came the dissolution of the coalition government and another general election. But there was no clear winner, and the coalition government was returned to power under Lloyd George.

On 28 June 1919, exactly five years after the assassination of Archduke Franz Ferdinand, Winston was at Versailles for the signing of the treaty that formally ended the war between Germany and the Allied Powers. While he was there he had a droll experience. He was staying at the Ritz in Paris when he was introduced to the twenty-nine-year-old divorcee Daisy Decazes de Glücksbierg,* the fiancée of his cousin Reggie Fellowes (Daisy and Reggie would marry later that year). Daisy invited Winston to come to her room to see her little child. It was perhaps because of the arrival of baby Marigold that he went along as she requested, only to find that the 'child' was Daisy, stark naked and lying on a tiger skin on the chaise-longue.[10] He left at once but he must have told Clementine about it, for years later she told a friend that she had quite forgiven Daisy because the seduction attempt was unsuccessful.[11]

Gladys Deacon had spent most of the war years in London – it had not been an especially hard time for her. She had not joined other women of her class in voluntary war work, although at the outbreak of war in Italy she spent a few months driving an ambulance. In 1915 she had become a naturalised British subject and from then on her life revolved around Sunny – she visited him frequently at Blenheim and he stayed with her in London. He was still as besotted as in the early days of their relationship. Sunny had the guardianship of his two boys until September 1915, after which they went to Consuelo, but he was able to visit them at Eton whenever he wished. Gladys went to Paris in spring 1916 to see her mother. During those war years it had not been the old Paris, but it had not been under siege either; many officers' wives, including Clementine while Winston was in the trenches, visited to meet a loved one on leave.

While Gladys was in Paris Sunny commissioned her portrait by Boldini, but a family friend who had not seen her for years was appalled to see the deterioration in her once perfect beauty. 'Her face has grown very full and heavy-jawed, and all her colours jar – hair too yellow, lips too red, eyes too blue. She looked

---

*Born Marguerite Decazes de Glücksbierg (1890–1962), she was the daughter of a German Duke and the heiress of the Singer sewing-machine company. Her first marriage in 1910 to Prince de Broglie ended when she discovered her husband in bed with the family chauffeur. Of her Broglie children the notoriously caustic Daisy once said, 'The eldest is like her father, only more masculine. The second is like me, only without the guts. And the last is by some horrible little man called Lischmann.'

deplorable . . . not a lady.'[12] She was still an attractive woman, but this was the first intimation of the awful damage that would eventually result from the facial surgery Gladys had undergone thirteen years earlier. The wax injected into the bridge of her nose had become unstable, and had begun to run down her face and neck causing blotches, and to settle around her jaw, making it lumpy. She attempted to disguise the disfigurement with 'clouds of tulle' around her neck, and she evidently discussed it with her mother, for the latter recommended facial massage to disperse the wax.

She continued to mix in the intellectual, artistic and high-bohemian circles in which she had always moved, and one friend she met in a café recorded an image of her sitting opposite him, elbows on the table, head resting on her hands, avidly absorbing the writer's admiration as he observed: 'I am being listened to by the most beautiful grown-up child in the world.'[13] In an era when many women dressed in drab colours to show they were patriotic and serious, Gladys favoured bright colours, feathers, large beads and veils and always made an impact in any company. When she returned to London and told Sunny that she was thinking of returning to France later that year, he became anxious that she might move back permanently. For him the days spent with Gladys were the only highlights in a life he regarded as full of care.

In the early days of the war Sunny had served as a lieutenant colonel on the General Staff. He was later appointed joint Parliamentary Secretary to the Board of Agriculture. But even with the insider privileges that accrued through these positions, like all great landowners he was now battling against financial difficulties because of new government taxation strategies. He also incurred losses through some bad investments recommended by George Cornwallis-West, as well as having to deal with the ongoing demands from the many family dependants who were beneficiaries under numerous complicated trusts, and from charities to which he was committed. His land agent had resigned to go to war and Sunny had been unable to fill the post because all suitable candidates were involved in the war effort. This was to have an inevitable adverse effect on returns from the land. All of these matters, added to the massive costs of running the estate, forced Sunny to consider the ultimate option of closing Blenheim. However, when one of Winston's friends, the brilliant Canadian Max Aitken, suggested he present Blenheim to the nation he was furious. And to his anxieties about Blenheim was now added the unbearable thought that he might lose Gladys.

Boldini and other arty friends were pressing Gladys to return permanently to Paris, but she did not want to lose Sunny either, despite the fact that her long relationship with him had brought with it a certain curtailment of her activities during her best years. To please him, instead of returning to Paris immediately she had spent the summer of 1916 in Brighton so that Sunny could visit her, then went to Paris in the autumn. Matters were not helped when he broke his foot, falling from his horse, and feared he might be left with a permanent limp. He knew that Gladys had a hatred of physical disability, and when he told her about his injury he suggested fearfully that this was her opportunity to end their relationship if she wanted to. She did not accept this escape route, apparently, and the couple spent some time together in Paris while he consulted specialists. They were in the same position as everyone else: it was difficult to see forward while the war was still going on.

Throughout 1917 Sunny hoped for the long-awaited change in the divorce laws that would enable him to divorce Consuelo on grounds of desertion after three years. This much discussed clause had been deferred because of the war, and many unhappy people longed for it to come on to the statute book. And there was a further irritation for Sunny – he quarrelled with Winston when the minimum wage was increased by 12.5 per cent. As an employer, this affected him so adversely that he vowed never to visit Winston and Clementine again. 'That 12½% I can never forgive,' he wrote to Gladys. 'It means another 150 millions a year more in wages. I wonder what the French would have done to their Minister of Munitions.'[14]

In the spring of 1918 he worried for the safety of his heir, Lord Blandford, serving in France as a second lieutenant in the Guards, but he worried even more when Blandford fell in love with a beautiful musical comedy actress while home on leave, and said he wanted to marry her. Sunny chose to attribute this 'looseness' in his son to the 'common blood' of his American mother, but the crisis was resolved when Blandford had to return to France and the relationship ended quite naturally. Soon after his return to his unit in the remote village of Jeancourt, the young officer was startled to receive an unexpected – 'avuncular', he described it – visit from Winston, who afterwards reported to Sunny that his son was well and happy. 'I thought you would like to know exactly how I found him,' he wrote. 'He lives in a weather-proof tin hut on the side of a hill, before which runs a road, deep in white mud and just below is the pan of the valley and the lines of the horse and the tents of the men . . . Blandford is in charge of about 80 Household Cavalrymen who live at this point and go up each night to dig trenches in or just behind the front line. In the event of an attack they would hold the village . . . just above them.' Blandford was one of only two officers on the site, Winston wrote, and he thought he might find it rather lonely. 'He doesn't like whiskey and he hasn't been able to get any port, so for the time being he is teetotal.'[15]

Gladys spent the winter of 1918–19 in France. Instead of returning to London after the Armistice as Sunny had hoped, she travelled down to the French Riviera and rented a house between Beaulieu and Nice, close to that of the now widowed Duke of Connaught, Leonie Leslie's long-time lover and the last surviving son of Queen Victoria. It was almost inevitable that the old man, who was something of a roué, would become obsessed with this attractive and intelligent young woman, and he did. Gladys enjoyed the innocent relationship, but eventually the two quarrelled irrevocably over a trifle. Gladys did not keep such relationships secret from Sunny.

Fearing that Gladys would get tired of waiting for him, Sunny sought new legal advice about divorcing Consuelo. By coincidence, Consuelo was staying in France not too far from Beaulieu at the time, and Gladys heard that she intended to build a house there; Consuelo was merely staying with her mother at Èze-sur-Mer to recover her strength after an attack of flu.* Given their earlier relationship, it is a surprise to read Consuelo's account of those weeks with Alva: 'We grew very close during those last years of her life, sharing each other's interests.' But by 1919 a new happiness had entered Consuelo's life. Not only had both her boys come safely through the war, but she had met the love of her life. He was Jacques Balsan.

Following her affair with Charles Castlereagh which had so damaged her reputation, Consuelo had been very discreet, although it is likely she had at least one serious affair (with Lord Curzon) and possibly another before the outbreak of war, with Harry Cust† (one of Jennie's former inamoratos). Marlborough was convinced Consuelo had also been the lover of his cousin Reggie Fellowes, though he could find no evidence. She had gradually built up a circle of other London friends, apart from the aristocrats whose lifestyle she shared at her regular Friday evening dinner parties and at country-house visits. After returning to England in August 1918 she involved herself in fund-raising for the Medical School for Women at the Royal Free Hospital, the only one in England at that time to allow women to practise medicine, and she helped to establish a delivery ward staffed entirely by women.

Consuelo had also worked with Jennie raising money for the two American-funded hospitals for officers in England, and she was the first woman to give one of the prestigious annual Priestley lectures: her topic was infant mortality.[16] When she mentioned that

---

*Millions were not so fortunate. The postwar flu pandemic – Spanish flu, as it was known, although it originated in China – may have claimed as many as 15 million lives world-wide. In Britain the deaths were 250,000, in France 400,000. In the USA some 28 per cent of the population caught the flu, and between 500,000 and 675,000 died. In common with the present-day swine flu, the Spanish flu was of the H_1N_1 virus strain, and those worst affected were the young and otherwise healthy members of the population.
†Tory politician and editor of the *Pall Mall Gazette*.

venereal disease was a major cause of death in infants, several well dressed matrons got up and left the hall. Consuelo was mortified, but she carried on and her speech was otherwise well received – by the newspapers too. Towards the end of the war she had bought a small country house in Surrey. Crowhurst Place was an exquisite fifteenth-century moated manor house and there Consuelo found a peace and happiness she had never known, disturbed only by her concern for her sons Blandford and Ivor who were still serving in France at that time. By then she had been persuaded to become a London county councillor as a 'progressive', known for tackling women's and children's issues in the poorest slum areas of the city.

She had first met Jacques Balsan in 1894 at her debut in Paris at the age of seventeen. He claimed he told his mother that night that he had met the girl he would like to marry, but he thought Mrs Vanderbilt would never allow it as he had been told Consuelo was earmarked for a German prince. The wealthy Balsan family were textile industrialists with factories in Châteauroux. In the nineteenth century they had made the cloth used exclusively for French Army uniforms called 'blue horizon' and had provided millions of uniforms since the time of Napoleon. Jacques's younger brother, the socialite playboy, polo player and racehorse breeder Étienne Balsan, was responsible for launching the career of Coco Chanel. He saw this young girl from a poor family working in a tailor's shop in Moulins, a small town about 180 miles south of Paris. After becoming her lover he introduced her to Parisian society, lavished clothes and jewels on her and provided her with a flat at an exclusive address, 160 Boulevard Malesherbes. There she began designing hats and, with Étienne's help, opened her first shop.

Moving in the same international circles, Jacques Balsan had seen Consuelo on a number of occasions in the intervening years. He had even been a house guest at Blenheim on several occasions when Consuelo was there. During the war he had sent her several postcards, in one of which he wrote that he did not believe he would return from one particularly dangerous mission and wanted to say goodbye to her. Jacques was rich and he played hard, but he was not merely a playboy; he had represented his family business on several successful international missions during his twenties. At an early age he had become fascinated by flying, and before the advent of powered flight it had been balloons that interested him. He held a balloon pilot's certificate (no. 90), and was soon setting height, distance and endurance records in his own balloon, the *St Louis*. In 1900 he was awarded the Exposition Universelle ribbon for high altitude. However, after the Wright brothers stunned the world with the first powered flight in December 1903 in North Carolina, he transferred his interest to aeroplanes. Although the Wrights were the first to succeed, there were other aviation pioneers in France at the time such as Voisin, Blériot and Farman, who had reached virtually the same stage of aeroplane development. In 1909, after Blériot flew the Channel, Jacques Balsan judged that planes were now beyond the experimental stage and were capable of sustained powered flight. So he purchased a Blériot and became the eighteenth man to hold a pilot's licence in France (Blériot himself held licence no. 1).

Balsan flew the first aircraft to be used in a military context (a single-engine Blériot) on a reconnaissance of guerrilla lines in Morocco in 1913. It was a dangerous mission, for early engines were unreliable: had he crashed and been captured by the Moors he would inevitably have been put to death. For this act of bravery he was awarded the Légion d'Honneur. When war was declared he volunteered immediately, was made a captain in the French Air Force and reconnoitred the Battle of the Marne from the air. In 1915, sponsored by Consuelo's father and two other Americans who deprecated American neutrality (they undertook to pay the fare of any American who wished to fight in the French Air Force), Jacques was involved in forming the Escadrille Lafayette, an elite squadron of volunteer airmen. By 1918 he was a lieutenant colonel, the equivalent of a wing commander, in charge of scout-plane squadrons.

Jacques had loved Consuelo from afar for years, without ever making his feelings known to her. But in 1917, when he was sent to London on a special mission, he began courting her. At the time Blandford was in love with his actress and attending her performances every night. One evening he found his disapproving mother sitting in the neighbouring box watching him, while 'being courted by Balsan'. It was not long before Consuelo realised that she loved Jacques. He had to return to his duties in France, but immediately the war ended she was to be seen in Paris on his arm at Armistice parties. Of course, she was not free to marry him. Furthermore, he was a Catholic and his family would never recognise a divorce, even if Consuelo could arrange one. Consuelo was then forty-one and Jacques forty-nine. He had been very briefly married, in a civil ceremony only, in 1903. This had ended in divorce in 1906, which his family apparently accepted; Consuelo's biographer suggests that this was probably a marriage of convenience to legitimise a child (who subsequently died).[17] Nevertheless, Consuelo decided that it was time to divorce Sunny, if he would agree. She knew that he longed to marry Gladys, and this gave her hope.

Although Sunny had been vicious in his condemnation of Consuelo since their separation, when her lawyers approached his with a formal request that they divorce he did not hesitate. It was now possible for a woman to divorce a man by providing evidence of unfaithfulness, which usually took the form of the husband spending a night in a hotel room with a professional co-respondent. No intercourse took place; the important pieces of evidence were the hotel bill and the fact that the two people were seen in the same bedroom together the following morning by a maid who was prepared to testify. Next, the husband had to leave the wronged wife, who then had to apply for restitution of conjugal rights; when the husband refused, a divorce was granted. In Sunny and Consuelo's case, in order to take advantage of this charade they needed to be seen living together for some weeks before the episode in the hotel. Appalling as this prospect was to both parties, each had their own agenda and so were willing to comply. Sunny spent some time in December 1919 at Crowhurst with Consuelo, with his sister Lilian*

---

*Lilian Grenfell was the younger of Sunny's two sisters (the elder was Norah Birt). Lilian had always liked Consuelo and named her own daughter after her. Consuelo was the child's godmother.

in attendance to leaven the inevitable awkwardness and provide a witness statement.

On 17 February 1920 they were both present at St Margaret's Church, Westminster, for the marriage of their elder son Lord Blandford to the Honourable Alexandra Mary Cadogan, daughter of Viscount Chelsea. They both approved of Mary, and were equally relieved that the relationship with the actress had ended quite naturally. With Blandford's wedding accomplished, the Marlboroughs' divorce proceedings went ahead. While waiting for the date of the hearing to be set, Consuelo received the news that her father had died in Washington on 22 July. She crossed the Atlantic and attended the private family funeral in the New York house where she had grown up, then accompanied the coffin to Staten Island, where he was interred in the family vault. New York papers had already got wind of the impending divorce and ran articles claiming that when she was free Consuelo intended to make her home in the USA. She stayed with her mother on Long Island, where Alva 'had built herself a medieval castle which dominated the Sound'.[18] Consuelo told her mother of her decision to live in France. Blandford was happily married; Ivor had returned to Oxford to complete his interrupted education, and showed no signs of marrying. If she waited until he did so, Consuelo thought Jacques might not wait for her.

At that point the Nineteenth Amendment to the American constitution needed only one more state to ratify it to gain the requisite number – three-quarters of the states – to give women the vote in America. It was no longer a matter of if, but when, and so with her crusading passion spent Alva decided to sell up in the USA and move to France too, to support Consuelo. Consuelo wryly observed that part of the attraction was the opportunity for Alva to build herself yet another grand house.

Consuelo returned to London in August 1920, put Sunderland House and Crowhurst on the market and tidied up her life in England before moving permanently to France. She leased a villa near Alva's property at Èze-sur-Mer, but she also had a town house in Paris, given to her by her father before his death, which made a convenient base when she travelled to England to visit her sons and to attend the divorce hearing, held on 9 and 10 November. For this event she dressed entirely in black but for strands of pearls around her long neck, and before she left the court she pulled a black silk scarf from her muff and tied it over her head, concealing her hair and face from the photographers waiting outside. The divorce was duly granted, although it would not become absolute for six months – in May 1921 – and Consuelo retired to the South of France to live quietly in the meantime.

On 1 June Gladys moved into Ivor Guest's Paris house and Marlborough inserted a betrothal notice in *The Times*. The press had its usual field day: all of Gladys's personal and family history – her father's manslaughter charge, her own rumoured relationship with the German prince as well as other 'engagements' attributed to her – was splashed about and commented upon, as was the canard that Gladys had been Consuelo's bridesmaid. Marlborough might have taken fright at this, but it was Gladys who hesitated, and this steadied him. Up to a point, being Marlborough's mistress had suited her perfectly; she enjoyed defying convention and she was not at all sure that she wanted to be his wife despite their having been happy together for so many years. Surprised, he commented that she had surely had enough time to make up her mind. On reflection, she decided that, after all, she would like to give the Duke a son – she was forty, but there was still time. The marriage went ahead in Paris.

Gladys had been raised a Roman Catholic and insisted on both a civil and a religious ceremony, even though the Catholic Church did not recognise Marlborough's divorce. There was some difficulty getting a clergyman to conduct the service in a private chapel at the Paris home of one of Gladys's friends. Five priests declined, but at the eleventh hour Sunny brought over the Blenheim chaplain. On 25 June the civil ceremony was held at the British Consulate, just as Randolph and Jennie's had been nearly fifty years earlier. Gladys knocked five years off her age on the marriage certificate, but this would not have fooled Sunny for it would have made her ten years old when he first met her. The church wedding was attended by over four hundred guests including Gladys's sister Princess Dorothy Radziwill,* the King of Greece, the Maharajah of Kapurthala, Marshal Foch, Anatole France and Elsie de Wolfe.† Sarah Wilson, who was also there representing the Churchills, reported that the bride was 'very beautiful', but not that the word 'obey' had been removed from the responses, at Gladys's insistence.

Anxious to avoid the publicity circus that had surrounded Sunny and Gladys's wedding, Consuelo and Jacques were married quietly in London a week later, on 4 July. At 9 a.m. there was a religious service in the Savoy Chapel, followed (to comply with French law) by a civil ceremony at Covent Garden register office at which the American Ambassador and Consuelo's cousin Cornelius Vanderbilt (banned by Alva from attending Consuelo's first marriage) were witnesses. Alva had remained in the United States so as to lull journalists into assuming the wedding was not yet imminent.

Did Consuelo think of the contrast between this quiet, happy day and her first joyless wedding? Of herself as little more than an unhappy child, walking up the aisle weeping behind her veil? At this second marriage ceremony she was no longer young – her hair was silver now and her sons were present. The small family party went on afterwards to Blandford's house at No. 1 Portman Square for the wedding breakfast. Consuelo discarded all the privileges of her rank and title with grace, and without a trace of regret. As Madame Louis-Jacques Balsan she looked forward confidently to many years in France with the man she adored and would continue to adore until his death. They left England for Paris soon afterwards – appropriately enough, travelling by air. The house overlooking the Eiffel Tower, given to Consuelo by her father, was to be their main home there. Only one factor marred the total happiness of the newly-weds: their marriage was not recognised by the Catholic Church, which meant that the Balsan family were unable to receive Jacques and his bride.

---

*The Radziwills were the richest and most influential family in Poland. Remarkably, newsreel coverage of this wedding can be found on an Internet site, with a skittish Gladys showing off her gown.

†An American interior designer whose clients included royalty and high society. She was married to the diplomat Sir Charles Mendl.

1921–4

Black Times

The year 1921 would prove to be a dark one for Winston and Clementine. A series of family losses and ill-omened incidents began with the death of Clementine's ninety-year-old grandmother, the matriarch Blanche, Countess of Airlie, in early January.

In February Winston was offered the post of Colonial Secretary – which looked promising, though it also included a poisoned chalice in the form of the newly created Middle East Department responsible for the affairs of the British-mandated lands in Palestine and Iraq. Early in the 1914–18 war, the Hashemite patriarch and Sharif of Mecca, Hussein ibn Ali, had allied with the British and French against the Ottoman Empire. His decision to do so was based on a written promise from the British High Commissioner in Egypt, Sir Henry McMahon,* which agreed that if the Arabs were successful in driving out the Turks from their lands the British government would support the establishment of an independent Arab state under Hashemite rule stretching from Damascus to the Arab peninsula.

The consequent Arab Revolt against the Turks in 1916, led by Hussein's son Sheikh Faisal and T. E. Lawrence, supported by the

---

*Known as the Hussein–McMahon letters, the agreement could not be made to stick because the wording of the promise by McMahon was open to interpretation, and Hussein could only speak for the Hashemite tribes, not other Arabs.

British and French armies, was successful. But the British had also made other agreements, which were allowed to override the promises made by McMahon. First, in 1916, the British and French made a secret deal known as the Sykes–Picot Agreement, whereby if the Ottomans were driven out, those areas formerly occupied by the Turks would be divided between themselves. Second, Foreign Minister Balfour declared British support for the establishment of a Jewish 'national home' in Palestine (known as the Balfour Declaration). This was later ratified in order to appease leading Jews who had financially supported the war in Europe.

The former Ottoman lands were divided into two and nominated as 'mandated land'. There were few natural borders in the form of rivers or mountains, so on the map straight lines were simply drawn across the desert, no account being taken of Arab tribal homelands. After the San Remo Conference of 1920, France took control of modern-day Syria and the British took the mandate of Palestine (consisting of Jordan, an area of Palestine which is now the Gaza Strip, the West Bank, Israel and Iraq). The Arabs were justifiably furious at this breach of promise by the British, which brought with it the loss of their right to self-determination. They were also concerned at the growing number of Jewish immigrants arriving from Europe and the threat of the establishment of a Jewish state, supported by the Balfour Treaty, to the disadvantage of their own influence. The Jewish National Fund subsequently purchased large swathes of land from absentee Arab landowners, and many Arabs who had lived for decades on the land were summarily evicted. It was this hotbed of Western political chicanery, Arab fury and Jewish ambition that Winston inherited, along with Colonial Office and responsibility for British dominions throughout the world.

In January, after the funeral of Clementine's grandmother, the Churchills had holidayed in Nice at the invitation of Sir Ernest Cassel. Winston returned to London, leaving Clementine to rest and regain her energy in the sun. They had moved to 2 Sussex Square by this time, and as well as his own ministerial work he was overseeing work Clementine had set in train before they left and keeping an eye on the children. 'All the kittens are for the moment blooming,' he wrote reassuringly to her. Randolph was at a boarding prep school, doing well. There would be no letters from him begging his father to visit: Winston made a point of visiting his son regularly, as often as he could. The two elder girls Diana and Sarah, now aged twelve and seven, attended day school in the city. And he wrote fondly about baby Marigold, the 'Duckadily' as he called her, in the nursery with Nanny. It is evident that within the constraints of his work Winston was a fond and attentive father.

During February he kept Clementine up to date with all the news. He had loaned Nellie £500 to open a hat shop. At that time he was responsible for three state departments, Air, Colonies and War, a record never beaten. He was writing a piece for the *Strand Magazine* about painting to earn money to pay off some debts.

And there was good news about his mother. Montague Porch, taken aback at how fast Jennie could get through money, had decided to return to the Gold Coast. He never remonstrated with her, but had merely decided quietly that he must go back to West Africa to boost their finances. This region was then spoken of as 'the white man's grave', and it was clear that an isolated life in the style of a memsahib would never be right for Jennie. Montague would go alone, then after he had built her a suitable house she would join him, for a while at least. Now Winston wrote that Jennie had managed to sell the refurbished house in Berkeley Square for £35,000 – 'A clear profit of £15,000,' he wrote admiringly. 'She has already taken a little house in Charles St. No need [now] to go abroad. All is well. I am so glad.'[1] But even Winston had little idea of the real extent of Jennie's debts.

He wrote to Clementine, about this time, that at a party held for the Prince of Wales he had noticed that the Prince was as besotted as ever by his long-term mistress Freda Dudley Ward, and had gazed adoringly at her. But people were generally bored with the relationship, he said: 'They think that a door should be open or shut.' His workload was obviously not proving too much, for he advised that he was 'booked almost every night for one of these tiny parties'. There was some good news too, when an unexpected inheritance* provided him with a capital sum and a potential annual income of £4000. To the eternal worrier Clementine this windfall came as a tremendous relief; now, no matter what happened they would always have this basic income on which to live.

Winston had been busy appointing staff to the new Middle East Department and was especially pleased to have persuaded T. E. Lawrence to join him, along with other more conventional experts such as Curzon. He had called a British–Arab Conference, to be held in Cairo in March, at the Mena House Hotel, at the foot of the Pyramids, and Clementine was to join him and the others on their ship at Marseilles, whence they would all continue on to Egypt.

The Cairo Conference was an important historical milestone, and Winston had gathered as many knowledgeable delegates as he could. Along with T. E. Lawrence he had invited the Middle East traveller Gertrude Bell, former Army officer and diplomat Sir Percy Cox, British Civil Commissioner in Baghdad Sir Arnold Wilson and Sir Kinkaid Cornwallis, British Ambassador to Iraq. He also called the Iraqi War Minister Ja'far Al-Askeri and the Minister of Finance Sasun Heskay to join them. At Lawrence's urging Winston recognised that the British had made certain promises to Sharif Hussein and that if they were to have any future credence in Arab countries they had to be seen to have kept at least some of them.

It was in this spirit that decisions were reached at the Cairo Conference that would form the basis of British administration in the Middle East for decades to come. First, the Hashemite sons of Sharif Hussein were made rulers of the regions in the British-mandated areas: Sheikh Faisal (who had led the Arab Revolt with Lawrence) took the throne of Iraq, and his brother Sheikh Abdullah was given Transjordan. Second, it was agreed that the British Army presence in Iraq would be reduced and the role of protection mainly overseen by Air Force squadrons. It has been stated in several

---

*Winston inherited under the will of his great-grandmother, Lady Londonderry, when two heirs with prior claims died childless. The last of these was Lord Herbert Tempest-Vane in a train crash at Abermule in Montgomeryshire, North Wales, on 26 January 1921.

biographies of Churchill that the decisions reached at this Conference have underlain the problems of the Middle East ever since, but in fact Churchill merely made the best of a bad job. His hands had been tied from the start by the promises, machinations and commitments already made by a bungling Foreign Office during the 1914–18 war.

The conference ended on 22 March when the Churchills and some of the delegates travelled on to Jerusalem, where Winston had meetings with other Arab and Jewish leaders. They travelled home slowly, stopping at Alexandria, Sicily and Naples, and arrived in London on 10 April relaxed after hard negotiation. Nothing could have prepared them for the events that were to occur. They had scarcely unpacked when, five days later, on 15 April, Clementine's brother, Nellie's twin Bill, shot himself in a hotel room in Paris. After the war he had left the Navy and gone into business, which had failed. He was a gambler, as were his mother and Nellie – it had been a way of life at Dieppe in their circle and all three had been sucked into it. Clementine alone had avoided the lure of the tables.

Lady Blanche's cousin Sydney Mitford (later Lady Redesdale) was staying with Blanche in Dieppe that month with her son Tom and her six daughters: Nancy, Pam, Diana, Unity, Decca and baby Debo. The first telegram merely spoke of Bill having shot himself. Clementine and Nellie were sent for and hurried over to Dieppe. They found Blanche 'so brave and dignified, but I do not think she will recover from the shock & the grief,' Clementine wrote. 'She sits in her chair shrunk and small. When we saw her she did not yet know that Bill had killed himself, but I saw by the look of agony & fear that she half guessed – Then she said, "No one must ever know – Winston will keep it out of the papers won't he?"'[2]

The younger Mitford children always remembered the pall of sadness that hung over their holiday with Aunt Natty. They were sent out on an excursion with their Nanny on the day of the funeral. The family had a struggle to find a clergyman who would allow a suicide to be buried in consecrated ground, and to help them Winston sent a letter by official messenger to affirm that Bill had been a hero and much loved, rather than a scapegrace disowned by his family. So a clergyman was found who would allow Bill's body to lie in the church and be honourably interred. 'Oh Winston my Dear,' Clementine begged, 'do come tomorrow & dignify by your presence Bill's poor Suicide's Funeral.'[3]

Many years later when asked by her daughter Decca, Sydney would state that Bill had shot himself because of gambling debts. In fact no evidence of any gambling debts was ever found, but such debts are seldom written down, and Sydney said that Winston had bailed Bill out on a number of occasions. When, soon afterwards, Nellie begged Sydney to loan her £8 to pay a gambling debt, Sydney refused and went straight to Lady Blanche to report the matter. The debt was honoured, Nellie was castigated and sent back to England. The younger Mitford children thought this was very mean of their mother, never connecting Bill's death and Nellie's small debt. Suicide was a deeply shameful subject and never spoken of.

Jennie, having sold her house for such an enormous profit, had paid the most pressing of her debts. Montague Porch left as arranged for West Africa on 8 March without her, and she went off to Italy to stay with friends. After he sailed, Porch found a note that Jennie had slipped into his pocket. It was addressed to 'My darling' and wished him 'au revoir'. She wrote that she loved him more than anything in the world and would try to accomplish all those things he wanted her to do in his absence. 'Love and think of me,' she finished.[4]

In Italy, with her new sense of relief from debt, Jennie was the star of the party, dancing the young to a standstill, going to the races and – as usual – shopping. With a dashing young husband and money in the bank, she was at her brilliant best. Before leaving England, she had gone flying with a young RAF officer in his biplane – she could easily understand Winston's fascination with aviation, she said. In those days foreign tourists often bought handmade shoes when in Italy, and among her purchases in Rome was a pair of pretty high-heeled evening slippers. She wrote to her sister Leonie that she was having such fun and Rome was very gay.

When she returned to England she went to stay with the Horner family at Mells Place. It was there, while hurrying down the stairs to dinner, wearing the new shoes, that Jennie slipped and fell, breaking the same ankle she had fractured many years earlier on a grouse moor. It was just a silly accident: the family blamed Jennie's maid for not roughing up the new leather soles, but Jennie was cross with herself. A doctor set the compound breaks, and after a few days she was able to travel to London to recuperate. Porch was advised by cable. 'My own darling – I am so terribly distressed,' he wrote. 'Your poor darling little foot . . . you will never be able to dance again . . . but I shall love you very very much to make up for all the pain & anguish you have suffered . . . Darling I am ready to come to you any day – this I have cabled to you. But my business would suffer v. much – my business* that has turned out an amazing success.'[5]

He had finished this letter but had not sealed it, when he received another cable from Winston telling him that blood poisoning had set in, followed by gangrene, and it had now been decided to amputate the leg. 'Jennie darling,' he added at the bottom of his letter before assuring her that the loss of her leg would not change his feelings for her, though he had been very shocked and made miserable by the news. 'I will help you to bear all this. How can I ever love you enough – I will be very good to you, considerate & faithful . . . Bless you sweet Darling – I send you all my love & kisses & more kisses for the poor little place where the stitches are.'[6]

Had Jennie not been so ill, nothing would have kept her or Winston from the Paris wedding of Sunny and Gladys on 25 June. At first after the amputation she had a very high temperature but after a few days she made a good recovery, although everyone knew there would be a long convalescence. That week Winston cabled Porch that the operation had been successfully carried out and Jennie was now out of danger. She was even able to have some visitors in her bedroom; propped up on pillows, she chatted brightly, joking that she would just have to put her best foot forward.

'My Own darling,' Porch wrote, 'Winston's last cable that "Danger was definitely over" was re-assuring – still I am often

---

*The details of Porch's business are sketchy – he termed it 'investment opportunities'.

frantic with apprehension & fear. I have no one in the world but You, that is no one I love, as I love you.' He told her that he had arranged to pay off her overdue tax bill, so that her income was now free of obligations; he had made the house in West Africa so nice for her and was sad that she might now never see it, but his business was doing amazingly well. 'I can never tell you too often that I love you & will devote my life to you. Your loving husband M.'[7] Jennie received this letter on 28 June and cabled a reply to him at once; she had not felt up to writing before then, and she knew he would be miserable at not hearing from her.

The following morning after breakfast she was sitting up in bed when she suddenly felt a gush of warm liquid on her good leg and told her nurse her hot water bottle had burst. When the bedclothes were pulled back they could both see it was a major haemorrhage: an artery above the amputation site had burst open. Her last words were to the nurse – 'I am feeling faint' – then she lapsed into unconsciousness. Winston and Jack were summoned and came fast. Winston lived a few streets away; as usual he had been working in bed and was still wearing his night clothes under his overcoat as he tore through the streets. But Jennie was near to death when he arrived, and she never spoke to her sons again.

Leonie, who was attending her daughter-in-law's labour, cabled their sister Clara (Clarita) in Sussex telling her to go to Jennie at once as she had been taken suddenly ill. By the time Clara's train pulled into Victoria Station the newspaper posters were already proclaiming 'Death of Lady Randolph'. Within minutes of Jennie's death Leonie's grandchild was delivered.

Jennie had lived in the very flame of life. For almost fifty years she had known everyone worth knowing in European and probably American society too – some of them intimately – and certainly in British politics. She had virtually pioneered the so-called Dollar Princess marriages to the British aristocracy. Winston's success had been the high point of her life and had made up for the disaster in his father's career. The tributes that poured in to comfort the stricken family spoke of her vitality and charm. After her death, when the lines had been smoothed away and the expression had relaxed, her bone structure had all the hallmarks of a Native American inheritance. Many family members remarked on this.

There was a memorial service on 2 July, and the private funeral was held at Bladon church near Blenheim later that same hot, cloudless day. Jennie was buried next to Lord Randolph in the family plot. The family mourners were joined by a few old friends including Jack's parents-in-law, Lady Sarah Wilson, Jennie's old love Hugh Warrender and his wife. Lord Howe, husband of one of Lord Randolph's sisters, attended as a representative of the royal family. They travelled down to Oxford by train with the coffin, bearing Porch's wreath on top of it, in a separate carriage; it would be another month before he could get home by ship from West Africa. With Sunny away on honeymoon there were no servants on duty; after the funeral, the mourners all walked over to Blenheim for a picnic lunch in the gardens.

It was Jennie's illness that prevented Winston and Clementine, and Jack and Goonie, from attending either Sunny's or Consuelo's wedding, and was one reason why Consuelo was able to marry Jacques Balsan without the press suspecting anything, since her wedding took place only two days after Jennie's funeral and there were few guests in the circumstances. With the exception of Sunny and Consuelo, they were all on visiting terms by that date. Consuelo had stayed with the Churchills on several occasions; she and Jennie had long ago settled their old argument, and during the war they had worked together fund-raising for hospital projects. Sunny and Winston were once again best friends, barring political disagreements from time to time.

Winston was inconsolable at his mother's death. It was Jack as executor of Jennie's estate, with the help of Montague Porch, who did what was necessary – for with all her abilities Jennie was never an administrator, and she died intestate. Although Porch had paid off many of her immediate debts after their marriage, she was still hugely overdrawn to the bank; and indeed, Porch had borrowed to launch his West African project with an overdraft of £4500 guaranteed by Winston. Porch's business was already in profit, but for the time being his money was tied up in West Africa, and for six months Winston was worried he might have to stump up for a shortfall of £1000 on the fixed-term loan. (This was a significant sum of money – £5000 would buy a small country estate at the time.) Almost all of Jennie's debts were covered by a spectacular auction sale of her house and contents.[8]

Porch wanted nothing from Jennie's estate; eventually he retired from Nigeria and settled in Somerset, where his family were small private bankers. After some years he married again, to an Italian noblewoman, Donna Giulia Patrizi, daughter of the Marchese Patrizi Della Rocca.*

Shortly before Jennie's accident Winston had found a house that he had fallen in love with. It was called Chartwell Manor, and overlooked the Weald of Kent, near Westerham. Jennie's illness had put this plan on hold, but now, perhaps as an antidote to his intense grief, he took it up again. Clementine liked 'the house on the hill', as she called it, too, but her compulsive worrying about money kicked in and after further inspection she became concerned about the amount of work called for to make it what Winston wanted it to be, as well as about their ability to run it within their income. Unlike Winston, she saw beyond the romantic old house and its superlative location to the problems of damp, dry rot and all the other dilapidations of a property that had lain unoccupied for several years (plus its several acres of wild rhododendrons that would need to be removed). So, writing to him on Diana's twelfth birthday, 11 July, she gently advised caution. She too longed for a country home, she wrote, somewhere they could have Goonie and Jack and the children to stay (Goonie had given birth eighteen months earlier to her last child, Clarissa), but it should be a place for Winston's relaxation, not another commitment for her already overworked husband.

The family summer holiday lay ahead, when they could hope to

---

*Montague Porch died in November 1964. He never spoke of his marriage to Jennie to anyone, but after his death when the new owners moved into his old house they found his room contained 'floor to ceiling' pictures of her. During the Second World War he applied to Winston to keep his Italian manservant out of an internment camp on his own cognisance. Winston complied.

recover from the blows they had suffered that spring. Almost as soon as the children came home, ten-year-old Randolph confided to his sister Diana that one of the junior masters at his school had made him touch him sexually. Randolph later wrote about it in his book *Twenty-One Years* without embarrassment, stating that he had not felt any distress and only realised that it was wrong when a maid came into the room and blushed scarlet while the master jumped to his feet and behaved oddly. Their nanny overheard the conversation between Randolph and Diana and told Clementine, who went to Winston and told him he must deal with it. Winston, of course, had vivid memories of being physically abused at school. 'I remember very well,' Randolph wrote, 'how my father sent for me one morning when he was still lying in bed and having his breakfast and asked me about the truth of the matter. I told him the truth as I have always done. I don't think I have ever seen him so angry before or since. He leapt out of bed, ordered his car and drove all across country – the round trip must have been well over two hundred miles.'[9] The man concerned was dismissed and Randolph was warned never to allow anyone ever to do this to him again.

At the beginning of August the children went off to the seaside to spend two weeks there with their nanny, following which they were to join their parents in Scotland. On 8 August Clementine set off for the north ahead of Winston in order to stay with friends en route. Her great talent was tennis, and she always enjoyed staying somewhere she could get a good game with challenging players – in this case Eaton Hall near Chester, the large country house of Bendor, the Duke of Westminster, who together with his second wife Violet* was to join the Churchills in Scotland later in the month. It was at Eaton Hall on 14 August, while preparing to leave for Scotland, that Clementine received an urgent cable from Nanny in Broadstairs to advise that Marigold was unwell.

Marigold was almost three. She had a tendency to colds and sore throats, just as her father had as a child. But the infection that began with a simple cold at Broadstairs rapidly developed into something

---

*He and Shelagh (his first wife, the sister of George Cornwallis-West) had divorced in 1919.

more serious and the little girl seemed unable to fight it off. Clementine rushed down to the south coast and sent the older children off to Scotland as planned, with her maid. It was evident that Marigold was in distress, and the doctor soon confirmed that the sore throat had turned into septicaemia. It would be another seven years before Sir Alexander Fleming discovered penicillin and at least twenty before antibiotics were available for clinical use. Clementine alerted Winston, who drove from London immediately. Both parents were with their youngest daughter when she died on 23 August 1921. Winston could not speak for grief and according to his secretary, Clementine 'screamed like an animal undergoing torture'. Stunned, they buried Marigold at Kensal Green cemetery.*

Clementine, always her own fiercest critic, carried the dreadful guilt that she had not been with her child when the infection started, and that had she been there she might have saved her. Winston had still not recovered from burying his mother, barely six weeks earlier, and this latest blow was even more difficult to bear. They travelled to Scotland to join the other three children, and when in September Clementine returned to London with them for the start of term, an abnormally subdued Winston went to visit the Duke of Sutherland before going on to Dundee to give a speech. His stay was hardly restful; the castle was the venue for the usual September fishing and shooting house parties. Among the guests that week were the Prince of Wales, his brother the Duke of Gloucester and the Dudley Wards. Winston found himself unable to join in the many pleasant pastimes that were available for the guests; instead he turned to solitary painting, near a quiet stream, and worked on his speech. He told Clementine she would have found it all too much. 'It is another splendid day: & I am off to the river to catch pictures – much better fun than salmon,' he wrote. 'Many tender thoughts my darling one, of you & yr sweet kittens. Alas I keep on feeling the hurt of the Duckadily – I expect you will all have made a pilgrimage [to the grave] yesterday.'[10]

---

*The simple headstone reads: Here lies Marigold dear child of Winston and Clementine Churchill Born Nov 15 1918 Died Aug 23 1921 RIP.

Nor was this the last of the bad news. While Winston was in Scotland Sir Ernest Cassel, his mentor and friend since his youth, died suddenly. Clementine was very moved when she wrote to tell Winston: 'I have been through so much lately that I thought I had little feeling left, but I wept for our dear old friend; he was a feature in our lives and he cared deeply for you . . . I took the children on Sunday to Marigold's grave and as we knelt round it . . . a little white butterfly . . . fluttered down & settled on the flowers which are now growing on it . . . the children were very silent all the way home . . . I wish so much I could be in Dundee to hear you [on] Saturday night. I much want to see you.'[11]

The postwar years brought changes for many members of the extended Churchill family. Reggie Fellowes, the banker son of Lord Randolph's sister Rosamund and once suspected by Sunny Marlborough of having an affair with Consuelo, had married Daisy, the French beauty who had attempted to seduce Winston in the Ritz in Paris. As well as being heiress to the Singer sewing-machine fortune she was a minor novelist and poet, later editor of *Harper's Bazaar* and a fashion icon in her own right. She was a major figure in between-the-wars Society and proved a colourful addition to the Churchill family when she married Reggie. She was to become a good friend of Clementine and Winston, and always managed to amuse him.

About this time, the seventeen-year marriage of Winston's cousin and long-time supporter Freddie Guest was looking precarious. Clementine had come to dislike visiting Freddie and Amy. They lived too extravagantly for her puritanical tastes, and the strong-willed Amy dominated her husband, which Clementine found embarrassing. She also disapproved of Freddie, who was a flirt. Winston, however, sybarite that he was, enjoyed the lavish comforts to be found at Burley-on-the-Hill. He was also fond of Freddie and Amy's teenage children, Winston, Raymond and Diana.

In the last days of 1921, after Christmas, Winston paid a short visit to Cannes with Lloyd George. The day after he left Sussex Square influenza swept through the house; Clementine, the children and all the servants caught it, and one of the servants died, thus bringing a dismal end to an unhappy year.

Winston was lucky to escape it. At his hotel in Cannes he met Freddie, now Secretary of State for Air, a post he had acquired via Winston's recommendation. Freddie told him he had fallen in love with the cool, svelte socialite Paula Gellibrand, and was seriously considering, he confided to Winston's unwilling ears, divorcing the forceful Amy. Paula Gellibrand was an unusual personality, not the sort of woman for whom men usually leave their wives. A top model – she has been described as a Modigliani come to life – she was neither beautiful nor pretty but she was extraordinarily striking, and with her angular figure and features she would frequently be seen in the contemporary images of the photographers Cecil Beaton and Baron de Meyer. At the time she was also being courted by the Cuban-Castilian Marqués de Casa Maury, a Bugatti-driving Grand Prix ace, whom she would later marry.

When Freddie imparted his news, Winston – evidently thinking on his feet – did not attempt to sermonise but simply remarked 'sepulchrally' that Miss Gellibrand seemed young enough to be Freddie's daughter, and reminded his cousin that another decade would carry both Freddie and himself towards the age of sixty. In reporting the conversation to Clementine, Winston added that he had told Freddie 'that he wd lose his office if he lost his Amy. So there's a problem!' In a postscript to Clementine he warned: 'Don't make chaff about it.'[12]

Later when he moved along the coast to stay with Adele, Countess of Essex, Winston could see from his window the hotel at Cap-d'Ail where he and Clementine had spent a last happy day picnicking with Jennie in January of the previous year when they were all staying near Nice. 'What changes in a year!' he wrote to Clementine. 'What gaps! What a sense of fleeting shadows! But your sweet love & comradeship is a light that burns the stronger as our brief years pass.'[13] He was there to work, and work he did, but he found the time to meet Clementine's mother Lady Blanche – now living in the South of France thanks to an allowance from Winston – who was an aficionada of the numerous casinos there. Not having Clementine's fear of gambling, Winston found Blanche amusing. She had won 400 francs one night when he accompanied her; he remarked, 'I think she enjoyed her evening. She is a dear.' Consuelo and Jacques Balsan had also made their home there, and as a belated wedding gift Winston gave them one of his paintings of Èze-sur-Mer that they had admired.

When Winston returned home to wintry London in mid-January 1922, he sent Clementine out to the Riviera with her cousin Venetia Montagu. He was too busy to stay there with her – 'My work will be very important next week – but how barren these things would be . . . if I had not a real home to come home to and a real sweet to await me there.' Clementine was pregnant again, and he was concerned about her health after the difficulties of the previous year. He thought the fine weather and a visit to her mother would help in 'recharging your accumulators'.* While there, Clementine attempted a hand of chemin de fer in a casino and won 15 francs. Playfully she suggested they should bet on whether the new baby's hair would be *rouge* or *noir*. Winston's aunt, Lady Sarah Wilson, who had been widowed during the war, was also staying there. Sarah appeared at every family occasion and was at the hub of the family's information exchange as ever: she was tolerated but not much liked.

Meanwhile, Winston dined three nights out of four with a group comprising Stanley Baldwin, F.E. Smith (now Lord Birkenhead, though always known as 'F.E.'), the Lord Chancellor and Max Aitken. So in the evenings they could all continue to work on the difficult Irish question over which, in the House, Winston had come up against a firebrand young Tory backbencher, Oswald Mosley. On his free evening Winston dined with Jack and Goonie, who told him that Asquith had accepted Goonie's invitation to dine the following week, but had imposed the condition that Winston should not be there. 'I have always been very courteous and considerate to the old man,' he wrote to Clementine. 'All the same I cannot forget the way he deserted me over the Dardanelles, calmly leaving me to pay the sole forfeit of the policy which at every angle

---

*An early form of battery.

he had actively approved.'[14] Clementine advised him to make the first move towards rapprochement – 'He has suffered more than we have by the War, by Death,' she wrote. 'People will only say "Look how nice Winston is."'[15]

During that summer a heavily pregnant Clementine joined Goonie and all the children at a rented seaside house in Devon. The two women were the closest of confidantes and Goonie was a safe ear when the pressures got too much for Clementine at home. With the assistance of a former schoolfriend, Lionel Rothschild, Jack had been made a partner of the leading stockbrokers Vickers Da Costa, and Winston was as busy as usual. Although he was engaged in the negotiations over Ireland, was running a ministry and appeared in the Commons each day, he was also working on the first volume of a book to be called *The World Crisis*.* As if this were not enough, he went dancing most evenings at summer balls, he reported to Clementine. At one ball, where Edwina Ashley (granddaughter of the late Sir Ernest Cassel) had danced all night 'in rapture' with her fiancé Lord Louis Mountbatten, Asquith had put in an appearance in a frail state and had to be helped up the stairs. Winston had danced eight times in a row – 'good exercise', he wrote. Perhaps the frenetic activity was a way of dealing with his losses, for he added that, in the midst of it all, 'I pass through again those sad scenes of last year when we lost our dear Duckadily. Poor lamb – it is a gaping wound, whenever one touches it.'[16]

The Churchills' fifth and last child was born on 15 September 1922, and they called her Mary. Despite Clementine's earlier misgivings about Chartwell, Winston went ahead and, without telling her, put in an offer for the old manor with its eighty acres of neglected hillside complete with stream and stands of old beech woods.[17] Possibly his rationale was to save his wife any worry at a difficult time, the last week of her pregnancy. More probably, that was how he justified to himself not telling her, because he wanted the house more than anything he had wanted for a long time and he knew that Clementine would try to talk him out of

---

*Volume I was published in 1923.

it. His first offer was not successful, but he finally purchased the house for £5000.*

While Clementine was still lying in he took Randolph, Diana and Sarah on a surprise day out, driving them down to Chartwell to show them round the property. They were impressed by the dank and gloomy house, which had a touch of the gothic about it, and they were allowed to run wild in the overgrown gardens. Their father's undivided attention for an entire day was undoubtedly a factor in their enchantment, and they begged him to buy it. Only when they reached Parliament Square on the return journey did he break the news to them that he had already done so. And then he had to tell Clementine. Not surprisingly, she felt he had been underhand with her. Years later she would confide to Mary that it was the only time in fifty years of marriage that he had acted 'with less than candour towards her'.[18] She never entirely forgave him for it; consequently Chartwell was always Winston's house rather than Clementine's home, although for the rest of their lives together she dutifully did her best to make it the home he always envisaged.

It was not a deep rift. They always made a point of 'never allowing the sun to go down on their wrath', and even while they were still in disagreement over Chartwell their letters show the same tenderness for each other. So Clementine had evidently decided to forget, if not forgive. Her concern was all financial, and it cannot have been any pleasure to her when she was later proved right to have been worried; although Winston was always confident that he would earn enough by his pen and his political efforts to keep his family, and Chartwell, in the manner to which a descendant of the great Duke of Marlborough should live. His vision of his place in the world was an essential part of Winston's character and of his successes.

Perhaps it worked in his favour that he was unwell at the time, complaining of abdominal pains, and he was also anxious about the fate of the government which was now in terminal decline. Clementine could hardly help being concerned about him and she was right to be so, for

---

*Winston was amused to discover that the vendor was a contemporary of his at Harrow, with whom he had regularly competed for bottom place in the fourth form.

soon afterwards he was rushed to hospital by ambulance in great pain and on 23 October his appendix was removed. This was not then a straightforward operation – mortality rates were high. So Winston was still prostrate, in conditions as close to aseptic as possible, when on 26 October the government fell, as he had feared it would.

He would not have been a good patient at the best of times, given the dietary regimen and the inactivity imposed on him, and now there was a general election to be fought. It was probably to keep him reasonably calm that in early November Clementine, with baby Mary, then just seven weeks old, travelled to Dundee to campaign for her husband. Winston joined her as soon as he was allowed to do so – certainly earlier than the requisite six weeks normally insisted upon after an appendectomy. He was carried to meetings in an invalid chair and delivered his speeches sitting down. The press gave good coverage to this human-interest story: mother and baby facing unsympathetic crowds on behalf of her sick husband, Churchill the gallant invalid struggling up from his sickbed. But the tide of opinion was wholly against the Liberal Party and Lloyd George.* The poverty and misery experienced in the great cities of the United Kingdom after 1918 did not reflect the anticipation of the men who had fought and won the war that they would return to 'a land fit for heroes'. The majority the Liberals had enjoyed in the postwar election was swept away on 15 November 1922 and the Tories were the overall beneficiary, but they managed only narrowly to form a government, under Andrew Bonar Law. It was impossible for anyone to disregard the fact that while the Liberals had achieved second position, having polled 5.5 million votes, some four million votes had been cast for the underdog third party, Labour. Bonar Law did not last long at No. 10; he resigned after six months, having been diagnosed with terminal cancer, and Stanley Baldwin took over the Tory leadership.

For the first time in over twenty years Winston found himself out

---

*Churchill did not always agree with Lloyd George, and there was considerable disharmony between the two men when Churchill attempted to involve Britain in a campaign against the Bolsheviks after the First World War.

of office. Even when he lost his ministerial post after the Dardanelles he had remained an MP. He was low and unwell. Later he would describe his position thus: 'In the twinkling of an eye I found myself without an office, without a seat, without a party and without an appendix.'[19] Clementine was tired after the birth of her baby, plus the effort and stress of the unsuccessful election campaign. They decided to go abroad for the winter, to recover their strength. They let the London house and rented a villa near Cannes. Called Rêve d'Or, it would feature in many of Winston's paintings during the six months they stayed there. He returned to England occasionally to escort the children to and from school and to oversee the renovations he had set in motion at Chartwell. Ninety years later, the difference between then and now in the lifestyle of the upper classes is epitomised by a minor detail: Clementine's insistence that the sewing room be large and airy, because '2 or 3 maids will sit & sew in there every day'.

When they returned to England Winston had time to work on Chartwell and to complete the first two volumes of *The World Crisis*. This subjective history of the 1914–18 war, including his passionate account of the Dardanelles campaign, was written in order to rehabilitate his status as a political thinker as much as to confirm his decisions as a war leader. His method of composition never changed. He dictated to a typist (or, later on, a team of typists), usually late at night, endlessly walking back and forth in his study, smoking a cigar and sipping at a brandy and soda. Inevitably, given Churchill's importance in history, this multivolume book has been pored over and dissected ever since. Scholars, as well as writers and politicians of far less ability than Churchill, have declared it to be not a wholly reliable account, although its place in literature was and is almost universally acclaimed. Published in the autumn of 1923, it did much to restore his reputation as a statesman.

Baldwin's tenure as Prime Minister did not last long. He called a general election for 6 December on a free-trade ticket but the electorate decided there were more important matters. The Conservatives retained the largest number of seats – 258 – but now the Labour Party had become the major party of Opposition, with 191 seats to the Liberals' 159. Baldwin formed a new government without an overall majority, then resigned a month later. On 22 January 1924 Ramsay MacDonald formed the first Labour government with the promised support of Asquith and the Liberals.

Winston was furious. This was not the Liberal Party he had crossed the floor to join – this was a party that supported Socialism, only one step removed from Bolshevism in his opinion. With his wonderful talent for a soundbite, he compared the Liberal support for Labour as 'not dissimilar from missionaries assisting cannibals'. However, although he was a free-trader he could not, he felt, rejoin the Conservatives because he was not in tune generally with the present aims of the party.

So a month later when the incumbent suddenly died and there was a by-election for the constituency of Westminster Abbey, he stood as an Independent Anti-Socialist (sometimes called Constitutionalist) and was defeated by only forty-three votes. It was an exciting campaign, in which leading Tories such as his friend Lord Birkenhead as well as Balfour supported his fight against the official – and ultimately successful – Conservative candidate. Freddie Guest organised his campaign and several other Liberal politicians worked tirelessly on his behalf. A-list celebrities such as Sunny Marlborough were coaxed into appearing to ensure maximum newspaper coverage, and Winston toured the small constituency on polling day driving a coach-and-four containing his young family. His defeat, rather than depressing him, seemed to reinvigorate him and in the next general election, held that autumn, he was elected as Member for Epping in North London with a large majority. Baldwin had ensured he was not opposed by a Conservative candidate.

In 1924, apart from campaigning Winston had concentrated on the huge amount of work yet to be done at Chartwell. He had employed as architect Philip Tilden, but at times he had almost the same relationship with him as Sarah Marlborough had had with Vanbrugh. On first sight, Tilden found Chartwell a dreary place: 'very close to the road' and so overhung by trees that the red bricks were 'slimed' with green. 'Only . . . the kernel of the old manor, floored and raftered in old oak, had withstood the ravages of wet; the rest was weary of its own ugliness so that the walls ran with moisture and creeping fungus tracked down the cracks and crevices.' Winston had a clear vision of what he wanted at Chartwell and simply expected Tilden to provide it. This involved transforming the interior of the ancient manor farm, with its high-ceilinged beamed rooms, into his personal domain – a huge study with a bedroom leading from it. This effectively turned the house around, so that instead of facing the shrubbery the front now commanded the best views of his land and the Weald beyond, with a run of French windows on the ground floor taking advantage of the magnificent views. He commissioned a new four-storey wing and a fair-sized terrace. And he envisaged lakes, dams and water gardens – perhaps even a natural swimming pool using the water from the Chart well, which rises on a hill above the house and from which it takes its name. Eventually, he got what he wanted; but just as the fictional Soames Forsyte's house vastly exceeded its original quotation, so did Chartwell. The original estimate of £7000 in 1922 culminated in bills for over £18,000, by which time architect and owner were barely on speaking terms.[20]

But he was now back in the Commons, where he belonged, and Baldwin wanted his expertise, even as an Independent. Winston was fully aware that in terms of parliamentary experience few in the House could beat him, but he had no sense of being courted. He told Clementine that if the Tories offered him a post it would have to be 'a great one' in order to tempt him back into the Tory fold. He had no intention of regressing, as he saw it, and intended to refuse any minor office. But when he was summoned to see Baldwin on 5 November he was dumbfounded to be offered his father's old post of Chancellor of the Exchequer. Not even in his dreams had he expected this. When Baldwin had asked him, 'Will you be Chancellor of the Exchequer?' Winston would later say he had felt like retorting: 'Will a duck swim?' Instead he answered formally that he would be proud to do so, and that as a matter of fact he still had his father's robes of office. These had been preserved for him by Jennie for almost thirty years. She was always convinced that Winston would need them one day.

On being asked to comment on his return to the Conservative front benches, he observed: 'Anyone can rat, but it takes a certain amount of ingenuity to re-rat.'

1921–31

The Twenties

On 28 July 1921 Gladys had gone to Blenheim for the first time as the wife of the 9th Duke. Despite having been a visitor there for almost twenty years, she did not slip easily into the role of chatelaine and nor was she popular with the tenants or with local society. Consuelo had won their hearts many years earlier, and Gladys was generally regarded as the reason why there had been no Duchess at Blenheim since 1908. Whereas Consuelo had tried hard to merge into what had been an alien environment for her and to do what was expected of a duchess, Gladys felt no such responsibility and simply lived her life as before, throwing parties and other entertainments. But her desire to shock and tease, which had been amusing and appealing in a beautiful young girl, could cause offence when it came from a middle-aged duchess. And though at first blissfully happy at having accomplished his much longed-for marriage, Sunny sometimes found himself squirming at his wife's behaviour. At their first house party she announced: 'If we have a daughter we shall call her Syphilis. Lady Syphilis Churchill is such a pretty sounding name.' One of the guests, Sonia Cubitt,* glanced quickly at Sunny and saw him wince.

In those days there were never fewer than forty indoor servants, probably the same number employed in the gardens, and another

---

*Younger daughter of Mrs Alice Keppel, Edward VII's mistress.

dozen men in the stables. All the footmen had to be over six feet tall in order to wear the uniform of maroon coat with silver brocade, and they still powdered their hair. Gladys told the sculptor Jacob Epstein that she had married a house rather than a man; and in as much as Sunny had sacrificed his life to Blenheim, that was true. He had used Vanderbilt money to shore the house up, refurbishing and renewing, replacing items plundered by previous Dukes, making the gardens beautiful and supporting a lifestyle that he considered suitable to his status. Throughout his adult life he ate off gold plates at Blenheim, even when dining informally. One of Jack Churchill's sons, a frequent visitor during his childhood, felt that this was an overrated privilege: 'I was always worried for fear some of the gold would chip off and get mixed with the vegetables.'[1]

Soon after Gladys's arrival, when invitations went out to the local gentry, more apologies than might have been expected were sent in reply. On the day of one such entertainment the Duke was riding past the house of a gentleman who had excused himself because he was going to be away. Unfortunately, Sunny could see that he was very much at home, relaxing in his garden. He never forgave the culprit for this slight.

Such pinpricks concerning his wife would eventually impinge on this proud man. But except when Gladys became pregnant in January 1922 and miscarried a few weeks later, life went on very much as before, though Sunny became increasingly short-tempered and argumentative. Within two years of their marriage, soon after another miscarriage when she was perhaps in low spirits, Gladys wrote in her diary that his rudeness to her was 'not very marked in public yet – but that will come. I am glad because I am sick of life here . . . we will separate perhaps before long and I will then go away for good and ever.'[2] It was almost as if she invited the conflict. Meanwhile they still rode together and performed the duties expected of them; they entertained most weekends when in Oxfordshire and travelled regularly in the Mediterranean countries, often gleaning ideas from the great houses in Italy for the gardens at home. The water gardens at Blenheim, the result of this joint research, were installed by Achille Duchêne who had designed and built Sunderland House for Consuelo. Sunny adored this project, spending hours each day overseeing every detail of the work. It took five years to complete. A flight of steps was marked by two large sphinxes, each with the face of Gladys.* Her first biographer, a contemporary, stated: 'This is the best likeness of her that will ever be seen.'[3]

Sunny had never appeared overtly religious. He had attended church as many Englishmen of his generation did because it was the right thing to do and *pour encourager les autres*. In 1923 he broke with the Anglican Church when as a divorcee he was publicly banned from attending the Oxford Diocesan Conference in his capacity as Lord Lieutenant of the County, an event he had no wish to attend anyway. Out of pique he began going to Catholic services as a non-communicant but a few years later, after taking a course of instruction from a Catholic priest,† he decided that, if possible, he would like to convert to Catholicism. His divorce was of course a hindrance to this ambition.

Coincidentally, Sunny's desire to convert was matched by Consuelo's to heal the breach within the Balsan family. Four years after Jacques and Consuelo's marriage there were members of Jacques's conservative family who still felt unable to receive the couple because they had been married outside the Church. There have been many instances throughout history of famous marriage annulments. Perhaps this is what persuaded Consuelo to take the first tentative step of consulting a Catholic lawyer about the possibility of having her first marriage annulled in order to allow her to marry Jacques in the Catholic Church. This was a totally selfless wish, she said in her autobiography, for she was perfectly secure in her Protestant marriage to Jacques and would have happily continued that way until she died. But she knew Jacques was saddened by the rift that their 'mixed marriage' had created within his family. The greatest risk, if her marriage to Sunny were to be

---

*The sphinxes can still be seen at Blenheim today.
†Father C. C. Martindale. For an account of the Duke's conversion, see W. S. Churchill and C. C. Martindale: *Charles, IXth Duke of Marlborough: Tributes.*

annulled, was the matter of the legitimacy of their sons Blandford and Ivor. However, investigation revealed that if the marriage was annulled by the Church, the legality of the children's birth would not be affected. It was a purely ecclesiastical matter and did not affect civil law.

A number of possible grounds existed for obtaining an annulment, such as a previous marriage, consanguinity or impotence, but the one that fitted the bill for Consuelo was that she had been under age when she was 'coerced' into the marriage by 'force and fear'. Sunny was as keen as she was to seek an annulment. Gladys had been raised as a Catholic anyway, and now Sunny made up his mind that he, too, would convert and marry in the Catholic Church. Consuelo claimed that the first move for an annulment had come from the Duke, but he immediately had his solicitors make a statement to the contrary. It hardly matters; but it is fair to say that the mutual loathing between Sunny and Consuelo made annulment acceptable to both parties.

Since her marriage to Jacques, Consuelo had known the first true happiness of her life. They both loved their Paris house and had spent months wandering the streets and quays finding beautiful antique furniture, old *boiseries* (pieces in decorated and carved wood), bibelots and Impressionist paintings to fill it. Money was no object, thanks to the trust fund of $2,500,000 left by her father as well as a massive personal bequest made before his death. Soon, exquisite Louis Quinze furniture stood on Aubusson carpets beneath paintings by Fragonard, Manet and Renoir. Gobelin tapestries hung in the halls lit by crystal chandeliers. Consuelo filled her home with fragrant flowers, and employed the best chefs. It was a jewel of a house, and as soon as the Balsans began entertaining they were quickly taken up by those who made up the Parisian *ancien régime*.

When the Paris house was finished they turned their attention to one near the medieval fortified hilltop village of Èze, overlooking St-Jean-Cap-Ferrat to the west of Monaco and close to Alva's house at Èze-sur-Mer on the Côte d'Azur. Here the Balsans built Lou Seuil, which they furnished in a *belle époque* style. They panelled some of the rooms to act as a foil for Consuelo's English furniture brought over from Crowhurst Place, and it was a great pleasure to them both to go hunting for items to furnish this winter home. It stood on a rocky hilltop, with Èze perched on a neighbouring hill-top across a deep ravine. When they bought it there was almost no land around it, but Jacques used his charm and his business acumen and 'bantered and bartered' for around fifty small adjoining plots belonging to local people. Consuelo said that only a Frenchman could have achieved it, as the bargaining process took years. Eventually the house was surrounded by beautifully tended terraced gardens. An army of gardeners ensured that drifts of flowers flour-ished under the olive trees on these terraces all year round.

Clementine stayed with the Balsans at Lou Seuil in March 1925, when Consuelo was nearing fifty. She wrote to Winston, 'My Darling, I am writing to you in bed in this marvellous scented nest – it is really almost too beautiful & too comfortable. One simply wallows. How I wish you were here with me to wallow, & to paint. Consuelo looks younger and more ethereal every year. Her hair is more silvery but on the other hand her cheeks are pinker and her eyes brighter. Her Jacques surrounds her with *petits soins* [little attentions] . . . the garden is a dream – carpets of purple, gold, and cream flowers on the emerald green grass.'[4] Churchill, too, was a frequent visitor to Lou Seuil over the years, and sometimes painted there. Consuelo and Jacques wanted everybody to share their obvi-ous happiness. 'One could see at once that it was a loved house,' said Consuelo's cousin Gloria Vanderbilt, when she visited.

When the application for the annulment of Consuelo's first marriage was heard, Alva – whose abhorrence for Sunny was only equalled by his for her – wrote a letter to the Catholic court of canon law which convened privately at Southwark in July 1926 to test the matter. She confirmed that she had coerced her teenage daughter into a marriage Consuelo had not wanted: 'I *ordered* Consuelo to marry the Duke . . . I considered myself justified in overriding her opposition, which I considered to be merely the whim of a young inexperienced girl,' she stated.[5] Her sister, Jenny Tiffany, recalled Consuelo being told that her mother had suf-fered a heart attack because of her refusal to marry the Duke, and that she might die if Consuelo continued to be obdurate. Alva's former secretary, a Miss Harper, verified these statements and confirmed that Consuelo had been in love with someone else at the time. To the court's inquiry, 'Do you consider that the constraint was simple persuasion or really coercion?', Alva's friend Mrs Lucy Jay affirmed on oath: 'Not persuasion at all, but absolute coercion.'

Consuelo appeared in person before the tribunal and offered in evidence a bundle of letters written to her by Winthrop Rutherfurd before her marriage. She had kept and treasured them throughout those unhappy years with Sunny. The Duke testified that Consuelo had arrived late for their marriage ceremony and appeared very upset. He said that about twenty days after the wedding he learned from his wife that she had contracted the marriage only because she had been forced to by her mother: 'She told me that her mother had insisted upon her marrying me; that her mother was violently opposed to her marriage with [Rutherfurd], and that every sort of constraint, pushed even to physical violence, had been employed to attain her end.'[6]

All the witness statements were delivered in strict privacy and the priests hearing the evidence were bound by the threat of excommunication to respect the secrecy of the court. When all the evidence was taken and gathered it was sent to the Rota in Rome, and within a few weeks the first marriage was annulled.

For some years, during the autumn shooting season the Balsans rented Grantully Castle in Perthshire. Clementine was staying with them in September 1926 when she wrote to Winston with startling news:

Private. Consuelo tells me that her marriage to Sunny has been annulled by the Pope! I was so staggered that I lost the chance of cross-examining her about it . . . however, after I had recovered from my embarrassment I asked her on what grounds she had suggested to His Holiness that He should operate the miracle – And she replied 'Coercion, being under age at the time.' She says Sunny is enchanted as rumour has it that he is to be received into the church

of Rome & will then be able to marry Gladys properly – I suppose
Jacques' family suggested it as they are strict Catholics & consider
him to be living in sin with Consuelo.[7]

Sunny was so delighted to have the marriage annulled that he
and Gladys went at once to Rome to be received in private audience
by the Pope. Perhaps it was this that alerted the press, or perhaps it
was a vicious quarrel that Alva had with a Roman Catholic bishop
in New York who decided to put certain information he had
gleaned into the public domain so as to get back at Alva. Either way,
the annulment was soon headline news in London and New York.
It caused a furore. Editors expressed themselves as 'shocked', and
accusations were made that the protagonists had only been able to
obtain such a dispensation because of their rank and fortune. There
were suspicions in New York that the annulment had been purchased with a large donation to the Church. Consuelo denied this
utterly. A spokesman for the Church, stung, retorted that Church
law was for tramps as well as dukes, and took the surprising decision to make the evidence of the tribunal public. Protestant
clergymen were up in arms – what right did the Catholic Church
have to annul the rites of another Church? In the USA bishops
wanted to know what right the Rota in Rome had to dissolve a marriage contracted and legalised twenty-five years earlier in the USA
under American law. Indeed, was *any* marriage now safe? Sunny,
who was still living on Vanderbilt money, was invited by several
sources to return the 'Vanderbilt millions' along with the original
marriage licence. Sunny was safe in his Blenheim fastness, but
Consuelo's house in Paris was besieged by reporters for weeks, until
the next big news story broke.

Consuelo and Jacques were duly married in the Catholic Church,
and shortly afterwards she was welcomed into the Balsan family; she
felt no resentment for the years of exclusion, she said. Sunny converted to Catholicism in a private ceremony at the Archbishop's
home at Westminster, after which his marriage to Gladys was
blessed. Goonie acted as one of the witnesses.

Soon afterwards the Balsans bought the house Consuelo loved

best of all her homes: a small moated chateau called Saint Georges-Motel, six miles north of Dreux in the Eure department. Deeply rural even today, surrounded by rich farmland, forests and rivers, it is a fairy-tale place,* and it would become a favourite house for Winston to visit and paint.

In early 1927 Winston was working on a further volume of *The World Crisis*. As usual, he wanted to escape the cold winter months by taking a holiday-cum-business trip to the sun. That year he decided on Italy, where Mussolini was holding sway. Winston took his brother Jack and fifteen-year-old Randolph, who was now at Eton (his father had given him the choice of Eton or Harrow). A precocious and entertaining talker, Randolph regularly joined the adults at dinner when he was at home. He absorbed from men such as F.E. Smith and Max Beaverbrook and political leaders like Lloyd George a wealth of information, as well as turns of phrase, which he remembered and used. He was allowed even to correct his elders, which he considered 'clever', and to drink wine. His father usually glowed with pride when Randolph held forth – in fact, he would silence the table so as to allow him to have his say, unable to see that his son was developing an unattractive arrogance. Clementine recognised what was happening, but felt it was not her territory. Perhaps she thought, or hoped, that he was simply displaying a youthful bravado and that he would grow out of it, but whenever she told Randolph off for being rude he would go to his father, who always forgave him instantly. Winston was 'incorrigible', she said, where Randolph was concerned. So she simply gave up.

On one occasion at Chartwell, as Randolph was returning to Eton his father asked him to take a stroll around the garden. Winston told him wistfully: 'Do you know dear boy, I think we have had more talk in these summer holidays than I had with my father in all his life.'[8] The emotional wounds of those years when Lord Randolph had neglected Winston had gone deep; in fact, he never entirely recovered from the hurt. The strange thing was that although Winston was a fond and caring parent who felt that he

---

*The author spent her honeymoon there in 1992.

was far closer to Randolph than he had been to his own father, he was frequently away from home or too busy to give the boy the time and attention he craved. When he did give Randolph his attention, though, it was undivided. The elder girls fared worse than Randolph who was Winston's favourite during those years. His son's showing off had begun, one family member thought, as a way of gaining more of Winston's attention and admiration.[9] By the time he was a teenager he had fallen into believing that he would be the youngest prime minister ever. With his background, ability and credentials, and his family contacts, he thought it should simply be a matter of time. He was never corrected.

On the trip to Italy together, Winston and Randolph were received by the Pope, and Winston had two meetings with the Fascist leader Mussolini. Clementine had stayed at home with Nellie and her two clever but unruly little boys, Giles and Esmond, and kept Winston updated with family news. In an attempt to make some money Nellie had written a novel called *Misdeal*, which was unashamedly a *roman-à-clef* of her own life. Clementine described it as 'hair-raising', and persuaded Nellie at least to use a pseudonym.* As soon as the Romillys left and her own girls returned to school, Clementine set off for Lou Seuil to visit Consuelo.

Although Winston still visited Sunny at Blenheim from time to time, he did not like Gladys and she did not like him. He was also made uneasy by the emotional tension between the two, so his visits tailed off – to his regret, for he treasured his link with the great house, always inextricably connected in his mind with his heritage and his deep love of England. But during Gladys's time the family Christmas parties at Blenheim, which had been such a feature of life for all the Churchills, were no more, so that it was Chartwell that became the family gathering place for the holidays in the late Twenties. 'Always a glorious feast,' his daughter Mary recalled.

Jack and Goonie and their three children Johnny, Peregrine and Clarissa were always there, as well as Nellie, her husband Bertram

---

*The book was published by Cassell & Co. in 1932 under the pseudonym Anna Gerstein.

Romilly and their two sons (inexplicably known as 'the lambs'). Sometimes close friends such as Winston's secretary Eddie Marsh would join them, but it was essentially a warm family occasion that all the children remembered. Johnny recalled that Uncle Winston adored children and that, unlike the other grown-ups, he seemed to enjoy playing with them. 'Charades, with their secrecy, dressing up and acting, particularly appealed to him. He was a generous uncle, and we in return always gave him the best presents we could afford . . . Some . . . such as a pair of braces or a toothbrush, struck me as dull, but . . . my uncle . . . always loved receiving presents. No matter how small and humble the gift he accepted it with surprise and pleasure . . . he would take the parcel into a quiet corner, open it carefully and examine the contents with the greatest possible interest.'[10] He would help visiting children to construct huge structures with Meccano in the dining room, irrespective of the fact that guests and staff had to duck under and around them to get to the table. Anything less like his own austere childhood would be difficult to envisage; but the one thing Uncle Winston was a stickler for, was table manners. Everyone at table was expected to contribute to good conversation. Once, after a dinner at which his nephew Johnny had been placed next to a very shy woman and had eventually given up trying to make conversation with her, Winston took him aside angrily. 'How dare you make no attempt to talk to your neighbour!' he fumed. 'Don't you know it is manners to make some kind of effort?'[11]

One memory of Johnny's visits to Chartwell paints a small and unusual picture of Churchill domesticity: 'It is a family idiosyncrasy to greet one another with the noises made by pets,' he wrote.[12] Winston and Clementine often meowed, wowed and woofed to each other, and the children also each had an animal sound. 'I think it all began with my uncle trying to talk to his swans, answering their greeting when he arrived to feed them.' But it is equally likely to have begun much earlier, when Winston and Clementine were first married and were always 'Pug' and 'Cat' to each other.

When it snowed, as it often did in the winters during those years, there was tobogganing down the many slopes at Chartwell, snow-men and igloos to build, and ice-skating on the lake. The snowfall was so heavy in 1927 that a tunnel had to be dug from the main road outside the estate to allow access. 'When we were all assembled on Christmas Eve', Mary recalled,

> the double doors between the drawing room and the library were flung open to reveal the Christmas tree, glowing with light, and radiating warmth, and a piny, waxy smell from a hundred real white wax candles. Electric lights can never distil for me the magic cast by the glimmering, sputtering beauty of the Christmas trees of my childhood days. Not surprisingly, one year the tree caught fire, and only Randolph's presence of mind, and speed in fetching an extinguisher, saved us from catastrophe.[13]

Winston had to work hard as Chancellor in those difficult post-war years. He was efficient, but he did not shine in the role, and Chartwell was his escape from the pressures of Westminster. There he worked on his estate, bricklaying and improving the gardens, painting and writing. Invariably, interesting people were to be found at his dinner table. Regular visitors included Professor Frederick A. Lindemann, always called 'the Prof',* one of the most brilliant scientific brains of his generation.

During the 1914–18 war Lindemann had worked at Farnborough, then in its infancy as an experimental aviation unit. In those days the biggest threat to airmen was not the enemy but an involuntary spin at low levels. No one had been able to work out how to recover from a spin, although a young pilot who survived one suggested that pushing the stick forward had appeared to make a difference. This seemed to defy all logic, so Lindemann set to work to prove mathematically that pushing the stick forward was indeed the correct procedure. No pilot could be found, however, who was willing to put this unlikely theory into practice, so Lindemann learned to fly and tested it himself at great personal risk. As a result of his heroic act numerous lives were saved. Furthermore, he had

---

*Physicist (1886–1957), later Lord Cherwell. He advised on scientific matters, especially on nuclear physics.

the gift of being able to reduce complicated scientific matters to simple terminology so that laymen were able to understand, which was a huge asset to Winston. Sometimes to amuse other diners the Prof would work out on his table napkin the answers to riddles such as how many bottles of champagne would fit into a railway carriage or how many bottles of champagne Churchill would consume in his lifetime. Clementine liked the Prof and Eddie Marsh, and they were regarded as almost family.

Other regular guests included Lord Beaverbrook and Brendan Bracken* (Clementine was wary of both for many years – eventually she accepted them, but she never entirely trusted Beaverbrook's motives), Sir Philip Sassoon, T.E. Lawrence, the artist Walter Sickert and his wife, and F.E. Smith, who was Winston's closest friend for many years. Family members who were regularly to be found at Chartwell included Clementine's cousin and close friend Venetia Stanley, and Tom and Diana Mitford, the children of her cousin David, Lord Redesdale. Tom, a brilliant pianist, was at Eton with Randolph and was regarded as having a calming influence on him. Diana was out-of-the-ordinary beautiful (Winston called her 'Dinamite'), and Randolph was enamoured of her from the age of twelve when he and his sisters had spent summer holidays at the Redesdales' Cotswold manor house. But the young were only invited as guests in their own right after they had passed the age of fifteen and were able to contribute to the conversation because – apart from Christmas, when Winston was happy to give unlimited time to children – he refused, he said, to have the house 'bunged up with brats'.[14]

Tom Mitford, brother of the Mitford sisters, recorded a Chartwell lunch that T.E. Lawrence attended in the guise of his alter ego, T.E. Shaw.† Dressed in the standard bulky unflattering

---

*Irish-born businessman who became a Conservative politician. On the strength of having spent three years in Australia as a youth, he returned to England claiming to be an Australian orphan related to the headmaster of Winchester College. He seems to have carried this masquerade off and was accepted as a former public schoolboy. It was his ardent anti-Nazi speeches and his frank admiration of Churchill that earned him a place at Chartwell.
†T.[Thomas] E.[Edward] Lawrence used several pseudonyms. As well as T.E. Shaw he used the name John Hume Ross, under which he published an account of life in the Air Force, *The Mint.*

uniform of an RAF aircraftsman, the formerly svelte-looking officer appeared – as the diarist Harold Nicolson noticed at about the
same time – squarer and stockier; 'a bull terrier in place of a
saluki'.[15] Churchill and Clementine liked Lawrence and he had an
open invitation to visit, but Tom Mitford was still at an age where
appearance is all:

> I am a little disappointed with Shaw. He looks just like any other
> private in the Air Force, is very short and he's in his five years of
> service become quite hardened. He isn't a bit like the Sargent portrait
> of him in his book. Last night I sat next to him at dinner and he had
> Winston on the other side. Winston admires him enormously. He
> said at one moment, 'If the people make me Prime Minister I will
> make you Viceroy of India.' Lawrence politely refused and said he
> was quite happy in the Air Force. When asked what he would do
> when, in five years' time he has to leave, he said simply, 'Join the
> dole I suppose.' It is curious that he should enjoy such a life with no
> responsibility after being almost King in Arabia. Some say it is
> inverted vanity; he'd have accepted a Kingship, but as he didn't get
> it he preferred to bury himself and hide away . . . This morning we
> flew over to see Colonel Gunnes at Olympia, about 80 miles away.
> We had a 7 man unit and flew in perfect formation over Brighton
> and the other resorts – very low to frighten the crowd. Lawrence was
> thrilled at flying: he said the Ministry had stopped him flying a year
> ago.* Winston drove his machine a little way. I hadn't realised he had
> done a lot of piloting before the war. We flew in arrow head forma-
> tion . . . and landed in a field . . . it took about an hour getting there
> and ¾ hour back, as we didn't return in formation.[16]

Despite having to give up flying, Winston had kept himself au fait
with developments in the fast-moving world of aviation. By the mid-
1920s aircraft were becoming reliable enough to operate short-hop

---

*The Air Ministry imposed conditions in agreeing to Lawrence's wish to remain in the Air
Force under his assumed name: he was not allowed to fly, and he was not to speak to anyone
of national importance (which would have included Churchill, F.E., Sassoon and Lady Astor –
many of the people he met at Chartwell).

scheduled passenger services, such as London to Paris, for daring travellers. In May 1927 Charles Lindbergh created an international sensation by flying solo across the Atlantic, a supreme test of man and machine. A year later aviation would play an important part in a surprising event touching the wider Churchill family.

Amy Guest had become devoted to air travel during her husband Freddie's tenure as Secretary of State for Air in the early Twenties. She was fascinated by the success of her compatriot Lindbergh, and although not a pilot, she was destined to play an important role in the history of flight. Immensely rich,* Amy was now a plump matron who thought that rules were for others and who rode rough-shod over other people's sensibilities (including her husband's). Although she was always a welcoming and extravagant hostess, useful to Winston in her financial support of aviation, she had totally alienated Clementine with her forthright feminism.

Although never a beauty, Amy had been a dashing young woman and an intrepid rider to hounds, hunting side-saddle and never seen to refuse even the highest fences. She was also an accurate shot, and in later years her fearlessness on safari in East Africa would impress the great white hunter Bror Blixen.[17] Amy had always yearned for adventure; as a teenager she wanted to be a nurse in the Spanish–American war of 1898, but had been thwarted by her clever grandfather. 'Do you really want to help our soldiers?' he had asked her. 'Or do you just want to go out there personally? Because if you really want to help the wounded, your mother and I will pay for two trained nurses to work at the army hospital for the duration of the war [instead of you].'[18] Several other dreams of adventure had been shattered by her parents and husband.

She was in New York in 1928 when she heard of an attempt to fly the Atlantic by a woman. Immediately she wanted to be the first woman to cross the ocean by air, but when her sons Winston and Ivor threatened to leave Yale University if she attempted such a foolish stunt, she decided instead to sponsor a young woman aviator called Amelia Earhart. Amy then sailed for England, and was in

---

*Amy's personal fortune at that time was rumoured to be $1.9 billion.

Southampton on 19 June to welcome Amelia and her crew after their successful flight.*

When Amelia's London hotel was besieged by the press and the curious, Amy invited her to stay at the Guests' Park Lane town house and, justifiably proud of this intelligent and attractive young countrywoman, she introduced her into Society. Amelia had brought no luggage for weight reasons and was persuaded to discard her riding breeches, shirt and pullover for a silk dress of Amy's which, commented one reporter, was 'noticeably large in places'. Amy bought Amelia a suit and took her to Royal Ascot, where the aviator was photographed with Lord Astor, the Prince of Wales and Winston and Clementine Churchill. Amy basked in her role in this great adventure – it was her time in the sun. But Clementine continued to dislike her, and the two families grew further apart.

Randolph's youthful crush on Diana Mitford was doomed to failure when she married Bryan Guinness, heir of the brewing family, in January 1929. Diana had been stimulated by her visits to Chartwell, though, and the political debate she heard around the dinner table spawned a lifelong interest in politics for which in later life she was to become notorious.

The Churchill children were growing up. Randolph was now eighteen and at Oxford, moving in a racy, port-imbibing set which included John Betjeman and Freddie Smith (son of F.E.). Diana and Sarah were twenty and fifteen – Sarah was still at boarding school and Diana was in Paris staying with a respectable family while she learned French (from where she wrote begging to be allowed to shingle her hair). Jack and Goonie's son Johnny was twenty, Peregrine was sixteen. Only the two youngest children – Clarissa and Mary, aged nine and seven respectively – remained at

---

*Amelia had no experience with multi-engine aircraft. The plane, the *Friendship*, was to be flown by a pilot and co-pilot, and it was agreed that only if they met with totally calm weather would Amelia be allowed to take the controls. In the event it was a rough passage and Amelia, as she stated frankly, was 'simply a passenger' on that 1928 flight. The *Friendship* landed in Burry Port, South Wales, where it refuelled before flying on to its destination Southampton where there was a seaplane 'runway' well marked out on Southampton Water. Four years later she would cross the Atlantic alone, becoming the first woman and only the second person (after Lindbergh) to fly solo across the Atlantic.

home. With or without the often outspoken guests, Chartwell was
a lively house at times, more often than not full of children and
teenagers because Jack and Goonie's family were inseparable from
Winston and Clementine's, and Nellie and her two boys Giles
and Esmond were also frequent visitors. Talk at the table would get
heated on occasion, especially when Randolph was there, arro-
gantly displaying his knowledge, repeating things he had heard
his father say, picking up on a remark of another one of his father's
visitors. Because Winston doted on him and because he was a
wonderfully attractive golden youth, he continued to be given more
than a fair degree of latitude. He often became so argumentative
that his sister Mary recalled 'Randolph would pick an argument
with a chair'.[19]

At the age of eighteen this trait was still capable of being corrected, for Randolph evidently recognised that he had a problem.
He told a contemporary at Oxford (Frank Pakenham, later Lord
Longford): 'I have an overwhelming urge to express myself, I am an
explosion that leaves the house still standing.'[20] It was after one turbulent weekend of debate and argument that Clementine – highly
strung, hating noise and discord, and driven to distraction – told
a startled Peregrine on the car journey to London: 'I just can't stand
it any longer.'[21] This remark, remembered by Peregrine for fifty
years, has been cited in some biographies as evidence of a serious rift
between Winston and Clementine, but it is abundantly clear from
their letters and from family members' recollections of the romantic and sentimental love that this couple retained for each other
throughout their lives that the incident was nothing more than
Clementine needing to let off steam after a difficult few days. Like
every couple they had moments of disagreement, and it is true that
at one point a few years later a distraught Clementine went to stay
with Goonie and spoke of getting a divorce because of the com-
bativeness between Winston and Randolph. Goonie comforted her
and Clementine was soon back at home with her Pug.

Clementine was a highly sensitive woman, not really equipped
emotionally or physically to deal with the hurly-burly of energy and
noise that Winston seemed to create effortlessly around him. She

coped, and she dealt with it, because she loved him. She provided him with a superbly run home filled with flowers and comfort, beautiful food efficiently served on time by well trained staff. Everything revolved around Winston's need to work, write, paint and occasionally to relax. But it took a great toll on her, and it became essential that several times a year she got away from Winston and the children so as to rest quietly and rebuild her reserves. Theirs was not a conventional union – how could it be? But Winston understood and was generally sensitive to her needs. There would be many holidays apart as the years went by, but these breaks were always punctuated by fond letters between them, Winston usually inquiring solicitously about her well-being. There can be no doubt where Clementine's love and sense of duty lay. As noted earlier, her children never came first, and she was content to consign them to a series of governesses and tutors. She once told her daughter Mary that it had taken all her strength and time just to keep up with Winston, explaining without apology that as far as her children were concerned, 'I never had anything left over.'[22]

The year 1929 saw the publication of another volume of Winston's history of the 1914–18 war, *The World Crisis*, which had occupied a good deal of his spare time for a decade. Not all of his spare time, however, because in those years he had also produced a large portfolio of oil paintings and several other books. But 1929 was most noteworthy for this political family for the fact that on 30 May the Conservatives were defeated in the general election. Winston had presented his fifth budget in April and had felt confident that it would be well received by the electorate. But as so often happens after a long period under the same administration, the electorate was in the mood for change. The election went well for Winston personally, with his attractive wife and appealingly wholesome family – Randolph a very promising eighteen-year-old and three pretty daughters (the youngest, Mary, a bright seven-year-old) – all campaigning alongside him and wearing their blue ribbons. But there was no convincing majority, and Baldwin resigned because he had no wish to head a minority administration and refused to head a coalition.

Instead Ramsay MacDonald formed the second Labour government with the support of the Liberals, and Winston was out of office from June, although he retained his parliamentary seat. He wondered at first if this signalled the end of his career, for he was now in his mid-fifties and in all likelihood it would be at least four years before the Tories could expect to form another government. There was no guarantee that an incoming prime minister would then be looking for ministers of sixty.

He was disappointed at the defeat of his party but not unduly upset, for unlike his enforced resignation after the Dardanelles this setback was not a personal defeat, merely the ebbing of a political tide. He decided to capitalise on having more time available by making a three-month tour of the USA and Canada, leaving in early August, to be funded by fees earned for speeches, articles and various book deals. Clementine was to have joined him, but as the departure date drew near she was still convalescing from a mastoid operation and was advised not to travel. He asked Jack to take Clementine's place, and then the two boys, Randolph and Peregrine, begged to join their fathers. Winston decided that it would be a wonderful experience for them, so it was an all-male Churchill party that toured the North American continent in a private railway carriage supplied by Canadian Pacific.

Winston loved America and the confidence of the people. And he was popular there, which felt good after the political defeat in England. Randolph, too, fell under the spell of the New World, and when on one occasion they were subjected at dinner to a boring speech by a local cleric, Randolph rose to his feet to deliver an unscheduled five-minute reply that had his audience agog with admiration. He knew exactly how far to go and how to win the sympathy of his audience, Winston told Clementine proudly, and he believed he could not have done it better himself.[23] Randolph kept a diary of the tour, and published part of it in his memoir *Twenty-One Years*.[24]

When the Churchill party reached California they stayed at San Simeon, the ranch of the newspaper publisher William Randolph Hearst. Even the extravagant hospitality the party had received throughout their tour failed to prepare them for the luxury of San Simeon and they were happy to wallow. It was there that Randolph lost his virginity, to Tilly Losch, the exquisite Hungarian dancer and actress.

Before leaving England Winston had taken advice from an expert and trusted financier about investing in Wall Street, which had been booming for over a year. Because he was going to be travelling and not always contactable, he had made arrangements for the broker to invest on his behalf without asking permission for each deal. He told the man blithely: 'I can usually lay my hands on two or three thousand pounds.' By September, when Winston examined his portfolio, he realised that the broker had invested about ten times more than he normally placed in the markets. But his concern was quickly dispelled when he saw that the new shares had already netted him a profit of £2000. Together with a large publisher's advance for his proposed biography of his ancestor the 1st Duke of Marlborough, royalties on his other books, some commissioned articles and lecture fees, he was feeling very confident financially. (This was despite the loss both of his ministerial salary and of the use of the Chancellor's official residence at 11 Downing Street.) Reckoning he had over £21,000 at that point (today, almost £700,000), he wrote to instruct Clementine to lease Venetia Stanley's house, as she wished to do anyway, and to hire enough servants for luncheon parties of '8–10 often, and dinner of the same size about twice a week. You should have a staff equal to this.'[25]

The first Wall Street crash began on 24 October 1929 when over twelve million shares were traded in one day, and over the next four trading days panic selling eventually caused the market to collapse. It was said that anyone who purchased stocks in 1929 and held on to them would pass most of their adult life before they reached parity. In one week alone some $30 billion was wiped off stock prices, resulting in the mass unemployment that was the other aspect of the Great Depression. On the day Winston and Jack Churchill reached New York to embark on their Atlantic crossing, the headlines announced the death of a ruined man who had leapt from the top of a skyscraper.

Winston lost over £10,000 (almost £300,000 sterling today) – half his wealth, hard-earned and carefully garnered. He was not wiped out, but it was a tremendous blow to him. He had two immediate concerns: first, that he would be able to hang on to, and still be able to live at, his beloved Chartwell. Second, how would he break the news to Clementine who, he knew only too well, had a horror of debt? She had spent the summer months with Nellie and the girls at Dieppe, then had gone to Italy in October. So she was rested and happy, still feeling the effects of the sunshine as she looked forward to Winston's return after their long separation. He intended to break the bad news gently.

On 5 November Clementine was at Waterloo Station to meet Winston off the Southampton boat-train (the boys had returned to England earlier, as they were due back at university). He kissed her but then, unable to bear pretending until a better time arrived that all was well, he blurted out the bad news there and then on the station platform. Clementine would never have made her reaction known in such a public place, but it is not difficult to imagine what a shock this would have been to her. For most of her life she worried about money, even in relatively good times – the legacy of her constant anxiety when young about her mother's fecklessness.

As they entered the Thirties – always recalled by Churchill as his 'wilderness years', for as well as his financial worries he was without office – they were living far more carefully. He worked hard at his writing and always earned enough to keep their finances ticking over, just. Often only a royalty cheque or an advance enabled him to clear his debts; but as noted earlier, although he was willing to economise to a certain degree, like Sunny, Winston was unable to lower his standards. The children were told to turn off lights and to keep telephone calls short but did not later recall real shortages. The couple entertained less often, reduced the number of servants, closed off all but a few rooms at Chartwell in which Winston could work on his money-earning books: four volumes of *Marlborough: His Life and Times* and *My Early Life*, as well as essays and lectures. And while in London they took furnished houses on short-term rentals, or stayed in a hotel. Clementine knew a thing or two about budgeting, and it was she who made sure that they survived the financial crisis. For several years, instead of living in the big house the family used a staff cottage in the grounds of Chartwell which Mary recalls as delightfully 'cosy'. It was only many years later, 'when I read my mother's letters and papers that I really began to understand: then I realised how fragile was the raft which supported that seemingly so solid way of life'. She was still in the care of a nanny, but her brother and sisters had begun to grow away from the family.

There was another blow for Winston to weather in September 1930, when his old friend Lord Birkenhead (F.E. Smith) died suddenly at the age of fifty-eight. The two men had been the closest friends for almost a quarter of a century, when they had entered Parliament in the same intake. A brilliant and charismatic man, F.E. enjoyed the same lifestyle as Winston, the same expensive drinks, food and cigars. Together they had founded the exclusive dining club known as 'the Other Club', and it was believed to be his excesses, especially drinking, that killed him before his time. When he received the news Winston wept openly, and Clementine remembered him saying repeatedly, 'I feel so lonely.'

He was still low because of this bereavement when Randolph, now nineteen and in his last year at Oxford, received – on the back of his visit with his father the previous year – an invitation to deliver a series of lectures in the USA. A lecture firm offered him the huge sum of $12,000 to make the tour. Against all parental, avuncular and tutorial advice, Randolph accepted the offer, leaving off his studies in October 1930. He justified his decision by saying he would return to Oxford (but he never did). Unlike his father, who had been so coldly treated as a schoolboy when he underperformed, Randolph had received only affection and understanding in the same circumstances. At Eton when he wrote to apologise to his father for 'having done so badly and [having] disappointed you so much', Winston – perhaps recalling how it felt to be lectured by a stern father – allowed him to drop Greek.[26] Randolph's will was done in this as in so many issues, and Clementine felt ever more uneasy about the latitude allowed to him, but without ever doing anything about it. She loved Randolph, but she did not share Winston's blind devotion for their son. In December, using some money Winston had given her to buy a small car, Clementine sailed to New York in order to visit Randolph, to whom she wrote, 'Papa is amused and rather outraged at the idea of me going to America without him!'[27]

He welcomed her warmly but she quickly discovered that, as she suspected, he had not been concentrating wholly on the lecture tour and that her instincts to check on him had not been at fault. He was spending money rapidly, and had fallen in love. He told Clementine that he intended to marry Kay Halle, an Irish-American girl from Cleveland, Ohio. Indeed, he had proposed to her several times but the personable Miss Halle had refused him. This news had just hit the headlines, and on her first morning in New York Clementine was surprised to read that she had travelled to America to put a stop to the wedding.

She attended one of Randolph's lectures and told Winston, 'Frankly, it was not at *all* good.' She felt Randolph *could* be brilliant if he would only give his full attention to his talks. But when she attempted to tell him this he had responded that it would go down well with most of his audience. 'So he won't take pains,' she wrote, '& this is a great pity. He delivers the same lecture everywhere, so he really ought to have got it good by now.' However, she had to admit that 'he has a most fascinating manner & delivery & the audience seemed spellbound – but I think it was his looks & his colossal cheek, chiefly!' On the subject of Miss Halle, Clementine wrote that she had met her and liked her, though she had pointed out to Randolph the dangers of marrying a woman eight years older than himself, and asked how he intended to support a wife. He was not interested in women of his own age, Randolph had replied, and he was confident his father would continue his allowance of £400 a year. Clementine pointed out that in three months he had already spent over £1000, or the equivalent of over £4000 a year. Nevertheless, she trod a diplomatic path because 'it would be madness to go against the idea, as I think he might try & rush into it. Much may happen . . . & Miss Halle may not come up to scratch.

She is, I think, very fond of Randolph but rather flustered & worried.'[28] These matters aside, she wrote that Randolph was a sweet and charming companion and that she was enjoying her holiday so much that she said she almost felt she was on a sort of honeymoon. Perhaps she was not unduly worried about the Kay Halle question because she noted that Randolph flirted shamelessly with other women he met while he escorted his mother around Washington and other cities.

Clementine went home in April 1931, and the following December she, Winston and Diana returned to New York, to which Randolph was already referring as his 'spiritual home'. Two days after their arrival Winston was hit by a car while crossing Fifth Avenue on his way to meet his friend Bernard Baruch.* Doctors told Clementine that had he not been so muffled up against the cold in a heavy fur-lined overcoat, he might have lost his life. As it was he was badly injured and was hospitalised, then bedridden for almost a month. It was another low point for Winston. In great discomfort, he had plenty of time to brood on his financial losses, his stagnant career and his son's problems, until Clementine took him to the Bahamas to recuperate for some weeks in the sun. He always revived in the sunshine. By February 1932 he was in Chicago writing to Bob Boothby† that he was lecturing every night despite discomfort following his accident, and a sore throat.[29] He met Kay Halle and her father and liked them both, but Kay firmly declined Randolph's frequent proposals of marriage, and wisely opted to remain a lifelong good friend.

Randolph, with his matinée idol looks and his considerable reservoir of charm (when he chose to exert it), had already realised that there were few women who could resist him. He was already on his way to becoming a womaniser, even in one instance getting a young woman invited to Blenheim without a chaperone by giving her the impression that there would be a house party there. To her dismay the party consisted of Sunny and Gladys (who were by then living

---

*Bernard M. Baruch (1870–1965) was an American financier, statesman and consultant to Presidents Wilson and F.D. Roosevelt on economic matters. He was also a successful racehorse owner and was renowned for his witty remarks.

†Robert Boothby (later Baron Boothby), 1900–86. A former stockbroker, he became a Conservative MP in 1924 and went on to hold a number of senior ministerial offices.

apart within the great palace), herself, Randolph and his schoolgirl cousin Anita Leslie. Sunny must have realised what was afoot, for when Gladys asked where the young woman was he told her that Randolph had taken her into the garden to seduce her. Anita Leslie recalled colourfully in her biography of Randolph how she and his intended victim had huddled under an eiderdown one night, in cold cream and curlers, while he sat on the bed endlessly talking after failing to bribe Anita to 'clear off' to her own bedroom. She remembered only that the phrase 'when I am Prime Minister' featured frequently in his long discourse before he gave up and returned to his room.[30] Anita, who was Leonie Leslie's grand-daughter, also remembered her mother telling her that, in her time, she had known of young women who were so bored and so cold while staying at Blenheim that they hiked into Woodstock village to send themselves telegrams urging an immediate return home.

The next time she met Randolph, Anita was a debutante herself, dining with a party at Quaglino's, the fashionable restaurant in Bury Street. It was the evening of the day Tilly Losch had lost her divorce case and Randolph, who was fortunate not to have been named as one of her lovers, was there with Tilly to celebrate and console. As he comforted a tear-stained and indignant Tilly 'in public', the other diners and even the waiters too enjoyed the spectacle. 'Alcohol – cigars – money – *and* Tilly Losch,' Anita wrote. 'Being nearly three years younger I could not say a word. I just admired.'[31]

In 1930 Winston had thrown a memorable coming-of-age dinner for Randolph at Claridge's. Most of those invited were in a position to be of use to the young lion: they included Admiral of the Fleet Lord Beatty, twenty-four-year-old Quintin Hogg, the Duke of Marlborough and Sir Oswald Mosley (then regarded as a possible Prime Minister in waiting).

It was hardly surprising, given the people to whom Randolph was continually exposed and the attentions he received, that great things were expected of him. Certainly, his estimation of himself knew no bounds.

1932–7

Changes at Blenheim

The first of Winston and Clementine's children to marry was Diana. This eldest child of theirs was always something of a misfit. She was well aware that Randolph was her father's favourite, that Sarah was her mother's, and that she came first with no one. She was timid in society, unlike her contemporary Diana Mitford, who 'took' immediately when the two girls came out together, Diana Mitford rapidly receiving a proposal from the Guinness heir. The latter's successful launch made Diana Churchill gloomy, and she was unhappy at home. Like most teenagers, she blamed her discontent on her parents and her home life. It was more in an attempt to get away from all this than from any sense of vocation as an actress that Diana badgered her parents until they agreed to allow her to apply for a place at the Royal Academy of Dramatic Art, where she spent five terms. She never shone on the stage, and when she acquired a suitor in the form of John Bailey, the son of Sir Abe Bailey, a rich South African who had been a friend of Winston's for many years, she accepted his proposal without any regret for her chosen career. Clementine was unhappy about the marriage; she thought Diana was far too young and immature, but the wedding went ahead at the end of 1932. Sunny loaned his London house for the reception.

Randolph was working as a journalist for various Rothermere publications, and Sarah was spending the obligatory few months in

Paris learning French before 'coming out' in 1933. Mary, regarded as still in the nursery, now attended day school, but she was cared for virtually exclusively by a cousin of Clementine's, Maryott Whyte.* Known as 'Moppet' in the family and 'Nana' by Mary, she was a trained Norland nursery nurse, the crème de la crème of English nannies. Cousin Moppet was with them for twenty years, arriving soon after Marigold's death, and it was she who provided stability for the Churchill children when Clementine and Winston made their several long trips abroad every year, often solo trips because they demanded different things of their leisure time. Winston had played his last game of polo in Malta in 1927, and though he still rode and occasionally hunted after that date, by the age of sixty his main interest, outside his almost never-ending projects at Chartwell and his writing, were painting, good conversation and playing cards.

Clementine had been a good horse-rider in the early days of their marriage and had hunted avidly alongside Winston, but as she grew older she turned to tennis – at which she was an above-average player – and skiing. These interests were important to her for she often became nervous in the highly charged atmosphere around Winston, especially when Randolph was present, and she took frequent holidays away from the family where she could play tennis and ski and just relax.

So for the children, and for Mary especially in these early years, no matter where their parents were, Cousin Moppet was always there providing loving care – to the extent that often, when Clementine made a suggestion Mary's first response was 'I must ask Nana.'[1] It was probably no coincidence that Mary was the only one of Churchill's children to evolve into a well adjusted adult. Her relationship with her mother she describes as 'admiring and respectful', until she reached the age of fourteen and was old enough to be taken on skiing holidays, when the two came to know each other better.

*

---

*Daughter of Lady Maude Ogilvy Whyte.

Winston had long looked at events occurring in Germany with an inquiring and jaundiced eye. His correspondence proves that he had never been happy with the way the 1914–18 war had ended, and he was always concerned about Germany's future direction. He had many contacts who lived in Germany or who visited the country, and he listened carefully to what they had to say. And in the early 1930s the sum of these reports was that the National Socialist Party leader, Adolf Hitler, was intent on revising existing treaties and rearming, contrary to the agreements that had been made at the end of the war.

In March 1932 Hitler polled 40 per cent of the vote in the presidential election and in July that year his party received the majority vote in the Reichstag elections. Six months later Hitler was elected Chancellor of the German Reich. His financial policies appeared to have substantially improved the German economy, at a time when the British economy was still in recession and unemployment had reached three million. Hitler's record was regarded with admiration by Lord Rothermere's* *Daily Mail*. 'I was disgusted,' Winston growled in a letter written to Clementine while he was holidaying at Château de l'Horizon, the home of an old friend, Maxine Elliott,† in the Golfe-Juan on the Côte d'Azur, 'by the D.M.'s boosting of Hitler. R[othermere] is sincerely pacifist. He wants us to be vy strongly armed and frightfully obsequious at the same time. Thus he hopes to avoid seeing another war. Anyhow it is a more practical attitude than our socialist politicians. They wish us to remain disarmed & exceedingly abusive.'[2] However, he was relieved, he said, that the German people had at least the sense not to vote Hitler in as President for life after the death of Hindenburg.

---

*Esmond Cecil Harmsworth, 2nd Viscount Rothermere (1898–1978), was from 1919 to 1929 Member of Parliament for Thanet. He served as ADC to the PM at the Paris Peace Conference of 1919. From 1932 until his death he was manager, president and director of the family-owned Associated Newspapers, which included the *Daily Mail*.

†Maxine Elliott was a rich American, formerly a classical actress who had made a fortune by taking the advice of her good friend the financier J.P. Morgan. She was about seventy at this time, and was always immensely kind to Churchill. Château de l'Horizon was a luxurious palatial villa on the Riviera. Built by Elliott in the early Thirties, it was close to villas owned by Max Beaverbrook and, later, the Duke and Duchess of Windsor.

That this matter was under regular discussion in the Churchill household from the late 1920s onwards is evident by occasional comments in letters between the couple. For example, in February 1931 Clementine wrote to Winston: 'I really do not think we must ever fight the Germans again – I'm sure they would win – Really we didn't beat them in 1918 – they were just stifled by numbers.'[3] She was already referring to Hitler in her letters as 'that Gangster', which was not the general perception of their class at that time. The name Hitler was yet to be associated with evil. There was admiration, albeit grudging in some quarters, for what he had achieved for the German people. Travel to Europe was generally restricted for reasons of cost to the middle and upper classes, and many who visited Germany wanted to meet Hitler. Churchill almost had the opportunity in summer 1932 when, together with Clementine, Sarah, Prof Lindemann and a few others, he decided to trace the route of the Duke of Marlborough's march in 1705 from the Netherlands to the Danube, as research for his biography of his ancestor. Randolph had been in Germany for some weeks before his parents arrived, researching a piece on the Nazi Party. He had observed a great deal, especially Hitler's charismatic influence on the populace, which he regarded as sinister: 'Let us make no mistake about it,' he had written in his *Daily Graphic* column on 3 March 1932. 'The success of the Nazi party sooner or later means war. Nearly all of Hitler's principal lieutenants fought in the last war . . . [and] they burn for revenge. They are determined once more to have an army. I am sure that once they have achieved it, they will not hesitate to use it.'

Randolph was anxious for his father to see how things were in Germany, and it is almost certainly he who suggested that Winston should take a look for himself. The research trip, which had to be made anyway, was probably the result. The Churchill party spent one day at the town of Blindheim (from which derives the name of Blenheim), then most of the rest of that week at a Munich hotel where they were approached by Ernst ('Putzi') Hanfstaengl, Hitler's foreign press chief public relations adviser cum propagandist. Hanfstaengl, a man of considerable charm and musical ability – he entertained the Churchill party by singing, accompanying himself on the piano – introduced himself as a friend of Randolph, to whom he had been introduced in London by Diana Guinness (née Mitford). Diana was also in Germany that summer, holidaying with her younger sister Unity and trying to persuade Hanfstaengl to introduce them to Hitler. The sisters were not successful in their ambition to meet the Führer on that first visit; Hanfstaengl eventually told them primly that they wore far too much make-up for him to even dream of presenting them to his leader.[4]

However, following his meeting with Winston, Hanfstaengl tried hard to persuade Hitler to call on the Churchills at their hotel. At one point Hitler appeared in the lobby after attending a meeting there, while the Churchill party were having a meal in the dining room. Hanfstaengl asked his leader if he would go in and meet them but Hitler hesitated, then said he did not know what he would say and also that he had not shaved.[5] The moment was lost, but when Churchill later recalled this incident he put Hitler's reluctance down to a conversation with Hanfstaengl, in which he (Churchill) had asked: 'Why is your chief so violent about the Jews? What is the sense of being against a man simply because of his birth? How can any man help how he is born?'[6] He assumed Hanfstaengl had reported this to his leader and that that was why Hitler refused to meet him. In the late 1930s when Hitler was at the acme of his powers he invited Churchill to visit him. On that occasion it was Churchill who excused himself.

One rare incident showed Randolph in a more favourable light than usual. In the summer of 1932 most of London Society had moved to Venice, where Randolph attended a lavish party given by Emerald Cunard for Diana Cooper's fortieth birthday. When one of the women guests was deliberately burned on the hand with a cigarette by a thwarted lover, Randolph 'sprang to her defence, and a dreadful fight ensued . . . the wives all clinging to their men to stop them joining in'.[7]

Sarah came out in 1932: she liked the business of being a debutante little more than Diana had. Her photographs show a rather solemn young woman, although Clementine found her far easier to dress than Diana had been. Unfortunately she told the girls this, which caused a family upset – Diana was hurt by the remark. Sarah attended as few functions as she could get away with. Clementine, having already been through the process once, was intensely bored at having to sit for hours on tiny gilt chairs with the other mothers and chaperones, through party after party, so she was probably only too happy to allow her daughter to skip as many events as she wished. Sarah had only one ambition, which was to dance professionally, and after a lot of unhappy lounging about, sighing, pleading and argument she finally wore her parents down and was allowed to enrol at a school of dance.

It was Winston and Clementine's silver wedding anniversary in 1933, and their letters show that they were as important to each other then as during the first years of their marriage. By contrast, the relationship between Sunny and Gladys had completely broken down by 1931. Gladys had converted rooms on the ground floor at Blenheim into her own apartment, while Sunny lived on an upper floor. They still encountered each other in the dining room, where Gladys would deliver endless cutting witticisms about Sunny and sometimes his guests, while he looked on alternately horrified, bored, scowling. Gladys was now engaged in the breeding of Blenheim spaniels and would eventually have up to fifty of them, all living in her rooms in the palace. Her arrival was always heralded, before she hove into view in the midst of her moving carpet of spaniels, by the clicking of a multitude of tiny claws on the polished floors.

The main problem, touched on earlier, appears to have been that Gladys was not cut out for the solemn formality of Blenheim, nor perhaps to deal with the man Sunny became whenever he was in residence there. She loved the cheerful bonhomie and bustle of cities, a sophisticated circle of artistic friends and smart highbrow conversation. She came to loathe the cavernous rooms at Blenheim, which were hardly filled even by the regular injections of weekend guests who, she complained, only ever wanted to talk about hunting and shooting. However, it must have been somewhat more invigorating than that would suggest, for the guests at Blenheim were often the same whose conversation glittered at Chartwell. Winston and Clementine were now only occasional guests at Blenheim, but the visitors' book reveals the presence there of the F.E. Smiths, Mrs Keppel, Shelagh Duchess of Westminster, Lytton Strachey, Edith Sitwell and Evelyn Waugh. And to these add top Hollywood stars such as Chaplin, Douglas Fairbanks and Mary Pickford. How was it possible for Gladys to be bored with such a guest list?

The marriage had started to go seriously wrong in 1923 when Gladys suffered her second miscarriage after falling over a stool during a violent quarrel with Sunny. She had been rather pleased when she miscarried the first time at the age of forty because she had been depressed during those early weeks of the pregnancy, but later she thought she might like a child and so was unhappy when the second miscarriage occurred. She became pregnant for a third time and lost that baby also, painfully, in January 1925, at which point all desire to conceive again appears to have evaporated. After this it seems that Gladys only came to life when she visited Paris, on one occasion slipping away from Sunny the moment they arrived there in order to wander about alone, and 'to . . . feel & hear . . . Paris itself'.[8]

Her Parisian friends on the Quai Voltaire wittily designated Blenheim 'Hyper-Boria' and issued frequent invitations to her to come to Paris and 'deBlenheimise'. There she transformed into the old bright, eager, fascinating Gladys. How curious that Sunny did not recognise that the minute she returned to Blenheim she lost her *joie de vivre* and slid into depression and increasing eccentricity. Today Gladys would almost certainly have been suspected of having bipolar disorder; even people who liked her increasingly regarded her as a little mad at times. Apart from her dogs the only pastime Gladys enjoyed was gardening – and that because it got her away from the house. Her low spirits, however, did not prevent her from holding her own with Sunny, and the house often rang with their loud quarrels, sometimes within earshot of visitors. One guest noted that Gladys was 'more than a match for the Duke', whom the writer 'always thought a very poor creature'.[9] Another factor in the deteriorating relationship was Gladys's determination not to become pregnant again just at the time of Sunny's conversion to Catholicism, when the Duke could no longer use contraception.

With no intimacy permitted, Sunny's temper became increasingly erratic. Gladys sought help from the Church on the grounds that his conversion had caused her husband a 'physical crisis'. She was advised, unhelpfully, that this often occurred after a conversion and would eventually resolve itself. One positive benefit from the Catholic remarriage was that Sunny was now totally rehabilitated in Society and could once again be received in royal circles, from which he had been excluded since his separation from Consuelo twenty years earlier. In 1928, Gladys organised a famous leap year's eve ball at their London home in Carlton House Terrace,* arguably one of the most prestigious non-royal addresses in London. It was the Society event of the year, attended by the Prince of Wales, and everyone of note turned up wearing fancy dress. Winston wore a Roman toga. Sunny was so delighted that Gladys reported to friends, 'For quite 3 days I was allowed to express several opinions a day and no taunt . . . was forthcoming.'

The only thing the couple shared with any enthusiasm, now, was the five-year construction project of the water gardens at Blenheim. But their rows had long been legendary, and at one dinner when Sunny was holding forth about politics Gladys shocked guests into silence by shrieking: 'Shut up! Shut up! You know nothing about politics. I've slept with every Prime Minister in Europe, and most Kings. You are not qualified to speak.' At one luncheon she arrived with a newly injured eye which slowly turned black during the meal. She took to sleeping with a loaded revolver on her bedside table in case Sunny should decide upon a night-time visit, and even occasionally placed it on the table at dinner parties. When one guest asked why she needed it there she replied that she might decide to shoot the Duke.

By 1931 Sunny could stand it no longer. He decided that his wife really was mad after she chased him around Blenheim with her gun when he demanded she leave. She refused to go, but since she hated the place her reaction appears to have derived from pique and a

---

*Overlooking the Mall and St James's Park. The Marlboroughs lived at No. 7, which retained its original Nash interior.

desire to annoy. One of the things that most distressed Sunny was Gladys's pack of spaniels which, apart from living in her rooms and sleeping on her bed, were allowed to eat, defecate and urinate wherever they liked in the palace. Watching the irreplaceable old carpets being thus damaged became a source of horror and revulsion to Sunny, who used to tour the house looking for new stains and other depredations such as small flaps cut into the great mahogany doors of the state rooms so that the dogs would not be impeded as they roamed the great building at will. Clarissa, daughter of Jack and Goonie, recalls visiting the palace as a child of ten or eleven in the early Thirties and finding dog cages in the Great Hall, which at that time smelled so pungently that one guest was reported to have fainted.

Why did Gladys not simply leave Blenheim and return to the bohemian life she clearly adored? After all, she was far happier in Paris. But it was not simply a desire to infuriate her husband that kept her at Blenheim. The most likely explanation is the 1929 crash. Gladys had been supported in luxury all her life by a trust fund set up by her father, which provided her and her sisters with up to $30,000 a year (about $350,000 today). But the trust fund had dried up in 1929 and from 1930 onwards Gladys was without private means – she was therefore wholly reliant on Sunny for even her simplest needs. As time went by Sunny refused to countenance this additional expense on his purse, and in an attempt to shame him into giving her an allowance Gladys took to wearing old court dresses that had been stored for years in Blenheim's huge cupboards. She would appear at dinner, and in public, in these or her oldest clothes, sometimes fastened with safety-pins.

The last time they were seen together in London was at Diana Churchill's wedding reception on 12 December 1932, held at the Marlboroughs' Carlton Terrace house. Gladys avoided having to stand next to Sunny by not attending the marriage service. Sunny sat in the church alone, dressed in a brown overcoat with a velvet collar, looking haunted and sad, next to Diana Guinness and her baby son. Gladys organised the reception with Clementine, but after that event was forbidden ever to come to the London house again. Finally, unable to stand Blenheim under Gladys's manage-ment, the Duke moved out of the home to which he had given his life and into Carlton House Terrace. When he visited Blenheim on business he stayed and ate at the Bear Hotel in Woodstock village. One can only guess what local people made of all this.

Gradually the number of servants at Blenheim dwindled to six, and at one point Gladys claimed that all she had in the world was £9. In May 1933 the Duke's solicitors served her with a formal notice to leave, advising unequivocally that the palace was to be closed down at the end of that month. Her own solicitors, Withers & Co., who also looked after the affairs of the royal family, protested at this 'unfair' treatment of the Duchess – where did the Duke expect her to go without any money? But as the appointed day drew near she had no alternative but to hire a removal van and some men, and move out with most of her belongings. Even that was made a more harrowing experience than necessary. Marlborough's agent, loyal to the Duke, of course, was determined to ensure that Gladys took nothing that belonged to Blenheim. He asked to inspect everything as it was loaded onto the van, and was so offensive to Gladys that she telephoned Withers & Co., for help. They hastily dispatched a man to Blenheim to protect their client against further 'insolence'.

When the Duke regained his palace he invited friends to inspect the physical damage that had been inflicted upon it. The stench was such that it was impossible to breathe comfortably in some of the rooms, and it was hard for anyone witnessing the squalor to side with Gladys. She sold or loaned out some of her dogs and stayed at the Carlton Hotel in the Haymarket for a few months, referring all the charges to Marlborough until the Duke publicly refused to pay any further bills incurred by his wife. Acting on the advice of her solicitors, while Sunny was visiting Blenheim Gladys moved into No. 7 Carlton House Terrace and squatted there. And there she stayed, behind locked doors and windows, while Sunny stormed and tried ineffectively to find some way of having her removed. She allowed a few visitors in to give the lie to Sunny's stories that she was insane.

Among these visitors was the twenty-two-year-old former Diana

Mitford, Randolph's first love. When Diana had married Bryan Guinness in 1929, the couple had seemed ideally matched. Then, in 1932, Diana met and fell deeply in love with the *enfant terrible* of the Tory Party, Oswald Mosley – later the leader of the hated 'Blackshirts' – who was married to Cynthia Curzon. A few months later, to the distress of her husband, her family and Society in general, Diana took her two small sons and left the marital home to live in a rented house in Eaton Square as Mosley's mistress. Diana Guinness and Gladys Marlborough were frequent visitors to each other's houses in those months; it was, as Diana remarked, a case of 'one social pariah visiting another'.[10] Harold Nicolson also mentions meeting Gladys at that time, on 21 June 1933. His diary entry reveals that he found her very easy to talk to. They discussed Proust and she recounted some personal recollections of him. There is no hint in this account of mental instability.

Sunny was forced to set up London headquarters at the Ritz while he found a way to evict Gladys. Eventually he sent three detectives to the Carlton House Terrace mansion to cut off the gas, electricity and telephone. Before locking themselves into the basement rooms which included the larders and pantries (where they lived off the food supplies), the men erected a barricade around the house to prevent friends visiting and supplying her with essentials. After four days Gladys was effectively starved out.[11] She returned to the Carlton Hotel in the Haymarket with no means of paying her bills, and there, between long stays at the houses of friends, she remained for almost a year. It is not entirely clear who did pay her Carlton Hotel bills; perhaps a friend stumped up, or Marlborough felt forced to pay for the sake of appearances. And Gladys was to have the last word, for Sunny's days were almost up. Less than a year later, in June 1934, he lay dying at Carlton House Terrace from cancer of the liver.

He had spent much of those last months of his life pitifully shrivelled, yellow-skinned and obviously seriously ill. His worry about the cost of overseeing the restoration at Blenheim and repairing the damage inflicted by Gladys was an added stress, but he worked feverishly to complete it. He succeeded so well that he was able to invite the Prince of Wales and Wallis Simpson to a weekend party there, which also included Duff and Lady Diana Cooper. But it was the final trump for this lonely and troubled man. Even before he was diagnosed with cancer he had contemplated handing Blenheim over to his heir Bert (Lord Blandford) and his wife Mary, and retiring to a monastery. He had only just learned of the death of his hated old adversary Alva, Consuelo's mother, after a stroke in January 1933* when he was told that his own illness was terminal. On the last evening of his life he held a tea party for his closest friends. Among them at his bedside was a desperately sad Winston. On 30 June the sixty-two-year-old Duke died painlessly, having slipped into a coma. Winston wrote enigmatically that his cousin had 'sacrificed much – too much – for Blenheim'.[12]

Gladys's life thereafter, and it was to be a long one, was marked by poverty, loneliness and increasing eccentricity. Sunny had cut her out of his will, leaving her penniless, and she was reliant on the generosity of friends, who gradually drifted away. Like Consuelo she had dropped the title 'Duchess', and this woman whose beauty and wit had once captivated the salons of the capitals of Europe slipped into obscurity, out of the society of those who might have assisted her. Somehow she managed to exist, for a time, but eventually she became unable to look after herself. In 1977 at the age of ninety-six she was in a care home, forgotten by all but a few ancient acquaintances who visited out of curiosity and pity, and a young biographer. She died on 13 October that year in her sleep.

Sunny and Consuelo's elder son Bert now succeeded to the title of 10th Duke, and with Duchess Mary took over the running of Blenheim. Consuelo had been forbidden to visit her former home for twenty years, but now she was welcomed back and was curious to see what changes had been made. Without Sunny's presence she found the palace less formidable and was touched when local people welcomed her with affection and made her feel wanted. She admired the wonderful water gardens that Sunny and Gladys had created, but mostly she enjoyed the change in ambience: 'How

---

*Alva died on 26 January at 9 Rue Monsieur, Paris, with Consuelo at her bedside.

rewarding are my memories of Blenheim in my son's time,' she wrote later. 'His life [there], with Mary and his children, was all that I wished mine could have been.'[13] Thereafter, Winston, Clementine and Consuelo all made regular visits to Blenheim and would spend the occasional Christmas there.

By the mid-Thirties Randolph had fallen in love with another Mitford cousin, a girl in fact, with the same blue eyes, fair hair and Madonna-like calmness as Diana (and also, incidentally, as Randolph's mother). This was Clementine Mitford,* and it was to her that Randolph poured out his political hopes and his despair when he was continually defeated at elections and thrown out of Chartwell by his mother, who had told him never to return because she could no longer tolerate the rows he caused. Clementine Mitford loved Randolph, but not as a potential husband: 'He was the *first clever* grown up person that I met,' she wrote. 'He was full of scintillating talk – quoting poetry and prose, and so funny and brave as a lion. All this, and added to it a great capacity for true affection, which he did not mind demonstrating. I think . . . that I filled a gap for him; he talked to me a lot about his relationship with his mother and father . . . the quarrels with Winston were so sad and both sides were upset.'[14]

When he was older Randolph could almost accept that his behaviour as a headstrong young man had often been inappropriate. He was always fired by an ambition to emulate his father and his grandfather; he once told Clive Irving, managing editor of the *Sunday Times*, that this was triggered by the realisation that he shared his birthday, 28 May, with the Younger Pitt. 'If he could be Chancellor of the Exchequer at twenty-three and Prime Minister at twenty-five I saw no reason why I shouldn't do the same,' he said.[15]

Randolph's rude, sometimes obnoxious, behaviour won him no friends. When the Conservative Party turned him down as a

---

*Later Lady Beit, Clementine Mitford was born after her father's death in action. Had she been a boy the child would have succeeded to the title of Lord Redesdale; as it was, her father's brother ('Farve' in Nancy Mitford's rollicking novels) was next in line.

candidate he stood as an Independent Conservative, backed financially by the multimillionairess Lady Houston. He stood three times between 1933 and 1935 at Wavertree, Norwood and Cromarty respectively ('More stags than Tories in Cromarty,' Brendan Bracken, Winston's staunchest supporter, had warned in a cable). Each time Randolph stood, he managed to split the Conservative vote between himself and the official Tory candidate so that Labour reaped the benefit, which made him a hated figure on the Tory benches. This odium spilled over on to Winston so that now, when he rose to his feet to address the House, he was often shouted down by irate men who should have been – and probably would otherwise have been – his supporters.

All this resulted in a bitter quarrel between Randolph and Clementine who blamed her son for endangering his father's career. Furious, she actually told him she hated him and would never forgive him. Randolph also quarrelled with his father when Winston refused to support him because he saw his son's course as perilous and because he saw how much it had upset Clementine. However, when Clementine was away on a cruise in 1935 and Randolph contracted jaundice, Winston forgot all the disagreements and rushed to the aid of his son, who was 'holed up', he reported, at the Ritz. Then he made excuses for him, writing to Clementine that in fact rather than having failed at the Cromarty election Randolph had done well to get as many votes as he had, because he had done it all alone without the backing of a party election machine. This was something of an exaggeration, since he had drawn heavily on Lady Houston's generous coffers and had been better-funded than Winston had ever been in his life.

Clementine had left Chartwell the week before Christmas 1934 to cruise around the Dutch East Indies (now Indonesia) aboard Lord Moyne's* yacht the *Rosaura*, which she joined in Sicily. Lord Moyne wanted to collect one of the indigenous 'dragon' (monitor)

---

*Lord Moyne (Walter E. Guinness, 1880–1944) was the father of Bryan Guinness who married Diana Mitford. A British statesman and businessman (CEO of the Guinness Brewery empire), he was a great friend of the Churchills, who took a number of cruises aboard the *Rosaura*, a converted 700-ton ferry.

lizards for London Zoo. It was a relief to Clementine to miss the usual family get-together. The previous Christmas most of her family had been at odds – her daughter Diana's marriage had failed within a year, and she was now as unhappy as ever; this had been forecast by Clementine, but it gave her no satisfaction to be proved right. Winston and Randolph were at loggerheads most of the time; the house rang with their disagreements. Nellie's son Esmond, now fourteen and rebellious of any authority, was proving more difficult than Randolph: he insisted on wearing a huge black wide-brimmed hat every waking minute and refused to dress for dinner, which annoyed Winston. But what really alarmed the family was that Esmond had espoused Communism (which annoyed Winston even more); and having run away from school several months before Clementine set off on her cruise, he was still missing at the time of her departure. All these troubling undercurrents submerged the arrangements Clementine had made for the usual Chartwell carol singing, tree lighting and present giving.

A few days after Clementine departed, Esmond was discovered living rough in an empty shop in London where a close friend visited him, describing him thus: 'He was at the height of his intolerant fanaticism, a bristling rebel against home, school, society . . . the world . . . He was dirty and ill-dressed, immensely strong for his age: his flat face gave the impression of being deeply scarred, and his eyes flared and smouldered as he talked.'[16] Esmond would spend Christmas Eve of 1934 in court, having been arrested after being found drunk in his dingy squat, where he was busy producing Communist propaganda. At the hearing Nellie told the judge that her son was 'uncontrollable' and he was committed to a six-week term in a remand home for delinquent boys, in what would prove to be a vain attempt to bring him back into line.

Winston, who was not keen on cruising and was anyway busy working on his Marlborough biography, had declined Lord Moyne's invitation. Seeing Clementine's disappointment, he had suggested she go without him. The letters written between Winston and Clementine during this long parting, now published, do not detail the fact that Clementine developed a romantic attachment for a fellow passenger,

Terence Philip. Initially there were only four aboard the *Rosaura*: Mr and Mrs Lee Guinness, Terence Philip and Clementine, and these four were alone for three weeks until joined by Lord Moyne and his long-term mistress Vera Broughton.

Clementine's only extramarital romance occurred during those three weeks of sybaritic sailing in tropical seas and visiting islands such as Bali, when there were no letters from Winston to remind her of home and the stresses there. The milestone of her fiftieth birthday came and went without any special notice. Sometimes she and Terence Philip picnicked alone on deserted islands while their fellow guests went deep-sea fishing. Clementine was still slender and desirable; Philip, who worked in the art world, was seven years younger, debonair and charming, and he became very fond of Clementine. Mary would relate in her biography of her mother that Clementine never stopped loving Winston, but for a few months she had surrendered to a romantic dream world far removed from the tumult that always surrounded her husband, and more specifically her son.

Many years afterwards Clementine admitted the relationship to her daughter, telling her that Terence Philip 'had never really been in love with her' before adding, 'But he made me like him.'[17] After her return – and her letters to Winston during the separation show that before the end of the cruise she longed to be reunited with him – Terence Philip visited her at Chartwell for a while and then went to live in the USA, where he worked until his death early in the war. It was an interlude about which she could feel tender and nostalgic during dark times. There was never any danger to her marriage, for Clementine belonged to the school that regarded marriage as a lifetime commitment, and it is impossible to believe that she was ever physically unfaithful to Winston. But perhaps the episode served to soften the attitude of a woman who had hitherto been a severe critic of those who strayed. There is certainly more than a hint of Winston beginning to worry about his wife's prolonged absence. 'I have not grudged you yr long excursion,' he wrote, 'but now I do want you back.' It is just possible he half-suspected his Kat might be having a romantic adventure of her own. 'Oh my darling Winston,' she replied from the Suez Canal on her way home, 'I send you this like

Sunny and Clementine dressed for foxhunting, on the steps of Blenheim. (Getty)

Clementine with Winston on army manoeuvres. (Churchill Archives)

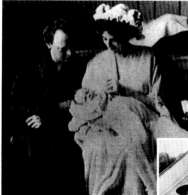

An unusually informal photo of Winston and Clementine with their first child, Diana, born in 1909. (Private collection)

Blenheim in 1911 when the Oxfordshire Hussars held a camp there. Sunny is on the left, Winston is standing and Jack is seated. (Churchill Archives)

Winston and Clementine on holiday just before the outbreak of war in 1914 (Churchill Archives)

Winston with Clementine in 1914 beside the Farman biplane in which he learned to fly. He enjoyed flying, but at Clementine's entreaty he gave it up.
(Getty)

Jack in the Dardanelles campaign in 1915.
(Imperial War Museum Q_013619)

Clementine with her mother-in-law Jennie, soon after the end of the First World War, at about the time of Jennie's third marriage. (Getty)

Jack's wife 'Goonie', beautiful and much loved by all the family. Here with her daughter Clarissa. (Private collection)

LEFT: Winston fought in the trenches during the war on his resignation from the Cabinet after Gallipoli. This is his trench gear. The helmet was given to him by a Frenchman. (Churchill Archives)

The 1921 Cairo Conference. Winston was Colonial Secretary and Clementine accompanied him to Egypt. She is wearing white and is on the first camel from the left. Next to her is Winston, then Gertrude Bell and T. E. Lawrence. (Churchill Archives)

Jennie was sixty-three when she married her third husband, Montague Porch. He was forty (younger than Winston), although he looks older in this press photograph taken as they left the register office. (Mary Evans Picture Library)

Consuelo and Jacques Balsan, the love of her life. (Getty)

The head of one of the sphinxes at Blenheim – said to be a very lifelike portrait of Sunny's mistress Gladys before her plastic surgery went awry (Author)

Sunny in 1900. He loved Gladys passionately for years. (Getty)

Duchess Gladys, soon after her marriage to Sunny in 1921. Even though they had been lovers for over a decade, their relationship began to fall apart shortly afterwards. (Getty)

The Churchill and the Mitford children often spent time at each other's homes. Here at Swinbrook, left to right, Ralph (a family friend), Unity, Jessica and Diana Mitford, Diana Churchill, Tom Mitford, Randolph and the imperturbable Lady Redesdale. (Private collection)

Randolph and Diana with their father at Chartwell. (Getty)

Winston playing at a polo match in 1923. He was a fine rider and played frequently. A dislocated shoulder sustained years earlier in India meant he always played with his right arm secured by a strap. (Corbis)

Clementine and Marigold, the Churchill daughter who died tragically as an infant.
(Churchill Archives)

A family group on Budget Day: Winston as Chancellor, carrying the famous red dispatch case, with Clementine, Sarah and Randolph. (Churchill Archives)

Winston specialised in landscapes, but he painted a few portraits, and this group painting demonstrates his ability to capture likenesses. From left to right: Winston (foreground), Thérèse Sickert, Diana Mitford, Edward Marsh, Professor Lindemann, Randolph, Diana Churchill, Clementine Churchill and Walter Sickert. Based on a photograph taken by Donald Ferguson, 29 August 1927.
(Curtis Brown © The Churchill Heritage/ The National Heritage)

Mary skating in Switzerland in the winter of 1937–8.
(Churchill Archives)

LEFT: Winston and his best friend, the utterly
brilliant F. E. Smith. After F.E.'s death Winston was
inconsolable. (Churchill Archives)

A rare photo of Clementine
with Terence Philip, her only
extra-marital romance. She
was his companion on a cruise
(pictured here in Madras in
January 1935) and later confided
in her daughter that 'he made
me like him'. (Churchill Archives)

At Chartwell. Left to right:
Tom Mitford, Winston
(unidentified), Clementine,
Diana, Randolph and Charlie
Chaplin. (Getty)

John the Baptist to prepare the way before me, to tell you I love you & that I long to be folded in your arms.'[18]

Meanwhile, the Conservative Party remained livid at Randolph's damaging and divisive attempts to win a seat as an Independent. Only at Norwood would the official Tory Party candidate, Duncan Sandys,* survive (although Randolph carved heavily into the majority there, too). The personable young Sandys had resigned a very promising career as a diplomat in the Foreign Office to enter Parliament. During the run-up to the election he had often met Diana and Sarah, who had been easily dragooned into working for their brother's campaign as an antidote to boredom at home. Diana, miserable in her failed marriage, fell headlong in love with Sandys and her feelings were reciprocated. Within a year she was divorced and on 16 September 1935, less than three years after becoming Mrs John Bailey, she married Duncan Sandys. Belonging to a generation that regarded divorce as a last resort, the Churchills could not be happy for their daughter. But although Winston had been prepared to dislike his new son-in-law, in fact Duncan Sandys supported him and shared the same political ideology; subsequently, their rapport was to excite Randolph's jealousy.

But Diana's emotional problems and the difficulties with Randolph were not the only worries that Winston and Clementine faced when she had returned home in May. Nellie was still distraught about Esmond. His espousal of Communism had begun when he wrote to his Uncle Winston requesting some information about Russia so that he could attack Russia in the school debate on the subject. Churchill replied that he was too busy to be of much help, but advised Esmond to consider that Russia had murdered millions of people during the Revolution. Blundering around, confusing pacifism with Communism while he researched the matter, Esmond came across the *Daily Worker* on his way to Dieppe to visit his mother. He was so intrigued with this new world, so different from the one he and his family inhabited, that he became a subscriber. He then began his own magazine called *Out of Bounds*,

---

*Sandys: pronounced 'sands'.

which when it was found and read by a master at Wellington was banned. This was enough to make it a bestseller, much sought after in other boys' schools as well as his own. After that his school career plummeted and he became a confirmed rebel. His bad behaviour and truancy caused him to be expelled, so he went on the run and lived rough until picked up by the police. Naturally, the newspapers got on to the story of this nephew of Churchill's to the distress of most of the family, especially Clementine. She blamed Nellie for not being firm enough with Esmond, but in fact nobody knew quite what to do with him.

At this point a crisis occurred closer to home that distracted Clementine's attention from Nellie and Esmond. Sarah's training at the discreet dance school run by two spinster ladies had unexpectedly led to her attending an audition for a role in a West End revue called *Follow the Sun*. The producer, C.B. Cochran, knew who Sarah was – he had known her grandmother, Jennie. 'Does your father know you are here?' he asked her. She replied disingenuously that he probably didn't because he wasn't especially interested in dancing. Clementine was shocked at the thought of her daughter being 'on the stage' as a dancing girl, and the fact that she would be appearing as one of C.B. Cochran's famous 'Young Ladies'* did little to soften the blow for a woman raised in the reign of Queen Victoria. Churchill, however, in reply to C.B. Cochran's letter requesting parental consent, remarked mildly that he hoped Cochran would give Sarah any role for which she seemed suited and that she was to be judged on her own merits. She was to have used a stage name, but since the press caught on immediately such a ploy would have been pointless. In his autobiography Cochran recalled Sarah's audition, at which she did some tap, ballet and modern dancing: she was so good, he said, that 'had she been merely Miss Jones or Miss Brown, or far less good to look at, she would have

---

*The Young Ladies were well-educated young women from good backgrounds who were always heavily chaperoned. Whenever they appeared in public they were obliged to wear very smart clothes including hats and gloves. Among the more famous were Anna Neagle, Jessie Matthews and Florence Desmond, whom I interviewed in 1987. She told me that the 'young ladies' were highly respected and considered 'as untouchable as debutantes'.

been engaged'.[19] But the name Churchill did no harm to her prospects.

Clementine was won round by Cochran's praise of her daughter's ability, and while she was a guest at the Christmas party at Blenheim that year she went to Manchester for the opening of the show. She wrote to Winston who was in Tangiers that Christmas, working on his Marlborough biography and painting: 'You really would have been proud of Sarah. The dancing performed by the chorus was difficult & intricate & she was certainly in the first flight. She looked graceful & distinguished. Blenheim was delightful & you were much missed. Tender Love to you my Darling. How is Vol: III & have you painted some lovely pictures?'[20]

Parental approval slipped when within weeks twenty-one-year-old Sarah announced that she had fallen in love with the star of the show, who was eighteen years older and married. Vic Oliver was a multitalented Austrian Jew who had lived and worked in the USA for some years and had an estranged wife in Austria. Since separating from his wife many years earlier he had been in a long-term live-in relationship, so in effect he now had two failed relationships behind him. Mr and Mrs Cochran both remonstrated with Sarah; everyone in the cast tried to make her change her mind. Her mother shied from actual dissuasion, cautioning Winston to write to Sarah, 'but not severely'. She reminded him of the effect the heavy-handed letter he had written to Randolph had produced five years earlier, as a consequence of which she feared their son had come close to marrying Kay Halle.

But Winston did not agree with Clementine. He decided to invite Vic Oliver for an interview, which he duly reported to her. 'He did not impress me with being a bad man; but common as dirt . . . a horrible mouth: . . . a foul Austro-Yankee drawl. I did not offer to shake hands.'[21] Oliver told Winston that he loved Sarah, but that he would not rush things. However, as he and Sarah were now openly seen to be in a relationship it might be better for them to be formally engaged while he obtained his freedom. After a difficult interview Winston conceded that if they would not see each other for a year and were still of the same mind at the end of that time he would withdraw his objections, provided that Oliver obtained American citizenship. Otherwise, he threatened, he would do everything he could to try to change Sarah's mind. He would tell her of their conversation, he said. At this stage, Winston related to Clementine, Oliver 'got up with gt emotion, not without some dignity, & said, "you don't need to do it. I will do it myself." Sarah [standing in the passage outside the door] followed him downstairs & I have not seen her since. But I put Diana on to her & I learn that the idea of an engagement is off . . . I don't think there is immediate cause to worry.'[22]

Clementine, who was on a skiing holiday at Zürs in the Arlberg Mountains of Austria when she received this letter, replied that it had 'riveted me with renewed horror at the possibility of such a marriage – Sarah must be more than stage-struck – In the middle ages it would be thought she was bewitched. . . . I agree with your diagnosis of Mr Oliver – not a bad man, but common.'[23] She had met Vic Oliver on the opening night in Manchester before the affair happened and had hardly noticed him, but now she found herself 'surprised at Sarah's lack of taste'.

After that the family trod carefully and concentrated on trying to encourage her to 'take time to think', and to Sarah's secret amusement Clementine ensured there was a regular supply of suitable young men invited to Chartwell whenever she visited for the weekend. When this had no effect, Clementine went so far as to privately offer Sarah a flat of her own in London, so that she 'could develop freely', as she put it. Sarah, who had been strictly brought up, was astonished that her prim mother was obviously prepared to accept her having a secret sexual liaison with Vic rather than contemplate her marrying him.

When the show ended, Vic Oliver returned to New York and Churchill summoned his daughter to the family's London flat, 11 Morpeth Mansions*:

---

*In 1932 Churchill acquired a long lease on this two-storey maisonette with four bedrooms. Half a mile from the House of Commons, it overlooks Westminster Cathedral. The family lived there until 1939.

He told me [Sarah wrote], in robust and ringing tones, as if he were addressing a public meeting, what a mistake I was making: to have worked so diligently at my chosen profession and then throw it away in marriage to a – er – to an 'itinerant vagabond' with whom I could not and should never hope to share in stage perform-ances . . . my father then seized his British passport, and waving it dramatically in front of me, said, 'If you marry this man who is not a British subject and he does not take American citizenship, in three or four years you may be married to the enemy and I shall not be able to protect you once you have lost this.'[24]

Diana, now in the ninth month of her first pregnancy, was at the flat that morning, and though she did not know what was said in the interview she recorded that soon afterwards her father bounded from the room, and 'changing from the stern parent to the cheru-bic innocent announced, "I think I have put her off."' But Diana had seen Sarah's face as she left, and she told him: 'On the contrary, I think you have chased her away.'[25]

Diana was correct; the interview had awakened Sarah's rebellious instincts, and when she heard in October that Vic's application for a British work permit had been refused she made her plans accord-ingly. Vic sent her a first-class one-way ticket to New York on the SS *Bremen*. On the day she was to sail (Mary's fourteenth birthday) Winston was abroad, so she confided in Mary, asked her to break the news to their parents, and left a letter for them with a friend before she bolted. The friend broke her confidence and told reporters, and Sarah soon discovered that her elopement was known about.

In those pre-terrorist days friends were allowed to embark with passengers on ocean-going liners to see them off and wish them bon voyage, and journalists habitually mingled with them. Sarah had to hide in the ship's cinema to avoid cameras while in port in Southampton and Le Havre. She then had two carefree days steam-ing towards her lover, but only until she received a cable: I AM ON THE QUEEN MARY. DO NOTHING UNTIL I ARRIVE. YOUR LOVING BROTHER RANDOLPH.[26]

The *Queen Mary* had departed Europe two days after the *Bremen*, but she was a larger, faster ship. When the *Bremen* ran into a hurricane and was forced to heave to, Sarah feared Randolph might overtake her and arrive in New York ahead of her, before she could speak to Vic. But the *Queen Mary* was also affected by the hurricane, and the *Bremen* arrived a day ahead, at which point Sarah faced a storm of publicity. Afterwards she angrily told her mother that this would never have happened had not Randolph been sent chasing after her. It would have been more tactful to ask one of their American cousins to meet her, she wrote, 'but Randolph's departure confirmed all the rumours and gave them a five day story'. As a result Vic had been pursued mercilessly before her arrival, and all sorts of speculative stories had been written under banner headlines such as 'Dash Across the Atlantic' and 'Brother Chases Cupid'.

Vic was allowed aboard before she disembarked, and he gave her an engagement ring. He had arranged for her to be transferred with as much privacy as possible, hoping to protect her from reporters, but instead Sarah took advice from fellow passenger Lady Astor, whom she knew well and who counselled Sarah to meet the press on her own terms and give them a prepared statement. Otherwise, the older woman warned, she would be hounded for weeks. So Sarah held a press conference in Lady Astor's huge state room, then left the ship to find her cousin Raymond Guest (son of Freddie and Amy) and his wife waiting at the bottom of the gangplank to take her to their Long Island home. 'We will look after you,' Raymond told her.

This was enough to rouse Sarah's Churchill fighting spirit. She had no desire to be 'looked after', she told them firmly. She was going to stay at the Waldorf Astoria and would visit them at the weekend. Next day, 'with a sisterly glint of satisfaction in my eye, at having arrived first', she fought her way through crowds of reporters waiting to meet Randolph as he disembarked. He soon saw that Sarah was determined to go her own way, and having done what he considered his fraternal duty he set off to cover the presidential election which was anyway the real purpose of his trip to the USA.

From then onwards Sarah and Vic saw each other every day, as discreetly as possible. She visited the Guests at Long Island at week-ends, and Vic arranged a work permit for her so she could join him in his new show *Follow the Stars*. Although her part in the show was a minor one, because she was headline news – dubbed 'The Dancing Debutante' – her name went up in lights, which caused some hostility amongst fellow cast members ('Is she a princess or something?'). Churchill tried through lawyers to find some legal hindrance to the marriage, but there was nothing he could do. Vic eventually obtained both a divorce and his American citizenship, but while they waited for all this to be finalised Sarah wrote some very bitter letters home which hurt her parents a good deal.

On Christmas Eve 1936 she and Vic were married, and immediately boarded the *Aquitania* to return to work in England. They spent their first weekend in England at Chartwell. Winston was away in the sunshine, but Clementine had agreed they could visit as she had no wish to be estranged from Sarah. In order to entertain the newly-weds she delayed her departure for a planned skiing holiday with Mary, Goonie, Clarissa, her cousin Venetia Montagu* and Venetia's daughter Judy. Curiously, when she reported to Winston she wrote that Sarah looked 'as virginal and aloof as ever'.

There had been other matters besides Sarah, Diana and Randolph diverting Churchill's attention during that year when Sarah fled to New York. King George V died on 20 January 1936 and the Prince of Wales, whom Churchill had known and liked for twenty years, ascended the throne. By the autumn, when Churchill returned after holidaying at Consuelo's chateau Saint Georges-Motel and at Château de l'Horizon,† he found himself embattled on many fronts. Sarah had left five days before their first grandchild, Diana's son Julian Sandys, was born, on 19 September. The new King Edward

---

*Née Venetia Stanley (of the Stanleys of Alderney), she was the young woman who had been the love of H.H. Asquith (see p. 296) until she married Edwin S. Montagu in 1915 after converting to Judaism. Her marriage to Montagu, who was Secretary of State for India from 1917 to 1922, was not happy, and she had a number of lovers including Beaverbrook. Her daughter Judith, born in 1923 shortly before Montagu's early death, is generally assumed not to have been Montagu's child though she bore his name.

†Clementine had been with him early on in the holiday but she returned home while he stayed on with Maxine Elliott at Château de l'Horizon.

VIII, who had also been a guest at Château de l'Horizon, had gone on to holiday aboard a chartered yacht, the *Nahlin*, taking Wallis Simpson with him. Although British papers held back from reporting this royal holiday, the rest of the world was agog at the romance, which had been developing for almost four years, but until 1936 in a reasonably discreet fashion. Among the guests on that voyage were Duff and Diana Cooper, who watched in astonishment as the King dropped to his knees to release the hem of Wallis's evening gown from under the leg of her chair. It seemed to them a blatant declaration of his feelings for her. By the end of that trip the King had begun telling his friends and advisers that he intended to marry Wallis or abdicate. To Winston, such an outcome was unthinkable; in his mind the King *was*, symbolically, England. This and his romantic nature led him to support the King in the ensuing imbroglio.

There was bizarre news, too, of Diana Guinness, the Mitford sister of whom Winston had been so fond when she was a teenager and with whom Randolph had been besotted. Having left her husband Bryan Guinness (son of their friend Lord Moyne) in 1932 to become the mistress of Oswald Mosley, when Mosley's wife died from peritonitis, Diana had now married Mosley. In the intervening years Mosley had formed his own extreme right-wing party, nicknamed 'the Blackshirts' by reason of their uniform, and as leader of the British Fascists had become very unpopular. To avoid unwelcome press attention the couple had married abroad. The wedding had been held on 6 June 1936 in the Berlin apartment of Josef and Magda Goebbels, with Adolf Hitler as guest of honour. It was the second (and last) time that Mosley and Hitler met; the first had been merely an introduction at a diplomatic reception a few years earlier, and they had no private conversation together at either meeting, but Churchill would not have known this. Any meeting between Mosley and Hitler would have appeared extremely sinister to him.

Churchill was increasingly concerned about events in Europe. In March 1935 Hitler had brought in conscription, which broke the terms of the Treaty of Versailles of 1919, but none of the countries involved in the treaty made a formal complaint. That summer the

German Ambassador in London, Ribbentrop, negotiated an Anglo-German naval agreement which gave Germany the right to build submarines; again, it was in breach of the Versailles Treaty. Finally, in 1936, having seen no opposition so far, Hitler denounced the Versailles Treaty outright and marched his troops into the Rhineland. The reaction of most French and British politicians was that the Germans were merely entering their own backyard. Churchill and a few others, however, regarded it as the opening move towards war. In Spain in 1936 General Franco received massive support from Hitler and Mussolini, which enabled him to launch an attack on the newly elected left-wing Popular Front government – an action that led to the Spanish Civil War. A few long-sighted commentators suggested that this was a rehearsal for another world war.

Churchill nagged away at this theme, but his fellow parliamentarians were so used to hearing his warnings that they no longer listened, and he simply gained for himself the reputation of a warmonger. Nor had his support of the King in his marriage difficulties been any more successful than had his opposition to Sarah and Vic Oliver. He suggested several alternative plans such as a morganatic marriage, which would make Wallis Simpson the King's legal wife without providing her with regal status. Prime Minister Stanley Baldwin would have none of it.

On 7 December 1936, a week after his sixty-second birthday, when Churchill rose to his feet in Parliament to request that 'no irrevocable step should be taken with regard to the King', he was howled down and forced to resume his seat without completing his speech. The blatant hostility of the House was a terrible blow to him; he had met with many objections to his policies in his forty-year parliamentary career, but never at this level. Brendan Bracken recalled: 'Winston stood there with folded arms, very pale but quite resolute. He was not going to give in to bullies. I went with him to the smoking room. Members pushed away from him . . . He was miserable beyond belief; to be howled down in the House of Commons was a disgrace.'[27] Winston not only felt totally humiliated, he was made to realise that he could not save the King; so in the midst of

all their family problems he and Clementine were particularly distressed when, on 11 December, the King abdicated. It is generally
believed that Churchill finessed or edited the moving abdication
speech broadcast over the wireless.

Randolph's political ambitions were forcibly put on hold towards
the end of 1936, leaving him, as his friend Freddie Smith remarked,
'unbowed, but bloody as usual'. One reason was the death of Lady
Houston (who, together with Amy Guest, in backing the Schneider
Trophy races was directly responsible for the development of the
Spitfire*); and with her death went also Randolph's source of electioneering finance. For the next few years he would use his position
as reporter for press barons Lords Rothermere and Beaverbrook to
promote his political agenda, which – like his father's – took the
form of constant but largely unheeded warnings about German
rearmament. During a visit to Munich in September 1937 he tried
to persuade his cousin Unity Mitford to introduce him to Hitler, for
she was then one of the favoured few with access to the German
leader. Randolph was cross when – always protective of the Führer –
she refused to help him.

As Spain became engulfed in a civil war, the family were startled
to hear that Esmond Romilly had run off to join the International
Brigade and fight against the Fascist regime. To Churchill's dismay,
Esmond publicly announced that he was a member of the Communist
Party. Among the upper classes at that time Communism was more
feared than Fascism. Indeed, some supported Hitler simply because
they regarded him and his Nazi troops as a bulwark against encroach-
ing Communism from Eastern Europe. Esmond's contacts in the public
school old-boy network enabled him to get a few commissions for
newspaper articles about the fighting in Spain, with headlines such
as 'Winston Churchill's Nephew sends Graphic Message'.

During 1937 the Churchills' finances had evidently recovered to
the extent that Winston was able to suggest to Clementine that they

---

*The Spitfire was a spin-off of the Supermarine Seaplane S6B, which won the Schneider
Trophy race at Calshot, Hampshire, in 1931, and a few weeks later set the world speed record
at 407.5 mph.

provide Sarah and Vic with a flat below Randolph's in Westminster Gardens. While Clementine was away Winston lived quietly, often visiting Blenheim or the homes of friends. But the cost of running Chartwell was a constant worry and in February he wrote to her that he had been told by an estate agent of a buyer looking for such a property. 'If I could see £25,000 I would close with it,' he confided. 'If we do not get a good price we can quite well carry on for a year or two more. But no good offer should be refused, having regard to the fact that our children are almost all flown, and my life is probably in its closing decade.'[28]

Winston did not appear depressed when he made this comment. On the contrary, his life was fuller than ever: he was producing some of his best writing and art, but he had always assumed he would die young and now he was approaching his mid-sixties. With no sympathetic indications from the Prime Minister, it was reasonable for him to suspect that his political career was winding down. Stanley Baldwin, he knew, was determined to resign after the coronation of George VI, and his place as leader of the party would be taken by Neville Chamberlain. There would be no support for Winston from this direction either. Winston spoke frequently in the House, invariably against Germany, but still nobody took notice. MPs on both sides would often pointedly leave the Chamber when he rose to speak. In a conversation with Bernard Baruch, who came to England at the request of President Roosevelt to learn what he could about German rearmament, Winston told him: 'Well, Bernie, the big war is coming. You will be in the forefront in America while I will be in the sidelines here.'[29]

His 'star', as he called it, in which he had always believed – and the great destiny that his mother had foretold for him – appeared to have been permanently eclipsed by the Dardanelles disaster. No one could have guessed at that point the great challenge that still lay ahead for this ageing man, one that would cement Churchill's reputation in British history as 'the greatest Briton' and surpass even the exploits of his most illustrious ancestor.

1938–9

Towards Armageddon

The *Anschluss* in the spring of 1938 merged Austria with Germany. The British government under Neville Chamberlain was now committed to rearming, but far too slowly for Churchill. When in September that year Hitler publicly promised to help the Sudeten Germans, who lived in parts of Czechoslovakia, by giving them *Lebensraum* (literally, room to live), the danger that Churchill had foreseen years earlier at last became transparent to others. France had a treaty that obliged her to aid the Czechs if they were attacked, and Britain was pledged to support France, which effectively meant that unless some diplomatic agreement could be reached, another major European conflict was inevitable.

Suddenly London was making ready for war. Trenches were dug in the parks, and air-raid shelters constructed. Over the next few months the civilian population was supplied with gas masks to combat what everyone now assumed was a fait accompli in the event of war – a chemical warfare attack from the air.

Chamberlain flew to Germany for discussions with Hitler, and concluded the infamous Munich Agreement in which Britain and Germany agreed not to go to war with each other and Hitler promised not to occupy the Sudetenland. Foolish as it appears with hindsight that Chamberlain believed Hitler, most historians agree that whatever else Chamberlain achieved or did not achieve at Munich, he gained a year of peace during which Britain made up for lost time in rearming herself and preparing for war. Neither Prime Minister Chamberlain nor any of his staff spoke German, so he was wholly reliant on an interpreter provided by the Germans. 'The impression left on me was that Herr Hitler meant what he had said,' he reported to the Cabinet. 'My view is that Herr Hitler is telling the truth.'[1]

Churchill was livid; his daughter Mary recalls that he 'throbbed with anger and emotion'. Lord Moyne,* Brendan Bracken, Robert Boothby, Duff Cooper and J.L. Garvin, editor of the *Observer*, were among his guests at Chartwell when on 29 September news was received of what Churchill regarded as Chamberlain's 'capitulation'. Lord Moyne recalled the scene: 'Winston ranted and raved, venting his spleen on the two government ministers present and demanding to know how they could support a policy that was "sordid, squalid, sub-human and suicidal".'[2]

A few weeks later during the Munich debate, Churchill made what was arguably the most powerful speech of his parliamentary life to date. He began by outlining why he believed that the Munich Agreement was an unmitigated defeat, rather than the triumph the government were claiming. Hitler had not been made to retract anything, and the terms that Chamberlain had achieved could have been made by ordinary diplomatic channels at any time during the previous few months. 'Silent, mournful, abandoned, Czechoslovakia recedes into the darkness,' he intoned sombrely. 'She has suffered in every respect from her association with the western democracies.' Britain and France had merely acceded to Hitler's demand for self-determination for the Germans in the Sudetenland. But while liberal Western democracies such as Britain and France were entitled to talk of self-determination, he said, 'such talk comes ill out

---

*Moyne, a member of the Other Club, was one of Churchill's greatest supporters in the 1930s when his warnings about Germany fell on mostly deaf ears. He was rumoured to have refused the offer from Adolf Eichmann, in charge of the Nazi deportation of Jews, to release a million Jews from the concentration camps in return for trucks and money from the Western Allies with the reply, 'What can I do with a million Jews?' He was probably not the man who made this remark; however, he was assassinated in November 1944 by a Jewish underground group.

of the mouths of those in totalitarian states [who refuse] the smallest element of toleration to every section and creed within their bounds'.[3] He forecast that Czechoslovakia would eventually have no alternative, with her banking, her industries and her infrastructure already in chaos, but to allow herself to be engulfed by the Nazi state.

> When I think of the fair hopes of a long peace which still lay before Europe at the beginning of 1933 when Herr Hitler first obtained power, and of all the opportunities of arresting the growth of the Nazi power which have been thrown away, when I think of the immense combinations and resources which have been neglected or squandered, I cannot believe that a parallel exists in the whole course of history.[4]

He listed the lost chances in those years when Hitler was testing the mettle of other nations as he pushed against the Versailles Treaty and found no objectors. Churchill now set out what he feared was their true position. The House listened intently to this inspired monologue, and when the MPs voted, thirty Conservative members refused to vote with their party in support of Neville Chamberlain.

However, although Winston's oratory swayed some MPs, the majority, like most other people in the country, were relieved that they were not being plunged into an immediate war. There were public celebrations. Tory MP Sir Henry 'Chips' Channon wrote in his diary, 'The whole world rejoices; only a few malcontents jeer.'[5] Consuelo from her chateau in France was one of those celebrating 'peace'; she wrote to Winston that she could not agree with him, for she wholeheartedly supported the spirit of the Munich Agreement.

But many of the malcontents referred to by Chips Channon had been making their way to Chartwell from the mid-1930s onwards, where Churchill had been creating an informal war dossier from information supplied to him from various knowledgeable sources. From these, as well as military intelligence from Europe, he was also kept advised of the activities of the two Mitford sisters, Diana and Unity, who had regular access to Hitler.

In fact Diana made frequent visits to Germany on behalf of her husband Oswald Mosley's British Union of Fascists (BUF) in the hope of gaining financial support for the organisation. Unity appeared to be a mere sensation seeker, making outrageous statements in the press in which she uncritically praised Hitler and his ideology. Diana was different: politically shrewd, she was the only person who knew both Hitler and Churchill at a personal level. It may seem surprising that she was still in touch with the Churchills and still regarded as part of the family even though she was a supporter, even a friend, of Hitler and senior members of the Nazi Party. Following her divorce from Bryan Guinness and her marriage to Mosley the previous year she was *persona non grata* as far as most of Churchill's friends were concerned, yet she was invited to Chartwell and to dine at Morpeth Mansions, where on one occasion she was joined by Lord Ivor (Consuelo's younger and favourite son) and Sarah Churchill. Sarah recalled that they all questioned her about Hitler and were 'simply fascinated, of course' by what she had to say. She suggested to Winston that he should meet him. 'Oh no,' he replied firmly. 'No!'[6]

Another Mitford sister had hit the headlines that year when seventeen-year-old Jessica ('Decca') eloped to Spain with Esmond Romilly, the family black sheep. In fact Winston and Clementine had not set eyes on Esmond for almost two years, since he defected from school at the age of fifteen. The elopement story was front-page news for several weeks in the UK because of the couple's connections and their ages (Esmond was slightly younger than Decca). In Germany, Hitler censored the story out of consideration for Diana and Unity, but at home the Mitford, Churchill and Romilly families were treated to a crop of headlines such as 'Peer's Daughter Elopes to Spain', 'Another Mitford Anarchist', 'Mixed Up Mitford Girls Confusing Europe'. Eventually the runaways were reported to be in Bilbao, and the Foreign Secretary Anthony Eden was persuaded to fire off a cable to the already beleaguered Consul there (who at the time had rather more on his plate than a couple of spoilt runaway aristocrats): FIND JESSICA MITFORD AND PERSUADE

HER TO RETURN. The Consul knew only too well where Decca was, because she and Esmond were hanging around his offices waiting for her visa to be issued. When tackled, Esmond himself composed a reply for the Consul to send: HAVE FOUND JESSICA MITFORD IMPOS-SIBLE PERSUADE HER TO RETURN. Next, the pair coolly hitched a lift on a British Navy* destroyer to Bayonne where they thought they could marry hurriedly, only to find that their age (both under eighteen) was against them without parental permission.

Decca's mother Lady Redesdale travelled to Bayonne, where she found her daughter already noticeably pregnant. She decided she could do nothing other than arrange a quiet wedding, and Nellie Romilly drove down to join her to watch their children marry.[7] Esmond and Decca returned to England after a winter living rough in France. Tragically, their infant daughter was to die of measles in May 1938.

The year 1938 was a bad one for Clementine's health. She spent most of the summer in France taking a cure at a spa, and when she felt better she joined Winston, in Paris on an official visit. There she broke her toe when she stumbled against a chair. She was already in low spirits on account of all the family troubles as well as the disturbing situation in Europe, so that when she was invited to cruise the Caribbean during that winter of 1938–9 aboard Lord Moyne's yacht the *Rosaura* she accepted with alacrity. Again, Winston was too busy to join her. He wrote to her on 19 December:

It seems an age since you left. Yet vy little has happened that matters. I have been toiling double-shifts at the English S.P.s[†] & our score tonight is 180,000 [words], or 30,000 above the tally of 1,000 a day from Aug. It is vy laborious: and I resent it, & the pressure . . . My life has simply been *cottage*[‡] & book . . . & I have only been to London for occasional Parl't Debates . . . Mary & I go to

*Sent to evacuate refugee women and children as the battle front moved along the coast during the Civil War.
† *History of the English-Speaking Peoples*, Churchill's four-volume history of Britain and her colonies, covering the period from 55 BC to 1914.
‡ He was building a cottage in the orchard to be used in time of crisis in case Chartwell itself became uninhabitable.

Blenheim on Saturday [Christmas Eve] . . . then I return here and think to stay until the middle of the month. I do not think war is imminent for *us*. Only further humiliations, in wh *I rejoice* to have no share. Darling do always cable every two or three days. Otherwise I get depressed – & anxious about you & yr health. Probably when this reaches you it will be in warm sunshine – How scrumptious.[8]

Ten days later Diana gave birth prematurely and easily to a baby daughter whom she called Edwina. 'The baby is tiny but perfect,' Winston reported, 'and by my latest news, thriving.' He and Mary had not overstayed their welcome at Blenheim and he had enjoyed playing bezique with Duchess Mary. 'Randolph made himself very agreeable all round . . . I have practically finished the brick-work of the cottage . . . I continue to lead my routine mechanically, reading the papers and letters, eating, building, correspondence, sleeping, dining and finally dictating until three o'clock in the morning.' There was news of Clementine's former fiancé, Sydney Peel, who had died suddenly, one of several of their contemporaries who died that winter, and the news had made Churchill feel old. 'It is quite astonishing to reach the end of life & feel just as you did fifty years before,' he added in a postscript. 'One must always hope for a sudden end, before faculties decay . . . I love to think of you in yr Sunshine. But I hope & pray that some solid gains are being made in yr poise and strength.'[9]

These letters never seemed to catch up with Clementine, who wrote to Winston almost daily. At each port she looked for letters from him, in vain. She gave him news of all the islands, reported that they had heartily cheered his name in Jamaica, and from Antigua she wrote about English Harbour:

Rodney, Hood & Nelson all were here. It is not deep enough for modern ships and the Navy gave it up about 50 years ago – Nelson served here as a young Captain of 25 . . . To while away the time he married a young Widow who lived in the neighbouring Island of Nevis. He re-visited Antigua in 1805 to refit his Ships after chasing

Villeneuve across the Atlantic – He then chased him back all the way home & got him at Trafalgar.

But she was depressed at not hearing from Winston.

My Darling – Do you know that I am starved for a letter from you . . . & I am rather miserable. You telegraphed that you had posted a letter by Air Mail leaving by Dec: 20th – This should have reached me at Antigua before we left there. And even if I had received it, my Darling, I had left home 4 weeks before – Do you think you could dictate a few words every day to a Secretary & she could send it off twice a week – Never mind about writing yourself – I used to mind about that, but I'm accustomed to typewritten letters now, & would rather have them than nothing. I feel quite, quite cut off – Your loving but sad, Clemmie. Ps: *Please* don't telegraph – I hate telegrams just saying 'all well rainy weather Love Winston'.[10]

Clementine had seen the obituary in *The Times* of the man to whom she had once been engaged:

Suddenly there was Sydney Peel looking at me . . . – A young photograph, as I used to know him – I closed my eyes . . . I lived again those four years during which I saw him nearly every day – He was good to me and made my difficult rather arid life interesting – But I couldn't care for him & I was not kind or even very grateful – And then my Darling you came, and in that moment I knew the difference – I am glad you wrote me about it, because at that moment I longed for you – I wanted to put my arms round you and cry and cry.[11]

By the time they made contact Winston was in the sunshine himself, staying with Maxine Elliott at Château de l'Horizon to escape the winter weather. Also visiting were the Windsors, and before their arrival one evening for dinner there was much discussion among the other guests on the thorny question of whether or not to curtsey to the Duchess. Winston, still a supporter of the former king, reported: 'All accounts show them entirely happy and as much in love with each other as ever.' Later he would visit the Windsors at their lovely villa. 'Everything [is] extremely well done and dignified. Red liveries, and the little man himself dressed up to the nines in the Balmoral tartan with dagger and jabot etc. When you think that you could hardly get him to put on a black coat and short tie when he was Prince of Wales, one sees the change in the point of view. I am to dine with him tomorrow night with only Rothermere.* No doubt to talk over his plan for returning home. They do not want him to come, but they have no power to stop him.'[12]

En route to the Riviera Churchill had stopped over in Paris, where, he told Clementine, he found the leading French politicians very anxious about Hitler and Mussolini; the general perception was that 'these two ruffians will be moving again quite soon'. He was pleased to hear that Roosevelt was echoing his own point of view. He described the chaos in London arising from new 'emergency' installations that had resulted in waterlogged trenches, which the authorities could not fill in but did not know how to drain, and which had to be guarded round the clock to prevent children falling in and drowning. There was great dissatisfaction in the newspapers about the arrangements for air-raid precautions (ARP), when the minister responsible was reported to be away skiing in St Moritz. In short, Winston commented, there was a total lack of drive, and the worst of it was that Chamberlain was probably not even aware of the extent of the neglect over which he presided. Without any trace of gloating over Chamberlain's growing unpopularity he added, 'I do not think it would be much fun to go and take these burdens and neglects upon my shoulders, certainly not without powers such as they have not dreamed of according.'[13]

Clementine's Caribbean cruise was not a great success: she was depressed by the poverty of the islanders and homesick – she missed Winston and Mary. Her tolerance was seriously challenged when

---

*Lord Rothermere was their neighbour at his villa, La Dragonnière.

one of her fellow diners attacked the anti-government faction – in other words, Churchill and his colleagues – though Winston was not actually named. Clementine immediately rose and left the table, apologised to Lord Moyne, packed and left the yacht, booking herself a passage on the next steamer home. Winston was 'enchanted' to learn of her early return.

In March, Hitler broke his promise to Chamberlain when German troops crossed into Czechoslovakia. A few weeks later Mussolini attacked and took possession of Albania. Winston, busy with his book a good deal of the time, watched from the back benches as the hapless British government debated what should be done. Sometimes he held court at Chartwell. His trusted confidants almost constituted a crisis Cabinet when it came to the international situation. They brought with them secret intelligence reports from a wide network of informants, which included senior Germans who risked their lives by visiting Churchill at Chartwell in an attempt to avert the war that they insisted was Hitler's intention. Major Desmond Morton, a former Army officer and a senior civil servant, was especially instrumental in providing Churchill with intelligence about German rearmament, which the latter used as a basis for his parliamentary attacks. The government wondered where Winston was obtaining his information, but – fortunately for Morton – the leak was never discovered.

Other visitors to Chartwell included the American Ambassador Joe Kennedy, the French Prime Minister Léon Blum, General Ironside (soon to be Chief of the Imperial General Staff), Sir Robert Horne, Max Beaverbrook, Sir Austen Chamberlain, Sir Edward Grigg, Anthony Eden, Lord Winterton and Sir Henry Croft. Brendan Bracken and 'the Prof' were always around; to Churchill they were trusted friends. Clementine still disliked Bracken intensely, just as she did Beaverbrook. She felt he was coarse and a poor influence on Churchill, and that Bracken used the connection with Winston to bolster his own reputation.

Later that month, thirty dissident Conservative MPs proposed a motion in favour of setting up an all-party coalition government. Among those promoting this, apart from Winston himself, were the usual suspects: Anthony Eden, Duff Cooper, Brendan Bracken and Harold Macmillan who told his constituency that this was a necessary move, not only to try to avoid an almost inevitable war with Germany, but even more importantly 'to avoid a defeat'. Winston demanded that a compulsory National Service register be set up – something that ought to have been done immediately after Munich, he thundered. He was starting to win points now. A Minister of Supply was appointed – something else that Winston had been advocating for several years – but still he could not sway the government from the policy of appeasement.

Bert and Mary Marlborough's daughter, Lady Sarah, came of age in July 1939. No one who knew Churchill could have been in any doubt that war was inevitable, so it was decided by the usually careful Duke and Duchess that this was no time for economies. The result was one of the most spectacular parties Blenheim has seen in modern times, redolent of the splendour and extravagance of the house during Churchill's Victorian and Edwardian youth. Lady Sarah's young guests – her contemporaries from the debutante world, including the young Kennedys who made such a mark on London parties in 1938 and 1939 – dined at tables on the terrace overlooking the lake. Consuelo came over from France; she joined Winston, Clementine and Anthony Eden at the family dinner in the saloon. Later they repaired to the water terrace – Sunny and Gladys's bequest to posterity – lit for the occasion by hundreds of Chinese lanterns and strings of coloured lights. They sat in the balmy summer night – the last summer of peace – with the strains of Viennese waltzes drifting through the open windows as they chatted over old times and the bad times that were coming. Consuelo now accepted that the war, about which Winston had been warning her for the last four years, was bound to happen, but even now she hoped for France's deliverance. It was fortunate that they were too deep in conversation to witness the spectacle of Randolph behaving badly towards a woman who had just spurned his advances. He had had too much to drink, began a noisy argument with another guest in defence of his father, and was eventually carted off.

It was the last fling of the old Blenheim that Winston had known from birth and that Consuelo had known as a young bride: foot-men in full livery with powdered hair, the best food and wines and a thousand beautifully dressed guests most of whom knew most of the others – at least those of their own generation. Diarist Chips Channon recorded: 'I was loath to leave but did so about 4.30am and took one last look at the baroque terraces with the lake below, and the golden statues and the great palace. Shall we ever see the like again? Is such a function not out of date? Yet it was all of the England that is supposed to be dead and is not. There were literally rivers of champagne.'*

That month the political tide was swinging in Churchill's favour as newspapers began a concerted campaign to get him into the Cabinet, a move supported within Parliament by a growing number of MPs from all parties. In August Churchill flew to France to visit the Maginot Line† at the invitation of one of France's most senior generals. From there he could see that the Germans were massing on their side of the border. To the ageing warrior this spelled only one thing: looming attack.

On 17 August he returned to Paris, and after a night at the Ritz he was driven to Dreux for a painting holiday with Consuelo and Jacques at their chateau Saint Georges-Motel. Clementine and Mary joined him there. During the journey he told the chauffeur that he believed Britain and France would be at war before the har-vest was gathered in. In such a climate of uncertainty he found it impossible to concentrate but he spent a few days painting the Moulin de Montreuil, a beautifully renovated house, one of two old

---

*Two months later Blenheim was in war mode: the polished wooden and marble floors cov-ered in protective linoleum, paintings and treasures packed safely away, windows covered in criss-crossed tape, temporary panelling erected to save precious features. Bert did what the Duke of Devonshire did at Chatsworth and decided that occupation by a school for the dura-tion of the war would be less damaging than occupation by the military. Malvern College had been commandeered by the government by then, so the four hundred pupils and staff moved in. Later, the school would be moved on to allow Blenheim to house various government departments, from MI5 to the Ministry of Supply.

†This much vaunted defence mechanism along the French–German border was to prove totally useless. The Germans simply marched around each end.

watermills beside the River Avre in the grounds of the chateau, with the French artist Paul Maze. On 20 August Maze noted in his diary that Churchill had said to him gloomily: 'This is the last picture we shall paint in peace for a very long time.'[14]

It was not a restful holiday. Churchill was fretful – they all were. Consuelo was busy with the 'countryside sanatorium' she had set up some time earlier for eighty children convalescing from surgery and some from tuberculosis, looked after by thirty nursing staff. She took Clementine and Mary on her daily rounds of the sanatorium and the isolation wards in the woods, and gave Mary an expensive leather bag, the sort Mary could never afford to buy for herself.

Increasingly anxious at being away from the centre of events, Churchill left two days later to fly from Paris to London, leaving Clementine and Mary to make their way home a few days afterwards by train and ship. As they changed trains in Paris at the Gare du Nord, Mary remembered, the station 'teemed with soldiers' and they realised that the French Army was mobilising. As soon as he arrived home Churchill hired a private detective, one W.H. Thompson, at £5 a week. 'I can look after myself during the daytime,' he told Thompson who had worked for him previously when Sinn Fein had vowed to kill him during the height of the Irish troubles. 'Will you protect me at night?' He gave Thompson his own Colt automatic. Thompson said that Churchill was a first-class shot and had a personal armoury of firearms with which he practised regularly, but apparently the Colt was Churchill's favourite gun.

On 26 August a state of emergency was declared and all reservists were called up. By the end of the month Churchill was at full stretch, attempting to complete the second volume of *A History of the English-Speaking Peoples*. He advised his publishers that he had completed 350,000 words* and was working every spare moment to try to complete it according to his contract. He knew that he would have no time for writing once war was declared. That same night, as he slept, the German Army invaded Poland. Thompson now

---

*By a rough rule of thumb this would be approximately 1000 pages of printed text.

became Churchill's government-employed shadow, because it was recognised that he was the number one target for assassination by the Nazi regime.

Next morning Churchill drove to Downing Street and was offered a Cabinet seat, without a ministry. He accepted it – how else could he be involved at the heart of the fight he knew was forthcoming? Chamberlain promised to announce the appointment, but failed to do so for several days: he was still trying to negotiate peace, still offering to ignore the incursions, if the Germans would even now withdraw from Poland.

Churchill based himself at Morpeth Mansions during these anxious days. One of his first acts as a Cabinet member was to write to the Prime Minister pointing out that the average age of the War Cabinet Chamberlain had detailed to him was 'over 64! Only one year short of the Old Age Pension! If however you included [Archibald] Sinclair (49) and Eden (42) the average comes down to 57½.'[15] Winston attended a parliamentary debate on 2 September, noting, 'There was no doubt that the temper of the House was for war. I even deemed it more resolute and united than in the similar scene on August 3, 1914, in which I had also taken part.'[16]

The next evening Chamberlain was finally forced, by a group of MPs who burst into Downing Street (through the garden door backing on to Horse Guards Parade) where he was dining with Lord Halifax, to send an ultimatum to Berlin. It stated that unless Germany halted its attack on Poland within three hours, Britain would consider herself at war with Germany. Chamberlain famously broadcast soon afterwards that 'No such undertaking has been received', and Britain declared war on Germany forthwith, quickly followed by a similar declaration by France.

Within minutes Londoners had their first experience of an air-raid warning. Clementine remarked sourly that it was typical of the Germans to be so prompt and efficient, and Churchill fortified himself with cigars and brandy before the couple hurried into an air-raid shelter. It was a false alarm – and just as well, for the nearest shelter, Churchill noted, was an ordinary basement room that was not even sandbagged. The mood of those in the shelter was cheerful and jocular, but Thompson watched Winston prowling around 'like a caged animal'.[17]

After the all-clear sounded Churchill rushed to Parliament, where he spoke eloquently, and it was exhilarating for him, after a decade of being the man to whom no one listened, once again to hold that institution in the palm of his hand. It was no longer, he told his rapt audience, a case of fighting for Danzig or Poland. Britain would now be fighting for herself, to save the world from Nazi tyranny 'and in defence of all that is most sacred to man'.[18] In short, it was a fight to establish on 'impregnable rock' the rights of the individual. More than a quarter of a century had passed, he reflected, and Britain was again threatened by the same enemy. There was no triumph for him in the fact that war had been declared, as he had so often forewarned, but he found some satisfaction in that all his warnings had turned out to be accurate.

Later that day, when Churchill was summoned to Downing Street again, he assumed and hoped that he was to be offered a ministerial post. Clementine went with him, waiting outside in the car during the short interview. Winston came hurrying back to her, delighted, saying as he got into the car, 'It's the Admiralty. That's a lot better than I thought.'[19] He did not wait for written confirmation (in fact he did not formally receive the Patent from the King until 5 September) but sent word to the Admiralty that he would take charge at once, and they might expect him at 6 p.m. As he entered the office of the First Lord – his old room – he recalled his 'pain and sorrow', almost a quarter of a century before, when he had been forced to quit it so ignominiously. There was his old chair and the wooden map case he had fitted up himself in 1911. In the following weeks he would find many of the furnishings he had formerly used, still in store, and he had them reinstated. According to his private detective, from that day onwards until the end of the war Churchill worked a regular 120-hour week.[20]

Immediately, the signal was flashed to all ships in the fleet – WINSTON IS BACK – and the words reverberated throughout the city on newspaper placards. It was a popular appointment among the professionals. And the Admiralty was reinvigorated, not least by

Churchill's confident approach which seemed to embody all the enthusiasm of his previous leadership. The lack of protection for 'the finest Navy in the world' made him angry, and when he visited Scapa Flow* he was horrified to note that it was almost undefended from air attack. But it was a German submarine, only a few weeks after war was declared, which penetrated Scapa and sank the battleship *Royal Oak* with the loss of 833 lives. This was – in his words – 'like a body blow' to Churchill.[21] He then visited all naval bases and establishments, 'prodding, goading, criticising and encouraging'.[22] He seemed to know instinctively what needed to be done to remedy the years of neglect, and where the priorities lay. Memoranda flew from his desk, invariably politely couched: 'Pray let me have the figures by tomorrow . . .', 'Pray let me know on a single sheet of paper the situation as it stands . . .' The recipients knew that despite the old-fashioned phraseology these were not requests but demands. Soon he was back at Scapa to check the new defences. While inspecting some dummy warships moored near HMS *Hood* to fool the German U-boats he noticed that there were no seagulls hovering around them. He ordered food to be thrown to the birds every day from the dummies to make them more life-like. No detail was too small to catch his attention.

The wilderness years were over. 'Had the Prime Minister in the first instance given me the choice between the War Cabinet and the Admiralty,' Churchill wrote in his memoirs, 'I should of course have chosen the Admiralty. Now I was to have both.'[23] He was sixty-four, but his star was back on track and moving confidently through the firmament. The destiny he had always believed was his, awaited him.

---

*This protected natural harbour in the Orkney Islands was used by the Vikings over a thousand years ago and was the main naval base for the British Navy during both world wars.

1939–40

'But You Don't Know Me'

The American journalist Virginia Cowles first met Randolph in
New York in the early Thirties. She next ran into him after the
Germans had occupied the Rhineland in 1936 when he was already
attacking the policy of appeasement in his newspaper columns. She
recalled:

I greatly admired the courage with which he launched his views;
nevertheless, going out with him was like going out with a time
bomb. Wherever he went an explosion seemed to follow. With a
natural and brilliant gift of oratory, and a disregard for the opinions
of his elders, he often held dinner parties pinned in a helpless and
angry silence. I never knew a young man who had the ability to
antagonise more easily.[1]

Randolph was very useful to Cowles, even, in February 1939,
arranging a Russian visa so that she could travel there in order to
report on the Soviet Union, something she had been trying to do
for over two years. One day in the late 1930s he took her to
Chartwell for tea where she found the family 'at home': Winston
dressed in a torn linen coat and a battered hat, pottering in the
grounds; Clementine, 'tall and handsome', presiding over all; Mary
looking after a newborn lamb. Cowles thought the most endearing
thing about the Churchill family was the affection they all showered

on Winston. This was totally understandable, she thought, for he had 'such a human touch' that one was instinctively drawn to him. As they entered the house Winston told Randolph *sotto voce* that he must not tell Clemmie that he'd forgotten to wear his galoshes, 'or she'll scold me'. When he showed Cowles around his studio he said to her, 'With all the fascinating things there are to do in the world, it's odd to think that some people actually while away the time by playing Patience. Just fancy!'[2]

During a second visit to Chartwell, in July 1939, she found Winston working hard at volume three of his *History of the English-Speaking Peoples.* 'But I'll never be able to finish it off before the war begins,' he told her ruefully. When that happened, he said, they planned to close Chartwell and move into the cottage he had built in the orchard, for which he had done much of the brick-laying and other work himself. 'You won't be living there,' Randolph interrupted indignantly. 'You'll be at No. 10 Downing Street.'

His father smiled. 'I'm afraid I haven't got the same fanciful ideas that you have,' he said.

'Well, at any rate, you'll be in the Cabinet,' Randolph retorted. Winston muttered that things would have to get very bad before that happened. The next time Cowles saw Winston, just weeks later, he was the First Lord of the Admiralty.[3]

Although Winston had for years publicly deprecated the government's lack of policy in developing and building aeroplanes and in building up munitions, he found the Navy, at least, in a good state to fight a war. This was mainly because Germany had been prevented from building ships for so many years and did not have the naval strength she had boasted in 1914, so Britain could still rule the seas. But Winston knew that the safety of Britain could no longer be wholly guaranteed by the Navy. Once Blériot had flown the Channel, the invulnerability that Britain had always enjoyed as an island was lost for ever. It was not only at sea but in the air that this coming war would be won, and Winston knew from his informants that, in numbers at least, the German Air Force was superior to Britain's. Yet at first even he did not envisage quite how that Air Force would be used to support the German Navy, to Britain's disadvantage at sea.

One of his first acts on assuming office was to summon Randolph to take part in a highly secret mission: to sail to Cherbourg aboard HMS *Kelly*, captained by Lord Louis Mountbatten, and bring back to England the Duke and Duchess of Windsor. In August, Randolph had joined his father's old regiment, the 4th Hussars; the old cavalry regiment had been officially mechanised but the promised tanks had not yet arrived, so there was no action. Kicking his heels in the boarding-school-like atmosphere of the camp, Randolph was thrilled to be given something important to do. Before going ashore in France to meet the former King, he made sure he was properly decked out in full dress uniform, right down to the spurs on his military boots. The Duke, who was eagle-eyed in matters of etiquette, had hardly stepped down from the train when he noticed that Randolph's spurs were upside down. And to the young Churchill's horror and embarrassment the former King insisted on stooping down to remove them and fit them correctly. Throughout the return voyage to Portsmouth Randolph was ragged mercilessly, until the Duke realised that he'd got all the mileage he could out of him. Turning to Mountbatten, he remarked that he was surprised that *he* hadn't noticed the error. 'Well Sir,' said Mountbatten implacably, 'of course I noticed it, but I didn't want to spoil your fun.'[4]

A week later, Randolph was on leave in London and found himself without a partner for dinner. He asked a married friend, Mary Dunne,* but she was already engaged that evening and suggested he invite a friend newly arrived from the country who was staying in a flat that Mary was renting to her. Pamela Digby was the nineteen-year-old, red-haired, blue-eyed daughter of Lord and Lady Digby of Minterne in Dorset; later, she would remember the conversation when she answered the telephone:

'This is Randolph Churchill.'

'Do you want to speak to Mary?'

---

*Formerly Lady Mary St Clair-Erskine, daughter of the Earl of Rosslyn. Her husband had just left to join his regiment.

'No – I want to speak to you.'

'But you don't know me.'

Down the phone Randolph explained that anyway he wanted her to come out to dinner, and at the same time Mary Dunne, who had just arrived, was nodding at her vigorously and encouraging Pamela to accept the invitation. So she did, telling Randolph to collect her at seven o'clock.

'What do you look like?' Randolph asked, before he ended the short conversation.

'Red-headed and rather fat, but Mummy says that puppy fat disappears.'[5]

At the age of twenty-eight Randolph had moved on from being attracted only to women who resembled his mother, such as Diana and Clementine Mitford. His women friends – and there were a good number attracted to this eligible and well placed bachelor, despite his explosive temperament – tended to be sophisticated types and were quite often married; Mary Dunne was one of them. Another was his present mistress, Clare Luce, a vivacious vaudeville star who visited Randolph at his regimental camp most weekends. Young debutantes (Pamela had made her debut at the age of eighteen in 1938 without 'taking') generally bored him. Yet it was from this pool that he would have to fish for a wife, and Randolph's various biographers agree that when war was declared he made up his mind that, as he was Winston's only son and stood a reasonable chance of being killed, he should marry and father a son as soon as possible so that 'the line' was continued.

This seems to be at least a partial explanation for the fact that, although he claimed to be deeply in love with Laura Charteris,* whom he had met in early 1939, within three days after that first dinner at 'Quags', as Quaglino's restaurant was known, Randolph Churchill and Pamela Digby announced their engagement. But Pamela's potent

---

*Frances Laura Charteris (1915–90) married Major Walter (Viscount) Long in 1933; they divorced in 1942. In 1943 she married William Ward, 3rd Earl of Dudley, divorced in 1954. Her third husband, whom she married in 1960, was Michael Canfield. In 1972 she married Bert, 10th Duke of Marlborough. Randolph remained in love with Laura for the rest of his life, but though she enjoyed his company the feeling was never reciprocated.

charm and sexual magnetism should not be underrated, even though at the time it was still a raw talent that was yet to be honed.

Pam was then girlishly pretty, with the captivating smile that is as characteristic a feature of the Digby family as the blue eyes are of the Mitfords. Her debutante portrait on the cover of *Tatler*[6] shows her unsmiling and thoughtful, however. 'Darling Daddie,' she wrote, 'I can't get over that picture in the *Tatler*. Do I really look as frightful as that? *It's terrible!*'[7] The mother of a fellow debutante wrote to Lady Digby: 'I really wanted to tell you how absolutely overcome I was by the beauty of your elder daughter. I've never seen anything so heavenly as that wonderful hair and looks, and apart from her beauty, such a perfectly charming expression. What a lovely creature she is. I felt I must write to you.'[8]

However, Pam was not considered one of the outstanding girls of her coming-out year: 1938 was 'a vintage year for beautiful girls', one 1938 debutante recalled, reeling off a list of names who had looks worthy of a Hollywood career and which included Clarissa Churchill.[9] Pam may not have been on this list of beauties but she managed what most of them had not – namely, a proposal of marriage from one of the most eligible men of that year, the dashing and handsome twenty-year-old Hugh Fraser,* younger son of Lord Lovat. For a few days the young couple discussed the matter: would their parents allow them to wed? They concluded they would almost certainly not, because of their ages and the fact that they would have very little money to live on. So they hatched a plan to elope, and it was Pam who was most grown-up about it, calling it off after a week or so. Fraser was very hurt, and it was nearly fifty years before he felt able to talk about the matter to Clarissa Churchill.[10]

Even at eighteen, Pam was an interesting conversationalist. Her smile lit up a room and she possessed a bubbly, friendly personality that was immensely attractive. She had travelled to Australia and Canada as a child, and spent time in Paris and Munich in 1937 living in with approved families while taking languages classes at

---

*(1918–84), MBE, soldier and Conservative MP. He was the first husband of Antonia Fraser (née Pakenham), who later married Harold Pinter.

finishing schools attended by fellow debutantes. There is a rumour
that Unity Mitford introduced her to Hitler, but there is no evidence of this meeting and it seems unlikely. Those who peopled her
letters home to her parents while she was in Munich were mainly
the same former boarding-school girl friends and Old Etonians with
whom she would mix in London at coming-out parties and at
country-house weekends. While in Munich she sometimes encountered Germans at parties; but, she told her mother, 'Between you
and me and the gatepost I hated the Germans . . . they were very
boring, I thought. I spent most of my time wondering when I
would be able to get home.'[11] She was strictly guarded by her tutors
(or so she reported to her parents) and claimed several longed-for
invitations had to be declined because a chaperone could not be
found. She wrote that she attended the opera and heard the Italian
tenor Beniamino Gigli sing in *Das Rheingold* and *Siegfried*, and
listened to a piano recital of pieces from *The Flying Dutchman*.
She took history of art lessons at the Pinakothek at her own request.
Lady Ravensdale (daughter of Lord Curzon and sister-in-law of
Oswald Mosley) introduced her to Pauline ('Popsie') Winn, Edwina
Drummond and Sarah Norton, and these three girls were to become
Pam's best friends. Making such useful contacts and acquiring some
international polish was what the exercise was all about.

A noted rider in both the hunting field and the show ring,* Pam
was as gregarious as Randolph, and she had a self-confidence and
flirtatiousness that almost matched his own. Furthermore, she had
been educated, as most young English girls of her class and time
were, to at least pretend to regard men as slightly superior beings.
Men were invariably attracted, and when she returned to England
she was a popular guest at weekend parties at Popsie's home, Leeds
Castle,† and at various Astor houses (Sarah Norton would marry an
Astor). But Pam was well brought up, and she was then conventional enough, for a while anyway, to remain a virgin despite

---

*She competed at international level at Olympia and at the Royal Bath and West Show, jump-
ing a pony called Stardust which could clear fences almost twice its own height.
†Then owned by the fabulously rich Olive, Lady Baillie, Popsie's mother.

numerous temptations. Her biggest problem at that time was her £200 annual allowance, which had to cover all her expenses including clothes. She abhorred debt, and would never contemplate exceeding her annual budget, but she often felt self-conscious beside her much richer friends who could spend £400 on a single cocktail dress by Molyneux or Hartnell. Sometimes she bought material and made herself a skirt or a blouse, and all her expenses were diligently listed in her accounts which she submitted to her parents, with explanations: 'a green evening dress . . . terribly *jeune fille*-ish, high at the back with a slightly cowled neck and a tiny sleeve, but the best part is its sash . . . I got the model because it fitted me and was much cheaper [only] £8. 8s.' There was also a navy blue crêpe de Chine dress 'that will go with anything and is dark enough to wear next winter'.[12]

Far from longing to get away from her home and her parents, as two of Pam's biographers have claimed, her surviving letters from the period provide solid evidence that she adored her parents and her childhood life at Minterne: 'I can't get over the thought of being at Minterne again – it is simply marvellous', '. . . longing to see you again, it is so near now, only ten days. I do love you so', 'Tell Daddie I shall die if he doesn't come and see me soon.' This is not to say that Pam didn't do what most of her contemporaries did, those small rebellious acts such as sneaking out through the French windows at a ball while the chaperones sat together drinking tea in the hall; then slip away to a nightclub, have a few forbidden drinks, and get back in again before the ball ended without being missed. At weekend parties she was a flirt, but she made no meaningful relationships with young men other than Hugh Fraser. At that time no man quite measured up to her father.

In September 1939 when she met Randolph, Pam was feeling very grown up, having just taken delivery of a Jaguar car. This was a nineteenth-birthday present from her parents, who were pleased with the way she had lived within her allowance. Having tasted life in London, she decided she did not want to spend the whole of the war at Minterne. Her father had been appointed an honorary guard to the King and her mother served as Commander of the Dorset branch of the women's Auxiliary Territorial Service (ATS). Sheila, her next sister, joined the Army, but that didn't interest Pam either. Instead, she found herself a war job with the Foreign Office through the introduction of a friend. She would be a French translator at a salary of £6 (£172 today) a week, out of which she had to pay £2 10s (£71.80p today) rent on her flat. With the allowance from her parents and given that men were expected to pay for dinners and dances in those days, Pam thought she could manage quite well.

Lord and Lady Digby, who never knew of the secret engagement to Hugh Fraser, were less than enchanted at the news of the sudden engagement to Randolph, for despite his illustrious connections he had the sort of reputation – brawling, womanising, gambling – with which no one would wish their teenage daughter associated. Lady Digby ('Pansy') had never been entirely happy with Pam's frequent visits to Leeds Castle, either. There her much-loved daughter inevitably mixed with a set considered by Pansy to be 'very fast'; indeed, she and Lord Digby came to believe that it was these early visits to Leeds Castle that set the tone of their daughter's future life.[13] Her brother Eddie, the present Lord Digby, was still at Eton at the time and recalls that Pansy simply had to rely on Pam's common sense and the good example of her own happy country home life. Pam was encouraged to bring these friends to Minterne, where Eddie was regularly star-struck by the girls: 'I fell in love constantly,' he admitted.[14]

Pam's father was a locally popular country squire. She wrote frequently to him when she was abroad during her 'finishing' process, sometimes about her visits to art galleries, the opera and concerts but more usually about hunting: 'I am enjoying myself . . . [but] I wish I was home now, and then I could have lots of hunts on Red Rogue.' It was not usual for children and parents of their class to have very close relationships, but her father was Pam's hero, and was almost certainly the reason she always felt so confident in her relationships with older men.

At the time Randolph proposed to Pam it was rumoured in their set that he was so desperate to marry and father a child before he was posted abroad that he had proposed to eight women in the past few weeks. Pam recalled that, at first, 'I was getting so terribly upset by seeing all my friends going off, as they dramatically thought, to be killed, and I thought how marvellous it was to be going out with somebody about whom I didn't give a damn.'[15] Her friends were almost unanimously opposed to the engagement, and warned her off Randolph to the extent that she began to waver. This was enough to send Randolph's courtship technique into overdrive, and Pam was flattered and excited by this powerful, mature man who for several days deluged her with phone calls begging her to marry him, and at once. She was also intrigued by his absolute certainty in himself; he believed the country was in for a long fight, and that therefore in the meantime they should enjoy every moment to the full.

But perhaps the deciding factor for Pam was meeting Randolph's father. Randolph took her to Chartwell, where a delighted Winston welcomed her warmly with an old-fashioned courtesy that touched her. It was a mutual, innocent attraction and in one sense at least she was probably more in love with Winston than with Randolph. Anyway, the entire proposition became more attractive with Winston, the father figure, as part of it. Winston and Clementine were down at Chartwell to close up the big house for the duration (though in fact it was used in the early part of the war to house evacuees), and Cousin Moppet who had brought Mary up was now installed in the former chauffeur's cottage with the two small Sandys children, Julian and Edwina, along with their nanny. The Morpeth Mansions flat was disposed of.

When they first took over Admiralty House in 1911, three years after they were married, Clementine had worried about their ability to afford living in the graceful Georgian mansion overlooking Green Park and Horse Guards Parade. Now, twenty-eight years later, she was still worried about their ability to afford living there, but she had learned a good deal about managing houses in the intervening time. The two top floors, formerly the nursery and attics, were converted by the Ministry of Works into living accommodation and the huge state rooms beneath them were to be closed off. When the Churchills had time to spend in the country they would be able to use the three-bedroom cottage built by Winston, with love, in the orchard at Chartwell.

Rushed weddings were in vogue; no one had time to organise huge white weddings when the bridegroom might be posted at any minute. Pam's parents told her they were worried she was too young, that she and Randolph had no money and nowhere to live. Winston – who had organised his own marriage to Clementine in under a month – blithely advised her that all they needed to be married was champagne, a box of cigars and a double bed. His father's overt approval of his choice of bride thrilled Randolph – at last he had got something right! Clementine was cool. It wasn't that she didn't like Pamela; she liked her very much, but she was unsure of Randolph's motives and so was not optimistic about the outcome. However, on reflection she thought that Pam, unlike Laura, was a nice, happy, uncomplicated girl without a past, and might make Randolph settle down. When the wedding date was set, a seemingly impossible three weeks away, she immediately contacted Pansy Digby and the two mothers set to work. The state rooms at Admiralty House were opened up and a reception organised. On 4 October 1939, just a month after war was declared, Randolph in the full dress uniform of a cavalry officer escorted his bride from St John's Church in Smith Square under an 'arch' created by the swords of his brother officers. Pam, beaming confidently, wore a deep-blue, fur-trimmed coat and dress and a matching velvet hat with a jaunty feather. The colours perfectly suited her fair skin and complimented her blue eyes and gold-red hair.

The Digbys met Randolph only once before the wedding. Eddie Digby remembers that he was 'very attractive and had great charm when he wanted to charm. But he loved putting the cat among the pigeons.'[16] A month after the wedding, since Winston had to go to Weymouth to inspect naval establishments there, he and Clementine took two days off – his first rest in months – and went to stay at Minterne with Pam's parents.

By the time the Churchill family met in London for Christmas everyone was already 'doing their bit'. As well as running things smoothly at Admiralty House, where Winston conducted much of his business across the dining table, Clementine had become involved in welfare work for Navy wives and in a maternity unit for the wives of serving men in all three services. Sarah and Vic Oliver, now assimilated into the family as a couple, were both still working on the stage – a much appreciated form of service in those sombre years. All theatres were closed when war was declared because of the initial fear of bombing, but by December they had opened again, and Sarah and Vic were appearing together in *Black Velvet* at the Hippodrome. Duncan Sandys had reported to his Territorial Army unit and was stationed in London with an anti-aircraft regiment; Diana was an officer with the Women's Royal Naval Service (the WRNS). But they were able to get leave and together with their two children Julian and Edwina, who had come up from the country, they joined in the Christmas festivities.

Mary, who had just left school, was doing some Red Cross work and helping in a canteen, while happily joining in the social life of the adults. The Prof and Brendan Bracken, the latter largely ignored by a jealous Randolph (because Winston seemed to give Bracken the sort of attention and affection he craved for himself), were there, too; their job was to support Winston in any way they could. It was still the time of the 'phoney war' and there was great apprehension. Most people had expected German activity in the skies as soon as war was declared, but when nothing happened they could only wait anxiously wondering when the conflict would begin.

Randolph was still stationed at the Army camp at Beverley in Yorkshire, where Pam had now moved into a guest house to be near him. She revealed years later that on their wedding night at Belton near Grantham, Randolph had insisted on reading out to her some extracts from Gibbon's *Decline and Fall*, though she did not remember which extracts or why he read them out. His intention was probably to illustrate some point about the course the war was taking, but it was not quite what the young bride expected. When, in the spring of 1940, Pam announced that she was pregnant there was no one in the Churchill family who was not thrilled. Pam's parents reacted with an affectionate letter of congratulations, thanking her for twenty years of being a wonderful daughter. Pam replied, 'You shouldn't have thanked me for my twenty years with you, that's for me to do, to thank you for putting up with my tiresome self so gallantly and for so long. Darling Mumsie, I do love you.' She added that everyone had been so sweet to her, especially Randolph, Vic and Sarah, while she was suffering horribly with morning sickness.[17]

When the Churchill family gathered at Admiralty House for that first Christmas of the war it was business as usual for Winston – he worked the same hours as ever, and he expected his staff to do the same, except that on Boxing Day he worked for only fourteen hours and then went to the cinema with Clementine. On Christmas morning he had received an anxious phone call from David, Lord Redesdale, father of the Mitford girls. Unity was still in Munich when war was declared on 3 September and her family could get no news of her, despite Churchill's inquiries through official sources. There was a rumour that Unity had been interred in a concentration camp for Czech women, 'which much as I deplore it has a sort of poetic justice,' her sister Nancy wrote.[18]

In October a note had arrived from a Hungarian friend of Unity in Budapest, which still had postal communications with Britain. The writer advised that Unity was in hospital, safe, but very ill. It was not until late November that news was passed from the American Embassy that Unity had shot herself in the head in a Munich park when she heard that the two countries she loved were at war, and that she was still recovering, but that the bullet could not be removed. The news inevitably leaked out, and in December the newspapers were full of stories about 'The Girl Who Loved Hitler' and even on one occasion 'Unity Mitford Dead'. Her old nanny was in London Christmas shopping – 'The shops were empty,' Nanny reported – when she saw this last headline written on a placard. She marched up to the astonished news vendor and told him vehemently, 'That's *not* true!'

It was late on Christmas Eve when the phone rang in the Redesdales' mews cottage in Knightsbridge. It was Unity, asking them weakly to come and get her. Hitler had arranged for her to be taken to Berne in neutral Switzerland in a specially fitted-out ambulance carriage attached to a train. She was accompanied by a doctor, a nurse and a friend. Although it was Christmas and all offices and government departments were closed, thanks to Winston the necessary travel permits and visas were obtained from the Foreign Office and two days later, on 27 December, Lady Redesdale and her youngest daughter, nineteen-year-old Debo, set off for Switzerland across a continent trembling on the brink of open warfare. It was midwinter, grey and freezing cold; no trains ran to schedule, but at least there was no fighting yet. They arrived on 29 December at the clinic where Unity was being treated. She was still very ill, had lost thirty pounds or so, her cheeks were sunken and her face was yellowish-white. 'Her hair was short and matted . . . and her teeth were yellow: they had not been brushed since the shooting,' Debo explained. 'She couldn't bear for her head to be touched. She had an odd vacant expression . . . the most pathetic sight.'[19]

When they finally got Unity home, itself a nightmare journey, they were besieged with press and newsreel journalists. Unity was reviled, but for a change and to Clementine's relief, the Churchill connection was not mentioned. Unity's brain was permanently affected by the shooting. She would live out the war, a tragic figure with a mental age of eleven or twelve, lovingly cared for by her mother, until in May 1948 she developed meningitis at the wound site, from which she died.

The phoney war came to an abrupt end in April 1940, when Germany invaded Norway and Denmark. Norway fought against the invader and asked Britain for help. Immediately, the truth of Churchill's warning about the superior strength of the German Air Force became apparent. After three weeks of fighting all British troops were withdrawn, apart from a few commandos who attempted, unsuccessfully, to take back the port of Narvik. With them was Nellie's son Giles Romilly.* He was a journalist for the *Daily Express*, reporting on the Army's first real action of the war when, in early May, he was taken prisoner. He was the first British captive to be

---

*Giles Bertram Romilly (1916–67) returned to journalism after the war and wrote several books. He suffered from depression and committed suicide in Berkeley, California, where he had gone to visit his former sister-in-law Decca.

regarded as a *prominente* (special) prisoner, because of his relationship to Churchill, and he was shipped to Colditz for the duration.*

Neither Giles's capture nor his whereabouts was known for some weeks. His father Bertram died on 6 May at his family home, Huntington Park, near Kington in Herefordshire, from the long-term effects of serious war wounds sustained in the First World War. During their childhood, Giles and Esmond Romilly knew their father mainly as a semi-invalid in constant pain. Their mother, in giving continual support to her husband, had largely ignored the two boys, who ran amok. The Communist Esmond was now in Canada, having joined the Canadian Air Force soon after the outbreak of war, leaving his pregnant wife Decca to live with friends in Washington DC. Nellie was quite alone facing her crisis, so Clementine, already overstretched and anxious about Winston, went to her sister's side. She stayed with Nellie for a few days, but immediately after the funeral rushed back to London.

During her absence the fighting had begun in earnest. In the early hours of 10 May German forces invaded Holland and Belgium. Randolph had phoned his father late on the 9th and Churchill obviously knew what was afoot, for he told his son quietly, 'I think I shall be Prime Minister tomorrow.'[20] Clementine had been torn, wanting to support her sister for whom she always had a strong maternal feeling, but her desire to be with Winston prevailed – she knew he would be working round the clock, relying on power naps to top up his energy. She arrived home just in time to catch him leaving for the Palace, only a two-minute drive down the Mall from Admiralty House. Churchill recorded the occasion:

I was taken immediately to the King. His Majesty received me most graciously and bade me sit down. He looked at me searchingly and quizzically for some moments, and then said: 'I suppose you don't

---

*The Germans would move the *prominente* prisoners from Colditz in March 1945, just ahead of the American advance. It was hoped to use them as hostages; the prisoners, mostly malnourished after years of imprisonment, were force-marched for eighty-six days to Lubeck. Giles Romilly was one of the survivors, as was John Winant, son of Churchill's friend Gil Winant.

know why I have sent for you?' Adopting his mood, I replied: 'Sir, I simply couldn't imagine why.' He laughed and said: 'I want to ask you to form a government.' I said I would certainly do so . . . I told the King that I would immediately send for the leaders of the Labour and Liberal Parties, that I proposed to form a War Cabinet of five or six Ministers, and that I hoped to let him have at least five names before midnight. On this I took my leave.[21]

All had not gone smoothly for Churchill in those first months of war at the head of the Admiralty. He had made many enemies during the previous decade and not all had been won over, even now. Some blamed him squarely for the defeat in Norway, yet Cabinet documents indicate that had Churchill had his way and been allowed to act instantly and boldly, as he recommended, Narvik could well have been in British rather than German hands in spring 1940. He was essentially an old-fashioned leader who thought on his feet and reacted with lateral solutions to unfolding events. This would have worked well in the eighteenth and nineteenth centuries, but he found he was constantly checked in Cabinet by Neville Chamberlain and Lord Halifax, who wanted to take days debating decisions that needed to be taken in hours. Clementine was terrified that Narvik might prove to be another Dardanelles for Winston.

Chamberlain had resigned after the withdrawal from Norway because he believed a coalition government supported by all parliamentary parties was essential to the war effort; but the Labour and Liberal parties would not join a government headed by him. He was publicly asked to resign by Leo Amery,* who quoted Oliver Cromwell's ringing demand to the Long Parliament which he considered unfit to conduct the affairs of the nation: 'You have sat too long for any good; Your troops are most of them old, decayed, serving men and tapsters . . . Depart, I say, and let us have done with

---

*Amery, a contemporary of Winston's at Harrow and a fellow journalist during the Boer War, had met Hitler several times and was violently anti-appeasement. He held no office at this time, but his speech was said to have decided the outcome of the debate.

you. In the name of God, go!' Churchill was not necessarily the natural successor. For most politicians the choice was between him and Lord Halifax, and even the King was not at first an outright supporter of Churchill; he and the Queen had not quite forgiven him for supporting brother David during the abdication crisis. What swung the balance was the level of support for Churchill among the people, and in the press. The politicians and even the King had to go along with public opinion.

On 10 May Churchill became Prime Minister, and in his memoir of that day he wrote: 'As I went to bed at about 3.a.m. I was conscious of a profound sense of relief. At last I had the authority to give directions over the whole scene. I felt as if I were walking with destiny and that all my past life had been a preparation for this hour and this trial.' It is extraordinary that Churchill, who had anticipated such a call all his life and almost given up on it, now, on the brink of old age, could be the right man at the right time. Among the hundreds of telegrams and letters of congratulation he received the next day was one he especially treasured. It was from his first love, Pamela Lytton: 'All my life I have known you would become PM, ever since Hansom Cab days! Yet now you *are* the news sets one's heart beating like a sudden surprise.'[22]

Three days later, when he rose to speak for the first time in the House of Commons as Prime Minister, he had already formed his coalition government. It was now that he made his famous 'blood, sweat and tears' speech. He could promise them only 'many long months of struggle and of suffering . . . You ask, what is our policy? I will say: it is to wage war by sea, land and air, with all our might and with all the strength that God can give us; to wage war against a monstrous tyranny, never surpassed in the dark, lamentable catalogue of human crime.'

It is easy for modern-day critics and academics, with the passage of time and from the safety of a relatively peaceful era in our history, to dissect and criticise individual decisions taken by Churchill under stress. But in the dark days of the Second World War most ordinary people believed that Churchill was a leader in whom they could safely entrust their uncertain future. He never lied to them and promised very little, but he welded the nation into a fighting machine as no one else could have done, and he imbued them with the spirit to fight the enemy to the death, if necessary. This scion of a noble house, who knew very little of the way working-class people lived, nonetheless correctly read the pulse of the nation. 'Winston will see us through' would become a popular saying, even after five years of unrelenting toil, shortages and loss of life. And reading the papers and letters of those times, it is at once evident that this was an honest man who, while calling on the nation for every last ounce of effort, never spared himself in the fight to save Britain from the hated enemy.

One of the first men Winston summoned into the Cabinet was Anthony Eden who had been a Conservative dissenter and a leading anti-appeaser in the late Thirties. Eden headed a group of men who, like Churchill, were opposed to dealing with Hitler, and who – because of Eden's good looks – were sometimes mockingly called 'the glamour boys', while Winston's supporters were known in the House as 'the old guard'. Winston wrote in his memoirs that he had lost sleep on the night Eden resigned, at the time of the Munich Agreement; now, the two men were to work closely together for the next fifteen years.

There was no honeymoon period: a few days after Winston was called to the highest office France capitulated after bombs fell on Paris and Lyons, and Brussels was captured. Until then he had made regular flights to France to meet the Supreme War Council in Paris. Before the last visit he had asked Thompson to return his Colt revolver, which he placed in his overcoat pocket. 'One never knows,' he told his detective reflectively. 'I do not intend to be taken alive.'[23] From then on he always had his revolver to hand.

Within a week German tanks had swallowed much of Europe and reached north-east France, cutting off the Allied force of almost 400,000 British, French and Canadian soldiers and leaving them with their backs to the Channel and no escape route. Hitler would have been justified in thinking he had already won the war. In Britain, although the full details were not generally released, news that the British Army faced annihilation was spreading. People cried openly in the streets, and church services were held for 'our soldiers in dire peril'.

Churchill called the events in France 'a colossal military disaster' and announced gravely: 'The House should prepare itself for hard and heavy tidings.' Then he introduced a plan, codenamed Operation Dynamo, which was a seemingly impossible attempt to rescue 45,000–50,000 men from the beaches of Dunkirk. Possibly he recalled how in the 1914–18 war he had overseen the massive transfer of the British Army to the French coast in two days without the loss of a single man. So he knew that, with reasonable luck, part of the Army might be recovered. In the event, what was otherwise a military rout was turned by 4 June into nothing short of a miracle, brought about when every craft that could float, from small yachts, fishing boats, trawlers, pleasure boats, river barges and ferryboats to naval destroyers, formed a great Armada of rescue vessels. Eventually a total of 338,000 men were picked up and returned to England, to fight another day. However, all their guns, tanks, vehicles and munitions had been left on the shores of France; a grave strategic loss.

To counteract jubilant headlines, Churchill warned, 'We must be very careful not to assign to this delivery the attributes of a victory. Wars are not won by evacuations. There *was* a victory in the deliverance, which should be noted.' Then followed his famous 'we shall fight on the beaches' speech.

Churchill received not only a first-hand account of what conditions had been like on the beaches, but also a clear visual impression. Jack's son Johnny had been one of the first men rescued from the Dunkirk beaches. As soon as his train got to Victoria Station he went to the Grosvenor Hotel to shave, then took a taxi to see his father who was living with Winston and Clementine. Jack was assisting Winston in his self-effacing way after his and Goonie's London home had been made uninhabitable by bombing; Goonie was presently being treated for cancer and living quietly in the country. Winston and Clementine were about to move to No. 10 Downing Street but were still at Admiralty House that day, and as it was scarcely 8 a.m. they hurried down in dressing gowns to greet their nephew.

The excitement and relief of the moment were overwhelming for them all, not least for Jack. Johnny was wearing his filthy battle-dress, still barely dried out from having waded out into the Channel to be picked up. 'Johnny!' Winston cried delightedly, 'I see you have come straight from battle . . . Have you come straight out of the sea?' 'Yes,' his nephew replied, 'and I will be pleased to go back again in a fast motorboat to give everyone encouragement.' Johnny, who had once tried his hand with a signal lack of success at his father's profession in the city, was a talented artist. He was quickly put to work to illustrate the events he had witnessed.

Later that month Mary joined her parents at 10 Downing Street, where an air-raid shelter had been constructed in the basement. Randolph, keen to see action, was at last posted overseas and his pregnant wife Pam also moved into No. 10. Jack's daughter Clarissa had grown into a striking young woman. After going through the finishing and debutante procedures in the same years as Pam Digby, she had very unusually decided to apply for Oxford University, where she read philosophy for two years. She had a first-class brain and saw Oxford as a way not only of continuing her education but of breaking away from Goonie's influence, which she found stifling.

Bert and Mary Marlborough, having turned over most of Blenheim to Malvern School, retreated with their family to rooms in the east wing. Duke Bert had become a military liaison officer. Despite giving birth to her fifth child (a surprise late pregnancy) in 1940, Duchess Mary, the possessor of extraordinary organisational skills, eventually became a senior officer in the ATS, thereby out-ranking her husband. During those years Bert always referred to Mary as 'the General'.[24] She was also President of the Oxfordshire Red Cross and the Women's Voluntary Service. Their daughter Lady Sarah, for whom the spectacular coming-of-age party had been held the previous year, became a machinist at the Morris Motor Company factory in nearby Oxford. Her immediate super-visor had formerly been a servant at Blenheim. Her siblings were too young to be involved in the war effort in the early war years. Her brother Lord Blandford was still at Eton.

Consuelo and Jacques were still living in the remoteness of Saint

Georges-Motel amid the forests of Eure, wondering what would happen to them and the children in their sanatorium if (or when) the Germans came. In her memoir Consuelo recalled how every day brought fear of invasion. As the Germans advanced rapidly across France the estate was overwhelmed with refugees, and Consuelo instructed her maid to pack an emergency valise and stow it under her bed. Eventually, when the Balsans had placed as many of their small patients as possible in safer accommodation, when the German troops were just an hour away they abandoned their lovely home and left for Pau, where they hoped to find accommodation for the remaining children. It was a hot, still day as they drove off down the drive: the pretty pink and white stone chateau with its blue slate roof was reflected in the still waters of the moat and the fountains were sparkling in the sunlight. Those children who remained, unaware of the gravity of the situation, were still playing happily in the gardens. Consuelo could only trust that the invaders would respect her beautiful historic chateau.[25]

When, that summer, France fell, Britain stood alone. Immediately the thoughts of the British naval chiefs flew to the French fleet, lying in the port of Oran on the coast of North Africa and preparing to demobilise under the terms of the armistice agreed between the French and the Germans. If this fleet fell into the hands of the enemy it would remove the single advantage Britain had over the Germans: superior naval power. It was a serious problem, and the Cabinet recognised that drastic action was called for. Hitler had announced that Germany had no intention of using the French vessels for its own purposes during the war. Yet, Churchill wrote, 'who in his senses would trust the word of Hitler after his shameful record and the facts of the hour?'[26] It was, he later admitted, the most hateful decision he ever had to make, 'the most unnatural and painful in which I have ever been concerned'. On 3 July French commanders were informed that they must sink their ships themselves before darkness fell, or they would be sunk. This signal was ignored. That evening with a heavy heart Winston approved the order and the British Navy opened fire on the French ships. Three battleships at Oran were sunk, and in other North African ports too the French

Navy was annihilated with the loss of 1297 French lives. It was a necessary act in the circumstances; but many Frenchmen would never forgive Churchill.

The following day Churchill reported to the House, giving a full account of the events, the effects and the outcome. At the end he was surprised by a response unique in his experience: he received a long standing ovation, the entire House cheering him. The action had made it clear to Germany, and to the world, that the British War Cabinet feared nothing 'and would stop at nothing'.

During these months Winston drove himself to breaking point, and he expected others to work at the same punishing pace. He was too busy to offer praise, was constantly irritable, and often found fault when his staff did not or could not measure up to his exacting standards. They appealed to Clementine who, following their lifelong practice when something was seriously amiss, broached the matter with him in a remarkable letter:

My Darling,

I hope you will forgive me if I tell you something that I feel you ought to know. One of the men in your entourage (a devoted friend) has been to me & told me that there is a danger of your being generally disliked by your colleagues & subordinates because of your rough sarcastic & overbearing manner – It seems your Private Secretaries have agreed to behave like schoolboys & 'take what's coming to them' & then escape out of your presence shrugging their shoulders – Higher up, if an idea is suggested (say at a conference) you are supposed to be so contemptuous that presently no ideas, good or bad, will be forthcoming. I was astonished & upset because in all these years I have been accustomed to all those who have worked with & under you, loving you – I said this & I was told 'No doubt it's the strain' –

My Darling Winston – I must confess that I have noticed a deterioration in your manner; & you are not so kind as you used to be. It is for you to give the Orders & if they are bungled – except for the King the Archbishop of Canterbury & the Speaker you can sack anyone and everyone – Therefore with this terrific power you must combine urbanity, kindness and if possible Olympic calm . . . I cannot bear that those who serve the Country & yourself should not love you as well as admire and respect you – Besides you won't get the best results by irascibility & rudeness. They will breed either dislike or a slave mentality . . . please forgive your loving devoted & watchful

Clemmie.[27]

In a postscript she added: 'I wrote this at Chequers last Sunday, tore it up, but here it is now.'

That Chequers weekend had been a typical one – family, friends and important contacts gathering for lunch and conversation. Jock Colville, one of Churchill's Private Secretaries, gives a fascinating description of it in his diaries. He tells how Winston filled every hour, discussing with Beaverbrook and Brendan Bracken the evacuation of the Channel Isles; then on to the need to increase aircraft production; then the position of the Duke of Windsor, who was presently in Madrid and attempting to impose conditions, 'financial and otherwise', about his return to England. Colville wrote:

> Winston proposes to send him a very stiff telegram pointing out that he is a soldier under orders and must obey. The King approves and says he will hear of no conditions, about the Duchess or otherwise . . . We had tea in the morning-room upstairs and while we were there the Sandyses arrived. Shortly afterwards came Randolph Churchill and his wife. I thought Randolph one of the most objectionable people I had ever met: noisy, self-assertive, whining and frankly unpleasant. He did not strike me as intelligent. At dinner he was anything but kind to Winston, who adores him . . . In reply to a request from the P.M., the Home Secretary sent a list of 150 'prominent people' whom he had arrested. Of the first three on the list two, Lady Mosley and Geo Pitt-Rivers,* were cousins of the Churchills – a fact which piqued Winston and caused much merriment among his children.[28]

---

*Second-in-command to Mosley at the British Union of Fascists.

Oswald Mosley had been taken into custody on 23 May. This could not have been a surprise because the party he had founded, the British Union of Fascists, was, rightly or wrongly,* regarded as sympathetic to Hitler, although Mosley denied this. He was arrested under the infamous rule 18B of the Emergency Powers Act, which had been rushed through Parliament in order to allow the Home Secretary to detain without trial anyone 'of potentially hostile origin or association' when it was considered necessary for the defence of the realm. Churchill had reluctantly agreed.†

The new government had decided to arrest and detain enemy aliens, known Fascists and Communists on the grounds that they were a potential security risk. Under an amendment (18B/1a) this was extended to include any member of an association which, in the view of the Home Secretary, was subject to foreign control or whose leaders were known to have had association with leaders of the enemy powers. The matter was regarded as justice by some, for although Mosley argued hotly and eloquently that his arrest and incarceration went against the rights of habeas corpus derived from Magna Carta, there is good reason to believe that had his own party ever come to power those rights would have been sacrificed by him for the sake of expediency. He had, after all, proposed similar legislation in 1931 to combat protesters against mass unemployment. In those days, however, he had still been 'respectable', a friend and colleague of Churchill.

But it was not Oswald Mosley about whom Winston was concerned so much as his wife, Diana. Winston had always been fond of Diana Mitford. He knew that she had given birth to a son only a few weeks earlier and must still be nursing him. When Mosley was arrested the Home Secretary was bombarded with letters about Diana, informing him that she was as dangerous as her husband. Three of these informants in particular stood out. One was Diana's

---

*For the argument about this matter see Lovell, *The Mitford Girls*, pp. 323–4.
†In a parliamentary debate in December 1946 Churchill would state: 'In time of war many things had to be done which were deeply regretted, particularly 18B. I have always regretted that, for which I take my share of responsibility. But great principles of habeas corpus can only be abrogated with the very greatest care, and in the most supreme crises of the State.'

sister Nancy (before she became a successful writer), who called on
Gladwyn Jebb* at his request to tell him what she knew of Diana's
frequent visits to Germany between 1932 and 1939. 'I advised him
to examine her passport,' she wrote. 'I also said I regard her as an
extremely dangerous person. Not very sisterly behaviour but in such
times I think it one's duty.'[29] Another informant was Lord Moyne,
one of Winston and Clementine's closest friends, who had been
Diana's father-in-law during her first marriage to Bryan Guinness.
Moyne wrote a two-page memorandum based on the testimony of
the nanny of Diana's two Guinness sons who were now living with
the Moynes in Ireland. The nanny had repeated to him things she
had overheard at Diana's house, and his covering letter stated that
he considered Diana 'an extremely dangerous person'. The last
informant was Irene, Lady Ravensdale (who had introduced Pam
Digby to Popsie Winn in Munich). She wrote saying more or less
the same: that in her opinion Diana was as dangerous, if not more
so, than Mosley. Of course one must view Lady Ravensdale's opinion with circumspection. One of the Curzon sisters, Irene
Ravensdale was Mosley's sister-in-law during his first marriage to
Lady Cynthia ('Cimmie') Curzon. Within weeks of Cimmie's death
she was Mosley's lover;[†] that relationship had ended when Diana
took Mosley from her.

The authorities felt they had sufficient evidence to arrest Diana –
in effect separating her without a moment's notice from her twelve-
week-old unweaned baby – and incarcerate her in Holloway prison.
As a politician Churchill knew a thing or two about the conditions
in Holloway, and though he did not approve of Diana's political
sympathies he was concerned about her plight and that of her abandoned baby. He attempted to ensure that she got at least one bath
a week – but even this proved impossible in practice.

---

*Hubert Gladwyn Jebb (1900–96) was in 1940 Assistant Secretary to the Minister of Economic
Warfare. Later a prominent civil servant and politician, he would become the first acting
Secretary-General of the United Nations.

†During his marriage to Cimmie, Mosley also had affairs with Cimmie's younger sister Lady
Alexandra (Metcalfe) and the sisters' stepmother, the American-born second wife and widow
of Lord Curzon.

Diana's mother Sydney Mitford (Lady Redesdale) visited Clementine to beg for assistance to get her released on compassionate grounds. Sydney had been one of Clementine's bridesmaids; the two families were not only cousins but had been friends for forty years. Clementine, as usual, had only one concern: Winston's position in the matter. Just as with Esmond Romilly, whenever the activities of Diana or her sister Unity were noticed in the press, their relationship to Clementine and Winston was always featured in headlines: Esmond was invariably 'the Red nephew of Mr Churchill' and Unity the 'Nazi-loving cousin of Mrs Churchill'. Clementine hated Winston's reputation to be sullied by constant association with the universally disliked Mosleys. She began the interview with Sydney carefully, remarking that Winston had always been 'so fond of Diana'. She then suggested that Diana and Mosley were probably better off in prison, for they would almost certainly be lynched by the mob if they were released. Sydney, who had been firmly in Chamberlain's appeasement camp and had come to regard Winston as a warmonger, replied frostily that they would be willing to take the chance. But she left, her mission unaccomplished.[30]

In the four years that Diana Mosley was incarcerated she never became accustomed to the squalor in which the women prisoners were obliged to live. She blamed Winston for this and for her imprisonment without trial, although wartime documents in the National Archives indicate that he did all he could to obtain her release and to mitigate the worst conditions for her. With some difficulty he eventually contrived to have the Mosleys reunited in a mixed prison, and later they were released under house surveillance (to howls of public protest), for none of which did Diana ever give Winston any credit.[31]

Since most people, like Colville, who worked for Churchill during the war years remained devoted to him, it would seem that Clementine's letter of gentle reprimand forced Winston to re-examine his behaviour. He *was* often overbearing, he did not bear fools gladly, and he overworked his staff as he overworked himself. But he was essentially a kind man. His impatience with others reflected his acute anxiety as the country faced the Luftwaffe, then the Battle of Britain, followed by blitzing raids on London and other major cities. From 7 September 1940 onwards London was bombed for fifty-seven consecutive nights. Randolph's wife Pamela, then heavily pregnant, had been staying at 10 Downing Street to be near a maternity unit, but that month she was sent away from the bombing to await her confinement at Chequers.

There, at the Prime Minister's official country residence, the Churchills spent most weekends – not relaxing, but at least Winston could work in a calmer environment. During September Randolph was invited to stand, unopposed, as MP for Preston. After having unsuccessfully fought three parliamentary contests, he found himself elected without difficulty. Winston (in tears), Clementine and Pam proudly watched him take his seat in the Chamber that his father and grandfather had dominated successively for seven decades. Two days later Randolph and Pamela's son, 'little Winston', was born. That weekend Pansy Digby stayed at Chequers to be with Pam, and Randolph and the Churchills had their first sight of the new baby. It was a joyous family occasion on which Winston and a still-dubious Clementine may have felt for the first time that things might at last come right for their difficult son. Randolph was married, had a pretty and charming wife and a healthy son, and he was a Member of Parliament as well as a serving officer. Pamela had always said that all he needed was to be 'given a chance'.

Cecil Beaton was asked to photograph the new infant and there was a huge public demand to see pictures of Churchill's namesake, who seemed to embody the country's hopes for the future. Churchill looked down at his new grandson and – always sentimental at such family moments – said with tears in his eyes: 'What sort of world are you being born into?'[32]

When Beaton took the proofs round to Clementine for approval before they were sent out to the press, he was taken aback to find her quite overwrought. She was disinclined to allow the photographs to be published, she told him, because in a recent article about her, in which his photographs of her had been used, it was implied that her marriage to Winston had been arranged by Lady Randolph. Without warning she suddenly attacked Beaton, blurting out that he must have known about this. To his astonishment, she was working herself into an almost hysterical state. 'Her face flushed, her eyes poured with tears,' he wrote. '"Really it's too damnable,"' Clementine had wept, sobbing to him that her life hadn't been an easy one. '"It hasn't, but when I married Winston he loved me" . . . I held her hand and comforted her,' Beaton wrote in his diary. 'But he *still* does . . . We all know that.' At this Clementine became even more upset, weeping uncontrollably and eventually confiding: 'I don't know why it is . . . I suppose my friends are not exactly jealous but they think that other people could do the job better and that I shouldn't have been married to Winston. After all he is one of the most important people in the world. In fact he and Hitler and President Roosevelt *are* the most important people in the world today.'[33] It was all too much for Beaton. He manfully brought the conversation around to the baby and, having received permission to publish the photographs, rushed off to a florist and purchased a huge bouquet to be sent to Clementine.

This was virtually the only public display of Clementine's insecurity and sense of inadequacy. But it was a constant thread running through her life. There are many hints of sympathy in Winston's letters to her. He loved her deeply and devotedly throughout his life (as she did him), but, as noted earlier, he had recognised in the early years of their marriage that Clementine found it hard to cope with the energy fields he created around himself. The sense of inadequacy that she suffered from was patently a delusion. One has only to consider her war work, the entertaining she did, and the style in which she met all the challenges that came her way to see that there could not have been a better wife for him. This outburst may have been cathartic for her, for there is no hint of anything similar in contemporary letters or diary entries of those in Churchill's entourage. And there is little doubt that Clementine was always the force behind Winston that made him the success he was; she was never afraid to tell him an unwelcome truth, she was somehow a link between him and ordinary people; and he knew that whatever else might happen, Clementine's love for him was steadfast.

*

Winston was now totally immersed in the battle not merely to survive the war but to win it, and one of his most important tasks was to motivate, to convince people that victory could be achieved. During the Blitz he sometimes went for walks around London, with his detective trailing him. He was given to visiting Regent's Park Zoo from time to time to see a lion called Rota,* which had been a gift to him from a visiting African dignitary as a symbol of Winston's attitude to life. On one of these occasions he walked out of Regent's Park and up Primrose Hill to look out over London. No observation was ever wasted. It was at this point that the phrase 'London can take it' was born; in the next speech he delivered to MPs, despondent about the bombing, he advised: 'Take a walk up Primrose Hill, and look over London.' A pause, a confident grin as he looked at them over the top of his spectacles: 'It's still there.'[34] One evening he went to inspect an underground shelter at Down Street near Piccadilly. It was an unused Underground station and was thought to be a safe place for the Prime Minister during air raids. He drove to it through a bombardment, and when he arrived was bemused to find it crowded with well dressed people drinking champagne and oblivious to the raid. His official biographer recorded how he marvelled at the relentless spirit of the British; he was later advised that he had walked in on the wedding reception for the daughter of the chairman of the London Underground service.

In December all the family gathered at Chequers for the second Christmas of the war: Pam and baby Winston, Diana and Duncan and their children, Sarah and Mary. On Christmas Eve Randolph and Vic arrived. The usual close friends, Cousin Moppet and Winston's private detective joined in the celebration, and despite the bombings and the terror of war it was the happiest Christmas Mary could remember. She wrote in her diary: 'I've never seen the family look so happy – so united.'[35]

It would be many years before they would all be together again.

---

*Rota sired three cubs, and after his death was stuffed as an exhibit; he is now housed in St Augustine, Florida.

Randolph was stagnating in a life that consisted either of hanging around at camp or engaged in whatever devilment he could come up with during bachelor sprees in town. He desperately wanted to prove himself in battle but suspected (as did everyone else) that the reason his unit was not ordered into battle was that his father was protecting him. This is probably true; Churchill had told Army chiefs that if Randolph was killed he would not be able to go on. So when Randolph heard of a unit being formed to train for special operations, No. 8 Commando, under David Stirling who would later become the founder of the SAS, he did not hesitate and got himself transferred. Soon after he left it, his old regiment was posted overseas.

It was February 1941 before No. 8 Commando got away from England. The unit was famously top-heavy in its ratio of officers to men – the lower deck was adorned with the slogan: 'Never before in the history of human endeavour have so few been buggered about by so many.'[2] One of his brother officers was Evelyn Waugh, who kept a diary of the voyage and wrote about the high-stakes gambling and carousing that went on in the mess when they were not training. They had been posted to Egypt where they were to do battle with the German–Italian enemy, but because of the danger of U-boats and the Luftwaffe cover of the Mediterranean it was not possible to sail there by a direct route. So they were sent the long way, around the Cape of Good Hope and up the East African coast through the Indian Ocean to the Suez Canal, a journey of nearly six weeks during which Waugh recorded: 'We did very little except PT and one or two written exercises . . . There was very high gambling, poker, roulette, chemin-de-fer, every night.'[3] To his wife Waugh added: 'At the last settling day for gambling, Randolph was £800 down [in two evenings]. Poor Pamela will have to go out to work.'[4]

Before he left England Randolph had been full of good intentions, telling Pam that his posting would mean they could live inexpensively, enabling them to pay off all his debts and even to save. Believing this, and hoping it was a new start for them, Pam lived as frugally as she could. There was no central heating in the chilly old rectory and it was bitterly cold that winter. She lived mostly in the kitchen, which was kept warm for the baby and his nurse, and wore a coat elsewhere in the house. She often went to bed at 6.30 to save on heating bills. She invited Diana Sandys to live with her to share costs, but there was hardly time for this to work out because a month or so after Randolph sailed Pam received a cable from him at Cape Town in which he confessed that he had lost £3000 gambling during the voyage. Unlike other debts, gambling debts to brother officers were debts of honour and must be paid as soon as possible. He instructed her to pay whatever she could at once, and to start paying off the balance at £30 a month to his various creditors from the annual £1500 salary that Lord Beaverbrook was continuing to pay him.

For twenty-year-old Pam, who suspected she might be pregnant again, it was a massive blow. For the past year she had lived with Randolph's profligate spending on tailoring, gambling, entertaining and mess bills. 'It simply never occurred to him to budget; if he saw or thought of something he wanted, he got it, did it, gambled on it. Pam had been brought up by my mother, who insisted that every bill must be paid immediately, and she had never had an overdraft,' Pam's brother Eddie recalled. 'Randolph thought that paying debts was an awful waste of money.'[5] Evelyn Waugh reported to his wife that Randolph had heard back from Pam via a letter carried out by a diplomat friend that she was 'very vexed with him'.[6] It is no exaggeration to say that Pam regarded debt as shameful. Winston had bailed Randolph out several times in the previous year because she had gone to him in tears. Now, not only did she shrink from taking this massive problem to him at a time when she knew he was under almost impossible pressures, but Randolph had ordered her not to. She was too humiliated to approach her own father. Instead, she went to Max Beaverbrook, one of little Winston's godfathers, and tearfully explained her predicament.

Beaverbrook was as busy as Churchill, in fact; without his colossal drive and dynamic leadership at the Ministry of Supply, the Battle of Britain would never have been won. Like Churchill he was the right man in the right place at the right time, and within a few months of taking over the ministry he had increased the number of operational aircraft by 65 per cent. In 1939 there were 430 operational

Spitfires and 500 Hurricanes; in 1940 under 'the Beaver', 1500
Spitfires and 2580 Hurricanes were available to fly.[7] Before he took
office there was no formal policy for aircraft repair, and when aircraft were damaged they were scrapped. Within twelve months
under Beaverbrook, the RAF repaired and restored 9000 damaged
aircraft and reclaimed 12,000 engines, restoring them to service.

Beaverbrook had not wanted office; he felt he had given his best
to the War Cabinet during 1914–18, and although his service then
had led to a peerage he felt he had been badly treated afterwards by
the then government. But Churchill wheedled, begged and even bullied him to lend an active hand; and once he joined, Beaverbrook
drove himself as hard as Churchill did, while nightly waiting anxiously for the phone call from his fighter-pilot son, young Max, to
say he was safe. This, and his overt Christianity, contributed an
unexpected human element to the dynamic Beaverbrook, who was
feared by many. He commented to a friend at this time: 'How many
of our young men do you think are swimming in the sea tonight?
How many of those pilots are on their rafts in the Ocean? Think of
the sufferings they endure. Think of the hunger. Think of the lack
of sleep and lack of hope. Crucifixion is an easier death than the
death those young men have sometimes to die.'[8]

That Beaverbrook found time to see Churchill's daughter-in-law
on a personal matter is remarkable. Pam was absolutely frank with
him, and asked if he would advance her enough of Randolph's
salary to allow her to pay off the debts. Beaverbrook knew
Randolph well, possibly better than Pam did, and he offered to
write her a personal cheque as an outright gift; but he could not
advance her a penny of Randolph's salary, he said. Pam knew what
her mother would advise: that she could not accept such a gift from
any man outside the family.* But she discussed options with
Beaverbrook and came to an arrangement with him. He would find
her a job in the London office of the Ministry of Supply. Baby

---

*Beaverbrook's reputation may have had something to do with how Pam felt her mother
would respond. When his son Max wanted to marry the actress Toto Koopman, Beaverbrook
objected strongly, then made Toto his own mistress. In a recent book it was hinted that
Beaverbrook may have had designs on Pam, too, but her family say this is untrue.

Winston and his nurse would move into Cherkley, Beaverbrook's chateau-style country house between Leatherhead and Dorking in Surrey. Pam would sublet the rectory at Ickleford, hopefully at a profit, and find herself somewhere cheap to live in London (many people had moved from London and were only too anxious to let their flats and houses). She hoped that by adopting this solution she would prevent Randolph's parents, of whom she was very fond, from finding out what had really happened. Then she went home and sold all her wedding presents, including some diamond earrings that had been a gift from her friend Popsie Winn's mother Lady Baillie, a diamond bracelet, and other jewellery given her by her mother.

With Beaverbrook's help she started working in a department that organised temporary hostel accommodation for groups of factory workers who were moved around the country to meet the exigencies of the moment. Initially she earned £12 a week – a sum that sounds small now, but most male factory workers with families to keep were paid between £4 and £8 a week at the time. The rectory was sublet at £3 a week to a nursery school that had been bombed out of London, and Pam rented a room at the Dorchester Hotel, at roof level. This was not quite as lavish as it sounds, at the relatively low cost of £6 a week for bed and breakfast (breakfast became her main meal of the day); few people wanted to live on the top floor of any tall building, with bombs dropping every night. She ate lunch in the office canteen, and was taken out most evenings or attended parties, quite a few of which were held at the Dorchester. Once a week she dined at No. 10, and she was able to save from her wages so that all Randolph's salary, together with occasional cheques from the Churchills and the Digbys, went to paying off his gambling debt.

Eventually, after some years, the debt was cleared, but there was a hidden cost. Years later she would tell her son that she realised very clearly during this period that if there was going to be any security for her and her baby she was going to have to provide it herself.[9] And she was never to forgive Randolph; eighteen months into their marriage he had already permanently forfeited all the respect and admiration Pam previously felt for him. The marriage was as good as over.

During this crisis Pam either miscarried or perhaps there was no pregnancy; there is no evidence either way. She had told almost no one and she was certainly at Chequers most weekends at that period. Jock Colville mentions her there in his diaries but he does not comment on her looking unwell or worried. Her angry letters* to Randolph at the time have not survived – and perhaps this is not surprising since they are unlikely to have been complimentary. The extent of Pam's distress, and her distaste for his gambling and running up debts, had probably not fully registered with Randolph, although it is true he was both annoyed with himself and remorseful that he had lost quite so much money in such a short time.

This chain of events and Pam's mood coincided with the arrival in London of President Roosevelt's personal representative on shipping and supply questions, Averell Harriman. The urbane and gentlemanly Harriman arrived in London on 18 March and the following day he dined at No. 10. After that he was a frequent visitor at Chequers and 10 Downing Street. Within a week of his arrival, a few days after her twenty-first birthday on 20 March, he was introduced to Pam at the weekly dinner party held by Emerald Cunard in her suite at the Dorchester. Harriman had a suite on the first floor and Pam was still living on the unpopular top floor. Pam would later recall her first impressions of him: 'Averell was just beautiful. He was absolutely marvellous looking, with his raven black hair. Very athletic, very tan[ned], very healthy.'[10] Harriman was slightly older than Pam's father, but, as mentioned earlier, Pam was always drawn to older men. The pair fell in love soon after their first meeting, despite the fact that both were married.

Wartime romances were two a penny, and were usually short-lived; all the old moral ground rules were swept aside amid the 'live now while you still can' atmosphere and heightened emotions

---

*Referred to by the writer Anita Leslie, granddaughter of Leonie (Jennie Jerome's sister) and Randolph's second cousin.

caused by frequent partings and uncertainty. Pam was still angry with Randolph for ruining her dreams of a cosy family home for little Winston. Averell had outgrown his wife (though in fact she was already involved with someone else, and was not concerned whether Averell strayed, provided he was circumspect about it). A surprising number of their acquaintances knew about Pam and Averell's affair from the start, and it appears that they were not very discreet.

Their meeting had coincided with the heaviest bombing raids of the war, and Averell offered Pam the protection of a sofa in his suite should she, *in extremis*, need it. This was not unusual; those living on the top floors often retreated to camp-beds in the public rooms on the ground floor, or asked one of the lower-floor guests occupying suites to let them camp there for the night. On the night of 16 April London suffered the worst raid ever, when 450 enemy planes rained bombs down on the city. The following morning, after breakfast, Jock Colville came upon Pam and Averell wandering along examining the devastation in the glass-littered streets near Whitehall. Diplomatically he made no comment in his diary, about them being together so early in the day, but it would have been difficult to avoid hearing the gossip and he had ample opportunity to watch them together, given that Pamela was a regular visitor to No. 10 and Chequers, often at the same time as Harriman. Winston liked both of them; with Harriman he could plan and plot to bring America into the war; and Pam petted him and called him Papa and patiently played bezique with him.

That same week Winston had been 'terribly upset', Colville reported,[11] when Diana's husband Duncan Sandys was injured in a bad car smash, and for some days it appeared that he might have to have a foot amputated. It evoked for Winston memories of his mother's death from an amputation.

That spring shortly before Averell and Pam met, Clarissa, the daughter of Jack and Goonie, abandoned her academic life at Oxford and moved to London. Clarissa had known Pam at boarding school when Pam was a plump, horse-mad redhead. Now, like Pam, she took advantage of the bargain rates for rooms on the top floor of the Dorchester during the worst days of the Blitz. The two young women had been debutantes together in 1938 and had run into each other frequently at parties and balls ever since, but Clarissa was not a close friend; nor was she a particular admirer of Pam. Years later she was amazed to learn from Hugh Fraser, a man she admired immensely, that he and Pam had planned to elope in 1938. 'He was one of the more sophisticated and dashing of the young men at parties in 1938, the year I came out,' Clarissa stated, while recalling that Pam was not regarded by 'most of the boys' as being particularly eligible.[12] It was Hugh Fraser who had nicknamed Clarissa 'Garbo', and indeed her high cheekbones and wistful beauty instinctively drew photographer Cecil Beaton to her and she became a favourite subject of his. But by 1941 when they were both Dorchester dwellers, Pam too had become svelte and glamorous; 'She combined a canny eye for chances with a genuinely warm heart. At any rate she was consistently kind and thoughtful to me, but she had no sense of humour,' Clarissa noted.[13] She recalled that the affair with Averell began in mid-April. 'One night Pam said she was fixing up to see Averell who had a suite on the 1st floor (we had always gone down to the foyer when an air raid was on) . . . This was when the affair began. A few weeks later she was showing me diamond bracelets.'[14]

In June, Kathy Harriman, Averell's daughter by a previous marriage, arrived in London having flown via Lisbon. Initially, Kathy stayed in her father's suite, but she and Pamela became friends and decided to rent a small house together and share costs. Kathy wrote to her stepmother, Averell's present wife, about Pam, praising her as 'a wonderful girl . . . my age, but one of the wisest young girls I've ever met – knows everything about everything, political and otherwise.'[15] They rented a flat in Grosvenor Square and a tiny cottage near Cherkley so that Pam could see more of baby Winston at weekends. Winston and Clementine were delighted that Pam had a friend to keep her company, and when Kathy subsequently discovered that Pam and her father were lovers she accepted it matter-of-factly.

'It seems a pity,' Churchill wrote innocently to Randolph in June, when he told him that Pam and Kathy were sharing a house, 'that the house at Ickleford is not available. Still, you are getting a very good rent [for it] . . . I see Pamela from time to time, and she gives me very good accounts of Winston. I have not seen him as he is living in Max's domains.' He added that he thought the baby safer where he was and went on to the main purpose of his letter, to introduce Averell Harriman to Randolph and ask Randolph to 'look after him' during Harriman's forthcoming visit to Cairo. When Evelyn Waugh returned briefly to England he reported back to Randolph that he had seen Pam in London, 'her kitten eyes full of innocent fun. She is showing exemplary patience with the Americans who now have the place in England which the Germans had in Italy in 1939.'[16]

Randolph was not enjoying himself in Egypt, having been told early on in no uncertain terms by a brother officer that he was heartily disliked by them all. Waugh wrote how Randolph had cried over this, for he had assumed he was a popular member of the regiment. However, Randolph was delighted by Averell Harriman; not only was he a good companion but he brought news of his parents and Pamela to him at a time when his family seemed a long way off. When he returned to London Averell carried two letters from Randolph, one of them to Pam, which read ingenuously: 'I found [Harriman] absolutely charming & it was lovely to be able to hear so much news of you & all my friends. He spoke delightfully about you & I fear that I have a serious rival.' Randolph had a long-term mistress and several nightclub hostess lovers throughout his time in Cairo, so this exchange does not carry the pathos it might otherwise have done. To his father he wrote:

It was indeed kind of you to suggest that I should be attached to the Harriman Mission. I have thereby not only obtained all the latest news of you and Pamela, and all my friends in London, but have also had a wonderful opportunity of learning about things out here. I have been tremendously impressed by Harriman, and can well understand the regard you have for him. In 10 very full and active days he has definitely become my favourite American . . . He got down to work out here with amazing ease and sure-footedness and has won the confidence of everyone . . . Thank you so much for your cheque [Churchill had sent him £100] & also for the very generous help you extended to Pamela. That has been a great help.[17]

Later that year Randolph was promoted to the rank of major and placed in charge of the press and Army information department at GHQ in Cairo, where he lived at the famous Shepheard's Hotel. Here his cousin (and his future biographer) Anita Leslie, who was serving with an ambulance company, saw him often. She recalled:

At one time he appeared at our camp with a flag flying from his car which only full Colonels were allowed. . . . One didn't like to ask too much about his postings . . . it was not long before my peppery chief, a former officer of the Army of India, was bursting into my room with cries of "This damned fellow Randolph Churchill – *your* friend! What the devil does he think he's doing?" He always remembered to salute senior officers but he could not cease trumpeting his opinions and older men could be seen turning purple with anger when he held forth in Shepheard's Hotel.

Anita observed that no one wanted to upset Winston, but it was extremely difficult for anyone to find a genuinely useful role for Randolph, given that he was generally held to be 'insufferable'.[18]

In August 1941 Winston paid his first wartime visit to the USA. Before he left, Goonie had died of cancer. She was much loved by everyone, and Clementine was especially hard-hit to lose her closest and most trusted confidante. This blow was followed closely by the breakdown of Sarah's marriage to Vic Oliver, which was a shock. While they had been opposed to the marriage at the start, both Winston and Clementine had come to respect this talented and gentlemanly son-in-law. Sarah claimed the break-up was triggered when Vic was ordered back to the USA by the American government. He was warned that non-compliance would mean losing his American citizenship, but when she refused to go with him, Vic stayed on, waiting and hoping Sarah would change her mind. In fact he remained throughout the war, and the simple truth was that Sarah had fallen out of love with him. She later claimed that the only favour she ever requested of her father was to ask him to arrange for her to join the services immediately, so that she could separate from Vic without it appearing obvious they had split up. Churchill had been 'flabbergasted', Clementine 'dismayed', and eighteen-year-old Mary (who had recently become informally engaged) wept when Sarah told them she was leaving Vic. Sarah was in the WAAF within forty-eight hours, which provided just the smokescreen she sought.

They were a high-profile couple and for today's media would have been A-list celebrities – Sarah because of her father, and Vic because he was not only a top West End star but also had become nationally popular via his regular appearances as a comedian on some of BBC radio's most popular shows, such as *Hi Gang!* He was a classically trained violinist, but on *Workers' Playtime* his act involved playing the violin tunelessly over a fast comic patter delivered in his unmistakable Austrian accent (a precedent for Victor Borge's act some time later). He also conducted a series of wartime light-classical concerts in the southern counties. But perhaps the best measure of his popularity was that he was the first guest on what would become BBC radio's longest-running programme, *Desert Island Discs*,* in January 1942. He was always aware that as a well known Jew his name was on the Nazi blacklist should Britain be invaded, but his love for Sarah and the fact that several close relatives were interned in Belsen persuaded him to stay on in England, helping the war effort in the best way he knew – boosting morale.

Throughout the war Sarah and Vic were seen together on her leaves, and she always made a point of going to his shows whenever she was in London; but at the end of the war there was a quiet, amicable divorce. Once at a dinner party attended by Vic, Churchill was asked to name someone he particularly admired. To everyone's surprise he answered, 'Mussolini.' When asked why, he

---

*Still going strong in 2011.

twinkled across the table at Vic, 'Because he had the good sense to shoot his son-in-law.'* This little incident illustrates Churchill's affection for Vic.

When Mary announced her engagement to someone of whom she did not approve, somewhat surprisingly, in view of the fact that she disliked him so much, Clementine went to consult Max Beaverbrook rather than bother Winston about it. Acting on his advice, she insisted on Mary waiting a year before announcing her engagement. Within months Mary realised she had made a mistake. Soon after her father's return from the USA she and her second cousin, Judy Montagu, joined the Auxiliary Territorial Service. In the meantime Clementine's letters to Mary provide the details of her increasingly busy life as she went about London, always wearing her trademark headgear, a headscarf tied as a smart turban: 'Yesterday I went to my Maternity Hospital & tried to buy a house for a Convalescent Home for the Mothers. But it was too expensive, so I am scratching my head and wondering what to do next . . . To-day for 3 hours I have been trudging round the Borough of St Pancras looking at A.R.P. Canteens & decontamination centres till I thought I should drop . . . the King and Queen lunched alone with Papa & me last Tuesday . . . Papa tried to interfere with the Menu but I was firm & had it my own way and luckily it was good . . . The King did not say much – He looked rather thin, & rather tired . . .'[19]

It was now almost Christmas – the third Christmas of the war – and although there had been a number of minor victories for the Allies the tide was not yet turning in Britain's favour; nor was there any end to the fighting in sight. On Sunday 7 December Winston was dining alone at Chequers with the American Ambassador John ('Gil') Winant and Averell Harriman. Clementine, worried about Nellie, had retired early, leaving the men to eat alone. As in every house in Britain, the wireless was switched on for the 9 p.m. news bulletin, and this was how the three men heard the momentous news that the Japanese had attacked American ships in Hawaii.

---

*Mussolini ordered his son-in-law Conte Ciano to be killed by firing squad on 11 January 1944.

Churchill recounted that he immediately put a call through to the White House:

> In two or three minutes Mr. Roosevelt came through. 'Mr. President, what's this about Japan?' 'It's quite true,' he replied. 'They have attacked us at Pearl Harbor. We are all in the same boat now.' I put Winant on the line and some interchanges took place, the Ambassador at first saying, 'Good. Good' and then, apparently graver, 'Ah!' I got on again and said, 'This certainly simplifies things. God be with you,' or words to that effect. . . . My two American friends took the shock with admirable fortitude . . . They did not wail or lament that their country was at war. They wasted no words in reproach or sorrow.[20]

One morning soon after Dunkirk, when there had seemed no possibility of defeating the Nazis, Churchill had been in his bathroom shaving and chatting with Randolph. 'I think I see the way we can win,' he had said. Randolph, incredulous, asked how. 'We must bring the Americans in,' Winston had told him. Now the strategy looked as if it might be accomplished. 'I thought of a remark,' Churchill wrote in his memoirs of the war years, 'which Edward Grey* had made to me more than thirty years before – that the United States is like "a gigantic boiler. Once the fire is lighted under it there is no limit to the power it can generate."' In December 1941 he rejoiced:

> So we had won after all! Yes, after Dunkirk; after the fall of France; after the horrible episode of Oran; after the threat of invasion, when, apart from the air and the Navy we were an almost unarmed people; after the deadly struggle of the U-boat war . . . after seventeen months of lonely fighting . . . we had won the war. England would live; Britain would live . . . How long the war would last or in what fashion it would end no man could tell, nor did I at this moment care . . . We should not be wiped out . . . Hitler's fate was sealed . . . I went to bed, and slept the sleep of the saved and thankful.[21]

---

*Foreign Secretary, 1905–16.

His euphoria was short-lived. Three days later the First Sea Lord telephoned to advise him that the battleship HMS *Prince of Wales* and the battlecruiser HMS *Repulse*, which had been sent to Singapore as a deterrent against Japanese aggression, had been attacked and sunk. 'I was thankful to be alone,' Churchill wrote. 'In all the war I never received a more direct shock . . . How many efforts, hopes, and plans foundered with these two ships. As I turned over and twisted in bed the full horror of the news sank in upon me. There were no British or American capital ships in the Indian Ocean or the Pacific, except the American survivors of Pearl Harbor who were hastening back to California. Over this vast expanse of water Japan was supreme and we were weak and naked.'[22]

On 12 December Winston left London for Washington with a delegation of eighty people. He need not have hurried: HMS *Duke of York* took ten days over the voyage because of relentless storms, and instead of steaming proudly up the Potomac as he intended, by the time they reached the American coast Winston was so impatient to see President Roosevelt that he jumped ship at Chesapeake with his doctor, valet and Max Beaverbrook, and flew to Washington DC, ordering his entourage to follow him by whatever means they could. As the small team flew into the capital that evening, the city looked like an illuminated fairyland to the English visitors used to a total blackout at home.

A few days before the news of Pearl Harbor, the family had received its own bad news. It was the reason Clementine had been too upset about her sister to dine with the American visitors and had gone to bed early on the night of 7 December. Five days earlier, Nellie's son Esmond had been posted officially missing over the North Sea while part of a nine-plane flight on an RAF bombing raid of Hamburg. Her other son Giles, who had been captured in the opening weeks of the war, was still a prisoner in Colditz. Widowed in the previous year, she was desperate with grief and worry, and Clementine suffered deeply with her.

Winston arrived in Washington on 23 December 1941 and he spent two full days in talks with the President discussing the progress of the lend-lease programme, and how Allied cooperation in North Africa now might turn the course of the war in Europe. On Christmas Eve he made a public appearance with the President, and some thirty thousand people gathered to see them light the White House Christmas tree, followed by carols. Knowing what Winston hoped to achieve on that mission, Clementine wrote that she was constantly thinking of him. With their children all in the armed forces – even Mary could not get leave – she planned to spend Christmas alone with Cousin Moppet at the Downing Street annexe. She was too unhappy to celebrate.

It was Christmas Day before Winston had any free time, and as soon as he could he dispatched a message to Esmond's wife Decca, who was living with friends at Seminary Hill just out-side Washington. He asked her to come and see him at the White House and, assuming that he could give her some news of Esmond, Decca duly arrived bringing their ten-month-old daughter.

She found him in bed surrounded by papers and books, with a secretary tapping briskly at a typewriter in an adjoining room – absorbed in his normal routine, in other words. He was working on the speech he was to deliver to Congress that afternoon, which included his famous sally: 'I cannot help reflecting that if my father had been American and my mother British, instead of the other way round, I might have got here on my own.' 'He looked mar-vellous,' Decca recalled, 'like some extravagant peacock in his bright silk dressing gown.'[23] All she knew for certain, through cables from the RAF, was that Esmond was missing. Now Winston told her that on Nellie's behalf he had had the most thorough inquiries made about Esmond's disappearance, and there was no longer any doubt that he was dead. He saw that this 'lovely young woman', sitting with her pretty baby in a white woollen suit, was crushed by what he had told her, and in an attempt to mask the emotion of the moment and to help her, he began awkwardly to talk about her family.

Decca was so stunned with the news that she could hardly take in what Winston was saying – until he mentioned Diana Mosley and explained that he had tried to help make Diana's life in prison a little more comfortable. Decca, herself a committed Communist by now (more so than Esmond had ever been), felt an uncontrollable anger sweep over her at the thought that while Esmond had been killed fighting Fascism her 'ghastly Fascist sister' was safe and being well looked after. Diana should be put up against a wall and shot, she exclaimed furiously. Churchill, realising it was time to be quiet, let her rage on, the tears spilling down her face. When she grew silent he told her he was full of admiration for Esmond and that he had died a hero's death. He advised her to remain in the USA for the remainder of the war, but that if she wished to return home to her family she was to let him know and he would facilitate it. As she rose to leave he handed her an envelope with her name written on it. Later she found it contained $500. As Decca wrote, 'It was a lot of money then.' Back in the UK a rumour went around the family that she had thrown the money in Winston's face, but this was not so. She took it and later, regarding it as 'blood money', she bought a pony for a friend's daughter and gave the rest to the Communist Party.

It had been a particularly difficult interview for Churchill, who was always emotional about any matter concerning his family, but he realised he could do nothing more to help Decca. Just as the Fascist sister Diana blamed him for her imprisonment and for parting her from her baby son, the Communist Decca would always regard him as personally responsible for Esmond's death. Back at home Winston would sigh as he reported the interview to Decca's brother Tom Mitford, reflecting, 'Decca is as fanatical a Communist as ever.'[24]

Churchill was engaged at this time in trying to merge the efforts of the British and American forces in North Africa against the German Army there. A few days later he left Washington accompanied by his doctor Sir Charles Wilson,* his Private Secretary John Martin and his private detective to spend five days resting in the Florida sunshine. He was in need of some rest, and having been loaned

---

*President of the Royal College of Physicians, Wilson was created Baron Moran in the New Year's Honours List of 1943.

an isolated cottage at Pompano near Miami by one of the President's administrators he could relax in the warmth of the Gulf Stream. 'Oranges and pineapples grow here,' Wilson noted in his diary. 'And the blue ocean is so warm that Winston basks half-submerged in the water like a hippopotamus in a swamp.'[25] So isolated was it that he was able to bathe naked (disregarding reports of a fifteen-foot shark in the area).[26]

While in Florida he visited Consuelo and Jacques at their Palm Beach home. Having made their way from France and Spain to Lisbon, the Balsans had been able to fly on a Transatlantic Clipper to New York, with seats arranged for them by Consuelo's brothers. After their arrival the Balsans bought houses on Long Island and Palm Beach and commuted between the two, living the life of rich Americans though always longing for their former life in France. Balsan was now seventy-four, but as a former national hero he was deeply uneasy at not being involved in the fight to save his country. He remained in the USA for Consuelo's sake, always hoping (until the Vichy government capitulated to the Germans) that Marshal Pétain would somehow save France. He tried unsuccessfully to persuade President Roosevelt to allow him to set up a sort of Foreign Legion of French exiles who would join in the fight. As he left the Balsans' house, after basking in peacetime luxury in the company of guests specially selected by Consuelo for his entertainment, Winston, who had observed Jacques's frustration, remarked under his breath to Wilson: 'Wealth, taste and leisure can do these things, but they do not bring happiness.'[27]

By the following year Jacques felt no longer able to remain on the sidelines. He got himself to London to join the Free French, but he was to face further aggravation when, ostensibly because of his well known love of children, the Free French deputed him to return to the USA to raise funds for the relief of poor French children. What he did not know was that Consuelo, afraid that Jacques would develop pneumonia during the harsh English winter, had initiated and financed this plan to return him to the USA, even involving Winston in the scheme.[28]

In mid-January 1942 after his short vacation in Florida, Winston flew home in a Boeing flying boat, having been away for five weeks, still unaware of the outcome of his talks with Roosevelt concerning US cooperation with the Allies in North Africa. The next weeks were probably the hardest of the war for him, with bad news piling in daily from Europe, North Africa, and now from the Far East as well.

At the end of February Mary wrote in her diary: 'Papa is at a very low ebb. He is not too well physically – and he is worn down by the continuous crushing pressure of events.'[29] Clementine took the brunt of this stress, trying to protect Winston where she could, and when in April she heard that Randolph had volunteered for an SAS mission, all her irritation for her difficult son overcame her and she began to despise him for the damage he was causing the family. In one of her letters to Winston:

> My darling, please don't think I am indifferent because I was silent when you told me of Randolph's cable to Pamela saying that he was joining a parachute unit . . . but I grieve that he has done this because I know it will cause you harrowing anxiety, indeed, even agony of mind. I feel this impulse of Randolph's is sincere but sensational. Surely there is a half-way house between being a Staff-Officer and a Parachute Jumper. He could have quietly & sensibly rejoined his Regiment & considering he has a very young wife with a baby to say nothing of a Father who is bearing not only the burden of his own country but for the moment [that] of an unprepared America.[30]

She wanted to cable Randolph and ask him to give up the scheme, but decided not to. She probably knew that Winston, who had seen Randolph during a brief visit to Cairo a few weeks earlier, would not have allowed it, anyway. But despite his anxiety for his son he would have fully understood Randolph's desire to see action, just as he had understood Jacques Balsan's frustration.

What Winston did not know was that, far from considering his young wife and baby, Randolph was behaving like an unattached bachelor. He was still in love with Laura Charteris, and his occasional brief letters and cables to Pam contrasted with the twenty or more love letters he wrote to Laura during 1942–3. 'Don't expect to hear from me for some time,' he wrote to Laura in one early letter, as he waited for the news that he was off to the Middle East. 'As I told you the other night it pains me deeply that I should not be in a position to say to you the things I would like to say.' A few days later he was writing while at sea, telling her he was on an exciting venture 'of which you will soon be reading more in the papers'. When he learned from Virginia Cowles that Laura had obtained a divorce from her first husband Lord Long and planned to marry the much older Earl of Dudley, Randolph persuaded Virginia to put his case to Laura. 'Randolph is here,' she wrote, 'and *you* are very much on his mind. He talks of nothing else. He is looking very thin and handsome and wishes you to think seriously before taking the plunge with the Earl! Life with Randolph I am sure would be far more glamorous and exciting . . . Why not *really* consider Randolph?'[31] Later Randolph would write again: 'You know what decision I pray that you will reach, although I think it would be wrong of me to press you to it. We could be divinely happy together.'[32]* Clearly, Pam was not even a consideration in his plans.

Randolph's SAS mission – a sabotage raid on a German supply depot at Benghazi in Libya – was a success, but during his return journey there was a road accident in which he dislocated his back, and he was shipped home to London to recover. Evelyn Waugh reported on a visit by Lord Digby who travelled to London to attempt to reconcile what Pam had told her father were 'differences' between her and Randolph. Pam and her father disappeared for a long time into the bedroom of Pam's flat to confer. 'Randolph was exuberant & vociferous. Panto [Pam] hates him so much,' Waugh reported, 'that she can't sit in a room with him but paced up & down the minute hall outside the door after her father had gone.'

---

*Laura married Lord Dudley. Randolph was deeply upset, but he sent her some nylons, as 'an un-wedding present'.

When at last Waugh persuaded her to come back into the room, 'she could not look at him & simply said over her shoulder in acid tones, "Ought you not to be resting?" whenever he became particularly jolly. She was looking very pretty & full of mischief,' he wrote.[33]

On 23 October 1942, the 8th Army under the command of Lieutenant General Montgomery attacked at El Alamein, delivering the heaviest artillery barrage of the war. After twelve days of heavy fighting they had taken thirty thousand prisoners and trounced the crack German and Italian desert troops of Field Marshal Rommel. Churchill always liked to say that it was the turning point of the war: 'Before Alamein we never had a victory. After Alamein we never had a defeat.' He wanted the church bells rung in celebration, but Clementine was worried it might lead to undue optimism. However, two weeks later when the victorious British captured Tobruk from the Vichy French, Churchill did not hesitate to order the bells rung as a sign that progress was being made after the long struggle.

Winston's sixty-eighth birthday on 30 November was a family occasion, and all those who could get to the Downing Street annexe, which was suitably decorated with masses of flowers, celebrated with him and Clementine: Diana, Sarah, Mary and Pam, brother Jack, Venetia Montagu and Brendan Bracken (Minister of Information since July 1941) gathered to toast Winston, who was dressed as usual in one of his signature one-piece 'siren-suits'* which Clementine had made up for him. For off-duty wear, some were made of velvet and other softer materials.

Pam had now been living at Grosvenor Square for almost a year (she said she was the only Englishwoman in 'Eisenhower-platz') and because of her friendships with top Americans from Eisenhower down – but particularly with Averell Harriman, who made frequent visits to London – she had become very Americanised in her

---

*The name 'siren-suit' was coined by Churchill. It has been described variously, from 'flying-suit' to 'rompers', depending what sort of spin the writer wishes to impose. It was a very efficient, comfortable garment in which to work, and Churchill had a wardrobe of them in various colours and materials.

opinions. She and Randolph quarrelled bitterly whenever he came home on leave: over the fact that, in his view, she worked far too much to allow her to see little Winston often enough; about his insistence on living a bachelor life whenever he wished; and not least because he now knew of her affair with Harriman. Sauce for the goose was not sauce for the gander, it seemed, but what most annoyed him was that a man he considered a friend of his had 'betrayed' him, as he put it. That he had himself conducted affairs with the wives of friends and brother officers, that he had recently all but proposed marriage to Laura – which could only take place after divorcing Pam – seemed not to occur to him. By the time Pam attended Winston's birthday party Randolph had formally left her. This was a relief to her, for it meant that she was not blamed for the parting.

When Pam saw Winston and Clementine to explain what had happened, they sided wholeheartedly with her. Mary believes that although this was mainly because they did not wish to lose touch with little Winston, they also genuinely loved Pam.[34] Only a short time earlier Winston had written to Randolph that Pam was 'a great treasure and a blessing to us all', and this 'favouritism', in Randolph's eyes, was the cause of much rancour between him and his parents. They invariably argued about it whenever he went to see them, and sometimes he was ordered to leave the house, not only by his mother but by Winston, too.

Pam's warmth and natural intelligence were recognised by others as well as by the Churchills. When her boring job at the Ministry of Supply came to an end and she began casting about for something more interesting to do in London, Brendan Bracken supplied the answer. The Churchill Club had been set up as a recreation club and morale-booster for all ranks, where Allied servicemen on leave could find relaxation and company in comfortable surroundings; they could also find books there, attend the odd concert and other cultural events. It was housed very near the Houses of Parliament in Ashburnham House, a fourteenth-century building that formed part of Westminster School – the boys had been evacuated since the outbreak of war. It was sponsored by top writers and politicians, including the Foreign Secretary, Anthony Eden, who would sometimes give talks there. What was lacking was the right person to run it.

Pam seemed made for the job, and before long she had become one of the reasons why people were drawn to the Churchill Club. She knew how and where to obtain spirits as well as food that was on ration, and it became one of the few places in London to obtain a decent dry Martini. In her mid-twenties, Pam was at the height of her considerable allure. 'Mummie' had been quite right: the puppy fat had disappeared. With her fresh colouring, red hair and blue eyes she seemed to glow. Her warm smile and innate kindness, her ability to charm men and make the club feel like a home from home, her knowledge of what top people expected to find in such an organisation, plus the fact that she knew so many celebrities who would come along and do an impromptu show for her, made the club a *succès fou*. There was no question of rank at the Churchill Club – although it was mainly patronised by officers, all men serving in the armed forces were welcome and everyone was supposed to be treated equally. Pam was as happy to flirt with or sit and listen to a young NCO as a five-star general.

She moved from the flat in Grosvenor Square that she had shared with Kathy Harriman and into her own at No. 49, again inexpensively sited on the top floor that other people didn't want. And it enabled her to bring two-year-old Winston and his nanny from Cherkley at last. The dormer windows overlooking Hyde Park provided the child with 'an almost nightly fireworks display'.[35] Little Winston recalled that he rather enjoyed air raids, not least being wrapped up and taken into a shelter at night when things got 'hot'.

When Averell was made Ambassador to the Soviet Union in October 1943, he and Pam were parted for several years. Their feelings for each other did not die – rather, they lay dormant. They wrote to each other constantly, and he arranged for regular luxury food parcels to be delivered to her. But she had always known he was a married man and had never expected their relationship to lead to anything permanent. After his departure she dated a number of men friends with whom, according to gossip, she slept with from time to time. In this she was very little different from other young married women of her class living in London during the war, but she had a lot more opportunity; while she was running the Churchill Club she was one of the most sought-after women in London.

Perhaps her affection for 'Papa' Churchill encouraged her at least to try to maintain some discretion. Her supposed lovers during the last two years of the war included, according to her unofficial biographer, the British Chief of Air Staff Sir Charles Portal, Edward R. Murrow, the famous CBS war correspondent, and William Paley, Murrow's colleague, as well as John ('Jock') Whitney, who would be US Ambassador to Britain in the late 1950s. A full listing would take up more space here than is available – but, tellingly, there is no evidence that Winston was ever embarrassed by his daughter-in-law's behaviour, or at least not in the way he and Clementine were by Randolph's. Perhaps he understood and looked the other way because he recalled his mother's numerous liaisons? As one friend put it, '[Winston] had not been brought up to be censorious about other people's sexual extravagances.'[36]

The most passionate of these affairs of Pam's was undoubtedly with radio journalist Ed Murrow. It was an unlikely pairing, for they sprang from very different worlds. He was a self-made man from a poor family on the wrong side of the tracks; almost socialist in his ideology, he deplored the rich young drones of the circles in which Pam had grown up, though he worshipped Churchill. He had worked his way through college, and by sheer effort and ability scrambled to his pole position as the most respected CBS journalist. Like Churchill he had spotted the Nazi threat long before it was widely acknowledged, and his impassioned live coverage of the *Anschluss* in March 1938 catapulted him to international fame. He was able to persuade leading European personalities to give him interviews, and his reports seriously rivalled the NBC news programmes that had hitherto commanded the largest audiences. He recruited the journalist William Shirer to do a similar job in Europe, and together these two men forged the profile of future radio news broadcasting.

Ed Murrow had been married to Janet (a journalist who became a friend of Clementine) for almost a decade when he became involved with Pam. By then his vivid reports of London under siege, delivered in his unmistakable slightly gravelly voice, had become a feature of the war on two continents. He always began with his signature opening line: '*This* is London' – emphasis on 'This', followed by a slight pause before 'is London'. He always ended with his own catch-phrase: 'Goodnight, and good luck.' He interspersed his news reports of the Blitz (often recorded during the height of the attacks from the top of a tall building and against a background of sirens, aircraft engines, exploding bombs, breaking glass, burning buildings and the shouts of anxious fire-fighters) with graphic coverage of the raids and of the personal heroism of individual London citizens. He flew on bombing raids over Germany. He punctuated his pieces with home-spun philosophy: 'Just because your voice reaches halfway around the world doesn't mean you are wiser than when it reached only to the end of the bar', 'No one can terrorise a whole nation, unless we are all his accomplices', 'I saw many flags flying from [flag]staffs. No one told these people to put out the flag. They simply feel like flying the Union Jack. [Pause.] No flag up there was white.' One of the great figures of the Second World War, he played a major part in the victory by involving Americans personally in the fight going on in Europe. President Roosevelt once sent him a cable that read: 'You burned the city of London in our houses and we felt the flames. You laid the dead of London at our doors and we knew that the dead were our dead . . . were mankind's dead, without rhetoric, without dramatics, without more emotion than needed be. You have destroyed the superstition that what is done beyond 3000 miles of water is not really done at all.'*

In 1944 Pam and Ed Murrow were moving in the same circles – Harriman's and Churchill's – and though it was an attraction of opposites it was a passionate relationship for all that. He was twelve years older than her: confident, successful, intelligent, powerful – all the elements that attracted Pam in a man. Money was useful, but it did not spark passion on its own. For the year that they were lovers Pam was as happy as she ever was in her life.

---

*Read out at a dinner to honour Murrow at the Waldorf Astoria in December 1941.

1943–5

Weathering the Storm

From 1943 Churchill's leadership took a different form. He was no longer the beleaguered ageing warrior leading a nation standing alone against the world. Following the Allied victories in North Africa the tide had turned favourably for Britain, but by then Winston's problems were changed rather than eased. He had worked relentlessly to bring the United States into the war, and when America – and Russia – joined Britain's fight, a lesser man than Winston might have lost control of the direction of events. Yet he still conveyed the impression that he was at least the equal of Roosevelt and Stalin, the other leaders of the Grand Alliance that convened in Tehran in November 1943, and even that it was his 'show'. It helped that he was a Victorian, for during his youth and young adulthood the British Empire was the greatest empire the world had ever known, four times the size of the Roman Empire, covering a quarter of the earth's surface. To Churchill, Britain was still essentially the mother of a great empire.

Winston had, though, been feeling the effects of age and stress when on 12 November he set off on this supremely important state mission aboard the battlecruiser HMS *Renown*. There was an element of royal progress about it: he was surrounded by a court of expert advisers such as the Foreign Secretary Anthony Eden, the commanders of the three services, backed by ambassadors and leading ministers and politicians. His personal team included his doctor and Private Secretary; and Sarah and Randolph, both in uniform, acted as his ADCs. He was unwell with a heavy cold when he set off, and spent most of the voyage in bed working on his papers, dispatches and speeches; he did not go ashore until they reached Malta five days later. Another big hitter, Harold Macmillan, had joined them at Gibraltar.[1] By the time they reached Cairo the rest and the warm air had revived Winston, and the British team joined the American delegation (which included Averell Harriman and US Ambassador Gil Winant) for talks with Chiang Kai-shek, China's Commander-in-Chief, about the war in the Far East. Then they all flew to Tehran, where Sarah felt that the affair was almost a gathering of old friends, since she had met so many of those present around the dining table at Chartwell.

When the gathering toasted Winston on his sixty-ninth birthday at the British Residence in Tehran, although he had not yet achieved his ultimate goal – victory over the enemy – he had reached a peak in both his life and his career. At that moment he had delivered all the promise of his star: he knew that, provided he, Roosevelt and Stalin could deal with each other, given time the war was all but won and it was his leadership that had put them in a position to achieve this. In his war memoir he reflected on the significance of his position as he hosted a dinner at the British Legation for the two other leaders:

> This was a memorable moment in my life. On my right sat the President of the United States, on my left the master of Russia. Together we controlled a large preponderance of the naval and three-quarters of all the air forces of the world and could direct armies of nearly twenty millions of men in the most terrible of wars that had yet occurred in human history. I could not help rejoicing at the long way we had come on the road to victory since the summer of 1940.[2]

Sarah wrote to Clementine to pass on her father's apologies for not writing. 'Papa's cold is much better and he loves the bright sun. He is working very hard . . . he really doesn't stop for one minute.'[3]

Despite his elation Winston was still weak. The previous year, a serious chest infection had lowered his spirits and drained him physically. His doctor had told Clementine that during the Washington visit in 1941 he had sustained a mild heart attack, but it was so mild that he had made the decision not to tell his patient. But now, because of the constant stress and the long hours he worked, it was possible that Winston could suffer another heart attack, especially if he undertook any long flights at high altitude. Clementine decided that, since he would not let up anyway, he did not need this extra worry and so should not be told. Apart from confiding in Mary, Clementine nursed this secret throughout the war, constantly anxious because Winston was in the air almost as often as in a car or a train. He always flew when possible, no matter the potential danger from the enemy, such as when he attended a conference in Algiers in May 1943. He had also, with Clementine, made a draining but necessary visit to Canada and the USA that summer, and they were in Washington DC on their thirty-fifth wedding anniversary when he told Clementine that he loved her more and more every year.[4] Because he refused to spare himself he became as prey to constant bronchial infections, as he was when a small boy.

Sarah had noted that her father was apprehensive until he reached Tehran, where a good deal of energy and friendly bombast were then required in order to dominate the proceedings; but somehow he found sufficient reserves. 'I have noted a curiously touching thing about the President when he is with Papa,' Sarah confided to Clementine. 'He forgets he cannot walk.* Once after some lunch, Papa sprang up from the table to go and arrange something . . . and the President very nearly got up too – he leant forward on the arms of his chair, just like a man about to rise quickly. It's this feeling [of energy] that Papa gives to everyone – this quality which he takes with him everywhere.'[5] Any feelings of jubilation over the agreements reached by the three leaders were blunted for Churchill when he learned that Roosevelt and Stalin had met together privately and made deals that did not include any British input.† Sarah saw that

---

*Roosevelt had contracted a paralytic illness in 1921 and suffered a permanent disability from the waist down. In private he used a wheelchair but in public he was always seen standing, supported by an aide.

†The same would happen at Yalta, when 'the Big Three' next met two years later.

her father felt wounded by this because he considered Roosevelt to be a personal friend. It was not just a personal hurt, however: Churchill worried about how these deals might affect Britain. In fact, as history shows, they had far-reaching effects that would dominate European history for almost half a century after 1945.

Also at Tehran, Sarah had noted a welcome change in Randolph's demeanour. During dinner 'a new restraint kept Randolph seated', she wrote to Clementine. 'I couldn't help thinking how a few years ago he would never have been off his feet! He is trying you know – there is a big change in him.'[6]

Churchill was a supreme military strategist who never found any glory in war and killing – his *raison d'être* was to preserve a way of life and a culture that meant everything to him. He wrote about this on a number of occasions, and it was vividly demonstrated at one dinner in Tehran. During the evening the subject was raised of what was to be done with the German military leaders when the war ended. Stalin stated that there were only about fifty thousand German military men and they should all be executed. Churchill was appalled. He retorted: 'I would rather be shot myself than agree to such a plan.' When a member of the American delegation appeared to support Stalin's suggestion Churchill rose and walked out of the room. He was only persuaded to return when he was assured that this was not a serious proposal.*

After Tehran the delegation flew to Cairo where, in a moving ceremony, Churchill inspected his old regiment, the 4th Hussars. Afterwards, the men were allowed to break ranks and crowd around him, chatting and shaking his hand – just as during the stop-over in Malta on the journey out, he had been mobbed by the Maltese. He also visited the Turkish mission to try to persuade them to end their position of neutrality, and that night as Sarah tucked in his mosquito net, Winston – 'looking just like a rubicund, naughty baby,' she wrote – said to her, '"The president of the Turks kissed

---

*His feelings about Hitler were not so tender; he regarded him as the apotheosis of evil. At one Cabinet meeting he insisted that if Hitler was captured he should be executed in 'the electric chair', adding wryly that they might be able to borrow such an appliance from the Americans under the lend-lease scheme.

me!"', and as he fell into a sound, contented sleep, he murmured, "'The trouble with me is that I'm irresistible.'"[7] What Sarah did not relate in her memoirs was that she and Ambassador Gil Winant had fallen in love during that tour. As they were both married they knew it was something that must never come to light; but others in their party knew of it, including Jock Colville, and it is inconceivable that Winston was not informed. The affair was the elephant in the room: no one spoke of this doomed relationship and Sarah knew that it could only continue in secret as yet another wartime romance.

While Winston was away the contentious Rule 18B was debated in Parliament with a view to amending it. He had been opposed to its introduction at the start of the war, but he had no power at the time to contest it. He loathed the fact that it overruled the right of a citizen not to be imprisoned without a trial, in contravention of the spirit of Magna Carta. He deprecated the fact that Diana and Oswald Mosley had been kept in captivity under this rule during the entire course of the war, with no trial and no opportunity to defend themselves in court. Now he wrote to Clementine that he burned to take part in the debate. 'If I were at home now I would blow the whole blasted thing out of existence. So long as Morrison* presents the case for exceptional treatment for Mosley naturally he is on difficult ground and people can cry "Favour!" He really would lose very little to sweep the whole thing away.'[8]

When he had carried out all his current duties, the willpower upon which Churchill had drawn so heavily seemed to evaporate. He was so exhausted that he collapsed, and his personal physician, Lord Moran (formerly Sir Charles Wilson), announced that his patient had been 'profligate of his resources'. As he rested, Winston and Randolph quarrelled over Randolph's failed marriage and who was responsible.

---

*Herbert Morrison's (1888–1965) move when Home Secretary, to repeal Rule 18B of the Emergency Powers Act, was unpopular because of the Mosleys. Majority public opinion held that they were fifth-columnists and that they should not be released. It was almost the only occasion in the war when Churchill's policies ran counter to the wishes of most ordinary people. The Mosleys were released, but lived under house arrest in their own home for the remainder of the war.

Winston still blamed his son – and as always, he found family problems far harder to cope with than complicated world matters.

On 12 December 1943 he flew on to Tunis to stay in Eisenhower's villa, the White House, near the ruins of ancient Carthage. There his condition worsened and within days he was diagnosed with pneumonia. Winston was so ill at this point that Lord Moran thought there was a chance he would not survive, and Winston himself evidently thought it was possible that he would lay his bones in Carthage. He told Sarah that she was not to worry about him. 'It doesn't matter if I die now, the plans of victory have been laid,' he told her. 'It is only a matter of time.'[9] But thanks to the new 'wonder drug' M&B, a precursor of antibiotics, administered by Lord Moran, Churchill slowly regained his health, and Clementine was flown out to join him in time for Christmas along with her confidential secretary Grace Hamblin.

On medical advice Churchill did not return to England for the worst month of the English winter. He and his retinue repaired to Marrakech to spend some weeks there while he regained his strength in the sun as the guest of the American Ambassador at Villa Taylor, a Moroccan palace set in its own superb gardens.* He had visited Marrakech previously with President Roosevelt, and had liked it. Not only was the climate generally mild, but the scenery immediately appealed to him as a subject for painting. He made a rapid recovery in the dry air, and the city was to become one of his favourite places for the rest of his life. An old friend, Diana, the beautiful wife of Duff Cooper† who had been posted to North Africa as Churchill's special representative, spent time with him there, and as Winston adored the company of beautiful and witty women he was kept gently amused until Max Beaverbrook unexpectedly joined the party. Winston rested for a good part of the day, reading Jane Austen novels almost exclusively, until he felt able to

---

*Villa Taylor was next door to the Mamounia Hotel, which Churchill would subsequently visit a number of times.

†In 1943, at the suggestion of Churchill and Anthony Eden, Duff Cooper was appointed British Representative in Algiers to the newly formed French Committee of National Liberation, with the prospect of becoming Ambassador in Paris after the war.

paint. The convalescent routine, which included hours of painting each day, relaxed him so much that he apparently made no objection when Brigadier Fitzroy Maclean* invited Randolph to join him in an active-service mission in Yugoslavia, behind the German lines. Winston had to be consulted because of the extraordinary situation that would arise should Randolph be captured. His reaction was to warn his son to take care *not* to be captured: 'The Gestapo would only try to blackmail me by sending me your fingers one by one,' he said. 'A situation I would have to bear with fortitude.'[10]

Thrilled to be actively involved again, Major Randolph Churchill flew off with his father's approval and, he thought, his open admiration. He wrote to tell Laura, now Countess of Dudley, about it. He told her too that his father had been 'a very unusual patient' who had spent Christmas presiding over an important military conference of the Supreme Military Commanders – namely, General Maitland Wilson, General Eisenhower, General Alexander and Admiral Cunningham. His father's energy, he wrote, was 'fantastic'. He signed off: 'My sweetest darling, I love you.'[11]

Duff Cooper visited Churchill from Algiers on 10 January 1944, flying in the specially fitted-out York that was the PM's private transport:

As soon as we went on board the steward offered us champagne cocktails, which were not refused. It was really a delightful journey. Perfect weather . . . and wonderful views of the Mediterranean and the Atlas Mountains . . . Clemmie and Sarah met us and took us straight to the villa where they are all living – a beautiful place . . . There we found Winston in his siren suit and his enormous Californian hat. When it got cooler he completed this get-up with a silk dressing gown . . . He has a huge staff here, including half-a-dozen cypher girls and a map room, with a naval officer permanently on duty . . . we were fourteen at dinner. Max Beaverbrook is here and

---

*Brigadier Fitzroy Maclean was in command of British aid to Marshal Tito and his Partisans. He attached a series of Allied 'missions' to local Partisan commanders and established a rear-guard HQ to provide the Partisans with food, general supplies and air support.

Lord Moran and his son. The rest are staff . . . we sat talking until after one. I have never known Winston in better form or more cheerful. Max on the other hand was very silent. He is never quite at ease except in his own house . . . Clemmie said she had given Winston a . . . lecture this morning on the importance of not quarrelling with de Gaulle. He had grumbled at the time, but she thought it would bear fruit.[12]

The Churchills returned to London on 18 January, Winston completely reinvigorated and ready to face what would be a momentous year ahead. That spring the Germans threw everything they had left into a bombing campaign on London. War-weary by now, Londoners found this battering hard to bear, while at the same time nurturing hope that very soon the Allies would begin an assault on the European mainland and drive the enemy back once and for all. Winston was everywhere: supervising, managing, organising, checking every minute detail. Almost nothing was too small to require his personal attention. Nothing must be allowed to go wrong. When the day arrived for the Allies to invade Europe and take it back from the Nazis, the British forces must not be found wanting. This long-awaited day, code-named D-Day, was set for 6 June, and right up to the first week in June Winston did the rounds of the encampments and ports of embarkation. His appearance was always a huge morale booster. He could not join in the planned Normandy landings as he wished, but he intended to watch the attack from the bridge of a warship in the Channel. Almost everyone was against this idea, even the King. And when the King's polite request turned into an order, Winston could not overrule it.

Given his critical role in the war that summer, he did not see a great deal of his grandson. But on one visit, the younger Winston recalled him down on his hands and knees playing with the second-hand train set that he and Clemmie had scoured London to find – no such thing being on sale in the shops during the war. Winston always tried to keep Randolph advised of his son's progress: 'Baby Winston is extremely well . . . Naturally, as he gets older he develops more personality, which takes the form of naughtiness. But his mother takes infinite pains with him . . . he is very handsome with a noble air.' Then, 'Baby Winston, as you will no doubt have been told by Pamela, has developed German Measles. I am ashamed to say I told him it was the fault of the Germans.'[13] As her son recovered, Pam contracted scarlet fever, a dangerous illness in an adult. She was quarantined, so little Winston went to live with the Churchills for over a month which, somewhat surprisingly, Clementine loved.

The battles in France were soon being consistently won by the Allies, but the enemy refused to give in. From mid-June through September, they launched in constant waves upon London the last weapons in their armoury – the top-secret V1 unmanned flying bombs, which the Londoners called 'doodlebugs', and the even more fearsome V2. But despite the fear that these weapons engendered there was a dogged sense that the war was all but over. Although diagnosed with a spot on the lung, Churchill insisted on sailing for Canada to attend the second Quebec Conference with Roosevelt, where he was welcomed as a hero.

In July Randolph had a serious accident. After leaving his parents in Morocco early in the year he had returned to England for training, later to be dropped secretly into Yugoslavia along with Evelyn Waugh and other friends such as Tom Mitford. There they helped to organise supplies to Marshal Tito's Partisans. Randolph was a passenger in a Dakota transport plane flying into Croatia to the rearguard HQ of his Commando unit, to take up his position as head of mission, when the plane crashed on landing and burst into flames. Ten people, including Randolph and Waugh, got out of the wreck alive. Waugh suffered concussion and Randolph had spinal and knee injuries, which, though not considered life-threatening, were largely to immobilise him throughout the summer. Waugh described how Randolph cried when he learned that his servant had been killed; and how, even as an invalid, he had dominated proceedings, roaring for morphine when in pain, calling for medical conferences about his condition, noisily demanding everyone else's medicine and 'attacking' the night nurse.[14] Eventually he was sent to convalesce in Algiers with Duff and Diana Cooper, where in August Winston briefly called to see him while en route to Italy. Recalling their last explosive encounters when they had quarrelled about Pam and little Winston, Churchill trod carefully, deciding not to give his son a letter from Clementine: 'No reference was made by either of us to family matters,' he explained to her. 'He is a lonely figure, by no means recovered as far as walking is concerned. Our talk was about politics, French and English, about which there was much friendly badinage & argument.'[15]

Clementine replied that she understood, though she thought her son would assume she was sulking. 'I agree that "where words are useless, silence is best",' she wrote. 'But I hoped that my few very mild & moderate words might turn out to be not quite useless. You see one shrinks from *saying* anything to Randolph because one wishes to avoid a scene. Consequently, he is not acquainted with one's point of view . . . I do think he ought to know this. Because then there is just the chance that he may be a little more considerate in future.'[16] What Clementine wanted him to know was that she was upset because little Winston had been removed from Chequers, where he had been staying while Pam was quarantined. As soon as Pam recovered she had wanted her son home with her.

Towards the end of that year Winston paid a visit to Russia, where he stayed with the US Ambassador Averell Harriman and his daughter Kathy. Again he was fêted with rapturous ovations wherever he went, but he was back in London for his seventieth birthday at the end of November. Here he solemnly toasted his beloved family and closest friends, telling them that he had been supported and comforted throughout the travails of war by their love.

During the last two years of the war Clementine somehow overcame her sense of inadequacy. She headed several fund-raising organisations, for which work she would eventually be honoured in England and Russia, but she found that her public morale-boosting appearances were almost as popular as Winston's. She had made it her life's work to be always there for Winston, watching over his health, ensuring that everything was just right to enable him to continue his work, and just as carefully supervising what we would these days call his public image. Churchill's daily routine included working lunches and dinners with Cabinet ministers, military leaders and overseas heads of state, all of which took a great deal of organisation. Their daughter Mary recorded that, family occasions apart, between January and September 1944 they gave seventy-five luncheon parties and nineteen dinners, and that Clementine's diary noted on only four occasions that year: 'dinner alone with Winston'.[17] Given this heavy workload, there were occasions when the stress became too great and she would give vent to her feelings. 'My mother always appeared calm and serene, as if she were coping with everything,' Mary explained. 'But she was a bomb waiting to go off and could just explode – as she once exploded with Cecil Beaton. She was highly combustible.'[18] Winston was invariably patient with these outbursts, always aware that his precious Kat, while loving him deeply, sometimes simply needed a rest from him. On one occasion after a disagreement she had flounced off angrily, witnessed by Jock Colville. Winston looked at Colville and announced dramatically, 'I am the unhappiest of men.' Colville wrote that this was so obviously the opposite of the truth that he burst out laughing.

Randolph was back in Yugoslavia by September 1944. His companion Evelyn Waugh recorded in his diaries that Randolph was drunk most days – and badly behaved every day, drunk or sober. In fact, his drunken ranting becomes a feature of virtually every diary kept by people who knew Randolph, such as Duff Cooper, and also in the biography of him by his cousin Anita Leslie – 'That was the trouble with Randolph, he didn't mean to rant and make people dislike him, but he did exactly that'. Waugh wrote that he found it irritating to have to tell Randolph everything twice: the first time, and then again when he sobered up. There were constant rows after which Randolph was sometimes apologetic. Once when he asked Waugh to be kinder to him, 'It left me unmoved,' Waugh wrote,

for . . . he is simply a flabby bully who rejoices in blustering and shouting down anyone weaker than himself and starts squealing as soon as he meets anyone as strong. In words he understands, he can dish it out, but he can't take it. I have felt less inclination to hide my scorn since his loss of self-control during the air-raid on Sunday. The facts are that he is a bore – with no intellectual invention or agility. He has a childlike retentive memory, and repetition takes the place of thought. He has set himself very low aims and has not the self control to pursue them steadfastly. He has no independence of character and his engaging affection comes from this. He is not a good companion for a long period, but the conclusion is always the same – that no one else would have chosen me, nor would anyone else have accepted him.[19]

Why did people tolerate Randolph? The main reason was his father, of course, but it seems that despite his many faults and his boorishness, at the best of times he could be brilliant and stimulating company. And he had some friends who were able to overlook his bad behaviour, among them Tom Mitford, who had been a close friend at Eton. It was one of the saddest events in Randolph's life when Tom was killed by a sniper in Burma in March 1945, just when most people considered the war was over.

Christmas 1944 was special in Britain. It was the sixth wartime Christmas and people believed they had weathered the worst. Although most families could name loved ones who were still away fighting, it was being called 'the last Christmas of the war' and much anticipation and preparation went into celebrating it in homes from the poorest to the wealthiest. The Churchills were no exception, and Clementine had made a special effort to make it a 'glowing' event, in her words, inviting all the family and close friends who could make it to Chequers for the holiday. Jack and his daughter Clarissa were there, with Nellie Romilly – often a sad figure now, since Esmond's death, and his brother Giles, as far as she knew, still a prisoner of war at Colditz. Diana and Duncan and their three children were there, along with two great friends of Winston who were almost family now, Prof Lindemann and Brendan Bracken. Jock Colville spent most of the holiday there, as did Gil Winant, who was still in love with Sarah and had recently become one of Clementine's close confidants.

Sarah and Mary were on duty on Christmas Day but planned to join the party on Boxing Day. Mary was now one of the officers with the Hyde Park Battery, an anti-aircraft gun site consisting of 230 women – 'Not so bad at 21!' Churchill had commented to Randolph. 'The Battery is to go to the front almost immediately, and will be under a somewhat stiffer rocket fire than we endure with composure here. Mary is very elated at the honour . . . when Mary sounded her girls out as to whether they wished to go over-seas, the almost universal reply was, "Not 'arf!"'[20]

When Nellie arrived at Chequers on 23 December she had found the house unexpectedly silent, Winston sitting disconsolately alone in the Hall. He welcomed her, then confided that it had suddenly become necessary for him to fly the following day to Athens where there had been a Communist uprising. When Clementine had been told, he explained, she had got very upset and had fled upstairs to her room. Nellie found her sister in tears: 'It was so rare for Clementine to give way,' Mary wrote. 'She was accustomed to sudden changes of plan, and had, in these last years especially, developed a strict sense of priorities.'[21] But the sudden news that Winston would not be there (for the second Christmas running) at this happily anticipated family gathering was more than Clementine could take. She had recovered by the time Winston and Jock flew off late on Christmas Eve, but it was an indication of how tightly she was stretched.

Randolph, who was still operating out of Yugoslavia, was given leave to join his father in Athens for a day or two,[22] and it was from there on 29 December that Winston cabled Clementine: DELIGHTED TO RECEIVE YOUR MESSAGE. I WAS FEELING LONELY. HOPE TO BE WITH YOU AT DINNER TOMORROW. TENDER LOVE.

When, later the following year, the family gathered to celebrate the peace, they assessed the cost of the war years on the family, though the eventual outcome was yet to occur in several cases.

Churchill's favourite daughter Sarah, as mentioned earlier, was quietly divorced from Vic Oliver in 1945. She had spent the later war years in Intelligence work as well as acting occasionally as an

ADC to her father. Her affair with Gil Winant had come to an end when her love for him waned. Gil often visited Chequers, and after her divorce in 1945 he would remain in London hoping to win Sarah back, but she sought acting jobs in Italy and the United States so as to avoid having to face him. In October 1947 he committed suicide, which was a great shock to Winston and Clementine, who had come to regard Gil as a valued friend.

Randolph and Pam would also be divorced (in December 1945). Days after the court hearing, Pam took young Winston down to stay with his Digby grandparents at Minterne in Dorset, before flying to New York, where – she told friends – Ed Murrow proposed to her and she accepted. Janet Murrow was still in London where she had given birth to a child, Casey, in early November. Murrow flew back to London, ostensibly to tell Janet that he wanted a divorce, and Pam flew to Palm Beach to stay with the Kennedys, whom she knew well from her debutante season when Joseph Kennedy had been American Ambassador to England. The Ambassador was not popular, but his good-looking, sociable children had made a great impression on the social scene and Pam became good friends with Kathleen, always called 'Kick', who was the same age.

Kick had recently suffered a tragedy. During her time in England before the war, when she was eighteen, she had fallen in love with twenty-year-old Billy Cavendish (Lord Hartington, heir of the Duke of Devonshire), but when war was imminent, in 1939, her father insisted Kick return with him and the rest of the family to the USA. She had little alternative but to obey. The couple still loved each other, and they wrote constantly for two years. The war, and Kick's parents' insistence that she must not marry out of the Catholic Church (the Cavendishes were staunch Church of England), seemed to put marriage out of the question. When in June 1943 Kick heard that Billy had become engaged to a niece of Lord Mountbatten's, she was convinced he was still in love with her. So she took matters into her own hands, joined a Red Cross war programme and sailed for England. Kick's hunch was correct; Billy still loved her and the pair became secretly engaged. At this point the Cavendishes, realising how much the couple still cared for each other after five years apart, withdrew their opposition. And without committing himself, Joseph Kennedy (who was in the middle of an adulterous affair) made a generous settlement on his daughter so that she need never be dependent on the Cavendish family. Kick's mother Rose, however, remained implacably against the proposed marriage on religious grounds.

Nonetheless, on 6 May 1944 and after many vicissitudes the couple married, with just one member of Kick's family in attendance, her elder brother Joe Kennedy Jnr who was serving with the USAF in England. Kick and Billy had just a few weeks' honeymoon before Billy returned to his regiment for the D-Day offensive, plus another few weeks when Billy got some leave. In August Joe Kennedy Jnr was killed while flying a top-secret mission.* Kick immediately wangled a place on a military flight to the USA so as to be with her parents. It was while she was there that she received news that Billy had been shot and killed while leading his men in a charge in Belgium. She and Billy had spent only five weeks together since their marriage.

It was five months afterwards that Pam visited Kick at Palm Beach. When she heard the news about Murrow's proposal, she was pleased for Pam. In the event, either Janet Murrow talked her husband round or when he saw her with their baby son he could not bring himself to ask for a divorce. About a week later, he sent Pam a cable which read simply, CASEY WINS.

But there is something in this account that doesn't quite add up. It appears that Murrow had already made his decision back in October, shortly before Casey's birth. Then he had written to Janet, apologising for taking her too much for granted, and (this was also written a few days before their tenth wedding anniversary) had added the words: 'Let's renew the contract . . . and I should like an indefinite option.'[23]

---

*Joseph Kennedy Jnr was piloting a plane packed with explosives, from which he was to have ejected (to be picked up later) before it reached its target on the enemy coast. However, the plane detonated in the air.

Pam, though, had evidently believed Murrow was serious when he asked her to marry him, for she had told her hosts about her engagement almost as soon as she arrived in Palm Beach, and her family knew about it too. So she was not only devastated to be abandoned by Murrow, but embarrassed. She left the Kennedys earlier than planned. But her visit had made more of an impact on them than she had realised at the time. She was a different person in 1945 from the plump eighteen-year-old they had met in London seven years earlier; she was now a beauty with an engaging personality, and as well as her Churchill connections she had acquired many important contacts in America, which made the Kennedy brothers regard her with renewed respect. Her relationship with the Kennedy family would provide one of the foundation blocks of her future life, but at the time Pam could think only of how cruelly she had been abandoned by Murrow.

When she arrived back in England she found Averell Harriman also there. He had recently ended his ambassadorial mission in Russia and Pam needed consoling. Within a fortnight their old relationship was reignited.

Mary, whom history would show to have been the real achiever of Winston and Clementine's children, had what was afterwards often referred to as 'a good war'. She began work in the Auxiliary Territorial Service quietly and without fuss, and she worked her way to the rank of junior commander (roughly the equivalent of major), never expecting or asking for advantageous treatment. Unlike Randolph she never traded on her father's position; indeed it is likely her parentage was a disadvantage with her superiors, who hesitated to promote her lest it appear they were currying favour. She served in England and Belgium, and eventually in Germany; the personification of a pretty young Englishwoman – intelligent, well mannered and extraordinarily wholesome. After meeting her in her tailor-made uniform, Laura Charteris said that Mary could easily be the perfect model for an ATS poster. For a good part of the war she was stationed with the anti-aircraft gun site in Hyde Park, where Churchill would sometimes pay informal visits. Little

Winston was also taken by his nanny to see this remarkable aunt who appeared to own four huge guns, and was thus to him a very important person indeed. Late in the war Mary's unit was moved to the Kent coast with a battery charged with providing the first line of defence against the flying bombs.

Devoted to her parents, the last 'kitten' in the nest, she returned to Chequers whenever she had leave. Only once or twice did Mary cause her mother any concern, and that was when she was attracted to men Clementine considered unsuitable. One was an English aristocrat to whom Mary became briefly engaged; and the other a handsome young Frenchman. But she was never rebellious like Sarah, so her mother's opinions were heeded instead of driving her in the opposite direction, and she quietly ended the relationships. When Clementine visited Russia for six weeks, to be thanked, fêted and decorated for the outstanding work she had done during the war as chairman of the Red Cross Aid to Russia Fund, she confidently left Mary in charge of Winston's care.

Consuelo and Jacques returned to France briefly soon after Paris was liberated. Their Paris house, which had been used by German officers, was now loaned to the British government as a rest house for British servicewomen. The chateau at Saint Georges-Motel was filled with several hundred displaced persons, who caused more damage in those few months than the Germans did during the entire war. But it was only cosmetic; the chateau and most of its furnishings and artwork – almost miraculously, it seemed – were preserved. Consuelo's biographer[24] suggests that this was mainly thanks to the Balsans' former major-domo, Basil Davidoff, a White Russian who before the war had run all their properties including the one in Paris and Lou Seuil.* He ensured that everything ran smoothly and luxuriously for family and guests, and no bedroom was ever without the favourite flowers or soap of the guest occupying it; bridge or golfing partners

---

*Lou Seuil was leased on a handshake between Jacques and an expat American in 1943. The tenant insisted they had agreed on ten years' occupancy, and after the war he refused to move out. The ever faithful Davidoff moved into the outbuildings there to keep an eye on the property.

of his or her level were always available to a visitor, no request was deemed too outlandish. A fierce supporter of the Tsar, Davidoff had himself been displaced by the Bolsheviks, and he hoped the Nazis would succeed in their attack on Russia. Meanwhile, he was happy enough to remain at the chateau, continuing to keep it running for the Luftwaffe officers who moved in within days of the Balsans' leaving. He won their confidence and even dined with them. However, he remained totally loyal to his employers and his chief aim throughout the Occupation, aided by Hoffman the butler who hailed from Luxembourg and spoke fluent German, was to preserve the chateau intact for the Balsans' return. Although Hoffman was once accused of being a spy,* no activities he might have engaged in affected the running of the house. The German occupants, many of whom were aristocrats or upper-class, were not disposed to allow it to be pillaged. Hermann Goering visited, and though he was notorious for picking up works of art he left Saint Georges-Motel empty-handed.

It is difficult to know what Consuelo expected, but she was deeply upset by her first postwar visit to France. Initially she refused to see the chateau, which must have disappointed Davidoff and Hoffman. She was never able to forget the way she and Jacques had had to leave it, and, she told her niece Diana Guest (daughter of Winston and Sunny's cousin Freddie Guest), she could never rid herself of the thought of 'jackboots in the corridors and Germans living in the rooms that she and Jacques had so lovingly furnished'.[25] She now had her favourite pieces removed from the chateau and shipped them to the USA, while a Renoir, *La Baigneuse*, was sold to aid poor and orphaned French children. She never returned to live at Saint Georges-Motel and it eventually passed to Diana Guest.† Consuelo and Jacques spent their remaining years in the USA, moving between their houses in New England and Palm Beach, each of which, decorated throughout in French

---

*In fact Louis Hoffman was anti-German and it is known that he passed on minor pieces of information to the local Resistance. He was briefly imprisoned but allowed to go free after an inquiry, aided by Davidoff's evidence. After the war he married Consuelo's maid, Anne.
†Parts of the property still remain in the ownership of the Guest family.

Diana's second marriage, to Duncan Sandys, lasted for many years until his womanising drove her to depression, with fatal results. (Getty)

Sarah meets Randolph as he disembarks from the *Queen Mary*, Sept 1936. (Getty)

Randolph's intervention failed and Sarah married Vic Oliver in December 1936, after which they sailed aboard the *Aquitania* for England. (Getty)

Winston and Jack with their sons John (at the back) and Randolph (foreground). (Getty)

Pamela Digby attracted men like a magnet.
(Mary Evans Picture Library)

Randolph and Pamela had only known each for a few days when he proposed. This was taken shortly after their marriage in 1939.
(Corbis)

Pamela and 'young Winston'. (Churchill Archives)

Winston during what he called 'the wilderness years' of the 1930s. (Churchill Archives)

Winston and President Roosevelt – the beginning of 'the special relationship' between the two nations. (Churchill Archives)

When people could not get home to listen to one of Winston's broadcasts, they would go to a pub or stand outside a radio shop. Here is one such group in Islington. (Churchill Archives)

Clementine and Eleanor Roosevelt. Both played important roles during the war. (Churchill Archives)

LEFT: Winston and Brendan Bracken leave No. 10. Initially, Clementine disliked Brendan when he failed to deny rumours that he was Winston's illegitimate son, but later he proved his loyalty and she came to trust him as a Churchill insider. (Churchill Archives)

All the Churchill children were involved in the war effort. Mary ran a gun emplacement in Hyde Park for most of the war. (Churchill Archives)

Mary accompanied her father to Canada as an ADC during the first Quebec Conference in 1943. Here they are pictured at Niagara Falls. (Getty)

Hundreds of thousands gathered on VE Day, all wanting to touch and cheer Winston. Within weeks he was voted out of power. (Getty)

Sarah with her husband Antony
Beauchamp in 1949. Her parents
disliked him intensely.
(Churchill Archives)

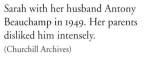

Randolph and Diana walking in Fleet Street,
London. (Corbis)

Randolph and Young Winston
represented Sir Winston when
he was made an honorary citizen
of the United States by President
Kennedy. Winston was only the
second person in history to be so
honoured; the first was Lafayette.
(Getty)

Clementine, Anthony Eden, Clarissa and Winston on
Clarissa's wedding day in the garden at Number 10.
(Getty)

Sarah found real happiness with
husband number four, Henry,
23rd Baron Audley, but their
marriage was destined to be
tragically short. (Getty)

Churchill returns from Moscow in August 1942 to be warmly greeted by Clementine. (Churchill Archives)

Winston and Clementine in the garden at Chartwell with their grandchildren. (Getty)

Winston and Clementine, travelling to the East End by launch during the Battle of Britain when the city streets were impassable. Their body language tells us all there is to know about what they meant to each other. (Churchill Archives)

Winston seems helpless with laughter in this informal shot taken at a meeting of the Woodford Conservative fête in 1956. (Churchill Archives)

The Churchills take the sun at La Pausa. (Getty)

Emery and Wendy Reves. A rare photo of the couple who ran La Pausa, their luxurious Mediterranean villa, around Winston's whims. (© University of Texas Press)

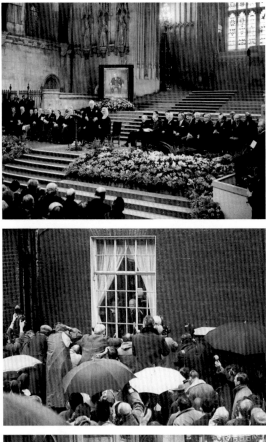

Westminster Hall. On Winston's eightieth birthday, members of Parliament presented him with a portrait by Graham Sutherland, one of the greatest living painters. Churchill loathed the painting and Clementine arranged for it to be secretly destroyed. (Churchill Archives)

Winston's ninetieth birthday – crowds of well-wishers called all day long. Winston, beautifully turned-out, waved but he was nearing the end of his long road. (Getty)

30 January 1965. Sir Winston's coffin is borne from St Paul's Cathedral after the funeral service. (PA/PA Archive/Press Association Images)

chateau style, was like a small piece of France; they invariably spoke French to each other and to their servants.

Consuelo's son Bert, the 10th Duke, was often described as having stepped from the pages of a P.G. Wodehouse novel. Essentially the product of an Edwardian upbringing, he dressed, acted and spoke accordingly, often adding 'What, what?' to the end of his sentences. Unlike his father, however, he made a very stable marriage, and the palace was filled during his stewardship of it with laughter and children playing. At the end of the Second World War the Ministry of Works provided a redecoration service, repainting and reflooring to repair the ravages of Blenheim's wartime occupation. When Bert and Mary began to entertain again, post-war rationing would not allow over-lavishness, and Noël Coward recalled that when he visited he was frozen the whole time because no coal was available for fires in the guest rooms. However, the main problem – for which the Ministry of Works abdicated responsibility – was the roof, which was so decrepit in places that rain poured into the attics. The south-east tower was also badly damaged. The estate could not afford the necessary repairs, and so the options available seemed to be either to hand the palace over to the National Trust (who could not afford it, either), or to sell it to the highest bidder.

It was Bert himself, Wodehousian caricature or not, who came up with a solution that suited the mid-twentieth century: he would open up the palace to the public. It would become a tourist attraction, and the half-crowns paid would help to keep the fabric of the palace in good repair. 'In such a way alone,' Consuelo wrote, 'could taxation be met and the upkeep of so large a house assured.' In the event it was almost five years before the property was restored to a state suitable to effect this plan, but it was a success from the start. Over a hundred thousand tourists visited Blenheim in the opening year. By the end of the twentieth century half a million visitors a year came to view the treasures that had once awed the young Churchill wives such as Jennie Jerome and Consuelo Vanderbilt. Part of it remains the home of the Marlborough family and the extended Churchill family.

*

Amidst feverish anticipation in Britain on 1 May 1945 that victory would be proclaimed at any minute, Jock Colville recorded in his diary that Churchill was dining that evening with Max Beaverbrook. 'In the middle of dinner I brought in the sensational announcement, broadcast by Nazi wireless, that Hitler had been killed today at his post in the Reich Chancellery in Berlin.'[26] At this moment of high excitement, Winston had a few family problems that he could only share with Clementine by letter, as she was still in Russia. First, he was upset and worried about his brother Jack, who had collapsed with a heart attack while visiting Weymouth Yacht Club with his son Peregrine. Second, Nellie had been to see him 'in deep anxiety about Giles', who with the other *prominenti* had been removed from the prisoner-of-war camp in Germany a few hours before the liberating Americans had arrived and taken to an unknown destination, no doubt as hostages. 'There is nothing to be done,' Winston wrote to Clementine. 'It would add to their danger if we show we minded.'[27]

By the following week it was discovered that Giles was safe, but although Jack was making some progress and Winston was able to spend time with him most days, he was still 'very ill', Winston reported, 'and the next few days are critical and possibly decisive'. This is almost certainly the reason behind his comment: 'It is astonishing that one is not in a more buoyant frame of mind in public matters. During the last three days we have heard of the death of Mussolini and Hitler; Alexander has taken a million prisoners of war; Montgomery took 500,000 additional yesterday and more than a million today . . . I need scarcely tell you that beneath these triumphs lie poisonous politics and deadly international rivalries.'[28]

Hostilities in Europe formally ceased on 8 May, which was declared Victory in Europe Day. Clementine had not been able to leave Russia to return as quickly as she had wanted to, much as she longed to be with Winston on this day of days. She had to content herself with a cable which read: ALL MY THOUGHTS ARE WITH YOU ON THIS SUPREME DAY MY DARLING STOP IT COULD NOT HAVE HAPPENED WITHOUT YOU.

At three o'clock that afternoon Winston broadcast to the nation from Downing Street, then drove to the House of Commons through the dense crowds who had gathered in their tens of thousands to see him and celebrate the victory. His open car had no need of its engine that day, propelled as it was by the pressure of the jubilant throng. Everyone wanted to shake his hand. He beamed, enjoying every minute. Just as he was about to leave Westminster to drive to the Palace he sent his detective scurrying back to Downing Street to get him a cigar. He did not wish to smoke it, he said, but he must have one – 'They expect it.'[29] Before climbing into the car he paused and lit it, while the crowds cheered themselves hoarse. After visiting the King he returned to Downing Street and appeared on the balcony at the Ministry of Health, where he told the roaring mass, 'This is *your* victory', then conducted them while they sang 'Land of Hope and Glory'. They could not get enough of him.

Later, when his car could not get through the crowds he ignored his detective's advice and walked to Whitehall, mobbed every step of the way until finally he had to climb on to the roof of a car. Later he appeared on the balcony once again. It was dark now, but even after he had delivered an impromptu speech to them the crowds would not let him retire. He had an inspiration. Signalling for a lull, he told them: 'Listen, I am going to recite a verse of "Rule, Britannia!" and then you are going to sing it.' Then he raised his arms and spoke the first lines. The crowd sang their hearts out, and as they finished Winston raised his hand in a V sign and retired. Theatre, yes; and Winston was as moved as anyone present.

On 18 May Churchill wrote to Clement Attlee, who had been Deputy Prime Minister during the last three years of the war, asking him to preserve the coalition government until the war in Japan was won. Three days later Attlee replied, refusing the request: he had no desire to continue in peacetime under an autocratic Churchill, any more than Winston wanted to enter once more into the knockabout of adversarial party politics where all too often nothing is achieved. Five days later Winston went to the Palace and tendered his resignation. The King then recalled him and asked him to form a Conservative government while a general election was called. There can be no question that Churchill was not only immensely popular and trusted, and viewed as the saviour of Britain – he was virtually idolised by more than half the population. But as leader of the Conservative Party he represented a way of life that was out of step with the times. The war had changed lives and expectations dramatically, and the working-class majority now believed that the Labour Party was more likely to provide them with a greater share of the good things in life than the old public-school class who led the Tory Party. Some voters did not even realise that by voting for a local Labour candidate they were voting Churchill out of office.

The country went to the polls on 5 July, but because many men and women were still serving abroad in the armed forces, three weeks were to be allowed for their votes to be returned for counting. Meanwhile Winston ran the country as before, now trying to win the peace. In June he replied to President Truman who had written complaining about de Gaulle, agreeing with him that 'after five long years of experience' of the belligerent Frenchman 'I am convinced [he] is the worst enemy of France in her troubles . . . I consider General de Gaulle is one of the greatest dangers to European peace. No one has more need than Britain of French friendship, but I am sure that in the long run no understanding will be reached with General de Gaulle.'[30]

Every pundit forecast that the Conservatives would win by between fifty and a hundred seats, and in confident frame of mind Churchill took Clementine and Mary, Jock Colville and Lord Moran on holiday to Hendaye in the South of France, near the Spanish border. They stayed at the luxurious seaside villa of Brigadier-General Brutinel, who owned the Château Margaux vineyard and had somehow managed to remain in France throughout the Occupation. Churchill spent the two weeks bathing from the sandy beach, Colville records, floating 'like a benevolent hippo in the middle of a large circle of French policemen who had duly donned bathing suits for the purpose',[31] and painting, while the rest of the party visited the local sights at St-Jean-de-Luz, Biarritz and Bayonne. The Duff Coopers joined them for a few days.

After attending what was to be the final meeting of the Big Three (the USA represented this time by Truman)* at Potsdam, with Mary in attendance, Churchill flew back to London on 25 July. When he, Mary and Clementine dined *en famille* at the Downing Street annexe he was low-spirited and anxious. Early next day he woke suddenly, 'with a sharp stab of almost physical pain,' he wrote. 'A hitherto subconscious conviction that we were beaten broke forth and dominated my mind.' In that moment he sensed that 'the power to shape the future would be denied me'.[32]

By the time he joined Beaverbrook and Brendan Bracken in the map room at the annexe, where arrangements had been made to flash up the election results on to a screen, the first results were already coming through. It was at once evident that the votes of those in the armed forces had veered left, giving an unexpected landslide victory to the Labour Party. Even Attlee was taken by surprise: he had expected, even hoped for, at best a Tory majority of about forty. Churchill retained his own seat, of course – the result was one of the first in – but Clementine immediately scented danger when his majority was reduced to 17,000, for she knew his opponent to be a very ineffectual man. Randolph and Duncan Sandys lost their seats at Preston and Norwood respectively – they embodied the type of MP that the working classes no longer wanted as their parliamentary representatives. Friends and family began arriving at the annexe looking 'dazed and grave'. Mary recalls the 'Stygian gloom' in which they lunched, everyone forcing their food down, including Brendan Bracken who had just learned he had lost his seat, and Sarah looking beautiful and distressed. Clementine 'maintained an inflexible morale'; Winston was 'robust and controlled' as he 'struggled to accept this terrible blow . . . not for one moment in this awful day did Papa flinch or waver. "It is the will of the people,"[33] he replied to anyone who attempted to commiserate.'

When Clementine, thinking about Winston's health and the stress under which he had been working, voiced her opinion that 'it may be a blessing in disguise', her hurt and disappointed husband growled:

---

*Franklin D. Roosevelt died 12 April 1945. Winston had seen him a few weeks earlier when he had been told by Dr Wilson (Lord Moran) that the President looked very ill and would not live much longer.

'At the moment it seems quite effectively disguised.'[34] He was feeling the pain of being rejected by a people to whom he had directed his every thought for the last five years. The Labour Party campaign had cleverly presented him as 'a great war leader', with the emphasis on war – with abilities not needed in peacetime. The war in the Far East was still unfinished. But Winston was now seventy, and he felt that from being one of the most powerful men in the world, all that lay ahead for him was a slide into a useless old age.

Clementine, sensibly, had considered what might happen if the Conservatives were not voted in. Months previously she had earmarked a possible future London base for them, at 28 Hyde Park Gate in Kensington. Winston had seen it and liked it. For her a period of frantic work would now begin to rebuild a normal home life for her shattered and weary husband. All Winston had to do was to make a final broadcast to the nation, to thank them for 'the unflinching, unswerving support which they have given me during my task, and for the many expressions of kindness which they have shown towards their servant'.[35]

The Aftermath

Traditionally, an outgoing Prime Minister must vacate 10 Downing Street within twenty-four hours. Not truly expecting to have to leave, the Churchills had not started packing, and on the morning after the result was announced there was much activity. But for Winston the most noticeable thing was the removal of the paraphernalia of power. 'The Map Room was deserted; the Private office empty; no official telegrams, no "red boxes".'[1] Jock Colville, in his capacity of Private Secretary to the Prime Minister (and now as much Churchill family friend), had been obliged to attend on the new PM.

Apart from Clementine, other family members attempted to offer love and support: Mary, Sarah, Diana and Duncan, and Jack – who looked wan and ill. Close friends and allies Anthony Eden and Brendan Bracken called in. But the fact was that Winston's career had come to a juddering halt; it was almost as shocking and grievous to him as when he was forced to quit the Admiralty during the Great War. Later, former staff, senior civil servants, chiefs of staff, secretaries, typists, cipher clerks, detectives, who had virtually lived with Churchill throughout the conflict, called to say their farewells. And it could only enhance the sense that this was a wake. The stream of callers continued at Chequers that weekend. Most were stunned and silenced by the events of the last few days, hardly able to find words of comfort. Fifteen people sat down to the final dinner at Chequers, and afterwards they all signed the visitors' book. Winston signed last of all, and under his signature he dramatically wrote the word 'Finis'.

He did not spend much time licking his wounds, and never did he do so in public. Everywhere he went he was still cheered and clapped, and when he and Clementine attended a Noël Coward play, at which he was noted in the press as 'roaring with laughter', he was given a prolonged standing ovation. There was no doubting the public affection for him, but he felt deeply the hurt of not being considered capable of running a peacetime government. The impish twinkle, which his friends knew preceded his famous sallies, was temporarily extinguished, but he always acknowledged the acclaim with a smile, if sometimes bleak, and raised his hand in the V-for-victory sign.

On 1 August he took his seat on the Opposition benches and prepared to oppose. He was back in the wilderness and with only occasional flashes of the old Churchill – which should, nevertheless, have warned his foes that the old man might be down, but he was not out. He consistently opposed what he considered were the excesses of the 'welfare state' being introduced despite the country being almost bankrupt; 'strength through misery,' he called it. 'What is the use of being a famous race and nation if at the end of the week you cannot pay your housekeeping bills?' His successor Attlee, whom he did not personally dislike although his meekness frequently irritated him, he described as 'a modest man, and I know no one with more to be modest about'. Of Sir Stafford Cripps, who filled the post of Chancellor of the Exchequer, a position Churchill had once held, he quipped: 'There but for the grace of God, goes God.'

On the day after the election defeat they woke up with nowhere to live, and Clementine knew it was up to her to sort out this problem. Diana came to the rescue. She and Duncan offered to move into a rented flat and lend Winston and Clementine their home in Westminster Gardens. This would enable the completion of the purchase of 28 Hyde Park Gate,* and for the necessary alterations

---

*The Churchills also purchased 27 Hyde Park Gate and made an internal link between the two houses. Number 27 became Churchill's secretariat. The top floor was furnished as a self-contained flat and rented out to provide income.

and decorating to be done there. Meanwhile, with Miss Hamblin and Cousin Moppet, Clementine began on Chartwell, where to her annoyance they discovered that mice had nested and eaten their way through damask cushions and that moths had attacked the hampers of curtains and linen so carefully packed away five years earlier. She was furious to learn, Mary said, that while humans had been strictly rationed, these fifth-columnist mice and moths had 'gorged themselves on our curtains'.[2]

Despite the mask of acceptance that Churchill presented to the world, Clementine found him hard to cope with during those months. She begged Mary, when it was rumoured that her regiment, which was serving in Germany, might be disbanded, to get a transfer into the War Office and come to live with them at Hyde Park Gate. 'I am very unhappy & need your help with Papa,' she wrote. 'I cannot explain how it is but in our misery we seem, instead of clinging to each other to be always having scenes. I'm sure it's all my fault, but I'm finding life more than I can bear. He is so unhappy & that makes him very difficult . . .'[3]

The Japanese surrender on 14 August, after the assault on Hiroshima and Nagasaki with the atom bomb, persuaded Churchill that he could now take a holiday. He went to the Italian Lakes with Sarah and they stayed in a marble villa with a few young officers as ADCs to keep them company. During this time Winston painted and swam and rested, never opened a newspaper, and within a few weeks this regimen seemed to put matters into perspective for him. As always, as soon as they were parted, Winston and Clementine missed each other. Sarah wrote that he frequently spoke of Clementine, and wished she were with them. His letters to her, in which he acknowledged that a great load had been lifted from him – 'It may all indeed be "a blessing in disguise",' he finally admitted – were especially affectionate: 'My darling I think a great deal of you, & last night . . . there came into my mind your singing to me "In the gloaming" years ago. . . . my heart thrilled w[ith] love to feel you near me in thought. I feel so tenderly towards you my darling, & the more pleasant and agreeable the scenes & days, the more I wish you were here to share them & give me a kiss.'[4]

Clementine managed to get Hyde Park Gate ready for Winston's return, and by some miracle she had also tweaked Chartwell into a semblance of pre-war life. Domestic help was impossible to find, with young people either still serving in the armed forces or working for better wages in factories, so this was no easy achievement. Rationing was tougher now than during the war years.* Churchill was appalled when first confronted with the weekly food allowance, for rationing had never touched him personally in the rarefied atmosphere of No. 10.

It was the following year that Lord Camrose, an old friend, learned that Churchill was being forced to consider selling Chartwell because he could no longer pay the costs of running it. Appalled that the man who had saved Europe might be driven out of the home he loved, Camrose approached some rich businessmen who anonymously put up the money to buy the property. The fund was placed in a trust to enable Winston and Clementine to live at Chartwell until the end of their lives, when it would be handed over to the National Trust. This was a relief to Clementine, but though Churchill was grateful for this solution to his problems there was a small worm in the apple for him because he had always intended Chartwell to go after his death to Randolph, and then on to little Winston – like a mini-Blenheim. The trust put an end to that dream.

Ironically, within a year or so, by his own efforts Winston became a rich man. He was commissioned to write a six-volume history of the Second World War, for which he received a massive advance and which, together with world syndication rights for his *History of the English-Speaking Peoples*, meant that the Churchills from then on would be able to live in the sort of luxury they had never previously envisaged. His impressive command of the English language allied to his grasp of the course of the war, plus the details of his personal concerns as the war unfolded, made this highly engaging series a bestseller for which he would be awarded the Nobel Prize for Literature in 1953. His prose was especially readable because he did

*Rationing did not end until the early 1950s. Food was rationed in Britain longer than in any other country.

not set out to write great literature, but to inform and entertain. 'Short words are best,' he once said, 'and the old words when short are best of all.' There is a story that he was once asked to read the draft of a speech written by an American general. He told the general that in his opinion there were 'too many passives and too many zeds' (such as 'systemize'). Asked to explain further, he replied: 'What if, instead of "We shall fight on the beaches" I had said, "Hostilities will be engaged with our adversary on the coastal perimeter"?' There were some adverse criticisms, of course: in his war memoirs he was accused of presenting a one-sided view of some incidents, to his own advantage. One wonders how many writers of memoirs do *not* present incidents from their own perspective. And anyway, surely anyone who bought Churchill's book wished to read about his experiences first-hand, rather than the accounts written by some of his contemporaries, who jumped into print to write history as they saw it from the sidelines?

Some years later, Winston would make much of his pride in the fact that he had earned his living 'by his pen'. His writing was to occupy him full-time during the immediate postwar years, and also saw him through many family dramas and traumas. Later, as neighbouring properties came up for sale, he was able to buy Chartwell Farm and Parkside Farm to the south of Chartwell, as well as Bardogs Farm on nearby Toys Hill, to increase his estate.

In 1946, while on a three-month visit to the United States,* he and Clementine paid a visit to Hyde Park, the former home of President Roosevelt, who had died a year earlier. Churchill was showered with public honours and given a ticker-tape parade in New York. They spent some weeks in Palm Beach, where they had been loaned a house. When they visited Consuelo there, even the Churchills found the Balsans' lavish French lifestyle astonishing after the grimness of postwar utilitarian Britain. And if Churchill noted the excess of it, it is certain that it was truly luxurious. When they returned home Mary had been demobbed and, to Clementine's relief, had decided to come

---

*At Fulton, Missouri, he delivered his stirring speech warning about the threat from Russia: 'From Stettin in the Baltic to Trieste in the Adriatic, an iron curtain has descended across the Continent . . .'

and live with them. Clementine was made a Dame Grand Cross of the British Empire in the Birthday Honours list, in recognition of her extensive work during the war.* She chose, however, not to use her title and preferred to be addressed as 'Mrs Churchill'.

Winston had recovered his confidence now, and was in attack mode in Parliament. With Anthony Eden as his heir presumptive, he prowled and threatened from the Opposition benches. The extremely able and thoroughly decent Eden had now become, to Randolph's dismay, a sort of substitute son. Randolph had assumed he would succeed to his father's position by 'birthright', he had let it be known, and now began to indulge in yet more displays of drunken excess, which caused Noël Coward to quip: 'dear Randolph, utterly unspoiled by failure'. Although his childhood fantasy of becoming Prime Minister still prevailed, almost everything he did and said made such an event ever less likely. Even the widespread affection for his father could not prevent him being blackballed when he applied to join the Beefsteak Club (an after-theatre dining club). He had stormed out of the Paris Embassy when Duff Cooper slapped him across the face twice for an ill-judged remark. When he accepted there was no hope of gaining a parliamentary seat, Randolph returned to journalism – for which he had a flair – visiting Russia to report on the Red Army parade. He had not given up trying to persuade Laura to marry him, and he knew her marriage was in trouble when he wrote to her in May 1946:

Laura darling,
This is just to thank you for last night . . . Every minute was . . . sheer enchantment. I only wish I could do one tenth as much for you as you did for me. I know beyond any doubt that I would like to spend my whole life with you. Please think about this before you make any plans. I love you my darling, more than ever . . . Bless you, your devoted, Randolph.[5]

---

*Clementine's wartime role, though overshadowed by Winston's, has been fully detailed in a remarkable biography of her written by her daughter Mary Soames. See *Clementine Churchill* (Penguin) 1981.

In the event, Laura's marriage to Lord Dudley would last in one form or another for a further ten years, but by then Randolph was not available and she subsequently married a young American, Michael Canfield. She would never have married Randolph anyway; she valued his friendship, and there is no doubt that she held him in great affection and was happy to sleep with him from time to time, but she told friends she was never in love with him and that he wanted and needed a mother rather than a wife. Yet eventually she *would* marry into the Churchill family.

Pam was out of the country at this time, which had its benefits; allowing little Winston, with his new governess twenty-year-old Kathleen Gilbert, to spend time at Chartwell and Minterne so that both sets of grandparents saw a good deal of him.

Although Winston kept a team of five secretary/typists busy all day and well into the night ('I shall need two women tonight,' he would tell his Private Secretary), Miss Gilbert recalled her surprise at how 'humble' the former Prime Minister seemed when he met her, shook hands with her and welcomed her to Chartwell. There were other signs of innate 'niceness' – after one visit he gave her his autograph for her father, and for herself the gift of a five-pound note: 'That was a fortune to me – like a hundred pounds today.'[6] One day when she was walking with Sir Winston and little Winston in the gardens, a small boy appeared. 'Hello, who are you?' Churchill asked. 'I'm the third gardener's son, Johnny.' 'Well, Johnny, I'm Winston Churchill; pleased to meet you.' And the great man solemnly shook the child's hand.[7] Little Winston, who used to help his Churchill grandfather bricklaying and pottering at Chartwell, and accompany his Digby grandfather – who was a dairy farmer – on a daily milk delivery round, claimed that had he ever been asked the occupations of his grandfathers, he would have answered that one was a bricklayer and one was a milkman.

When not with his grandparents – in the absence of his mother, whose busy social life and frequent visits to the USA meant she was away from home a good deal – little Winston was cared for at Grosvenor Square by Kathleen Gilbert and the cook. Besides her maid who travelled with her, Pamela employed a dresser and a daily help. Averell Harriman sometimes loaned her his butler, and eventually the butler would come to work for Pamela full time. One of the first things Pam told Kathleen Gilbert about little Winston was 'Don't let him think he is important just because his name is Winston Churchill.'[8]

That summer Sarah had a successful London run in the melodrama *Gaslight*, after which she received an offer to appear in a film in Italy. She was tempted because her entanglement with Gil Winant was still causing her some embarrassment. The affair was long over as far as she was concerned, but she felt unable to tell Gil because he was such a close friend of Winston and Clementine. She hesitated because the Italians had so recently been the enemy. When she sounded out her father on this point, he told her: 'Go ahead, it is part of the victor's job to help the defeated.'[9] She had been there a month and had just completed ten days of shooting when she was struck down with a kidney infection. Her high temperature did not fall, and after a week the British Embassy notified the Churchills. Mary was asked to travel to Rome to care for her sister.

Mary, now twenty-four, privately thought her sister might have been safer without the benefit of her limited nursing skills, but – although she was delighted at the idea of an 'unexpected jaunt' – there was a situation of which her parents were not yet aware. During a recent visit to the British Embassy in Paris when she had accompanied her father, Mary had met Christopher Soames, an officer in the Coldstream Guards who was Assistant Military Attaché. There had been an instant attraction, and they arranged to meet in London during his next leave. This leave coincided with the date of Mary's departure for Rome, so Christopher offered instead to meet her in Paris, where she was to change trains. He put her on the Italian train and got into her compartment to chat, and to her confusion did not get out when the train began to move off. Confidently he told her that he was accompanying her to Rome. By the time they reached the Simplon Tunnel he had proposed – a curious re-enactment of the event in 1908 when, after becoming engaged to Clementine, as she left Oxford to go and tell her mother, Winston decided he could not be parted from her and jumped aboard the train.

Sarah recalled: 'When Mary arrived [in Rome], her flushed cheeks and excitement outdid what was left of my fever. She told me in breathless sentences that she had fallen in love.'[10] Sarah was over the worst of her infection, but her recovery was slow and she spent most days in bed. Mary knew she would have to stay on with her for some time but Christopher had to return to Paris within a few days, so they had only that brief time to get to know each other. The magic of being in Rome (where no food rationing was in force), free of the conventions that would have inevitably applied in London, where she was instantly recognisable, clearly speeded up what might otherwise have been a much longer courtship. After the dutiful grind of the war years, during which Mary had never put a foot wrong, she was suddenly catapulted into days of wine and roses with a handsome young officer, who sent flowers to both sisters and wrote a poem for Sarah. By the time Christopher left for Paris all doubts had resolved themselves; Sarah was captivated and Mary was left with the sticky problem of writing to tell her parents that she was engaged to be married to someone they had never met, and whose parents they did not know. Sarah wrote to them too, in sisterly support.

When Mary left for London Sarah went back to work, and celebrated her thirty-second birthday on the set. On the same day Vic married his third wife, Natalie. To her father Sarah wrote, 'Remember Chequers – when we knew all was finished finally and legally with Vic? You called me across the room and whispered in my ear: "Free!" I had no answer – for already I knew, already I was not.'[11] But the Winant affair, too, was now finally over – and although she does not say so in her memoirs, she must have written to tell him so. *Sinfonia fatale*, the film in which Sarah starred, won an Italian prize at the Lugano Festival, and she felt she could return to England. There she met Pam and Averell Harriman who were visiting Chartwell. Their relationship was now causing harmful gossip, and in September Max Beaverbrook took Pam aside and strongly recommended she part from Averell in order not to damage his career. He more or less ordered her to fly out to Jamaica and spend some time at his estate there.

In February 1947, Mary married Christopher Soames at the same church in Westminster where her parents had married almost forty years earlier. Although Clementine had been apprehensive about the proposed marriage, she had soon realised that Mary was not prepared to give Christopher up as she had with her previous relationships. Clementine and Winston soon took to him, indeed he quickly became a favourite with them both, his common sense and his good humour providing a mutually rewarding father–son relationship that had long been lacking in Churchill's life. Despite all that had happened over the years, Churchill had what he called 'a deep animal love' for Randolph, but by now even he was forced to acknowledge his son's many faults. 'Every time we meet we seem to have a bloody row,' he reflected.[12] Randolph once told his cousin Anita that he could not help his rages; the anger seemed to rise from his feet and take him over. If he could stop the process by total concentration, before this tide reached his knees, he told her, he could control himself, otherwise not. Alcohol, of course, destroyed any chance of self-control and also fuelled his sense of thwarted destiny. Christopher, by contrast, was uncomplicated; he admired his father-in-law unreservedly, without ever being too overawed to speak his mind.

While on honeymoon Christopher became ill with a duodenal ulcer, and Clementine flew out to help Mary care for him and bring him home. There were lots of jokes about mothers-in-law on honeymoons, but the episode helped to seal the relationship between Christopher and Clementine. His condition eventually necessitated his resignation from his regiment, and it was decided that he and Mary would move to the farm at Chartwell and run it, and that Christopher should enter politics. He and Winston would become very close friends and political allies. Jock Colville wrote that, without any malice or intrigue, or indeed any intention on Christopher's part, he stepped into the shoes 'so long destined for Randolph'.[13]

It was Christopher who encouraged a new passion in Winston's life: horse-racing. Winston would become a highly successful racehorse owner, and from 1949 he always had horses in training, racing under his father's old colours of pink and chocolate. It was a sport that he followed with enormous interest until the last year of his life. However, it was with the first horse he ever purchased, Colonist II, that Winston achieved his most spectacular successes. Colonist was a real stayer, and became one of the most popular horses in the country, every housewife following 'Winnie's horse'. The big-hearted grey powered his way to thirteen wins, including the prestigious Jockey Club Cup, the Winston Churchill Stakes and the Ribblesdale Cup at Royal Ascot; he was entered and placed twice in the Ascot Gold Cup. When, after the 1951 flat season, Colonist's trainer Walter Nightingale suggested that it was time to retire the horse and send him to stud, Winston is said to have replied: '[What?] . . . and have it said that the Prime Minister of Great Britain is living on the immoral earnings of a horse?'[14] Colonist was sold at auction in December that year and became a successful sire. When Churchill was once asked whether Colonist was still racing, he replied: 'No, he has given up racing. He is now rogering.'[15] One of Winston's greatest treats was to be invited to watch the racing from the Royal Box, which became a frequent occurrence.

At about the time of Mary's marriage Jack's health deteriorated dramatically. His doctor – the same who had treated Jennie in her final illness – was seventy-six years old, and Johnny unsuccessfully tried to persuade his father to call in a younger man. But Jack had great faith in the old physician, and would not have it. The fact was that although the family knew of Jack's heart condition, no one knew how ill he had been over the last decade, and it was a shock to them all when the doctor told them that Jack had suffered an aneurysm which could only be managed for a short time, and that his imminent death was inevitable. Three weeks after Mary's wedding, Johnny and Winston were with Jack as he lay dying one Sunday night – all three were in tears as they said goodbye. At the last, Johnny left his father and uncle together. For Winston, his brother's death was one of the great emotional blows of his life, and it is remarkable that he was able to perform his duties that week. He told Johnny that when his own father died he had been 'prostrate for a whole day and night'. And then, seeing his nephew's distress he said, 'Johnny, I will take your father's place. Come to me if you are in trouble. I will be your father.'[16]

In September that year Pam spent a holiday at Lismore, County Waterford, at the romantic Irish castle that had once belonged to Sir Walter Raleigh and now formed part of the Duke of Devonshire's estate. Among the fellow guests were Kick and Jack Kennedy, Hugh Fraser (who had once proposed to Pam) and Sir Anthony Eden. Kick, the widowed Marchioness of Hartington, was now living in England and had fallen in love with the multimillionaire Peter Fitzwilliam (the 8th Earl Fitzwilliam). A former SOE hero who had been awarded the DSO, Fitzwilliam also had an estate in Ireland. He was married, albeit by that time unhappily, for his wife was an alcoholic, but this was not considered sufficient grounds for divorce. Jack was the only member of the Kennedy family who knew about the relationship. Pam, having enjoyed an amusing flirtation with David Niven – to whom she always playfully referred as 'Niv the Spiv'[17] – was now involved in a casual affair with the devastatingly handsome Prince Aly Khan. She was a welcome and supportive confidante to Kick throughout that winter – and Kick needed a friend after she told her family that she was going to marry Fitzwilliam as soon as he could obtain a divorce. She met with a stony resistance. With the exception of her brother Jack and her father Joseph, who conceived a plan to ask the Pope for a dispensation, most of the family were appalled that Kick, who had already married out of the Catholic Church when she married Billy Cavendish, was now proposing to marry a divorced man – which was just as bad. Her mother turned her face from her and the two were never reconciled.

It was at Whitsun in mid-May 1948 that Pam drove Kick and Peter Fitzwilliam to Croydon Airport, where he had chartered an eight-seat, twin-engined De Havilland Dove. He and Kick had arranged to fly down to Cannes for the long weekend, and they pressed Pam to accompany them – at least as far as Paris, where they were meeting Beaverbrook's son Max and his wife Jane for lunch while the plane was serviced. But Pam had made other engagements for the holiday and had to decline the invitation. The following day, she heard on the radio that Peter and Kick had been killed instantly when their plane, en route from Le Bourget to Cannes, had crashed in low cloud during a storm in the Rhône valley. Peter, who was piloting the plane, had been advised by radio to turn back, but having flown in far worse conditions during the war he had evidently decided to press on to the good weather that was forecast not far ahead of their position. It was assumed at the inquest that he became disoriented and had flown into the side of a mountain (near the town of Privas).[18] Kick's mother's shocking remark on hearing of her death was that the fatal crash was 'God's way of pointing His finger at Kick and saying No!' The Devonshires, who had come to love Kick dearly, recovered her body and organised her burial in Edensor churchyard at Chatsworth in Derbyshire. The Duchess decided on the movingly brief epitaph: 'Joy she gave, Joy she had found'.

Pam attended the funeral, deeply distressed. It seemed somehow worse that Kick had managed to survive the war only to be cut down when she had found a new life. Randolph was there too, and when the mourners repaired to Chatsworth he tried to persuade Pam 'to give him a second chance'. Perhaps because she was distressed, Pam made the unlikely decision to do so. Her love affair with Aly Khan was coming to a natural conclusion by then; it had always been clear to the realist Pam that it would not last for ever, and Randolph found Pam wrong-footed. One short weekend at the country home of friends was enough to bring her rapidly to her senses; she returned to London, to collect little Winston and take him to his Digby grand-parents before flying to Château de l'Horizon.* She was still there in late summer, after Aly Khan had been introduced to the stunning movie star Rita Hayworth and fallen headlong in love with her. Pam felt no jealousy; she continued to visit the villa from time to time, and it was there that she met a new man, Giovanni ('Gianni') Agnelli, grandson of the founder of the Fiat motor empire.

---

*Winston enjoyed a number of painting holidays there during the Thirties, and Clementine visited a few times. The owner Maxine Elliott died in 1940 and at the end of the war the property was purchased by Prince Aly Khan.

Gianni turned up at Château de l'Horizon one day in a speedboat, found Pam alone, sunbathing, and the attraction was mutual and explosive. Unusually, for a woman who generally preferred older men, Gianni was slightly younger – twenty-seven to her twenty-eight – but Pam's relationship with the good-looking Italian playboy would last for over five years, longer than the time she had been married to Randolph. 'Pam adored Gianni', her brother Eddie told me, and despite agreeing to terminate a pregnancy by him in the first year of their relationship she believed they would eventually marry. Indeed, she converted to Catholicism and obtained an annulment of her marriage to Randolph, pleading the same mitigation as Consuelo: that she had been very young at the time of the marriage and that her unease about Randolph beforehand (confirmed by witness statements) had been overcome by his persuasion. Coincidentally, Gianni made a large donation to the Church at about the same time as the annulment was granted. However, he would never marry Pam: he was an orphaned Italian with four possessive sisters, the eldest of whom regarded Pam as a sort of she-devil, and they made it clear to him that, given Pam's reputation, she was not marriageable material.

For those five years Pam was Gianni's wife in all but name. She did not merely live with him as a mistress; she ran his homes, furnished them and presided over them as chatelaine, filling them with designer furnishings, works of art and banks of fresh flowers, and she entertained their guests. She knew almost everyone worth knowing throughout Europe, and she spoke fluent and accentless French. Many of those she invited to stay would never have met Gianni in the ordinary course of events, but would later prove to be invaluable contacts for him. He and Pam were seen everywhere together, and everywhere they were regarded as a couple. Although Pam was not accepted by Gianni's family, the Digbys liked and befriended him. Pam's two biographers were at pains to point out that everything she did during these years was financed by Gianni, that she 'got out of him' the money for the fabulous homes, the designer clothes, the jewels. In fact, it seems evident that he behaved exactly as any rich husband would have done, footing the bills for a wife who ran his homes beautifully and whom he wanted to see dressed and adorned in a manner that reflected his wealth and status.

Pam's brother would reflect that her education, like most girls of her class, focused entirely on how to look after and entertain men.[19] Pam was supreme at creating an impressive home that was also comfortable and welcoming. Gianni loved this. Entertaining was so natural to Pam that she could cater for a room full of people at an hour's notice and appear beautifully coiffed, gowned and totally unruffled. The pair did not spend their time exclusively in each other's company; Gianni had the family business to run in Turin, where his family made Pam feel very unwelcome. Pam, too, had her own commitments, not least to little Winston;* and she had a social life in Paris, where Gianni had bought an apartment. During these separations Gianni was not entirely faithful, but if she was aware of this Pam had decided not to notice. Her brother insisted, however, that whatever her two biographers suggested, 'while she was actually in a relationship Pam was never unfaithful to her lovers – in most cases it was the man who strayed while Pam was entirely focused on that man'. Towards the end of his life Gianni told Eddie that the years he spent with Pam were probably the happiest and most carefree of his life,[20] but because of his family's disapproval he never regarded her as marriageable.

The affair ended after Pam returned to their villa on the Riviera unexpectedly one night in the early hours and discovered Gianni with another woman. There was a spectacular row, and Gianni left hurriedly to drive his companion home. The two had met at a party where they had been drinking heavily and, Pam believed, Gianni had taken cocaine. As he drove at high speed along the Lower Corniche in the darkness, he ploughed into an unlit cart near the

---

*Her biographers implied that Pamela abandoned her son to enjoy her liaison with Gianni. This is not entirely true. Although young Winston certainly spent long holidays with his two sets of grandparents and with his father and stepmother, he also had regular holidays with his mother in Paris, on the Riviera at Gianni's villa, Château de la Garoup, and during the winter at St Moritz. Pam also visited young Winston at Le Rosey, his boarding school in Switzerland, chosen for its air, because he suffered from bad hay fever.

entrance to the Cap Roux tunnel. He and his passenger, as well as the driver of the cart, were seriously injured.[21]

A shocked Pam stayed with Gianni in the hospital at Cannes and oversaw his treatment over the next weeks. When septicaemia and ultimately gangrene set in – a scenario reminiscent of Jennie's final illness – he was told one of his legs must be removed. But unlike Jennie, Gianni was young and healthy; furthermore, antibiotics were now available. He refused amputation, opting instead for months of agonising treatments while the affected flesh was cut away. When he was moved to Florence, Pam was not allowed – since she was not his wife – to stay in the hospital, so she moved into a nearby hotel in order to be with him during the day. Meanwhile, his sisters did everything they could to exclude her. When Gianni was at last discharged from the hospital, his sisters collected him and took him to the family home in Turin to convalesce. Pam tried to visit but as usual was frozen out by Gianni's family. The sisters made a point of constantly introducing him to Italian girls whom they considered more suitable; eventually he fell in love with one of them and married her.*

By then Pam had regretfully accepted that they had come to the end of their relationship, but they were, at least, able to discuss it amicably. Gianni made a generous settlement, which included the deeds to an apartment adjoining his own in Paris.† Allegations by Pam's biographers that this arrangement was forced upon him by a weeping and desperate Pam seem to have emanated from his sisters. In fact, Pam *was* distressed by the break-up, but the couple were to remain affectionate friends for the remainder of her life. Later one of his sisters came to recognise that Pam was a true friend and a

---

*Princess Marella Caracciolo di Castagneto, an elegant half-American half-Neapolitan noblewoman once regarded as one of the best-dressed women in the world. She married Gianni on 19 November 1953 and gave birth to their only son Eduardo seven months later. Eduardo was never interested in Fiat, and grew into a sensitive and spiritual man. He committed suicide in Turin in 2000.

†Gianni died in January 2003 of prostate cancer. He owned the majority shareholding in Fiat and at one time controlled almost 5 per cent of Italy's GDP. He was renowned for his impeccable taste and dress sense (*Esquire* magazine once named him as one of the five best-dressed men in the world). His marriage did not curtail his womanising and he had many glamorous mistresses thereafter, including the film star Anita Ekberg and the American fashionista Jackie Rogers.

good influence on Gianni, and she used to stay with Pam. Gianni was a frequent guest at Pam's various homes: after her death he continued to visit her family in Dorset until shortly before he died.[22]

In December 1947, when Winston wanted to finish off a book without interruption and do some painting, he longed for warm sunshine and the well-being induced by a hot climate. Clementine, however, wished to spend Christmas in England with the family, so with full blessings, each did what they wanted to. Winston and Sarah went to Marrakech and stayed at the Mamounia Hotel, while Clementine stayed at home with Mary and Christopher, taking little Winston to a pantomime and lunching with Pam. The following year, unwilling to be parted from Clementine, Winston compromised on his hatred of the English winter cold by spending the Christmas of 1948 at Chartwell, then immediately afterwards leaving with Clementine and Sarah for the Hôtel de Paris at Monte Carlo.

When Sarah had arrived at Chartwell that December she had some surprising news to impart. Soon after the war she had met the war artist and photographer Antony Beauchamp in London. While she was successfully touring in the United States with *The Philadelphia Story* in the leading role, she had met him again and they had fallen in love. He was invited to join them in Monte Carlo. When he arrived on 2 January 1949, Winston and Clementine disliked him on sight, feeling he was not right for Sarah. The atmosphere was so bad whenever he was with them that to save Sarah's feelings Clementine made excuses and returned home early. Winston, Mary recalled, was 'resolutely hostile',[23] and the fact that he had caused Clementine to leave early and thus spoilt the holiday was yet another black mark against Antony.

Sarah stayed on with her father after Clementine left, and after a few days Antony departed. A few days later Winston went home too, after he and Sarah quarrelled. As a result of this unfortunate affair Sarah took umbrage against her parents, and they heard little from her throughout the spring and summer. So they were stunned in the autumn of that year to read in the newspapers that Sarah and Antony had married at Sea Island, Georgia. Sarah had been their favourite daughter, but several months were allowed to drift by before Clementine wrote to attempt a rapprochement by inviting Sarah and Antony to Chartwell.

The welcome was warm according to Sarah, and both Winston and Clementine worked overtime to make Antony feel part of their family; but they never took to him, and after a while Winston could not keep up the pretence. Clementine attempted to compensate for their estrangement by arranging for the trust set up by Winston from the proceeds of his writing to buy a house in Ebury Street in London that Sarah and Antony could use whenever they visited the UK. But for the next few years most contact between the Beauchamps and the Churchills would be by letter and phone. Sarah made a few flying visits to the UK, but she was kept fully occupied by her film, stage and TV work in America.

In January 1950 Winston and Clementine were on holiday in Madeira when news broke that a dissolution of Parliament had been announced in London. He returned home at once, by flying boat, while Clementine finished her holiday and came home later. Hardly was Churchill back than he plunged into preparations for a general election. In the event the Conservative Opposition, led by Winston, slashed the Labour majority from 168 seats to 6. This was not a governing majority; it was simply a matter of time before the country was forced to go to the polls again. At the next election on 26 October 1951, the Conservatives fought under the slogan 'A Strong Free Britain'.

Although there was a great sense of discontent – rationing remained in force and the country was tired and dispirited – at first the results were too close to call, and it was thought that the Labour Party might have again held on with a narrow majority. But as the returns from the provinces began coming in it was clear the Conservatives were making steady gains, and at 5.30 in the evening Attlee conceded defeat.

At the age of almost seventy-seven Winston became the second-oldest Prime Minister in the country's history, outstripped only by William Gladstone during Lord Randolph's time, who led his last government in 1892.

1952–5

A New Era

Three years before his father became Prime Minister for the second time, Randolph had remarried. His wife was June Osborne, daughter of Colonel Rex Osborne DSO MC. She was fair, fragile and a typical English beauty with the same colouring as Clementine. At twenty-six June was Randolph's junior by eleven years, and although never previously married she had been intimately involved with several literary figures.* After Randolph had accepted that Laura was never going to marry him he was a lonely man, desperate for a ménage of his own. So he went looking for a wife, just as he had before the war when he met Pam.

Although more mature than Pam had been, June was far less able to cope with Randolph's boisterous nature. She was a vulnerable and needy girl–woman, who evidently believed she saw in Randolph a strong male figure who would provide her with some stability. Randolph never ceased to love Laura, but he thought he could make marriage to June work. His friends looked on anxiously throughout an exceptionally stormy three-month courtship, during which at one point June, high on Benzedrine and wine (a mixture unwittingly administered by Randolph, who thought he was helping her over a cold), threatened to commit suicide and rushed off towards the Thames. When Randolph caught up with her on the

---

*Peter Quennell, Alastair Forbes and Cyril Connolly, among others.

Embankment, she attacked him, then called the police and accused him of indecent assault. They managed to recover from this incident, Randolph taking all the blame. At his request, Evelyn Waugh – who alternately loved and loathed Randolph (he claimed that once a year they broke off relations for ever) – wrote to June to tell her that he had known Randolph since before she was born 'and have always felt that he had a unique capacity for happiness, which one way and another has never been fully developed. I am sure you will be able to do this for him.' He finished with a perceptive observation: 'He is essentially a domestic and home-loving character who has never had a home.'[1]

Clementine may have had some sympathy with this view. She did not actually hate her son but she was never able to cope with his rude, unruly and argumentative nature, and there were times when she disliked his behaviour very much. She could not bear to be around him. A good deal of what his mother termed 'heated argument' Randolph would have dismissed as mere 'discussion': Winston could always tolerate a degree of this, although he liked it less as he grew older and his energy diminished. But Clementine's only defence was to see as little of Randolph as possible, and she often retired to the peace of her own room when her son visited. Randolph had been ordered to leave the house countless times after tempestuous scenes, and banned from ever returning on one or two occasions. He had himself stormed out several times, swearing never to return. He always did return, of course; at bottom, both parents still loved this difficult child.

It was on Randolph's behalf that Clementine wrote to Winston, who was staying with the Duke and Duchess of Windsor at Château de la Croë, Cap d'Antibes. Winston and Clementine had gone there together to celebrate their fortieth wedding anniversary, but Clementine had returned home early leaving Winston to paint and rest. It was a few years earlier that, with the income from his war memoirs, he had set up a trust for his children and grandchildren to compensate them for the loss of Chartwell. Now, in her capacity as chairman of the trust (the Prof and Brendan Bracken were two of the trustees), Clementine wrote to Winston saying that she wished to discuss 'the plan for the Chartwell Literary Trust to buy Randolph a house'. Randolph had just told her about his forthcoming marriage, that he hoped they would have children, and that he would also need room for little Winston to visit. This letter was written four weeks before Randolph's marriage to June at Caxton Hall on 2 November 1948. Winston and Clementine attended the wedding, and welcomed June warmly into their family. For these two ageing parents the hope was still alive that June could make a home for Randolph and introduce some peace into his unsettled life.

Randolph and June honeymooned in Biarritz at the home of a friend. When Diana Cooper went over to lunch with them, she saw at once that this couple were not attuned to each other. 'What did either of them do it for?' she asked Evelyn Waugh. 'Is security so precious to her? Of course it's not security. And he? Love doesn't seem to be a part of it at all.' But Evelyn replied that he had heard conflicting reports of the honeymooners, and other friends 'spoke of bliss'.[2] They returned to live in Catherine Place in Westminster, and Randolph continued to work as a journalist. But he had a dream of living in the country, and in the anticipation that the trust would buy him somewhere suitable, viewing country houses became a regular feature of their lives. Eleven months later, June produced a baby girl as beautiful as herself, to whom they gave a traditional Churchill name, Arabella.* Even before the child was born the marriage was tempestuous, and it would become worse, almost as though the couple fed on discord. There are glimpses of this strife throughout Evelyn Waugh's diaries and letters: 'Mrs Randolph Churchill is said to be treating him slightly more kindly. He is abject.'[3] Even Clementine became involved: 'Dearest June,' she wrote, 'I was very sad after I had read your letter and seen Randolph. Marriage strikes deep roots, and I pray that with you

---

*Said to be Winston's favourite granddaughter, Arabella Churchill became deb of the year in 1967. Later, as a convert to Buddhism, she married a professional juggler called Haggis and lived as what she called 'a hippy'. She was infinitely more comfortable helping to organise the Glastonbury Festival than as part of London's Society scene. She died in December 2007 from pancreatic cancer, aged fifty-eight.

both, in spite of storms, that these roots may hold. Do not hesitate to come and see me if you think I could help.'[4]

Fortunately, Randolph was away a good deal during 1950, travelling in Korea as a war correspondent to report on the conflict there.[*] Seventeen Western war correspondents were killed in Korea during the course of this conflict and Randolph was in the thick of it, electing to accompany men on patrols in order to be able to send home punchy stories. On one of these patrols he was seriously wounded in the leg by shell fragments which also injured a number of the soldiers he was with. Randolph refused emergency treatment until he had written his report. He then organised for the copy to be given to the crew of a plane about to depart for Hong Kong, with instructions on how to file it.[5]

He was, though, as Waugh reported to Nancy Mitford, physically 'in a bad way'[6] and had to be repatriated for treatment. That December Waugh told friends that he had 'heard terrible accounts of Randolph's violence and melancholy but [I] met him at dinner . . . and he behaved modestly and calmly. But by all accounts this is unusual and he is losing his reason.'[7] Four months later Randolph was still undergoing treatment for a wound that would not heal, which naturally made him even more short-tempered than usual. Waugh visited him in hospital where he noted that there was 'no sign of June at the bedside'. Randolph told him his financial difficulties were 'huge'. He needed to recover quickly in order to work his way out of them. 'I must say I lead an awfully dull life,' Waugh commented, 'but when I see the alternative I am consoled.'[8]

After his father's return to power, and encouraged by the Conservative resurgence, Randolph thought it would be a good time to return to politics. When he was well enough he contested the marginal seat of Devonport, Plymouth, for the Conservatives, against Michael Foot, the Labour contender. Perhaps he was still unwell, but all his natural ebullience seemed to drain from him on

---

[*]A friend of the author, a former BOAC air hostess, wrote an account of how Randolph had become drunk and abusive on a flight at this time. Because of his father he was treated kindly: the crew covered for him and got him off the plane at the first opportunity – 'However, I am sure everyone in First Class would have known.'

this occasion, and although his father spoke on his behalf in February 1952 Randolph lost by 2390 votes. He put on a brave front when he conceded defeat, but he was utterly crushed. He had seen Christopher, Mary's husband, a complete newcomer to politics, gain a seat with apparent ease, and many of Randolph's friends who had lost out in the postwar drubbing of the Tories were now back in Parliament. He, though, with all his knowledge of politics and political history, his family background and his numerous contacts, could not manage it. In fact, the only time he had ever gained a seat was when no opposition was offered. Waugh saw him immediately after this defeat and reported to Nancy Mitford that nothing Randolph had ever done deserved such a terrible punishment.

In the following summer one of Randolph's first serious loves, the former Clementine Mitford, invited him and June to stay at Russborough House, a stunning Palladian house in the hills of County Wicklow in Ireland, that she and her husband had recently bought. Clementine had married Sir Alfred Beit in 1938,* and though there were no children it was a very happy marriage and the Beits loved to entertain their friends. They had always regarded Randolph as a friend for whom they felt vaguely sorry, and privately they always referred to him as 'poor Randolph'. Immediately Randolph and June arrived at Russborough they began quarrelling, and continued to do so throughout their visit. Sir Alfred had warned Clementine that Randolph would behave badly, so he had the dubious satisfaction of being able to say, 'I told you so.'[9] Such behaviour was probably typical of the couple, and it says more for the patience and loyalty of their friends than for the manners of Randolph and June that they were still being invited to house parties.

Randolph had noted the peace and contentment of his parents at Chartwell in the postwar years, when financial worries were a thing of the past and even Clementine had come to terms with the house and was happy there. He had been keenly disappointed to

---

*Sir Alfred Lane Beit, 2nd Baronet (1903–94), was a Conservative politician, art collector and philanthropist. He had inherited a great fortune from his father, including an art collection that included works by Vermeer, Gainsborough, Rubens and Goya, displayed at his mansion in Kensington Palace Gardens.

learn that he could not inherit Chartwell, but had come to believe that if he could leave London and live in the country, he too would find contentment. This aspiration intensified after Mary and Christopher moved into the farm and started their family. Randolph could not help but be envious. He also wanted to write the official biography of his father, but he knew that it was unlikely to be feasible at present, so it was a goal he set himself for the future.

Earlier that year, on 6 February 1952, the fifty-six-year-old King George VI had died in his sleep after suffering a coronary thrombosis, although he had been ill with lung cancer and frail for some time. Winston had formed a close bond with the King during the war years, and it is no exaggeration to suggest that the romantic side of his nature accorded his sovereign a loyalty not far removed from that offered to a liege lord by a medieval knight. Jock Colville* heard the news when he arrived at No. 10 that morning. He found the Prime Minister sitting alone in his bedroom weeping. 'I had not realised how much the King meant to him,' Colville wrote. 'I tried to cheer him up by saying how well he would get on with the new Queen, but all he could say was that he did not know her, and that she was only a child.'[10]

The next weeks were frantically busy. There was the King's funeral, and a row between Prince Philip and the government over the name Windsor – the Prince had wanted to adopt the surname Mountbatten for Prince Charles and children-to-be, but had been overruled. Then followed a foreign affairs debate (in which Churchill and Eden squashed the Opposition), a major defence debate, and also a budget, which slashed food subsidies but provided fresh incentives for hard work and overtime and lowered the bottom rates of income tax. And all this after an exceptionally demanding diplomatic trip to the USA the previous month.

Clementine worried that it was all proving too much for Winston; and sure enough, on 21 February he suffered, in the words

---

*Colville was summoned back by Winston in 1952 to be joint head of his private office at No. 10. Lord Moran – Winston's doctor for almost twenty-five years – would say of Jock Colville: 'I know no one who understood with such intuitive sympathy this baffling creature [Winston] who is so unlike anyone else in everything he says and does.'

of Lord Moran, 'a small arterial spasm'. He warned Clementine and Colville that this might be the precursor of a major stroke if the pressures of the PM's life were not significantly reduced. He was, after all, seventy-seven years old and the constant stress since he took office had aged him noticeably. After speaking to Clementine, Lord Moran wrote Winston a letter to this effect and Winston took things somewhat easier for a while. But all thoughts Winston had about resigning in favour of Anthony Eden were forgotten when a local by-election showed the Labour Party gaining ground. Everyone had hoped the Conservatives would be able to relax food rationing, but it remained in force and for some items it was almost as stringent as during the war. The overwhelming response of a nation that had now suffered twelve years of shortages was probably best summed up as 'A plague on both your houses.'

Colville's concern about Winston's reaction to the poor polls was mitigated by the fact that he could not see how Eden could succeed Winston, anyway. 'He has no knowledge or experience of anything except foreign affairs,' he wrote in his diary.[11] Of Churchill, he would note in the following weeks that he was low. 'Of course the Government is in a trough, but his periods of lowness grow more frequent and his concentration is less good. The bright and sparkling intervals still come, and they are still unequalled, but age is beginning to show.'[12] One indication of this was that for the first time in his life Winston delivered a speech written for him by someone else – by Colville, in fact.

It was in August 1952 that the highly intelligent Clarissa, the thirty-two-year-old daughter of Jack and Goonie, announced that she was engaged to Anthony Eden and that they were to be married two days later at Caxton Hall. The family was stunned; only Winston and Clementine had been forewarned, and they were pleased for them both. Anthony was Winston's trusted political heir apparent, and Clarissa his beloved brother's only daughter for whom Winston regarded himself as standing *in loco parentis*. He correctly foresaw a media fuss once the announcement was made, and invited Clarissa to move into 10 Downing Street for the week of the wedding, where she could take advantage of the security facilities. She was fond of her Uncle Winston and Aunt Clementine without being close enough to them to discuss personal matters.[13] At the time, Clementine was on holiday in Rome with Mary Marlborough, but Clarissa had written to her before she broke the news to Winston. Clementine received the letter with mixed feelings; she believed Clarissa was far too independent to make a successful marriage. All the same, she wished her well, and returned to Downing Street in time to organise the wedding reception, for 14 August.

No one quite expected the degree of 'fuss', in Colville's words, that erupted – least of all Clarissa, who had to negotiate 'banks of photographers' as she moved into Downing Street. Jock Colville favoured neither bride nor groom; he thought Clarissa 'very beautiful but . . . strange and bewildering, cold if sometimes witty, arrogant at times and understanding at others. Perhaps marriage will change her and will also help to calm the vain and occasionally hysterical Eden. W[inston], who feels avuncular to his orphaned niece, gave her a cheque for £500 and told me he thought she had a most unusual personality.'[14]

Clarissa had first met Eden when she was a teenager at a country house party, and it would have been difficult to ignore his matinée-idol looks. She saw him again at a dinner party ten years later. But it was not until 1948 that they began seeing each other regularly, and their relationship, based on many shared interests, had developed quietly without raising suspicions. In 1950 he obtained a divorce from his wife Beatrice whom he had married in 1923. The couple had one son, Nicholas, upon whom they doted, but Beatrice did not enjoy politics; indeed she found political life boring and moved to the United States in 1946, thereby enabling Eden to claim desertion as the reason for their divorce. At that time the Church of England would not marry a divorced person, hence the need for a register office wedding, but in any case Clarissa had been raised by Goonie as a Catholic and marriage to a divorced person was proscribed.

Evelyn Waugh, a fellow Catholic, was outraged that Clarissa had chosen to ignore the laws of the Church, and he and Randolph quarrelled about it; Randolph took the line that as Waugh was not an archbishop, nor the editor of the Catholic newspaper *The Tablet*, nor even her cousin like him, what business was it of Waugh's? But Waugh thought it *was* his business and wrote to Clarissa that he was appalled. Of Randolph's defence of her he added: 'I know and love Randolph too much ever to think better or worse of him.'[15]

All the Churchills attended, and Winston was the principal witness. After a few photographs the wedding party drove to Downing Street where Clementine had filled the room with flowers from Chartwell. The following day the couple flew to Portugal for a short honeymoon.

If one had to describe Anthony Eden in as few words as possible, the most succinct description would be: 'He was a decent man.' Utterly honest and sincere, he was a natural diplomat, though he lacked a sense of humour. In Churchill's new administration he was once again given the Foreign Office, which he ran under the ethos 'Be firm, be friendly, be fair.' When negotiating he seemed to realise unerringly when a goal became unachievable, and instead would ask for something less than the opposition expected, which seemed to wrong-foot his opponents and nearly always worked in his favour. Some of the agreements he brokered helped to maintain peace in a united Europe during the Cold War years, and certainly prevented Russia from gobbling up more German territory.

Churchill did not allow his deteriorating health to prevent him from doing whatever he felt must be done. Determined to mitigate the Russian threat and convinced that American assistance was the only way of ensuring this, he made another visit to the United States in January 1953, aboard the Cunard liner *Queen Mary*. Despite his waning physical powers he still retained a total grasp of world affairs, and during the voyage he confided in Colville. 'He said that if I lived my normal span,' Colville wrote, 'I should assuredly see Eastern Europe freed of Communism. He also said that Russia feared our friendship more than our enmity.' Winston told Colville that after Eisenhower won the presidency (in 1953) he (Winston) was obliged to expunge a good deal of material from volume six of his war memoirs to avoid offending him. The United States, he said, had given away vast tracts of Europe to Russia (land the Russians had occupied) because they were suspicious of Churchill's pleas for caution. He had been too sidetracked by the 1945 election, he went on, to prevent Truman from underwriting such land distribution, but he could not blame Truman, who had been a mere novice at negotiation. Had FDR lived and been in good health, he said, he would have seen 'the red light' and checked this American policy.[16]

After his talks in Washington, Churchill went on to Jamaica to join Clementine and Sarah, Mary and Christopher, for a vacation. While there, he worked at correcting volume six, the final part of *The Second World War*. Beaverbrook was on the island too, and the break recharged Churchill. He would need that renewed energy. As well as a double workload caused by the absence of Eden who was seriously ill, by the time Winston returned to London the country was gearing itself up for the coronation. For a short time, and mainly for a privileged few, the glittering and glamorous life that had vanished with the declaration of war in 1939 briefly resurfaced. But even for the masses of less privileged citizens the coronation offered a glorious moment of respite in a very bleak period. Winston and Clementine were in demand at numerous coronation balls and dinners, and they held a party at No. 10, Winston wearing the Garter star that had belonged to Lord Castlereagh in the time of Winston's great-grandfather. Then, dressed in his uniform as Lord Warden of the Cinque Ports,* he stood in for Anthony Eden and threw the Foreign Secretary's banquet for 150 people at Lancaster House, which had been restored to its former glory, after bomb damage, at huge public cost.

On 2 June, the day of the coronation, Winston,† dressed in his full Garter robes, acknowledged the cheering crowds with his famous victory sign from a carriage that was part of the official

---

*An appointment made in 1941 by the King.
†He was now Sir Winston, having received the Order of the Garter from the Queen in her coronation year, on 24 April 1953. He had declined this honour after his political defeat in 1945, but with the new acclamation 'by the people' he felt it was appropriate to accept. It was the more acceptable because everyone knew the late King had wished it bestowed on him.

procession. Next to the royal family he was probably the most popular person in this historic pageant; and the fact that he had begun his public life in the service of this young sovereign's great-great-grandmother was not lost on him or TV commentators. His son and grandson were also involved in the ceremony. Young Winston acted as page to Lord Portal, who had been Chief of Air Staff from 1940–6. Randolph was a Gold Staff Officer.* Members of the Marlborough family also took part. The Duke and Duchess – Bert and Mary – were seated among the peers, but their daughter Lady Rosemary Spencer Churchill, granddaughter of Consuelo, had postponed her wedding to act as one of the six maids-of-honour who bore the Queen's train. When the televising of the ceremony was first proposed Winston, backed by the Cabinet and the Archbishop of Canterbury, formally advised the Queen to make things easier for herself and avoid the heat of the lights and the intrusion of the television cameras. But the Queen, advised by Prince Philip, wisely overrode this advice in order that all her subjects would be able, for the first time ever, to feel as though they were somehow participating in the historic event.

The work and the entertaining took an inevitable toll on Winston, who ate many sumptuous dinners and took little exercise. On 23 June, three weeks after the coronation, he and Clementine held a dinner at No. 10 for the Italian Prime Minister. Winston made a brilliant short speech about the Roman conquest, and the diners had just moved to the drawing room when he was taken ill. He was helped to a chair by Christopher Soames, but when it became clear that he was unable to move from it, the guests were told that their host was very tired and they all departed earlier than planned. After a while Winston was able to get to his bedroom, leaning heavily on Jock Colville's arm. The following morning he insisted on being taken downstairs to the Cabinet Room, where he was seated before anyone else arrived. He then presided over a

---

*An appointment peculiar to coronations. The Earl Marshal of England appoints several Gold Staff Officers to assist wherever necessary; for example, in 1953 ushering the eight thousand peers and other invited guests to their allocated seats and dealing with other marshalling and security matters.

Cabinet meeting during which, to Colville's surprise, no one noticed anything wrong with the PM – except for Rab Butler,* who noted that Winston was 'more silent than usual'.[17] That evening his speech became slurred and he lost the use of his left leg and arm. It was evident that he had suffered a stroke. The next day he was driven down to Chartwell, to be treated in private. He had been due to leave for Bermuda for a meeting with President Eisenhower at the end of June; this was cancelled, and it was announced that the Prime Minister had been overworking and had been advised to take a complete rest.

Sarah was summoned from New York. She was warned at the airport by Mary that their father was in a bad way. Even so, she was shocked at his appearance – it was, she wrote, like seeing 'a great oak felled . . . My father was in a chair. I went over to him quickly and kissed him on the brow, then said, "Darling, Wow!" [a childhood nickname for their father] . . . his eyes flashed brilliantly, but of course he could not answer and his face was [un]naturally distorted on the left.'[18]

At first, Winston was so ill that Lord Moran warned Clementine and Colville that he might not survive the weekend. He had suffered what Moran termed 'a slow leak', which could gradually get worse, and this accounted for the fact that he was able to carry on for the first twenty-four hours rather than being brought down in one blow. Because of this diagnosis Colville secretly discussed the matter with Party leaders Lord Salisbury and Rab Butler, and Sir Alan Lascelles† on behalf of the Palace. They proposed a caretaker government under Salisbury for six months, during which time they could decide whether Eden (who had undergone major gall-bladder surgery on the very day of Winston's stroke and was expected to have to convalesce for six months) or Butler should lead the government.

But Churchill was far from finished. After a week of total rest he began to make an astonishing recovery, although there were periods

---

*Richard A. Butler (1902–82), Tory politician, generally known as 'Rab'. He served as Chancellor of the Exchequer, Home Secretary and Foreign Secretary, but never achieved the premiership.
†A Private Secretary to the sovereign 1943–53.

of depression and tetchiness and he tired very easily. As usual, it was the devoted Clementine who pulled him through, but even Winston wondered if he could continue as Prime Minister. The decision to confine news of his illness, and allow him to remain in office if he felt able to do so, was coloured by Eden's ill-health. Winston instructed Colville to ensure that no hint of what he called his own 'temporary incapacity' was leaked, and that the administration should continue as though he were in full control. Beaverbrook, Brendan Bracken and Lord Camrose between them somehow prevented the press from even hinting at the nature of the Prime Minister's condition. The Queen knew, of course: she expressed a wish to visit Winston at Chartwell, but Clementine decided that a royal visit would lead people to assume Winston was dying, so this was postponed. He still had the use of his right hand and was able to scrawl messages to Clementine – he wrote that she must tell the Queen that he would see her at the St Leger in September. And he did. Luck played a part, too: the media were kept fully occupied for a month when the story of the relationship between Princess Margaret and Captain Peter Townsend broke (after she had been seen to casually brush a piece of cotton off his jacket lapel.)

Four weeks after suffering the stroke, Winston was well enough to travel to Chequers, where he began to take up some light work. The few in the know were amazed at his resilience, especially when on 18 August he presided over a Cabinet meeting. Slowly, steadily, he took up his workload and was seen in public at the races, despite Clementine's misgivings. During this time he was greatly helped by Christopher Soames who, Colville noted – not for the first time – 'now held the place in Churchill's heart so long reserved for Randolph who had been incapable of filling it'.[19] As Parliamentary Private Secretary, Christopher did not have security clearance to read Cabinet papers or secret documents, but Colville bent the rules. It was an emergency, and he later concluded: 'In the event the shrewdness of his comments, combined with his ability to differentiate between what mattered and what did not, was of invaluable help in difficult days.'[20]

Jock Colville gives Brendan Bracken – who was distraught at the thought that Winston might die – much credit for his remarkable recovery. Bracken's 'confident predictions were so convincing that he restored Winston's spirits and helped to raise him from what his doctor feared was a deathbed,' Colville recalled. 'He galvanised [Winston's] will and convinced him that as the world did not have the slightest inkling of the seriousness of his illness he had plenty of time to recuperate.'[21]

Before the end of July Winston was 'sufficiently restored to take an intelligent interest in affairs of state', Colville wrote. 'Christopher and I then returned to the fringes of power, having for a time been drawn perilously close to the centre.'[22] In September Mary and Christopher accompanied Winston to Beaverbrook's Riviera villa, where he was able to rest and eventually take up his painting. On 21 September 1953, three months after the stroke, he wrote a long handwritten letter to Clementine, which reveals that at this stage he had still not decided whether or not he would resign:

> My darling one . . . I do not think I have made much progress tho' as usual I eat, drink & sleep well. I think a great deal about you & feel how much I love you. The kittens [Mary and Christopher] are vy kind to me, but evidently they do not think much of my prospects . . . I still ponder on the future and don't want to decide unless I am convinced . . . *Please continue to love me* or I shall be vy unhappy . . . Ever your loving & as yet unconquered, W.[23]

The same week, while speaking at a Foyle's literary luncheon on the subject of 'the standards of Fleet Street', Randolph had hit the headlines by attacking the newspaper magnate Lord Rothermere (a friend of his parents as well as his own erstwhile employer). He had had a few drinks before he spoke, got carried away, and accused the *Daily Mail* of gaining sales by vicarious methods such as the use of sexy pictures and headlines. 'I have known Lord Rothermere all my life, but I confess myself baffled that so rich and cultivated a man should hire people to prostitute a newspaper in this way – it must be a case of pornography for pornography's sake.' He got enough publicity from this outburst to encourage him to develop the theme, and used it on another public occasion, this time accusing Rothermere of 'power without responsibility; the prerogative of the harlot throughout the ages'. His parents were embarrassed, but a few days later Rothermere called on Winston, who reported: 'Esmond [Rothermere] came to luncheon yesterday and was very friendly & not a bit vexed about poor Randolph's performance.'[24] Clementine followed up: 'Randolph lunched here & is with me now. I don't think he has any idea of what we all think of his ill-natured blunder – He is such good company when in a good mood, & we have played highly competitive croquet . . . which we both enjoyed.'[25]

One of his friends elaborated on this characteristic of Randolph's to his cousin Anita, explaining that what others would call 'rage' Randolph regarded as 'warming to the subject . . . By normal standards he would appear to be in the throes of a blood row [sic], but if you came in during one of these performances to say lunch was ready, he would turn it off like a tap, and by the time we got to the dining room he would be talking about something else.'[26] It seems his love of controversy, of shocking people, and his desire to take centre stage in any arena overrode any common sense or regard for others. And yet many of his friends, such as Diana Cooper, were devoted to him and wrote of his 'warmth'. The plain fact was that the Randolph one could like for himself was a different man from the Randolph who had taken a few drinks.

There was evidently a leak while Winston was in the South of France, for newspapers began printing articles about 'the Prime Minister's health', querying whether he would be fit to resume work on his return from holiday and whether he might be considering retirement. Perhaps this was the spur Winston needed: in early October he addressed the Conservative Party Conference at Margate, delivering a long address that was incisive and amusing, betraying no hint of infirmity. A few days later while Clementine was in Paris he dined with Pam for the first time in years. 'How agreeable she is!' he wrote.[27] He had always enjoyed Pam's company and henceforward she became a regular visitor whenever she was in

England. Indeed, she would be the last visitor he would have to lunch, on his final day at No. 10.

By December when he flew to Bermuda to attend the conference cancelled earlier in the year, Winston was back to dealing with his normal workload. The matter of his stroke came to light only in the summer of 1954 when he referred to it casually during a speech in Parliament. Meanwhile, Christopher accompanied him to Bermuda, and the support and confidentiality provided by this favourite son-in-law gave Churchill a tremendous sense of security.

When the family had gathered at Chartwell at Christmas 1953 it was not Winston who was below par, but other members of the family. Diana was very low-spirited (and would go on to suffer a nervous breakdown), Clarissa was diagnosed with a duodenal ulcer, and Clementine was to suffer agonising pain from an attack of neuritis, not helped by the exceptionally cold winter. She spent the spring months of 1954 at a spa in Aix-les-Bains (which has specialised since the time of the Romans in the treatment of rheumatic complaints). As usual during any time that the Churchills were apart, tender letters flew between them.

Diana had always felt cut out of her parents' affection by Sarah, whose constant ill health following glandular fever as a child had made her particularly needy of parental time. Moreover, Winston had clearly favoured Sarah, the more outgoing and daring of his daughters. When she grew up tall and slender it was easy to make her look presentable as a debutante. Diana had never been able to forget Clementine's wounding comment: 'Sarah is *so* easy to dress.' Diana's marriage, although outwardly happy, was not an easy one. Duncan was immersed in his successful career and he was also serially unfaithful to her.

Diana's nervous breakdown at the end of 1953 was the result of her anxiety about her marriage. At one point Randolph was called to deal with her because she had run amok with a carving knife and was hiding near her house in some bushes. He told Laura afterwards that it was 'like disarming a butterfly'.[28] In the Fifties there were no effective drug treatments for depression and other psychiatric disorders; clinical observation in a hospital was available if you had the means, and therapy of the pull-yourself-together school. Beyond that there was only the horror of electric shock treatment (electrotherapy). Diana had suffered bouts of depression all that year. Churchill, who understood the condition, had tried to help her early on, but at that point he had become occupied with the coronation preparations, then was himself ill. Naturally, all Clementine's energies (and she too had been unwell) were concentrated on Winston. As usual Diana's problems took a back seat. Eventually she snapped.

The person who could best have helped Diana was Sarah, to whom she was always very close. But Sarah was living in the USA, and her infrequent visits to Chartwell were always stiff and awkward on account of Winston's antipathy towards Antony. The Beauchamp marriage was, in fact, over in all but name, but Sarah had not yet told her parents; she had intended to, when her father's stroke intervened.

Randolph had achieved one of his ambitions by 1954. He had known for some time that he needed to leave London and get away from clubs such as White's, where he could never stop himself running up huge gambling debts. For a while in 1953 he and June had lived in Oving House near Aylesbury courtesy of the Churchill Trust. There he worked on the authorised biography of Lord Derby,* who had died in February 1948. Randolph imaginatively called him 'the King of Lancashire'. He was lucky enough to get a good research assistant and aide in Alan Brien (later the celebrated journalist) to do all the necessary paperwork with which Randolph could not have coped, but the writing was Randolph's and the result was a very readable and critically acclaimed book. Evelyn Waugh wrote to the recently widowed Diana Cooper – Duff Cooper had died in January 1954 – that Randolph had been 'tremendously patronising since a lunatic gave him £3000 to write the life of the late Lord Derby. "You

---

*Edward George Villiers Stanley, 17th Earl of Derby (1865–1948), was a professional soldier, politician (Secretary of State for War), diplomat (Ambassador to France) and racehorse owner.

must study the market, Evelyn",' Randolph told him grandly. "'It is no good writing to please yourself.'"[29]

Randolph hoped that the trustees of the Churchill Literary Trust would note this literary success and approve him to write his father's biography, but he could never quite bring himself to ask directly – especially when the trustees made it clear that after he had completed the Lord Derby project he must move from Oving House, as it was too costly for them to pay for him to remain there. Finally, after years of searching, he and June found the sort of country property of which he had dreamed; and to his relief, the trustees agreed to purchase it for him. It was Stour House in the village of East Bergholt, Suffolk. Not far from Colchester, East Bergholt lies in the shade-dappled, gently rolling countryside of the beautiful Stour valley. It was the birthplace and sometime home of that most English of painters, John Constable.* Stour House is a short stroll from Flatford Mill and Willy Lott's cottage (which appears in *The Hay Wain*), and across the river is Dedham church, another of Constable's subjects. There was much to do in the lovely Georgian house and garden, which had fallen into neglect during the war years, but Randolph left the running of the house to June; a room on the top floor overlooking Dedham church was allocated as a nursery for their small daughter Arabella.

Randolph envisaged restoring the seven-acre garden but it is clear at first, at least, he had no idea of how to set about it. He had seen his father 'pottering' at Chartwell, where things seemed to get done, but he did not recognise that Winston had a feel for nature and was happy to labour alongside the men he employed. Still, Randolph loved Stour. This, he decided, was what he had always lacked in his life: a home of his own. If enthusiasm alone could have achieved what he wished to achieve, it would have gone smoothly. At Stour, Randolph felt, he could write in peace, with none of the temptations of London. But not much really changed: the terrible domestic rows continued as before, and Evelyn Waugh continued

---

*John Constable (1776–1837) had his first studio in East Bergholt, of which he wrote: 'I love every stile and stump and lane.' His father owned the flour mill at Flatford.

to note from time to time that Randolph had blacked June's eye or that she had gone to stay with friends.

There are snippets in diaries and letters detailing, for instance, the time June flung her clothes out of a window, screaming that she was leaving him. There was a huge falling-out at Chartwell on one occasion after Randolph, drunk, had upset everyone at dinner by his familiar extreme rudeness. He called Christopher Soames 'a shit' and Eden 'a jerk'. Winston was so 'shaken with fury' that Clementine and June feared he would suffer a seizure – according to June, it was a 'gruesome' scene. Later Randolph stormed up to his bedroom, vowing that he was leaving and would never see his father again. He forced June to start packing, setting off another noisy row between the two of them. Eventually, at 1 a.m., Winston came plodding wearily along the corridor in his pyjamas to tell them: 'I am going to die soon. I cannot go to bed without composing a quarrel and kissing [you] both.'[30] Then there were the wild scenes at London parties where physical injury sometimes resulted. Once, in a restaurant, a drunken Randolph had silenced the other diners by yelling at June a string of abuse amongst which he called her 'a paltry little middle-class bitch always anxious to please and failing owing to her dismal manners'.[31] By the summer of 1954 June was unable to take any more. She took Arabella and left Randolph for good.

Soon after Pam broke up with Gianni, she began another relationship. Cynthia Gladwyn in her *Diaries* recalls an incident when she was lunching at the British Embassy in Paris where the Duke of Windsor was a guest. When the Duke accidentally spilled his coffee over one of the ladies he made profuse apologies, and was relieved to discover that she was a Rothschild and could therefore afford another dress. In an attempt to cover his gaffe he asked her brightly: 'Can you tell me which is the Rothschild with whom Pamela Churchill is having an affair?' The woman replied: 'Sir, that's worse than the coffee. That's my husband!'[32]

For Churchill, who was eighty years old in November 1954, those few years of his last administration were anything but golden: the lives of all his children, except Mary, were in acute disharmony. Worshipping his Clemmie as he still did, and in the peace and happiness he always enjoyed at Chartwell, it was a puzzle beyond his understanding how the children could fail to make happy marriages for themselves.

Nor were family troubles his only ones. Carrying an immense load as Prime Minister, he half decided to celebrate his birthday, then retire the following April, standing down at the forthcoming general election. But having made this decision he immediately became truculent and complained that he was being hounded out of office by Eden. The truth was that he could not bear to contemplate the end of his career – he had made some spectacular comebacks, but he knew that when he stood down this time there was no coming back. It was Christopher Soames who finally persuaded him that it was in the best interests of the country that he hand over the problems and stresses of office to younger men.

At times now he would be bad-tempered and fractious – 'like a spoilt and naughty child,' his daughter Mary said. But whereas his colleagues made allowances for his outbursts, Clementine was just as critical as she had always been when he behaved rudely, and 'would burst forth as soon as they were in private . . . But for all that he sometimes deserved her scoldings,' Mary wrote. All the same, 'there were periods now when she really harried him too much'.[33] These quarrels never lasted long and were invariably followed up with an affectionate note: 'Darling, Fondest love. I am so sorry I was awkward at dinner. My heart was full of nothing but love, but my thoughts were wayward. Your ever devoted, W.'[34] Other touching notes would tell her about his pets – he kept pets throughout his life and he was devoted to them – how 'the little cat' was sitting on his papers as he worked, and how his pet budgie Toby, which he even took with him on his constant travels, would sit on the rim of his glass, then hop across his desk as he worked. Sometimes he enclosed a tiny yellow feather – 'a present from Toby'. But Clementine too was under pressure – simply looking after Winston and enabling him to carry on required greater effort than ever. Furthermore, she was in constant pain from the neuritis that afflicted her throughout those years, and earlier that year she had lost the closest member of her own family when Nellie died of cancer.

Winston's eightieth birthday celebrations were a triumph, however. No. 10 was deluged with flowers and tributes. To mark the occasion, Winston had set aside £25,000, a large sum for those days (worth over £570,000 today), towards the founding of a new Cambridge college which was to bear his name.* That day he addressed the House of Commons: 'I have never accepted what many people have kindly said: namely that I inspired the nation,' he said in a confidential tone. And then, raising his voice, 'It was the nations and the race dwelling all round the globe that had the lion's heart.' A pause, then an apparent afterthought: 'I had the luck to be called upon to give the roar.' It was a supreme performance, and later, as the cheers died down in a crowded Westminster Hall, blue curtains were pulled back to reveal the gift of both Houses of Parliament – a full-length portrait of Winston by Graham Sutherland. Winston had been shown the painting two weeks earlier, and had hated it on sight. But he did not wish to spoil the occasion, so he looked at it for a second or two as though seeing it for the first time, then said pointedly, 'This is a remarkable example of modern art.' The assembled company hooted. Winston could still hold an audience, but although he could perform for great occasions he was ageing fast and he no longer had the physical resources to govern.

But even now, he hated the thought of retirement. Anthony Eden, his friend and trusted colleague during the Thirties and Forties, had long been promised the premiership. Now, Churchill regarded Eden as looking at the top post with 'hungry eyes' (hardly surprisingly, given that he'd been in the wings so long and was ageing himself). He became resentful of Eden. He had earlier promised him he would go after his birthday, but Eden then heard that Winston had confided in Nehru's sister that he wouldn't go

---

*Churchill College, Cambridge, houses Churchill's papers and those of some of his contemporaries.

until he dropped down dead. That Winston knew very well what effect these changes of mind were having on Eden is nicely illustrated in an exchange with Colville, who suggested that Winston go to Marrakech for that year's Christmas holiday. He replied: 'No. If I'm going to be a dog in the manger, I'd better stay in the manger.'[35]

It was a tricky situation and even Colville, who admired and loved Churchill, was torn:

> He could still make a great speech . . . indeed none could rival his oratory or his ability to inspire. But he was ageing month by month and was reluctant to read any papers except the newspapers . . . the preparation of a Parliamentary Question might consume a whole morning . . . and yet on some days the old gleam would be there, wit and good humour would bubble and sparkle, wisdom would roll out in telling sentences and still, occasionally, the sparkle of genius could be seen in a decision, a letter, a phrase. But was he the man to negotiate with the Russians and moderate the Americans? The Foreign Office thought not; the British Public would, I am sure, have said yes. And I, who have been as intimate with him as anybody during these last years, simply did not know.[36]

By spring 1955 Eden had become extremely bitter, not helped by Randolph (who had long been jealous of Eden's place in his father's affections) taking pot shots at his abilities in newspaper articles. Randolph was to continue this hate campaign – mainly in the *Evening Standard* – even after Eden became Prime Minister, always implying that his leadership was weak and ineffective. And because Randolph was a good writer, it did Eden a good deal of harm at the time and has arguably affected his reputation today. However, when it looked as though Churchill might once again change his mind, Eden behaved with impeccable good manners in public, despite complaining privately in a cold rage to Colville.

Eventually, though, what Eden had waited so long for had to come. On 4 April 1955 the Churchills held a retirement dinner at Downing Street for fifty guests including the Queen and Prince Philip, which was a signal honour. Anthony and Clarissa Eden were there. No. 10 would become theirs the following day – assuming, Colville reflected privately, that the PM did not change his mind yet again overnight. At one point Randolph took Clarissa aside and told her frankly, 'I suppose you know I am against the new regime.' Winston told the Queen that she was 'right to put complete confidence in Anthony Eden'. After the other guests had left, Jock Colville went upstairs to find Winston sitting on his bed wearing the Garter decoration, the Order of Merit and court knee-breeches. 'For several minutes he did not speak and I, imagining that he was sadly contemplating that this was his last night at Downing Street, was silent. Then suddenly he stared at me and said with vehemence: "I don't believe Anthony can do it."' Colville could only reflect uneasily that Winston's prophecies, all too often, had been borne out by events.[37]

The following day Winston presided over his final Cabinet meeting. Then, dressed in the frock-coat and top-hat he always wore to royal audiences, he went to the Palace to tender his resignation formally. The Queen offered him a dukedom. It was no surprise; he had been approached about it some days before. He had been deeply touched by the compliment, and had thought hard about it. On the one hand it would give him parity with his illustrious forebear John, 1st Duke of Marlborough, and it would be a fitting crown to his sixty-year career. But on the other, he reasoned (almost certainly with Clementine's input), there was insufficient money to support a dukedom, and furthermore he wished to remain a member of the House of Commons until age – or his constituents – prevented it. He declined the Queen's offer, and said to Colville later: 'What good would a Dukedom be to Randolph? It might ruin his and little Winston's political careers.'[38]

1955–63

Safe Harbour

On 5 April 1955 Winston left Downing Street quietly and unobtrusively for Chartwell. He had requested no fuss; it would have been more than he could deal with emotionally. Within days he, Clementine, the Prof and Jock Colville were in Sicily, but it was not a happy time for any of them. It rained every day, Winston was in low spirits, and Clementine was having to inject herself with pethidine to cope with the pain from the neuritis in her right shoulder and arm.[1]

After the holiday Winston fought another general election and was returned again as the Member for Woodford, with a huge majority. In July the Edens invited them to luncheon at No. 10, but Clementine was unable to accept. 'She sounded terribly flat and piano on the phone,' Clarissa wrote in her diary, 'in pain all the time, and no hope of anyone curing her.' Winston attended alone. Now there was no longer any rivalry, his old affection for Anthony had returned in full. Clarissa, though, noted a 'great deterioration' in her uncle.[2]

Having been in agonising pain for months Clementine took herself off to St Moritz for a series of spa treatments, which gave her some relief, and Mary was able to join her there. Winston wrote to her often, sometimes in his 'own paw', tender notes, often with a small sketch of a pig or a dog, to boost her. He had taken up *A History of the English-Speaking Peoples* again, the four-volume work he had begun in the Thirties and put aside when war was declared, then put aside again when he became PM for the second time. Now he found solace in this work, and in his painting; it would occupy him for the remainder of the year despite his suffering two small 'spasms' (minor strokes). Clementine read the manuscript and was thrilled with it, writing to him that it would encourage people to read about history.

In September they went together to Max Beaverbrook's villa at Cap-d'Ail. It was a good time for them both. Even though Clementine usually found life on the Riviera cloying she greatly enjoyed this holiday. Winston had cheered up, and her obvious happiness added to his own. But he knew that Clementine did not like accepting hospitality from people of whom she did not approve (in particular she feared that Winston might be compromised), and it was probably the success of this holiday that gave him the idea that she might be prepared to spend more time on the Riviera with him if they had their own villa. He could then look forward to spending every winter painting in the sunshine he loved, with Clementine at his side. It seemed the best of all worlds. After she left for London, leaving Winston to paint, he began a search for a suitable property.

The idea filled Clementine with dismay, in fact, for although she could cope with a short holiday there now and then for Winston's sake, she disliked the South of France and its glitzy society. But worse, she never lost her fear of poverty, and even now, with all Winston's success, she genuinely feared that with three homes to keep up they might run out of money. To her, the only favourable aspect of such a scheme was that Winston would no longer be reliant on the generosity of others. He could, of course, have afforded to stay in the best hotels, but he was of a generation and a class to which hotel life was acceptable only for short visits; he enjoyed the life one experienced in a well run and well staffed private home. Furthermore, he was too famous to have been able to stay comfortably in any public place.

The topic of 'the villa' would provoke heated discussions for several years, involving the whole family; eventually, Mary concluded that 'Clementine made too much of the difficulties, and it was easy to sympathise with Winston's wish for a holiday home in the sun.'[3] Winston forged ahead with his plan anyway, and spent much time reconnoitring suitable properties. Any visiting family member was roped in on these jaunts. In a letter Sarah wrote to Clementine while she was staying with her father she mentioned that they had been 'villa hunting', then hastened to assure her mother that she was confident Winston would not buy anything without her, Clementine's, approval. 'I don't think he even wants to [buy] really,' she consoled, 'but he does love the sun so.'[4] Clementine, though, could never quite forget that Winston had bought Chartwell without telling her.

In January 1956 Winston paid what would be the first of ten long visits to La Pausa at Roquebrune-Cap-Martin, on the Côte d'Azur between Menton and Monaco. The magnificent white marble villa had been built in the 1920s by Bendor, Duke of Westminster, for his mistress Coco Chanel, and it was bought in 1954 by the millionaire publisher and art collector Emery Reves. Set among olive groves and lavender fields in Haute Provence, La Pausa was the epitome of luxury and hedonism, and in the hands of Reves and his stunning blonde Texan mistress Wendy Russell* (a former *Vogue* model) it quickly became a hub of Riviera society. Apart from Churchill and various members of his family, other guests included Greta Garbo, Prince Rainier and Princess Grace of Monaco and the Duke and Duchess of Windsor.† Reves owned one of the finest collections of Impressionist and post-Impressionist paintings in the world, as well as a famed collection of Renaissance jewellery. It was not a huge house, but well proportioned and surrounded by lawns and simple landscaping. Once inside, the iron gates were locked to create an utterly private world. Every visitor to La Pausa had the soles of their shoes cleaned by the major-domo as they entered the house, and women had to remove their shoes.

---

*They lived together from 1948 and married in 1964.
†Winston came to accept that he was wrong to have supported the Duke during the abdication crisis, describing him later to Montague Browne as 'an empty man. He showed such promise. Morning Glory.'

Winston had known Emery Reves since 1937, when the two men were introduced by Austen Chamberlain.* Reves, a Hungarian Jew, then known by his original name Imre Revesz, was the owner of *Cooperation*, a European magazine with an anti-Nazi stance, founded four years earlier. Revesz published a number of Winston's articles at a time when Winston needed a voice in Europe. During the war Winston used Revesz's multilingual abilities and important contacts in a number of Intelligence projects, and to disseminate favourable propaganda, especially in the United States.[5] By the end of the war Revesz had anglicised his name and in 1945 wrote an acclaimed book *The Anatomy of Peace*, which was endorsed by Albert Einstein.

Already a rich man, Emery Reves made further millions in commissions from the sale of the foreign publishing rights of Churchill's war memoirs† and his other books. Knowing well how Winston blossomed in the sunshine, Reves now invited his best client to stay at La Pausa. Winston went out alone that January, intending to look at villas for rent while he was there – a compromise arrived at with Clementine in lieu of his proposal that they should buy a property. Clementine had arranged to go cruising around Ceylon in February with a friend, Sylvia Henley,‡ but meanwhile she went into hospital to be treated for a recurrence of the neuritis. While in hospital she caught an infection and was so ill for several weeks that she could not even write to Winston. When she did, her letters were addressed, as ever, to 'My darling one', as were Winston's to her, suggesting that their disagreement concerning a Riviera villa was not a serious one.

In his letters Winston tried to keep Clementine informed and entertained: 'Reves and Wendy are most obliging,' he informed her. 'They ask the guests I like and none I don't. A few people have written, & so we had last night Daisy Fellowes & her young man

*First Lord of the Admiralty under Ramsay MacDonald and stepbrother to the subsequent Prime Minister Neville Chamberlain.
†In his book *In Command of History* (2005), David Reynolds claims that these rights were sold for a figure worth up to $60 million in today's currency.
‡Elder sister of Venetia Montagu, Clementine's former best friend, who had died in 1948.

Hamish Edgar. Daisy was vy sprightly . . . She is wonderfully well-maintained & kept us all agog.'[6] It was Daisy who, as a young woman, had unsuccessfully attempted to seduce Winston at the Ritz in Paris in 1919, later marrying his first cousin Reggie Fellowes (a former lover of Consuelo). Daisy had also been Duff Cooper's lover for a while, and though she was sixty-six when Winston mentioned her in this letter she was still able, evidently, to captivate a room. She lived on minute helpings of grouse, iced carrot juice and vodka, and still thought nothing of spending thousands on a single dress. Conversation about mutual acquaintances was likely, with Daisy, to be maliciously amusing (one friend reported that she was afraid to leave the room for fear of what might be said about her in her absence).[7] Winston enjoyed Daisy's company in small doses.

In his next letter, on 17 January, he advised that 'Randolph brought Onassis (the one with the big yacht) to dinner last night. He made a good impression upon me. He is a vy able and masterful man & and told me a lot about whales. He kissed my hand!'[8] Aristotle Onassis (who insisted on being called 'Ari') would become a good friend, one of Winston's best in those sunset years, although the cultivated Reves privately considered that the Greek millionaire was vulgar.

'I spend the days mostly in bed [working] & get up for lunch and dinner,' Winston wrote, and he related that when he was up and about Reves instructed him about modern art by showing him around his collection of Impressionists. 'Also they have a wonderful form of gramophone wh plays continuously Mozart . . . on 10-fold discs.'[9] He tried to persuade Clementine to come out and be pampered by Wendy, or to join him aboard the Onassis yacht *Christina* – named after Ari's daughter – to and from which Winston was ferried by a Piaggio amphibian plane.* But Clementine did not like the sound of all this, and replied:

---

*Alexander, the only son and heir of Aristotle Onassis, would die at the controls of this aircraft, which crashed on take-off at Ellinikon International Airport, Athens, in January 1973.

If Mr Onassis invited you & a party, you could have a little Easter cruise with Mr Reves and Wendy & Mary & Christopher etc. But somehow I don't want to be beholden to this rich powerful man & for the news to be blazoned. Similarly, tho' to a lesser degree, I don't want to stay at La Pausa, though one day I should like to meet Wendy . . . please forgive me; but you can't teach an old dog new tricks – But I *am* happy that you should be there in the sunshine.[10]

That summer Winston paid another solo visit to La Pausa. He was there on 9 June when Noël Coward was one of the many guests, along with Edward Molyneux the couturier and Somerset Maugham (invited so as to keep Winston amused and stimulated). Coward wrote in his diary: 'To Roquebrune to lunch with Emery Reves, Wendy Russell, the most fascinating lady, Winston Churchill, Sarah [Churchill] and Winston's secretary'. Winston, he noted, was 'absolutely obsessed with Wendy Russell. He followed her about the room with his brimming eyes and wobbled after her across the terrace . . . I doubt if . . . Churchill has ever been physically unfaithful to Lady Churchill but, oh, what has gone on inside that dynamic mind?'[11]

Churchill liked nothing better than to sit under an umbrella in the garden painting while Wendy sat chattering brightly by his side and dispensing champagne. And it was true, as Wendy observed some years later, that 'Winston never had a Black Dog day at La Pausa'.[12] But what is the truth about Winston's relationship with Wendy? Did he fall in love with her, as Noël Coward suggested?

Something similar had happened several years earlier, when at the end of the war Winston had lunched one day with the Duff Coopers at the Paris Embassy and was introduced to the attractive widow Odette Pol-Roger.* Her late husband Jacques had been head of the famous champagne-producing company, and Pol Roger was

---

*Odette Pol-Roger, née Wallace, was one of the three daughters of Major General Wallace, who were known as 'the Wallace Collection'.

Winston's favourite champagne.* ('In defeat I need it,' he said, mis-quoting Napoleon, 'and in victory I deserve it'.) Cases of it travelled with him, even during the war years. 'What a *beautiful* name' were his first words on meeting her. Thereafter, he developed a fondness for Odette, saw her often and entertained her in England whenever she visited. But it was a perfectly innocent relationship, accepted by Clementine, and all the family knew that Winston adored Odette. From the date of their meeting, every year until his death, on Winston's birthday in November Odette never forgot to send him a case of his favourite vintage.† In return, he sent her a set of his war memoirs with the inscription: '*Mise en bouteille* Chateau Chartwell'.‡ Odette became a great friend to all the Churchills.

But his relationship with Wendy was somehow different. When she finally visited La Pausa, Clementine could not help but see that Winston was drawn to the fragile, long-legged beauty of Wendy. She was not jealous, exactly – she knew Winston would not be unfaithful to her at this stage in his life – and he had never been a womaniser, even when young and virile. Still, she was discon-certed and uneasy to see how he relied on Wendy, who petted and mildly flirted with him. Nothing was too good for him; nothing was too much trouble, and in fact the entire palatial edifice revolved around him. Winston's last Private Secretary, Anthony Montague Browne, who always enjoyed the lotus-eating visits to La Pausa, sug-gested that Noël Coward's assertion that Winston was 'absolutely obsessed with a senile passion for Wendy'[13] was no more than bitchiness because Coward believed Winston had played a part in his omission from the honours list. Or he might have heard Winston's off-the-cuff remark about another homosexual, that 'buggers can't be choosers'.[14] Montague Browne agreed that there

---

*It was reckoned that in his lifetime he consumed five hundred cases of it.

†She put aside all bottles of 1928 vintage for Churchill until it ran out in 1953, and after that always sent him the finest vintage available. He named one of his racehorses after her. He once told her that if she would invite him to Épernay during the grape harvest he would tread some grapes himself. A decade after his death, Pol Roger launched a new label: the Cuvée Sir Winston Churchill.

‡After Churchill's death in 1965 Odette decreed that a black border was to be added to all bot-tles of Pol Roger sold in the UK.

was a form of affection between Winston and Wendy but that it owed nothing to the prurient insinuations of Coward. However, Diana and Nancy Mitford, Beaverbrook and others in their circle believed that Winston *was* infatuated with Wendy, and even Winston's doctor noted in his records 'the uplift' in Winston's spirits whenever he visited La Pausa. So the answer is probably that Winston did fall in love with Wendy in a way, and his feelings were reciprocated. But it was never a sexual relationship and it never affected Wendy's relationship with Emery, or Winston's deep visceral love for Clementine. It did, though, keep the Churchills apart for a while, because he so enjoyed himself at La Pausa where he was spoiled and never corrected. Winston was experiencing the octogenarian equivalent of a teenage crush; and Wendy, idol worship.

There is an incident that allegedly took place in the same year as the Coward meeting. As Winston was leaving the men's room at the Carlton Club it was pointed out to him that his flies were undone. Winston glanced down, made the appropriate adjustment, and commented with a sigh: 'Dead birds don't fall out of trees.'*

It was also about this time that Clementine quietly disposed of the Sutherland portrait. Probably, she burned it. Winston loathed the fact that it depicted him as a querulous old man; his opinion was that its 'force and candour . . . made me look half-witted, which I am not', and there is no doubt that in a photograph of him at the unveiling of the portrait he appears far more youthful and vital than the Sutherland image propped on an easel behind him. A few years later the portrait would have been a more defining image of a great man in old age, but this peep into his future haunted Churchill, and it was certainly not the way he wished to be remembered by posterity. When he worried about it, Clementine made him a promise that the portrait 'would never see the light of day', and she was as good as her word: it was never seen again. She mentioned it once in a letter to Max Beaverbrook: 'This gift which was meant as the expression of the affection and devotion of the House of Commons caused him great pain & it all but ruined his 80th

---

*Confirmed by Mary Soames to author.

birthday – It wounded him deeply that this brilliant . . . painter with whom he had made friends while sitting for him should see him as a gross & cruel monster.'[15] It was not the first occasion that a portrait of Winston of which Clementine did not approve went missing: in 1927 a sketch by her old friend Walter Sickert was given away,* and in 1944 a cartoon for a portrait by Paul Maze mysteriously disappeared.

For Consuelo, 1956 was a dreadful year. In the late summer her younger son Ivor was diagnosed with an inoperable brain tumour. He had helped her three years earlier with the various phases of publication of her memoir *The Glitter and the Gold.* The book sold well, though so much of it had been edited out by members of the family in order not to hurt tender feelings that it is curiously flat – apart from the section where Consuelo vividly described how she was hectored into marriage by Alva. Even then, Winston was concerned at some of the things Consuelo had written about Sunny – he had loved them both – but most British reviewers thought the book would have been improved had Consuelo been *less* discreet about the Duke.

Randolph reviewed the book in *Punch*: 'Madam Balsan indulges herself in many criticisms of a man who has been dead for twenty years, and who was the father of her two sons; and it is painful to record that after a lapse of sixty years she finds it decent to criticise even his table manners.' Consuelo had never liked Randolph and the animosity over the book did not improve the relationship; but after Winston read it he wrote to her from Blenheim to congratulate her, saying that the book had brought back many happy memories of a golden age now long forgotten.

Ivor had married Elizabeth Cunningham after the war and eight years later, in 1954, they had a son, Robert. In the two years since then Consuelo had seen little of Ivor because he hated flying, while her ageing husband Jacques had developed Alzheimer's disease and she could not bear to leave him. Perhaps she thought Ivor had

---

*It is now in the National Portrait Gallery.

longer to live than he had; she kept hoping he would come to her because Jacques was now so frail, but Ivor died in September, and was buried at Bladon. A few weeks later Jacques, aged eighty-eight, was discovered on a golf course in a state of collapse. He died on 4 November; his body was flown to Paris to be interred in the family tomb in Montmartre.

Relations between Britain and Egypt had been deteriorating throughout 1955–6. Affairs came to a head with the Suez crisis in October 1956. Some months earlier, Britain and the USA had withdrawn an offer to fund the Aswan Dam following Egypt's recognition of the People's Republic of China at a time of great tension between China and Taiwan. When Nasser then announced his intention to nationalise the Suez Canal, Britain and France supported Israel – dependent on the Canal for the shipping of goods – and sent a tripartite military force to invade Egypt. Winston watched critically from afar, writing to Clementine from La Pausa, 'I am very glad the burden does not rest on me.'[16]

The burden rested very much with Anthony Eden, who had more experience in high-level foreign affairs than any man alive, yet he was dogged by ill-health, and probably lacked the robustness needed to deal with his many critics and political opponents, as well as his advisers, who refused to accept the decline of Britain's influence in the Middle East. 'I listened to Anthony last night,' Winston wrote to Clementine at one point. 'It was hard to hear but I'm afraid I was disappointed by what I did hear – There was no inspiration.'[17] Eden overestimated the support for him in Washington, and he was eventually forced to withdraw troops from Egypt when the Americans applied pressure. Apart from Britain's loss of face, the result was public fury and a 40 per cent increase in fuel prices. Eden's reputation as a statesman was in shreds. On medical advice, he took a short holiday in November at Ian Fleming's house, Goldeneye, in Jamaica, in an attempt to regain his health and soldier on as Prime Minister. Noël Coward, in contact with Anthony and Clarissa there (she was an old friend of his), wrote that he had been told that Eden 'has wakened in the night

screaming several times and sent for the Guard'.[18] In fact Eden was
desperately ill. He was subsequently told by doctors that if he did not
retire from the stress of his office, he would soon die. While all
this was occurring, in Eden's absence, Harold Macmillan and Rab
Butler were busy working on a palace coup, and Eden found himself
outmanoeuvred. He resigned in January 1957, in Macmillan's favour,
but it was a case of did he fall or was he pushed? Clarissa was left to
pick up the pieces and to try to nurse her shattered husband to health.

Winston spent most of 1957 with the Reveses at La Pausa. At various times he had members of his 'court' with him: one or other of
his children, his butler, his detective, his Private Secretary Anthony
Montague Browne, two secretaries and – always – his budgie Toby.
He returned to London in April to celebrate Clementine's seventy-
second birthday at a party at Hyde Park Gate, but a month later on
21 May he was back in the South of France accompanied by Sarah
and Montague Browne. 'Darling,' he wrote to Clementine, 'We
arrived today and all is well . . . the skies are without a cloud . . .
Your visit to me the night before I left was vy precious . . . Wendy
was obviously disappointed to learn that you wd not come, but
would see you at Capponcina [Beaverbrook's villa] in September.'[19]
A visit to Beaverbrook's villa in the coming September was the only
way he could persuade Clementine to join him in the South of
France, for by now she had resolutely set her face against Wendy. It
was awkward for him, but Winston promised Wendy that after
Clementine returned to London he would return to La Pausa,
which was what he did.

In mid-June he went home to attend the annual Garter ceremony at Windsor. His short time in England was punctuated by
unwelcome news. He had been home only a few weeks when word
came that the Prof – Professor Lindemann – his trusted friend for
thirty years, had died in his sleep on 3 July. On 7 August, Sarah
arrived in England from America. She and Antony had been virtually separated for two years, and she had decided to tell him that
she felt it was no longer worth trying to make their marriage work.
Having arranged to see Antony the next day to discuss the matter,

she spent the night anxiously pacing up and down a friend's apartment, going over what she should say. At seven the next morning the phone rang. It was Clementine. 'We never beat about the bush in our family,' Sarah recalled. 'I heard my mother's crisp voice . . . "Sarah, you should know – Antony Beauchamp has committed suicide."'[20] He had taken an overdose of sleeping pills.

The news hit Sarah very hard: it was, of course, reminiscent of Gil Winant's suicide. Sarah had to identify the body, attend the inquest and make the funeral arrangements, helped by Diana, the only member of the Churchill family to attend the funeral. Directly after the service Sarah flew to California, where she had a TV film to make in Hollywood. She rented a small cabin for herself at Malibu – then an isolated beach village – which was the last thing she ought to have done. Desperately unhappy, after filming she would return each evening to the beach and seek oblivion in alcohol.

In September Winston and Clementine departed for Beaverbrook's La Capponcina, as planned. Two years earlier Christopher Soames had been offered a ministerial post under Anthony Eden, and was subsequently appointed Secretary of State for War. Consequently, he and Mary felt they could no longer run the two farms, Chartwell and Bardogs. So the farms had been sold and Mary and Christopher moved to Hamsell Manor near Tunbridge Wells, Kent, leaving just the original estate around Chartwell itself.

The Churchills were at home for Christmas 1957. The family gathered at Chartwell as usual, but Winston left again for La Pausa on 12 January. Two days later, headlines announced that Sarah had been arrested at Malibu, charged with being drunk. Winston and Clementine were stunned and shocked: Clementine, especially, hated the headlines and the photographs. Randolph was dispatched to his sister's aid and Clementine tried to forget about it all by taking her grandchildren to pantomimes in London and lunching with Pamela and young Winston (now seventeen).

Winston's solution was to invite Sarah to come to him at La Pausa, and she flew there to spend a week on 18 February, deeply grateful for the reticence and understanding he showed.[21] Towards the end of her visit – before she departed for England and what would prove to be the first of many drying-out sessions – Clementine was to fly out to join them; Winston had arranged to meet her in the Reveses' car at Nice airport.

On the day before Clementine's arrival Winston and Emery Reves lunched with Onassis aboard the *Christina* in Monte Carlo harbour, eating and drinking as usual, afterwards playing chemin de fer for high stakes. Winston had only recently recovered from a bad cold, but he seemed in good form, if a little excitable. Later that afternoon, however, he reported feeling 'all in' and was taken back to La Pausa to rest. The following morning his face was white and he was shivering violently. The plan for him to meet Clementine was abandoned, and by the time she arrived at the villa she could see for herself that the problem was serious. Winston had suffered three previous attacks of pneumonia, and recognising the symptoms, Clementine wasted no time in telephoning Lord Moran. Moran took the next flight out and treated Winston with massive doses of antibiotics for pneumonia and pleurisy. Clementine's week turned into a month as Winston fought back, often bad-tempered with everyone out of frustration, and not least because of increasing deafness.

They arrived back at Chartwell on 3 April, in time for the Easter holiday. Lord Moran took his son John and daughter-in-law Shirley to Chartwell to meet Churchill. As they left, Moran heard John say to Shirley: 'Think of it, that hand you shook today held a sabre at Omdurman.'[22]

From this date onward Winston always had at least one male nurse in attendance, and in retrospect Mary believes that this very serious illness marked a major turning point in her father's health – he was never really robust again. When the Queen heard of this latest deterioration in Winston's health, she discussed the matter with Prime Minister Harold Macmillan, and it was decided that when the end came he was to have a state funeral. Some writers have suggested that Winston planned much of his funeral himself, but this is not true: he said he was 'unwilling to address my mind to the subject' – in fact, his sole input was his request to be buried at Bladon, close to his parents, instead of at Chartwell as he had previously intended.

During January 1958, but overshadowed by Sarah's arrest, June had quietly obtained a divorce from Randolph. Within a few weeks Randolph was also seriously ill with bronchopneumonia, and he was still convalescing at Stour House at Easter. But his life had now changed. A year earlier he had met the second great love of his life in the most unlikely circumstance. Had the incident not been detailed by an impeccable witness, it would seem almost too fantastic to be true.

Randolph's friend Patrick Kinross* was staying with him at Stour when they were visited by a neighbour. Natalie, wife of a naval officer, 'Bobby' Bevan, was an old friend of Lord Kinross, so when she heard he was in East Bergholt she drove over to see him. Kinross opened the door to her knock, and Randolph came into the hall behind him to see who the caller was. Kinross recalled that he felt he might as well not have been there, for a *coup de foudre* struck Randolph and Natalie. After staring at her for what seemed minutes without saying a word, Randolph took her hand and led her out into the rose garden where he told her without any preamble that he had been waiting for her 'for so long. I love you.' And then he kissed her – not in a flirtatious way, but gently and affectionately. He knew immediately that this was to be a great love, as great as his long, unrequited love for Laura, and so it would prove. Natalie, not least because she was married to Bobby, was not as certain about it as Randolph, but she felt the same instinctive recognition at the first sight of him; and whenever she thought about it later, she always recalled the scent of roses.[23] That year, she would write in her diary, was 'the most golden' of her life.[24] As the affair developed she told her husband about her feelings for Randolph, and rather than

---

*John Patrick Balfour, 3rd Baron Kinross (1904–76), was a prolific writer whose best-known works were his biography of Ataturk and books on Islamic history. His first wife, whom he married in 1938, was Angela Culme-Seymour (formerly married to Randolph's cousin Johnny Spencer Churchill). They divorced in 1942 because Kinross was homosexual. Angela married several more times, and was Nancy Mitford's model for 'the Bolter' in *The Pursuit of Love*.

break up his marriage he decided to accept the situation and see where it led. A few years later, after three days of intense discussion about their relationship, Randolph begged Natalie to marry him: 'I want you to be my wife as soon as possible,' he wrote. 'Whatever you decide I shall love you, now and forever. Please help me to make us both happy.'[25]

By then Natalie had been thoroughly accepted by the Churchill family as Randolph's partner. She had holidayed aboard the *Christina* with Winston and Clementine, spent weekends at Chartwell and often dined with them at Hyde Park Gate. In short, she came to love them, and they became a significant part of her life. But she could not bring herself to divorce Bobby, who also loved her and had stood by, waiting patiently. She thought deeply about it, then told Randolph gently that he would simply have to accept – as Bobby did – that their relationship must continue as it was. He had no option but reluctantly to agree. When a friend told him that 'after a certain age people don't really fall in love', he rounded on her. 'Age has nothing to do with it,' he retorted. 'I am more in love now than I ever have been in my life before.'[26] Many years later his first love, the former Diana Mitford, would recall: 'Randolph changed a great deal after he met Natalie . . . we were all so pleased [for him].'[27]

But there was another element to the remarkable transformation in Randolph, and that was the realisation of his great ambition. One day after Natalie had kissed him goodbye, she had started to drive off when he came tearing out of the house after her, waving a telegram. She stopped the car. 'He's *asked* me!' he panted. 'He's asked me, at last.' He was so out of breath he could not continue, but Natalie knew what he meant. Winston had asked his son to write the official biography, as Winston had once written his own father's story. Nothing else he could have done or said could have pleased Randolph half as much. He wrote to his father about how proud and happy the commission had made him: 'Since I first read your life of your father, 35 years ago, when I was a boy of 14 at Eton, it has always been my greatest ambition to write your life.'[28]

*

By mid-summer 1958 Brendan Bracken was dying of a particularly painful cancer which caused him virtually to starve to death. He and Winston had met nearly forty years earlier, in 1923, and it was a considerable blow to Winston to lose another of his oldest and closest friends. Overcoming his intense dislike of hospitals, he visited Brendan twice, and was very distressed by his old friend's emaciation and intubation. For many years, Clementine had disliked Brendan, had mistrusted him (especially when it had been widely rumoured that he was Winston's illegitimate son, and Brendan had done nothing to contradict this). But during the difficult war years she came to recognise that he was a true and loyal friend to Winston, and thereafter she was always happy to welcome him as one of the most frequent visitors to their various homes. She was as upset as Winston when Brendan died, on 8 August.

The next weekend they stayed at Blenheim, where family celebrations were held to mark the fiftieth anniversary of their engagement. The Golden Wedding day, three weeks later, was spent quietly at La Capponcina with Max Beaverbrook. Randolph and Arabella were the only family members able to spend that day with them. Randolph arrived with a bouquet of fifty gold roses, and presented the family gift – a collection of gold rose bushes, these to form an avenue at Chartwell,* together with an album of rose paintings, each individual flower painted by a leading artist of the day. Before she returned to England, Clementine – unwilling to part from Winston at such a happy time – paid one of her rare visits to La Pausa (she went there only four times); but she could not enjoy it, and found the life claustrophobic, according to Mary. Winston fell into his well oiled routine there: he worked in bed all morning, painted or rested in the afternoon, and in the evenings he dined, chatted and played bezique until bedtime. The grounds were too steep for Clementine to take walks on her own, and to go further afield she had to ask for a car and a driver. So she felt that she was 'really the prisoner of kindness, and of other people's plans'.[29]

---

*Now called the Golden Rose Walk, it runs through the original kitchen garden and circles the sundial.

Despite the smiles and pleasantries she felt she had very little in common with her hosts. Realising that Winston had all he wanted there, including a devoted Wendy to grant his every wish, she decided that she would far rather be in England and leave him to enjoy himself. Her life, still devoted to Winston, involved keeping his homes running smoothly, ready for him to occupy whenever he wanted to; standing in for him in the constituency; and carrying on with her own work (she was in great demand to open hospitals and other public buildings).

During November and December 1958 Randolph published six articles in the *Daily Express* about the Suez crisis and Eden's handling of it. They were noticeably vindictive, and probably imbued with Randolph's old jealousy of Eden. He dismissed Eden's part in the abortive invasion of Egypt, calling it 'ill-planned, ill-timed . . . tragedy on an almost classical scale'.[30] The book he wrote soon afterwards, *The Rise and Fall of Sir Anthony Eden*, was liked by few politicians, and statements were made against it in the House – which only helped its sales. Clarissa, furiously protective of Anthony, was livid; even Evelyn Waugh, no particular friend of Eden, described Randolph's attack as contemptible.[31] In November Randolph gatecrashed a dinner at the British Embassy in honour of Winston, who was in Paris with Clementine to receive the Croix de la Libération from President de Gaulle. Randolph had not been invited and the other guests held a collective breath when he arrived, for it was known that Clementine had not been on speaking terms with her son for two years. However, all went well, and Clementine even referred to him as 'dear boy'.[32] After dinner, Winston sat in an armchair in the Blanc et Or salon and the ladies ranged themselves around him, some sitting at his feet. One friend described him as 'a pasha in heaven'.[33]

Winston and Clementine went to Morocco, staying at the Mamounia Hotel in Marrakech during the first weeks of 1959, before boarding the *Christina* for a three-week cruise. Afterwards, Winston went on alone to La Pausa to spend a month with the Reveses. In March, while he was there, Sarah hit the headlines again when she was arrested for drunken behaviour in Liverpool, where she had been playing the lead in *Peter Pan*. Winston tried to make excuses for her, but clearly her parents recognised by now that Sarah was a fully fledged alcoholic, for Clementine reported that her doctor had begged her, as soon as she finished her present theatrical tour, to 'do a serious cure'. Sarah replied that she would rather die.[34]

It is difficult to know what part these constant barbs of worry about his children played in Winston's state of health. He had just returned to London in April when he suffered another slight stroke, but against Moran's advice he insisted on carrying on with a planned trip in May to Washington. It was his first flight in a jet, a de Havilland Comet,* and despite his obvious frailty he refused to allow Lord Moran to accompany him because, he said, he did not want to look like an invalid. He had his trusted Private Secretary, Anthony Montague Browne, as essential support. After a taxing visit to Washington, where Eisenhower devoted a presidential address to him, he toured Gettysburg, then flew on to New York where he stayed with his old friend Bernard Baruch. He was so exhausted when he arrived at Baruch's apartment that he went straight to bed. A statement was made to waiting journalists that Sir Winston would not be seeing anyone else until his departure. However, on the day he was due to leave for home he somehow mustered the energy to visit Consuelo in her New York home for tea. Winston was now eighty-four and Consuelo was eighty-two; both knew that it might be their last meeting – perhaps Consuelo recalled the opportunity she had missed with Ivor.

Clementine, now in her mid-seventies, had dared to hope that Winston would not stand for Parliament in another general election, but in October 1959 she could not bring herself to suggest retirement. She knew what his role as an MP meant to him; it was virtually all he had left, and he made sure he was always kept au fait

---

*The Comet was as novel and prestigious in design as the Concorde would be thirty years later, but early models suffered from metal fatigue, causing a number of fatal crashes, and it was withdrawn from service. Although a later model enjoyed a safe career for over thirty years, the Comet's reputation made it unpopular as a commercial airliner. The current RAF Nimrod derives from the original design, and is expected to remain in service into the 2020s.

with political developments. So she turned out again and fought alongside him in what was to be Winston's last campaign. It was the fifteenth election they had fought together, and he was re-elected as the Right Honourable Member for Woodford. He achieved a resounding majority, though slightly smaller than that of the 1955 election. Clementine secretly believed that young people must have felt they were not properly represented.

That winter of 1959–60 Emery Reves suffered a heart attack, so Onassis suggested that instead of paying his usual early spring visit to La Pausa, Winston and Clementine should both come cruising in the Caribbean aboard the *Christina* with him and his wife Athena ('Tina'). They embarked in March at Tangiers and cruised for a month in the West Indies. Clementine much enjoyed this holiday, especially showing Winston around the islands she had first seen aboard Lord Moyne's yacht, years earlier. Ari and Tina were generous hosts and could never do enough for them. Ari almost worshipped Winston, and once, when he asked him what he would like to be in another existence, Winston replied, 'A tiger. What about you?' Ari smiled and replied, 'I would like to be your budgerigar, Toby.'

The two couples got on well because Clementine especially liked Tina. But not long after this trip Onassis and Tina would part, after Tina had boarded the *Christina* unexpectedly and discovered Onassis and his most famous mistress, the soprano Maria Callas, having sex in the saloon beneath an El Greco. Tina divorced Ari the following year, 1961, but although the Churchills no longer met her aboard the *Christina*, they were not to lose touch. On 23 October 1961, after her divorce, she married Bert's son Lord Blandford (another Sunny Marlborough), who became stepfather to the Onassis children.* On hearing this news Churchill is said to have smiled and said, 'So, Ari and I are now related.'

---

*Athena (née Livanos, 1929–74) married Onassis in 1946 and they had two children, Alexander and Christina. She divorced Onassis in 1960. Her third husband, after her divorce from Sunny Marlborough in 1971, was Stavros Niarchos, her sister Eugenia's widower. When her twenty-four-year-old son died in a plane crash she never recovered from the shock and died soon afterwards, aged forty-four, of a drug overdose.

After their West Indies cruise the *Christina* returned to Monte Carlo. Emery had recovered his health, and he and Wendy confidently expected Winston to ask to come and stay. He did not; instead he stayed in a suite at Ari's Hôtel de Paris in Monaco, after which Ari had him flown back to London in a private plane. Winston was now an old man. The small strokes he had suffered sometimes made him tire easily, and at such moments he became confused. Probably not realising how much his condition had deteriorated since his last visit, the Reveses took offence at what appeared to them a serious slight. It was the second – the first had occurred not long before when Clementine had refused to accompany Winston on the *Christina* if Emery and Wendy were fellow guests. Even though the Reveses had already accepted the invitation, Ari had had to ask them to withdraw because Winston so much wanted Clementine to join him. The hurt was bad enough the first time, but they found it quite unacceptable the second. When Winston cabled them in August proposing to visit La Pausa in October and saying how much he wanted to see them both, Emery replied bitterly that his dismissal of them earlier in the year made them feel that they 'had done something, or behaved in a manner which prevented you from returning to us'.[35] Someone had intrigued against them, he believed, and he virtually accused Winston of totally disregarding their feelings. In any case, he said, the affair had made Wendy ill, and they were leaving in October for the USA.[36] Winston was shocked and upset, and asked Clementine to write and explain that 'there were no intrigues; and we are all deeply grateful for the hospitality we have enjoyed with you'.[37] When Winston wrote to Wendy, apologising and telling her that the times he had spent at La Pausa were 'among the brightest of my life', she too informed him that she felt he had treated them badly.[38]

There were no further visits to the Reveses after that; there were letters about literary matters and very occasional lunches and dinners at Cap-d'Ail and London, but it was friendship at a distance. Instead of 'Pausaland' Winston and Clementine stayed at the Hôtel de Paris in Monaco that autumn, and all Winston's future visits to the Riviera would be spent there in the luxurious suite that Onassis always made available to him, with his own private staff laid on.[39] Clementine thought it might be easier there for her than at La Pausa, but one visit convinced her that she still disliked the Riviera: it was 'a ghastly place . . . fine if one was a florist or a waiter'. And she wrote to Mary: 'I am suffocated with luxury and ennui, as you feared.'[40] She also disliked Winston's frequent visits to the casino, although he never gambled huge sums. On one occasion she woke in the night to hear a curious rustling on her counterpane. When she investigated she found that Winston had stolen quietly into her room and covered her bed with French franc notes – his winnings at the gaming tables.

At the end of November, back in London, Lord Moran visited Winston on his birthday, taking a pound of caviar as a gift. He knew Winston was feeling low, for several people had reported that he had told them he wanted to die. But occasionally someone would say something that caught his attention, a light would appear in his eyes and he would join the conversation. Now, though, he was becoming increasingly isolated by his deafness. 'I do not want to do anything any more,' he told Onassis. 'I have had enough of power, but I should not like to lose touch altogether.'[41] Winston fell at Hyde Park Gate and broke a vertebra in his neck, but he was back in Parliament before the end of January 1961. In Monaco a few weeks later he was deeply upset when Toby the budgie flew out of an open window and was never recovered. This little creature had held a disproportionately large place in Winston's heart, and although there were suggestions of another budgie, Winston refused. Toby could never be replaced.

That winter he and Clementine went on another cruise in the Caribbean aboard the *Christina*, with Ari. In March when they reached the Grenadine Archipelago, the Edens came aboard for lunch. For about a year after Eden's resignation, he and Clarissa had lived in a cottage with no phone and no electricity, at Friendship Bay on the delightfully remote island of Bequia in the Windward Islands, which notwithstanding the absence of any doctor had contributed to Eden's long haul back to health. Despite Randolph's attacks he retained much of his personal popularity and was created Earl of Avon in 1961, but he felt very acutely the stigma of the Suez shambles, for which he had been wholly blamed, just as Churchill had once shouldered all the responsibility for the Dardanelles. When in England, the Edens lived in Clarissa's tiny cottage at Broad Chalke in Wiltshire, but they loved the Caribbean and would later own an old plantation house in Barbados for some years.* The *Christina* cruise ended in New York, where Winston met Bernard Baruch for what would be the last time. The party flew home in April, and Winston was in Monaco again in late May when he heard that Bert's wife Mary, Duchess of Marlborough, had died of cancer. He returned to England in June for just four days to participate in the Garter Procession and to watch one of his horses run at Ascot; then travelled back to the Riviera.

In July Sarah was arrested again. It was the fourth time since Antony Beauchamp's suicide four years earlier that she had been picked up by the police for being drunk and disorderly. On this occasion she was remanded in Holloway Prison for ten days for a medical report. Winston and Clementine bore the headlines stoically. 'Never explain, never apologise' was Clementine's attitude, but privately they were both extremely upset. When the ten days were up Sarah appeared before a magistrate, was fined again, and released on condition that this time she would seek further help for her drink problem at the Maudsley Hospital.†

For once she did as she was told, and when the therapy was over she decided to go and live quietly in Spain. At the end of 1961 she found a villa for rent in Marbella, at that time an insignificant beach village between Gibraltar and Malaga. There was a half-decent hotel there, where the handful of expats met for sundowners and socialising. It was there in early March 1962 that she met Henry, Baron Audley.‡ Six feet tall and red-haired, forty-nine-year-old Audley had served in India and the Far East during the war. His first marriage had not been a success, and he was divorced when Sarah met him.

---

*Villa Nova subsequently became a luxury hotel and more recently a conference centre.
†The Maudsley Hospital in South London provides mental health care and help for substance-abuse cases.
‡Henry Tuchet-Jesson, 23rd Baron Audley of Heleigh (1913–63), had succeeded to the title from a cousin in 1942.

He was also disabled, having sometime earlier suffered a massive stroke during his sleep and woken up to find himself paralysed and blind. With time he had recovered his sight, and with treatment he was able to walk with varying degrees of success. He then travelled to Spain for the climate, and to her astonishment Sarah and he fell in love at first sight. (Members of the Churchill family seemed to fall in love in this way with an inexplicable regularity.)*

Henry moved into Sarah's villa within days, and almost as quickly they were discussing marriage. She wrote to Clementine to warn her parents before someone in Marbella alerted the press, and she seemed dazed by the delight of it all: 'I never ever believed I would ever find anyone ever again who could make me take heart and believe that happiness & love were yet ahead of me.'[42]

A week later they flew to London, where Randolph did a little research and established that Henry's title was the fourth-oldest in England. 'That puts the Marlboroughs in their place,' he quipped. Then the couple drove down to Chartwell to meet Winston and Clementine and tell them of their intention to marry immediately in Gibraltar, because London held 'too many ghosts' for them both. Clementine took to Henry at once. Winston was too old to make new friends but, seeing joy back in her face after many years of unhappiness, he rejoiced for his favourite daughter. Diana flew back to Spain with them and acted as matron of honour when on 26 April they were married at the Gibraltar register office. After a wedding breakfast at the Rock Hotel, they set off on 'an enchanted honeymoon journey' touring Morocco. By the time the honeymoon was over and they returned to their new villa in Marbella, Sarah had driven four thousand miles. Her old life, the stage and her drink problems were all behind her.

*

---

*The condition of 'love at first sight' has been known throughout recorded history. Plato suggested that primitive men and women were matched double creatures (as in 'soulmates'), and that their modern counterparts spent their lives searching for their 'missing half'. When lovers are fortunate enough to find that part of themselves, he stated 'they are both so intoxicated with affection, with friendship, and with love, that they cannot bear to let each other out of sight for a single instant'.

In June 1962, Winston had been in Monaco for only two days when he had a dizzy spell which caused him to trip and fall, breaking a hip. In great pain, he was so worried that he might die there that he got an RAF Comet to fly him home. He was in hospital in England for almost two months, and Sarah and Henry flew to London to spend some time at his bedside.

Winston had always made a point, whenever possible, of spending the big occasions such as Christmas, Easter and Whitsun with Clementine and the family at Chartwell, even if, in later years, he subsequently disappeared off to the sunshine within a day or so. The Churchills now had ten grandchildren (two Churchills, three Sandyses and five Soameses) and he enjoyed watching them all grow. When in England he still attended sessions at the House and each June he had always attended the Garter ceremony, but after 1962 this was no longer a date enshrined in his diary because he found the procession too tiring and hot and his mobility was affected permanently after the hip operation. He still enjoyed dinners at the Other Club; in fact this, and his occasional appearances in the House, were what he lived for. His frailty was concealed from the world by his personal courage; also, 'All his outings and public appearances were carefully prepared and stage managed,' Mary explained, 'so that, impeccably attired, he gave a debonair impression.'[43] Usually Mary's husband Christopher gave him an arm, and Winston somehow summoned hidden reserves of energy and the inevitable quip – he never forgot how to play to the gallery. At home at Hyde Park Gate Clementine had arranged for a lift to be installed and his bedroom was changed, so that he had no stairs to climb. During the summer of 1962 Clementine never left Winston's side as he recovered from his operation. But the job of carer took a toll on her own health – she was then seventy-seven and still insisted on supervising the running of the house around Winston. At Christmas that year she had four generations to lunch one day, and the next day took Mary's children and Arabella to the circus.

In 1963, after spending a holiday in Monaco with Clementine, Mary and Christopher, Winston was somehow able to make one final visit to Washington. His doctor was convinced the trip would kill him, but in fact the excursion seemed to energise him, for his daily routine had become very boring to him. He followed this journey with his eighth and last cruise aboard the *Christina*. He was now an old, old man, seldom even bothering to paint. Clementine and the family were always watchful and worried about him, and they had held their breaths collectively while he was in America. His main problems, though, were the familiar effects of old age – mild depression and deafness.[44] The deaths, one by one, of his old contemporaries also saddened him greatly; Max Beaverbrook died in June 1963. He could still make an effort, show flashes of the old Winston, but he often sank into long silences, though he hated to be left alone. Mary recalled in her biography of her mother how he would sometimes, after one of these periods of silence, suddenly put out an affectionate hand and say apologetically to his visitor: 'I'm sorry I'm not very amusing today.'[45]

It was in July 1963, while Sarah and Henry were visiting Granada, that tragedy struck. They had only just checked into their hotel room, and Henry was resting on the bed while Sarah was in the bathroom brushing her teeth. The couple were chatting to each other when Sarah suddenly realised Henry had not answered a question. When she popped her head around the door to ask 'Did you hear me?' it was obvious straight away that he was dead. Doctors diagnosed a heart attack, but later it would be confirmed that it was a sudden and massive cerebral haemorrhage that had killed him instantly, between one heartbeat and the next.

Apart from the shock and the grief – they had been happily married for just over a year – there were the inevitable doctors, police, post-mortem and death certificates to cope with, all in Spanish. It was an appalling few days for Sarah until Diana arrived, calmly assured, to take over and allow Sarah to fall into an exhausted sleep, and then begin the grieving process. The following day they discussed the funeral and Sarah deliberated whether she should ship Henry's body back to England. But Diana was a rock: 'Remember,' she said firmly, 'we are the daughters of a soldier. Where we fall, there we rest.' Diana knew the British Consul at Malaga, who suggested that the British naval cemetery there would be a suitable resting place for Henry. So it was all arranged. Sarah was told: 'We have chosen a very beautiful place where there are two slim trees, a pepper and a fir.' Sarah placed her wedding ring in the earth that she sprinkled on the coffin. Within a few days she flew to England and drove down to Chartwell. Winston met her at the front door and they stared silently at each other. It must have been so difficult for him to know what to say that could offer his daughter any comfort. But then he took her hand and held it, and said simply, 'We must close ranks and march on.'[46]

A few weeks later, in September 1963, Clementine collapsed with a nervous breakdown. It was surprising she had not done so before. One friend had spotted her decline before it happened, and wrote to Mary: 'She really is worn out. Winston dislikes being left alone all day with his nurses, and dislikes having meals alone; Clemmie found it a strain having to talk loudly to make him hear . . . My view is that . . . Clemmie . . . is worn out and needs rest.'[47] She had always been highly strung, living on her nerves, and to this was added the strain not only of being a carer but also of maintaining her own impossibly high standards. Then there were the various problems concerning her children – not least, Henry's death just when Sarah seemed to have her life back on the rails. Such events, which always made headlines, were all the more distressing for someone who hated her personal life being exposed. She was admitted to hospital, heavily sedated, and underwent several electrotherapy sessions. While this was happening, another family tragedy occurred.

After Diana flew to England following Henry's funeral, Sarah had returned to the Marbella villa that she and Henry had bought after their marriage. She was still there some weeks later when her neighbour called round. Sarah had no telephone and her neighbour took calls for her from England. This time she advised Sarah to prepare herself for bad news when she went to the phone. 'I couldn't imagine what else could have happened,' Sarah recalled, and she suspected it was going to be news about Winston. She went to the telephone and heard Mary's voice say: 'Darling Sarah, Diana has died. There's to be an inquest.'[48]

1963–78

Crossing the Bar

Diana had never got over losing Duncan. For some years before their divorce the two had lived apart, and well before that she had lived with the knowledge that her marriage was far from stable. Whether it was cause or effect, her life had been punctuated for many years with periods of depression. Duncan had made a success of his parliamentary life, had worked closely with 'the Prof' promoting secret weapons, and had been appointed Financial Secretary at the War Office. After that he held Cabinet posts in successive Tory governments for the remainder of his career. Clementine had never taken to Duncan, so his visits to Chartwell were infrequent, but Winston liked him a lot and was upset that Diana's marriage had failed. After the divorce Winston asked Jock Colville to invite Duncan to dinner at the Other Club: 'I should so much like to see him again, but if I asked him to luncheon or dinner, Clemmie would be upset.'[1]

Diana underwent several intensive electrotherapy treatments, which seemed to leave her just as depressed and confused as before. Perhaps only Winston really understood her deep despair: having himself suffered from the same affliction, he was able quietly to offer sympathy and comfort. Recently, though, Diana had appeared far more serene, and had even become a Samaritan in order to try to help others with similar mental problems. When she flew to Spain in July to help Sarah she had taken over the funeral arrangements for Henry with a calm assurance. This is remarkable in view of the fact that from March to July 1963 Diana had suffered a more than usual amount of stress. In March the sensational divorce case of the Duchess of Argyll* was heard in London and Duncan Sandys was named as one of her lovers. The case and the rumours and accusations rumbled on through the early summer at exactly the same time as the Profumo scandal. John Profumo admitted that he had lied to the House of Commons about his affair with Christine Keeler and resigned in early June. Later the same month, Duncan, who was Minister of Defence at the time, under extreme pressure from the media, confessed in a stormy Cabinet meeting to being the 'headless man'. Another sex scandal, coming so soon after Profumo's resignation, could easily have toppled the Macmillan government, so Duncan was persuaded not to resign, and instead an inquiry was ordered, headed by Lord Denning, Master of the Rolls. Diana had all this to contend with when she flew to help Sarah. But when on 19 October Diana learned that Duncan's new wife had just given birth to a son, it was evidently more than she could tolerate. She took an overdose of sleeping pills.

Clementine was still under sedation, a feature of the treatment for her condition, and it was Mary who had to break the news about Diana to Winston. He seemed stunned at the death of his eldest child, but he said very little. By now he spent long periods in silence every day, remote from those around him. It was difficult to know whether he was deep in thought, or bored because he could not hear what was going on, or whether he had begun to slide into the vacant realms of dementia. But it is evident from the diary entries of those closest to him that there were still brief moments when light would come back into his eyes and the old Winston would shine forth.

---

*Margaret Campbell, third wife of the 11th Duke of Argyll. The divorce case made headlines when the prosecuting counsel introduced as evidence several Polaroid images of the Duchess, naked but wearing her pearls. In one photo she was performing a sex act on a man whose head had been cut off by the camera angle. He was known as 'the headless man' and it was widely suspected that it was Duncan Sandys, Minister of Defence – who had access to the only Polaroid camera in the country at the time. Subsequently it was proved that there were two men in the photographs; the other was Douglas Fairbanks Jnr, who was identified by his handwriting on the reverse of the photos.

Eventually Mary was able to tell her mother about Diana's death. Because Clementine was still lightly sedated, the information filtered only gradually through to her over a period of days, without causing huge shock. But both she and Winston were too upset, and too unwell, to attend the funeral. Instead they attended the memorial service on 31 October.

In the spring of 1964 Randolph was seriously ill again with bronchopneumonia. Evelyn Waugh visited him and wrote to Diana Cooper: 'I have become reconciled with R. He looked so pathetically thin and feeble and when he tried to shout a whisper came. So 12 years [of] enmity are expunged.'[2] After exploratory surgery for suspected lung cancer later that year, Randolph had part of his lung cut away. The tissue underwent a biopsy but no cancer was found. Waugh could not resist telling their friends that the surgeons had cut out the only part of Randolph that was not malignant. But his hell-raising days were behind him – he spent all his time now working on the great opus that was his father's life story.

The entire family was thrilled when in June twenty-four-year-old Winston, who would go on to make a career in politics, married his childhood sweetheart Minnie d'Erlanger. His grandfather was unable to attend the wedding but the couple called on him afterwards at Hyde Park Gate. A few weeks later, on 27 July 1964, Winston made his final appearance in the House of Commons. His first day there, as an ambitious twenty-six-year-old, had been 14 February 1901, shortly after the death of Queen Victoria when the London streets were filled with horse-drawn buses and hansom cabs and illuminated by gas lamps. On 28 July, a deputation consisting of the Prime Minister and other leaders and elders of the House called on him at Hyde Park Gate and presented Winston with a formal vote of thanks for a lifetime of service, following a resolution passed that day in the House.[3]

Clementine had recovered from her breakdown by this time, and although much relieved at Winston's retirement – indeed, she had engineered it – she also agonised that it had removed from him his only incentive for getting up each day. He still managed to attend dinners at the Other Club, which he greatly looked forward to.

Despite the family difficulties they'd had to overcome in recent years the deep love of this couple for each other never faltered, and on his ninetieth birthday in November 1964 at a party at Hyde Park Gate Clementine gave Winston a small gold heart engraved with the numerals '90'. It was to hang on his watch chain, alongside the gold heart with the ruby that she had given him when they became engaged fifty-seven years earlier.[4]

Brushed and spruced up, Winston had made a public appearance at the window of the drawing room at Hyde Park Gate, where a crowd had appeared in the street below to sing 'Happy Birthday'. As usual he rose to the occasion, and press photographs depict him waving, making the victory sign, smiling broadly and looking remarkably well. That evening there was a family party attended by Randolph and Arabella, Mary and Christopher and their children, Sarah, young Winston and Minnie, and a few very close friends such as Anthony Montague Browne and his wife. As they toasted Winston's health Mary felt the poignancy of the occasion, for her father was now very fragile, 'and often so remote'.

A week later Consuelo died quietly at her house Garden Side, in the Hamptons, Long Island, aged eighty-seven. Her son Bert, the 10th Duke, flew over to be with her when summoned, but he arrived too late. The funeral service was held in the church where she had so unwillingly married Sunny Marlborough almost seventy years earlier. She was interred at Bladon in the Churchill plot: Bert and his family, with Clementine, Randolph, Sarah and Mary, attended the ceremony. Winston was unable to be there.

Pamela, now married to the Hollywood producer and agent Leland Hayward,* was still living the life of international jet-setter, and would visit Winston whenever she flew into London. For years he had paid her a small pension, to make up for Randolph's failure to do so. Pam still adored her former father-in-law, and her visits seemed to offer him some cheer. Soon after Consuelo's death, when

---

*Among Leland Hayward's (1902–71) successes were *The Sound of Music, South Pacific, Spirit of St Louis, The Old Man and the Sea* and *Gypsy*. His clients included stars such as Fred Astaire and Ginger Rogers, James Stewart, Greta Garbo and Katharine Hepburn.

she was sitting holding his hand, he said wistfully: 'Why can't I just die?' Not realising that he said the same to other visitors, she understood it to be a private confidence and it haunted her for years. But Winston's family and closest friends had become accustomed to hearing those words. The man who had once believed he would die young, and so had always been in such a fervour to justify his existence before it was too late, had done everything there was for him to do. Thirty years earlier he had written, 'One must always hope for a sudden end, before faculties decay . . .' But this grace was not given to him.

Soon after the New Year of 1965 Winston caught a cold which he could not shake off. On 11 January Clementine phoned Mary and told her that her father seemed to have suffered another 'spasm' and was far from well. Lord Moran, who had now treated Winston for twenty-four years, came and checked his patient. He told the family that Winston had suffered a cerebral thrombosis, and although he had pulled through such attacks on previous occasions he believed he was too feeble to weather this one. When Mary saw him that evening she felt he did not recognise her. The following morning he woke up, but seemed 'very remote and said nothing'. In the afternoon Christopher sat with him, and to encourage him to talk, asked him, 'Would you like a glass of champagne?' Winston regarded him vaguely, and delivered his last coherent sentence: 'I'm so bored with it all.'

He could still move his right arm and for a while it seemed there was a chance that, despite what Lord Moran had said, he might yet recover. However, Moran warned that if he did survive he would be terribly 'impaired', which left the anxious family not knowing what to hope for.

By the 15th Winston fell into deep unconsciousness and it was agreed that a formal announcement of his condition should be made. It read: 'After a cold, Sir Winston has developed a circulatory weakness and there has been a cerebral thrombosis.' Sarah was summoned from Rome and arrived next day. The house was swamped with telegrams and flowers and a small crowd gathered quietly outside the house despite the freezing weather. There would always be knots of people outside the house now, keeping vigil, until the end. Initially these were swelled by groups of reporters and cameramen, but Clementine requested that they move away because the noise, arc lights, flashbulbs and chatter were disturbing. Without a word and within minutes they had withdrawn respectfully to a distant corner, where they could still be on hand to watch members of the family as they came and went each day, and to catch the daily health bulletins.

Through all the family visits Winston slept on, apparently tranquilly. He had taken no sustenance since 14 January, and all the family could do was keep his mouth and lips moistened with water and glycerine, and speak to him. Once, when young Winston was alone with him he was so worried that his grandfather might be thirsty that he disobeyed instructions and gave him a sip of orange juice. Sometimes Winston's right hand would move as though he were painting, and once it seemed he was attempting to smoke an invisible cigar. A good deal of the time Clementine sat quietly holding his hand, while Winston's beloved marmalade cat lay curled at his feet on the bed. Clementine appeared serene, only once – briefly – breaking down. She seemed surprised that she could maintain a calm demeanour and told Mary she did not know where all her tears had gone. Always immaculately dressed and coiffed, she seemed to have withdrawn into herself, while mechanically checking the scores of messages and flowers that arrived daily, running the house as impeccably as always and organising meals for visitors. 'There had never been any room in her life for slipshod ways,' Mary recorded.[5] On Friday the 22nd Randolph looked in to report that Minnie had safely given birth to a son whom she and young Winston had named Randolph.

Two days later, shortly after 8 a.m. on 24 January, after a few deep sighs Winston died. Most of the people he loved, Sarah, Mary, Diana's daughter Celia, Randolph and young Winston, were at his bedside with Clementine and Anthony Montague Browne. Lord Moran was in attendance. 'Nobody moved or spoke,' Mary recorded. 'Presently, Clementine looked up at Lord Moran. "Has he gone?" she asked. He nodded . . . One by one we all got up and silently left the room. I went back and remained with my mother for some little time. Then we both kissed his hand and then his brow and left him.'[6]

Soon after, Randolph went to find a book to check something that had occurred to him. He came back to tell them that Winston had died seventy years to the exact day, and almost to the hour, after his father's death, for Lord Randolph had died at 6.15 a.m. on 24 January 1895. Perhaps, with his great sense of history, Winston had somehow played a deliberate part in this remarkable coincidence.* Jock Colville could not help recalling a morning some years earlier when Churchill was still at the height of his powers: 'I went to his bedroom,' he wrote, 'to talk to him about some business matter while he was shaving. "Today," he said to me, "is the twenty-fourth of January. It is the day my father died. It is the day that I shall die too."'[7]

It is not too fanciful to say that grief enveloped Britain. Winston had dozens of political opponents, but as a person he was deeply loved by the people, and it seemed that the nation almost stopped in its tracks at the news. Prime Minister Harold Wilson postponed a major speech in the House of Commons, and ceremonies to commemorate the seven-hundredth anniversary of the first Parliament were postponed for six months. Winston's customary place, the corner seat by the gangway, was left vacant out of respect for the man who was arguably the greatest parliamentarian during all of those seven centuries.

It had already been agreed some years earlier to accord Winston a state funeral, and the codename for this operation was 'Hope Not'. Immediately the news was out, the great panoply of state swung into motion under the direction of the Duke of Norfolk, who as the Earl Marshal of England† was responsible for organising such national occasions. The plans for this funeral had been laid twelve years earlier.

Churchill's body lay in state at Westminster Hall for three days, the coffin draped in the Union flag upon which lay his Garter decoration.

---

*It is common for coma patients to live to a special, much looked-forward-to date such as Christmas, the birth of a child or a family marriage, and then die quietly immediately afterwards.
†This great office of state dates back to the twelfth century and has been held on a hereditary basis by the Norfolk family since 1672.

Four Guardsmen took up their stations at the corners of the catafalque, heads bowed in symbolic grief, hands clasped on the hilts of their drawn swords. Every twenty minutes the guard changed, silently; no commands were issued. Clementine and the family were able to gain access whenever they wished through a side door, and stood watching the surreal scene as the line of people, who had queued for hours in the freezing weather day and night to pay their last respects, silently and respectfully filed past the coffin. A carpet had been laid there, so no sound disturbed the quiet of the great candlelit hall. The line snaked back over two miles throughout the three days; the family were later told that 320,000 people had passed through.

On 30 January the coffin was loaded on to a naval gun-carriage and, drawn by ratings, set out from Westminster for St Paul's Cathedral. It was an intensely cold day as Winston made his final journey, through hushed streets. The men of the family, led by Randolph, Christopher and young Winston, marched behind the gun-carriage. Knowing there was an hour's walk ahead of them in the biting wind young Winston worried about his father, who was not fully recovered from his lung surgery some months earlier. The ladies and other family mourners rode in five carriages from the royal mews, equipped with lap rugs and hot-water bottles; they could only faintly hear the band and the ninety-gun salute at St James's Park.

Heralds in colourful medieval tabards, carrying Churchill's Garter emblems draped in black, accompanied the coffin to the bier in front of the altar. The Queen set aside the order of precedence* in favour of Clementine and the family, and after the solemn service the coffin was borne to Tower Hill for another cannon salute and a parade of the Yeomen of the Guard, whose Elizabethan uniforms provided a colourful contrast to the sombre black bearskins and dark winter greatcoats of the Guards. At Tower Pier the coffin was placed on a motor launch, with Winston's pennant as Lord Warden of the Cinque Ports flying at the mast. The coffin was

---

*Under the order of precedence, the sovereign is the most important person present at any occasion.

ferried to Festival Pier, to be placed aboard a special train waiting at Waterloo. The short voyage upriver was rendered even more poignant when the booms of all the dockside cranes were lowered as the launch passed by. Lightning Jets of Fighter Command dipped their wings as they roared overhead, offering a reminder of how far aviation had advanced since those early days when Winston had learned to fly in aeroplanes made of wood, string and canvas.

The train that bore Winston's body home was pulled by a Battle of Britain-class steam engine bearing the name *Sir Winston Churchill*. From the country railway station and all along the Oxfordshire lanes to the village of Bladon which lies within sight of Blenheim Palace, silent crowds stood four or five deep as the coffin, now guarded by Winston's old regiment the 4th Queen's Own Hussars, proceeded on the last miles of its journey. Men removed their hats: not a sound was heard in the thin, cold air. At Clementine's request no press were present at the church.

Only his beloved family was with him, as Winston Spencer Churchill was buried close to his parents and his brother in Bladon churchyard. His grave bore the simplest of headstones. That night as she went up to bed Clementine told Mary that it had been not a funeral, but a triumph.

There is a small, little known footnote to history about that day. At Bladon churchyard Captain Barry de Morgan was the officer in charge of the bearer party. He recalled: 'The coffin was very heavy and the strain on the bearer party was considerable; so much so that in order to keep a grip on the straps each of the bearers had to dampen their gloves to avoid the risk of a runaway . . .' During the measured lowering of the coffin, the strain on the clothing of the bearers was so intense that in the case of one – Sergeant Webb – the pin holding his medals beneath his greatcoat gave way and dropped into the grave. Captain de Morgan heard a 'clunk' but with his mind on the important task in hand he ignored it. As they were about to board the train to return to London the sergeant told him that his medals were missing, and the clunk was explained. Captain de Morgan immediately notified the officer in charge of the railway station for the day, Major Ronnie Ferguson,[*] who rapidly despatched a guardsman to recover the medals before the grave was filled in.

In the weeks that followed, one of Clementine's first acts was to hand Chartwell over to the National Trust. Although under the terms of the Chartwell trust it was hers for her lifetime, it had always been Winston's house and she knew she would never be happy living there alone. She also put the two adjoining houses at Hyde Park Gate on the market, and would later buy a flat at nearby Prince's Gate. In February, with Mary and Christopher she sailed on the *Queen Mary* to Barbados, where old friends Ronald and Marietta Tree[†] had invited them to come and stay at their West Coast mansion, Heron Bay. Ten days later, they flew on to Jamaica to stay with the widowed Bert Marlborough and several members of his family near Montego Bay. The kindness of friends, the peace, the light and the colour, and the balmy Caribbean air, all helped Clementine through those days.

Randolph had the biography of his father to work on, and he applied all his considerable literary ability to the task. Family and friends have said that his work on this project after his father's death, his poor health notwithstanding, provided him with a hitherto unknown contentment. Another factor was Clementine's regular visits to Stour House. All his life he had craved his mother's attention and demonstrations of her love for him, but while Winston was alive Randolph had always taken a back seat. Now Randolph was enchanted to be consulted by Clementine for his opinions and advice. He was still incorrigible, still steam-rollering his way to something he wanted, or wanted done. Rules were not

---

*Father of Sarah Ferguson, former wife of Prince Andrew.

†Arthur Ronald Lambert Field Tree (1897–1976) was MP for Harborough in Leicestershire, a journalist and an inventor. He had a British father and his mother was the American heiress of Marshall Field's department store. One of Winston's political allies, Tree owned Ditchley Park, an eighteenth-century stately home in Oxfordshire; during the Second World War, in clear weather whenever bombing raids were expected, he made Ditchley available to Winston and Clementine (Chequers was considered to be an easy target). Marietta, his second wife, was known for her famous lovers, who included Adlai Stevenson and John Huston.

made for Randolph Churchill, and there would still be the occasional explosion when everything did not go his way. But far more often now the charm of the man came to the fore.

Less than eighteen months after Winston's death Lord Moran published *Winston Churchill: The Struggle for Survival*. It is a large book and had clearly been started a considerable time before Winston's death. Moran had raised the matter of his writing a book in 1964, during the last summer of Winston's life, when it was no longer possible to involve Winston in discussion about it for fear he would be upset. At the time Clementine made it quite clear to Moran, in writing, that she could not approve the project. 'I always supposed that the relationship between a doctor and his patient was one of complete confidence,' she wrote. 'Had you been writing your own biography with passing reference to Winston, it would have been understandable, though I would have hoped you would tell us what you intended to say.' She pointed out politely that Lord Moran's career had already been considerably enhanced by his association with Winston, implying that this should perhaps have been sufficient for him. There was no reply to this letter, and Clementine assumed he had dropped the matter.

One year to the day after Winston's death, Lord Moran wrote Clementine a long letter saying that few authors would allow others to see their manuscripts, that he had finished the book (to be published that summer), and he requested permission to use a specific portrait of Winston in it. Permission was withheld.

In April 1966 the *Sunday Times* ran the first of a six-part serialisation of the book, for which Lord Moran received £30,000. There is no doubt that this book caused huge distress to Clementine, and members of the family were outraged. Apart from the breach of confidentiality, Moran's harrowing descriptions of Winston in extreme old age were not how Clementine wished Winston to be remembered – any more than the Sutherland painting had been. A storm of controversy broke, involving many eminent public figures who had known and worked closely with Churchill, and leading physicians who questioned the morality of Moran's exposing his patient's illness to the world without gaining the permission of the family. The question most asked was, 'How can it be ethical of Dr Moran to contravene his Hippocratic oath?'

Moran claimed that the information was taken from his own diaries. Yet friends who had been closest to Churchill in his last decade, such as Colville and Montague Browne, pointed out that the book contained many factual errors indicating that parts of it were at best the result of retrospective editing after many years, rather than contemporary diary entries. Moran referred, for example, to a journey to New York with Winston on the *Queen Elizabeth*. The voyage was actually taken on the *Queen Mary* – an error which, at a distance of years, would be easy to make – whereas had Moran been keeping a daily diary, as he claimed, he would hardly have mistaken the name of the ship on which he was sailing. Moreover, conversations were quoted and events referred to at which the doctor claimed to have been present, whereas from diaries kept by others it was evident that he had merely joined the company afterwards, when Churchill had mentioned the matters in passing. There were also demonstrable misquotations as well as quotations taken out of context.

It was claimed by the *Sunday Times* and the publishers that Moran and Winston were intimate friends, and Moran quotes him as thanking him for keeping him alive for so long. More contentiously, he claimed that Winston had known of his intention to write the book and had approved, and that Brendan Bracken had actively encouraged it. The family and his really intimate friends denied these assertions. Winston *had* regarded Lord Moran as a friend, though not as an intimate. He had trusted him utterly as his doctor and allowed him to see him in a totally relaxed state – sometimes, necessarily, when he was ill and vulnerable. Had he suspected that his words were being recorded, Clementine believed, Winston would never have done so. Furthermore, Winston, who had no secrets from Clementine and few from Mary, Christopher and the others, had never mentioned to anyone the major matter of Moran's proposed book. Indeed, he took the issue of his historical legacy so seriously that he had agonised for years over whether to allow his own son to write about him – so was it likely that he would ever have sanctioned an unedited version by his doctor so soon after his death? But of course, neither Winston nor Bracken could be called as a witness, and Moran defended himself by stating that any study of Winston's last twenty-five years would be inaccurate without knowing the state of his health and the 'exhaustion of mind and body that accounted for much that is otherwise inexplicable'.[8]

There is no question that the book was and remains a fascinating document. Nor is there any doubt that a good deal of what Moran placed in the public domain was accurate. However, the image conveyed of Churchill, from as early as 1943, was of a man in almost constantly failing health. This, clearly, is not wholly correct, though it could be explained by the fact that Moran only ever saw his patient when he needed a doctor. In the end Moran was censured by the Medical Ethics Committee of the British Medical Association, but the fact remained that considerable hurt was caused to Winston's family and the genie could not be put back in the bottle.

The rumpus sent sales sky-high. Diana Mosley – who had known Winston all her life but had fallen out with him over her imprisonment during the war years – was fascinated by the book. She wrote to her sister Nancy Mitford (who had given away many family secrets under the guise of fiction):

I'm deep in Lord Moran, it has made my eyes ache because one can't stop reading. I can't imagine what the fuss is about (it seems people come to blows over it). Imagine if he really had been gossipy & spilled the beans – Wendy at Monte Carlo, Randolph vile & making him cry, Diana getting electric shocks for her hysteria, Sarah in & out of the cells etc. The doctor must have known all, with knobs on, yet there is never a hint (he does say once there was 'an uplift' in Winston's spirits when he visited the Reveses . . . It reminds me of old Beaverbrook saying to me once: 'Why can't they leave him with Wendy where he's happy?).[9]

In May 1965 while the Moran row was still raging, Clementine was made a life peer. She assumed the title Baroness Spencer Churchill of Chartwell, which gave her a seat in the Upper House.

Although she never spoke in the Lords she often attended and voted.

Randolph's health was poor after the operation in 1964 to remove part of his lung, but he devoted all his energy to his book, and by the summer of 1968, three years after Winston's death, two hefty volumes had been completed as well as half a dozen companion volumes containing the transcripts of hundreds of letters and papers (for which he has earned the hearty gratitude of hundreds of subsequent Churchill researchers). The project had taken eight years at that point. Randolph had originally said that 'the Life' would consist of five volumes, each of 200,000 to 300,000 words (plus the companion volumes), but he could not work alone on this mammoth undertaking. He had a team of brilliant young historians as research assistants, plus secretaries and typists. One of the 'young gentlemen' researchers, as he referred to them, was Martin Gilbert,* who was told that it would be his job to call at the various great houses around the country, explain his credentials and seek out any papers on Churchill that might be of interest.

While working on his *magnum opus* Randolph had taken to spending part of his winters in Marrakech and sometimes made trips to Switzerland. In the summer he enjoyed visits to Monte Carlo, when Natalie invariably accompanied him as his muse. He seldom drank any more, and though he still behaved with the arrogance of Louis XIV he was less explosive. It was the long years of abuse to his digestive system, especially his kidneys, that destroyed him in the end. He ate like a bird now and was emaciated, his skin hanging in folds. Anita Leslie, who visited him at that time, said that she could hardly bear to look at him when she recalled what he had once been: 'He would suddenly raise his head and catch me turning away and he knew why I [had] turned.' But, she said, 'perhaps the most striking thing was his sense of wonder. He never lost it. He lived in a magic world where every day amazed and excited him.'[10] Natalie spent most days

---

*He subsequently took over from Randolph as Churchill's official biographer, producing a further six volumes, plus companion books (see the Bibliography).

with him and usually saw him into bed before returning each night to her own house.

Randolph was alone when he died during the night of 7 June 1968 aged fifty-seven. His doctor said later that he had worn out every organ in his body. One of his researchers found him the next morning when he took him a cup of tea. Mary noticed that at Randolph's funeral Clementine was wrapped in the remote silence she always adopted in sorrow; of her five children – the 'puppy-kittens', as she and Winston had always called them – only Mary and Sarah now remained.

Clementine's life during the years after Winston's death was busy and fulfilled, and thanks to good friends and staff she was never alone, even though her daughters were seldom able to be with her. Sarah had returned to the United States and was working there. Christopher was made Ambassador to France soon after Randolph's death, so the Soameses moved to Paris. Clementine was able to visit them several times a year, always travelling by boat-train. She had known and loved Paris all her life, so this was a treat. It came to an end only when, four years later, Christopher was recalled and appointed one of the two first Commissioners to the European Economic Community. Released from the onerous duties of an Ambassador's wife, Mary was now able to spend more time with her mother.

When she was able to read Randolph's published volumes Clementine was delighted with them. Once, near the end, she told Mary that she missed Winston more now than in the days immediately after his death. On the centenary of his birth, 30 November 1974, she was taken in a wheelchair to his grave by young Winston. She laid some flowers and whispered: 'I hope I shall not be long now.'[11]

As time passed Mary worried increasingly that her mother might have to face pain or a further major trial at the end of her life, but she need not have been concerned. Her death came on 12 December 1977. Clementine had lunched in her flat at Prince's Gate with her trusted friend and secretary, Nonie Chapman. She enjoyed the meal, but afterwards there was a sudden change in her breathing. Her two Filipino maids were summoned and they all helped her into her bedroom to lie down. There was no panic, or pain, and within a few minutes Clementine's life eased gently away, as though on an ebb tide. She was interred quietly with Winston, in the churchyard of St Martin's at Bladon.

At the service of thanksgiving for her life, held on 24 January 1978, the thirteenth anniversary of Winston's death, extracts were read from the marriage service of Winston and Clementine held almost seventy years earlier. It ended with the words: 'May your lives prove a blessing each to the other and both to the world, and may you pass in the Divine mercy from strength to strength and from joy to joy.' Seldom can a more apposite blessing have been given to any bride and groom.

In the opening chapter of this book I wrote of the first Duchess of Marlborough: 'Sarah never regretted the marriage, for theirs was that enviable partnership, a genuine love match, though Sarah's fiery temperament ensured that their years together were never humdrum.' Winston Spencer Churchill not only matched and bettered his illustrious ancestor's record in battle, he also matched John Churchill's good fortune in finding the perfect life partner.

Family and Friends

Mary and Christopher Soames Having enjoyed an impressive career in government during which he achieved Cabinet rank and was admitted to the Privy Council, Christopher was created a life peer in 1978 as Baron Soames. From 1979 to 1981, under Margaret Thatcher, he was Lord President of the Council and Leader of the House of Lords, in tandem with his duties as the last Governor of Southern Rhodesia (originally a Harold Wilson appointment). Christopher died in 1987 of pancreatitis at the age of sixty-six and was buried in the Churchill plot at Bladon. Mary, who had helped him throughout his career, was honoured for her public services, notably in Southern Rhodesia, and was created a Dame Commander of the Order of the British Empire. In 2005 she was appointed a Lady Companion of the Order of the Garter, the honour which her father regarded as one of the greatest of the many tributes heaped upon him.

Today she is a successful and highly regarded writer in the Churchill genre, and is noted especially for her affectionate but frank biography of her mother (*Clementine Churchill*, published in 1979). She has also published a book of the letters between her parents, *Speaking for Themselves*, which has been a source of invaluable information to many Churchill researchers. When I interviewed her for this book in her London house, she was eighty-nine and busy writing her memoirs. A friend who accompanied me on this occasion and was introduced to Lady Soames for the first time, was startled into blurting: 'My goodness! You are *so* like your father' (my friend may not thank me for revealing this). Lady Soames was simply amused.

Of Mary's five children the best-known is Nicholas Soames, former Conservative Shadow Secretary of State for Defence. He has been an MP since 1983 and has held a number of high positions. He is also a former equerry to the Prince of Wales and has worked in a number of roles in the City.

Sarah Churchill   In the years following her mother's death, Sarah was in poor health. She died in her sleep, aged sixty-seven, in 1982. Cause of death was given as renal failure. She is buried at Bladon in the Churchill plot.

Albert ('Bert'), 10th Duke of Marlborough   Only six weeks before his death in 1972, Bert married, as his second wife, Laura Charteris (1915–90), by then the widow of the American publishing heir Michael Temple Canfield and sister-in-law of the novelist Ian Fleming. She had been the lodestar of Randolph Churchill's adult life – the unattainable woman he always wanted. It is ironic that she should have eventually married into the Churchill family. Laura also fended Bert off for a long time because she had no wish to live in 'gloomy' Blenheim, stared at by tourists from behind a cordon whenever she ventured outside to play croquet. But he wore her down by singing romantic old love songs to her. Harsh things have been said about Bert: he was described by some as 'a bore' and as 'stupid', but he saved Blenheim for the nation and protected the inheritance of the Marlboroughs from the Inland Revenue.[1] He thereby fulfilled the primary duty of a Duke of Marlborough. He was interred in the chapel vault in Blenheim.

John ('Sunny'), 11th Duke of Marlborough   Bert was succeeded in 1972 by his son John (inevitably called 'Sunny') who had married, first, Susan Hornby from whom he was divorced in 1961. His second wife was Tina Onassis; they divorced in 1971. He married a third time, to Dagmar Rosita Douglas Stjemorp, daughter of Count Carl Ludwig Douglas, a Swedish nobleman and diplomat who was the Swedish Ambassador to Brazil. When his father Bert died, John and Rosita became the 11th Duke and Duchess.

Although, according to his friend, Cynthia Gladwin, Bert bullied Sunny 'all the time', Sunny had shared the running of Blenheim with his father for many years and so the change-over was a smooth one. The death duties were dealt with by donating an archive of over 30,000 documents, of inestimable value, to the nation; these, the Blenheim Papers, are now at the British Library where scholars, academics, historians and visitors from all over the world have open access. Blenheim itself is a World Heritage site and is now run as a business, a popular tourist destination, especially for overseas visitors. Sunny and Rosita were divorced in 2008 and the Duke is now married to the former Lily Mahtani.

Clarissa and Anthony Eden   In early January 1977 the Edens were in Florida when Sir Anthony was given two weeks to live. Clarissa was unable to get him home because of a strike by British Airways. The Prime Minister Jim Callaghan, having been asked to provide RAF transport, at first demurred because of the cost, but his aides pointed out that it would reflect badly on him if he refused to 'help and honour' a former Prime Minister who was still popular with the public. A jet was duly sent and Eden came home to England, to die on 14 January, in his eightieth year. Clarissa (Lady Avon) still lives in London and published her autobiography in 2009.

Emery and Wendy Reves   After their rift in 1960, contact between Churchill and Emery was restricted to literary matters. Sarah remained in contact with the couple, though, and after Winston's death Clementine wrote twice to them in response to their letters of condolence. Emery died in 1981, and Mary wrote to Wendy to tell her of Sarah's death a year later. Wendy devoted the remainder of her life to philanthropy, making extensive charitable endowments in the fields of education, medical research and the arts. She died at the age of ninety in March 2007 at a hospital near La Pausa.

Winston S. Churchill (young Winston)   Churchill adored his namesake grandchild, who, some might say, had the misfortune to have two extremely strong and self-centred parents. If one recalls Lord Randolph and Jennie Jerome, it seems almost a case of history repeating itself. Sir Winston was as close to the boy as his own demanding career and his grandson's schooling allowed, and he was thrilled when young Winston married his childhood sweetheart Minnie d'Erlanger in 1964. This marriage produced two daughters and two sons, the elder of whom was born two days before Sir Winston's death and was predictably christened Randolph. The marriage ended in 1997, to his mother Pam's disapproval, for like everyone in the family she adored Minnie. Winston married Luce Engelen soon afterwards.

The younger Winston was a competent MP for over twenty-six years, but he lived in the shadow of his famous grandfather whose shoes were impossible to fill (which had caused him to be bullied at school). Although he would never admit it, he too suffered from the fallout of his father's reputation because Randolph had offended so many people. Young Winston was unfailingly robust in defence of both his grandfather and his father whenever pejorative comments were made in the House or in the press about either. Several people interviewed for this book described young Winston as bumptious and suffering from Churchill arrogance, but when I met him in aviation circles many years ago I found a man with a charming – boyish – eagerness about him. After his father died in 1968, he hoped that he might be allowed to take over as official biographer of Sir Winston, but the trustees decided to ask Martin Gilbert, who had worked as Randolph's research assistant from the start, to continue the work. Young Winston might well have obtained a ministry under Margaret Thatcher, but after he voted against sanctions on Rhodesia she felt she could no longer wholly rely on his support. She may have been right in her assessment, for he would later attack her in the House, claiming she had done less for defence than Harold Wilson.

He made newspaper headlines several times in later years, notably after the tabloid press discovered his two-year love affair with Soraya

Khashoggi, former wife of a Saudi Arabian arms dealer, and later when he sold his grandfather's papers to the nation. Many people felt that because these papers were part of the nation's history they should have been gifted, not sold. However, it could also be argued that they were the product of Sir Winston's pen just as his published writings were. The Churchills have never been a rich family, and the papers were a realisable asset. This issue coincided with a change of constituency boundaries as a result of which the constituency that Winston represented disappeared. He did not seek re-election.

In spring 2009, the day before I was due to meet him over lunch to ask him some questions for this book, he was diagnosed with terminal cancer. We communicated by email briefly during the early stages of this illness, and he fought hard for his life for a year, supported lovingly to the end by Luce. He died on 2 March 2010.

Pamela Digby Churchill Harriman   At the time of Churchill's death Pam had been married for three years to the Hollywood and Broadway impresario and producer Leland Hayward, whose greatest hit was *The Sound of Music*. Until Leland's death in 1970 they lived in luxury at his country estate Haywire in Westchester County, New York. It was a happy marriage and Pam ensured that everything revolved around her husband, even to the detriment of his children. During Leland's lifetime Pam's relationship with her stepchildren was cordial enough, but after his death it became extremely acrimonious and Pam's stepdaughter wrote a bitter memoir entitled *Haywire*, which in essence accused Pam of robbing Leland's children of items left by their father.

By 1971 Pam had met up again with her first real love, Averell Harriman, now seventy-nine and also recently widowed. Pam and Averell resumed their old relationship soon after Leland's death, and were married six months later when she became a citizen of the United States. It was during this marriage that she became active in Washington society and in particular within the upper echelons of the Democratic Party. This was another happy marriage, but again there were stepchildren problems when the children of Averell's previous marriage felt ousted by Pam, which created deep antagonism.

Following Averell's death in 1986 Pam became embroiled for years in legal arguments over his will. She had been left $65 million and Harriman's children accused her of 'wasting' $30m of their trust fund in ill-advised investments, leaving them only $3 million.

But in her own right Pam was a mover and shaker, running successful fund-raising campaigns and a political action committee, Democrats for the 80s (and later, Democrats for the 90s). She was named Woman of the Year in 1980; in 1993, for her help in his presidential campaign (it was said he would never have succeeded without Pam's stamp of approval), President Clinton sent her to Paris as United States Ambassador. She was a stunning success.

On 5 February 1997, while swimming in the pool at the Ritz in Paris, she suffered a brain haemorrhage and died some days later. I had met her briefly a few weeks earlier to interview her about a book I was working on at the time. She was bright, vital, full of laughter and looked twenty years younger than her age.

President Clinton sent Air Force One to collect Pam's body from Paris and return it to Washington, where it was received with full military honours before being given a state funeral. No previous American Ambassador had ever been so honoured.

It was Pam's misfortune to have two biographers who appear to have disliked her a good deal. The first biography had begun as a cooperative venture: Pam would supply the information and documentary materials and the professional biographer was to do the writing. Some months into the work Pam's brother Eddie and one of her sisters persuaded her to pull out of the project as they believed it would reflect unfavourably on her position as American Ambassador. The biographer went on to write an unauthorised biography of Pam anyway. The context could not be described as sympathetic. The second biography, perhaps taking its cue from the first, was also an unflattering portrait, concentrating on Pam's numerous love affairs and the evidence of her disaffected stepchildren – the equivalent of writing a biography of Kennedy or Clinton via their bedroom conquests as told by the lovers' husbands and children.

Men were indeed important milestones in Pam's life, and she learned much from most of them about art, wine and music – all this she regarded as part of her education. But apart from her indisputable abilities as a courtesan – and I do not use this word in any pejorative sense – she was a success above the ordinary in her own right. Ask any Parisian about Pam's achievements as American Ambassador to France and you will more often than not receive a glowing commendation. In Washington she was revered as a political hostess by Democrats and highly respected, albeit grudgingly, by Republicans. Her former lovers remained on good terms and were still welcomed by her family as friends years after the affairs had ended.

Lord Randolph Churchill and the Diagnosis of Syphilis

It has long been accepted by historians and biographers that Lord Randolph Churchill died of syphilis. This was accepted at the time by the patient himself and his closest family, including Winston Churchill, who discussed the matter with his father's doctor and had access to his medical file. Winston's son Randolph, who also had access to the file, also believed the diagnosis was correct. However, many years later another grandson, Peregrine (son of Jack Churchill), who was born long after Lord Randolph's death, contested it.

In the pre-antibiotic days of the nineteenth century, syphilis was such a common affliction that every doctor in general practice knew its symptoms extremely well. Lord Randolph consulted Dr Thomas Buzzard, the renowned specialist in venereal disease. Other opinions were also sought so that several physicians were involved in the diagnosis and treatment of Lord Randolph's condition, and there appears to have been a concurrence of expert medical opinion.

This does not prove that the illness *was* syphilis, of course. An article by a doctor published in the United States and used as a thesis in a recently published book[1] claims that the same symptoms could have been caused by an undiagnosed brain tumour. Peregrine Churchill preferred to accept this alternative diagnosis as the cause of his grandfather's death.

The acceptance of the original diagnosis by those most concerned *at the time* seems to make that one more likely to be right, especially given that Lord Randolph was known to have had an affair in Paris, before the onset of his illness, with a professional courtesan, and that he himself did not query the diagnosis. He clearly had some grounds for accepting the possibility that he was suffering from venereal disease.

Winston was not the only family member to suspect there was more to his father's illness than they were being told at the time. Leonie Leslie and Clara Frewen, Jennie's sisters, found out about it from Jennie. Randolph's sister Cornelia (Lady Wimborne) wrote to Dr George Keith, who had accompanied Randolph and Jennie on their trip around the world, and asked him to describe his symptoms and the prognosis. Dr Keith initially replied that it 'would only cause you a great deal of grief if I told you what Lord Randolph does and says as it is too painful for words to see a man like Lord Randolph in the progress of this disease. I have had a doctor to see him here and he has confirmed me in every detail. We have no doubt what is the matter with Lord Randolph and none as to the inevitable end.'[2] After conferring with the family doctor Robson Roose, Dr Keith wired Lady Wimborne in November 1894 to the effect that her brother would not live longer than six months. Even the Prince of Wales had heard rumours, and wishing to learn the facts, he contacted Dr Buzzard a few weeks before Randolph's death. Buzzard obligingly confided Randolph's condition and symptoms to him.

Dr Buzzard's case notes show that he had first been consulted by Randolph in October 1885 (four years after the Marlboroughs left Ireland) at the request of Dr Roose, but later stated that he could not be sure whether this was the first time he had seen Randolph or not. Drs Buzzard and Roose clearly anticipated, from the start, what would inevitably happen to Lord Randolph as the disease progressed. Dr Buzzard had noted:

It was in the early summer of 1893 . . . if not before that I came to the conclusion that there was in all probability commencing G.P. [General Paralysis]. His articulation became slurred, and his tongue tremulous . . . Beginning of September symptoms were slowly changing, becoming apathetic, occasionally a loss of co-ordination, slight delusions. Appetite good, sleeping well. On September 23rd left hand became numb, and there was a decided loss of power in the arm. He became sleepy and confused. In that evening left hand became almost useless. Next morning seemed much as usual. October 3rd: nearly assaulted one of his valets; violent dislike of him. October 11th: another attack, speech became very bad, loss of coordination very marked. Followed by unusually good temper . . . Nov 4th: Has been violent and apathetic by turns; Lower lip and chin seem to be paralysed. Gait staggering and uncertain. November 16: Speech slow and uncertain . . . voice weak. Takes little interest in things. Face losing its expression. Altogether he is well into the 2nd stage of G.P.[3]

Most of these symptoms (although not the haemorrhaging reported by Dr Keith) could have been caused by a brain tumour. However, they are also all typical of the final stages of syphilis. The patient would have presented at the first stage with a rash or ulceration of the genitals. The tertiary symptoms in isolation would not have automatically suggested syphilis, but could easily have been what doctors then termed 'an inflammation of the brain'. But the fact that Randolph suddenly ceased all sexual relations with his young wife sometime after Jack's birth in 1880 would appear to be not unconnected.

Having consulted several doctors and compared symptoms, and taken into account the surviving letters and documentation of the time, I lean towards Winston Churchill's belief that his father died of syphilis. However, it is too long ago to be entirely sure; only DNA could now provide incontrovertible evidence. The story of the nature of Lord Randolph's illness was resurrected in the 1920s with the publication by the notorious Frank Harris of his scurrilous bestselling memoirs, *My Life and Loves*. This book was banned in Britain because of its sexual content, but it was freely available in the United States and France. There is little doubt that its publication harmed Winston's career at a critical time for him.

NOTES

Full details of all publications cited in the text are provided in the Bibliography.

Abbreviations used in the notes
AL – Anita Leslie
BL – British Library
CA – Churchill Archives, Churchill College, Cambridge
CB – Consuelo Balsan (formerly Vanderbilt, Duchess of Marlborough)
CHAR – Chartwell Papers, Churchill College Library, Cambridge
CHUR – Churchill Papers, Churchill College, Cambridge
CSC – Clementine Spencer Churchill
JC – Jennie Churchill
CV – Companion volumes to the official biography of Sir Winston Churchill
MS – Mary Soames
PH – Pamela Harriman (formerly Pamela Digby Churchill)
RSC – Randolph Spencer Churchill
TKP – Tarka King Papers
WSC – Sir Winston S. Churchill

I

1 Information from Simon Bird.
2 Goa in India was another.
3 Manley: *Secret Memoirs*, p. 81.
4 Thompson: *The First Churchill*, p. 19.
5 Green: *Sarah, Duchess of Marlborough*, p. 35.
6 WSC: *Marlborough*, pp. 110–11, 121–8.
7 Hibbert: *The Marlboroughs*, p. 14.
8 Henrietta Spencer Churchill: *Blenheim and the Churchill Family*, p. 101.
9 Ibid., p. 92.
10 BL Add. 61457 (f.103) 18 July 1723.

2

1 Henrietta Spencer Churchill: *Blenheim and the Churchill Family*, p. 109.
2 Harriet Arbuthnot: *The Journal of Mrs Arbuthnot 1820–1832*, pp. 304–5.

3 Author's conversation with Lord Digby, January 2007.
4 A.L. Rowse: *The Later Churchills*, p. 110.
5 Henrietta Spencer Churchill: *Blenheim and the Churchill Family*, p. 137.
6 Ibid., pp. 139–41.
7 CHAR 28/112. Correspondence between Eton and the 7th Duke of Marlborough, December 1863.
8 CB: *The Glitter and the Gold*, p. 26.
9 AL: *The Fabulous Leonard Jerome*, p. 166.
10 AL: *Jennie*, p. 21.
11 Ibid., pp. 27–8.
12 Ibid., pp. 25–6.
13 RSC: CV1/1, p. 12.
14 RSC: *Winston S. Churchill*, vol. 1, p. 19.
15 Ibid., p. 14.
16 CVI/i, p. 11.
17 AL: *Jennie*, p. 27.

18 Peregrine Churchill and Julian Mitchell: *Jennie, Lady Randolph Churchill*, p. 23.
19 AL: *Jennie*, p. 31.
20 CHAR 28/41. Randolph to 'Madame Jerome', 10 September 1873.
21 *Dictionary of National Biography*, vol. II Supplement (Chippendale-Hosle), 1901 (Supplement), p. 10.
22 CHAR 28/41. Leonard Jerome to Marlborough, 9 April 1874.
23 BL, Duke of Marlborough to Lord Randolph, 14 April 1874; and RSC: *Winston S. Churchill*, vol. 1, p. 23.
24 TKP: Leonie Jerome to 'Gertrude', 21 April 1874.

16 AL: *Jennie*, p. 76.
17 John S. Churchill: *A Churchill Canvas*, p. 284.
18 Virginia Woolf: *Biography of Roger Fry*. This was the last book written by Woolf before her suicide. Her description of St George's School was derived from letters sent to his parents by Fry.
19 Ibid.
20 CVI/i, pp. 94–5.
21 Ibid., p. 88.
22 Ibid.
23 Henrietta Spencer Churchill: *Blenheim and the Churchill Family*, p. 153.
24 Ibid. p. 153

3

1 Mrs Cornwallis-West: *Reminiscences of Lady Randolph Churchill*, p. 57.
2 Ibid., p. 61.
3 Benjamin Disraeli to Queen Victoria, 22 May 1874, quoted in RSC: *Winston S. Churchill: Youth*, p. 15.
4 Anthony Trollope: *Phineas Finn*, p. 44 (first published 1869).
5 Mrs Cornwallis-West: *Reminiscences*, p. 39.
6 TKP: 21 October 1873.
7 AL: *The Fabulous Leonard Jerome*, p. 18.
8 Mrs Cornwallis-West: *Reminiscences*, p. 37.

4

1 AL: *Edwardians in Love*, p. 88.
2 Ibid., p. 88.
3 Ibid., p. 90.
4 Peregrine Churchill and Julian Mitchell: *Jennie*, p. 90.
5 Ibid. p. 91.
6 AL: *Edwardians in Love*, p. 91.
7 Peregrine Churchill: *Jennie*, p. 91.
8 Ibid., p. 93.
9 *The Times*, 12 May 1876.
10 CVI/i, p. 69.
11 Mrs Cornwallis-West: *Reminiscences*, p. 70.
12 Celia and John Lee: *Winston and Jack*, p. 28.
13 CV V/iii, p. 267.
14 WSC: *My Early Life*, pp. 12, 13.
15 Ibid., p. 13.

5

1 Lord Rosebery, quoted in AL: *Jennie*, p. 97.
2 TKP: JC to her mother, 21 November 1880.
3 AL: *Jennie*, p. 97.
4 CHAR 28/7/6–7.
5 AL: *Edwardians in Love*, p. 195.
6 *New York Times* obituary, 10 November 1892.
7 Ibid.
8 CHAR 28/98/38–9.
9 CHAR 28/98/f28–8.
10 AL: *Jennie*, p. 87.
11 John S. Churchill: *A Churchill Canvas*, p. 23.
12 AL: *Jennie*, p. 93.
13 Ibid., p. 82.
14 WSC: *My Early Life*, pp. 21–2.
15 CVI/i, p. 256. (WSC to Jack).
16 AL: *Jennie*, p. 93.
17 Wilfrid Scawen Blunt papers: unpublished ms 28, 'Secret Memoirs' (1975), vol. 4, Fitzwilliam Museum, Cambridge
18 Letter from Henry Labouchère to Lord Rosebery dated 25 November 1885, quoted in R.F. Foster: *Lord Randolph Churchill*, p. 217.
19 AL: *Jennie*, p. 89.
20 RSC: *Winston S. Churchill: Youth*, p. 72.
21 Ibid., p. 73.
22 Ibid., p. 75.
23 AL: *Jennie*, p. 107.

24 CVI/i, p. 214.
25 Ibid., p. 518.
26 Ibid., pp. 113, 127.
27 CHAR 28/42 8 September [1886].
28 CHAR 28/42 10 September [1886].
29 CHAR 28/42 26 September [1886].
30 Peregrine Churchill and Julian Mitchell: *Jennie*, p. 154. Fanny Churchill to JC, 19 November 1886.
31 George Cornwallis-West: *Reminiscences*, p. 141.
32 R.F. Foster: *Lord Randolph Churchill*, p. 319.

6

1 Peregrine Churchill and Julian Mitchell: *Jennie*, p. 161. Letter from JC to Lord Randolph Churchill dated 21 February 1887.
2 Ibid., p. 160. Letter from JC to Lord Randolph Churchill dated 15 February 1887.
3 Ibid., p. 160. Letter from JC to Lord Randolph Churchill dated February 1887; p. 162.
4 Ralph Martin: *Lady Randolph Churchill*, p. 218.
5 AL: *Jennie*, p. 138.
6 BL. Blenheim Papers. Also quoted in Martin: *Lady Randolph Churchill*, p. 219.
7 AL: *Jennie*, p. 172.
8 John Colville: *The Churchillians*, p. 19.
9 CVI/i, p. 386.
10 CHAR 28/14/53-4.
11 CVI/i, p. 424.
12 Ibid., p. 566.
13 Ibid., p. 496.
14 Ibid., p. 591.
15 TKP.
16 Ibid.
17 CVI/i, p. 531.
18 Anthony Montague Browne: *The Long Sunset*, p. 122.
19 CVI/i, p. 547.
20 Ibid., p. 502.
21 WSC: *My Early Life*, p. 36.
22 John Colville: *The Churchillians*, p. 18.
23 Lord Randolph Churchill: *Churchill: Youth*, pp. 62, 74.
24 Ibid.
25 Ibid., p. 50.

26 CVI/i, p. 545.
27 AL: *Jennie*, p. 178.
28 RSC: *Churchill: Youth*, p. 255.
29 Ibid.
30 CVI/i, p. 559.
31 AL: *Jennie*, p. 178

7

1 CVI/i, p. 578.
2 CB: *The Glitter and the Gold*, p. 28.
3 Author interview: Julia Budworth, recalling conversation with Lady Sydney Redesdale.
4 CHAR 28/42/23. 29 July 1894, p. 4.
5 Elliott Roosevelt and James Brough: *An Untold Story*, pp. 109–10.
6 CB: *The Glitter and the Gold*, p. 33.
7 *The World*, 16 February 1895.
8 CB: *The Glitter and the Gold*, p. 36.
9 Ibid.
10 Ibid.
11 Ibid., p. 37.
12 Ibid., p. 40.
13 RSC: *Churchill: Youth*, p. 267.
14 CVI/i, p. 600.
15 Ibid.
16 Transcript of speech on NATO website. Quoted in RSC: *Churchill: Youth*, p. 282.
17 RSC: *Churchill: Youth*. p. 282.
18 Ibid., p. 270.
19 *New York Herald*, 7 November 1895.
20 CB: *The Glitter and the Gold*, p. 46.

8

1 CB: *The Glitter and the Gold*, p. 52.
2 Ibid., p. 53.
3 Lady Angela Forbes: *Memories and Base Details*, pp. 84, 87.
4 WSC: *My Early Life*, p. 92.
5 RSC: *Churchill: Youth*, p. 276.
6 CB: *The Glitter and the Gold*, p. 55.
7 Ibid., p. 55.
8 Ibid., p. 57.
9 CVI/i, p. 503.
10 CB: *The Glitter and the Gold*, p. 59.
11 Ibid., p. 60.
12 Ibid., p. 76.
13 Ibid., p. 84.
14 Ibid., p. 93.
15 CHAR CA1/8/107. Dated 21 September 1897.

16 Hugo Vickers: *Gladys, Duchess of Marlborough*, p. 12.
17 Daphne Fielding: *The Face on the Sphinx*, p. 4.
18 Hugo Vickers: *Gladys, Duchess of Marlborough*, p. 41.
19 Ibid., p. 42.
20 CB: *The Glitter and the Gold*, p. 98.
21 Ibid., p. 99.
22 Ibid., p. 99.

9

1 RSC: *Churchill: Youth*, p. 297.
2 Ibid., p. 318.
3 Ibid., pp. 352–3.
4 Ibid., pp. 296–7.
5 *Observer*, Sunday 9 November 2003, article about auction of Pamela Plowden's letters.
6 RSC: *Churchill: Youth*, p. 320.
7 CHAR. 28/24/20 19/1/1898.
8 Jennie to WSC, 3 March 1897, CVI/ii, p. 743.
9 WSC to JC, 28 January 1898, CVI/ii, p. 743.
10 CHAR 28/152/145. WSC to Jack Churchill, 16 February 1898.
11 CVI/i, p. 676.
12 AL: *Jennie*, p. 214.
13 Ibid., p. 194.
14 CVI/i, p. 256.
15 CVI/ii, p. 1232.
16 CHAR 28/26/2. 11 January 1899.
17 George Cornwallis-West: *Edwardian Hey-days*, p. 102.
18 CHAR 28/64/19. Prince of Wales to JC.
19 WSC: *My Early Life*, pp. 195–9.
20 AL: *Jennie*, p. 222.
21 Ibid., pp. 223–4.
22 RSC: *Churchill: Youth*, p. 452.
23 Ibid.

10

1 J.B. Atkins: *Incidents and Reflections*, p. 122.
2 WSC: *My Early Life*, p. 257.
3 J.B. Atkins: *Incidents and Reflections*, p. 107.
4 WSC: *My Early Life*, p. 274.
5 Ibid., p. 273.
6 RSC: *Churchill: Youth*, p. 483.

7 WSC: *My Early Life*, p. 274.
8 Ibid., p. 311.
9 CVI/ii, p. 506.
10 Ibid., p. 507.
11 WSC: *My Early Life*, p. 355.
12 RSC: *Churchill: Youth*, p. 510.
13 Maria Theresa von Hochberg: *Daisy, Princess of Pless*, p. 72.
14 WSC: *My Early Life*, pp. 320–21.
15 CVI/ii, p. 507.
16 CVI/ii, p. 510.
17 CVI/ii, p. 512.
18 WSC: *My Early Life*, pp. 366–7.
19 Lady Sarah Wilson: *South African Memories*, p. 99.
20 Ibid., p. 100.
21 *Daily Mail*, 26 March 1900.
22 Lady Sarah Wilson: *South African Memories*, p. 106.
23 Quoted in Earl of Birkenhead: *Churchill*, p. 114.

11

1 CHAR 28/26/59–60.
2 Peregrine Churchill and Julian Mitchell: *Jennie*, p. 225.
3 Seymour Leslie: *The Jerome Connection*, p. 55.
4 Peregrine Churchill and Julian Mitchell: *Jennie*, p. 225.
5 Ibid.
6 AL: *Jennie*, p. 263.
7 *Peterborough Examiner*. Undated article on WSC's stay in Peterborough, Ottawa on 1 January 1901.
8 WSC: *My Early Life*, p. 377.
9 RSC: *Churchill: Youth*, p. 544.
10 CHAR 28/26/22.
11 RSC: *Winston S. Churchill: Young Statesman*, p. 2.
12 Ibid., p. 7.
13 Earl Winterton: *Churchill the Parliamentarian*, p. 51.
14 Peregrine Churchill and Julian Mitchell: *Jennie*, p. 220.
15 CHAR 28/35/62.
16 CVI/ii, p. 1043.
17 CHAR 28/35/62.
18 John Colville: *The Churchillians*, p. 112.
19 AL: *Jennie*, p. 264.
20 Ibid., p. 264.
21 CVI/ii, p. 1209.

22 Blunt, Wilfrid Scawen: *My Diaries 1900–1914*, pp. 74–5.

23 Violet Bonham Carter: *Winston Churchill as I Knew Him*, p. 18.

24 Ibid., p. 19.

25 Quoted in William Manchester: *The Last Lion*, p. 367.

26 CHAR 8/16. RSC: *Churchill: Young Statesman*, p. 127.

27 Amanda Mackenzie Stuart: *Consuelo and Alva*, p. 248.

28 Hugo Vickers: *Gladys, Duchess of Marlborough*, p. 67.

29 Ibid. And Amanda Mackenzie Stuart: *Consuelo and Alva*, p. 256.

30 Princess Daisy of Pless: *My Private Diary*, p. 69.

31 CB: *The Glitter and the Gold*, p. 134.

32 Amanda Mackenzie Stuart: *Consuelo and Alva*, pp. 262–3.

33 MS: *Speaking for Themselves*, p. 3.

34 Birkenhead: *Churchill 1874–1922*, p. 112

12

1 Cynthia Gladwin: *Diaries*, p. 230.

2 RSC: *Churchill: Young Statesman*, p. 249.

3 MS: *Speaking for Themselves*, p. 5.

4 CVII/i, p. 331.

5 CVII/i, pp. 455/6.

6 RSC: *Churchill: Young Statesman*, p. 81.

7 Ibid., p. 83.

8 CVII/i, p. 388.

9 George Cornwallis-West: *Edwardian Hey-days*, p. 119.

10 CVII/i, p. 341.

11 CVII/i, p. 393. Cornelia Wimborne to WSC.

12 CVII/i, p. 409.

13 RSC: *Churchill: Young Statesman*, pp. 141–2.

14 Edward Marsh: *A Number of People: A Book of Reminiscences*, pp. 148–9.

15 CHAR 28/128/27. JC to George Cornwallis-West.

16 Quoted in Amanda Mackenzie Stuart: *Consuelo and Alva*, p. 269.

17 CVII/i, p. 588. CHAR 28/27/63. WSC to JC, 13 October 1906.

18 CHAR 28/78/44. JC to WSC.

19 CVII/i, p. 588/9 (October 1906).

20 CVII/i, p. 593 (20 October 1906).

21 CHAR 1/57/9. 21 October 1906.

22 CHAR 28/78/45.

23 CHAR 1/57/27.

24 B.H. Friedman: *Gertrude Vanderbilt Whitney: A Biography*, p. 230.

25 CHAR 1/57/18. c. October 1906.

26 CHAR 1/65/1. 4 January 1907.

27 CHAR 1/65/8–10. 31 January 1907.

28 CVII/ii, p. 691.

13

1 King Edward VII to WSC, 6 April 1907, quoted in RSC: *Churchill: Young Statesman*, p. 211.

2 John S. Churchill: *A Churchill Canvas* (Little, Brown, Boston, 1961), p. 16.

3 CVII/ii, p. 704. Jack Churchill to WSC 21 November 1907.

4 Cynthia Asquith: *Remember and Be Glad*, p. 88.

5 CVII/ii, p. 677.

6 Ibid., p. 679.

7 Hugo Vickers: *Gladys, Duchess of Marlborough*, p. 114.

8 CVII/ii, pp. 695–7.

9 CVII/ii, pp. 705–6.

10 CVII/ii, p. 738.

11 Quoted in RSC: *Churchill: Young Statesman*, pp. 231–3.

12 CVII/ii, p. 707.

13 CVII/ii, p. 706.

14 CVII/ii, p. 723.

15 CVII/ii, p. 729.

16 RSC: *Churchill: Young Statesman*, p. 236.

17 George Cornwallis-West: *Edwardian Hey-days*, p. 119.

18 CVII/ii, p. 738.

19 RSC: *Churchill: Young Statesman*, p. 256.

20 CVII/ii, pp. 754–6.

21 Ibid.

22 Margot Asquith to WSC, 28 March 1908. Quoted in CVII/ii, pp. 756–7.

23 CVII/ii, pp. 781–2; RSC: *Churchill: Young Statesman*, pp. 251–2; MS: *Speaking for Themselves*, p. 7.

24 MS: *Speaking for Themselves*, p. 8.

25 Quoted in RSC: *Churchill: Young Statesman*, p. 257.

26 Ibid., p. 260.

27 CVII/ii, pp. 798–9.

28 Ibid.

29 Ibid.
30 Wilfrid Scawen Blunt: *My Diaries*, vol. 2 (14 August 1908).
31 CVII/ii, pp. 804–5.
32 CVII/ii, p. 804.
33 Wilfrid Scawen Blunt: *My Diaries*, vol. 2 (12 September 1908).
34 CVII/ii, pp. 804–5.
35 CHAR 28/27/86. CVII/ii, p. 819.

14

1 The final sentence in WSC: *My Early Life*.
2 John Colville: *The Churchillians*, p. 20.
3 Ibid., p. 21.
4 MS: *Clementine Churchill*, p. 93.
5 CVII/ii, p. 902.
6 MS: *Speaking for Themselves*, p. 20.
7 Ibid., p. 23: and CVII/2, p. 893.
8 Ibid., p. 24.
9 Ibid., p. 28.
10 Ibid., p. 29.
11 Ibid., p. 30.
12 Daisy, Princess of Pless: *My Private Diary*, p. 163.
13 CHAR 28/78/74.
14 CVII/ii, p. 901.
15 Ibid., p. 915.
16 Ibid., p. 916.
17 MS: *Speaking for Themselves*, pp. 37–8.
18 Andrew Rosen: *Rise Up, Women!*, p. 126.
19 *The Times*, 30 March 1912.
20 CVII/ii, pp. 1082–3.
21 CVII/ii, p. 1083.
22 Theodore Roosevelt to Whitelaw Read, in Henry Pringle: *Theodore Roosevelt*, and quoted in Hugo Vickers: *Gladys, Duchess of Marlborough*, p. 108.
23 CB: *The Glitter and the Gold*, p. 154.
24 Ibid., p. 156.
25 Ibid., p. 157.
26 CHAR 28/78/73.
27 Peregrine Churchill and Julian Mitchell: *Jennie*, p. 234.
28 MS: *Speaking for Themselves*, p. 53.
29 Ibid., p. 54.
30 RSC: *Churchill: Young Statesman*, p. 531.
31 Quoted in ibid., p. 528.
32 MS: *Speaking for Themselves*, pp. 72–3.
33 WSC: *The World Crisis*, p. 104.

34 Quoted in RSC: *Churchill: Young Statesman*, p. 697.
35 Ivor Courtney, WSC's instructor, quoted in ibid., pp. 697–8.
36 Quoted in RSC: *Churchill: Young Statesman*, p. 699.
37 Ibid., p. 703.
38 Ibid., pp. 704–5.
39 Peregrine Churchill and Julian Mitchell: *Jennie*, p. 240.
40 Quoted in Amanda Mackenzie Stuart: *Consuelo and Alva*, p. 359.

15

1 Quoted in RSC: *Churchill: Young Statesman*, pp. 682–3.
2 Ibid., p. 681.
3 MS: *Speaking for Themselves*, pp. 69–71.
4 Quoted in RSC: *Churchill: Young Statesman*, pp. 710–11.
5 Ibid., pp. 714–15.
6 CHAR 28/33/4–5.
7 Ibid.
8 Ibid.
9 CHAR 28/135.
10 Ibid.
11 MS: *Speaking for Themselves*, p. 98.
12 Quoted in Elisabeth Kehoe: *Fortune's Daughters*, p. 297.
13 Peregrine Churchill and Julian Mitchell: *Jennie*, p. 248.
14 AL: *Jennie*, p. 307.
15 Peregrine Churchill and Julian Mitchell: *Jennie*, p. 249.
16 Lady Fortescue: *There's Rosemary*, pp. 69–70; and quoted in Amanda Mackenzie Stuart: *Consuelo and Alva*, p. 282.
17 MS: *Speaking for Themselves*, p. 71 (7 February 1913).
18 CHAR 13 (Admiralty Papers). Churchill to Sir John French on 11 January 1915.
19 Quoted in Martin Gilbert: *Winston S. Churchill: The Challenge of War*, vol. 3, p. 447.
20 John S. Churchill: *A Churchill Canvas*, p. 33.
21 Quoted in Earl of Birkenhead: *Churchill*, pp. 400–1.
22 WSC: *Thoughts and Adventures*, p. 326.

23 Minnie Churchill: *Sir Winston Churchill's Life through His Paintings*.
24 Seymour Leslie: *The Jerome Connection*, p. 83.
25 Draft letter 29 October, WSC to Asquith. Quoted in Earl of Birkenhead: *Churchill*, p. 403.
26 Max Beaverbrook: *Politicians and the War*, p. 5.
27 WSC: *Thoughts and Adventures*, p. 105.
28 MS: *Speaking for Themselves*, p. 113.
29 Ibid., p. 114.
30 Ibid., p. 172.
31 Ibid., p. 118.

16

1 WSC: *The World Crisis*, p. 708.
2 MS: *Speaking for Themselves*, p. 206.
3 Anne Sebba in conversation with the author.
4 Peregrine Churchill and Julian Mitchell: *Jennie*, p. 261.
5 Ibid.
6 Anne Sebba: *American Jennie*, p. 312.
7 TKP: undated notes by Shane Leslie for AL.
8 MS: *Speaking for Themselves*, p. 212.
9 Ibid., p. 216.
10 Anthony Montague Browne: *The Long Sunset*, p. 224.
11 John Colville: *Fringes of Power*, vol. 2, p. 339.
12 Hugo Vickers: *Gladys, Duchess of Marlborough*, p. 145.
13 Ibid., pp. 147–8.
14 Ibid., p. 155.
15 Henrietta Spencer Churchill: *Blenheim and the Churchill Family*, p. 176.
16 Amanda Mackenzie Stuart: *Consuelo and Alva*, p. 362.
17 Ibid., p. 383.
18 CB: *The Glitter and the Gold*, p. 188.

17

1 MS: *Speaking for Themselves*, p. 225.
2 Ibid., pp. 236–7.
3 Ibid., p. 237.
4 Peregrine Churchill and Julian Mitchell: *Jennie*, p. 263.

5 Ibid., p. 264.
6 Ibid., p. 265.
7 Ibid., pp. 266–7.
8 Celia and John Lee: *Winston and Jack*, p. 302.
9 RSC: *Twenty-One Years*, pp. 24–5, and AL: *Cousin Randolph*, p. 7.
10 MS: *Speaking for Themselves*, p. 242.
11 Ibid., pp. 242–3.
12 Ibid., p. 244.
13 Ibid., p. 245.
14 Ibid., p. 250.
15 Ibid., p. 253.
16 Ibid., p. 261.
17 National Trust: *Chartwell*, p. 13, and MS: *Speaking for Themselves*, p. 262.
18 MS: *Clementine Churchill*, p. 319.
19 WSC: *Thoughts and Adventures*, p. 213.
20 National Trust: *Chartwell*, pp. 16–18.

18

1 John S. Churchill: *A Churchill Canvas*, p. 22.
2 Henrietta Spencer Churchill: *Blenheim and the Churchill Family*, p. 178.
3 Daphne Fielding: *The Face on the Sphinx*, p. 59.
4 CHAR 1/179/5.
5 *New York Times*, 25 November 1926, p. 1.
6 F.J. Heed: Ms: A transcript of the Tribunal hearing and Acta Apostolicae Sedis 1926, Library of Congress Card number 59–10656.
7 MS: *Speaking for Themselves*, p. 299.
8 AL: *Cousin Randolph*, p. 12.
9 Ibid., p. 13.
10 John S. Churchill: *A Churchill Canvas*, pp. 24–5.
11 Ibid., p. 263.
12 Ibid., p. 277.
13 MS: *Clementine Churchill*, p. 340.
14 AL: *Cousin Randolph*, p. 9.
15 Harold Nicolson: *Diaries and Letters, 1930–1939*, p. 154.
16 Chatsworth House archives: Tom Mitford to Lady Redesdale, 17 August 1930. Quoted in Mary S. Lovell: *The Mitford Girls*, pp. 115–16.
17 The late Beryl Markham to the author.

18 Mary S. Lovell: *Amelia Earhart – The Sound of Wings*, pp. 115–17.
19 Lady Soames in conversation with the author, 9 September 2009.
20 AL: *Cousin Randolph*, p. 16.
21 John Pearson: *Citadel of the Heart*, p. 213.
22 MS: *Clementine Churchill*, p. 343.
23 MS: *Speaking for Themselves*, p. 344.
24 RSC: *Twenty-One Years*, pp. 72–85.
25 CHAR 1/188/61. WSC to CSC, 19 September 1929.
26 CHAR 1/188/61–3.
27 Winston S. Churchill (the younger): *His Father's Son: The Life of Randolph S. Churchill*, p. 75.
28 MS: *Speaking for Themselves*, p. 353.
29 Robert Boothby: *Recollections of a Rebel*, p. 85.
30 AL: *Cousin Randolph*, p. 23.
31 Ibid., p. 25.

19

1 MS: *Clementine Churchill*, p. 360.
2 MS: *Speaking for Themselves*, pp. 359–60.
3 CSC to WSC, 12 February 1931. Quoted in MS: *Speaking for Themselves*, p. 351.
4 Mary S. Lovell: *The Mitford Girls*, pp. 159–62.
5 Ernst Hanfstaengl: *Hitler: The Missing Years*, pp. 184–6.
6 WSC: *The Second World War: The Gathering Storm*, p. 65.
7 Artemis Cooper: *Mr Wu and Mrs Stitch*, p. 12.
8 Hugo Vickers: *Gladys, Duchess of Marlborough*, p. 205.
9 Ibid., p. 207.
10 The late Diana Mosley (formerly Guinness), taped interview with the author in Paris, January 2000.
11 *Time*, 21 August 1933. Foreign News section.
12 WSC and C.C. Martindale: *Charles, IXth Duke of Marlborough: Tributes*, 1934.
13 CB: *The Glitter and the Gold*, p. 236.
14 AL: *Cousin Randolph*, p. 37.
15 RSC: *Twenty-One Years*, p. 117.
16 Philip Toynbee: *Friends Apart* (MacGibbon & Kee, 1954), p. 18.

17 MS: *Clementine Churchill*, p. 385.
18 MS: *Speaking for Themselves*, pp. 398–9.
19 Quoted in Sarah Churchill: *Keep on Dancing*, p. 55.
20 MS: *Speaking for Themselves*, p. 403.
21 Ibid., p. 412.
22 Ibid.
23 Ibid., p. 413.
24 Quoted in Sarah Churchill: *Keep on Dancing*, p. 67.
25 Ibid.
26 Ibid., p. 72.
27 Bracken to Moran, quoted in Lord Moran: *Winston Churchill: The Struggle for Survival*, p. 744.
28 MS: *Speaking for Themselves*, p. 426.
29 Bernard Baruch: *A Birthday Letter*, p. 162.

20

1 William Manchester: *The Caged Lion*, p. 339.
2 D.A. Wilson: *Dark and Light: The Story of the Guinness Family*, pp. 222, 227.
3 Martin Gilbert: *Winston S. Churchill: The Wilderness Years*, p. 237.
4 Ibid., p. 238.
5 H. Channon: *Chips: The Diaries of Sir Henry Channon*, p. 173.
6 Mary S. Lovell: *The Mitford Girls*, p. 205.
7 The full story of this elopement is told in Mary S. Lovell: *The Mitford Girls*, pp. 217–61.
8 MS: *Speaking for Themselves*, p. 442.
9 Ibid., pp. 443–4.
10 Ibid., pp. 444–5.
11 Ibid., p. 449.
12 Ibid., pp. 448–9.
13 Ibid., p. 448.
14 Martin Gilbert: *Winston S. Churchill: The Wilderness Years*, p. 261.
15 WSC: *The Second World War: The Gathering Storm*, p. 317.
16 Ibid., p. 318.
17 W.H. Thompson: *I Was Churchill's Shadow*, p. 18.
18 Martin Gilbert: *Winston S. Churchill: The Wilderness Years*, p. 267.
19 Ibid., p. 267, and W.H. Thompson: *I Was Churchill's Shadow*, p. 20.

20 W.H. Thompson: *I Was Churchill's Shadow*, p. 21.
21 Ibid., p. 23.
22 Ibid., p. 23.
23 WSC: *The Second World War: The Gathering Storm*, p. 320.

21

1 Virginia Cowles: *Looking for Trouble*, p. 113.
2 Ibid., p. 115.
3 Ibid., p. 251.
4 Winston S. Churchill (the younger): *Memories and Adventures*, p. 4.
5 Author's interview with Lord Digby.
6 *Tatler*, 22 June 1938.
7 PH to Lord Digby, 17 October 1936, Minterne Archives.
8 Letter signed 'Doris' to Lady Digby, 15 June 1935, Box 29a, Minterne Archives.
9 Deborah Devonshire: *Home to Roost*, p. 79, and correspondence with the author.
10 Clarissa, Countess of Avon, to the author, October 2009.
11 PH to her mother, 19 June 1937, Minterne Archives.
12 Ibid.
13 Lord Digby to the author.
14 Ibid.
15 Winston S. Churchill (the younger): *Memories and Adventures*, p. 5.
16 Lord Digby to the author.
17 PH to her mother, 20 March 1940, Minterne Archives.
18 Mary S. Lovell: *The Mitford Girls*, p. 300.
19 The Duchess of Devonshire (now the Dowager Duchess) to the author.
20 AL: *Cousin Randolph*, p. 48.
21 WSC: *The Second World War: The Gathering Storm*, pp. 525–6.
22 Martin Gilbert: *Winston S. Churchill: Finest Hour*, vol. 6, p. 321.
23 W.H. Thompson: *I Was Churchill's Shadow*, p. 57.
24 Henrietta Spencer Churchill: *Blenheim and the Churchill Family*, p. 202.
25 CB: *The Glitter and the Gold*, p. 239.
26 WSC: *The Second World War: Their Finest Hour*, p. 205.
27 MS: *Speaking for Themselves*, p. 454.

28 John Colville: *Fringes of Power*, vol. 1, p. 207.
29 Charlotte Mosley: *Love from Nancy: The Letters of Nancy Mitford*, p. 132.
30 Mary S. Lovell: *The Mitford Girls*, p. 378.
31 Ibid., p. 380.
32 Hugo Vickers: *Cecil Beaton*, p. 244.
33 Ibid.
34 'Travel', *Christian Science Monitor*, 28 January 2004.
35 MS: *Clementine*, p. 433.

22

1 Winston S. Churchill (the younger): *Memories and Adventures*, p. 14.
2 Evelyn Waugh: *Letters*, p. 150.
3 Evelyn Waugh: *Diaries*, p. 493.
4 Evelyn Waugh: *Letters*, p. 150.
5 Lord Digby to author.
6 Evelyn Waugh: *Letters*, p. 151.
7 Peter Howard: *Beaverbrook*, p. 125.
8 Ibid., p. 130.
9 Winston S. Churchill (the younger): *Memories and Adventures*, p. 18.
10 Elizabeth Bumiller, 'The Remarkable Life of . . . Pamela Harriman', *Washington Post*, Supplement, 12 June 1983, p. 1.
11 John Colville: *Fringes of Power*, vol. 1, p. 443.
12 Clarissa, Countess of Avon, to the author, October 2009.
13 Clarissa Eden: *A Memoir*, p. 59.
14 Clarissa, Countess of Avon, to the author, October 2009.
15 Quoted in Christopher Ogden: *Life of the Party*, p. 129.
16 Evelyn Waugh: *Letters*, p. 154.
17 Quoted in Winston S. Churchill (the younger): *Memories and Adventures*, pp. 20–1.
18 AL: *Cousin Randolph*, p. 54.
19 MS: *Clementine*, p. 445.
20 WSC: *The Second World War: The Grand Alliance*, p. 538.
21 Ibid., pp. 539–40.
22 Ibid., p. 551.
23 Mary S. Lovell: *The Mitford Girls*, p. 348.
24 Ibid., pp. 348–50.
25 Moran, Lord: *Winston Churchill: The Struggle for Survival*, p. 21.

26 W.H. Thompson: *I Was Churchill's Shadow*, p. 84.
27 Lord Moran: *Winston Churchill: The Struggle for Survival*, p. 22.
28 Interview notes, Diana Guest.
29 MS: *Clementine*, p. 452.
30 Ibid., p. 453.
31 AL: *Cousin Randolph*, p. 73.
32 Ibid., p. 77.
33 Evelyn Waugh: *Letters*, p. 160.
34 Mary Soames to the author. Interview, October 2009.
35 Winston S. Churchill (the younger): *Memories and Adventures*, p. 25.
36 John Colville: *The Churchillians*, p. 15.

23

1 Letter to the author from Lady Soames.
2 'Churchill's Memoirs', *Life Magazine*, 22 October 1951, p. 103.
3 Sarah Churchill: *Keep on Dancing*, p. 117.
4 MS: *Clementine*, p. 487.
5 Sarah Churchill: *Keep on Dancing*, p. 121.
6 Ibid., p. 122.
7 Ibid., p. 123.
8 MS: *Speaking for Themselves*, p. 487.
9 Ibid., p. 493.
10 AL: *Cousin Randolph*, p. 93.
11 Ibid., p. 77.
12 John Julius Norwich: *Duff Cooper Diaries*, p. 288.
13 Winston S. Churchill: (the younger): *Memories and Adventures*, p. 29.
14 Evelyn Waugh: *Diaries*, p. 573.
15 MS: *Speaking for Themselves*, pp. 497–8.
16 Ibid., pp. 498–9.
17 MS: *Clementine*, p. 502.
18 Lady Soames in interview with the author, October 2009.
19 Evelyn Waugh: *Diaries*, p. 587.
20 Winston S. Churchill (the younger): *Memories and Adventures*, p. 32.
21 MS: *Clementine*, p. 518.
22 AL: *Cousin Randolph*, p. 102.
23 Quoted in Sally Bedell Smith: *Reflected Glory*, p. 124.
24 Amanda Mackenzie Stuart: *Consuelo and Alva*, p. 477.

25 Author's interviews with Diana Guest Manning, Palm Beach 1991; and at Saint Georges-Motel, 1992.
26 John Colville: *Fringes of Power*, vol. 2, p. 242.
27 MS: *Speaking for Themselves*, p. 528.
28 Ibid., p. 530.
29 W.H. Thompson: *I Was Churchill's Shadow*, p. 157.
30 National Archives, Kew, Secret Cabinet Papers. WSC to President Truman, 7 June 1945.
31 John Colville: *Fringes of Power*, vol. 2, p. 258.
32 WSC: *The Second World War: Triumph and Tragedy*, p. 583.
33 MS: *Clementine*, p. 550.
34 WSC: *The Second World War: Triumph and Tragedy*, p. 583.
35 Ibid., p. 584.

24

1 MS: *Clementine*, p. 551.
2 Ibid., p. 555.
3 Ibid., p. 557.
4 MS: *Speaking for Themselves*, p. 537.
5 Quoted in AL: *My Cousin Randolph*, pp. 109–10.
6 Interview with Mrs Kathleen Dunn (née Gilbert), 17 March 2010.
7 Ibid.
8 Mrs Kathleen Dunn to the author, 18 March 2010.
9 Sarah Churchill: *Keep on Dancing*, p. 142.
10 Ibid., p. 153.
11 Ibid., p. 159.
12 CV VIII, p. 308.
13 John Colville: *The Churchillians*, p. 29.
14 Martin Gilbert: *Winston S. Churchill: Never Despair*, p. 488n.
15 Anthony Montague Browne: *The Long Sunset*, p. 151.
16 John S. Churchill: *A Churchill Canvas*, p. 247.
17 Mrs Kathleen Dunn to the author.
18 Mary S. Lovell: *The Mitford Girls*, pp. 410–11.
19 Lord Digby to the author, November 2009.
20 Ibid.
21 Ibid.

22 Lord Digby to the author.
23 MS: *Speaking for Themselves*, p. 550.

25

1 AL: *Cousin Randolph*, p. 116.
2 Artemis Cooper: *Mr Wu and Mrs Stitch*, p. 103.
3 Evelyn Waugh: *Letters*, p. 307.
4 MS: *Clementine*, p. 588.
5 AL: *Cousin Randolph*, p. 119.
6 Evelyn Waugh: *Letters*, p. 343.
7 Waugh quoted in *Mr Wu and Mrs Stitch*, p. 113.
8 Evelyn Waugh: *Letters*, p. 349.
9 AL: *Cousin Randolph*, p. 117.
10 John Colville: *Fringes of Power*, vol. 2, p. 294.
11 Ibid., p. 300.
12 Ibid., p. 303.
13 Lady Eden to the author.
14 John Colville: *Fringes of Power*, vol. 2, pp. 309–10.
15 AL: *Cousin Randolph*, p. 121.
16 John Colville: *Fringes of Power*, vol. 2, p. 316.
17 Ibid., p. 328.
18 Sarah Churchill: *Keep on Dancing*, p. 235.
19 John Colville: *Fringes of Power*, vol. 2, p. 330.
20 Ibid.
21 John Colville: *The Churchillians*, p. 44.
22 John Colville: *Fringes of Power*, vol. 2, p. 330.
23 MS: *Speaking for Themselves*, pp. 572–3.
24 Ibid., p. 572.
25 Ibid., p. 573.
26 AL: *Cousin Randolph*, p. 129.
27 MS: *Speaking for Themselves*, p. 575.
28 John Pearson: *Citadel of the Heart*, p. 368.
29 Quoted in Waugh: *Mr Wu and Mrs Stitch*, p. 190.
30 Evelyn Waugh: *Diaries* (refers to an earlier letter from June Churchill), p. 732, and AL: *Cousin Randolph*, p. 133.
31 AL: *Cousin Randolph*, p. 133.
32 Cynthia Gladwyn: *Diaries*, p. 229
33 MS: *Clementine*, pp. 626–7.
34 Ibid., p. 627.
35 Clarissa Eden: *A Memoir*, p. 181.

36 John Colville: *Fringes of Power*, vol. 2, p. 377.
37 Ibid., p. 379.
38 Ibid.

26

1 MS: *Clementine*, p. 593.
2 Clarissa Eden: *A Memoir*, p. 217.
3 MS: *Clementine*, p. 653.
4 Ibid., p. 654.
5 CHAR 2/386.
6 MS: *Speaking for Themselves*, p. 601.
7 Private information.
8 MS: *Clementine*, p. 657.
9 MS: *Speaking for Themselves*, p. 603.
10 Ibid., p. 605.
11 Graham Payne and Sheridan Morley, *The Noël Coward Diaries*, p. 323.
12 Duchess of Devonshire (now the Dowager Duchess) to the author, 25 August 2009.
13 Anthony Montague Browne: *The Long Sunset*, p. 218.
14 Ibid., p. 220.
15 MS: *Clementine*, p. 716.
16 MS: *Speaking for Themselves*, p. 612.
17 Ibid., p. 611.
18 Barry Day: *The Letters of Noël Coward*, p. 626.
19 MS: *Speaking for Themselves*, p. 616.
20 Sarah Churchill: *Keep on Dancing*, p. 257.
21 MS: *Clementine*, p. 660.
22 Lord Moran: *Winston Churchill: The Struggle for Survival*, p. 741.
23 AL: *Cousin Randolph*, p. 151.
24 Ibid., p. 152.
25 Ibid., p. 154.
26 Ibid., p. 155.
27 Lady Mosley to the author.
28 Martin Gilbert: *Winston S. Churchill: Never Despair*, p. 1313.
29 MS: *Clementine*, p. 656.
30 AL: *Cousin Randolph*, p. 145.
31 Artemis Cooper: *Mr Wu and Mrs Stitch*, p. 271.
32 Cynthia Gladwyn: *Diaries*, p. 229.
33 Ibid.
34 MS: *Speaking for Themselves*, p. 629.
35 Martin Gilbert (ed.): *Winston Churchill and Emery Reves: Correspondence 1937–1964* (University of Texas) 1997, p. 387.

36 CHUR 2/532 a-b.
37 Ibid.
38 Martin Gilbert: *Winston S. Churchill: Never Despair*, p. 1315.
39 MS: *Clementine*, p. 656.
40 Ibid., p. 657.
41 Lord Moran: *Winston Churchill: The Struggle for Survival*, p. 768.
42 MS: *Clementine*, p. 681.
43 Ibid., p. 678.
44 Ibid., p. 659.
45 Ibid., p. 680.
46 Sarah Churchill: *Keep on Dancing*, p. 315.
47 MS: *Clementine*, p. 682.
48 Sarah Churchill: *Keep on Dancing*, p. 316.

27

1 John Colville: *The Churchillians*, p. 26.
2 Artemis Cooper, *Mr Wu and Mrs Stitch*, pp. 306–7.

3 MS: *Speaking for Themselves*, p. 647.
4 MS: *Clementine*, p. 694.
5 Ibid., p. 698.
6 Ibid., p. 701.
7 John Colville: *The Churchillians*, p. 19.
8 Lord Moran, letter to *The Times*, 25 April 1966.
9 Charlotte Mosley: *The Mitfords: Letters between Six Sisters*, p. 462.
10 AL: *Cousin Randolph*, p. 203.
11 MS: *Clementine*, p. 736.

APPENDIX 1

1 John Pearson: *Citadel of the Heart*, p. 433.

APPENDIX 2

1 Celia and John Lee: *Winston and Jack: The Churchill Brothers*. See Bibliography.
2 CVI/i, p. 536.
3 Ibid., pp. 542–3.

BIBLIOGRAPHY

All books published in the UK unless otherwise noted.

Arbuthnot, Harriet: *The Journal of Mrs Arbuthnot 1820–1832* (Macmillan) 1951
Asquith, Cynthia: *Remember and Be Glad* (Scribner, New York) 1952
Atkins, J.B.: *Incidents and Reflections* (Unwin) 1921
Balsan, Consuelo: *The Glitter and the Gold* (Heinemann) 1953
Baruch, Bernard: *A Birthday Letter in Tribute to Winston S. Churchill* (Cassell) 1954
Beaverbrook, Max: *Politicians and the War* (Thornton Butterworth) 1928
Bedell Smith, Sally: *Reflected Glory* (Touchstone, New York) 1997
Birkenhead, Earl of: *Churchill* (Harrap) 1989
Blunt, Wilfrid Scawen: *My Diaries 1900–1914* (Alfred A. Knopf, New York) 2 vols 1921
Bonham Carter, Violet: *Winston Churchill as I Knew Him* (Eyre & Spottiswoode) 1965
Boothby, Robert: *Recollections of a Rebel* (Hutchinson) 1978
Channon, H. *Chips: The Diaries of Sir Henry Channon* (Weidenfeld & Nicolson) 1967
Churchill, Jennie *see* Cornwallis-West, Mrs
Churchill, John S.: *A Churchill Canvas* (Little, Brown, Boston), 1961
Churchill, Minnie (with David Coombs): *Sir Winston Churchill's Life through His Paintings* (Chaucer Press) 2003
Churchill, Peregrine, and Julian Mitchell: *Jennie, Lady Randolph Churchill* (Collins) 1974
Churchill, Randolph S.: *Twenty-One Years* (Weidenfeld & Nicolson) 1964
—— *Winston S. Churchill: Youth* (Heinemann) 1966
—— *Winston S. Churchill: Young Statesman* (Heinemann) 1967
Churchill, Sarah: *Keep on Dancing* (Coward, McCann & Geoghegan, New York) 1981
Churchill, [Sir] Winston S.: *My African Journey* (Hodder & Stoughton) 1908
—— *The World Crisis* (Penguin) 2 vols 1931
—— *Marlborough: His Life and Times* (Harrap) 4 vols 1933–8
—— *My Early Life* (Macmillan) 1944
—— *The Second World War: The Gathering Storm* (Cassell) 1948
—— *The Second World War: Their Finest Hour* (Cassell) 1949
—— *The Second World War: The Grand Alliance* (Cassell) 1950
—— *The Second World War: The Hinge of Fate* (Cassell) 1951
—— *The Second World War: Triumph and Tragedy* (Cassell) 1954
—— *The Second World War: Closing the Ring* (Cassell) 1956
—— *History of the English-Speaking Peoples* (Cassell) 4 vols 1955–8
—— *Thoughts and Adventures* (Muller, Delaware) 2009
—— and C.C. Martindale: *Charles, IXth Duke of Marlborough: Tributes* (Burnes, Oates & Washbourne) 1934

Churchill [the younger], Winston Spencer: *Memories and Adventures* (Weidenfeld & Nicolson) 1989
—— *His Father's Son: The Life of Randolph S. Churchill* (Weidenfeld & Nicolson) 1996
Colville, John: *Footprints in Time* (Michael Russell) 1976
—— *The Churchillians* (Weidenfeld & Nicolson) 1981
—— *Fringes of Power* (Sceptre) 2 vols 1987
Cooper, Artemis: *Mr Wu and Mrs Stitch: The Letters of Evelyn Waugh and Diana Cooper* (Hodder & Stoughton) 1991
Cornwallis-West, George: *Edwardian Hey-days* (EP Publishing) 1975
Cornwallis-West, Mrs: *Reminiscences of Lady Randolph Churchill* (Edward Arnold) 1908
Cowles, Virginia: *Looking for Trouble* (Hamish Hamilton) 1941
Culme-Seymour, Angela: *The Bolter's Granddaughter* (Writersworld) 2001
Day, Barry: *The Letters of Noël Coward* (Methuen Drama) 2007
Devonshire, Deborah, Duchess of: *Home to Roost* (John Murray) 2009
Eden, Clarissa (ed. Cate Haste): *A Memoir* (Weidenfeld & Nicolson) 2007
Fielding, Daphne: *The Face on the Sphinx* (Hamish Hamilton) 1978
Forbes, Lady Angela: *Memories and Base Details* (Hutchinson) 1921
Fortescue, Lady: *There's Rosemary* (Blackwoods) 1939
Foster, R.F.: *Lord Randolph Churchill* (Oxford, Clarendon Press) 1981
Friedman, B.H.: *Gertrude Vanderbilt Whitney: A Biography* (Doubleday, New York) 1978
Gilbert, Martin: *Winston S. Churchill: The Challenge of War* (Heinemann) 1971
—— *Winston S. Churchill: The Prophet of Truth* (Minerva) 1976
—— *Winston S. Churchill: The Wilderness Years* (Macmillan) 1981
—— *Winston S. Churchill: Never Despair* (Macmillan) 1988
Gladwyn, Cynthia: *Diaries* (Constable) 1995
Green, David: *Sarah, Duchess of Marlborough* (Heron Books) 1967
Hanfstaengl, Ernst: *Hitler: The Missing Years* (Arcade, New York) 1994
Hibbert, Christopher: *The Marlboroughs* (Penguin) 2002
Hochberg, Maria Theresa von: *Daisy, Princess of Pless* (John Murray) 1937
Howard, Peter: *Beaverbrook* (Hutchinson) 1964
Kehoe, Elisabeth: *Fortune's Daughters* (Atlantic Books) 2005
Lee, Celia and John: *Winston and Jack: The Churchill Brothers* (privately published) 2007
Leslie, Anita: *The Fabulous Leonard Jerome* (Hutchinson) 1954
—— *Jennie* (Hutchinson) 1969
—— *Edwardians in Love* (Hutchinson) 1972
—— *The Gilt and the Gingerbread* (Hutchinson) 1981
—— *Cousin Randolph* (Hutchinson) 1985
Leslie, Seymour: *The Jerome Connection* (John Murray) 1964
Lovell, Mary S.: *Amelia Earhart – The Sound of Wings* (Hutchinson) 1989
—— *The Mitford Girls* (Little, Brown) 2002
Manchester, William: *The Caged Lion* (Michael Joseph) 1988
—— *The Last Lion* (Laurel) 1989
Manley, Mrs de la Riviere: *Secret Memoirs* (New Atlantis) vol. ii 1709
Marsh, Edward: *A Number of People: A Book of Reminiscences* (Harper & Brothers, New York) 1939
Martin, Ralph: *Lady Randolph Churchill* (Cassell) 1969
Montague Browne, Anthony: *The Long Sunset* (Cassell) 1995
Moran, Lord: *Winston Churchill: The Struggle for Survival* (Constable) 1966

Mosley, Charlotte: *Love from Nancy: The Letters of Nancy Mitford* (Sceptre) 1993
—— *The Mitfords: Letters between Six Sisters* (Fourth Estate) 2007
National Trust: *Chartwell* 1992
Nicolson, Harold: *Diaries and Letters, 1930–1962* (Collins) 3 vols 1966–8
Norwich, John Julius: *The Duff Cooper Diaries* (Weidenfeld & Nicolson) 2005
Ogden, Christopher: *Life of the Party* (Little, Brown) 1994
Payn, Graham and Sheridan Morley: *The Noël Coward Diaries* (Macmillan) 1982
Pearson, John: *Citadel of the Heart* (Macmillan) 1991
Pless, Princess Daisy of: *My Private Diary* (John Murray) 1931
Pringle, Henry: *Theodore Roosevelt* (Jonathan Cape) 1932
Roosevelt, Elliott and James Brough: *The Roosevelts of Hyde Park: An Untold Story* (W. H. Allen) 1974
Rosen, Andrew: *Rise Up, Women!* (Routledge & Kegan Paul) 1974
Rowse, A. L.: *The Later Churchills* (Macmillan) 1958
Sebba, Anne: *American Jennie* (W.W. Norton, New York) 2007
Soames, Mary: *Clementine Churchill* (Penguin) 1981
—— *A Churchill Family Album* (Penguin) 1985
—— *Speaking for Themselves* (Doubleday) 1998
Spencer Churchill, Henrietta: *Blenheim and the Churchill Family* (Cico Books) 2005
Stuart, Amanda Mackenzie: *Consuelo and Alva* (HarperCollins) 2005
Thompson, George Malcolm: *The First Churchill* (Secker & Warburg) 1979
Thompson, W.H.: *I Was Churchill's Shadow* (Christopher Johnson) 1951
Trollope, Anthony: *Phineas Finn* (Panther) 1968
Vickers, Hugo: *Gladys, Duchess of Marlborough* (Weidenfeld & Nicolson) 1979
—— *Cecil Beaton* (Weidenfeld & Nicolson) 1985
Waugh, Evelyn: *Diaries* (Weidenfeld & Nicolson) 1976
—— *Letters* (Weidenfeld & Nicolson) 1980
Wilson, D.A: *Dark and Light: The Story of the Guinness Family* (Weidenfeld & Nicolson) 1998
Wilson, Lady Sarah: *South African Memories* (Edward Arnold) 1909
Winterton, Earl: *Churchill the Parliamentarian: Churchill by His Contemporaries* (Hutchinson) 1955
Woolf, Virginia: *Biography of Roger Fry* (Harcourt Brace, New York) 1940

OTHER BOOKS READ DURING RESEARCH

Bardens, Dennis: *Portrait of a Statesman* (Frederick Muller) 1955
Barrow, Andrew: *Gossip: A History of High Society 1920–1970* (Hamish Hamilton) 1978
Beaverbrook, Lord: *Men and Power* (Hutchinson) 1916
Boothby, Robert: *I Fight to Live* (Victor Gollancz) 1947
Collier, Peter and David Horowitz: *The Kennedys* (Secker & Warburg) 1984
Cooper, Diana: *The Rainbow Comes and Goes* (Rupert Hart-Davis) 1958
—— *The Light of Common Day* (Rupert Hart-Davis) 1959
Eade, Charles (ed.): *Churchill by His Contemporaries* (Reprint Society) 1953
Eden, Anthony: *Memoirs* (Cassell) 2 vols 1960–5
Enright, Dominique (ed.): *The Wicked Wit of Winston Churchill* (Michael O'Mara Books) 2001
Farrer, David: *G for God Almighty* (Weidenfeld & Nicolson) 1969

Fisher, Clive: *Noël Coward* (Weidenfeld & Nicolson) 1992

Fowler, Marian: *Blenheim* (Penguin) 1989

Green, David: *Sarah Duchess of Marlborough* (Heron Books) 1967

Halle, Kay: *Randolph Churchill: The Young Unpretender* (Heinemann) 1971

Hardwick, Joan: *Clementine Churchill* (John Murray) 1997

Hough, Richard: *Winston and Clementine* (Bantam) 1990

Howarth, Patrick: *When the Riviera Was Ours* (Century) 1988

James, Robert R.: *Bob Boothby* (Hodder & Stoughton) 1991

Kishlansky, Mark: *A Monarchy Transformed* (Allen Lane) 1996

Lash, Joseph P.: *Eleanor and Franklin* (New American Library, New York) 1973

—— *Roosevelt and Churchill* (W.W. Norton, New York) 1976

MacColl, Gail and Carol McD. Wallace: *To Marry an English Lord* (Sidgwick & Jackson) 1980

Marchant, Sir James (ed.): *Winston S. Churchill: Servant of Crown and Commonwealth* (Cassell) 1954

Miles, Alice C.: *Every Girl's Duty* (André Deutsch) 1992

Montgomery-Massingberd, Hugh: *Great British Families* (Michael Joseph) 1988

Moorehead, Alan: *Gallipoli* (Hamish Hamilton) 1956

Morgan, Janet: *Edwina Mountbatten* (HarperCollins) 1991

Redesdale, Lord: *Memories* (Hutchinson) 2 vols 1915

Spencer, Charles: *The Spencer Family* (Penguin) 1999

Sykes, Christopher: *Nancy* (William Collins) 1972

Taylor, A.J.P.: *Beaverbrook* (Hamish Hamilton) 1972

Thomson, George M.: *The First Churchill* (Secker & Warburg) 1979

Trevor-Roper, Hugh: *The Last Days of Hitler* (Pan) 1947

Wrigley, Chris: *Winston Churchill: A Biographical Companion* (ABC-CLIO, Santa Barbara, Calif.) 2002

Young, Kenneth: *Churchill and Beaverbrook* (Eyre & Spottiswoode) 1966

Ziegler, Philip: *Diana Cooper* (Alfred Knopf, New York) 1982

—— *Mountbatten* (Book Club Associates) 1985

ACKNOWLEDGEMENTS

I am lastingly indebted to the following, who made time to provide me with information that could not be found in books or papers: Clarissa, Countess of Avon; Simon Bird; Judith Brown (of Adelaide, Australia); Julia Budworth; Winston S. Churchill Esq. ('young Winston', d. 2010); Mark Culme-Seymour; Deborah, Dowager Duchess of Devonshire; Edward, Lord Digby; Dione, Lady Digby; the late Robert Ducas*; Mrs Kathleen Dunn, governess to young Winston; the late Diana Guest*; Julian Guest; the late Lord Hankey*; the Hon. Jacquetta James; Richard ('Tarka') King; the late Diana, Lady Mosley*; Charlotte Mosley; Lady Mary Soames; C.H.B. Watts; Emeritus Professor Trevor Wilson; Lord Wimborne.

I should like to thank the archivist and staff at the Churchill Archives Centre, Churchill College, Cambridge, for their help, especially Sandra Marsh, Daisy Davies, Madelin Terrazas, Bridget Warrington and Caroline Herbert; the counter staff at Western Manuscripts, Bodleian Library, Oxford; and Anne Hammond and the staff at Rosetta Cottage, Cowes.

While researching for earlier books I interviewed a number of people, now dead, who provided me with information that has proved relevant to this book on the Churchill family. These sources of information are marked above with an asterisk. The interviews were conducted long before I conceived a book on the Churchills, and had I been able to interview them specifically for this book I would have asked more – and probably different – questions.

Other people helped me in various ways during the research. My friend Anne Biffin nobly assisted me when the first draft was completed in the tedious job of checking citations and page proofs. Pamela Cornwell accompanied me to Cowes to visit Rosetta Cottage (Villa Rosetta during the Jeromes' time) when I was too unwell to travel alone. Bernadette and Maureen Rivett arranged for us to visit the *Dollar Princess* exhibition at the American Museum, Bath. I met fellow biographer Anne Sebba in 2008, some years after I had researched Jennie Jerome and Randolph Churchill. We had probably been working on many of the same sources at approximately the same time, but I had to take two years out because of illness in May 2006, and in the meantime Anne went on to publish her book *American Jennie*, to deserved acclaim. In 2009, when I met Anne again, she told me of some information that had come her way, too late for her to use it, about Jennie's third husband Montague Porch.

With characteristic generosity she sent me her notes, and I have included some of the the information here.

I would also like to thank Minnie Churchill for the generous gift of a signed copy of her book, *Sir Winston Churchill's Life through His Paintings.*

Books are not produced by authors alone. When the writing process ends, the editorial and production teams kick in, and I should also like to thank those who were part of that team:

Editors: Star Lawrence at W.W. Norton in New York, Richard Beswick and Vivien Redman at Little, Brown in London.

Copyeditor: Sue Phillpott
Proofreader: Dan Balado
Picture researcher: Linda Silverman
Jacket designer: Hannah Clarke
Production: Marie Hrynczak
Family tree and map: John Gilkes
Index: Mark Wells

Last, but certainly not least, my thanks to my literary agent, Louise Ducas, who is always on hand in a crisis.

COPYRIGHT CREDITS

Note: Although I have been granted appropriate copyright permission, as above, I have been asked to make it clear that this does not indicate any form of authorisation by the Churchill family for the views or opinions expressed in this book.

Also:
Huchinsons & Co Ltd., for extracts from *Cousin Randolph* and *Jennie: The Life of Lady Randolph Churchill*.
Hodder & Stoughton for extracts from *The Fringes of Power*.
Orion Publishing Group for extracts from *The Churchillians, The Letters of Evelyn Waugh, The Diaries of Evelyn Waugh* and *The Diaries of Duff Cooper*.
Charlotte Mosley for extract from *The Mitfords: Letters between Six Sisters*.
Tarka King Esquire, for extracts from letters of the Jerome and Leslie families.
Constable & Robinson Ltd for extracts from *Winston Churchill – The Struggle for Survival*.
Quotations from *The Glitter and the Gold* by Consuelo Balsan (which was first published in book form in 1952 and which is still available in paperback) appear by kind permission of George Mann Books.

The author has made strenuous attempts to find the present copyright holders, heirs and assigns for extracts, and to obtain written permission. The author apologises for any inadvertent oversights in this respect. Although the appropriate citation should identify the probable owner, any copyright owner who is affected should immediately contact the publishers who will correct the matter in any future editions.

AUTHOR'S NOTE

Quotations: Although extracts used in this book are reproduced as originally written, I have very occasionally felt it necessary to add a comma or some other form of punctuation in order to make the sense more easily understood.

INDEX